BUSINESS ETHICS

SAGE LIBRARY IN BUSINESS AND MANAGEMENT

BUSINESS ETHICS

VOLUME 1
Ethical Theory, Distributive Justice,
and Corporate Social Responsibility

Edited by
FRITZ ALLHOFF
and
ANAND VAIDYA

SAGE Publications
London • Thousand Oaks • New Delhi

Introduction and editorial arrangement © Fritz Allhoff and
Anand Vaidya 2005

First published 2005

SAGE Publications Ltd
1 Oliver's Yard
55 City Road
London EC1Y 1SP

SAGE Publications Inc
2455 Teller Road
Thousand Oaks, California 91320

SAGE Publications India Pvt Ltd
B-42, Panschsheel Enclave
Post Box 4109
New Delhi 110 017

British Library Cataloguing in Publication data

A catalogue record for this book is available from the British
Library

ISBN 1-4129-0254-1 (set of three volumes)

Library of Congress Control Number: 2004096763

Typeset by PDQ Typesetting, Newcastle-under-Lyme
Printed and bound in Great Britain by TJ International Ltd,
Padstow, Cornwall

CONTENTS

Appendix of Sources   xi
Editor's Introduction   xix

VOLUME 1
Ethical Theory, Distributive Justice, and Corporate Social Responsibility

Preliminaries: Why Business Ethics?

1. Excerpts from "Business Ethics: Widening the Lens"
   Clarence C. Walton   1

Unit One: Ethical Theory and Business Ethics

Perception

2. Excerpts from "The Parable of the Sadhu" *Bowen H. McCoy*   11
3. The *Rashomon* Effect *Patricia Werhane*   18

Strategy

4. Excerpts from "The Prince" *Niccolò Machiavelli*   28
5. Excerpts from "The Art of War" *Sun Tzu*   32

Perspectives

6. Utilitarianism and Business Ethics *Milton Snoeyenbos and James Humber*   34
7. Victims of Circumstances? A Defense of Virtue Ethics in Business *Robert C. Solomon*   48
8. Virtue Ethics, the Firm, and Moral Psychology *Daryl Koehn*   68
9. A Kantian Approach to Business Ethics *Norman E. Bowie*   85

Unit Two: Distributive Justice

Classical Theories of Contracts, Property, and Capitalism

10. Excerpts from "Leviathan" *Thomas Hobbes*   103
11. The Justification of Property *John Locke*   114

12. Excerpts from "The Wealth of Nations" *Adam Smith* 120
13. Alienated Labor and Private Property Communism *Karl Marx* 126

Contemporary Theories of Distribution and Property

14. Excerpts from "A Theory of Justice" *John Rawls* 145
15. Excerpts from "Anarchy, State, and Utopia" *Robert Nozick* 160
16. Capitalism and Morality *James Q. Wilson* 175
17. Illusions about Private Property and Freedom *Gerald A. Cohen* 189
18. Excerpts from "Ethics and Society" *Milton Fisk* 203

Intellectual Property

19. Justifying Intellectual Property *Edwin C. Hettinger* 211
20. Trade Secrets and the Justification of Intellectual Property:
    A Comment on Hettinger *Lynn Sharp Paine* 229

Unit Three: Corporate Social Responsibility

The Central Debate

21. The Social Responsibility of Business Is to Increase Its Profits
    Milton Friedman 247
22. A Stakeholder Theory of the Modern Corporation
    R. Edward Freeman 253
23. Economics, Business Principles, and Moral Sentiments *Amartya Sen* 265
24. The Normative Theories of Business Ethics: A Guide for the
    Perplexed *John Hasnas* 278
25. Arguments For and Against Corporate Social Responsibility
    N. Craig Smith 303
26. Smith and Friedman on the Pursuit of Self-interest and Profit
    Harvey S. James, Jr. and Farhad Rassekh 310
27. Does Business Ethics Make Economic Sense? *Amartya Sen* 320
28. New Directions in Corporate Social Responsibility *Norman Bowie* 329

Globalization and its Ethical Significance

29. Globalization and its Impact on the Full Enjoyment of All
    Human Rights *Preliminary Report of the Secretary-General* 344
30. Rights in the Global Market *Thomas J. Donaldson* 360
31. International Business, Morality, and the Common Good
    Manuel Velasquez 381
32. The Great Non-Debate Over International Sweatshops
    Ian Maitland 395
33. Should Trees Have Standing? Toward Legal Rights for Natural
    Objects *Christopher D. Stone* 410
34. The Place of Nonhumans in Environmental Issues *Peter Singer* 424
35. At the Shrine of Our Lady of Fatima, or Why Political Questions
    are Not All Economic *Mark Sagoff* 431
36. A Defense of Risk-Cost-Benefit Analysis *Kristin Shrader-Frechette* 444

VOLUME 2
Fairness and Justice in the Workplace

Unit One: Rights and Obligations of Employers and Employees

Employment at Will

37. Employment at Will and Due Process *Patricia H. Werhane and Tara J. Radin* 3
38. In Defense of the Contract at Will *Richard A. Epstein* 10

Work-Life Balance

39. Work in the Family and Employing Organization *Sheldon Zedeck and Kathleen L. Mosier* 20
40. Work/Family Border Theory: A New Theory of Work/Family Balance *Sue Campbell Clark* 43

Whistleblowing

41. Whistleblowing and Professional Responsibility *Sissela Bok* 63
42. Whistle Blowing *Richard T. De George* 72

Drug Testing

43. Drug Testing in Employment *Joseph DesJardins and Ronald Duska* 82
44. Drug Testing and the Right to Privacy: Arguing the Ethics of Workplace Drug Testing *Michael Cranford* 98

Employees' Rights to Privacy

45. The Ethics of Genetic Screening in the Workplace *Joseph Kupfer* 112
46. Computers and Privacy *Stacey L. Edgar* 121
47. Privacy, Polygraphs and Work *George G. Brenkert* 145

Employees' Rights to Safety

48. The Employer-Employee Relationship and the Right to Know *Anita M. Superson* 155
49. Human Rights, Workers' Rights, and the 'Right' to Occupational Safety *Tibor R. Machan* 168

Unit Two: Justice and Fair Practice

Affirmative Action

50. Regents of University of California v. Bakke, 438 U.S. 268 (1978) 177
51. Why Bakke Has No Case *Ronald Dworkin* 188
52. Affirmative Action: The Price of Preference *Shelby Steele* 197
53. What Is Wrong with Reverse Discrimination? *Edwin C. Hettinger* 205

Sexual Harassment

54. The Definition of Sexual Harassment *Edmund Wall* 218

55. A Feminist Definition of Sexual Harassment *Anita M. Superson*   232

Bluffing

56. Is Business Bluffing Ethical? *Albert Z. Carr*   250
57. Business and Game-Playing: The False Analogy *Daryl Koehn*   260
58. Second Thoughts About Bluffing *Thomas Carson*   268
59. Business Bluffing Reconsidered *Fritz Allhoff*   276

VOLUME 3
Professional Ethics

60. Just Another Day at the Office: The Ordinariness of Professional
    Ethics *Don Welch*   1
61. Professional Responsibility: Just Following the Rules? *Michael Davis*   8

Unit One: Ethical Issues in Advertising

Truth and Deception in Advertising

62. Deceptive Advertising *John J. McCall*   21
63. Advertising: The Whole or Only Some of the Truth?
    Tibor R. Machan   30
64. The Making of Self and World in Advertising *John Waide*   41

Creation of Desire

65. Advertising and Behavior Control *Robert L. Arrington*   50
66. Persuasive Advertising, Autonomy, and the Creation of Desire
    Roger Crisp   63

Is Targeting Ethical?

67. Children as Consumers: An Ethical Evaluation of Children's
    Television Advertising *Lynn Sharp Paine*   71
68. Marketing to Inner-City Blacks: PowerMaster and Moral
    Responsibility *George G. Brenkert*   85

Consumer Risk

69. The Ethics of Consumer Production *Manuel G. Velasquez*   103
70. Strict Products Liability and Compensatory Justice
    George G. Brenkert   114

Unit Two: Ethical Issues in Accounting and Finance

71. Earnings Hocus-Pocus: How Companies Come Up with the
    Numbers They Want *Nanette Byrnes, Richard A. Melcher
    and Debra Sparks*   123

72. The Ethics of Creative Accounting *Oriol Amat, John Blake and Jack Dowds*   132
73. Ethics in the Public Accounting Profession
    Mohammad J. Abdolmohammadi and Mark R. Nixon   146
74. The Ethics of Insider Trading *Patricia H. Werhane*   162
75. What is Morally Right with Insider Trading *Tibor R. Machan*   168
76. Justice and Insider Trading *Richard L. Lippke*   176

Unit Three: Ethical Issues in Journalism
77. The Ethical Responsibilities of Journalists *David Detmer*   193
78. The Intervention Dilemma *Susan Paterno*   203
79. Ethically Challenged *Lori Robertson*   215
80. Ethical Boundaries to Media Coverage *Raphael Cohen-Almagor*   226
81. Truth, Neutrality, and Conflict of Interest *Judith Lichtenberg*   237
82. Media Culpas *Kelly Patricia O'Meara*   247

Unit Four: Ethical Issues in Law
83. Professional Responsibility of the Criminal Defense Lawyer:
    The Three Hardest Questions *Monroe H. Freedman*   255
84. The Adversary System Excuse *David Luban*   269
85. Pure Legal Advocates and Moral Agents: Two Concepts of a
    Lawyer in an Adversary System *Elliot D. Cohen*   307
86. Can Virtue be Taught to Lawyers? *Amy Gutmann*   320
87. Confidentiality and the Lawyer-Client Relationship
    Bruce M. Landesman   333
88. A Lawyer's Duty to Represent Clients, Repugnant and
    Otherwise *Charles W. Wolfram*   354

Unit Five: Ethical Issues in Medicine
89. The Hippocratic Oath   377
90. The Virtuous Physician and the Ethics of Medicine
    Edmund D. Pellegrino   379
91. Four Models of the Physician-Patient Relationship
    Ezekiel J. Emanuel and Linda L. Emanuel   385
92. Legal and Ethical Myths about Informed Consent
    Alan Meisel and Mark Kuczewski   399
93. Truth and the Physician *Bernard C. Meyer*   409
94. Lies to the Sick and Dying *Sissela Bok*   420
95. Standards of Competence *Allen E. Buchanan and Dan W. Brock*   436
96. Surrogate Decision Making for Incompetent Adults: An
    Ethical Framework *Dan W. Brock*   443

Appendix of Sources

Grateful acknowledgement is made to the following sources for permission to reproduce material in this book.

1. Excerpts from "Business Ethics: Widening the Lens", *Clarence C. Walton*
   Enriching Business Ethics (New York and London: Plenum Press, 1990). Reprinted with permission of Springer-Verlag GmbH.

2. Excerpts from "The Parable of the Sadhu", *Bowen H. McCoy*
   Harvard Business Review (September/October, 1983) pp 182–7. Copyright © 1997 by the Harvard Business School Publishing Corporation. All rights reserved.

3. "The *Rashomon* Effect", *Patricia Werhane.*
   Laura Hartman, *Perspectives in Business Ethics* (McGraw Hill/Irwin, 1996).

4. Excerpts from "The Prince", *Niccolo Machiavelli*
   Translated by David Wootton. Copyright ©1995 Hackett Publishing Co. Reprinted by permission.

5. Excerpts from "The Art of War", *Sun Tzu*
   Sun Tzu, *The Art of War,* translated by Thomas Cleary (Boston, MA: Shambhala Publications, 1988). Copyright © 1988. Reprinted with permission of Shambhala Publications, Inc., Boston, MA., www.shambhala.com.

6. "Utilitarianism and Business Ethics", *Milton Snoeyenbos and James Humber*
   Robert E. Frederick (ed.), *A Companion to Business Ethics* (Oxford: Blackwell Publishers, 2002). Reprinted with permission of the publisher.

7. "Victims of Circumstances? A Defense of Virtue Ethics in Business", *Robert C. Solomon*
   Business Ethics Quarterly 13 (1) (2003): 43–62.

8. "Virtue Ethics, the Firm, and Moral Psychology", *Daryl Koehn*
   Business Ethics Quarterly 8 (1998): 497–515.

9. "A Kantian Approach to Business Ethics", *Norman E. Bowie*
   Robert E. Frederick (ed.), *A Companion to Business Ethics* (Oxford: Blackwell Publishers, 2002). Reprinted with permission of the publisher.

10. Excerpts from "Leviathan", *Thomas Hobbes*
    Edwin Curley (ed.), *Leviathan* (Indianapolis, IN: Hackett Publishing, 1994). Reprinted with permission of Hackett Publishing company, Inc. All rights reserved.

11. "The Justification of Property", *John Locke*
    John Locke, *The Second Treatise of Government* (New York: Macmillan, 1956, first published, 1764). Reprinted with permission of Simon & Schuster.

12. Excerpts from "The Wealth of Nations", *Adam Smith*
Adam Smith, *The Wealth of Nations*, Books I and IV (Chicago, IL: Chicago University Press, 1976, first published 1776). Copyright ©Adam Smith 1776.

13. "Alienated Labor" and "Private Property Communism", *Karl Marx*
Karl Marx, *Selected Writings*, Lawrence H. Simon (ed.) (Indianapolis, IN: Hackett Publishing, 1994). Reprinted with permission of Hackett Publishing Company, Inc. All rights reserved.

14. Excerpts from "A Theory of Justice", *John Rawls*
John Rawls, *A Theory of Justice: Revised Edition* (Cambridge, MA: Harvard University Press, 1999). Copyright © 1999 by the President and Fellows of Harvard College.

15. Excerpts from "Anarchy, State, and Utopia", *Robert Nozick*
Robert Nozick, *Anarchy, State, and Utopia* (New York: Basic Books, Inc., 1974). Reprinted by permission of Perseus Books Group.

16. "Capitalism and Morality", *James Q. Wilson*
The Public Interest 121 (Fall, 1995): 42–61. Reprinted with permission of the author. © 1995 by the National Affairs, Inc.

17. "Illusions about Private Property and Freedom", *Gerald A. Cohen*
John Mepham and David-Hillil Rubin (eds), *Issues in Marxist Philosophy, IV* (Atlantic Highlands, NJ: Humanities Press, 1979). Reprinted by permission of Prometheus Books.

18. Excerpts from "Ethics and Society", *Milton Fisk*
Milton Fisk, *Ethics and Society* (New York: New York University Press, 1980). © Milton Fisk.

19. "Justifying Intellectual Property", *Edwin C. Hettinger*
Philosophy and Public Affairs 18 (1989): 31–52. Copyright © 1989 The Johns Hopkins University Press. Reprinted with permission of The Johns Hopkins University Press.

20. "Trade Secrets and the Justification of Intellectual Property: A Comment on Hettinger", *Lynn Sharp Paine*
Philosophy and Public Affairs 20 (1991): 247–63. © 1991 Philosophy and Public Affairs.

21. "The Social Responsibility of Business Is to Increase Its Profits", *Milton Friedman*
New York Times Magazine, September 13, 1970. Copyright © 1970 by The New York Times Company.

22. "A Stakeholder Theory of the Modern Corporation", *R. Edward Freeman*
Excerpts from R. Edward Freeman, 'The Politics of Stakeholder Theory', in *Business Ethics Quarterly* 4 (1994): 409–21. Published by the Society for Business Ethics. Reprinted with permission.

23. "Economics, Business Principles, and Moral Sentiments", *Amartya Sen*
Georges Enderle (ed.), *International Business Ethics* (Notre Dame, IN: University of Notre Dame Press, 1999), pp. 15–29.

24. "The Normative Theories of Business Ethics: A Guide for the Perplexed", *John Hasnas*
Business Ethics Quarterly 8 (1) (1998): 19–43. Published by the Society for Business Ethics. Reprinted with permission.

25. "Arguments For and Against Corporate Social Responsibility', *N. Craig Smith*
N. Craig Smith, *Morality and The Market* (New York: Routledge, 1990), pp. 69–76. Published by Taylor & Francis Ltd (www.tandf.co.uk/journals). Reprinted with permission.

26. 'Smith and Friedman on the Pursuit of Self-interest and Profit', *Harvey S. James, Jr. and Farhad Rassekh*
Laura P. Hartman (ed.), *Perspectives in Business Ethics*, 3rd edn (New York: McGraw-Hill, 2002), pp. 248–56.

27. "Does Business Ethics Make Economic Sense?", *Amartya Sen*
Business Ethics Quarterly 3 (1) (1993): 245–51. Published by the Society for Business Ethics. Reprinted with permission.

28. "New Directions in Corporate Social Responsibility", *Norman Bowie*
Business Horizons 34(4) (July-August, 1991): 56–65. Copyright © 1991 with permission from Elsevier.

29. "Globalization and its Impact on the Full Enjoyment of All Human Rights", *Preliminary Report of the Secretary-General*
United Nations General Assembly 31 (2000): 1–12. © United Nations General Assembly.

30. "Rights in the Global Market", *Thomas J. Donaldson*
R. Edward Freeman (ed.), *Business Ethics: The State of the Art* (Oxford: Oxford University Press, 1991).Copyright © 1991. Used by permission of Oxford University Press, Inc.

31. "International Business, Morality, and the Common Good", *Manuel Velasquez*
Business Ethics Quarterly 2 (1) (1992): 27–40. Published by the Society for Business Ethics. Reprinted with permission.

32. "The Great Non-Debate Over International Sweatshops", *Ian Maitland*
British Academy of Management Annual Conference Proceedings (September, 1997): 240–65. © 1997 Ian Maitland. Reprinted with permission of the author.

33. "Should Trees Have Standing? Toward Legal Rights for Natural Objects", *Christopher D. Stone*
Southern California Law Review 45 (1972): 240–7.

34. "The Place of Nonhumans in Environmental Issues", *Peter Singer*
K.E. Goodpaster and K.M. Sayre (eds), *Ethics and Problems of the 21st Century* (Notre Dame, IN: University of Notre Dame Press, 1979), pp. 191–8.

35. "At the Shrine of Our Lady of Fatima, or Why Political Questions are Not All Economic", *Mark Sagoff*
The Economy of the Earth Philosophy, Law and the Environment, 1988: pp13–162. Copyright © Cambridge University Press, 1981. Reproduced with kind permission of the author and publisher. Notes deleted.

36. "A Defense of Risk-Cost-Benefit Analysis", *Kristin Shrader-Frechette*
Louis P. Pojman (ed.), *Environmental Ethics: Readings in Theory and Application*, 3rd edn (Stamford, CT: Wadsworth, 2001).

37. "Employment at Will and Due Process", *Patricia H. Werhane and Tara J. Radin*
John R. Rowan and Samuel Zinaich (eds.), *Ethics for the Professions* (Stamford, CT: Wadsworth, 2003).

38. "In Defense of the Contract at Will", *Richard A. Epstein*
University of Chicago Law Review 34 (1984): 275–83. Reprinted with permission of The University of Chicago Law Review.

39. "Work in the Family and Employing Organization", *Sheldon Zedeck and Kathleen L. Mosier*
American Psychologist 45 (2) (1990): 240–51. Published by the American Psychological Association.

40. "Work/Family Border Theory: A New Theory of Work/Family Balance", *S. Campbell Clark*
Human Relations, 53 (6) (2000): 747–70.

41. "Whistleblowing and Professional Responsibility", *Sissela Bok*
New York University Education Quarterly 11 (1980): 2–7. Published by New York University Education Quarterly.

42. "Whistle Blowing", *Richard T. De George*
Richard T. De George (ed.), *Business Ethics* (New York: Macmillan, 1986).

43. "Drug Testing in Employment", *Joseph DesJardins and Ronald Duska*
Business and Professional Ethics Journal 6 (3) (1986): 101–11. © Business and Professional Ethics Journal 1986. Reprinted with permission.

44. "Drug Testing and the Right to Privacy: Arguing the Ethics of Workplace Drug Testing", *Michael Cranford*
Journal of Business Ethics 17 (1998): 1805–15. Published by Springer-Verlag.

45. "The Ethics of Genetic Screening in the Workplace", *Joseph Kupfer*
Business Ethics Quarterly 3 (1) (1993): 240–5. Published by the Society for Business Ethics. Reprinted with permission.

46. "Computers and Privacy", *Stacey L. Edgar*
Stacey L. Edgar, *Morality and Machines: Perspectives in Computer Ethics* (Sudbury, MA: Jones and Bartlett Publishers, 1997).

47. "Privacy, Polygraphs and Work", *George G. Brenkert*
Business and Professional Ethics Journal 1 (1) (1981): 19–35. © Business and Professional Ethics Journal 1981. Reprinted with permission.

48. "The Employer-Employee Relationship and the Right to Know", *Anita M. Superson*
Business and Professional Ethics Journal 3 (4) (1983): 185–93. © Business and Professional Ethics Journal 1983. Reprinted with permission.

49. "Human Rights, Workers' Rights, and the 'Right' to Occupational Safety", *Tibor R. Machan*
Gertrude Ezorsky (ed.), *Moral Rights in the Workplace* (Albany: State University of New York Press, 1987).

50. Regents of University of California v. Bakke, 438 U.S. 268 (1978)

51. "Why Bakke Has No Case", *Ronald Dworkin*
    New York Review of Books 24 (18) (1977): 11–15. © New York Review of Books, 1977.

52. "Affirmative Action: The Price of Preference", *Shelby Steele*
    Shelby Steele, *The Content of Our Character: A New Vision of Race in America* (New York: St. Martin's Press, 1991).

53. "What is Wrong with Reverse Discrimination?", *Edwin C. Hettinger*
    Business and Professional Ethics Journal 6 (3) (1986): 431–41. © Business and Professional Ethics Journal 1986. Reprinted with permission.

54. "The Definition of Sexual Harassment", *Edmund Wall*
    Public Affairs Quarterly 5 (4) (1991): 140–50. Published by University of Illinois Press.

55. "A Feminist Definition of Sexual Harassment", *Anita M. Superson*
    Journal of Social Philosophy 24 (1) (1993): 150–62. Published by Blackwell Publishing.

56. "Is Business Bluffing Ethical?", *Albert Z. Carr*
    Harvard Business Review 46 (1) (1968): 4–10. Copyright © 1968 by the Harvard Business School Publishing Corporation; all rights reserved. Reprinted by permission of Harvard Business Review.

57. "Business and Game-Playing: The False Analogy", *Daryl Koehn*
    Journal of Business Ethics 16 (1997): 1447–52. Published by Springer-Verlag.

58. "Second Thoughts About Bluffing", *Thomas Carson*
    Business Ethics Quarterly 3 (4) (1993): 506–12. Published by the Society for Business Ethics. Reprinted with permission.

59. "Business Bluffing Reconsidered", *Fritz Allhoff*
    Journal of Business Ethics 45 (2003): 283–9.

60. "Just Another Day at the Office: The Ordinariness of Professional Ethics", *Don Welch*
    Professional Ethics 2 (1993): 3–14.

61. "Professional Responsibility: Just Following the Rules?", *Michael Davis*
    Business and Professional Ethics Journal, 18 (1), 1999, pp 62–9. Published by the Center for Applied Philosophy and Ethics in the Professions.

62. "Deceptive Advertising", *John J. McCall*
    Joseph R. DesJardins and John J. McCall (eds.), *Contemporary Issues in Business Ethics*, 3rd edn (Stamford, CT: Wadsworth, 1996).

63. "Advertising: The Whole or Only Some of the Truth?", *Tibor R. Machan*
    Public Affairs Quarterly 1 (4) (1987): 336–42. Published by University of Illinois Press.

64. "The Making of Self and World in Advertising", *John Waide*
    Journal of Business Ethics 6 (1987): 73–9. Published by Springer-Verlag.

65. "Advertising and Behavior Control", *Robert L. Arrington*
    Journal of Business Ethics 1 (1982): 3–12. Published by Springer-Verlag.

66. "Persuasive Advertising, Autonomy, and the Creation of Desire", *Roger Crisp*
Journal of Business Ethics 6 (1987): 413–18. Published by Springer-Verlag.

67. "Children as Consumers: An Ethical Evaluation of Children's Television Advertising", *Lynn Sharp Paine*
Business and Professional Ethics Journal 3 (3/4) (1983): 119–25. © Business and Professional Ethics Journal 1983. Reprinted with permission.

68. "Marketing to Inner-City Blacks: PowerMaster and Moral Responsibility", *George G. Brenkert*
Business Ethics Quarterly 8 (1) (1998): 1–18. Published by the Society for Business Ethics. Reprinted with permission.

69. "The Ethics of Consumer Production", *Manuel G. Velasquez*
Manuel G. Velasquez, *Business Ethics: Concepts and Cases*, 3rd edn (Upper Saddle River, NJ: Prentice Hall, 1992), pp. 277–92.

70. "Strict Products Liability and Compensatory Justice", *George G. Brenkert*
Michael Boylan (ed.), *Ethical Issues in Business* (Fort Worth, TX: Harcourt Brace, 1995).

71. "Earnings Hocus-Pocus: How Companies Come Up with the Numbers They Want", *Nanette Byrnes, Richard A. Melcher and Debra Sparks*
Business Week 5 (1998): 134–42. Published by McGraw-Hill, Inc.

72. "The Ethics of Creative Accounting", *Oriol Amat, John Blake and Jack Dowds*
Economics Working Paper (1999): http://econpapers.hhs.se/paper/upfupfgen/349.htm Published by Taylor & Francis. Reprinted with permission.

73. "Ethics in the Public Accounting Profession", *Mohammad J. Abdolmohammadi and Mark R. Nixon*
Robert E. Frederick (ed.), *A Companion to Business Ethics* (Oxford: Blackwell Publishers, 2002). Published by Blackwell Publishers. Reprinted with permission.

74. "The Ethics of Insider Trading", *Patricia H. Werhane*
Journal of Business Ethics 8 (1989): 841–5. Published by Springer-Verlag.

75. "What is Morally Right with Insider Trading", *Tibor R. Machan*
Public Affairs Quarterly 10 (2) (1996): 239–44. Published by University of Illinois Press.

76. "Justice and Insider Trading", *Richard L. Lippke*
Journal of Applied Philosophy 10 (2) (1993): 244–54. Published by Blackwell Publishing.

77. "The Ethical Responsibilities of Journalists", *David Detmer*
Samuel Zinaich and John Rowan (eds.), *Ethics for the Professions* (Stamford, CI: Wadsworth: 2002). © Copyright David Detmer. Reprinted with permssion of the author.

78. "The Intervention Dilemma", *Susan Paterno*
American Journalism Review 20 (2) (1998). © 1998 American Journalism Review.

79. "Ethically Challenged", *Lori Robertson*
American Journalism Review 1 (2001) © 2001 American Journalism Review.

80. "Ethical Boundaries to Media Coverage", *Raphael Cohen-Almagor*
    Australian Journal of Communication 26 (1999): 11–34. Published by the University of
    Queensland. Reprinted with permission.

81. "Truth, Neutrality, and Conflict of Interest", *Judith Lichtenberg*
    Business and Professional Ethics Journal 9 (1990): 65–78. © Business and Professional Ethics
    Journal 1990. Reprinted with permission.

82. "Media Culpas", *Kelly Patricia O'Meara*
    Insight December 11, 2000: 10–12, 29. Washington Times Corp.

83. "Professional Responsibility of the Criminal Defense Lawyer: The Three
    Hardest Questions", *Monroe H. Freedman*
    Michigan Law Review 27 (1966): 1469–85. © 1966 Monroe Freeman. Reprinted with
    permission of the author. See Monroe Freeman and Abbe Smith, *Understanding Lawyers'
    Ethics*, 3rd edn (New York: Matthew Bender, 2004) for an updated and expanded analysis.

84. "The Adversary System Excuse", *David Luban*
    David Luban (ed.), *The Good Lawyer: Lawyers' Roles and Lawyers' Ethics* (Totowa, NJ: Rowman
    and Allanheld), pp. 83–122.

85. "Pure Legal Advocates and Moral Agents: Two Concepts of a Lawyer in an
    Adversary System", *Elliot D. Cohen*
    Criminal Justice Studies 4 (1) (1985): 38–48. Published by Taylor & Francis Ltd (www.tandf.co.
    uk/journals). Reprinted with permission.

86. "Can Virtue be Taught to Lawyers?", *Amy Gutmann*
    Stanford Law Review 45 (1993): 1759–71. Published by Stanford Law School.

87. "Confidentiality and the Lawyer-Client Relationship", *Bruce M. Landesman*
    Utah Law Review (1980): 765–86. Published by the University of Utah.

88. "A Lawyer's Duty to Represent Clients, Repugnant and Otherwise",
    Charles W. Wolfram
    David Luban (ed.), *The Good Lawyer: Lawyers' Roles and Lawyers' Ethics* (Totowa, NJ: Rowman
    and Allanheld), pp. 214–35.

89. "The Hippocratic Oath"
    Owesi Temkin and C. Lilian Temkin (eds.), *Ancient Medicine: Selected Papers of Ludwig Edelstein*
    (Baltimore, MD: Johns Hopkins Press). Copyright © The Johns Hopkins University Press.
    Reprinted with permission.

90. "The Virtuous Physician and the Ethics of Medicine", *Edmund D. Pellegrino*
    Earl E. Shelp (ed.), *Virtue and Medicine: Explorations in the Character of Medicine* (Dordrecht:
    Reidel Publishing Company, 1985).

91. "Four Models of the Physician-Patient Relationship", *Ezekiel J. Emanuel and
    Linda L. Emanuel*
    Journal of the American Medical Association 267 (1992): 2251-6.

92. "Legal and Ethics Myths about Informed Consent", *Alan Meisel and Mark
    Kuczewski*
    Archives of Internal Medicine 156 (1996): 2521-6.

93. "Truth and the Physician", *Bernard C. Meyer*
    E. Fuller Torrey (ed.), *Ethical Issues in Medicine* (New York: Little, Brown and Company, 1968),
    pp. 161–77.

94. "Lies to the Sick and Dying", *Sissela Bok*
    Sissela Bok, *Lying: Moral Choice in Public and Private Life* (New York: Pantheon Books, 1974),
    pp. 220–41. Copyright © 1978 by Sissela Bok. Used by permission of Pantheon Books, a
    division of Random House, Inc.

95. "Standards of Competence", *Allen E. Buchanan and Dan W. Brock*
    Allen E. Buchanan and Dan W. Brock, *Deciding for Others: The Ethics of Surrogate Decision-
    Making* (Cambridge: Cambridge University Press, 1990), pp. 48–57. Copyright © 1990
    Cambridge University Press. Reproduced with the permission of the authors and publisher.

96. "Surrogate Decision Making for Incompetent Adults: An Ethical Frame-
    work", *Dan W. Brock*
    The Mount Sinai Journal of Medicine, Vol. 58, no. 5 (1991), pp. 388–92.

Introduction
Fritz Allhoff and Anand J. Vaidya

Introduction to Ethical Theory

Before beginning our discussion of *business ethics*, we might first wonder what *ethics* itself is. Presumably, there is some broader area of ethics, of which business ethics might be considered to be one aspect. Broadly speaking, ethics is the field of philosophy concerned with how we *ought* to act. While different philosophers might disagree as to what is the proper criterion of right action, they would nevertheless agree that the goal of their discipline is to provide such a criterion.

Technically, philosophers would divide ethics into three 'branches': meta-ethics, normative ethics, and applied ethics. Normative ethics is the branch concerned with the issues discussed in the preceding paragraph, which largely have to do with the notion of moral obligation. Meta-ethics is the most amorphous of the areas of ethics and includes topics in a wide range of issues: the metaphysics of morality, moral epistemology, the linguistic analysis of moral claims, the nature of moral motivation, etc. Applied ethics covers a number of different topics as well: business and professional ethics, biomedical ethics, environmental ethics, etc. In the first part of this introduction, we will focus on normative ethics given its relevance for our upcoming forays into business and professional ethics.

As we said above, different philosophers would disagree as to the proper criterion of right action. In these volumes, you will notice that many of the contributors presuppose disparate moral theories. Of course, the differing theories will affect the results that these writers derive, and much of the debate on specific issues (e.g. corporate social responsibility) derives from the different theories with which the authors begin. In this part of the introduction, we would like to discuss the two most prevalent theories that you will encounter in these volumes.[1] From the outset, you should think about which theory you find the most attractive since your allegiance to one will most likely dictate the stance that you will take on particular issues.

Utilitarianism

One of the most canonical of the moral theories is *utilitarianism*. This theory has a long historical tradition, which begins with the Epicureans of classical Greece (c. 300 B.C.E.), continues through the British empiricist David Hume (1711–1776), and receives its central modern formulations in Jeremy Bentham (1748–1832) and John Stuart Mill (1806–1873). The central thesis of utilitarianism is that actions are right if and only if they maximize total aggregate happiness. So, according to the utilitarian, when we are deliberating about how to act, we must choose the action that will bring the most happiness into the world. If, for example, we are trying to decide whether to show up to teach our classes or else stay at home and watch television, we would have to apply various utility forecasts to determine what to do. If we stayed at home, we might have fun watching television and our students might be moderately relieved that they did not have to sit through a lecture. If we went to class, we might have fun teaching philosophy, and our students might derive tremendous pleasure from expanding their horizons. Or else, they might find philosophy to be a miserable bore and be terribly unhappy that they have to endure it. Regardless, the idea is that the right action, attending the class or staying home, would be dictated by which action produced more happiness, and this determination would be affected by empirical considerations.

Because utilitarianism attempts to predicate right action upon empirical results, some of its adherents have maintained that it offers a 'scientific approach' to ethics. To figure out which actions are right and wrong, we would have to go out into the world and *measure* the amounts of happiness produced, and this empirical foundation gives utilitarian ethics a scientific basis. There are, of course, going to be methodological and epistemic hurdles (i.e., *how* to measure happiness and how to *know* what quantity of happiness would be produced) but, conceptually, it would still be an empirical matter.

Pushing further, we might look at the various elements that would be used to measure happiness. Bentham proposed seven elements of the so-called *hedonic calculus*: intensity, duration, certainty, propinquity, fecundity, purity, and extent. Let's take these in turn. All else equal, more *intense* pleasures are preferably to less intense pleasures. If watching a basketball game makes you really happy and watching a football game only makes you somewhat happy then, all else equal, you would be morally required to watch basketball. Again, all else equal, we must choose pleasures that have longer *duration*. If watching a television show only satiates you for an hour but an hour of studying philosophy could reward you for the rest of your life, then you must choose philosophy! Next is *certainty*: more certain pleasures are desirable to less certain pleasures. If you had a 10% chance of winning $50 or a 20% chance of winning $50, you should obviously opt for the latter. And note how certainty and intensity could simultaneously be facets of the same deliberation: would you choose a 10% chance of winning $20 or a 20% chance of winning $15? Why?

Another factor is *propinquity* (or nearness): we should prefer utilities that are temporally close to those that are temporally far. For example, imagine that you could receive $10 now or its equivalent in 2020. You should take the money now since you might not still be around in 2020, you might not need the money in 2020, etc. *Fecundity* holds that, all else equal, we should prefer pleasures that give rise to further pleasures over those that do not (or do so to a lesser degree). Exercising, for example, leads to better health, better self-confidence, better attractiveness, etc., and would therefore be comparatively fecund. Conversely, *purity* maintains that we should not choose pleasures that lead to pains. Drug use, for example, might be relatively pleasurable in the short term but leads to various problems (e.g. economic, social, health) in the long term and therefore suffers on considerations of purity. Lastly, the utilitarian would say that we have to invoke these above considerations for everyone who would be affected by actions; this is the element of *extent*. For example, if I were to make a decision between saving one drowning person or saving five drowning people then, all else equal and assuming these were lives of positive utility, I should save the five over the one.

So the idea behind utilitarianism is that we would apply this hedonic calculus to determine which, of the actions available to us, would maximize total aggregate happiness. An idea implicit in this one is that of *impartiality*: we add up the total happinesses of all people affected by any action, and none of those happinesses is weighted more than any others. This might be contrasted with partisan ethical theories, such as egoism, which might hold that the right action is the one that maximizes *my* happiness. On this view, my happiness would receive infinite weight (or, equivalently, other happinesses would receive zero weight). But utilitarianism thinks that all happiness is equally morally important, regardless of whose it is. For example, the utilitarian could not say that a mother should save *her* child as against someone else's since the weightings of the children should be equal. When Bentham and Mill were proposing the theory, this was taken to be a very progressive feature of it since, in Victorian England, the interests of the elite few were commonly taken to be more relevant than the interests of the many. Another consequence of the impartiality feature of utilitarianism is that the theory need not be anthrocentric: any sentient being capable of pleasure and pain would factor into the hedonic calculus. Those concerned with animal welfare, for example, often adopt utilitarianism as their normative theory since it directly affords moral status to any non-human animal capable of pleasure and pain.

This discussion has set out the central tenets of utilitarianism, but let us address one concern often expressed by those who first encounter the view: pragmatic applicability. Some people might say that this theory sounds all well and good but could be very skeptical about their ability to apply it in the real world. After all, how can we tell what utilities will be manifested by some action? Should we save the drowning person or not? S/he might be the one who would deliver the cure to cancer, or s/he might be the next Hitler. The utilitarian would hold that the right action (saving or not saving) would be predicated upon the answers to these questions, and these answers are certainly not available to the prospective moral agent. In responding to this objection, we might draw a distinction between a *decision procedure* and a *standard of right and wrong*. What utilitarianism provides us is a standard of right and wrong: actions are right if and only if they, out of the options available to the agent, maximize total aggregate happiness. This claim is logically distinct from a decision procedure which would tell us *which* actions maximize total aggregate happiness. If we think that the goal of moral philosophy is to provide a criterion of right and wrong, then it is irrelevant whether utilitarianism would suffer problems (e.g. epistemic) of application. The utilitarian might offer another decision procedure as the one that fallible humans should adopt, and these could include intuition, rules of thumb, heuristics, etc.

There are many objections to all ethical theories, and utilitarianism is no exception. Rather than catalog this litany of objections, I would like to elucidate one that will be most relevant to selections in these volumes: the notion of *rights*. Remember that, for the utilitarian, the right action is the one that maximizes total aggregate happiness. If, for example, happiness would be maximized by torturing or killing someone, then utilitarianism would require it. Some people would want to argue that we have rights against being tortured or killed, and that these rights are insensitive to considerations of utility. This view (often called deontology) will be discussed shortly, but one comment might be helpful. It is true that, for the utilitarian, rights would not have *primary* moral status since we would only ascribe to a system of rights (or, more cynically, 'rights') insofar as it contributed to happiness. In cases where happiness were maximized by violating those rights, utilitarianism would require us to do so. But Mill talks about rights, and he says that, in the vast majority of cases, protections of life, liberty, etc. will tend to promote happiness and, consequently, would be maintained under his theory. The critic could still complain about the derivative nature of those rights, but a utilitarian might (with some exceptions or in some particular cases) generate a similar system of rights as the deontologist.

Deontology

Alongside utilitarianism, deontology is one of the most dominant moral theories. Etymologically 'deontology' is the study of *rights* and *duties*: according to the deontologist primary moral consideration should be afforded to rights and duties instead of the utilitarian's happiness. The deontologist does not hold the (implausible) position that happiness is morally irrelevant, but s/he denies its *primacy* in moral reasoning. The deontologist could hold that, ceteris paribus, we should maximize happiness, though he would go on to say that we *cannot* aim at happiness if doing so requires rights violations. To take a simple example, imagine that someone asks you whether you like the birthday present she gave you, and further imagine that you do not. What should you do? An innocent lie might surely maximize happiness: the gift giver would then be pleased that the present was well-received and you, let us assume, would not be overly ridden with guilt (and perhaps even derive pleasure at contributing to another's happiness). So, according to the utilitarian, we might imagine that the morally required action is to lie. But the deontologist could disagree: he might argue that you have a *duty* not to lie and, furthermore, that the giver of the present has a correlative *right* not to be lied to. Thus, for the deontologist, you might be required to tell the truth and risk offending the gift-giver.

So we now understand that deontology is an ethical system consisting of rights and duties. But which rights? Which duties? It is not enough to merely assert that *some* rights and duties exist: we need to also know what they *are*. In answering these questions, we might turn to Immanuel Kant (1724–1804), one of the most famous of all deontologists. Kant's philosophy is very complicated, but we should be able to get through some of the main ideas without too much strife. According to Kant, all actions are guided by *maxims*. A maxim is a 'rule of action', and is of the form: In conditions C, I perform action A in order to achieve end E. So, for example, a maxim might be 'When I am thirsty, I drink water in order to satisfy my thirst'.

For Kant, a maxim must have all these elements. Every time we act, it is against some background conditions, and these are (or at least can be) morally relevant. For example, imagine that I am debating whether to eat a loaf of bread. This action might be contemplated against two sets of hypothetical background conditions. In the first, let us imagine that my consumption of the bread will lead to the starvation of someone else (and let us further imagine that my consumption of the bread is not necessary to allay my own starvation). In the second, let us imagine that my consumption of the loaf of bread is necessary to allay my own starvation and that nobody else would be adversely affected by the action. In both cases, the *act* is *exactly* the same: I eat the bread. What is different is the background conditions. And these make all the moral difference in the world: the consumption is impermissible in the former case and permissible (or perhaps even obligatory) in the latter. So the important lesson is to recognize that, whenever specifying your maxim, you must include the background conditions.

Relatedly, you must include the end at which your act aims. Again, consider two hypothetical maxims. In the first, imagine that, in some arbitrary conditions C, I lie to my mother-in-law *in order to* hurt her feelings (by, for example, telling her that I do not like a present that I in fact do). In the second, and in the same arbitrary conditions C, I lie to my mother-in-law *in order to* spare her feelings (by, for example, telling her that I do like a present that I in fact do not). Again, in both cases, the *act* itself is identical: I lie to my mother-in-law. And, by stipulation, the background conditions are the same. What is different is the *goal* of the action, and this is certainly morally relevant since the latter action more morally laudable than the first. (Remember, though, that *some* deontologists might hold that both are impermissible.)

So now that we know what a maxim *is*, we can look at Kant's ideas regarding which maxims are morally permissible. Kant's general strategy is going to be to offer a test that we will apply to individual maxims. Maxims that pass the test will be morally permissible and maxims that fail the test will be morally impermissible. (And, furthermore, maxims whose negations fail the test will be morally *required*.) This test is often referred to as the 'categorical imperative test' and is based upon Kant's notion of the categorical imperative.

Kant makes a distinction between what he calls hypothetical imperatives and categorical imperatives. Hypothetical imperatives tell an agent how to achieve some end that he finds desirable. For example, if we want to do well in school, then we ought to study; this maxim relates some antecedent desire that we have with a necessary means to that end. But what if we have no desire to do well in school? Then this hypothetical imperative would exert no force upon me. Turning to morality, Kant was worried about its governance by hypothetical imperatives. Why? Well, the maxims would go something like this 'If A wants to be moral, then A will φ' (where φ is some generic action required by morality). But what if A has no desire to be moral? Then this hypothetical imperative would be motivationally impotent against me. And this worried Kant: he did not think that the demands of morality should be only contingently applicable to agents who happened to have an interest in being moral. Rather, he thought that moral edicts should apply to *everyone*, regardless of their desires. Hence the categorical imperative. These imperatives bind everyone *categorically*, which is to say that they take no inputs (e.g. contingent desires) and apply universally. Categorical imperatives are therefore of the form 'Do φ' as opposed to 'If ψ, then do φ'.

Kant thinks that the categorical imperative is synonymous with the moral law, though he thinks that this moral law can be expressed in different formulations. He offers four formulations, though only two are commonly discussed. (It is worth noting that, since these are supposedly all formulations of the same moral law, they should be equivalent, though they certainly do not appear to be; this purported equivalence is an important issue in Kantian scholarship.) The first, the so-called 'Law Formulation' says 'act only on that maxim that you can simultaneously will to be universal law'. And the second, the so-called 'Humanity Formulation', says 'always treat humanity, whether yourself or others, as an end, and never as a means only'. While the humanity formulation deserves much discussion, we will concentrate on the law formulation because of easy applicability for the categorical imperative test.

So remember that the basic idea is that maxims which pass the test are permissible and maxims which fail the test are impermissible. This test, which makes use of the law formulation, has three steps. First, you must formulate a maxim. Secondly, you must universalize the maxim, which means that you apply it to all the moral agents of the universe. Finally, you search for 'a contradiction' (i.e. two statements that cannot simultaneously be true). If there is a contradiction, the maxim is impermissible and, if there is none, then it is permissible. Certainly this all sounds daunting, but let's consider elucidating examples. A fairly straightforward one is: 'When I want money, I rob a bank in order to acquire money'. Hopefully, this will come out impermissible. Since we have the maxim, we now universalize it: 'Whenever anyone wants money, s/he will rob a bank in order to acquire it'. Now we must try to find a contradiction. Think about what would happen if everyone who wanted money went around robbing banks. Most likely, one of two things would happen: people would succeed and banks would go bankrupt or else banks would tire of being robbed and enact impenetrable defenses. Either way, future robberies would fail. And now we can generate a contradiction. If banks are commonly robbed, then prospective robberies will undoubtedly fail. Therefore, nobody will end up robbing a bank. But remember that my maxim involved the element of *my* robbing a bank. However, if *nobody* can rob a bank, then certainly *I* cannot rob a bank: an entailment of the universalization of my maxim is inconsistent with the maxim itself. So we have located a contradiction, and the maxim is therefore impermissible. If the contradiction is between the maxim and an entailment of the universalization, we say that we have located a *contradiction of conception.* We ascribe this label because we cannot *conceive* of a world wherein the universalization of the maxim attains. For example, we cannot imagine a world wherein everyone who wants money robs a bank in order to get money for the aforementioned reasons.

We are almost finished with Kant, but for one more important idea. There are, unfortunately, types of contradictions other than contradictions of conception. Imagine another putative maxim: 'Whenever someone is drowning, I will fail to provide aid in order to not inconvenience myself'. Again, this should come out impermissible. So we universalize the maxim: 'Whenever someone is drowning, *nobody* provides aid in order to prevent inconvenience'. Any contradiction yet? Is this universalization conceivable? Yes, it is. So we have to press further in order to derive the contradiction. Next, we invoke the so-called 'standing intention' (i.e., an intention which we always have): 'I will all means necessary to achieve my ends'. Intuitively, this should make sense as we are rationally required to will all necessary means to our ends. For example, if I wanted to get married, and getting married required the finding of a potential spouse, then it would be irrational to say that, while I wanted to get married, I did not want to find a potential spouse. Now we can generate the necessary contradiction in the previous example. Imagine that we live in the (conceivable) world wherein nobody saves drowning people. Furthermore, imagine that *I* begin to drown and need saving. Whatever ends I might have, continued survival must be a necessary condition to their attainment (e.g. I cannot go fly a kite if I drown) – Kant famously argued against the permissibility of suicide – so I must will that *someone save me*; this is required by the standing intention. But one feature of the universalization of my maxim was that nobody was saving anyone! Hence, nobody would be saving me. Since, according to Kant, I am committed to all logical entailments of my universalization, we have the contradiction: I am simultaneously willing that nobody saves anyone and that somebody saves me. If the contradiction is located between an entailment of the universalization and an entailment of the standing intention, we say that we have located a *contradiction in will.* Finally, Kant argued that we have *perfect duties* to perform the negation of maxims which lead to contradictions in conception and that we have *imperfect duties* to perform maxims whose negations lead to contradictions in will. If there is a conflict between the two (can you create one?), perfect duties trump imperfect duties.

We have now come a long way through a lot of hard and abstract moral theory. In the chapters that follow, you will realize that most of the authors adopt either utilitarian or deontological approaches to ethics, and you will now hopefully understand the foundational differences among these views. When disagreements ensue, you should realize that the disagreements are as likely to have to do with the normative theories underlying the respective views as they are at some more applied level. Which theory do you find more compelling? Are you a deontologist or a utilitarian? Certainly your allegiance to one view over another will affect your stances on many of the issues discussed in these volumes.

Business Ethics and Professional Ethics and Objections

Now that we have considered what ethics is, what branches of ethics there are, and some of the most important normative theories still in use today it will be useful to consider some objections that are often offered against business and professional ethics. These objections are aimed at undermining the ethical project of both of these areas of applied ethics. In addition, these objections are not specific to these areas of applied ethics – they are often offered against any area of applied ethics.

First, I will say a bit about business and professional ethics. Business ethics is distinguished from professional ethics by the fact that professional ethics is specific to the established professions, such as medicine, law, and accounting. Business ethics is more general and pertains to issues dealing with business, such as employee rights, corporate obligation, advertising, and intellectual property. In some sense professional ethics, in so far as the professions are businesses, can be seen as a sub-field of business ethics; but the prevailing trend has been to keep them separate.

The criticisms that both of these applied fields face are the following:

- Business ethics is *useless* because individuals upon reaching the age at which they will enter the workforce already have ingrained habits and procedures for deciding what is the morally correct thing to do in a specific situation.
- Business ethics is *valueless* because it is *indeterminate.* Ethicists disagree over which normative theory is the correct normative theory, and since different normative theories give different answers to specific problems, business ethics is indeterminate.
- Business ethics is *beside the point* because for the most part we already know what is the morally correct thing to do, what we want is to figure out how to get people to *behave* morally; since business ethics focuses on what is the morally correct thing to do it is beside the point.

Each of these criticisms is in a sense naïve; however, exploring why they are wrong shows a lot about the nature moral psychology, moral theory, and moral reasoning.

The main reason why business ethics, and professional ethics in particular, is not *useless* is because people do not have *static* moral psychologies or personalities. In general, people do change the way in which they evaluate a moral problem. The explanation for this is quite clear. More often than not people undergo experiences that force them to change their moral beliefs, and when those moral beliefs change, how they subsequently evaluate a moral problem changes. In addition, in a world in which most us are uncertain about the future it is rational to attempt to gain the most accurate information when making a decision. One component of the information gathering process will be acquiring the best model for evaluating moral problems. Acquiring the best model will require that one changes whatever moral assumptions are in the model that do not maximally fit with other information available to the agent.

Moreover, it is just bad psychology to think that people cannot or would not change their behavior because their behavior has already been determined at the age at which they enter the work force.

The second criticism is a bit more astute. The criticism can be formulated as the following argument:

1. Business ethicists disagree over first principles.
2. If theorists in a field of inquiry disagree over first principles, then there are no determinate answers within that field.
3. If there are no determinate answers within a field, then the field of inquiry is valueless.
4. So, business ethics is without value.

The argument gets its force from what was discussed above in the sections on normative ethics. There are competing normative theories. And in many cases these normative theories give different answers to specific applied questions. As a result one can become frustrated with business ethics. The goal was to go to business ethics to find answers to specific problems, and instead one finds a host of inconsistent answers. This leads some to think that business ethics is valueless.

It is important to note from the beginning that this argument is thoroughly general. We could replace premise (1) with the claim that economists disagree over first principles, and arrive at the conclusion that economics is without value. And it is true that there are different schools of economic thought, and as a consequence there are different answers to specific questions depending on which school you consult. But we are less inclined to say that economics is without value.

The way to assuage the pressure of this argument is to argue that premise (3) is false. The reason why indeterminacy over first principles does not render a discipline valueless is because debates over first principles are themselves valuable. Their value lies in the fact that innovation is made possible through these debates, and clarity over first principles is often gained. Scientific revolutions serve as a great example of how debates over first principles lead to innovation. In addition, it false to assume that the indeterminacy over first principles means that disparate theories do not converge in the answers they give in certain cases.

The third criticism is that we already know what the morally right thing to do is in most situations, and thus the real issue is over how to get people to behave the right way. And since the real issue is over behavior we ought to consult psychology, rather than business and professional ethics.

There is a grain of truth to this criticism. Corporate culture plays a big role in how one behaves. If one's peers at work more or less are immoral in their behavior, one will be more prone – through peer pressure – to behave in an immoral fashion. So, the question is how to get people to behave morally, so that we have the appropriate corporate culture.

However, there are two misconceptions underlying this criticism. First, it is not true that we already know what is the morally correct thing to do in every situation. Genetic engineering would not be a hot topic if we already knew that it was morally permissible/impermissible. More to the point, as technology advances new ethical questions come with it. In fact some of the problems of the past, such as nuclear arms, have been caused by technology advancing far beyond our ethical reasoning. Ethics needs to stay at the cutting edge of technology. In addition, we don't want to answer novel ethical questions by just consulting what happened in the most similar case in the past. We want the novelty of the technology and the time in which it was developed to play a role in determining what is the ethically correct decision. So, in general it is not wise to assume that we already know what the ethically correct thing to do is in every situation.

Second, it is false to think that studying case studies and moral theories cannot change one's ethical outlook, or aid one in moral decision making. The whole point of the case study approach to business ethics is that by seeing how things went wrong in a well defined setting, which is not so uncommon, we can learn from our past mistakes. Case studies show us how people reasoned in the past, what they did, and what were the consequences; those are exactly the ingredients of what makes a person want to decide if they want to act in a similar way. Furthermore, learning to reason effectively about morality provides one with confidence about the moral decisions they are making. It turns out to be the case that we are most confident about the decisions we are making when we understand the reasons that go into them. So, since business ethics and professional ethics provide us with a spectrum of reasons, and theories, we can be assured that it is effective in having the capacity to motivate us to act appropriately.

The Central Debate in Business Ethics

The central debate in business ethics is over what moral obligations corporations have; often this topic is called corporate social responsibility (CSR). The reason why this is the central debate is because many of the other topics in business ethics relate in one way or another to what obligations corporations have.

On one side of the debate we have those that argue that the sole moral obligation of a corporation is to maximize the profit of its shareholders. This position was originally argued for by the Nobel Laureate economist Milton Friedman. On the other side, we have those that argue that corporations have a moral obligation that includes shareholders, but extends to stakeholders, individuals who have a vested interest in the corporation because of how they are affected. Stakeholders generally include distributors, employees, suppliers, and customers. Those that are of the stakeholder persuasion generally maintain that corporations have a wider net of responsibilities.

The general idea is that if corporations only have obligations to share-holders, then if it is to the advantage of the shareholders to close down a factory that has been in operation for as long as the company has been in operation, there is no moral consideration that holds the corporation back from making this decision. The mere fact that the community which is dependent on the factory will break down – due to the lack of jobs – does not present a moral problem for the corporation. Stakeholder theories of corporate social responsibility maintain that the detrimental effect to the community does count as a serious consideration that the corporation from a moral standpoint must attend to.

One novel wrinkle in this debate is whether or not the two theories are really distinct, and if so how to distinguish them. If it turns out to be the case that respecting the rights of groups other than the shareholders actually is more profitable than not respecting the interest of these groups the two theories would seem to prescribe the same things. One way of separating the two theories is by thinking of what the motivation is for the action. This approach is discussed by several authors who think about corporate social responsibility.

The Contents of the Series

The three volumes on business and professional ethics contain an extensive list of classic pieces as well new pieces in each field. We have broken down the three volumes so that each one represents a set of closely related ideas.

Volume 1: *Ethical Theory, Distributive Justice, Corporate Social Responsibility* was created for those interested in getting a firm foundation in both the central topic of business ethics as well as the background that goes into doing good business ethics research. Unit 1: *Ethical Theory and Business Ethics* introduces the dominant normative theories, such as deontology, utilitarianism, and virtue theory; as well as some non-classical sources of business thinking, such as Sun Tzu's *Art of War*. The point of this section is to introduce to the reader the background ethical theories that are necessary for doing good business ethics. Unit 2: *Distributive Justice* adds to the background information that one needs for doing business ethics. Though ethical theory is central to good research in business ethics, distributive justice play a prominent role because its central issue is what constitutes a just distribution of goods. The section contains both classical sources, such as Hobbes' *Leviathan* and excerpts from Rawls' *A Theory of Justice*; as well as contemporary discussions of intellectual property. Unit 3: *Corporate Social Responsibility* moves on to the central debate in business ethics. The section contains the classic articles by Friedman and Freeman, as well as more contemporary discussions by Sen. In addition, this section contains articles on topics such as sweatshops and environmental responsibility.

This volume not only provides the background for business ethics as well as good coverage of the central debate, but also the tools for understanding a deeper level topics covered in Volumes 2 and 3.

Volume 2: *Fairness and Justice in the Workplace* was created for those interested in all the ways in which fairness and justice pervade the business world. Unit 1: *Rights and Obligations of Employers and Employees* canvasses all the central issues that arise between employers and employees, such as: employment at will, drug testing, privacy, work/life balance, and safety. In addition, the popular topic of whistle blowing has been included in this area. Unit 2: *Justice and Fair Practice* also includes topics that relate to the relation between employees and employers, such as affirmative action and sexual harassment, but it also includes more general business related issues such as the permissibility of bluffing in business negotiations.

The articles in this volume will helpful to those wanting to do research in specific areas of business ethics, as well as topics that stretch out in general ethical theory. For example, though affirmative action and sexual harassment are specific topics in business ethics they are also very important general topics in ethical theory. In addition, there will be various links between themes in articles from this volume to the central debate, corporate social responsibility, discussed in Volume 1.

Volume 3: *Professional Ethics* was created for those interested in doing research on any of the following professions: law, medicine, accounting, and journalism. The section on accounting is *new*, most other anthologies do not offer it. It was primarily introduced because of the recent growth in interest in this field due to the accounting scandals of the 2002. However, it also contains articles of general interest on the ethics of insider trading. The section on legal ethics and medical ethics shares in common the topic of confidentiality, attorney–client and doctor–patient, but each topic in each section is discussed in its own particular way. The volume will provide non-researchers also with a good forum to understand some of the more general ethical issues that arise in the profession they are interested in. So, on the one hand, while the articles are good for those interested in research on the topics, the articles are not so abstract that a person looking for a good understanding of ethical issues in, say journalism, would be lost.

1 While we will only discuss utilitarianism and deontology, it should be noted that *virtue ethics* completes the standard triumvirate of moral theories. We will omit it here not because it is unimportant, but rather because hardly any of the articles in these volumes adopts a virtue-theoretic stance toward business or professional ethics. We expect to see a greater industry in these approaches in upcoming research but, for now, virtue theory has not made substantial contributions to the topics of these volumes.

To Our Parents

1

Excerpts from "Business Ethics: Widening the Lens"

Clarence C. Walton

Whe the field of business ethics is discussed, critics call it soft and muddled–even pale in the shadow-gray world it so often depicts. What critics overlook, however, is the ability of moral philosophers to help them *think through* critically important value issues. A mode of thinking that is better than other forms of moral analysis is what ethicists seek to promote. From its critics, however, ethicians hear fusillades that sound something like this: Business ethics is *useless, irrelevant, dangerous,* and *confused.* By such standards, business ethics should never have been conceived. If these descriptives were accurate, moral philosophers would find their feet in ankle-high canons of scholarship. It is well, therefore, first to address each of the charges before considering the main task, namely, learning: what other social sciences can offer to business ethicists.

I. The State of Business Ethics

A. The "Useless" Argument

Influential people like Wall Street guru Felix Rohaytn and MIT Dean Lester Thurow have stated publicly that teaching business ethics to adults makes little sense: People learn values at their mother's knee, or they never learn them. It is a comforting thought–without substance. In the light of so many corporate aberrations, parents either do not teach or cannot teach–or many of their offspring are abysmal learners. The fact is that all life is a moral journey. New experiences provide new challenges, and new responses require new insights. To say, therefore, that the moral life is lived without moral learning runs counter to reality. There is, furthermore, empirical evidence from psychologists that shows that roughly between ages 18 and 30 significant advances are made in

Source: *Enriching Business Ethics* (New York and London: Plenum Press, 1990).

moral understanding.[1] So it is time to dismiss the "useless" argument as useless.

B. The "Irrelevant" Argument

No one conversant with the literature on business ethics can fail to be impressed by the recurrent use of an argument made over 20 years ago in the pages of the *Harvard Business Review*.[2] The proposition was advanced by Albert Z. Carr who wrote that business, like poker, had its own rules. The trick is to learn the rules, obey the rules, and pledge total fealty to the organization. Moral codes for one's personal life were salutary but "in their office lives managers cease to be private citizens; they become game players who must be guided by a somewhat different set of ethical standards."[3] It should be noted that Carr was more circumspect than many of his followers who came to believe that the development of other rules for either market operations or for business careers might well produce ethical schizophrenics.

Here again, critics overlook an important point. Individuals do not automatically shed their moral codes the moment they enter office doors. If no effort is made to sharpen moral insights, the result is a business world peopled by moral eunuchs where a Gresham's Law of morality develops: Bad ethics drive out good ethics. The relevance of honesty, truth, and fairness to the efficient operation of the market system (and to organizations operating within it) is demonstrably true. To conclude in this fashion is not to say that there are no rules of the game in business. It is to say that without moral rules the game turns nasty.

A variant of the "irrelevant" theme has been made by economist Milton Friedman who argues that business ethics provides two criteria– and two only: (1) use resources efficiently and (2) obey the law.[4] By doing so, all other blessings will come. But efficiency and equity do collide, and laws can be ineffective or poorly administered. It is lawful to peddle pornography. It is legal to pay minimum wages to the nonunionized. It is legal to lead a takeover assault–even when the takeover artist has absolutely no interest in promoting stockholder interests. It is legal to engage in leveraged buyouts by management when the game strategy is solely to preserve the boss's job. The litany goes on. What is lawful can be unethical.

C. The "Dangerous" Argument

Many who subscribe to high levels of morality for business are nonetheless skeptical of business ethicists. They fear that philosophers are less interested in education and more in indoctrination. Business deans have been sensitive to this charge, often pointing out that courses in business ethics first flourished in church-related institutions. At this point an historical footnote is worth recalling. Twenty-five years ago (when the Carnegie and Ford reports on reforming the business curricula appeared), quality faculties faced the issue of business ethics and its role in the professional curriculum. What the Columbia business faculty did was symptomatic of those times: It discussed and debated, created task forces, and heard detailed reports–but it circled the problem quite circumspectly. The nearest the faculty came to business ethics was its pioneering program, Conceptual Foundations of Business. A fascinating effort, the course dealt with the origins of private property and contract, the evolution of unions and corporations, and so on. But the course was overwhelmingly descriptive. Its analytical content dealt overwhelmingly with the need for economic efficiency. Questions of equity came slowly, and often indirectly.

Because senior executives generally favored a substantial component of ethics in the business curriculum, it appears in retrospect that deans and faculties missed the boat. And the one on which they are now asked to embark worries some of them. Is the vessel of ethics to be called the *Crusader*? What port will it visit? How much will the sailing cost?

D. The "Confused" Argument

The most telling criticism of business ethicists is that they themselves neither agree on the kind of moral reasoning that is most logical nor on the criteria most relevant for specific acts or policies. Raised here is the specter of endless quibblings between the deontologists who believe with Kant that morality consists in doing one's duty according to principles established *a priori* by the mind[5] and the utilitarians who subscribe to John Stuart Mill's maxim that ethics consists of doing things that promote the greatest good of the greatest numbers.[6]

The confusion has been exacerbated by the popularity of Cambridge Professor G. E. Moore who, in 1903, startled his contemporaries by flatly denying that good was definable: "goodness, like yellowness, is a subjective assessment [resting] on a form of perception, not on inference."[7] Moore would have us believe that practical moral principles are inaccessible to the mind and that seeking to establish them has little relevance to actual conduct. The debates continue. Stephen Toulmin recently assured us that because the truth or falsity of moral judgment can be determined by the accurate possession of facts, Moore is, therefore, wrong. One can make valid inferences that lead to valid moral judgments.[8] Whereas Toulmin concentrated on specifics, another respected philosopher, R. M. Hare, stressed universals–a command or imperative reached syllogistically on the basis of inductive analysis.

> All men are mortal
> Socrates was a man
> Socrates was mortal[9]

Hare feels that ethics has two essential features: It is prescriptive (a person should do so-and-so), and it has universality (all are obliged to follow a common norm). In sum: There is some truth in the charge that business moralists have much to do to put their house in order. But to cease seeing value in ethical inquiry is like ceasing to see value in legal or economic inquiry; Learned judges reverse other learned judges; respected economists critique other respected economists–and so on. The utility of ethical inquiry, like the value of other forms of critical investigation, is found in the way individuals learn the art of moral reasoning, an art demanding the same levels of analytical sophistication that are found in other of the nonphysical sciences.[10]

II. The Art of Moral Reasoning

What, then, are managers and students to make of all this? Are moral judgments the results of gut reactions? Is one person's morality as good as another's? Pleasant though an affirmative answer may be (it removes from our mental shoulders the heavy freight of hard thinking), its results are a form of moral relativism that threaten an organization's success and a government's effectiveness. Carried to extremes, moral relativism negates a basic purpose of university education, namely stimulation of the student's reasoning faculties on all aspects of reality.[11]

So managers and managed, as well as pupils and pedagogues who enter the moral thicket, sense that a word made famous by Rene Descartes is the name of the game: *cogito,* "I think." Critical thinking about moral issues releases people from the bondage of dogmas and ideologies. Individuals so involved may seek resources for their business philosophies in diverse places– Puritanism or Confuciousism, Judaism or Islamism, Catholicism or Protestant- ism, Kantianism or Benthamism.[12] The attempt is to reconcile individual and societal needs–what philosophers call the *One* and the *Many.* So a learner may find a inspiration in a single major philosopher–Aquinas or Anselm, Bentham or Kant; on the other hand, mentoring may come from many–Aquinas and Anselm, Bentham and Kant. Sorting out the best from each may be the best we can do. Whether the approach is toward synthesis or sorting, it demands the cogito element.

A. The "Sidgwick Circle"

An example of the *cogito* effort can be found in Henry Sidgwick, a late nineteenth-century English philosopher whose great contribution to managers and students was a clear description of his own intellectual odyssey.[13] It was a struggle that moved from conviction to confusion and back again to conviction. Sidgwick was first attracted to the Intuitionists, a badly split group heavily influenced by Kant, who claimed that through the union of understanding and sense-acquired knowledge one could discover canons of morality.[14] Finding Intuitionism quite unsatisfactory (they were hopelessly loose in their definitions and axioms, said Sidgwick), he became a Utilitarian because Bentham and Mill struck him as having made a good case for the argument that an act was good when it promoted the greatest good of the greatest number. He then began to build his own logic for supporting Utilitarianism, but construction was halted when Sidgwick discovered flaws in Bentham's and Mill's reasoning. One that particularly upset him was the ambiguous meaning they attached to *happiness,* a key concept in their vocabulary. So Sidgwick retraced his steps to intuition via Aristotle's theory of commonsense morality (veracity and good faith are the authentic ethics) and Kant's principle of justice.[15] By combining the two he constructed Utilitarianism on different principles: "I was a Utilitarian again, but on an Intuitional basis...and I could find no real opposition between the two."[16]

Divorced from jargon, Sidgwick's reasoning goes something like this: A duty ethic of Kant (do no harm) is a good place to begin. However, because harm is the consequence of an action, concern for consequences cannot be dismissed. What consequences are, therefore, to be sought? Bentham, speaking for the Utilitarians, has a quick answer: the greatest good of the greatest number. So far, so good. But consequences of what sort, asks the increasingly frustrated inquirer? *Pleasure* is the utilitarians' reply. But problems persist: is it not possible that one person's pleasure is another's pain? Is it not possible to contribute the greatest good of the greatest number while harming a minority, especially a helpless minority? Finally, is it possible to be sure that actions intended to serve the greatest number are what the greatest number will deem to be in their best interests at some future date?

Uncertain answers to one or all questions begin to dampen enthusiasm for total acceptance of Bentham's argument. So back to Kant, aware that you have already found his ethic deficient. Nevertheless, his do-no-harm ethic involves not simply action and result: It also involves the motive that precedes the act, not simply the consequence that follows the act. Motive is important. Emerging is a possible combination of criteria from Kant and Bentham, a Kan-Ben ethic that says: Will no harm and do no harm but, in addition to avoiding harm, do things that help the large majority of the community. Willing no harm eliminates casual hurting any minority. Willing a "good" means serving others effectively. What Kan-Ben ethics stresses are the rights of others. The I-Thou maxims must remain secure. Sidgwick's journey may be repeated by those who seek to sharpen their modes of moral thinking. It is likely that "cogito" managers and students will run full circle before breaking out to develop their own moral logic. In the so-called real world, they know that recipe answers to different moral questions are hard to come by. They also know that answers have to be made. In the response process, comfort comes from the fact that some logical defenses are more trustworthy than others, but they have to be discovered, ironically enough, in what are often called "self-evident" truths.[17]

B. Closing the Circle

To end with analogy: Ethical reasoning is like a tourist taking the Circle Line river tour around New York. Schedules and piers are published, and after a leisurely 2-hour cruise visitors return to the same dock. But they are not exactly the same people. Different perspectives of the skyline have resulted in different perceptions of the metropolis. The urban image becomes more complex–and more exciting. Perspective sharpens perception. Consider, for example, the story told by A. A. Achenbaum (then a senior vice president and director of marketing services at the J. Walter Thompson advertising agency) who described his experience at a meeting on general semantics and information flow.

> At that meeting, a group of twenty executives were told to sit in a circle. The group leader asked us to describe an apple, and passed one to the first person he came to. The obvious answer of the first person was to say that it was red. The next–following the color lead–said it was also yellow; another said it had green in it; the next said it was mostly red.
>
> There then followed a whole series of descriptions on its shape (some saying it couldn't be measured) until someone remarked that we were only talking about the outside. How about cutting it in half and describing the inside? Once more, someone mentioned its color and said it was white; the next person said it had pits which were brown and black. This was followed by statements that it had a peel, it felt moist, it was cold, it contained water, it was pulpy. And then someone realized that the apple's color had changed. In the half hour we handled that poor apple it turned somewhat brown and a bit grey on the inside. The dynamics of this began to play a rote in the description. Now we noticed that it was softer than before, it lost its stem, etc. It was well over an hour, after hundreds and hundreds of descriptions–this was truly a creative group, none of whom ever wrote a piece of copy to my knowledge–and not one thought of tasting the apple, or trying to describe its taste, or how it could be used or eaten.
>
> But once that subject was brought up, another plethora of descriptions came forth until the question of nutrition was raised. And off we went on another track. The exercise, I must tell you, continued for two hours. In that time, over four thousand words or phrases were used to describe the apple, or trying to describe its taste, or how it could be used or eaten.
>
> My point (and the point of the exercise in perception) is quite simple. Any tangible item has an almost infinite number of descriptions, and to commu-nicate ...all of them is virtually impossible.[18]

If difficulties mark efforts to describe a small fruit, one can imagine what difficulties attend the search for descriptions of such intangibles as truth and beauty, right and wrong, responsibilities and rights, intuitions and judgments. Like the observers of the apple and the excursionists on the Hudson tour, perceptions change with perspectives. A widened lens helps make a wiser moralist and all of us, after all, are moralists who need large perspectives.

III. Perspectives From Religion

Unlike many European countries whose governments had formal ties to particular churches, Americans subscribe to a separation-of-church-and-state doctrine. With their utilitarian bent, however, the people–or at least their leaders–see religion as a stabilizing force in society's need for a certain moral seriousness. When Americans differ on points of doctrine they fall back on a "civil" religion to hold them together in a moral consensus. The civil religion rests on the people's belief in three things: (1) belief in a God-Creator, (2) belief in themselves as a "chosen people," and (3) belief in public schools as the primary instrument for socializing their children.[19] Because traditional churches are challenged by the civil religion, a question arises: Are they really relevant to today's world? This very question merits a response.

A. Jewish Traditions

So accustomed are American ears to hearing that Western civilization has been shaped by Judaic-Christian beliefs we neglect to ask what father Abraham, lawgiver Moses, and Jesus the Christ really mean to our ways of thinking and behaving. Take, as a first instance, our Jewish ethical traditions: What are they? What do they signify? Not much to many Jews.

UNIT ONE
ETHICAL THEORY AND BUSINESS ETHICS

2

Excerpts from "The Parable of the Sadhu"

Bowen H. McCoy

T his parable is based on the true experience of the author, Bowen McCoy, a senior executive from Morgan Stanley who decided that he needed a sabbatical from the hectic life he had created. His answer was an extended trek through the Himalayas. The goal of this trek was to reach Muklinath, an ancient holy village on the other side of an 18,000-foot ice-covered pass. The parable offers McCoy's reflections upon his return from the experience.

Last year, as the first participant in the new six-month sabbatical program that Morgan Stanley has adopted, I enjoyed a rare opportunity to collect my thoughts as well as do some traveling. I spent the first three months in Nepal, walking 600 miles through 200 villages in the Himalayas and climbing some 120,000 vertical feet. On the trip my sole Western companion was an anthropologist who shed light on the cultural patterns of the villages we passed through.

During the Nepal hike, something occurred that has had a powerful impact on my thinking about corporate ethics. Although some might argue that the experience has no relevance to business, it was a situation in which a basic ethical dilemma suddenly intruded into the lives of a group of individuals. How the group responded I think holds a lesson for all organizations no matter how defined.

The Sadhu

The Nepal experience was more rugged and adventuresome than I had anticipated. Most commercial treks last two or three weeks and cover a quarter of the distance we traveled.

My friend Stephen, the anthropologist, and I were halfway through the 60-

Source: *Harvard Business Review*, September/October, 1983, pp 182–7.

day Himalayan part of the trip when we reached the high point, an 18,000-foot pass over a crest that we'd have to traverse to reach the village of Muklinath, an ancient holy place for pilgrims.

Six years earlier I had suffered pulmonary edema, an acute form of altitude sickness, at 16,500 feet in the vicinity of Everest base camp, so we were understandably concerned about what would happen at 18,000 feet. Moreover, the Himalayas were having their wettest spring in 20 years; hip-deep powder and ice had already driven us off one ridge. If we failed to cross the pass, I feared that the last half of our "once in a lifetime" trip would be ruined.

The night before we would try the pass, we camped at a hut at 14,500 feet. In the photos taken at that camp, my face appears wan. The last village we'd passed through was a sturdy two-day walk below us, and I was tired.

During the late afternoon, four backpackers from New Zealand joined us, and we spent most of the night awake, anticipating the climb. Below we could see the fires of two other parties, which turned out to be two Swiss couples and a Japanese hiking club.

To get over the steep part of the climb before the sun melted the steps cut in the ice, we departed at 3:30 a.m. The New Zealanders left first, followed by Stephen and myself, our porters and Sherpas, and then the Swiss. The Japanese lingered in their camp. The sky was clear, and we were confident that no spring storm would erupt that day to close the pass.

At 15,500 feet, it looked to me as if Stephen were shuffling and staggering a bit, which are symptoms of altitude sickness. (The initial stage of altitude sickness brings a headache and nausea. As the condition worsens, a climber may encounter difficult breathing, disorientation, aphasia, and paralysis.) I felt strong, my adrenaline was flowing, but I was very concerned about my ultimate ability to get across. A couple of our porters were also suffering from the height, and Pasang, our Sherpa sirdar (leader), was worried.

Just after daybreak, while we rested at 15,500 feet, one of the New Zealanders, who had gone ahead, came staggering down toward us with a body slung across his shoulders. He dumped the almost naked, barefoot body of an Indian holy man—a sadhu—at my feet. He had found the pilgrim lying on the ice, shivering and suffering from hypothermia. I cradled the sadhu's head and laid him out on the rocks. The New Zealander was angry. He wanted to get across the pass before the bright sun melted the snow. He said, "Look, I've done what I can. You have porters and Sherpa guides. You care for him. We're going on!" He turned and went back up the mountain to join his friends.

I took a carotid pulse and found that the sadhu was still alive. We figured he had probably visited the holy shrines at Muklinath and was on his way home. It was fruitless to question why he had chosen this desperately high route instead of the safe, heavily traveled caravan route through the Kali Gandaki gorge. Or why he was almost naked and with no shoes, or how long he had been lying in the pass. The answers weren't going to solve our problem.

Stephen and the four Swiss began stripping off outer clothing and opening their packs. The sadhu was soon clothed from head to foot. He was not able to walk, but he was very much alive. I looked down the mountain and spotted below the Japanese climbers marching up with a horse.

Without a great deal of thought, I told Stephen and Pasang that I was concerned about withstanding the heights to come and wanted to get over the pass. I took off after several of our porters who had gone ahead.

On the steep part of the ascent where, if the ice steps had given way, I would have slid down about 3,000 feet, I felt vertigo. I stopped for a breather, allowing the Swiss to catch up with me. I inquired about the sadhu and Stephen. They said that the sadhu was fine and that Stephen was just behind. I set off again for the summit.

Stephen arrived at the summit an hour after I did. Still exhilarated by victory, I ran down the snow slope to congratulate him. He was suffering from altitude sickness, walking 15 steps, then stopping, walking 15 steps, then stopping, Pasang accompanied him all the way up. When I reached them, Stephen glared at me and said: "How do you feel about contributing to the death of a fellow man?" I did not fully comprehend what he meant.

"Is the sadhu dead?" I inquired.

"No," replied Stephen, "but he surely will be!"

After I had gone, and the Swiss had departed not long after, Stephen had remained with the sadhu. When the Japanese had arrived, Stephen had asked to use their horse to transport the sadhu down to the hut. They had refused. He had then asked Pasang to have a group of our porters carry the sadhu. Pasang had resisted the idea, saying that the porters would have to exert all their energy to get themselves over the pass. He had thought they could not carry a man down 1,000 feet to the hut, reclimb the slope, and get across safely before the snow melted. Pasang had pressed Stephen not to delay any longer.

The Sherpas had carried the sadhu down to a rock in the sun at about 15,000 feet and had pointed out the hut another 500 feet below. The Japanese had given him food and drink. When they had last seen him he was listlessly throwing rocks at the Japanese party's dog, which had frightened him.

We do not know if the sadhu lived or died.

For many of the following days and evenings Stephen and I discussed and debated our behavior toward the sadhu. Stephen is a committed Quaker with deep moral vision. He said, "I feel that what happened with the sadhu is a good example of the breakdown between the individual ethic and the corporate ethic. No one person was willing to assume ultimate responsibility for the sadhu. Each was willing to do his bit just so long as it was not too inconvenient. When it got to be a bother, everyone just passed the buck to someone else and took off. Jesus was relevant to a more individualistic stage of society, but how do we interpret his teaching today in a world filled with large, impersonal organizations and groups?"

I defended the larger group, saying, "Look, we all cared. We all stopped and gave aid and comfort. Everyone did his bit. The New Zealander carried him down below the snow line. I took his pulse and suggested we treat him for hypothermia. You and the Swiss gave him clothing and got him warmed up. The Japanese gave him food and water. The Sherpas carried him down to the sun and pointed out the easy trail toward the hut. He was well enough to throw rocks at a dog. What more could we do?"

"You have just described the typical affluent Westerner's response to a problem. Throwing money—in this case food and sweaters—at it, but not solving the fundamentals!" Stephen retorted.

"What would satisfy you?" I said. "Here we are, a group of New Zealanders, Swiss, Americans, and Japanese who have never met before and who are at the apex of one of the most powerful experiences of our lives. Some years the pass is so bad no one gets over it. What right does an almost naked pilgrim who chooses the wrong trail have to disrupt our lives? Even the Sherpas had no interest in risking the trip to help him beyond a certain point."

Stephen calmly rebutted, "I wonder what the Sherpas would have done if the sadhu had been a well-dressed Nepali, or what the Japanese would have done if the sadhu had been a well-dressed Asian, or what you would have done, Buzz, if the sadhu had been a well-dressed Western woman?"

"Where, in your opinion," I asked instead, "is the limit of our responsibility in a situation like this? We had our own well-being to worry about. Our Sherpa guides were unwilling to jeopardize us or the porters for the sadhu. No one else on the mountain was willing to commit himself beyond certain self-imposed limits." Stephen said, "As individual Christians or people with a Western ethical tradition, we can fulfill our obligations in such a situation only if (1) the sadhu dies in our care, (2) the sadhu demonstrates to us that he could undertake the two-day walk down to the village, or (3) we carry the sadhu for two days down to the village and convince someone there to care for him."

"Leaving the sadhu in the sun with food and clothing, while he demonstrated hand-eye coordination by throwing a rock at a dog, comes close to fulfilling items one and two," I answered. "And it wouldn't have made sense to take him to the village where the people appeared to be far less caring than the Sherpas, so the third condition is impractical. Are you really saying that, no matter what the implications, we should, at the drop of a hat, have changed our entire plan?"

The Individual vs. The Group Ethic

Despite my arguments, I felt and continue to feel guilt about the sadhu. I had literally walked through a classic moral dilemma without fully thinking through the consequences. My excuses for my actions include a high adrenaline flow, a superordinate goal, and a once-in-a-lifetime opportunity—factors in the usual corporate situation, especially when one is under stress.

Real moral dilemmas are ambiguous, and many of us hike right through them, unaware that they exist. When, usually after the fact, someone makes an issue of them, we tend to resent his or her bringing it up. Often, when the full import of what we have done (or not done) falls on us, we dig into a defensive position from which it is very difficult to emerge. In rare circumstances we may contemplate what we have done from inside a prison.

Had we mountaineers been free of physical and mental stress caused by the effort and the high altitude, we might have treated the sadhu differently. Yet isn't stress the real test of personal and corporate values? The instant decisions executives make under pressure reveal the most about personal and corporate character.

Among the many questions that occur to me when pondering my experience are: What are the practical limits of moral imagination and vision? Is there a collective or institutional ethic beyond the ethics of the individual? At what level of effort or commitment can one discharge one's ethical responsibilities?

Not every ethical dilemma has a right solution. Reasonable people often disagree; otherwise there would be no dilemma. In a business context, however, it is essential that managers agree on a process for dealing with dilemmas.

The sadhu experience offers an interesting parallel to business situations. An immediate response was mandatory. Failure to act was a decision in itself. Up on the mountain we could not resign and submit our résumés to a headhunter. In contrast to philosophy, business involves action and imple-mentation—getting things done. Managers must come up with answers to problems based on what they see and what they allow to influence their decision-making processes. On the mountain, none of us but Stephen realized the true dimensions of the situation we were facing.

One of our problems was that as a group we had no process for developing a consensus. We had no sense of purpose or plan. The difficulties of dealing with the sadhu were so complex that no one person could handle it. Because it did not have a set of preconditions that could guide its action to an acceptable resolution, the group reacted instinctively as individuals. The cross-cultural nature of the group added a further layer of complexity. We had no leader with whom we could all identify and in whose purpose we believed. Only Stephen was willing to take charge, but he could not gain adequate support to care for the sadhu.

Some organizations do have a value system that transcends the personal values of the managers. Such values, which go beyond profitability, are usually revealed when the organization is under stress. People throughout the organization generally accept its values, which, because they are not presented as a rigid list of commandments, may be somewhat ambiguous. The stories people tell, rather than printed materials, transmit these conceptions of what is proper behavior.

For 20 years I have been exposed at senior levels to a variety of corporations and organizations. It is amazing how quickly an outsider can sense the tone and style of an organization and the degree of tolerated openness and freedom to challenge management.

Organizations that do not have a heritage of mutually accepted, shared values, tend to become unhinged during stress, with each individual bailing out for himself. In the great takeover battles we have witnessed during past years, companies that had strong cultures drew the wagons around them and fought it out, while other companies saw executives, supported by their golden parachutes, bail out of the struggles.

Because corporations and their members are interdependent, for the corporation to be strong the members need to share a preconceived notion of what is correct behavior, a "business ethic," and think of it as a positive force, not a constraint.

As an investment banker I am continually warned by well-meaning lawyers, clients, and associates to be wary of conflicts of interest. Yet if I were to run away from every difficult situation, I wouldn't be an effective investment banker. I have to feel my way through conflicts. An effective manager can't run from risk either; he or she has to confront and deal with risk. To feel "safe" in doing this, managers need the guidelines of an agreed-on process and set of values within the organization.

After my three months in Nepal, I spent three months as an executive-in-residence at both Stanford Business School and the Center for Ethics and Social Policy at the Graduate Theological Union at Berkeley. These six months away from my job gave me time to assimilate 20 years of business experience. My thoughts turned often to the meaning of the leadership role in any large organization. Students at the seminary thought of themselves as antibusiness. But when I questioned them they agreed that they distrusted all large organizations, including the church. They perceived all large organizations as impersonal and opposed to individual values and needs. Yet we all know of organizations where people's values and beliefs are respected and their expressions encouraged. What makes the difference? Can we identify the difference and, as a result, manage more effectively?

The word "ethics" turns off many and confuses more. Yet the notions of shared values and an agreed-on process for dealing with adversity and change–what many people mean when they talk about corporate culture–seem to be at the heart of the ethical issue. People who are in touch with their own core beliefs and the beliefs of others and are sustained by them can be more comfortable living on the cutting edge. At times, taking a tough line or decisive stand in a muddle of ambiguity is the only ethical thing to do. If a manager is indecisive and spends time trying to figure out the "good" thing to do, the enterprise may be lost.

Business ethics, then, has to do with the authenticity and integrity of the enterprise. To be ethical is to follow the business as well as the cultural goals of the corporation, its owners, its employees, and its customers. Those who cannot serve the corporate vision are not authentic business people and, therefore, are not ethical in the business sense.

At this stage of my own business experience I have a strong interest in organizational behavior. Sociologists are keenly studying what they call corporate stories, legends, and heroes as a way organizations have of transmitting the value system. Corporations such as Arco have even hired consultants to perform an audit of their corporate culture. In a company, the leader is the person who understands, interprets, and manages the corporate value system. Effective managers are then action-oriented people who resolve conflict, are tolerant of ambiguity, stress, and change, and have a strong sense of purpose for themselves and their organizations.

If all this is true, I wonder about the role of the professional manager who moves from company to company. How can he or she quickly absorb the values and culture of different organizations? Or is there, indeed, an art of management that is totally transportable? Assuming such fungible managers do exist, is it proper for them to manipulate the values of others?

What would have happened had Stephen and I carried the sadhu for two days back to the village and become involved with the villagers in his care? In four trips to Nepal my most interesting experiences occurred in 1975 when I lived in a Sherpa home in the Khumbu for five days recovering from altitude sickness. The high point of Stephen's trip was an invitation to participate in a family funeral ceremony in Manang. Neither experience had to do with climbing the high passes of the Himalayas. Why were we so reluctant to try the lower path, the ambiguous trail? Perhaps because we did not have a leader who could reveal the greater purpose of the trip to us.

Why didn't Stephen with his moral vision opt to take the sadhu under his personal care? The answer is because, in part, Stephen was hard-stressed physically himself, and because, in part, without some support system that involved our involuntary and episodic community on the mountain, it was beyond his individual capacity to do so.

I see the current interest in corporate culture and corporate value systems as a positive response to Stephen's pessimism about the decline of the role in the individual in large organizations. Individuals who operate from a thoughtful set of personal values provide the foundation for a corporate culture. A corporate tradition that encourages freedom of inquiry, supports personal values, and reinforces a focused sense of direction can fulfill the need for individuality along with the prosperity and success of the group. Without such corporate support, the individual is lost.

That is the lesson of the sadhu. In a complex corporate situation, the individual requires and deserves the support of the group. If people cannot find such support from their organization, they don't know how to act. If such support is forthcoming, a person has a stake in the success of the group, and can add much to the process of establishing and maintaining a corporate culture. It is management's challenge to be sensitive to individual needs, to shape them, and to direct and focus them for the benefit of the group as a whole.

For each of us the sadhu lives. Should we stop what we are doing and comfort him; or should we keep trudging up toward the high pass? Should I pause to help the derelict I pass on the street each night as I walk to the Yale Club en route to Grand Central Station? Am I his brother? What is the nature of our responsibility if we consider ourselves to be ethical persons? Perhaps it is to change the values of the group so that it can, with all its resources, take the other road.

3

The *Rashomon* Effect

Patricia Werhane

T he abstract of this article offers background to the piece. Consider how perspective alters judgment. Can you think of times when your perspective may have altered your judgment? What does this say of our justice system? What does it say of our information system as a whole? Do you obtain most of your news from (and therefore base your judgments on) television news shows? the newspaper? How might you ensure that your judgment is based on the most broad and unbiased perspectives?

The Academy Award winning 1960s Japanese movie *Rashomon* depicts an incident involving an outlaw, a rape or seduction of a woman, and a murder or suicide of her husband told from four different perspectives; that of the outlaw, the woman, the husband, and a passerby. The four narratives agree that the outlaw came upon the woman and her husband, the outlaw tied up the husband, sex took place between the woman and the outlaw in front of the bound husband, and the husband was found dead. How these events occurred and who killed the husband (or whether he killed himself) differs with each narrative.

Applied ethics uses case stories to illustrate ethical issues, and it evaluates the stories or cases through moral theories and moral reasoning. The way we present cases or stories or describe the "facts," that is, the narratives we employ and the mental models that frame these narratives, affect the content of the story, the moral analysis, and subsequent evaluation of events. Indeed, we cannot present a case or tell a story except through the frame of a particular narrative or mental model. When one narrative becomes dominant, we appeal to that story for the "facts," taking it as representing what actually happened. Yet we seldom look at the narrative we use nor are we often aware of the "frame" or mental model at work. If my thesis is not mistaken, then, it is just as important, morally important, to examine different narratives about the cases

Source: *The Rashomon Effect* by Patricia Werhane from "Perspectives in Business Ethics" ed Laura Hartman (McGraw Hill/Irwin) 1997.

we use as it is to carry out the ethical analysis.

To demonstrate what I am talking about, I am going to recount narratives of a well-worn case, the Ford Pinto. I shall illustrate how different commentators present what one of them has called "independently supportable facts" (Schmitt and May, 1979, p. 1022). In each instance I cite, the commentator claims that he is presenting facts, not assumptions, commentary, or conjecture. Yet, for some reason, these "facts" seem to differ from each other. The accounts of the case I shall use are Mark Dowie's "Pinto Madness" from September/October 1977 *Mother Jones*, later revised and printed in *Business and Society*; "Beyond Products Liability" by Michael Schmitt and William W. May from the *University of Detroit Journal of Urban Law*, Summer 1979; Manuel Velasquez's treatment of Pinto in his book *Business Ethics* (second ed.); Dekkers L. Davidson and Kenneth Goodpaster's Harvard Business School case, "Managing Product Safety: The Ford Pinto"; Ford Motor Company's statements from their law suit, *State of Indiana v. Ford Motor Company*; and Michael Hoffman's case/essay "The Ford Pinto," printed in *Taking Sides*. It will become evident that one narrative, Mark Dowie's, one of the earliest accounts of the case, becomes the dominant one.

> There is one indisputable set of data upon which all commentators agree. On May 28, 1972, Mrs. Lily Gray was driving a six-month old Pinto on Interstate 15 near San Bernardino, California. In the car with her was Richard Grimshaw, a thirteen-year-old boy.... Mrs. Gray stopped in San Bernardino for gasoline, got back onto the freeway (Interstate 15) and proceeded toward her destination at sixty to sixty-five miles per hour. As she approached Route 30 off-ramp, . . . the Pinto suddenly stalled and coasted to a halt in the middle lane . . . the driver of a 1962 Ford Galaxie was unable to avoid colliding with the Pinto. Before impact the Galaxie had been braked to a speed of from twenty-eight to thirty-seven miles per hour.
>
> At the moment of impact, the Pinto caught fire and its interior burst into flames. The crash had driven the Pinto's gas tank forward and punctured it against the flange on the differential housing.... Mrs. Gray died a few days later.... Grimshaw managed to survive with severe burns over 90 percent of his body. (Velasquez, 199, p. 122; *Grimshaw v. Ford Motor Co.*, p. 359).

In 1978 a jury awarded Grimshaw at least 125 million dollars in punitive damages. *Auto News* printed a headline "Ford Fights Pinto Case: Jury Gives 128 Million" on February 13, 1978. The number $125 million is commonly cited and is in the court records as the sum of the initial punitive award. This award was later reduced on appeal to $3.5 million, a fact that is seldom cited.

What is the background for the development of the Pinto? According to public statements made by Lee Iacocca, then CEO of Ford, to meet Japanese competition Ford decided to design a subcompact car that would not weigh over 2,000 pounds nor cost over $2,000 (Davidson/Goodpaster, 1983). According to Davidson/Goodpaster, Ford began planning the Pinto in June 1967, ending with production beginning in September 1970, a 38-month turnaround time as opposed to the industry average of 43 months for engineering and developing a new automobile (Davidson/Goodpaster, 1983, p.4). Mark Dowie claims that the development was "rushed" into 25 months (Dowie, p. 20); Velasquez says it occurred in "under two years" (Velasquez, p. 120); Hoffman claims that Ford "rushed the Pinto into production in much less than the usual time" (Hoffman, p. 133). While the actual time of development may seem unimportant, critics of the Pinto design argue that because it was "rushed into production" Pinto was not as carefully designed nor checked for safety as a model created over a 43-month time span (Dowie, Velasquez).

The Pinto was designed so that the gas tank was placed behind the rear axle. According to Davidson/Goodpaster, "At that time almost every American-made car had the fuel tank located in the same place" (p. 4). Dowie wonders why Ford did not place the gas tank over the rear axle, Ford's patented design for their Capri models. This placement is confirmed by Dowie, Velasquez and some Ford engineers to be the "safest place." Yet, according to Davidson/Goodpaster other studies at Ford showed that the Capri placement actually increased the likelihood of ignition inside the automobile (p. 4). Moreover, such placement reduces storage space and precludes a hatchback design. Velasquez argues that "[b]ecause the Pinto was a rush project, styling preceded engineering" (p. 120), thus accounting for the gas tank placement. This fact may have been derived from Dowie's quote, allegedly from a "Ford engineer who doesn't want his name used," that "this company is run by salesmen, not engineers; so the priority is styling, not safety" (p. 23).

Dowie argues that in addition to rushing the Pinto into production, "Ford engineers discovered in pre-production crash tests that rear-end collisions would rupture the Pinto's fuel system extremely easily" (p. 18). According to Dowie, Ford crash-tested the Pinto in a secret location and in every test made at over 25 mph the fuel tank ruptured. But according to Ford, while Pinto's gas tank did explode during many of its tests, this was because, following government guidelines, Ford had to test the car using a fixed barrier standard wherein the vehicle is towed backwards into a fixed barrier at the speed specified in the test. Ford argued that Pinto behaved well under a less stringent moving-barrier standard, which, Ford contended, is a more realistic test (Davidson/Goodpaster; *State of Indiana* v. *Ford*).

Ford and the commentators on this case agree that in 1971, before launching the automobile, an internal study was conducted that showed that a rubber bladder inner tank would improve the reliability of Pinto during tests. The bladder would cost $5.08 (Dowie, p. 29; Schmitt and May, 1979, p. 1023), $5.80 (Davidson/Goodpaster) or $11 (Velasquez, p. 120). The $11 figure probably refers to a design adjustment that Ford would have had to make to meet a later new government rollover standard (see below). However, the idea of this installation was discarded, according to Ford because of the unreliability of the rubber at cold temperatures, a conjecture no one else mentions. Dowie also contends that Ford could have reduced the dangers from rear-end collisions by installing a $1 plastic baffle between the gas tank and the differential housing to reduce the likelihood of gas tank perforation. I can find no other verification of this fact.

All commentators claim that Ford did a cost/benefit analysis to determine whether it would be more costly to change the Pinto design or assume the damages for burn victims, and memos to that effect were evidence at the Grimshaw trial (*Grimshaw* v. *Ford Motor Co.*, 570). However, according to Davidson/Goodpaster and Schmitt/May, this estimate was done in 1973, the year *after* the Grimshaw accident, in response to evaluating a proposed new government rollover standard. To meet that requirement would cost $11 per auto, Ford calculated. Ford used government data for the cost of a life ($200,000 per person), and projected an estimate of 180 burn deaths from rollovers. The study was not applicable to rearend collisions as commentators, following Dowie's story, claimed.

There are also innuendoes in many write-ups of this case that the $200,000 figure was Ford's price of a human life. Dowie says, for example, "Ever wonder what your life is worth in dollars? Perhaps $10 million? Ford has a better idea: $200,000." In fact, it was the U.S. government's 1973 figure.

How many people have died as a result of a rear-end collision in a Pinto? "By conservative estimates Pinto crashes have caused 500 burn deaths to people who would not have been seriously injured if the car had not burst into flames. The figure could be as high as 900," Dowie claimed in 1977 (p. 18). Hoffman, in 1984, repeats those figures word for word (p. 133). Velasquez, more cautious, claims that by 1978 at least 53 people had died and "many more had been severely burnt" (p. 122), and Schmitt and May, quoting a 1977 article in *Business and Society Review*, estimate the number at "at least 32" (p. 1024; May, p. 102 at 16). Davidson/Goodpaster claim that by 1978 NHTSA estimated there were 38 cases which involved 27 fatalities.

There was a second famous Pinto accident that led the State of Indiana to charge Ford with criminal liability. The facts in that case upon which all agree are reported by Hoffman as follows:

> On August 10, 1978, a tragic automobile accident occurred on U.S. Highway 33 near Goshen, Indiana. Sisters Judy and Lynn Ulrich (ages 18 and 16, respectively) and their cousin Donna Ulrich (age 18) were struck from the rear in their 1973 Ford Pinto by a van. The gas tank of the Pinto ruptured, the car burst into flames, and the three teenagers were burned to death. (p. 132)

There are two points of interest in this case, points that helped to exonerate Ford in the eyes of the jury in the Indiana trial. First, in June of 1978 Ford recalled 1.5 million of its Pintos to modify the fuel tank. There is some evidence that the Ulrich auto had not participated in the recall (*State of Indiana* v. *Ford Motor Company*). Secondly, Ulrich's Pinto was hit from behind at 50 miles an hour by a van driven by a Mr. Duggar. Mr. Duggar, who was not killed, later testified that he looked down for a "smoke" when he then hit the car, although the Ulrichs had their safety blinkers on. Found in Duggar's van were at least two empty beer bottles and an undisclosed amount of marijuana. Yet this evidence, cited in the *State of Indiana* v. *Ford Motor Co.* case, are seldom mentioned in the context of the Ulrich tragedy, nor was Duggar ever indicted.

The point of all this is not to exonerate Ford nor to argue for bringing back the Pinto. Rather, it is to point out a simple phenomenon–that a narrative–a story–can be taken as fact even when other alleged equally verifiable facts contradict that story. Moreover, one narrative can become dominating such that what it says is taken as fact. Dowie's interesting tale of the Pinto became the prototype for Pinto cases without many of the authors going back to see if Dowie's data was correct or to question why some of his data contradicts Ford's and government claims. Moreover, Dowie's reporting of Grimshaw becomes a prototype for the narrative of Ulrich case as well, so that questions concerning the recall of the Ulrich auto and Mr. Duggar's performance were virtually ignored. Such omissions not only make Ford look better. They also bring into question these reports and cases.

Let me mention another set of stories, those revolving around the more recent Dow Corning silicone breast implant controversy. From the volumes of reports there are a few facts upon which everyone agrees. Dow Corning has developed and manufactured silicone breast implants since 1962. It is one of a number of manufacturers that include Bristol Myers Squibb, Baxter, and 3M. In 1975 it changed the design of the implant to a thinner shell that, according to the company, was more "natural," thus less likely to harden over time. Out of the almost 2 million women who have had implants, at least 440,000 have joined class action suits or brought individual law suits claiming to have experienced a variety of illnesses, including autoimmune diseases such as lupus and rheumatoid arthritis, connective tissues diseases, scleroderma, cancer, and various other malaises such as pain, fatigue, insomnia, memory loss, and/or headaches (*New York Times*, 1995, p. C6; Angell, p. 18).

Since this is an evolving case not all the positions and narratives have sufficiently solidified to make exhaustive comparisons. But let me focus on three points. First, there is a very simple question, Do silicone breast implants cause cancer and other diseases, in particular, connective tissue or auto-immune diseases? Second, did the industry, and Dow Corning in particular, cover up or not inform physicians or women patients of the risks of implantation? Third, did Dow Corning fail "to acknowledge and promptly investigate signs of trouble?" (See bibliography for citations.)

The first question is the most simple and the most puzzling. A seldom cited fact in the case is that pacemakers and a number of other implants are made from silicone, because silicone is thought to be the most inert of all possible implant substances. Yet pacemaker wearers have not sued for illnesses that allegedly result from that implant. According to pathologist Nir Kossovsky, however, silicone breast implants can affect the immune system and cause a variety of harms to the system. This is particularly acute when an implant ruptures (Taubes, 1995). Yet in numerous independent epidemiological studies investigators have been unable to establish any but the weakest correlation between breast implants and cancer, connective tissue disease, or autoimmune diseases (Sanchez-Guerrero et al., 1995; Giltay et al., 1994; McLaughlin and Fraumeni, 1994). The most extensive of these is a longitudinal study by Brigham and Women's Hospital of 87,318 women nurses from the ages of 30 to 55 covering their medical records over a 14-year span. This study, partly funded by the NIH, is the basis for what will be a larger study of 450,000 women. (It should also be noted that silicone breast implants were withdrawn from the market by the FDA, not because they were proven to be harmful but because the FDA concluded that the evidence was not strong enough to show they were not harmful.) Despite what an overwhelming number of scientists consider to be overwhelming evidence, a number of lawsuits have been won by claimants who argue they became ill because of implants.

The second question–Did Dow Corning cover up evidence?–is also equally puzzling. Dow Corning claims, of course, that they did not. This is partly because they instigated their own studies that found no conclusive link between implants and disease, and partly because from the very beginning they did in fact inform physicians about risks of implants, including possibility of rupture or hardening in some patients. It is only recently, since 1985, that Dow Corning has developed brochures to be distributed to candidates for implantation.

The third question seems to become moot if implants do not cause disease. Yet more is at stake here. Dow Corning and other silicone breast implant manufacturers depended on the narratives of science. They imagined that scientific evidence and only scientific evidence would count as evidence in the courts, that the media would not print a story to the contrary when such scientific evidence was conclusive, and that the emotional fact that women with implants became ill would become a dominant factor in what appeared to be a matter of science. We have here a number of narratives: the scientific evidence reports, Dow Corning's defense of their consent procedures, and lawsuits that focus on the illnesses. There is also a set of media narratives that focus on the emotional reactions of ill women (not all media narratives do this), the dominating examples of which are the *Business Week* article "Informed Consent" (Byrne, 1995) and John Byrne's book, which was produced from this reporting. This article focuses on the emotional trauma of Colleen Swanson, the wife of a Dow Corning manager, John Swanson, who recently resigned from Dow Corning after 27 years of employment. Colleen Swanson had had implants 17 years ago and has been suffering from a variety of illnesses almost since the end of the operation. While Byrne focuses on Colleen's emotional suffering he cites the epidemiological evidence but puts that evidence in doubt by stating:

> Recent studies from Harvard Medical School and the Mayo Clinic, among others, have case doubt on the link between implants and disease. But critics have attacked these studies on numerous grounds–among them that they look only for recognized diseases such as lupus, rather than the complex of ailments many recipients complain of. (Byrne, 1996, p. 116)

Again I am not trying to whitewash this case. But it is interesting how the fact of illnesses in women with implants has been conflated with the causal claim of "illnesses caused by silicone breast implants." Perhaps it is the notion of causality that should be brought into question. The dominating emotional narratives have simply overshadowed the scientific ones. It is no wonder that Dow Corning cannot figure out what happened since they focused primarily on the scientific narratives. Moreover they seemed to assume that physicians performing implant surgery were all reasonable professionals who would inform their patients uniformly and thoroughly about the risks of implantation. (One cannot even with good conscience construct a narrative that claims that scientists are male-dominated and thus biased in their data analysis, because these studies have been conducted by men and women of a variety of scientific and medical backgrounds and nationalities.)

What can we say about the role of narratives? As I have argued elsewhere (Werhane, 1991, 1992) human beings do not simply perceive the data of their experiences unedited, so to speak. Each of us orders, selects, structures, and even censors our experiences. These shaping mechanisms are mental models or schema through which we experience the world. The selection processes or schema are culturally and socially learned and changed, and almost no perspective or model is permanent or unalterable. But we never see the world except through a point of view, a model, or framing mechanism. Indeed, narratives that shape our experiences and influence how we think about the world are essential to the facts of our experience. At the same time, these mental models or schema and these narratives are not merely subjective. They represent points of view that others share or can share, and they are, or can be, what Amartya Sen calls "positionally objective." Sen writes:

> What we can observe depends on our position vis-a-vis the objects of observation.... Positionally dependent observations, beliefs, and actions are central to our knowledge and practical reason. The nature of objectivity in epistemology, decision theory, and ethics has to take adequate note of the parametric dependence of observation and inference on the position of the observer.

Position-dependency defines the way in which the object appears "from a delineated somewhere." This "delineated somewhere," however, is positionally objective. That is, any person in that position will make similar observations, according to Sen. I would add that the parameters of positionality are not merely spatial but could involve a shared schema. For example, managers at Ford had access to a lot of the same data about the Pinto. Ford's decision not to recall the Pinto despite a number of terrible accidents could be defended as a positionally objective belief based on the ways in which managers at Ford processed information on automobile crashes. (Gioia, 1991) Similarly, Dow Corning's reluctance to stop manufacturing silicone implants could be construed as positionally objective from their focus on scientific evidence and reliance on responsible surgeons. Colleen Swanson and other ill recipients of implants also adopt a positionally objective view, from their perspective as very ill people with implants.

However, a positionally objective point of view could be mistaken in case it did not take into account all available information. Thus, as Sen points out, in most cases one need not unconditionally accept a positionally objective view.

Because of the variety of schema with which one can shape a position, almost any position has alternatives, almost every position has its critics. I would qualify that further. Even allegedly positionally objective phenomena are still phenomena that have been filtered through the social sieve of a shared mental model or schema.

As I have just demonstrated, some narratives are more closely based on actual experiences; others are taken from the narratives of others which we have accepted "as true"; still others are in the form of stories. For example, the movie *Wall Street* tells a story about Wall Street that reshapes our perception of investment banking. These perspectives are necessarily incomplete, they can be biased, or they can be constituted by someone else's framing of experience. So, for example, as E. H. Gombrich the art historian relates, following Albrecht Durer's famous etching of a rhinoceros, for a very long time naturalists as well as artists portrayed rhinos with "armored" layers of skin, when in fact, a simple look at a rhino belies that conclusion (Gombrich). Similarly, Dowie's portrayal of the Pinto case became the prototype for other case descriptions. Byrne's *Business Week* article and his subsequent book on the Dow-Corning breast implant controversy appear to be becoming the prototype factual bases for analyzing that case. What happens in these instances is that "life imitates art," or the "grammar," the alleged data of the narrative creates the essence of the story.

Does this mean that one can never arrive at facts or truths? The short answer is "yes" or "no." The longer answer is more complicated. The thesis that experience is always framed by a perspective or point of view is closely related to another thesis, Wittgenstein's claim that "*[e]ssence* is expressed by grammar" (Wittgenstein, § 1953, 371), that is, in short, that all our experiences are framed, organized, and made meaningful only through the language we employ to conceive, frame, think, describe, and evaluate our experiences. Whether or not all experiences are linguistically constituted is a topic for another essay. What is important is what Wittgenstein does not say, that "essence is *created* by grammar" (Anscombe, 1976, p. 188). Nor did he hold that view, as I have argued in detail elsewhere (Werhane, 1992). To put the point in more Kantian terms, there is data or "stuff" of our experience that is not created or made up (although sometimes we can and do make up the content of our experiences when we envelop ourselves in fantasy) and, indeed, the distinction between "reality" and "fantasy" may be just that—that we do not make up the content of our experience. Nevertheless, that data or content or "stuff" is never pure—it is always constituted and contaminated by our perspective, point of view, or mental model.

At the same time, we are able to engage in "transpositional" assessments or what Sen has called a "constructed 'view from nowhere.' " A trans-positional view from nowhere is a constructed critique of a particular conceptual scheme, and no positionally objective view is merely relative nor immune from challenge. This sort of assessment involves comparing various positionally objective points of view to see whether one can make coherent sense of them and develop some general theories about what is being observed. These transpositional assessments are *constructed* views, because they too depend on the conceptual scheme of the assessors. From a trans-positional point of view conceptual schemes themselves can be questioned on the basis of their coherence and/or their explanatory scope. Although that challenge could only be conducted from another conceptual scheme, that assessment could take into account a variety of points of view. Still, revisions of the scheme in question might produce another conceptual scheme that more adequately or more comprehensively explained or took into account a range of phenomena or incidents. Together, studying sets of perspectives can get at how certain events are experienced and reported, and even, what mental models, schemes, or narratives are at work in shaping the narratives about these experiences. While one can never get at those from a pure *tabula rasa*, nevertheless one can achieve a limited, dispassionate view from somewhere.

Near the end of *Rashomon* the narrator of the tale, who is also the bystander, decries the lack of trust in society engendered from the impossibility of ascertaining the truth. The cases we develop must be done with care. In using others' cases and narratives one should study not just the facts as presented in the case narratives. Rather, we need to examine the ways in which the facts are constituted to make a story or a case, and one should become aware of how some of those cases can become prototypical narratives that we imitate. The so-called "classics" like Pinto need to be revisited or they will become cliched prototypes. And we need to be wary of assumptions generated by these prototypes such as the assumption that Dow Corning caused egregious harms, perhaps even deliberately, to the over 2 million women who have their breast implants. While we cannot arrive at The Truth we can at least approximate it more fully. Only then will we who teach and write in applied ethics become, in the words of Henry James, "finely aware and richly responsible" (Nussbaum, 1990).

Bibliography

Angell, Marcia. 1995. "Are Breast Implants Actually OK?" *The New Republic*, September 11, 17–21.

_____. 1996. *Science on Trial.* New York: W. W. Norton & Co.

Anscombe, G. E. M. 1976. "The Question of Linguistic Idealism." *Essays on Wittgenstein in Honour of G. H. Ron Wright*, Acta Philosophica Fennica, Vol. 28. ed. Jaakko Hintikka. Amsterdam: North Holland Publishing Co., 181–215.

Byrne, John A. 1995. "Informed Consent." *Business Week*, October 2, 104–116.

_____. 1996. *Informed Consent: A Story of Personal Tragedy and Corporate Betrayal.* New York, McGraw-Hill Companies.

Davidson, Dekkers, and Kenneth E. Goodpaster. 1983. "Managing Product Safety: The Ford Pinto." Harvard University Graduate School of Business Administration Case #9-383-129. Boston: Harvard Business School Press.

Dowie, Mark. 1977a. "Pinto Madness." *Mother Jones*, September/October, 18–32.

_____. 1977b. "How Ford Put Two Million Firetraps on Wheels." *Business and Society Review*, 23: 46–55.

"Ford Fights Pinto Case: Jury Gives 128 Million." 1978. *Auto News*, February 13, 1.

Gabriel, S. E., et al. 1994. "Risk of Connective-Tissue Diseases and Other Disorders after Breast Implantation." *New England Journal of Medicine*, 330: 1697–1702.

Giltay, Erik J., et al. 1994. "Silicone Breast Protheses and Rheumatic Symptoms: A Retrospective Follow up Study." *Annals of Rheumatic Diseases*, 53: 194–196.

Gioia, Dennis. 1991. "Pinto Fires and Personal Ethics: A Script Analysis of Missed Opportunities." *Journal of Business Ethics*, 11: 379–389.

Gombrich, E. H. 1961. *Art and Illusion.* Princeton: Princeton University Press.

Grimshaw v. Ford Motor Co. 1978. No. 197761. Super CT. Orange County, CA, February 6.

Hoffman, Michael. 1984. "The Ford Pinto." Rpt. in *Taking Sides*. Ed. Lisa H. Newton and Maureen M. Ford. Dushkin Publishing Group, 132–137.

Kolata, Gina. 1995. "Proof of a Breast Implant Peril Is Lacking, Rheumatologists Say." *New York Times*, October 25.

McLaughlin, Joseph K., and Joseph E Fraumeni Jr.1994. "Correspondence Re: Breast Implants, Cancer, and Systemic Sclerosis." *Journal of the National Cancer Institute*, 86: 1424.

Nussbaum, Martha. 1990. *Love's Knowledge.* New York: Oxford University Press.

Sanchez-Guerrero, Jorge, et al. 1995. "Silicone Breast Implants and the Risk of Connective-Tissue Diseases and Symptoms." *New England Journal of Medicine*, 332: 1666–1670.

Schmitt, Michael A., and William W. May, 1979. "Beyond Products Liability: The Legal, Social, and Ethical Problems Facing the Automobile Industry in Producing Safe Products." *University of Detroit Journal of Urban Law*, 56: 1021–1050.

Sen, Amartya. 1993. "Positional Objectivity." *Philosophy and Public Affairs.*

State of Indiana v. *Ford Motor Co.* (179), No. 11–431, Cir. Ct. Pulaski, IN.

Taubes, Gary. 1995. "Silicone in the System." *Discover*, December, 65–75.

Velasquez, Manuel. 1988. *Business Ethics*, 2d ed. Englewood Cliffs: Prentice-Hall, Inc.

Werhane, Patricia H. 1991. "Engineers and Management: The Challenge of the Challenger Incident." *Journal of Business Ethics*, 10: 605–616.

_____._____. 1992. *Skepticism, Rules, and Private Languages.* Atlantic Highlands, NJ: Humanities Press.

_____. 1998. "Moral Imagination and Management Decision-Making." *New Avenues of Research in Business Ethics.* Edited by R. Edward Freeman. New York: Oxford University Press.

Wittgenstein, Ludwig. 1953. *Philosophical Investigations.* Trans. G. E. M. Anscombe. New York: Macmillan and Co.

4

Excerpts from "The Prince"

Niccolò Machiavelli

Niccolò Machiavelli (1469–1527) was born to a Florentine family distinguished by its history of political prominence. Unfortunately for Niccolò, his father (an unsuccessful lawyer) and his immediate family were beset by chronic financial woes. Machiavelli held significant positions in the government of Florence. As an ambassador, he was able to gather information about the chaotic world of international and Italian politics. He was also a military technician responsible for overseeing the city's military preparedness. As the defense minister, he was known for substituting a citizen's militia for the mercenary system. His power and influence ended in 1512, when the Spanish, in league with the pope, attacked Florence.

Machiavelli's writings were shocking and highly controversial. *The Prince* was banned by the pope; some critics contend that he led to modern totalitarianism. But Machiavelli saw *The Prince* as a realistic account of the qualities necessary for political success. He believed that although some common virtues (e.g., moderation, clemency, chastity, gentleness, generosity, vigor, religion, and devotion) might be praiseworthy, they were not what the real world required. A person with these virtues would be good–but too good for this world, and a disastrous leader. Instead, a leader would need qualities like energy, boldness, and shrewdness. Compare this philosophy to that of Lao Tzu, who wrote in *Tao Te Ching*:

> A leader is best
> When people barely know that he exists.
> Of a good leader, who talks little,
> When his work is done, his aim fulfilled,
> They will say, "We did this ourselves." (Chapter 17)

Machiavelli believed in divorcing ethics from politics, contending that "a weak Christian makes a better president than a strong one.... [A president] needs to

---

Source: Translated by David Wootton. Copyright © 1995 Hackett Publishing Co. Reprinted by permission.

be unscrupulous, without strong standards and beliefs." Since public acts often have unforeseen consequences, Machiavelli believed that a political agent may be excused for performing certain acts that would be ethically indefensible in private life.

...Going further down our list of qualities, I recognize every ruler should want to be thought of as compassionate and not cruel. Nevertheless, I have to warn you to be careful about being compassionate. Cesare Borgia was thought of as cruel; but this supposed cruelty of his restored order to the Romagna, united it, rendered it peaceful and law-abiding. If you think about it, you will realize he was, in fact, much more compassionate than the people of Florence, who, in order to avoid being thought cruel, allowed Pistoia to tear itself apart.[1] So a ruler ought not to mind the disgrace of being called cruel, if he keeps his subjects peaceful and law-abiding, for it is more compassionate to impose harsh punishments on a few than, out of excessive compassion, to allow disorder to spread, which leads to murders or looting. The whole community suffers if there are riots, while to maintain order the ruler only has to execute one or two individuals. Of all rulers, he who is new to power cannot escape a reputation for cruelty, for he is surrounded by dangers. Virgil has Dido say:

> Harsh necessity, and the fact my kingdom is new, oblige me to do these things,
> And to mass my armies on the frontiers.[2]

Nevertheless, you should be careful how you assess the situation and should think twice before you act. Do not be afraid of your own shadow. Employ policies that are moderated by prudence and sympathy. Avoid excessive self-confidence, which leads to carelessness, and avoid excessive timidity, which will make you insupportable.

This leads us to a question that is in dispute: Is it better to be loved than feared, or vice versa.[3] My reply is one ought to be both loved and feared; but, since it is difficult to accomplish both at the same time, I maintain it is much safer to be feared than loved, if you have to do without one of the two. For of men one can, in general, say this: They are ungrateful, fickle, deceptive and deceiving, avoiders of danger, eager to gain. As long as you serve their interests, they are devoted to you. They promise you their blood, their possessions, their lives, and their children, as I said before, so long as you seem to have no need of them. But as soon as you need help, they turn against you. Any ruler who relies simply on their promises and makes no other preparations, will be destroyed. For you will find that those whose support you buy, who do not rally to you because they admire your strength of character and nobility of soul, these are people you pay for, but they are never yours, and in the end you cannot get the benefit of your investment. Men are less nervous of offending someone who makes himself lovable, than someone who makes himself frightening. For love attaches men by ties of obligation, which, since men are wicked, they break whenever their interests are at stake. But fear restrains men because they are afraid of punishment, and this fear never leaves them. Still, a ruler should make himself feared in such a way that, if he does not inspire love, at least he does not provoke hatred. For it is perfectly possible to be feared and not hated. You will only be hated if you seize the property or the women of your subjects and citizens. Whenever you have to kill someone, make sure you have a suitable excuse and an obvious reason; but, above all else, keep your hands off other people's property; for men are quicker to forget the death of their father than the loss of their inheritance. Moreover, there are always reasons why you might want to seize people's property; and he who begins to live by plundering others will always find an excuse for seizing other people's possessions; but there are fewer reasons for killing people, and one killing need not lead to another.

When a ruler is at the head of his army and has a vast number of soldiers under his command, then it is absolutely essential to be prepared to be thought cruel; for it is impossible to keep an army united and ready for action without acquiring a reputation for cruelty. Among the extraordinary accomplishments of Hannibal, we may note one in particular: He commanded a vast army, made up of men of many different nations, who were fighting far from home, yet they never mutinied and they never fell out with one another, either when things were going badly, or when things were going well.[4] The only possible explanation for this is that he was known to be harsh and cruel. This, together with his numerous virtues [*virtù*], meant his soldiers always regarded him with admiration and fear. Without cruelty, his other virtues [*virtù*] would not have done the job. Those who write about Hannibal without thinking things through both admire the loyalty of his troops and criticize the cruelty that was its principal cause. If you doubt my claim that his other virtues [*virtù*] would have been insufficient, take the case of Scipio.[5] He was not only unique in his own day, but history does not record anyone his equal. But his army rebelled against him in Spain.[6] The sole cause of this was his excessive leniency, which meant his soldiers had more freedom than is compatible with good military discipline. Fabius Maximus criticized him for this in the senate and accused him of corrupting the Roman armies. When Locri was destroyed by one of his commanders,[7] he did not avenge the deaths of the inhabitants, and he did not punish his officer's insubordination. He was too easygoing. This was so apparent that one of his supporters in the senate was obliged to excuse him by saying he was no different from many other men, who were better at doing their own jobs than at making other people do theirs. In course of time, had he remained in command without learning from his mistakes, this aspect of Scipio's character would have destroyed his glorious reputation. But, because his authority was subordinate to that of the senate, not only were the consequences of this defect mitigated, but it even enhanced his reputation.

I conclude, then, that, as far as being feared and loved is concerned, since men decide for themselves whom they love, and rulers decide whom they fear, a wise ruler should rely on the emotion he can control, not on the one he cannot. But he must take care to avoid being hated, as I have said.

Notes

1 In 1501.

2 Virgil, *Aeneid,* I, 563–4.

3 Cicero, *De officios,* bk. 2, ch. 7, § 23–24.

4 Hannibal (ca. 247–183 B.C.) campaigned in Italy from 218 to 203 B.C. Machiavelli's source is Polybius, bk. 11, ch. 19.

5 Scipio (ca. 236–183 B.C.) defeated Hannibal at Zama in North Africa (202 B.C.).

6 In 206 B.C. Livy, bk. 28, chs. 24–29.

7 In 205 B.C.

5

Excerpts from "The Art of War"

Sun Tzu

I s business another form of war? Can business practitioners learn from strategic analysis utilized in combat? Consider the application of the following statements by Master Sun Tzu and his disciples to traditional business decision making and strategic planning.

1: Strategic Assessments

MEI YAOCHEN

Whether you live or die depends on the configuration of the battleground; whether you survive or perish depends on the way of battle.

MASTER SUN

Therefore measure in terms of five things, use these assessments to make comparisons, and thus find out what the conditions are. The five things are the way, the weather, the terrain, the leadership, and discipline.

DU MU

Five things are to be assessed–the way, the weather, the lay of the land, the leadership, and discipline. These are to be assessed at headquarters–first assess yourself and your opponent in terms of these five things, deciding who is superior. Then you can determine who is likely to prevail. Having determined this, only then should you mobilize your forces.

***

MASTER SUN

The Way means inducing the people to have the same aim as the leadership, so that they will share death and share life, without fear of danger.

Source: Sun Tzu, *The Art of War*, translated by Thomas Cleary (Boston, MA: Shambhala Publications, 1988).

CAO CAO
This means guiding them by instruction and direction. Danger means distrust.

ZHANG YU
If the people are treated with benevolence, faithfulness, and justice, then they will be of one mind, and will be glad to serve. The *I Ching* says, "Joyful in difficulty, the people forget about their death."

***

DU MU
Also, if a general lacks the planning ability to assess the officers and place them in positions where they can use the best of their abilities, instead assigning them automatically and thus not making full use of their talents, then the army will become hesitant.

Huang Shigong said, "Those who are good at delegating responsibility employ the intelligent, the brave, the greedy, and the foolish. The intelligent are glad to establish their merit, the brave like to act out their ambitions, the greedy welcome an opportunity to pursue profit, and the foolish do not care if they die."

If your own army is hesitant and confused, you bring trouble on yourself, as if you were to bring enemies in to overcome you.

***

MASTER SUN
So only a brilliant ruler or a wise general who can use the highly intelligent for espionage is sure of great success. This is essential for military operations, and the armies depend on this in their actions.

DU MU
It will not do for the army to act without knowing the opponent's condition, and to know the opponent's condition is impossible without espionage.

6

Utilitarianism and Business Ethics

Milton Snoeyenbos and James Humber

This chapter states and clarifies act and rule utilitarian principles, enumerates several advantages of employing utilitarianism as an ethical theory in business contexts, and discusses the main difficulties with utilitarianism in such contexts.

Utilitarianism is a consequentialist ethical theory. It is an ethical theory because it is concerned with whether human actions are right or wrong; it is consequentialist because it tells us that an act's rightness or wrongness is determined solely by the act's consequences and not by any feature of the act itself. For example, if I make a promise to you and then act in such a way as to break it, my act has the feature of breaking a promise, and many people would claim my act was wrong because it has that feature. However, according to utilitarianism, that feature does not make the act wrong for that feature is irrelevant to whether the act is right or wrong. For the utilitarian, whether breaking a promise is right or wrong depends entirely on the act's consequences. The intuitive idea behind utilitarianism is that we should act to bring about the best consequences and, hence, whether an act is morally right or wrong depends on whether the act does or does not bring about the best consequences. Of course, we will have to say more about what we mean by "best consequences," but for now let us just use our ordinary concepts of benefit and harm to make sense of the notion. Of two acts, one of which causes you pleasure and the other pain, we would ordinarily say the former benefits you and the latter harms you, and that the former is better for you than the latter. Again, of two acts, one of which increases dividends and the other of which bankrupts a firm, we would commonly say the former benefits and the latter harms shareholders, and that the former is better than the latter for shareholders.

According to one version of utilitarianism, act utilitarianism, an act is morally right if and only if it maximizes utility, i.e., if and only if the balance of benefit to harm calculated by taking everyone affected by the act into

Source: Robert E. Frederick (ed.), *A Companion to Business Ethics* (Oxford: Blackwell Publishers, 2002).

consideration is greater than the imbalance of benefit to harm resulting from any alternative act. Although we will have to modify it slightly, this statement of act utilitarianism best enables us to see how the act utilitarian goes about determining which act is right in typical situations. In deciding to act, the act utilitarian will:

1 set out all the relevant alternative acts that are open to him or her;
2 list all the individuals who will be affected by the alternative courses of action, including oneself if affected;
3 assess how the individuals will be affected by the alternative acts, computing the balance of benefit to harm for each individual affected by each act; and
4 choose that act which maximizes utility, i.e., which results in the greatest total balance of benefit to harm.

Suppose, for example, that a person P_1 faces a situation in which there are four possible courses of action (A_1, A_2, A_3, A_4) and assume there are four people who will be affected by at least some of these acts (P_1, P_2, P_3, P_4). Assume, furthermore, that the balance of benefit to harm for each person affected by each act can be expressed quantitatively, with a positive value indicating an overall benefit and a negative value indicating an overall harmful effect. Finally, assume a calculation yields the following result:

Persons

		P_1	P_2	P_3	P_4	Totals
Acts	A_1	+6	+2	−7	+4	+5
	A_2	+5	−4	0	+6	+7
	A_3	−12	−1	−6	+15	−4
	A_4	−3	−1	−2	+7	+1

Here it may be that P_2 is both benefitted and harmed by A_1 (for example, P_2 benefits +7 but is harmed −5), but on balance he or she benefits to the extent of +2; similarly, P_3 may receive some benefits from A_3 (say, +1), but also some harm (say, −7), so that on balance he or she is harmed to the extent of −6. In the situation represented by the above chart, the act utilitarian will choose act A_2 because it provides the greatest total balance of benefit to harm (+7) when everyone affected by the acts is considered.

Using the chart, we can further clarify act utilitarianism and distinguish it from other consequentialist theories. First, act utilitarianism differs from ethical egoism in that, for the latter, an act is morally right if and only if, of all available acts, it provides the greatest balance of benefit to harm for the person performing the act. Accordingly, P_1, acting as an ethical egoist, will do A_1 because A_1 produces the greatest benefit to harm ratio for P_1 (+6), whereas P_1 acting as an act utilitarian would do A_2, since A_2 maximizes utility. Furthermore, act utilitarianism is not altruism. The altruists do not consider themselves in the benefit to harm calculation; they act to produce the greatest benefit to harm ratio when only others affected by the acts are considered. Accordingly, P_1, acting as an altruist, will select A_3 as the right act, since it produces a balance of +8 when considering the effects on P_2, P_3, and P_4, and this balance is greater than those for A_1 (−1), A_2 (+2) and A_4 (+4), whereas P_1 acting as an act utilitarian will do A_2. Of course, there will be many occasions on which the act required by ethical egoism will be the same as that required by act utilitarianism, and for that matter altruism. For example, CEOs may maximally benefit themselves by a singular focus on profit maximization, but at the same time maximally benefit customers, employees, shareholders, and society as well. Yet act utilitarianism, as a general ethical theory, is distinct from egoism and altruism; in calculating benefits and harms, the act utilitarians consider themselves equally with others, no less but no more.

Second, act utilitarianism is not the principle that we should maximize total benefits, rather, one should maximize utility. If we calculate just benefits, A_3 provides +15 and A_2 provides +11, hence A_3 would be the right act. However, in calculating utility, it is important to consider harms as well as benefits, which act utilitarianism does in judging A_2 to be the right act.

Third, the act utilitarian is not concerned solely with short-term benefit-to-harm ratios; long-term consequences also have to be calculated. However, this requirement is consonant with good business practices; research and capital expenditures are aimed at long-term benefits.

Fourth, act utilitarianism is not the theory that an act is morally right if its overall benefits outweigh its harms. A_4's benefits outweigh its harms (by +1), but A_2 is the right act according to act utilitarianism, and all the other alternative acts, including A_4, are morally wrong.

Fifth, act utilitarianism is not the principle that an act is right if and only if it provides the best consequences for the greatest number, where this means that to be right an act must maximize utility and, at the same time, maximize the number of individuals who realize a positive benefit to harm ratio. In our charted example, A_2 maximizes utility but A_1 maximizes the number of individuals who realize a positive balance of benefit to harm, since three individuals benefit (P_1, P_2, P_4) from A_1 but every other act benefits at most two individuals. Since none of the acts in our example satisfies the best consequences for the greatest number principle, none of the acts listed is morally right according to that principle, an odd result, since if we are consequentialists we would expect that one of these acts is right and, of course, A_2 is right according to act utilitarianism. This criticism of the best consequences for the greatest number principle also enables us to see a defect in our formulation of act utilitarianism. Suppose a person has three acts available, two of which produce the same overall utility, say +9, and a third which yields − 4. In this case, since no one act maximizes utility, none of the acts is right. Accordingly, we have to revise our statement of act utilitarianism to read: an act A is morally right if and only if no other alternative act has greater overall utility than A. Thus, the result in the above example would be that both +9 acts would be morally right.

Since act utilitarians focus on maximizing benefits and minimizing harms, we now need to consider what they regard as benefits and harms. We shall discuss three major utilitarian value theories: hedonistic, pluralistic, and preference.

Hedonistic act utilitarians claim that pleasure (or happiness, construed as long-term pleasure) is the only intrinsically good thing, i.e., the only thing that is good in and of itself. Other things, when they are good, are good instrumentally, i.e., they are good as a means to other things. Money for example, is not always instrumentally good, but when it is good it is good as a means to other things; it is instrumentally, not intrinsically, good. The English act utilitarian Jeremy Bentham (1748–1832) attempted to establish a method for determining quantities of pleasure by listing seven criteria for pleasure and (what he took to be) its opposite, pain: other things being equal, of two pleasures P_1 and P_2, P_1 is greater than P_2 if P_1 is

1 more intense than P_2, or
2 of greater duration than P_2, or
3 more certain of realization than P_2, or
4 nearer in time than P_2, or
5 such that it will lead to other pleasures that P_2 does not lead to, or
6 purer, i.e., less mixed with pain than P_2, or
7 such that more people can realize it than P_2.

The idea is that we can assign numbers to each dimension of pleasure. To simplify matters, consider pleasurable experiences having only the dimensions of duration and intensity. We might say that a pleasurable experience of one hour duration is assigned +1, two hours +2, and so on. A pleasure of a certain intensity is assigned +1 and a pleasure twice as intense is +2. Accordingly, a three-hour pleasurable experience of intensity +4 is assigned +12 (+3 x +4). In this way, pleasures can be measured and compared. Bentham's follower John Stuart Mill (1806–73) further developed the former's "hedonistic calculus." Among other things, Mill was concerned that Bentham's approach would allow beer guzzling to be better than doing philosophy, so he argued that the type of pleasure should be included as well as Bentham's factors, with "higher" pleasures being accorded higher values than "lower" pleasures. So, doing philosophy might be assigned +60, beer drinking +5. Accordingly, one hour of doing philosophy of intensity +2 ($1 \times 2 \times 60 = +120$) would be better than four hours of more intensely pleasurable (+3) beer drinking ($4 \times 3 \times 5 = +60$).

Although we might agree that Bentham's criteria are factors that should be considered in weighing alternative courses of action, it is questionable whether they allow us to make the precise, mathematical calculations utilitarians envisage. Duration can be calculated rather precisely, say, in seconds, but it is often difficult to say just when a pleasurable experience begins and/or ends. We can and do say that one pleasurable experience is more intense than another, one pain more intense than another, but we do not say that one experience is nine times more intensely pleasurable than another and it is doubtful we can attain such quantitative precision. If duration and intensity are not quantifiable, then the other five of Bentham's criteria, which depend on these two, are not quantifiable. Mill's proposal faces these difficulties, plus two more. His proposal requires us to rank pleasures (e.g., doing philosophy is "higher" than drinking beer) and then assign them numerical values. However, some people will rank drinking beer higher than doing philosophy; in fact, if we were to take a vote, more people might well rank beer drinking higher than doing philosophy. So how can Mill justify his belief that intellectual pleasures always must be ranked higher than physical pleasures? Even if we can rank doing philosophy as higher than beer drinking, what argument can be employed for assigning +60 to doing philosophy and +5 to beer drinking? Neither question has been answered satisfactorily.

Given these measurement and comparison problems with the concept of pleasure, act utilitarians have four main options. First, they can continue the pleasure quantification quest; after all, at one time we used "hot" and "cold" but we now have precise temperature concepts. Perhaps someone will devise a pleasureometer. Second, they can retain hedonism but abandon quantification, claiming that, even if we cannot measure pleasure with mathematical precision, we all know that some experiences are quite pleasurable and that some pleasures are greater than others, as we know that boiling water is hot, and hotter than ice. If, in some cases, rough judgments and comparisons are all that can be obtained, they are, nonetheless, useful and often adequate. Third, since utilitarianism can be construed as the claim that we should maximize that which is intrinsically good – and the theory itself leaves open what is intrinsically good – act utilitarians can claim that other things in addition to pleasure should be added to the list of things intrinsically good: knowledge, freedom, beauty, fairness, friendship, generosity, etc. In fact, some act utilitarians, known as pluralistic act utilitarians, have developed this approach. However, this strategy does not alleviate our measurement and comparison problems. How do we measure friendship and compare it with pleasure? Furthermore, if we allow different persons to weight (in some manner) these intrinsic goods differently, then overall utility calculations will differ. Which should we accept?

In this century, a fourth strategy, preference act utilitarianism, has been developed. If pleasure seems subjective and unmeasurable, our preferences, linked to our desires, choices and behavior, are more objective and may offer a firmer basis for a theory of value. If you prefer celery over pork, you behave in certain ways; you typically choose celery when presented with the two alternatives. So, we can say that celery has more value for you than pork, if you exhibit more preference for celery than pork. Economists have devised methods for assigning numbers to a person's preferences; hence, if we can determine how many people prefer celery over pork, we have a way of totaling preferences, i.e., a general method for determining which acts maximize total preference satisfaction.

Preference act utilitarianism has three major advantages over its hedonistic relative:

1 As noted, it handles the measurement and comparison problems better than hedonism.
2 It admits a greater range of values than hedonism: what is valuable to you is anything you prefer.
3 It is more tolerant than hedonism: other things being equal, the hedonistic act utilitarian will claim it is right to restrict what you prefer, if doing so will maximize happiness in the long run, whereas preference act utilitarianism is based on whatever you actually prefer.

The third advantage raises the main difficulty for preference act utilitarianism understood as a general moral theory. Some people prefer heroin to celery, and we commonly think this preference is wrong even if the choice of heroin affects no one else. Of course, some preferences do affect others, and we say that a manager acts wrongly in preferring to sexually harass an employee rather than treating him or her fairly. So the concept of preference, important as it seems to be in the development of an economic theory adequate to explain and predict actual market behavior, is initially problematic as a basis for value in an adequate moral theory. We seem to need the concept of an "acceptable" preference, i.e., a morally acceptable preference, but it is not clear whether such a concept is even consistent with the notion of preference construed as a fact, and it seems to undercut the fact-based advantages preference act utilitarians claim their theory offers over hedonistic act utilitarianism. Moreover, although some preference act utilitarians argue that "unacceptable" preferences should not count in utility calculations because they interfere with others' "acceptable" preferences, it seems more plausible to say that such unacceptable preferences should count in the calculation; it is that they simply lead to unhappiness. The conclusion is that they should be factored into a hedonistic utility calculation. Some preference act utilitarians suggest the concept needed is that of "informed preference," roughly, the preferences a person would have, if fully informed about the relevant facts related to preference alternatives. However, critics argue that such preferences would simply be those that maximize happiness – we try to satisfy our preferences and those of others because doing so maximizes happiness. If so, the theory again seems to reduce to hedonistic act utilitarianism. Preference act utilitarianism also has difficulties with simple distributional issues. If you prefer X which costs 40 cents per unit, and I prefer Y which also costs 40 cents, and we have only 55 cents to distribute, pure preference act utilitarianism has no answer as to how the 55 cents should be distributed. Hedonistic act utilitarianism does: we figure out who would be made happier by getting what he or she wants. Finally, preference utilitarianism is not as simple as it seems. Our preferences change over time: some are added, some dropped. Should I maximize those I have now but will not have later? It would seem not, but how can I know now which preferences I will drop? Should I seek to maximize only the unchanging preferences? What are they? And how will this enable me to add new preferences? Surely, in some cases, it is rational to change preferences, but accounting for this will require a much more complex theory than one based simply on the preferences people do in fact now exhibit.

Although the measurement problems for act utilitarianism are severe, if they could be overcome the theory would have distinct advantages as an ethical theory in business contexts. First of all, as a thoroughgoing consequentialist theory, it has a commonsense plausibility. If your manager tells you to treat customers with respect, he or she probably adds that doing so will benefit the two of you: your firm, and your customers. In other words, we standardly base and explain our moral judgments on acts' overall consequences. In addition, unlike ethical egoism, act utilitarianism is impartial in that it takes into account each individual affected by the acts considered and requires that act which maximizes utility irrespective of who benefits. As an act utilitarian, businessmen will not seek to just maximize their utility or their firm's utility; they consider equally everyone affected by their acts. This squares with our commonsense idea that the "best" business transaction is one in which the "best result" is achieved when both buyer and seller are considered and benefitted. Moreover, act utilitarianism provides a definite method for determining which act is right. It cautions us not to act on our mere intuitions as to what is right and wrong, and requires us to enumerate alternatives, consider all their consequences, calculate utilities, and then act to maximize utility. Now businesses certainly engage frequently in this type of calculation. In considering whether to relocate a plant, alternative sites are listed and the consequences for the firm, stockholders, employees, customers, and the communities affected are analyzed in terms of benefits and harms. Act utilitarianism simply requires the businessperson to act to maximize utility.

Act utilitarianism also accounts for why certain business practices are held to be immoral. Breaking a contract is generally wrong because doing so, typically, does not maximize utility. If you promise your employees a wage increase, other things being equal, you should keep your promise, because doing so will generally lead to better consequences than breaking it. However, moral rules, such as "keep your contracts," are not inviolable. If you sign a contract to build a plant, but then discover that doing so will destroy an ecosystem and not maximize utility, you should break the contract. And if you have promised your employees a wage increase but your company suddenly loses money, maximizing utility may morally require you to break your promise. So, act utilitarianism can account for the moral rules we employ in business, while also permitting business the flexibility to break such rules when morality requires it.

Because it is universalistic, provides a definite method for determining which acts are right, and permits flexibility in adhering to moral rules we use in business, act utilitarianism has decided advantages in international business contexts. In some countries, bribery is prohibited; in others, it is permitted, while in yet others it may be required to do business. Which rules should a business follow? Well, all such rules are merely rules of thumb according to act utilitarianism. Following the rule "never bribe" may typically have utility in one society, while following the rule "always bribe" may typically have utility in another society. All such rules are breakable, and we are obligated to break them when utility maximization requires it.

Act utilitarianism also provides a basis for economics and social policy. Assuming that

1 value is based on preference and is measurable,
2 price is the exchange value of one good in terms of another, and
3 the "rational economic person" will act to maximize his or her own self-interest (i.e., his or her own utility),

economists are able to explain price behavior in a competitive market and show that the "free market" would enable consumers to maximize their own utility. A long line of economists, from Adam Smith to Milton Friedman, argue that the best way to organize the exchange of goods is to let people trade freely with whatever resources they possess, because doing so maximizes overall utility. These economists provide a utilitarian justification for the free market. In effect, Smith and Friedman make an efficiency claim for the free market: the market is said to be the most efficient means to maximize utility. However, the ordinary notion of business efficiency as applied to the individual firm also has a utilitarian basis. The efficient firm maximizes outputs in relation to inputs, which squares with the utilitarians' argument that one should act to maximize benefits and minimize costs. Profit, which in one sense is just a measure of efficiency, thereby has a utilitarian justification. Act utilitarians also argue that their theory provides the best basis for governmental and social policy. Given a set of policy alternatives, which should be chosen? Act utilitarians say we should choose the one that provides the greatest overall benefits at the least cost, the one that maximizes utility.

Act utilitarianism is also attractive to businesspersons because it provides the foundation for cost-benefit analysis, which in its purest form calculates benefits and costs in terms of money. Of course, the market itself places a monetary value on many goods, services, and activities; in addition, utilitarians have devised ingenious methods of placing a price on such seeming unmeasurables as aesthetic value, health, even human life. For instance, we can determine the value you place on your own life by examining the risks you do or would take and the insurance premiums you pay or would be willing to pay. We can also calculate the value of your life by discounting to the present your expected earnings in the future, or by calculating the losses others would experience from your death. Given that we can legitimately make such calculations, the basic strategy of cost-benefit analysis is straightforwardly utilitarian: enumerate alternative courses of action A_1, . . ., An, calculate the benefits and costs of each alternative in monetary units, and if A_2's benefits outweigh its cost and A_2's balance of benefits to costs is greater than any other alternative, then A_2 should be done.

Finally, although some act utilitarians claim their theory supports the shareholder conception of corporate responsibility and others claim utilitarianism supports the stakeholder conception, all agree that utilitarian considerations are the sole basis for resolving the dispute. Briefly, utilitarians favoring the shareholder theory argue that maximizing shareholder interests (typically profit maximization) will, via Adam Smith's "invisible hand," tend to maximize overall utility. "Maximize profits" is thus a general rule of thumb, to be violated only if doing so is required by the utilitarian principle. Advocates of the stakeholder theory argue that all stakeholders (shareholders, employees, customers, suppliers, society, etc.) should be taken into consideration directly in the utilitarian calculation. In any case, act utilitarians agree the dispute is to be resolved by determining which approach actually maximizes utility.

In spite of its advantages in business contexts, act utilitarianism faces severe criticisms in addition to those involving the measurement of utility. Many critics focus on the utilitarians' claim that the only morally relevant feature of an act is its consequences, namely, its utility; according to act utilitarians, no feature other than utility even contributes to an act's rightness. So, if my alternatives involve keeping or breaking a promise and keeping it is morally right, then that act is right solely because it produces more utility than breaking the promise. If breaking the promise has more utility than keeping it, no other feature is morally relevant and breaking it is morally right. Critics point out that one intrinsic feature of an act of keeping a promise is that one is keeping a promise and one intrinsic feature of an act of breaking a promise is that one is breaking a promise. So consider two acts, A_1, and A_2, and features of these acts (where we assume the utility/disutility of keeping/breaking promises are factored into both utility calculations):

Features of acts

		F_1	F_2
Acts	A_1	+85 utility	keeping a promise
	A_2	+86 utility	breaking a promise

Utilitarians claim A_2 is morally right; A_2 maximizes utility, which is the only morally relevant feature. Some critics claim A_1 is morally right, believing that a small increase in utility should not override one's obligation to keep a promise. At the very least, critics claim, promise-keeping and promise-breaking are morally relevant features in determining which act is right and, since act utilitarianism does not regard them as relevant, the theory is defective. Now, clearly, promise-keeping is very important in just about every sort of business transaction, and if act utilitarianism does not provide a plausible account of the role and importance of promise-keeping in business, it is inadequate as an ethical theory for business.

Critics also allege that act utilitarianism does not adequately take into consideration individuals' rights when determining whether an act is morally right. For example, suppose executive X in company Q has worked for months to secure a contract between Q and another company D. Whether the contract is signed depends heavily on what X does, for negotiations are at a crucial stage. If the contract is signed, Q and D will increase profits and new jobs will be created. During final negotiations, Q's president by chance discovers that X has embezzled $50,000 from Q. The president knows Q will be audited tomorrow and knows the auditors will discover X's theft. Q's president confronts X, who explains that the money was needed to pay for an emergency operation for a close relative, but notes that this relative has died and never again will X be pressed to steal money from Q. Also, X says that if the theft is made known to the negotiating team in D, they will no longer trust X and the deal will fall through. Since X's theft will be detected by the impending audit, the president says there is little that can be done. As luck would have it, however, there is a middle-manager, Y, in Q, who has had bad relations with his or her supervisors and is about to be fired. X suggests that Q's president make it appear as though Y embezzled the $50,000. When Y is fired, the company will not press charges, and X will quietly repay the money stolen. The question then is this: should Q's president frame Y for the embezzlement actually committed by X? If, as it appears, doing so would maximize utility, then the act utilitarian would answer yes. However, framing Y seems morally wrong: it violates Y's right to be treated fairly and Y's right not to be falsely accused. Similar cases can be developed to show that managers, acting as utilitarians, would be required to trample on individuals' rights to privacy, due process, safe working conditions, and perhaps even the right to life. Such rights violations pose powerful counterexamples to act utilitarianism.

In addition to difficulties with promising and rights, critics claim that act utilitarianism permits social injustice. For example, the following sort of utility calculation could be employed to "justify" what we would regard as an unjust act of enslavement:

		Persons				
		P_1	P_2	P_3	P_4	Totals
Acts	A_1	+33	+27	+30	−49	+41
	A_2	+10	+10	+10	+10	+40

It is conceivable that the enslavement of P_4 via act A_1 would produce slightly greater total utility than act A_2, which does not involve enslavement and also results in a more equitable distribution of happiness. Since the act utilitarian is committed to holding that A_1 is morally right, but A_1 seems morally wrong because it is unjust, act utilitarianism seems to be an inadequate moral theory.

In response to these three sorts of criticism, act utilitarians claim the counterexamples are contrived and not indicative of real-world situations. They claim that slavery would not maximize utility, so the value assignments in the enslavement counterexample do not reflect reality. Framing the innocent manager is contrived because, in the real world, there surely would be other alternative acts that could be selected. Finally, the promise-breaking case is either contrived because the full negative consequences of breaking a promise are not reflected in the utility calculation, or it is not contrived and the utility values are adequately represented, in which case the only morally relevant feature is utility and A_2 is morally right.

Other utilitarians, convinced these sorts of criticisms are decisive against act utilitarianism, have changed the theory to try to answer them. Although it has been formulated in a variety of ways, this type of theory, called rule utilitarianism, is based on two convictions:

1   Utility maximization plays a central role in an adequate moral theory.
2   Rules play an important role also, a more important role than is accorded them by act utilitarianism.

These two convictions are combined in the idea that we should employ the principle of utility maximization to determine which rules everyone should follow, and then, when faced with a decision as to which act is right in a particular circumstance, we simply determine which act is required by the rule everyone should follow. So, overlooking some terminological technicalities, according to one version of rule utilitarianism an act A in circumstance C is morally right, if and only if the utility of everyone acting according to the rule "If you are in C, then do A" is at least as great as the utility of everyone acting according to any alternative rule applicable to C.

To see how this principle works, suppose you are in a circumstance C in which you have made a promise and you have only two alternative acts available: A_1 (keep your promise) and A_2 (break your promise). Assume A_2 produces more utility than A_1. The act utilitarian will claim A_2 is morally right. The rule utilitarian will consider the rules applicable to this circumstance. Consider two rules: R_1 (If you made a promise, then keep it.), i.e., (If C, then A_1), and R_2 (If you made a promise, then break it.), i.e., (If C, then A_2). The rule utilitarian asks which rule, if followed by everyone, would maximize utility. Of these two rules, it seems clear that R_1 would maximize utility if it were followed by everyone, since if everyone broke his promises chaos would result. Accordingly, the rule utilitarian would claim A_1 is morally right. So, it seems that act and rule utilitarianism sometimes yield different results as to what is morally right, and that rule utilitarianism is sometimes more in accord with our ordinary notion of what is right. Consider another example, our earlier case in which corporation Q's president is to decide whether to frame the innocent Y for X's theft. Assume the president has a choice of two acts: A_1 (frame Y) and A_2 (do not frame Y), and assume that of these two acts A_1 produces more utility than A_2. According to act utilitarianism, A_1 is morally right, but this, as we noted, seems to violate Y's rights and seems intuitively wrong. According to rule utilitarianism, we should examine the rules applicable to this circumstance. Consider two such rules: R_1 (If you are in C, then frame the person.), and R_2 (If you are in C, then do not frame the person.). If, as seems plausible, everyone's following R_2 would maximize utility and everyone's following R_1 would not, then the act in accord with R_2, namely A_2, is morally right. In this manner, rule utilitarians claim their account establishes a central place for both the principle of utility maximization and for moral rules, and combines them into a theory that is able to meet the criticisms of act utilitarianism.

Critics of this version of rule utilitarianism claim that, in the case of the president framing the innocent employee, there is another rule which must be considered: R_3 (if you are in C, then do not frame the person unless doing so maximizes utility.). The critics point out that more utility would be produced by everyone's following R_3 than by everyone's following R_2; indeed, everyone's following R_3 will maximize utility whereas everyone's following a rule such as R_2 will not, since R_2 requires that one never frame a person in C, even when framing that person would maximize utility. So, by his or her own moral principle, the rule utilitarian is committed to R_3. However, applying R_3 to the president's circumstance will produce exactly the same result as applying the act utilitarian principle directly to the circumstance: on both, the morally right act is to frame the innocent employee. This argument is easily generalized. In any circumstance C, the rule that will maximize utility, if followed by everyone, essentially will be: "In C, act to maximize utility." However, when this rule is applied to a particular C, the act recommended as morally right will be exactly the same act recommended by the act utilitarian principle. Since there seem to be very good counterexamples to the act utilitarian principle that make it unacceptable to many people as a moral theory, and the same counter-examples apply to this version of rule utilitarianism, it also seems unacceptable.

Recently, several rule utilitarians have offered revised theories to meet the above criticism, one being Richard Brandt's optimal code utilitarianism. Instead of focusing on the utilities of individual rules, Brandt focuses on the utilities of entire moral codes. Roughly, a moral code (MC) for a society S is a set of shared desires and aversions, along with a complete set of moral rules governing what should be done in all circumstances that may arise in S. Brandt's basic idea is that although any one of a number of moral codes (MC$_1$ or MC$_2$ or . . .) could be employed in S, one such code would have more utility than the others if it were widely accepted in S. This is S's optimal moral code (MC$_0$). According to optimal code utilitarianism, then, an act A in society S is morally right if, and only if, A is not prohibited by the MC$_0$ for S. So, right acts in S are those permitted by the moral code optimal in S, and the optimal code in S is the code that, if it were widely accepted, would maximize utility. Since the optimal code for S will presumably prohibit framing an innocent employee, this theory seems to meet the counterexamples that undercut other versions of utilitarianism.

To the criticism that the optimal moral code for S would consist of one rule (MU) "Maximize utility," and hence the optimal code utilitarian principle yields the same results as the act utilitarian principle, Brandt replies that the critics would have to show that no code could have higher utility if widely accepted than the code which consists solely of MU, and he claims this is highly implausible. Some codes, if widely adopted, would undoubtedly produce high utility but, if MU were widely accepted, it probably would not. If your employees faced a moral problem and inquired about the rule governing such cases, you could only say "Maximize utility," and if they requested more specific advise you could only repeat "Maximize utility." MU is so abstract that if it were the only rule widely accepted in S, uncertainty and confusion would probably result; hence broad adoption of MU probably would not maximize utility. On the other hand, among all the codes consisting of relatively specific rules, there will be one which, if widely accepted, would maximize utility and allow you to provide specific advice to your employees. Hence, Brandt claims that optimal rule utilitarianism will not yield the same counterintuitive results as does act utilitarianism.

Still, optimal code utilitarianism is not defect free in business contexts. The theory rests on the notion of a "society," but any society will consist of subgroups, e.g., physicians, businesspersons. Do businesspersons constitute a society? Well, it is commonly said that they operate by their own set of rules, a set somewhat distinct from ordinary morality. If businesspersons do constitute a society, then the optimal code for the society of businesspersons may permit an act that is prohibited by the moral code optimal for the general society. When such a conflict occurs, what principle can be employed to resolve it? In addition, since the code optimal for S (the code that would maximize utility if it were widely accepted) is probably very different from the code that is actually widely accepted in S, a person following the optimal code may be at a serious disadvantage in a society in which only a few follow it. If the optimal code permits only strict truth in advertising, those who follow it will probably not prosper in a society in which puffery is widely accepted and practiced.

With a history of over two hundred years, utilitarianism has proven to be a durable and resilient ethical theory which is also an important foundation for economics and social policy. Although severe criticisms have been directed at the theory in recent years, the newer versions of rule utilitarianism may provide the basis for an adequate moral theory and even those who believe that no version of utilitarianism will be able to handle the rights and justice criticisms will have to acknowledge that utilitarian considerations must be included as a part of any adequate moral theory.

Bibliography

Alston, W. P. 1967: Pleasure. In P. Edwards (ed.), *The Encyclopedia of Philosophy*, Vol. 6, New York: Macmillan, 341–7.

Bayles, M. D. (ed.) 1968: *Contemporary Utilitarianism* Garden City, NY: Doubleday & Co.

Bentham, J. 1789: *The Principles of Morals and Legislation.* Oxford: Oxford.

Brandt, R. B. 1967: Happiness. In P. Edwards (ed.), *The Encyclopedia of Philosophy*, Vol. 3, New York: Macmillan, 413–4.

Brandt, R. B. 1979: *A Theory of the Good and the Right.* Oxford: Clarendon.

Brandt, R. B. 1992: *Morality, Utilitarianism, and Rights.* New York: Cambridge University Press.

Feldman, F. 1978: *Introductory Ethics.* Englewood Cliffs, NJ: Prentice-Hall.

Glover, J. (ed.) 1990: *Utilitarianism and its Critics.* New York: Macmillan.

Gorovitz, S. (ed.) 1971: *Mill: Utilitarianism – Text and Critical Essays.* Indianapolis: Bobbs-Merrill.

Hooker, B. (ed.) 1994: *Rationality, Rules and Utility: New Essays on the Moral Philosophy of Richard B. Brandt.* Boulder: Westview Press.

Jackson, J. 1993: *A Guided Tour of John Stuart Mill's Utilitarianism.* Mountain View, Ca.: Mayfield Publishing.

Lyons. D. 1965: *The Forms and Limits of Utilitarianism.* Oxford: Clarendon.

Lyons. D. 1994: *Rights, Welfare, and Mill's Moral Theory.* New York: Oxford University Press.

McInerney, P. K. and Rainbolt, G. W. 1994: *Ethics.* New York: Harper Collins.

Mill, J. S. 1957: *Utilitarianism.* Indianapolis: Bobbs-Merrill.

Miller, H. B. and Williams, W. H. (eds) 1982: *The Limits of Utilitarianism.* Minneapolis: University of Minnesota Press.

Mishan. E. J. 1982: *Cost-Benefit Analysis.* 3rd edn. London: Cambridge University Press.

Plamenatz, J. 1958: *The English Utilitarians.* Oxford: Blackwell Publishers.

Quinton, A. 1989: *Utilitarian Ethics.* London: Duckworth Press.

Ross. W. D. 1930: *The Right and the Good.* Oxford: Oxford University Press.

Ross, W. D. 1939: *Foundations of Ethics.* Oxford: Oxford University Press.

Sen, A. and Williams, B. (eds) 1982: *Utilitarianism and Beyond.* New York: Cambridge University Press.

Sidgwick, H. 1902: *Outlines of the History of Ethics.* 5th edn. London: Macmillan.

Sidgwick, H. 1922: *The Methods of Ethics.* London: Macmillan.

Smart, J. J. C. 1961: *An Outline of a System of Utilitarian Ethics.* Melbourne: Melbourne University Press.

Smart, J. J. C. 1967: Utilitarianism. In P. Edwards (ed.) *The Encyclopedia of Philosophy.* Vol. 8, New York: Macmillan, 206–12.

Smart, J. J. C. and Williams, B. 1973: *Utilitarianism: For and Against.* London: Cambridge University Press.

7

Victims of Circumstances?
A Defense of Virtue Ethics in Business

Robert C. Solomon

Abstract

S hould the responsibilities of business managers be understood independently of the social circumstances and "market forces" that surround them, or (in accord with empiricism and the social sciences) are agents and their choices shaped by their circumstances, free only insofar as they act in accordance with antecedently established dispositions, their "character"? Virtue ethics, of which I consider myself a proponent, shares with empiricism this emphasis on character as well as an affinity with the social sciences. But recent criticisms of both empiricist and virtue ethical accounts of character deny even this apparent compromise between agency and environment. Here is an account of character that emphasizes dynamic interaction both in the formation and in the interplay between personal agency and responsibility on the one hand and social pressures and the environment on the other.

Business ethics is a child of ethics, and business ethics, like its parents, is vulnerable to the same threats and challenges visited on its elders. For many years, one such threat (or rather, a family of threats) has challenged moral philosophy, and it is time it was brought out in the open in business ethics as well. It is a threat that is sometimes identified by way of the philosophical term, "determinism," and though its status in the philosophy of science and theory of knowledge is by no means settled, it has nevertheless wreaked havoc on ethics. If there is determinism, so the argument goes, there can be no agency, properly speaking, and thus no moral responsibility. But determinism admits of at least two interpretations in ethics. The first is determination by "external" circumstances, including pressure or coercion by other people. The second is

Source: *Business Ethics Quarterly,* 13 (1) 2003, 43–62.

determination within the person, in particular, by his or her character. In the former case, but arguably not in the latter, there is thought to be a problem ascribing moral responsibility.[1]

The argument can be readily extended to business ethics. Versions of the argument have been put forward with regard to corporations, for instance, in the now perennial arguments whether corporations can be or cannot be held responsible.[2] One familiar line of argument holds that only individuals, not corporations, can be held responsible for their actions. But then corporate executives like to excuse their actions by reference to "market forces" that render them helpless, mere victims of economic circumstances, and everyone who works in the corporation similarly excuses their bad behavior by reference to those who set their agenda and policies. They are mere "victims of circumstances." They thus betray their utter lack of leadership. Moreover, it doesn't take a whole lot of research to show that people in corporations tend to behave in conformity with the people and expectations that surround them, even when what they are told to do violates their "personal morality." What (outside of the corporation) might count as "character" tends to be more of an obstacle than a boon to corporate success for many people. What seems to count as "character" in the corporation is a disposition to please others, obey superiors, follow others, and avoid personal responsibility.

In general philosophy, Kant tried desperately to separate determinism and moral responsibility, defending determinism in the domain of science and "Nature" but preserving agency and responsibility in the domain of ethics. "I have found it necessary to limit knowledge to make room for faith" as he put in one of his most concise but rather misleading *bon mots*. Other philosophers were not so bold. They were willing to accept determinism (even if conjoined with skeptical doubts) and somehow fit agency and responsibility into its domain. David Hume and John Stuart Mill, the two most illustrious empiricist promoters of this strategy, suggested that an act is free (and an agent responsible) if it "flows from the person's character,"[3] where "character" stood for a reasonably stable set of established character traits that were both morally significant and served as the antecedent causal conditions demanded by determinism. Adam Smith, Hume's best friend and the father of not only modern economics but of business ethics too, agreed with this thesis. It was a good solution. It saved the notions of agency and responsibility, it was very much in line with our ordinary intuitions about people's behavior, and it did not try to challenge the scientific establishment. So, too, a major movement in business ethics, of which I consider myself a card-carrying member, is "virtue ethics" which takes the concept of character (and with it the related notions of virtue and integrity) to be central to the idea of being a good person in business. Among the many virtues of virtue ethics in business, one might think, is that, as in Hume and Mill, it would seem to keep at bay the threat of situational ("external") determinism.

Such a solution seems particularly appropriate for business ethics because the concept of character fills the void between institutional behaviorism ("organizational behavior") and an overblown emphasis on free will and personal autonomy that remains oblivious to context, the reality of office work, and the force of peer and corporate pressures. It provides a locus for responsibility without sacrificing the findings of "management science." But I have mixed feelings about the empiricist solution. On the one hand, it seems to me too weak. It does not account (or try to account) for actions "out of character," heroic or saintly or vicious and shockingly greedy behavior, which could not have been predicted of (or even by) the subject. And it does not (as Aristotle does) rigorously hold a person responsible for the formation of his or her character. Aristotle makes it quite clear that a wicked person is responsible for his or her character not because he or she could *now* alter it but because he or she could have and should have acted differently early on and established very different habits and states of character. The corporate bully, the greedy entrepreneur, and the office snitch all would seem to be responsible for not only what they do but who they are, according to Aristotle's tough criterion.

On the other hand, however, the empiricist solution overstates the case for character. (This is what some psychologists, and Gilbert Harman, refer to as the "attribution error.") The empiricists make it sound as if character is something both settled and "robust" (the target of much of the recent psychological literature). Character consists of such traits as honesty and trustworthiness that are more or less resistant to social or interpersonal pressures. But character is never fully formed and settled. It is always vulnerable to circumstances and trauma. People change, and they are malleable. They respond in interesting and sometimes immediate ways to their environment, their peers and pressures from above. Put into an unusual, pressured, or troubled environment, many people will act "out of character," sometimes in heroic but more often in disappointing and sometimes shocking ways. In the corporate setting, in particular, people joke about "leaving their integrity at the office door" and act with sometimes shocking obedience to orders and policies that they personally find unethical and even downright revolting.

These worries can be taken care of with an adequate retooling of the notion of character and its place in ethics, and this is what I will try to do here. But my real worry is that in the effort to correct the excesses of the empiricist emphasis on character, the baby is being thrown out with the bath toys. In recent work by Gilbert Harman and John Doris, in particular, the very notion of character is being thrown into question.[4] Indeed, Harman suggests that "there may be no such thing." Doris entitles his book, tellingly, *Lack of Character.* Both Harman and Doris argue at considerable length that a great deal of what we take as "character" is in fact (and demonstrably) due to specific social settings that reinforce virtuous conduct. To mention two often-used examples, clergy act like clergy not because of character but because they surround themselves with other clergy who expect them to act like clergy. So, too, criminals act like criminals not because of character but because they hang out with other criminals who expect them to act like criminals. Harman argues vehemently against what he calls the illusion of "a robust sense of character." Doris argues, at book length, a very detailed and remarkably nuanced account of virtue and responsibility without character. The conclusion of both authors is that virtue ethics, construed in terms of character, is at best a mistake, and at worst a vicious political maneuver.

It is worth saying a word about this "vicious political maneuver" that is the political target of Harman's and Doris's arguments. I share in their concern, and I, too, would want to argue against those who, on the basis of an absurd notion of character, expect people to "pick themselves up by their own bootstraps," blaming the poor, for instance, for their own impoverishment and thus ignoring social and political (not to mention medical and racial) disadvantages that are certainly not their fault. I, too, reject such a notion of character, but I am not willing to dispense with the very notions of character and the virtues in order to do this.

So, too, in business ethics, there is a good reason to be suspicious of a notion of character that is supposed to stand up to overwhelming pressures without peer or institutional support. I would take Harman's and Doris's arguments as a good reason to insist on sound ethical policies and rigorous ethical enforcement in corporations and in the business community more generally, thus maximizing the likelihood that people will conform to the right kinds of corporate expectations. Nevertheless, something extremely important can get lost in the face of that otherwise quite reasonable and desirable demand. It is the idea that a person can, and should, resist those pressures, even at considerable cost to oneself, depending on the severity of the situation and circumstances. That is the very basis on which virtue ethics has proven to be so appealing to people in business. It is the hope that they can, and sometimes will, resist or even rise up against pressures and policies that they find to be unethical.

So whatever my worries, I find myself a staunch defender of character and the indispensability of talk about character in both ethics and business ethics.[5] To quote my friend and colleague Ed Hartman, "the difference between Peter Hempel [one of the most wonderful human beings we ever met] and Richard Nixon is not just a matter of environment." In both everyday life and in business, there are people we trust, and there are people we do not, often on the basis of a substantial history of disappointments and betrayal. And we trust or distrust those people in much the same circumstances and under much the same conditions. To be sure, character is vulnerable to environment but it is also a bulwark *against* environment. Character supplies that familiar and sometimes uncomfortable or even uncanny resistance to untoward pressures that violate our "principles" or morally disgust us or are damaging to our "integrity." It is character and not God or the Superego that produces that nagging inner voice called "conscience." (It has been suggested that conscience produces character rather than the other way around, but apart from religious predilections there seems to be little sound philosophical argument or empirical research to defend this.) One person refuses to obey a directive to short-change his customers while another refuses to cheat on her expense account despite the fact that everyone around her is doing so. It is character that makes the difference, though not, to be sure, *all* the difference.

Some of my concern with this issue is personal. Like most conscientious people, I worry about my integrity and character, what sorts of temptations and threats I could and would withstand. I feel ashamed (or worse) when I give into those temptations and humiliated when I succumb to (at least some of) those threats. I am occasionally even proud about those temptations and threats I have withstood. Philosophically ("existentially"), I worry about how we view ourselves when the balance of accounts is shifted over to causal and statistical explanations of behavior instead of a continuing emphasis on character, agency, and responsibility. Will that give almost everyone an excuse for almost everything? And professionally, I have made something of a reputation for myself as a "virtue ethicist" in business ethics, in the twisted tradition of Aristotle and Nietzsche, and virtue ethics requires a solid notion of character. *But not a fixed and permanent notion of character.* To be sure, many writers about the virtues, perhaps betraying their own insecurity, tend to describe good character and integrity in terms of rock and stone metaphors, suggesting that the truly virtuous person is capable of standing up against anything. (A handful of mostly legendary examples provide the paradigm.) But I for one never said that virtue ethics requires a strong sense of autonomy, the ability to cut oneself off from all influences and pressures from other people and institutions and ignore one's personal "inclination" and make a decision on the basis of one's "practical reason" alone. On the contrary, I have argued that one's inclinations (one's emotions, in particular) form the essential core of the virtues, and I have argued that so do Aristotle and (more obviously) Nietzsche. And one's emotions are largely *reactive*, responsive to other people and the social situations in which one finds oneself. Virtue ethics need not, and should not, deny any of this.

The "New Empiricism" Virtue Ethics and Empirical Science

Behind the attack on character and virtue lies *another* commendable motive. John Doris puts it well. Virtue ethics, he says, can be traced back to the momentous writings of Aristotle, 2500 years ago. Unfortunately, however, the social psychology on which virtue ethics rests is also 2500 years old. Even the work of Hume, Mill, and Adam Smith is pressing on 250 years, ancient times in the scope of modern psychology. As both Doris and Harman properly point out, there has been a great deal of research in the social sciences, much of it within the last 50 years, that ought to be taken into account. And this, they think, seriously undermines the claims of virtue ethics and its emphasis on character.

As so often in these discussions, there is an easy, but wholly misleading, analogy with physics. Paul Griffiths, for instance, compares our present "folk psychology" to Aristotle's obviously erroneous category of "superlunary objects," an arbitrary grouping wholly determined by ancient ignorance of astronomy.[7] So, too, Harman juxtaposes our ordinary intuitions about morality with the findings from scientific research, arguing (by analogy) that just as we are wrong in our intuitions about classical mechanics so, too, we can be wrong in our moral intuitions. But I think there are very real questions about the extent to which modern empirical studies of human behavior have in any sense replaced rather than merely supplemented or possibly deepened our age-old "folk psychology" in anything like the way that modern astronomy and physics have introduced revolutions in the way we see the world. I do not doubt that many of our moral intuitions are erroneous or archaic, left over from earlier phases of human culture and no longer practical (what Nietzsche once called "the shadows of God"). Nor do I doubt that many of our moral judgments are based on hypocrisy, self-deception, and wishful thinking. But our moral intuitions are not *like* our intuitions in physics. There is no "matter of fact" independent of our intuitions and attitudes. (Against the moral realists of his day, Nietzsche insisted that "there are no moral facts," and contemporary authors such as Simon Blackburn have argued for a "quasi-realism" in which our personal intuitions and attitudes are ineliminable from moral concerns.[8]) The social sciences, our ordinary intuitions, and moral philosophy are all of a piece. There is no easy separation of "facts" about personal character and evaluations of moral merit.[9] Character traits and virtues–honesty, trustworthiness, and a sense of fairness–are normative. They are not mere behavioral tendencies. *All* psychology, if it is psychology at all, is one or another version of "folk psychology" ("the only game in town," according to Jerry Fodor).

Harman and Doris attack virtue ethics in general and the concept of character in particular on the grounds that they do not survive experimental findings in the past few decades. Exhibit number one for both of them is the infamous Stanley Milgram experiments in which people with supposedly good character performed the most despicable acts when encouraged to do by an authority (the experimenter). But though empirical research in social psychology can on occasion shock us, surprise us, annoy us, and sometimes burst our illusions, it all gets weighed and accounted for, whether well or badly, in terms of our ordinary folk psychology observations and the ordinary concepts of belief, desire, emotion, character, and interpersonal influences, interactions, and institutions. There are no Copernican revolutions and no Michelson-Morley experiments. The Milgram and other experiments such as those by Darley and Batson that play a central role in Doris's and Harman's arguments get rationalized and explained in all sorts of ways, but none of them in violation of the basic forms of psychological explanation that Aristotle would have found perfectly familiar.[10] Of course, there remains a debate about the relative influence of "external" (environmental) and "inner" factors (character), but the debate, which ever way it goes, remains within the framework of folk psychology and our ordinary psychological concepts.

We might be disturbed, for example, that so many subjects followed the instructions of an authority figure to the point of (what they thought was) the torturing of another human being, but the various explanations in terms of "obedience to authority" or the unusual circumstances of the experiment (how often are most of us told to punish anyone?) do nothing to challenge our ordinary moral intuitions. It just reminds us of something we'd rather not remember, that ordinary people sometimes act very badly in group and institutional situations. This should come as no surprise to those of us who do corporate and organizational ethics.

I would not want to rest my argument on a general and contentious claim about the social sciences, however. On the contrary, what is disturbing to me is Harman's and Doris's juxtaposition of virtue ethics *against* the social sciences. One of the virtues of virtue ethics, I have always thought, is its utter compatibility with the social sciences. It rests on (one or another) theory of human nature, and it is unashamedly a theory about how people *are*, not how they ideally ought to be. Kantian ethics is explicitly not so. Its main thrust lies in the domain of autonomy and it matters only marginally what people in fact want to do or normally do. In virtue ethics, by contrast, what people want to do and normally do makes a great deal of difference. And learning what people want to do and normally do is always relevant, even if only as a warning that our practices and institutions are offering up the wrong kind of role models and encouraging the wrong kinds of desires, ideas, and behavior. (Utilitarianism is also rigorously empirical and shares this virtue with virtue ethics, but it tends to emphasize the consequences of behavior and thus ignore the intentions and motives–and thus the character–of the agent.)

I have long been an advocate of cooperation between moral philosophy and the social sciences in business ethics. I think that the more we know about how people actually behave in corporations, the richer and more informed our moral judgments and, more important, our decisions will be. In particular, it is very instructive to learn how people will behave in extraordinary circumstances, those in which our ordinary moral intuitions do *not* give us a clue. All of us have asked, say, with regard to the Nazi disease in Germany in the Thirties, how we would have behaved; or how we would behave, think, and feel if we worked for a tobacco company. But even in an ordinary corporation (which is not the same as a university in which there is at least the illusion of individual autonomy and "academic freedom"), the question of "obedience to authority" comes front and center.

Thus an experiment like the Milgram experiment is shocking precisely because it does not seem to presuppose any extraordinary context. Milgram's experiment, which would certainly be prohibited today, has to do with subjects inflicting potentially lethal shocks to victim-learners (in fact the experimenter's accomplices). Even when the victim-learners pleaded for them to stop, the majority of subjects continued to apply the shocks when ordered to do so by the authorities (the experimenters). One could easily imagine this "experiment" being confirmed in any corporation.[11] But I find the use of such research to undermine the notion of character not at all convincing.[12] Harman, for example, argues that

> Empirical studies designed to test whether people behave differently in ways that might reflect their having different character traits have failed to find relevant differences. It is true that studies of this sort are very difficult to carry out and there have been few such studies. Nevertheless, the existing studies have had negative results. Since it is possible to explain our ordinary belief in character

traits as deriving from certain illusions, we must conclude that there is no empirical basis for the existence of character traits.[13]

But in addition to leaping from "very few studies" that are "difficult to carry out" to the conclusion that there is "no empirical basis for the existence of character traits" the whole weight of the argument comes to depend on the *possibility* of explaining our ordinary belief in character traits as "deriving from certain illusions." But what would such an explanation consist of? What illusions are we talking about? And what is our "ordinary belief in character"? I will argue that it does not require the "robust" notion attacked by Harman.

Doris is much more cautious and painstaking in his conclusions. He admits that empirical psychological studies are deeply flawed and limited especially in the fact that the studies he employs describe only particular behavior in particular (artificial) situations and not long-term patterns of behavior–which is what character is all about. He admits that "meaningful generalization outside of the laboratory is "questionable."[14] He even says, borrowing from Churchill on democracy, "I'll readily admit it: experimental psychology is perhaps the worst available method for understanding human life. Except, I hasten to add, for all of the other methods" (including the use of moral "intuitions" of armchair moral philosophy).[15] His main objection to those who champion virtue ethics, however, is that "they presuppose the existence of character structures that actual people do not very often possess" (12, 42, 68). But unless such structures are supposed to be indefensibly wooden and the "not very often" means "very rarely" this is a fairly weak claim that is perfectly compatible with what virtue ethicists require in terms of character.

What Is a Virtue and Whence Character?

Harman does a nice job of delimiting the ordinary notions of virtue and character, namely those that are most relevant to business ethics. He distinguishes character from various psychological disorders (schizophrenia, mania, depression). More dubiously, he distinguishes character from "innate aspects of temperament such as shyness or being a happy or sad person."[16] Kant, oddly enough, quite correctly insists that being happy (though an "inclination") can be a virtue, as it makes us more inclined to do our duty. But Harman is not just attacking the virtues. He is after character traits in general. Shyness, for example, is a non-moral example of a character trait. Harman considers this a prime example of "false attribution." But I think Jean-Paul Sartre has his eye on something very important when he refers to the citing of such a character trait as "bad faith," namely, where we point to a causal syndrome where we should be talking about decisions and the cultivation (in a very strong sense) of character.[17] There is a certain element of such Sartrianism (an insistence on existential choices rather than robust character) in Harman's argument (with which I quite agree), but this is a very different set of reasons for questioning or qualifying the concepts of character and the virtues.[18]

Harman then considers such Aristotelian traits as courage, cowardice, honesty, dishonesty, benevolence, malevolence, friendliness, and unfriendliness. (Although it is not clear, contra Hume, that benevolence and malevolence are virtue and vice, respectively. Doing and not merely wishing, beneficence and maleficence, are the virtues in question.) Aristotle describes "the ordinary conception of such character traits" as relatively long-term dispositions to act in certain ways. (We might note again that Aristotle was describing the ordinary conception of his Mediterranean peers twenty-three hundred years ago.) Doris calls this long-term disposition to act in certain ways "globalism" which involves (a) consistency of character traits, (b) stability of character traits, and (c) the integration of various such traits, what in Aristotle is usually called "the unity of the virtues." It is what he ultimately claims to be "empirically inadequate."[19] Character traits involve activity, not just "possession," habits and operative desires and not just skills. Skills and knowledge may well be involved but are not sufficient for the attribution of the virtue (or vice). Furthermore, character traits must be *broad based* rather than narrow dispositions. (A particular fear does not signify cowardice.)

But the attribution of virtue (or vice) and the ascription of character traits are particularly tricky notions in Harman's and especially in Doris's discussions. To deny that a particular fear or phobia entails cowardice is not yet to leap to the "global" hypothesis that a virtue or character trait must be all-pervasive in one's personality. Doris discusses "local traits" (honesty in particular) and observes that people are sometimes honest in one sort of situation but not in another (108). This, of course, is no surprise. (Alfred Carr, among others, has often noted the inappropriateness of the virtues in at least some business settings.[20]) But in the defense of the virtues one need not insist on global virtues (or vices) any more than one should insist that each and every bit of behavior is the reflection of a virtue (or lack thereof). Doris's dramatic postmodern conclusion, "The Fragmentation of Character," the idea that there is no single "core of character" that alone explains our social behavior, is on the one hand (like most postmodern rhetoric) enormously overblown. On the other hand, it is just a bland description of what we all recognize, when we are not being blindly moralistic or overly philosophical, that the virtues are contextual and only rarely "global" in nature.

In the ordinary conceptions of character traits and virtues, Harman and Doris tell us, people differ in their possession of such traits and virtues. People are different, and these differences explain their differences in behavior. Harman: "We ordinarily suppose that a person's character traits *help* to explain at least some of the things the person does" (italics mine). But, he says, "the fact that two people regularly behave in different ways does not establish that they have different character traits. The difference *may* be due to their different situations rather than differences in their characters" (italics mine). But notice that there is no inconsistency whatever between insisting that a person's character traits *help* to explain their behavior and insisting that a difference in behavior *may* be due to the different situations in which two people find themselves. So, too, Doris's objection to globalism is that people (in experimental situations) fail to display the consistency and stability that explanations in terms of character require. But, again, the short-term experiments that he cites do not undermine our more ordinary long-term judgments about personal propensities and dispositions. At best, they force us to face some hard truths about ourselves and consider other propensities and dispositions that may not be virtuous at all.

In our "ordinary conception" two people (one honest, one dishonest) in the same situation (discovering a lost wallet in the street, encountering a person in apparent desperate need, being ordered by an experimenter to "keep on punishing") will very probably act differently. But any philosopher worthy of his or her debating trophies will quickly point out that no two situations are sufficiently similar to make that case. It is only a very thin description of "the situation" (the experimental set-up) that makes it seem so. Subjects come from different backgrounds and different social classes. They are different genders. They may as a consequence have very different senses of the situation. I would not join Joel Feinberg in claiming that those students who do not stop for a stranger in need (in Darley and Batson's much-discussed "Good Samaritan" experiment) have a "character flaw" but neither would I conclude (with Doris) that their behavior is largely "situational."[21] The student's way of seeing and being in the situation may be very different, and this, of course, is just what Aristotle says about character. It is, first of all, a kind of perception, based on good up-bringing. Thus I think Harman is being a bit disingenuous when he argues that "they must be disposed to act differently in the same circumstances (as they perceive those circumstances)." The question of character begins with how they perceive those circumstances.

In his subsequent discussion, Harman follows Nisbett and Ross (1991) in arguing that "people often choose the situations to which they are exposed."[22] "Thus clerics and criminals rarely face an identical or equivalent set of situational challenges. Rather they place themselves, or are placed by others, in situations that differ precisely in a way that induce clergy to look, feel, and act consistently like clergy and that induce criminals to look, feel, and act consistently like criminals" (Nisbett and Ross, 19). Furthermore, in the presence of their peers, people "sometimes feel *obliged* even committed to act consistently (ibid, italics in original). True enough (and Jean-Paul Sartre could not have put it better). Corporate managers and employees feel obliged and committed to act in conformity with corporate pressures and policies even when they are questionable or unethical, and they learn to rationalize accordingly. The question is, does any of this imply that we should give up or give in on character? Or should we say that character is both cultivated and maintained through the dynamic interaction of individuals and groups in their environment and they in turn develop those virtues (and vices) that in turn motivate them to remain in the situations in which their virtues are supported, reinforced, and not threatened?

In Milgram's famous "shocking people" experiment in the early 1960s (just as America was getting more deeply involved in the morass of Vietnam), the experimental data were indeed shocking, even to Milgram and his colleagues who expected no such result. In the social context of the times, questions about obedience to authority (left over from the Nuremberg trials not so many years before) had a special poignancy, especially in the face of the soon to be challenged American "innocence" of the time. It was very upsetting to find that good, solid, ordinary middle-class people could be ordered (but not coerced) to act so brutally (whether or not they had severe misgivings about their behavior at the time–a matter of no small importance here). The facts of the experiment are beyond dispute. But what the experiment *means* remains highly controversial, and it does not deserve the central place in the attack on character that it is now receiving. Doris claims that "Milgram's experiments show how apparently non-coercive situational factors may induce destructive behavior despite the apparent presence of contrary evaluative and disposi-tional structures." Accordingly, he "gives us reason to question the robustness of dispositions implicated in compassion-relevant moral behavior."[23]

Well, no. The disposition (virtue) that is most prominent and robust in this very contrived and unusual situation, the one that virtually all of the subjects had been brought up with and practiced everyday since childhood, was doing what they were told by those in authority. Compassion, by contrast, is a virtue more often praised than practiced, except on specially designated occasions (giving to the neediest at Christmas time) or stretching the term to include such common courtesies as restraining one's criticism of an unprepared student or letting the other car go first at a four-way intersection. (I would argue that such examples betray a lack of understanding of what compassion is.) Most often, people display compassion by "feeling sorry for" those much worse off than they, a very small expenditure of effort even when it is sincere. It seems to me that what the Milgram experiment shows–and what subsequent events in Vietnam made all too painfully obvious–was that despite our high moral opinions of ourselves and our conformist chorus singing about what independent individuals we all are, Americans, like Germans before them, are capable of beastly behavior in circumstances where their *practiced* virtues are forced to confront an unusual situation in which unpracticed efforts are required. In the Milgram experiment as in Vietnam, American subjects and soldiers were compelled by their own practiced dispositions to follow orders even in the face of consequences that were intolerable. Obedience may not always be a virtue. But that is not what is being challenged by Harman and Doris. They are denying (contrary to the empirical evidence) that people have robust dispositions. I would say, no. They are just looking at the wrong disposition.

In discussions of Vietnam, those who were not there (especially politicians) like to talk about the virtue of courage as the defining trait of the American forces. What they ignore, of course, is the very nature of the war. In several important memoirs by soldiers who served there, Bill Broyles and Tim O'Brien, it becomes clear that courage was just about the last thing on most of the soldiers' minds.[24] They were terrified of losing legs and arms. They were moved by camaraderie and a sense of mutual obligation. (The virtue-name "loyalty" misses the mark.) The only discussion of courage in O'Brien's book has to do with a single heroic figure, a Captain Johansen whom he likens to Hector in Homer's *Iliad*. But this one character is exemplary in precisely the fact that he alone talked about and exemplified true courage. But the absence of courage (which is not to imply anything like cowardice on the part of the American troops) had a great deal to do with the nature of this particular war. It lacked any sense of purpose or progress. It lacked any sense of meaning for most of the men. And so, in that moral vacuum, all that was left for most soldiers was the worry about their own physical integrity and their keen sense of responsibility for each other. The atrocities at My Lai and Thanh Phong followed as a matter of course. There was no context in which either character or courage could be exercised.

Which brings us back to the misgivings and feelings of discomfort experienced by some (not all) of the subjects and the "grunts" in Vietnam. Feelings of compassion (and other moral sentiments) may not be definitive in motivating behavior, especially if one has not faced anything like the awful situation in which the subjects and soldiers found themselves. But it does not follow that there is nothing more for virtue ethics to say about such cases. Experiments such as Milgram's are no longer allowed on college campuses, and for good reason. The feelings provoked in the subjects were too painful, and often with lasting damage. [25] And this is nothing, of course, compared to the post-traumatic experiences of many of those who served in Vietnam. The robustness of compassion must be measured not simply in terms of whether the subjects refused to continue with the experiment or not (most did) or whether the soldiers continued to do as they were ordered but by how powerful and upsetting the feelings they experienced both during and after the experiment. It is worth noting that there were a few sadists who actually enjoyed cruelty. There were others that were brutalized by the experiment and many who were brutalized by the war. That, it seems to me, should not be discounted. Bosses today are once again being forced to lay off thousands of their managers and employees. ("Market forces" is the inescapable explanation.) But there is all the difference in the world between those monsters like the infamous Al "Chainsaw" Dunlap who took such evident pride in cross the board cuts and virtual saints such as Aaron Feuerstein who felt so badly about having to lay off workers (after a fire gutted his factory) that he kept them on the payroll until the company got back on its feet.[26]

The Milgram Experiment Revisited: A Model of Corporate Life?

Is corporate life nothing but the vectors of peer pressures, leaving very little or even no room for the personal virtues? Does social psychology show that this is not the case only for corporate grinds but for all of us? Empirically-minded philosophers love to find a single experiment, or perhaps two, that make this case for them, that is, which provide the basis for speculative excursions that go far beyond the (usually rather timid) findings of the social psychologists themselves. Harman's appeal to the two famous experiments by Milgram and by Darley and Batson are illustrative. Doris takes in a much wider swath of the social science literature, but even he is forced to admit, throughout his admirable book, that there are profound reasons for not generalizing from particular experiments to a good deal of "real life."

Regarding the Milgram experiment, Harman (following Ross and Nisbett) rejects as implausible any explanation in terms of a "character defect" and suggests instead the "step-wise character of the shift from relatively unobjectionable behavior to complicity in a pointless, cruel, and dangerous ordeal." I think that this is indeed part of the explanation. Milgram's subjects needed to have their callousness cultivated even as they dutifully obeyed the authorities (like the proverbial frog in slowly boiling water). The subjects could not have been expected to simply shock strangers on command. But where Harman adds that we are tempted to make the "fundamental attribution error" of blaming the subjects' destructive obedience on a personal defect, I would say instead that what the Milgram experiment shows is how foolish and tragic the otherwise important virtues of conformity and obedience can be. There is no "personal defect" on display here precisely because what the experiment shows is the consistency and stability of *that* virtue. And the fact that it is (like all virtues) not always a virtue is no argument against its status as part of the core of the explanation of the subjects' behavior. The rest of the explanation involves not just the incremental but also the disorienting nature of the situation.

But one third of the subjects in the Milgram experiment *did* quit. And those who did not were indeed confused. Is there no room for character in a complete explanation? Or do the differences between the subjects and their behavior and feelings *demand* such an explanation? Where are all of those studies on individual differences that would explain the differences (without necessarily taking anything away from the importance of the situation and the importance of the authority of the experimenters)? What about that voluminous literature not in social psychology but in the (artificially competing) field of personality theory, from Freud, Gordon Allport, David McClelland, and more recently, Costa and McRae? At the University of Minnesota, just a few blizzards away from Doris's previous base in Ann Arbor, the continuity and stability of character has become something of a minor industry.[27] If we want to play off moral philosophy and virtue ethics against the social sciences, let's make sure that all of the social sciences are represented and not just social psychology, which tends to define itself (artificially again, in competition with personality theory) as the study of the social dimensions of human behavior.

The other often-used case for "lack of character" is the case of the "good Samaritan" designed by Darley and Batson. Seminary students, on their way to give an assigned lecture (on "the good Samaritan") were forced to confront a person (an accomplice of the experimenter) on their way. Few of them stopped to help. It is no doubt true that the difference between subjects and their willingness to help the (supposed) victim can be partially explained on the basis of such transient variables as the fact that they were "in a hurry." And it is probably true as well (and not at all surprising to those of us who are not pushing "faith-based initiative" these days) that people who were (or claimed to be) religious or who were about to talk on a religious topic of direct relevance to the experience did not act so differently as they would have supposed. But does it follow that character played no role? I would say that all sorts of character traits, from one's ability to think about time and priorities to one's feelings of anxiety and competence when faced with a (seemingly) suffering human being all come into play. Plus, of course, the sense of responsibility and obligation to arrive at an appointment on time, which once again slips into the background of the interpretation of the experiment and so blinds us to the obvious.

As in the Milgram experiment, how much is the most plausible explanation of the case precisely one that the experimenters simply assume but ignore, namely the character trait or virtue of promptness, the desire to arrive at the designated place on time? It is not lack of character. It is a *conflict* of character traits, one practiced and well-cultivated, the other more often spoken of than put in practice. Theology students have no special claims on compassion. They just tend to talk about it a lot. And as students they have had little opportunity to test and practice their compassion in ways that are not routine.

In his discussion, Harman argues that people often choose the situations to which they are exposed. But on what basis do they make such choices? Surely part of the explanation is their wanting to act as they believe they ought to, with the knowledge that they are prone to temptation and peer pressure. A more obvious aspect of their choice is their judgment that they would feel more comfortable in one situation rather than another and that their comfort depends, in part, on their virtues. Thus clerics and criminals place themselves, or are placed by others, in situations that differ precisely *because* they induce clergy to look, feel, and act consistently like clergy and induce criminals to look, feel, and act consistently like criminals. None of this eliminates situational factors as an explanation of behavior. On the contrary, it furthers them and explains why people "feel *obliged* and even committed to act consistently." None of this implies that we should give up or give in on character but rather tells us that circumstances and character cannot be pried apart and should not be used competitively as alternative explanations of virtuous or vicious behavior.

Harman notes that employers mistakenly think that they can gain useful information from interviewing potential employees. But such interviews, Harman argues, only add "noise" to the decision process. This may explain, by the way, Princeton's peculiar (and so far as I know unique) policy of hiring new professors without interviews, on the basis of the written work alone. But I doubt that it has much justification in social science. First of all, it is a falsification of the interviewing process to think that what it provides is more *information.* Rather it provides an opportunity for employers (or their chosen representatives in "Human Resources") to "get the feel" of a candidate, see how much "in sync" they are, in order to anticipate how they will "get along." This explains why most interviewers describe themselves as typically having made a decision for all intents and purposes within the first minute or so, which would make little sense if the purpose of the interview was to gather "more information." Second, of course, there are people who have the skill (not necessarily a virtue) to interview well and others who do not. This can indeed be misleading, and it is all the worse if the candidate is also skillful at deception, hiding his or her crasser motives and intentions in order to "make a good impression." But none of this undermines the importance or intelligibility of the interviewing process. It just means that interviewers should be on their toes and learn to ferret out insincerity and deception, skills on which most of them already pride themselves.

What is not debatable, it seems to me, is that people present themselves differently, whether or not their presentations accurately represent their virtues and vices (which longer exposure is sure to reveal). I have long argued that the subject of explanation is not just the behavior of an agent but the behavior of an *agent-in-situation* (or some such odd locution). In business ethics, in particular, the behavior in question is the behavior of an "*individual-within-the-organization*," which is not for a moment to deny that this context may not be the only one of relevance in moral evaluation. Context is essential but it isn't everything. Virtues and vices are important for our explanations of human behavior, but they make sense only in the context of particular situations and cultural surroundings. There is no such thing as courage or generosity in abstraction, but it does not follow that there is no such thing as courage or generosity.

Conclusion: In Defense of Business Virtue Ethics

Virtue ethics has a long pedigree, going back to Plato and Aristotle, Confucius in China, and many other cultures as well as encompassing much of medieval and modern ethics–including, especially, the ethics of Hume, Adam Smith, and the other "Moral Sentiment Theorists." But we would do well to remind ourselves just why virtue and character have become such large concerns in the world today–in business ethics and in politics in particular. The impetus comes from such disparate sources as the Nuremberg trials and American atrocities in Vietnam, teenage drug use and peer pressure, and the frequently heard rationalization in business and politics that "everyone is doing it." The renewed emphasis on character is an attempt to build a personal bulwark (call it "integrity") against such pressures and rationalizations and (though half-heartedly) to cultivate virtues other than those virtues of unquestioning obedience that proved to be so dominant in the Milgram experiments and in Vietnam atrocities such as My Lai.

Nevertheless, I share with Harman and Doris a concern that virtue ethics and talk about character is being overused and abused. Too often preachers of the virtues praise (in effect) their own sterling personalities without bothering to note how little there has been in their lives to challenge their high opinion of themselves. Too often, people are blamed for behaving in ways in which, given the situation and their personal backgrounds, it is hard to see how they could have acted or chosen to act otherwise. In contemporary politics, in particular, the renewed emphasis on character is prone to bullying and even cruelty, for example, as way of condemning the victims of poverty and racial oppression for their behavior and insisting that such people "boot-strap" their way to respectability. Thus I could not be more in agreement with Harman when he throws suspicion on the American conservative William Bennett. But Nietzsche beats him to it, a full century before *The Book of Virtues*:

> Then again there are those who consider it a virtue to say, "virtue is necessary"; but at bottom they believe only that the police are necessary.[28]

I think that Harman's and Doris's ultimate aim is to take moral philosophy away from such vicious moralism and give it back to the good old empirical social engineer. Indeed, B. F. Skinner is never far from these new empiricist accounts, although neither Harman nor Doris would accept the absurdities of strict behaviorism. But once we have downplayed character and with it responsibility and put all of the emphasis back onto the environment, the "situation", all that is left is to design circumstances conducive to desirable behavior. To be sure, such design is important and essential and almost totally ignored by too many virtue ethicists today. If we are to combat intolerance, encourage mutual forgiveness, and facilitate human flourishing in contexts plagued by ethnic hatred, for instance, there is no denying the need for mediating institutions that will create the circumstances in which the virtues can be cultivated. Closer to home, the cultivation of the virtues in much-touted moral education also requires the serious redesign of our educational institutions. And much of the crime and commercial dishonesty in the United States and in the world today is due, no doubt, to the absence of such designs and character-building contexts. (The market, said the late great "Buddhist" economist E. F. Schumaker, "is the institutionalization of non-responsibility."[29]) We need less moralizing and more beneficent social engineering.

I could not agree more with these aims. But the existentialist twist to which Harman alludes (that we *choose* our circumstances) and the postmodern turn encouraged by Doris (that we acknowledge that for the most part our circumstances make us) convince me not that we should eliminate talk of the virtues and character but fully acknowledge both the role of the social sciences (all of the social sciences) and stop preaching the virtues without due emphasis upon *both* personal responsibility and the force of circumstances. Like Doris, we should appreciate more such "out of character" heroic and saintly behavior (he mentions Oscar Schindler in particular) and the exigencies of context and circumstances. But we should insist, first and foremost, that people–at any rate, people *like* us–are responsible for what they do, and what they make of themselves.

Notes

1. See, for example, Robert Young, "The Implications of Determinism," in Peter Singer, *A Companion to Ethics* (London: Blackwell, 1991). I am not considering here the post-Freudian complications of determination by way of compulsion or personality disorder.

2. E.g., Kenneth Goodpaster and John B. Matthews, Jr., "Can a Corporation have a Conscience?" *Harvard Business Review*, Jan.–Feb. 1982; John Ladd, "Morality and the Ideal of Rationality in Formal Organizations," *The Monist*, Oct. 1970; Peter A. French, *Collective and Corporate Responsibility* (New York: Columbia University Press, 1984), Peter A. French, "Responsibility and the Moral Role of Corporate Entities," in R. Edward Freeman, ed., *Business as a Humanity* (*Ruffin Lectures II* (New York: Oxford, 1994); Peter A. French, "The Corporation as a Moral Person," *American Philosophical Quarterly* 16: 3 (1979). Manuel G. Velasquez, *Business Ethics* (Engelwood Cliffs, N.J.: Prentice-Hall, 1982 and further editions).

3. David Hume, *An Enquiry Concerning Human Understanding*, 2nd ed. L. A. Sleby-Biggee, ed. (Clarendon: Oxford University Press, 1902). John Stuart Mill, *A System of Logic* 8th ed. (New York: Harper & Row, 1874). Adam Smith, *Theory of the Moral Sentiments* (London: George Bell, 1880).

4. Gilbert Harman, "Moral Philosophy Meets Social Psychology: Virtue Ethics and the Fundamental Attribution Error," *Proceedings of the Aristotelian Society* 99 (1998–99): 315–331. Revised version in Harman, G., *Explaining Value and Other Essays in Moral Philosophy* (Oxford: Clarendon Press, 2000), 165–178. See also, "The Nonexistence of Character Traits," *Proceedings of the Aristotelian Society* 100 (1999–2000): 223–226. John Doris, *Lack of Character: Personality and Moral Behavior* (New York: Cambridge University Press, 2002).

5. Two philosophical defenses of character are Joel Kupperman, "The Indispensability of Character," in *Philosophy*, April 2001, 76(2): 239–250, and Maria Merritt, "Virtue Ethics and Situationist Personality Psychology," in *Ethical Theory and Moral Practice* 3 (2000): 365–383.

6. The fight against the pervasiveness of excuses is something I learned early on from Jean-Paul Sartre and pursue in some detail in my series, *No Excuses: Existentialism and the Meaning of Life* (The Teaching Company, 2000).

7. Paul Griffiths, *What Emotions Really Are* (Chicago, 1997).

8. Simon Blackburn, *Essays in Quasi-Realism* (New York: Oxford University Press, 1995).

9. Alasdair MacIntyre, *After Virtue* (Notre Dame, 1984).

10. I would plea for something of an exception in the case of the fascinating flow of neuropsychiatric research of the last thirty or so years, which does indeed go beyond folk psychology, not only in its particular findings but in the very vocabulary and structure of its explanations. Nevertheless, what is so dazzling in much of this research is precisely that way in which neurological anomalies violate our ordinary "folk psychology" explanations. I will limit my references to two. The first is a wonderful series of studies published by Oliver Sachs over the years, including *The Man Who Mistook His Wife for a Hat and Other Clinical Tales* (Touchstone, 1998). The second is the recent research of Antonio Damasio, esp. in *Descartes's Error* (Putnam, 1994).

11. Stanley Milgram, "Behavioral Study of Obedience," *Journal of Abnormal and Social Psychology*, vol. 67, 1963; Obedience to Authority (New York: Harpercollins, 1983).

12. I have argued with both Harman and Doris that they have made selective use of

social science research. In particular, they have restricted their appeals and references almost entirely to social psychology and have been correspondingly neglectful of counter-arguments in personality theory. The differences in perspective–and consequently the tension–between these two branches of empirical psychology are extremely significant to the argument at hand. See, e.g., Todd F. Heatherton (ed.), Joel Lee Weinberger, (ed.), *Can Personality Change?* [edited book] (Washington, D.C.: American Psychological Association, 1994), xiv, 368. A. Caspi, and B. W. Roberts (1999), "Personality Continuity and Change Across the Life Course" in L. A. Pervin and O. P. John (eds.), *Handbook of Personality: Theory and Research*, 2nd ed., (New York: Guilford), 300-326. Thomas J. Bouchard, Jr., "The Genetics of Personality," [chapter], Kenneth Blum (ed.); Ernest P. Noble, (ed.) et al., *Handbook of Psychiatric Genetics* (Boca Raton, Fla.: CRC Press, Inc. 1997), 273–296.

13. Gilbert Harman, "Moral Philosophy Meets Social Psychology" (web version), 1.

14. P. 67, p. 24 (all page numbers are to the unpublished manuscript, courtesy of John Doris.)

15. Doris, 15-6.

16. But see a similar distinction defended by Ed Hartman, "The Role of Character in Business Ethics," in J. Dienhart, D. Moberg, and R. Duska, *The Next Phase of Business Ethics: Integrating Psychology and Ethics* (Amsterdam: JAI/Elsevier, 2001), 341–354.

17. Jean-Paul Sartre, *Being and Nothingness*, trans. H. Barnes (New York: Philosophical Library, 1956), see for instance 104f.

18. An essay that uses the Milgram experiment to talk about "excuse" is A. Strudler and D. Warren, "Authority, Heuristics, and the Structure of Excuses," in J. Dienhart, D. Moberg, and R. Duska, *The Next Phase of Business Ethics*, 355–375. My own view is that "everybody's doing it" is NO excuse, or at best a mitigating one. See my *No Excuses: Existentialism and the Meaning of Life*. See also the now classic essay by Ron Green, "Everybody's Doing It," in *Business Ethics Quarterly* 1(1): 75–94.

19. Doris, 41-2.

20. Alfred Carr, "Is Business Bluffing Ethical?" *Harvard Business Review* (Jan.-Feb. 1968).

21. J. M. Darley and C. D. Batson, "From Jerusalem to Jericho: A Study of Situational and Disposition Variables in Helping Behavior," *Journal of Personality and Social Psychology* 27, 1973.

22. Nisbett and Ross, *Human Inference: Strategies and Shortcomings of Social Judgment* (Prentice-Hall, 1980).

23. Doris, 69.

24. William Broyles, Jr., *Brothers in Arms* (New York: Knopf, 1986) and Tim O'Brien, *If I Die in a Combat Zone Box Me up and Ship Me Home* (New York: Delacorte, 1973). Both books are discussed by Thomas Palaima in "Courage and Prowess Afoot in Homer and in Vietnam" in *Classical and Modern Literature*, 20/3/(2000).

25. See Milgram, *Obedience to Authority*.

26. See my discussion in A *Better Way to think about Business* (Oxford, 1999), 10.

27. For a good summary of the debate and the differences between the two approaches, see D. T. Kenrick, and D. C. Funder, 1988. "Profiting from Controversy: Lessons from the Person-Situation Debate," *American Psychologist* (43): 23–34, and David C. Funder, "Personality," *Annual Review of Psychology*, 2001, vol . 52: 197–221.

28. *Thus Spoke Zarathustra*, Part II, "On the Virtuous," trans., Kaufmann (New York: Viking, 1954), 207

29. E. F. Schumaker, *Small is Beautiful* (Harper and Row, 1973).

References

Blackburn, Simon. 1995. *Essays in Quasi-Realism* (New York: Oxford University Press.

Bouchard, Thomas J., Jr. 1997. "The Genetics of Personality" [chapter]. Kenneth Blum (ed.), Ernest P. Noble, (ed.) et al. *Handbook of Psychiatric Genetics.* Boca Raton, Fla.: CRC Press, Inc., 273–296.

Broyles, William, Jr. 1986. *Brothers in Arms.* New York: Knopf.

Carr, Alfred. Jan.-Feb. 1968. "Is Business Bluffing Ethical?" *Harvard Business Review.* 143–153.

Caspi, A., and B. W. Roberts. 1999. "Personality Continuity and Change Across the Life Course" in *Handbook of Personality: Theory and Research* 2nd ed. L. A. Pervin and O. P. John (eds.) New York: Guilford, 300–326.

Damasio, Antonio. 1994. *Descartes's Error.* New York: Putnam.

Darley, J. M., and C. D. Batson. 1973. "From Jerusalem to Jericho: A Study of Situational and Dispositional Variables in Helping Behavior." *Journal of Personality and Social Psychology* 27.

Doris, John. 2002. *Lack of Character: Personality and Moral Behavior.* New York: Cambridge University Press.

French, Peter A. 1984. *Collective and Corporate Responsibility.* New York: Columbia University Press.

_____. 1979. "The Corporation as a Moral Person." *American Philosophical Quarterly* 16(3).

_____. "Responsibility and the Moral Role of Corporate Entities." 1994. In *Business as a Humanity (Ruffin Lectures II).* R. Edward Freeman (ed.). New York: Oxford.

Funder, David C. 2001. "Personality." *Annual Review of Psychology.* 52: 197–221.

Goodpaster, Kenneth, and John B. Matthews, Jr. Jan.-Feb. 1982. "Can a Corporation Have a Conscience? *Harvard Business Review.*

Green, Ronald. "Everybody's Doing It." *Business Ethics Quarterly* 1(1): 75–94.

Griffiths, Paul. 1997. *What Emotions Really Are.* Chicago University of Chicago Press.

Harman, Gilbert. 1998–99. "Moral Philosophy Meets Social Psychology: Virtue Ethics and the Fundamental Attribution Error." *Proceedings of the Aristotelian Society* (99): 315–331.

_____. 1999–2000. "The Nonexistence of Character Traits." *Proceedings of the Aristotelian Society* (100): 223–226.

_____. 2000. *Explaining Value and Other Essays in Moral Philosophy.* Oxford: Clarendon Press, 165–178.

Hartman, Edwin M., ed. 2001. "The Role of Character in Business Ethics." in *The Next Phase of Business Ethics: Integrating Psychology and Ethics.* J. Dienhart, D. Moberg, and R. Duska (eds.). Amsterdam: JAI/Elsevier, 341–354.

Heatherton, Todd F. and Joel Lee Weinberger (eds.). 1994. "Can Personality Change?" [edited book]. Washington, D.C.: American Psychological Association, 368.

Hume, David. 1902. *An Enquiry Concerning Human Understanding,* 2nd ed. L. A. Sleby-Biggee (ed.). Clarendon: Oxford University Press.

Kenrick, D. T., and Funder, D. C. 1988. "Profiting from Controversy: Lessons from the Person-Situation Debate." *American Psychologist* (43): 23–34.

Kupperman, Joel. April 2001. "The Indispensability of Character." *Philosophy* 76 (2): 239–250.

Ladd, John. Oct. 1970. "Morality and the Ideal of Rationality in Formal Organizations." *The Monist.*

MacIntyre, Alasdair. 1984. *After Virtue.* Notre Dame: Notre Dame University Press.

Merritt, Maria. 2000. "Virtue Ethics and Situationist Personality Psychology." *Ethical Theory and Moral Practice* (3): 365–383.

Milgram, Stanley. 1963. "Behavioral Study of Obedience." *Journal of Abnormal and Social Psychology* 67.

Milgram, Stanley. 1983. *Obedience to Authority.* New York: HarperCollins.

Mill, John Stuart. 1874. *A System of Logic.* 8th ed. New York: Harper & Row.

Nietzsche, Friedrich. 1954. *Thus Spoke Zarathustra.* Trans., Kaufmann. New York: Viking, 207.

Nisbett and Ross. 1980. *Human Inference: Strategies and Shortcomings of Social Judgment.* Engelwood Cliffs, N.J.: Prentice-Hall.

O'Brien, Tim. 1973. *If I Die in a Combat Zone Box Me up and Ship Me Home.* New York: Delacorte.

Palaima, Thomas. 2000. "Courage and Prowess Afoot in Homer and in Vietnam," in *Classical and Modern Literature* 20(3): 1–22.

Sachs, Oliver. 1998. *The Man Who Mistook His Wife for a Hat and Other Clinical Tales.* New York: Touchstone.

Sartre, Jean-Paul. 1956. *Being and Nothingness.* Trans. H. Barnes. New York: Philosophical Library.

Schumaker, E. F. 1973. *Small is Beautiful.* New York: Harper and Row.

Smith, Adam. 1880. *Theory of the Moral Sentiments.* London: George Bell.

Solomon, Robert C. 1993. *Ethics and Excellence.* New York: Oxford University Press.

———. 1999. *A Better Way to Think about Business.* New York: Oxford University Press.

Strudler, A., and D. Warren. 2001. "Authority, Heuristics, and the Structure of Excuses" in *The Next Phase of Business Ethics.* J. Dienhart, D. Moberg, and R. Duska (eds.), 355–375.

Velasquez, Manuel G. 1982. *Business Ethics.* Engelwood Cliffs, N.J.: Prentice-Hall.

Young, Robert. 1991. "The Implications of Determinism" in *A Companion to Ethics.* Peter Singer (ed.). London: Blackwell.

8

Virtue Ethics, the Firm, and Moral Psychology[1]

Daryl Koehn

Abstract

Business ethicists have increasingly used Aristotelian "virtue ethics" to analyze the actions of business people and to explore the question of what the standard of ethical behavior is. These analyses have raised many important issues and opened up new avenues for research. But the time has come to examine in some detail possible limitations or weaknesses in virtue ethics.[2] This paper argues that Aristotelian virtue ethics is subject to many objections because the psychology implicit within the ethic is not well-suited for analyzing some problematic forms of behavior. Part One offers a brief overview of the firm and of the good life from a virtue ethics perspective. Part Two develops a number of criticisms of this perspective.

Part One

The firm from a virtue ethics perspective

Every firm has one or more corporate purposes. The manager's role consists of helping the firm to achieve its objectives. Since many of these objectives require the voluntary cooperation of members of the firm, the manager inevitably will need to consider how best to engender this cooperation.[3] So, at one level, the managerial task is purely instrumental: The bottom line requires that the manager try to elicit cooperation. But, in another sense, virtue ethics views this managerial task of building community as intrinsically moral. As Hartman has argued, to say that a stance, position, or world-view is *moral* just is to say that stance reflects an awareness that the individual is a part of a community. The moral agent acknowledges that there is a "we," as well as an

---

Source: *Business Ethics Quarterly* 8 (1998), 497–515.

"I," whose interests need to be respected.[4] Moral agents are inclined to work with their fellow citizens because they see these others as part of a larger whole to which they, too, belong.[5]

Insofar, then, as a firm is morally good, it aims at eliciting the collaboration needed to achieve communal purposes thought to be in the interest of the members of the relevant community. Of course, the same could be said of any cabal. So the question becomes: How does a morally good firm set about encouraging cooperation? Good management tries to cultivate a milieu in which people want to work with each other.[6] While a manager might try to force people to cooperate, this strategy is likely to prove counterproductive in the long run. So, for prudential reasons, the manager aims at voluntary cooperation. In addition, the good manager refuses to resort to coercion because she understands coercion to be intrinsically immoral. The coercing party behaves as if there were only one interest in the world–the coercer's. This stance ignores the existence of the "we," the perception of which lies at the heart of an moral perspective and, therefore, must be judged immoral.

Good managers differ from leaders of cabals because they refuse on both moral and prudential grounds (which are not rigidly separated by virtue ethics[7]) to resort to force or threats to get people to cooperate. Furthermore, virtuous managers understand that what people (including the manager!) take to be in their self-interest may actually be detrimental to the self. The good manager is sensitive to the lessons to be learned from the prisoners' dilemma and from the problem of the commons. Such dilemmas, discussed at length by Hartman,[8] demonstrate that agents sometimes pursue what they take to be their self-interest to the detriment of the larger public interest. As a result, these agents undermine the "we" that is the ground of the ethical, human "I," thereby subverting their own individual humanity. They may even harm their self-interest in a narrow prudential sense (e.g., they may overgraze the commons to the point where there is no grass left for their own flocks[9]).

In order to avoid these undesirable outcomes, good management strives to establish incentives encouraging individuals to consider other people's interests at the same time as they pursue their own interests and happiness. (Again, virtue ethics does not rigidly separate self-interest and happiness.) Virtuous managers know that there is no "natural" or "innate" concept of self-interest. How people conceive of their self-interest depends upon how they are taught to understand it.[10] Not surprisingly, we see a wide range in people's conceptions. Some people look out only for themselves, while other agents make their individual happiness contingent upon the well-being of other people (e.g., friends, lovers, spouses, children). As a leader in the firm, the good manager tries to shape employees' ideas about self-interest by instituting incentives rewarding cooperation and reinforcing the pleasure people take in collaborating with each other.[11]

But establishing incentives is not enough. People can and do alter their ideas about the character of self-interest in light of objections posed by other people. We are less inclined to equate "self-interest" with "whatever the self happens to desire" after thinking about self-destructive behaviors such as heroin addiction or overeating or about instances in which people are induced to desire some object as a result of brainwashing. Since the brainwasher may intend his victim harm, it is naive to accept the victim's desires as being in the victim's self-interest simply because the victim happens to think them so while under the influence of the brainwasher. Reflection itself appears to be in our self-interest because it enables us to refine our concept of self-interest. Therefore, good managers set an example by approaching crises and policy-making in a reflective manner and encouraging others to imitate them.

We cannot predict exactly what conclusions people will draw as a result of reflection. Nor does virtue ethics provide us with an universal measure or rule by which to judge whether an envisioned action is good or even in our self-interest.[12] What we *can* say is that the more virtuous persons are, the more they will move back and forth between their intuitions and their principles, taking into account the objections of other people and modifying their positions over time.[13] The good stance is not one that conforms to some rule or set of hypernorms.[14] Rather it is one in which the particulars 1) have been examined from a number of perspectives using a variety of principles having currency within the community; and 2) have been evaluated with the understanding that how particulars are portrayed is a function of the concerns, values and character of those doing the analysis.

Although there is no univocal measure or rule for assessing the goodness or rightness of an action, there certainly are better and worse choices. Better choices are those that reflect the thoughtfulness that would be brought to bear by an experienced adult who is willing to accept responsibility for his or her actions. Thus, the manager who accepts at face value an employee's accusation that another employee is embezzling funds is less virtuous than the manager who investigates the charge and discusses it with both the accuser and the accused. The latter manager's actions show that she understands that "facts" are reported by someone to somebody. The accuser may have an axe to grind or may simply have misunderstood the character of some financial transaction. The manager's willingness to investigate also operates as a check on a bias she may have against the accused party. Indeed, the virtuous manager may enlist other colleagues' help with the investigation so that she will be less likely to act out of "groupthink" or prejudice or to overlook some salient feature of the situation.[15] The second manager's choice is better because it reflects more of an awareness of the complicated forces of motive, representation, and fallibility that come into play in human judgments. This choice is more in line with the reality of the human condition and is less likely to result in a solution ill-suited to the problem at hand. Since it better reflects the real problem, the choice is more apt to respect the objective interests of persons who are involved in the crisis. This respect, in turn, leaves the manager better positioned to enlist his employees' cooperation.

The good life as a fulfillment of our distinctively human nature

For Aristotle, the good life is that form of life that expresses and realizes our distinctively human nature. Human beings are, by nature, rational and social. In order for us to live the good life, we need to fulfill our *rational and social* capacities. This claim is equivalent to saying that living the good life requires acquiring the virtues because the human virtues are the excellences of these distinctively human capacities. Since the human life is an active life, we must act well to live well. Acting well demands that we excel in practical deliberation. That is, we need to become adept at considering our options and doing so in a timely fashion. Furthermore, since what we take our options to be depends upon what we take the situation to be, we must also excel at representing the situation accurately in order to judge it well. Excellence in such deliberation is a fulfillment of our *rational* being.

Aristotle insists that our decisions in ethical matters rest with perception (*aisthesis*) of the "that." Our perception is sound only if we have had the right upbringing. Having the right upbringing means having come to see the value of being courageous, temperate, liberal, witty and just and having striven to acquire these traits. All of these virtues constitute a realization of our *social* nature. Each virtue has its own proper domain. For example, courage is the trait of fearlessly and knowingly facing what is most to be feared–death, especially death on the battlefield; while temperance involves indulging in the right pleasures to the right extent, at the right time, with the right person, etc. In another sense, though, all of the virtues share the same domain. They all involve acknowledging and respecting other people as "other selves." The courageous person does not simply use other people to further her own ends. She is so committed to the desirability of a life of human excellence that she will willingly die for her community in order that this way of life will endure for her fellow human beings. The liberal person freely gives to other people because he understands that there is more to human relations than mutually using one another to meet our needs. The gesture of the gift signifies or points to a form of life oriented toward virtue–i.e., toward a beauty (for Aristotle, the good is beautiful) that we desire to emulate and wish to have in our lives simply because it is beautiful. A present to another person makes this human potentiality "present" to giver and recipient alike.

If people of practical wisdom are virtuous, then there is no need to fear that they will be bigots or harassers. For, as Aristotle insists, the virtuous person has the "that"–i.e., this person will be able to correctly perceive the "facts" of the situation. So we do not have to worry about the case of a courageous, temperate anti-Semite because the good person will not "see" Jews as especially cunning vermin. Since the virtuous person views other people as "second selves," she will not reduce them to vermin or offal. Furthermore, since such a person deliberates well, she would recognize the contradiction inherent in thinking of the Jews as brilliant rats plotting to take over the world through a series of complicated financial transactions. Rats do not tally figures or make loans.

Similarly, a virtuous manager would not attempt to evade responsibility for what happens to the employees he manages by saying to himself, "These employees can always leave if they are unhappy." While it may be true that a harassed employee has a "right of exit," the manager will not tolerate harassment in the first place. The harasser fails to treat the other as a "second self." Since the manager desires to operate within an organization capable of fostering virtue, he will act to curtail the harasser's abuse.

In more general terms, the Aristotelian will assure us that the truly good manager or employee will always act well because his or her perception has been appropriately formed by virtue. The virtuous person always has the correct perception of the "that" and is willing to act upon that perception; those who don't share this perception of the "that" fall short in virtue. But matters are not so simple. To see why, I want to briefly analyze four cases of business behavior. These cases suggest that the picture Aristotle paints of human character, choice and desire is blind to several important dimensions of choice.

Part Two

Problems with the moral psychology implicit in Aristotelian Virtue Ethics

Four examples drawn from business to show why even this Aristotelian understanding of the firm and of human choice is not adequate.

Case 1: The weak-willed manager

In a 1995 survey of clients conducted by the Ethics Resource Center, a leading think tank for business ethics, nearly one-third of respondents confessed to having personally observed behavior in violation of the law or the company's own ethical standards. Yet fewer than one-half of these persons reported the violations to appropriate personnel within (or without) the corporation.[16] How are we to understand these persons' failure to whistle-blow?

This case appears to perfectly illustrate virtue ethics' understanding of the difference between the virtuous and those lacking in virtue. According to Aristotle, the virtuous person chooses well because her character has been appropriately shaped and because that character, in turn, informs her judgment. She wants to be just and has the courage to follow through on her convictions. So, if she discovers that her company is illegally dumping toxic chemicals into the community's water supply, she will do the right thing and report the violation. Even if there were no law prohibiting such dumping, she will still be inclined to look after the well-being of her fellow citizens and act to stop this potential threat to their health and well-being. Since very few people are thoroughly vicious, those surveyed employees who knew of the dumping and other illegal acts but who did not report it must be deemed "weak-willed" (the Greek term is *akratic*). That is to say, such agents know what the right thing to do is. Their wrongdoing is not unwitting. Instead, the wrongdoing is a sign of a lack of virtue. In particular, the weakness of will shows the person has failed to achieve the distinctively human excellence of choosing well.

But why has the akratic person failed to achieve this excellence? The problem is to understand why, knowing the right course, the employees fail to act upon this knowledge. Aristotle's answer is complex. But it is fair to say that Aristotle attributes that failure to defective reasoning. The weak-willed agent has the words "This is wrong" and may even repeat them like an actor. The reasoning lacks compulsion, however, because of the way in which the agent represents the situation to herself (henceforth, I will refer to this way as a "mode of representation"). Since Aristotle himself contends that pleasure is most responsible for corrupting choice, it is helpful to think of weakness of will first in the context of bodily appetite and then to extend the analysis to the corporate context.

The weak-willed differ from the vicious in being conflicted about their pleasures. Unlike the vicious person, the weak-willed person freely acknowledges that prohibitions apply to him or her and will say or think, "Perhaps I ought not to do this thing." While the vicious, intemperate person wolfs down the second piece of cake without a moment's hesitation, the akratic person who has a weight problem tells herself that she should not eat the second piece of cake. Nevertheless, she goes ahead and does so. Aristotle argues that such a person fails to correctly perceive the particular–the second piece of cake.[17] Although she may say, "Oh, the cake is fattening and, therefore, I should avoid it because I do not want to be fat," she does not really bring her reasoning to bear in a full way on this second piece of cake. She is repeating words she may have heard elsewhere (e.g., discussions of fat on news programs). Her rote mode of representation discourages further deliberation. Precisely because it is so rote, she does not stop to ask herself why fat is bad and how being obese will affect her day-to-day life.[18] At best, she may have some vague idea that being thin is a good idea. Nothing, though, in her representation suggests any way of acting on the prohibition and so it loses its practical force.

The person who is on the road to becoming virtuous, by contrast, does not settle for repeating the prohibition against eating the second piece of cake in a purely formulaic way. Instead, she acts as the practically wise person would, enlisting others' opinion regarding the wisdom of eating this second piece of cake. She looks to others for inspirational stories and for support. She reminds herself that she will be imposing a burden on relatives if she destroys her health. She tells herself that being obese can lead to additional health problems down the way and make it difficult for doctors to operate if she were to need surgery. She tries to understand why she sees the cake as so desirable in the first place. The intellectual curiosity she brings to bear in an effort to comprehend the prohibition against consumption makes it less rote and more of a living force. This mental activity, which, Aristotle thinks, *is* in her control, functions to give her a sense that she can do something about her eating habits. This sense, in turn, imbues the prohibition with a still greater practical force. The strengthened prohibition leads her to explore still other strategies for checking her desire. For example, she may submit to rituals imposed by others (e.g., Jenny Craig, Weight Watchers) in order to break her old eating habits.

If we ask, "How does the agent move from being akratic to more virtuous?" the answer is simple: through "choice." Choice encompasses not only 1) the formulation of a course of action; but also 2) the mode of representation the agent employs in this formulation; and 3) the interplay between this mode and the strategies for action the mode either inspires or precludes. To say, as Aristotle does, that choice is an originating principle or *arche* simply is to say that it is the cause of an action. There is no point in seeking that which determines choice since that fine of reasoning will only involve one in an endless regress–i.e., there will be some further cause that determines that which determines choice. To think to enlist friends and to go to Jenny Craig workshops is an expression of freedom, the freedom that is the human being.

In this sense, Aristotle's account of good and bad agency is quintessentially ethical.[19] By this I mean that Aristotle distinguishes among the types of human being solely in terms of their choices understood as the exercise of the freedom that makes them human beings instead of merely social animals like bees or ants.[20] If we summon our reason to help us figure out how to do what we think we should, we habituate ourselves to both this summoning and this reasoning and thereby preserve our humanity. If, on the other hand, we adopt representations of our situation and of our self that lead us to fail to summon our reason and to settle for doing what feels good to us at the time, we sacrifice a bit of our humanity. Since what feels good to us may be totally arbitrary, we slide a bit toward the bestial life, an existence marked by bizarre and unintelligible pleasures. This slide is itself habituating and over time results in a loss of our human power to bring reason to bear upon our situation in a full way. In this sense, we lose our human freedom. When this freedom is no longer present–when the choosing that is the mark of human being is destroyed through free choice itself– then the human being, too, has disappeared. We are left with a beast.

Keeping this discussion in mind, we are now in a position to understand how Aristotelian virtue ethics would view the employee who fails to whistleblow: Virtue ethics would see the employee as an akratic agent using a defective mode of representation. When the employee dumps waste into the water supply or watches others do so, she tells herself that such dumping is wrong but she does not elaborate to herself why the act is wrong. She does not, as it were, activate her sense of justice. She sees chemicals going into the water but she does not reason a step further and say, "These chemicals are entering the water supply. My family and I drink this water as do the folks downstream. The body metabolizes the water. If there are foreign substances in the water, these substances may be taken up into our bodies in such a way as to damage them. This damage may lead to extreme pain. Sure, I may lose my job in the short run by whistle-blowing but, in the long run, I may lose my job anyway if I get cancer or leukemia. Moreover, I may be harming the very people–my friends, the fellow members of my congregation–on whom I rely for support during sickness or other crises." Aristotle believes that, if she were to reason in this way, she would find the courage to follow through on her perception of wrongdoing. However, since she settles for saying "This is wrong," she never activates virtue and virtue is an activity of choosing well. It is not that the pleasure of keeping her job and making money "trumps" her commitment to do the right thing. Rather her "commitment" never attains the status of a true commitment–i.e., a belief binding an agent to action. From Aristotle's perspective, it would be more accurate to say that the perceived pleasure of making money/keeping her job is allowed to become more controlling than it should be because the agent's mode of representing the situation to herself does not engage her reason.

While the mode in which we represent various situations to ourselves clearly is important, this analysis misses several important dimensions of the ethical problem. First, whether or not reason becomes active depends on communal or social attitudes and practices as well as upon reason itself. Aristotelian virtue ethics tends to treat reason as if it were a completely transcultural, ahistorical, entirely autonomous activity. But this account of reason does not accord with Aristotle's own description of how we acquire excellences. We model our behavior on what others do and think. Reasoning is a practice or *energeia* learned within a community. If so, then reason inevitably has a social dimension. Once this point is acknowledged, the "moral failure" to whistleblow looks rather different. Corporations place a premium on being a "team player." Viewed cynically, this emphasis encourages people to "go along to get along." Employees are trained to suppress doubts in the name of the greater good of corporate morale. In other words, the wider corporate culture sanctions and supports attitudes that lead the employee to use one mode of representation rather than another. Which representation is used (or not used) is not purely a matter of autonomous choice. To the extent judgment takes its bearings from communal standards, we should think of an act of whistle-blowing (or a refusal to whistleblow) as a communal act, not just an individual act.

Second, and equally importantly, since, in many contexts, this strong sense of "the team" is a genuine good, this corporate habituation in favor of cooperation is not necessarily bad. This sense of the team helps, for example, to curb the human propensity to become self-righteous. Such self-righteousness is always a danger, especially because the whistle-blower may begin to think of himself as a "holy crusader" destined to save the world. Persons in this state of mind frequently neglect to take steps to double-check their own perceptions. Perhaps the discharged chemicals are not dangerous. Or perhaps they have already been neutralized by means of some treatment the whistle-blower has failed to make herself aware of. An agent's alleged "failure to whistle-blow" may actually be a thoughtful response to a complex situation instead of weakness of will. Virtue ethics' character typology and its idealization of the practically wise person can produce a rather large blind spot in our moral vision because the theory assumes a virtuous response (e.g., blowing the whistle) and then characterizes other responses as defective without examining the particular merits of the individual's reasoning. Instead of combating bigotry, the theory may introduce its own form of bigotry– bigotry concerning the "sound" vs. "defective" form of reasoning.

Case 2: The virtuous, truthtelling company

The second case I wish to consider is that of Dow Corning. During the 1970s, Dow Corning was lauded for creating a culture that appeared to meet Aristotelian criteria for ethical goodness.[21] The firm created and widely distributed codes of conduct. These codes were not mere statements of legal duties or compliance documents but codes designed to foster integrity and respect for persons. Corporate executives regularly cited the code, and the code was used in evaluating performance. The company took pains to run ethics seminars not merely at the home office but also in foreign operations. All of these measures would seem to be good because they identify humanly virtuous practices and institute incentives for employees to realize these virtues. Yet, despite these measures, the company has recently come under attack for its decision to manufacture and distribute silicon breast implants and for its reluctance to immediately withdraw these implants from the market when it began to receive complaints from women with implants that the product was causing them health problems. The press and some portions of the medical community have portrayed this recalcitrance as a massive moral failure to respect customers.

This type of case poses something of a conundrum for Aristotelian virtue ethics. First, why, if the Dow Corning culture was so good, did the employees, especially senior management, act badly when it came to pulling the implants from the market? After all, if people's upbringing and education within the relevant communities is good, then they should have the "that"–i.e., sound perception of the situation and what should be done about it. The Aristotelian answer is: If there was indeed an ethical failure here, it was due to the employees' bad use of their freedom to make autonomous choices. Even when our education is good, it still falls to us to interpret what we are taught. We are free to either activate or not activate our reason to shape our choices. Dow Corning's insensitivity to their customer complaints must be attributed to management's failure to desire what the thoughtful person would desire. Members of management had not fully realized their humanity; they were not truly virtuous and had not become excellent in deliberation and making choices.

Yet it is not clear that Aristotelian virtue ethics would judge the managers' judgment truly defective. Management at Dow Corning consisted largely of scientists. The scientists within the company have steadfastly maintained that they acted with integrity in not pulling the product. They argued it would be disrespectful to women to urge them to have the implants removed when the available evidence suggested the silicon was an inert substance. On their view (a view supported by some other researchers who have investigated the implants and discovered no causal link between the implants and the sorts of diseases implantees claimed to be experiencing), the danger of removing the implants was greater than leaving them in. By refusing to advocate removal, the scientists arguably acted as persons of practical wisdom and reasoned desires. Moreover, management could and did claim it would be unjust to deny implants to women who have had mastectomies and who need these implants to bolster their self-esteem. Surely the scientists demonstrated courage in standing up for these women's rights. If we adopt virtue ethics' view of reason as completely autonomous, the scientists and Dow Corning must be judged praiseworthy. They seem to embody the virtues of justice and truthtelling and courage to a greater extent than the women complainants and their personal injury attorneys who "hysterically" circulate rumors and unsubstantiated horror stories about life-threatening implants.

Although this response tries to resolve the first difficulty by dissolving away the ethical problem–i.e., the scientists were virtuous; they therefore correctly perceived the situation and the appropriate response; they had the courage and justice to act upon this perception; and therefore the company acted ethically throughout the implant furor–this response brings a second difficulty in its wake. The scientists' response looks virtuous, prudent and rationally sound *when judged from the scientists' perspective.* Why, though, should their perspective be decisive? The scientists at Dow Corning have tried to make the issue of the ethical goodness of their response to customer complaints turn on the question of whether silicon is a biologically inert substance. From a feminist perspective, this maneuver is itself ethically suspect. By focussing attention on this issue, the employees of Dow Corning have tried to relieve themselves of moral responsibility for helping to create demand for the product in the first place. The company worked with plastic surgeons who lobbied to have small breasts defined as a disease.[22] Even if implants prove to be biologically inert, it is questionable whether Dow Corning's marketing strategy, designed to make women anxious about their bodies and to fuel demand for the implants, genuinely respected women. If we ask why this rhetoric was tolerated within the company, then we are driven to consider the issue of power, social structures, and social dynamics. If there had been women in positions of power and authority at Dow Corning, the product might never have been manufactured and marketed. But there weren't such women because the company had not promoted women into these positions.

The Dow Corning example shows the danger of relying on virtue ethics to assess the actions of corporate agents. Dow Corning's employees displayed many of the virtues in this case. But their judgment was both skewed and reinforced in its bias by a culture that could not hear women's voices, in part because that culture had contributed to silencing women by failing to promote any into positions of authority. We will not be able to form accurate ethical judgments of others' behavior simply by looking to whether the people exhibit virtues realizing their human nature. *We need to acknowledge the possibility of systemic biases and examine the ways in which existing power structures may prevent us from hearing from people who are adversely affected by our judgments.* To the extent virtue ethics downplays or ignores power structures and systemic biases, it indirectly fosters unethical behavior.

Case 3: The virtuous but thoughtless actor

A third type of case involves apparent evil yet the agents' behavior is not well understood in terms of either virtue, vice or weakness of will. Consider the following case: For many years, airline pilots would routinely jettison fuel to lighten their planes before landing. This practice continued until one airline pilot–W. Lain Guthrie–thought to protest this polluting practice. When Guthrie refused to dump fuel, other members of pilots' union eventually supported him and, in the end, the airlines stopped the dumping.[23] While few would disagree that fuel dumping failed to respect the environment or the people who lived in the areas where the pollution was occurring, the more interesting ethical issue centers on how we are to understand the willingness of all these pilots to dump fuel over a period of many years.

The Aristotelian would have us question the pilots' virtue, but this line of questioning is not very promising. It seems unlikely that all of these pilots were lacking in virtue. Airlines recruit heavily from the military, so no doubt some of these pilots had flown dangerous combat missions during WW2 or the Vietnam war. Moreover, flying large passenger planes is hardly a job for the weak in spirit. Therefore, the pilots' courage is not in question. Nor is there any reason to doubt the pilots' justice, temperance, truthfulness or generosity. It is tempting to try to salvage the Aristotelian approach by, on the one hand, conceding that the pilots certainly were not vicious but arguing, on the other hand, that they were weak-willed. However, there is no evidence to support this hypothesis either. The pilots did not say to themselves, "Oh, I should not dump this load of fuel" and then proceed to do so. Rather it appears they just failed to think about what they were doing. The pilots were trained to perform a series of steps as part of landing–flaps up, landing gear down, dump fuel at this point, etc. They mechanically went through these steps without a second thought until one pilot one day woke up to what he was doing and realized that this fuel was being dumped somewhere and was affecting people on the ground below.

Aristotelian virtue ethics does not deal well with evil caused by simple thoughtlessness. It locates evil in the corruption of reason by pleasure. But the pilots' blameworthiness does not stem from the fact that their desires have been corrupted by pleasure and are consequently out of line with what a prudential person would desire. The ethical problem in this case is not one of desire at all. The problem is that the pilots were, so to speak, on "autopilot." They internalized these "scripts" provided by corporate trainers and mechanically went through the motions of life without giving any thought to the import of their practices. Asking that corporations emphasize the acquisition and exercise of virtue will not necessarily serve as a wake-up call to those functioning as automatons. On the contrary, creating corporate incentives to elicit virtuous responses may produce agents who are very concerned with acting acceptably. Such agents are eminently trainable. They want to do things right in the eyes of others who seem to be good judges of the matter at hand. But notice that the pilots fell into precisely this class. They were rewarded by their company and society (which has historically esteemed airline pilots) for adhering strictly to generally accepted procedures. And therein lay the problem. The widely accepted procedures were themselves defective. What was needed in this case was a shock to the pilots' system, something akin to a paradigm shift. But nothing in Aristotelian virtue ethics supports such shifts.

This case gives us cause to wonder whether good judgment and virtue necessarily move along the same track. Aristotelian ethics places them on the same track when it conceives of the virtuous person as an agent who, through training within the community, has acquired right desire and correct perception. Aristotle locates the source of ethical error in a failure to apply correct ethical teachings known within the community. This failure, in turn, stems from the agent's reliance on modes of representation that do not encourage the agent to bring these teachings to bear in a practical way. Aristotelian virtue ethics never comes to terms with the possibility that sheer thoughtlessness about a community's accepted, yet possibly defective, practices is a major cause of evil.

Case 4: The good bigot

The final case returns us to the problem of prejudice. Singer and Wooten tell the intriguing story of a highly inventive manager who revolutionized industrial management.[24] This manager argued for "participative" organizations with "collegial decision-making, fluidity of organizational structure,...and industrial self-responsibility" for local managers. He pioneered "management by objectives," linking rewards to achievement of these objectives and to individual initiative. Furthermore, he believed in flexible organizations in which employees would be encouraged and empowered to innovate in order to solve problems. He anticipated many other managerial innovations as well, relying upon project management techniques and matrix management to improve employee effectiveness.[25]

Most of us would praise the manager for improving communication and effectiveness within the corporation and for encouraging individual initiative. We probably would even judge the manager virtuous. For the virtues support communal living and cooperation, and the manager in question clearly understood in some rather profound ways the sources of human motivation. He got people to work together, and the industry he supervised became "one of the most productive and efficient industries known to man."[62] But therein lies the problem. For the manager was none other than Albert Speer, Hitler's Minister for Armaments and War Production. His practical success resulted in horrible suffering for the millions the Germans attacked.

This case is worth thinking about because it is not entirely clear how virtue ethics would have us think about Speer's character. Speer is probably not vicious by Aristotelian standards. As I have argued elsewhere, the vicious person is someone who has destroyed his or her power to choose.[27] The vicious can and do reason but their reasoning takes the form of mere cunning– i.e., selecting means to ends. Their reasoning is not such as to bring the ends themselves into question. They simply pursue whatever seems to be of immediate advantage. Speer does not appear to be vicious because he cared for his community. Moreover, he wanted to help people to realize their full creative and innovative potential. As Keeley notes, Speer seemed to be concerned not only about his managers but also about the working conditions of the captive labor force.[28] Unlike many Nazis, Speer did not seem particularly obsessed by the need for order *per se*. He was more interested in the human capacity for "organized improvisation" and apparently was willing to allow persons (including members of the captive labor force) considerable freedom and latitude in making their own plans and executing them. Speer's actions are intriguing as well as shocking precisely because his desires appear praiseworthy in many respects even though his cause strikes most of us as evil.

The excellent manager Speer is a variant on the worrisome case of the virtuous bigot discussed earlier. I disagree with those who think that our horror at Speer's behavior shows that the primary ethical lesson to be drawn from the example of Speer is "that organizational goals and their attainment are not, in the final analysis, our most important private concerns."[29] There is another equally important lesson here–namely, we need to explore whether virtue ethics, which thinks of the good as that which extends and fulfills human capacities, has correctly understood goodness. In "de-bureaucratizing industry," Speer did expand the scope for human choice and even instilled a degree of courage in employees. Speer supported them in their attempts to take some risks and to innovate. What Speer did not do was fight for the political rights of the Jews and POW's employed by the industries he managed. Speer apparently could not "see" these workers as having much individual potential. Instead, they appeared to him to be expendable: If one worker died, there was another to take his or her place. We cannot blame Speer for having an unrealistic perception. Speer's perception was only too accurate: *The Jews and other workers were expendable because the Nazis had made them such.*

To condemn Speer for cruelty is beside the point. What we need to wrestle with is the fact that our perception of the "that" is frequently a politicized perception. We will not be inclined to realize other people's distinctive human potential if the situation is structured by the community and its regime in such a way as to ensure 1) that some people are not seen as having any potential; and 2) that no opportunity is ever given to these "dehumanized" people to prove this assumption false. In a certain sense, Speer's own emphasis on *individual* innovation blinded him to the political forces that affected human behavior and perception but were beyond the ability of any single individual to control. The same charge applies to Aristotelian virtue ethics: By seeing choice largely as a human capacity that is realized or destroyed through *individual* initiatives and actions, virtue ethics is continually in danger of overlooking the larger forces responsible for making practical situations appear in a certain light in the first place.[30]

Conclusion

In summary, while virtue ethics has many strengths, the theory in its present form does not provide a sufficiently nuanced account of desire or of evil. The problems are:

1. The theory overlooks how politicized our perceptions of situations frequently are. It fails to pay sufficient attention to systemic biases and to imbalances in power, both of which may make apparently "virtuous" responses ethically suspect. Judgments and choices are treated as free-floating apolitical determinations. Yet a choice, such as a decision to resist evil or to become a whistle-blower, may depend upon the law and wider cultural values. An example from military law helps to illustrate my concern: Courts have held that soldiers have a duty to resist superiors' orders if and when these orders are "manifestly unlawful." "Unlawful" here has been held to mean "naturally unjust" as well as "conventionally unlawful."[31] Either way, the central idea is that the *glaringly* immoral quality of an order or law justifies holding a soldier responsible for failing to resist the order. Yet if the larger social setting and legal framework is itself largely corrupt, then no single command is going to stick out as *manifestly* immoral. And, if it does not, then we must again face the question of what justifies holding the person who obeys orders responsible for the evil committed. Virtue ethics sidesteps this second sort of issue by treating the faculty of choice as autonomous.

2. The theory is in some ways quite conventional. Virtuous agents are those who bring to bear ethical teachings and insights already present (explicitly or implicitly) within the culture. The theory fails to acknowledge the possibility that generally accepted practices or procedures may themselves be suspect and that the agent may need to make a radical change in his or her thought in order to be able to do the right thing.

3. The theory's typology of virtuous, vicious and weak-willed agents may blind us to behaviors that do not neatly fall into any of these categories. Some evil seems due to simple thoughtlessness, not, as the theory posits, to corrupt desire. I would add that some vice seems to coexist with virtue. David Messick and others have argued that experimental data show that people are willing to act on a combination of "greed tempered by justice, or justice contorted by greed. Greed and justice fuse into an ungainly shape that resists explanation by one principle alone."[32] Other theorists have found that there appears to be an almost systematic incoherence in the way in which people weigh the relative importance of justice versus other factors when evaluating job offers.[33]

Virtue ethics needs to be revised to take these problems into account. If it is not coupled with a richer, more complex individual and social psychology, managers and employees who are trying to live virtue ethics' version of the good life will find their actions frustrated and perhaps even counterproductive.[34]

Notes

1 I am indebted to Ed Hartman, Wayne Eastman, Tim Fort and two anonymous reviewers for their helpful comments on an earlier draft of this manuscript. I profited as well from some objections John Dienhart and Ron Duska raised when I first began thinking about the relationship between moral psychology and virtue ethics.

2 Donaldson has offered some criticisms of virtue ethics from a deontological perspective. Thomas Donaldson, "The Language of International Corporate Ethics," *Business Ethics Quarterly* vol. 2, no. 3 (July 1992): 271–281. This paper attempts to critique virtue ethics, more on its own terms by exploring possible weaknesses stemming from the moral psychology implicit within the ethics.

3 In this section, I have drawn heavily upon Hartman's recent work on the character of the firm. While I would argue that Hartman's ethical stance is more autonomy-based than Aristotle's is, many of the issues Hartman raises are very much in the spirit of Aristotle. Moreover, his insistence that the virtuous person, rather than a rule or hypernorms, serves as the ethical standard is thoroughly Aristotelian. See Edwin Hartman, *Organizational Ethics* (Oxford: Oxford University Press, 1996).

4 Hartman, 15–16; 69–70.

5 Hartman is well aware of the sort of problems Michael Keeley identifies with any attempt to construe the firm in purely descriptive instrumental terms. See Michael Keeley, *A Social Contract Theory of Organizations* (Notre Dame: University of Notre Dame Press, 1988). Hartman understands the firm as a normative human enterprise. He likely would agree with Aristotle's contention that anyone who can live apart from a lawful community is either a beast or god. Or, as Aristotle puts it, the human being is by nature political. The virtuous person is someone who sees things as they truly are and thus understands this political nature of human beings.

6 Hartman, 82. See also 113n14: "The moral problem for management is to get people with differing interests to cooperate; the only real solution is to get them to do so voluntarily. That management characteristically orchestrates common tasks requiring cooperation does not necessarily undermine rights."

7 Hartman, for example, distinguishes between a merely prudential point of view and a moral one. However, he correctly notes that virtue ethics, unlike deontological ethics, does not treat these two points of view as mutually exclusive. For confirmation of Hartman's point, see NE 1106a19–24 where Aristotle argues that the virtue of something makes the thing good in itself and instrumentally good. Hartman's insistence that no one is required to become an ethical martyr is consistent with virtue ethics, which does not recognize supererogatory actions. Hartman, 82.

8 Hartman, 7, 10, 24, 32n42, 75–76, 80, 88n.17, 88n.19, 112n.6.

9 In the short run, the overgrazer may think overgrazing is in his interest. After all, it is better to have some grass for his flocks than none. But in the long run, Hartman's point still holds–the overgrazer will have acted against his own interests (prudentially understood) if he now has no grass while he could have had some grass through, say, cooperation with his fellow grazers.

10 Indeed, Hartman understands culture, be it the national or organizational, as those beliefs, values, expectations and behavior that shape life within the culture. Hartman, 149.

11 Hartman makes the point that desires are vulnerable to pleasures. Hartman, 149.

12 I concur with both Nussbaum and Hartman that Aristotle is a foundationalist only in a limited sense of that term. Hartman, 119n60; Martha C. Nussbaum, *Love's Knowledge: Essays on Philosophy and Literature* (New York: Oxford University Press, 1990),

56–66. Aristotle does provide a ground or basis for judging acts and agents good. The prudent agent is the good agent and the good act is done as the prudent person would do it. But what considerations the prudent person chooses to advance may vary from situation to situation.

13 Wiggins captures this interplay rather nicely. He characterizes Aristotle's ethic as "a conceptual framework which we can apply to particular cases, which articulates the reciprocal relations of an agent's concerns and his perception of how things objectively are in the world; and a schema of description which relates the complex ideal the agent tries in the process of living his life to make real to the form that the world impresses, both by way of opportunity and by way of limitation, upon that ideal." David Wiggins, "Deliberation and Practical Reason," in Amelie Oksenberg Rorty, *Essays on Aristotle's Ethics* (Berkeley: University of California Press, 1980), 221–240. Hartman would presumably agree since he argues that we must continually move back and forth between intuitions and principles, rethinking each. Hartman, 104.

14 Hartman rejects hypernorms on a number of grounds, all of which Aristotle would likely agree with. Hartman, 97–98.

15 Again, there is no absolute rule as to what the good manager would do in this sort of case. Much would depend on the particulars of the case. While the virtuous generally do consult with other people, confidentiality requirements might preclude such conferences in some cases.

16 Gary Edwards, "False Comfort: Corporate Compliance and the Board of Directors," *Director's Monthly*, vol. 20, no. 11 (November 1996): 1–6.

17 Aristotle *NE* 1147a5–9.

18 Aristotle compares the incontinent person to an actor who simply repeats lines written by others at *NE* 1147a24.

19 It is not surprising that Aristotle's treatment of choice should be ethical and not psychological because Aristotle believes that ethics and psychology are discrete disciplines with an integrity of their own. Like Plato, I doubt that the ethical can be divorced from the psychological, in part for the reasons given in this paper.

20 The purely ethical quality of Aristotle's understanding of choice is apparent in his discussion of bestiality. He concedes that some people are bestial through disease but insists that others become bestial through choice. Aristotle *NE* 1145a25-35.

21 During the 1980s, *Harvard Business Review* wrote a set of glowing case studies about ethics at Dow Corning. These are discussed in John A. Byrne, *Informed Consent* (New York: McGraw Hill, 1996), 36.

27 Byrne, 62.

23 "Airline Pilot Who Refused To Dump Fuel," *Chicago Tribune*, March 31, 1997, Section 2, p. 4.

24 Ethan A. Singer and Leland M. Wooten, "The Triumph and Failure of Albert Speer's Administrative Genius: Implications for Current Management Theory, *Journal of Applied Behavior Sciences*, no. 12 (1976): 79–103.

25 Singer and Wooten, 80–88.

26 Singer and Wooten, 85–88.

27 Daryl Koehn, "A Role for Virtue Ethics in the Analysis of Business Practice," *Business Ethics Quarterly*, vol. 5 (July 1995): 533–540.

28 Keeley, 8. Page 5t2

29 Keeley, 8.

30 I am reminded of the story David Grossman tells about the young son of his neighbor. Grossman and the boy passed a Palestinian women on her knees cleaning the floor in their apartment complex. Grossman stopped to speak with the woman and the

boy was visibly surprised. As they moved out of earshot from the woman, the boy asked if the woman was "a little bit a person and a little bit a dog, right?" When Grossman probed as to why the boy thought this, the boy responded, "She is a little bit a dog because she always walks on all fours. And she is also a little bit a person, because she knows how to talk." The boy's question was quite reasonable given that the political structures in Israel resulted in the Palestinians doing much of the menial work and little else. David Grossman, *The Yellow Wind* (NY: Farrar, Straus, Giroux), 214–215.

31 See, e.g., the way the Israeli military court interpreted the requirement. It contended that "a feeling of lawfulness...lies deep within every human conscience [including those] who are not conversant with the books of laws." The court thus refused to equate "lawfulness" with conventional law. It went on to refer to "an unlawfulness glaring to the eye and repulsive to the heart, provided the eye is not blind and the heart is not stony and corrupt." Quoted by Hannah Arendt, "Personal Responsibility under Dictatorship," *The Listener*, August 6, 1964, 187.

32 David Messick, "Why Ethics Is Not the Only Thing That Matters," *Business Ethics Quarterly* vol. 6 (April 1996), 224.

33 A. Tversky, S. Satta, and P. Slovic, "Contingent Weighting in Judgment and Choice," *Psychological Review*, vol. 95, 371–384. Of course, such data are descriptive and do not tell us how people should proceed when making a judgment. Nevertheless, it would be a mistake to invoke the normative versus descriptive distinction and to dismiss this data. At a minimum, the data suggest that we will be misled if we try to distinguish among character types on the basis of whether or not they summon reason to help them combat licentiousness and to grapple with the particulars of the decision they face. It looks as if somewhat licentious people can and do reason. Moreover, they apparently appeal to a variety of principles and considerations, including some which the virtuous person would cite (e.g., issues of justice and equity). In general, people's preferences appear to be quite sensitive to whether options are considered in groups or individually. If the relative weighting of principles is indeed highly responsive to how the agent groups options, this sensitivity is a psychological fact that will need to be reflected in the ethicist's account of choice and the good manager. It means that the good manager must become a student of psychology and must try to make people aware of the need to reflect on how they are evaluating their options.

34 M. H. Bazerman, H. A. Schroth, P. P. Shah et.al., "The Inconsistent Role of Comparison to Others and Procedural Justice in Reactions to Hypothetical Job Descriptions: Implications for Acceptance Decisions," *Organizational Behavior and Human Decision Processes*, vol. 60, pp. 326–352.

9

A Kantian Approach to Business Ethics

Norman E. Bowie

E ven the most cursory foray into business ethics will bring one face to face with Kantianism. Indeed Kant's influence on that branch of ethical theory known as deontology is so strong that some writers simply refer to deontology as Kantianism. Despite the fact that Kant's name is often invoked in business ethics, as of 1997 there was no published book that systematically applied Kantian theory to business. (However, Bowie (1999) fills this gap.) Kant is best known for defending a version of the "respect for persons" principle which implies that any business practice that puts money on a par with people is immoral, but there is much more to a Kantian approach to business ethics than this. In this essay, I focus on five key aspects of Kant's moral philosophy. I begin by showing some of the implications of Kant's three formulations of the fundamental principle of ethics. I then show why Kant's emphasis on the purity of our intentions in acting morally has created problems for a Kantian theory of business ethics. I conclude with a brief discussion of Kant's cosmopolitan and optimistic outlook, and show the relevance of those ideas to contemporary business practice.

Background

Kant was born in 1724 in Konigsberg in East Prussia, not far from the Baltic Sea. He spent his entire life within 26 kilometers of Konigsberg and died there in 1804. Today, Konigsberg is located in a small strip of Russian territory between Poland and Lithuania, and is called Kaliningrad. Kant's major writings on ethical theory occurred between 1785 and 1797. Kant argued that the highest good was the good will. To act from a good will is to act from duty. Thus, it is the intention behind an action rather than its consequences that make that action good. For example, for Kant if a merchant is honest so as to earn a good reputation, these acts of being honest are not genuinely moral.

Source: Robert E. Frederick (ed.), *A Companion to Business Ethics* (Oxford: Blackwell Publishers, 2002).

The merchant is only truly moral if he or she is honest because being honest is right (one's duty). Persons of good will do their duty because it is their duty and for no other reason. It is this emphasis on duty, and the lack of concern with consequences that makes Kant the quintessential deontologist.

But what does Kantian morality think our duties are? Kant distinguished between two kinds of duty (imperatives). Sometimes we do something so that we may get something else. We go to work to earn money or study to earn good grades. If you want good grades, you ought to study. Kant referred to this kind of duty as a hypothetical imperative because it is of the form if you want to do x, do y. The duty to study is dependent on your desire for good grades.

Other duties are required *per se*, with no ifs, ands or buts. Kant described these duties as categorical and referred to the fundamental principle of ethics as the categorical imperative. He believed that reason provided the basis for the categorical imperative, thus the categorical imperatives of morality were requirements of reason. Although Kant spoke of "the" categorical imperative, he formulated it in many ways. Most commentators focus on three formulations:

1 Act only on maxims which you can will to be universal laws of nature.
2 Always treat the humanity in a person as an end, and never as a means merely.
3 So act as if you were a member of an ideal kingdom of ends in which you were both subject and sovereign at the same time.

Kant believed that only human beings can follow laws of their own choosing (i.e. act rationally). Human beings are the only creatures that are free, and it is the fact that we are free that enables us to be rational and moral. Our free will is what gives us our dignity and unconditioned worth.

Kant's ethics then is an ethics of duty rather than an ethics of consequences. The ethical person is the person who acts from the right intentions. We are able to act in this way because we have free will. The fundamental principle of ethics, the categorical imperative, is a requirement of reason and is binding on all rational beings. These are the essentials of Kant's ethics. Let us see how they apply, specifically, to business ethics.

The Self-defeating Nature of Immoral Actions

Kant's first formulation of the categorical imperative is "Act only on that maxim by which you can at the same time will that it should become a universal law." Although the phrasing is awkward, Kant is providing a test to see if any proposed action, including actions in business, is moral. Since Kant believed that every action has a maxim, we are to ask what would happen if the principle (maxim) of your action were a universal law (one that everyone acted on). Would a world where everyone acted on that principle be possible? One example Kant used to illustrate his theory was a business one.

Suppose you desperately needed money. Should you ask someone to lend you money with a promise to pay the money back but with no intention of paying it back? Do your extreme financial circumstances justify a lying promise? To find out, Kant would require us to universalize the maxim of this action: "It is morally permissible for anyone in desperate financial circumstances to make a lying promise, that is, to promise to repay borrowed money with no intention of doing so." Would such a universalized maxim be logically coherent? Kant (1990, p. 19) answers with a resounding no.

> And could I say to myself that everyone may make a false promise then he is in a difficulty from which he cannot escape? Immediately I see that I could will the lie but not a universal law to lie. For with such a law there would be no promises at all, inasmuch as it would be futile to make a pretense of my intention in regard to future actions to those who would not believe this pretense or- if they over hastily did so- would pay me back in my own coin. Thus my maxim would necessarily destroy itself as soon as it was made a universal law.

Notice what Kant is *not* saying here. He is not saying that if everyone made lying promises, the consequences would be bad – although they would. Rather, Kant is saying that the very concept of lying promises, when adopted as a principle by everyone, is incoherent.

Thus the categorical imperative functions as a test to see if the principles (maxims) upon which an action is based are morally permissible. The action can only be undertaken if the principle on which the action is based passes the test of the categorical imperative. A business manager who accepts Kantian morality would ask for any given decision, does the principle on which the decision is based pass the test of the categorical imperative, that is, can it be willed universally without contradiction? If it can, then the decision would be morally permissible. If it cannot, the action is morally forbidden.

Let us consider two other examples to illustrate Kant's point. First, theft by employees, managers, and customers is a major problem in business. Suppose that an employee, angry at the boss for some justified reason, considers stealing from the firm. Could a maxim which permitted stealing be universalized? It could not. Because goods and services are in limited supply and universal collective ownership is impossible, the institution of private property has developed. If a maxim that permitted stealing were universalized, there could be no private property. If everyone were free to take from everyone else, then nothing could be owned. Given the practical necessity of some form of private property, a universalized maxim that permitted stealing would be self-defeating. Thus, if the employee steals from the boss, the theft is morally wrong.

Another example found in the press concerns companies that try to renegotiate contracts. A favorite ploy of General Motors, especially with Jose Lopez in charge, was to demand price reductions from negotiated contracts with suppliers. In this way, General Motors cut costs and contributed to its bottom line. Would such a tactic pass the test of the categorical imperative? No, it could not. If a maxim that permitted contract breaking were universalized, there could be no contracts (and contracts would cease to exist). No one would enter into a contract if he or she believed the other party had no intention of honoring it. A universalized maxim that permitted contract breaking would be self-defeating.

Now consider an objection to Kant's no self-contradiction requirement raised by Hegel, Bradley, and several others. Simply put the argument runs like this: If there is a practice of private property, then a maxim that permitted stealing would be self-contradictory. However, there is nothing self-contradictory about a world without the practice of private property. So Kant's argument fails.

But as Christine Korsgaard (1996, p. 86) has argued, this criticism misses Kant's point. Kant is simply arguing that if there is a practice of private property then a maxim that permitted stealing would be logically self-contradictory. In all capitalist societies, and indeed in most societies, we do have private property and so a maxim that permitted stealing in societies with private property would be self-contradictory.

We can see this when we consider an example that does not have the ideological baggage that accompanies a term like private property. Take the practice of lining (queuing) up. There is nothing inconsistent about a society that does not have such a practice. However, in a society that does have the practice, cutting into line is morally wrong. The maxim on which the act of line-cutting is based cannot be made a universal law. An attempt to universalize line-cutting destroys the very notion of a line.

What is helpful about Korsgaard's response on behalf of Kant against Hegel and his other critics is that it allows the first formulation of the categorical imperative to work for the rules of any institution or practice. Indeed the test of the categorical imperative becomes a principle of fair play. One of the essential features of fair play is that one does not make an exception of oneself. For example, Kant (1990, p. 41) says:

> When we observe ourselves in any transgression of a duty, we find that we do not actually will that our maxim should become a universal law. That is impossible for us; rather the contrary of this maxim should remain as the law generally, and we only take the liberty of making an exception to it for ourselves or for the sake of inclination, and for this one occasion. Consequently, if we weighed everything from one and the same standpoint, namely reason, we would come upon a contradiction in our own will, viz., that a certain principle is objectively necessary as a universal law and yet subjectively does not hold universally but rather admits exceptions.

Thus the categorical imperative captures one of the key features of morality. Unless the principle of your action can be universalized, to make an exception for yourself is immoral.

I have frequently used these arguments with executives who may find them theoretically persuasive but who, nonetheless, think that their practical application is limited in the real world of business. They point out that, in the real world, contracts are often "renegotiated" and yet business people still engage in contract-making.

These executives raise an interesting point. However, an examination of what goes on in the business world does more to vindicate Kant than to refute him. Consider the following real-world situations.

- When on vacation in Ocean City, Maryland, my favorite seafood outlet had a large sign on the wall saying, "We do not cash checks and here is why." Below the sign and nearly covering the entire wall were photocopies of checks that had been returned with "Returned: Insufficient Funds" stamped in large letters. At least in this retail outlet, a threshold had been crossed. A sufficiently large number of customers wrote bad checks so that it was no longer possible to use checks in that retail store. Suppose a maxim permitting writing checks without sufficient funds in the bank to cover them was really universalized. There would be no institution of check writing.
- While lecturing in Poland in 1995, I was informed that, shortly after the fall of communism, there was a bank collapse because people did not pay on their loans. And experts generally agree that one of the impediments to the development of capitalism in Russia is the failure of various parties to pay their bills. A supplier is reluctant to provide a product if it is not known if and when payment will be received.
- Finally, there has been considerable speculation regarding the future of capitalism in Hong Kong now that the Chinese have regained sovereignty there. As business commentators have pointed out, Hong Kong had developed a legal system that enforced business contracts and limited the influence of politics. In China, political influence plays a much greater role. If the tradition of legal enforcement that has been developed is undermined, can Hong Kong survive as a thriving prosperous major center of business practice? A Kantian would agree with the economists here. Hong Kong would lose its premier standing as a commercial center and would suffer economically.

There are positive stories that illustrate Kant's point as well. By that I mean there are stories showing that when a certain threshold of morality is reached, certain institutions that, until then, were not feasible become feasible and develop. The development of a Russian stock market provides one such example. Russia had difficulties developing a stock market because company spokespersons would not provide accurate information about their companies. As a Kantian would expect, investors were not forthcoming. Gradually, a few companies including Irkutsk Enerego, Bratsky LPK, and Rostelecom were able to establish a reputation as truth tellers. These companies were then able to attract investors and have done well. The success of these honest firms has led other firms to be more honest to the point where the Russian stock market is thriving. The March 24, 1997 *Business Week* reported that the Russian stock market was up 127% in 1996 and had already gained 65% at that point in 1997. (Since 1997, the Russian stock market has plunged. However, the reasons for that plunge are completely consistent with the arguments made here.)

Thus the categorical imperative is not irrelevant in the world of business. If a maxim for an action when universalized is self-defeating, then the contemplated action is not ethical. That is Kant's conceptual point. And when enough people behave immorally in that sense, certain business practices like the use of checks or credit become impossible.

Treating Stakeholders as Persons

Since human beings have free will and thus are able to act from laws required by reason, Kant believed they have dignity or a value beyond price. Thus, one human being cannot use another simply to satisfy his or her own interests. This is the core insight behind Kant's second formulation of the categorical imperative: "Always treat the humanity in a person as an end and never as a means merely." What are the implications of this formulation of the categorical imperative for business?

First, it should be pointed out that the "respect for persons" principle, as I shall call it, does not prohibit commercial transactions. No one is used as merely a means in a voluntary economic exchange where both parties benefit. What this formulation of the categorical imperative does do is to put some constraints on the nature of economic transactions.

To understand Kant fully here, we need to draw a distinction between negative freedom and positive freedom. Negative freedom is freedom from coercion and deception. Kant scholar Christine Korsgaard (1996, pp.140–1) has put it this way.

> According to the Formula of Humanity, coercion and deception are the most fundamental forms of wrongdoing to others – the roots of all evil. Coercion and deception violate the conditions of possible assent, and all actions which depend for their nature and efficacy on their coercive or deceptive character are ones that others cannot assent to...Physical coercion treats someone's person as a tool, lying treats someone's reason as a tool. That is why Kant finds it so horrifying; it is a direct violation of autonomy.

However, simply refraining from coercive or deceptive acts is not sufficient for respecting the humanity in a person. Additional requirements can be derived from Kant's view of positive freedom. Positive freedom is the freedom to develop one's human capacities. For Kant, that means developing one's rational and moral capacities. In interacting with others, we must not do anything to diminish or inhibit these uniquely human capacities.

Thus, treating the humanity in a person as an end, and not as a means merely, in a business relationship requires two things. First, it requires that people in a business relationship not be used, i.e. they not be coerced or deceived. Second, it means that business organizations and business practices should be arranged so that they contribute to the development of human rational and moral capacities, rather than inhibit the development of these capacities. These requirements, if implemented, would change the nature of business practice. A few examples are in order.

American have been deeply concerned about the massive layoffs created by the downsizing of corporations in the early and mid-1990s. Are these layoffs immoral? A naive Kantian response would label them as immoral because, allegedly, the employees are being used as mere means to enhance shareholder wealth. However, that judgment would be premature. What would be required from a Kantian perspective is an examination of the employer/employee relationship, including any contractual agreements. So long as the relationship was neither coercive nor deceptive, there would be nothing immoral about layoffs.

What is highly contested is whether or not the standard employer/employee relationship is coercive and/or deceptive. Employers tend to argue that employees are well aware of the possibility of layoffs when they take a position and, furthermore, that employees have the right, which they frequently exercise, to take positions elsewhere. There is neither deception nor coercion in either standard labor contracts or in the implicit norms governing the employer/employee relationship. On the other hand, many employees argue that, in times of relatively high unemployment and job insecurity, employees really must accept job offers on management terms. You take what you can so as to eat, but you do not accept the threat of a layoff to enhance shareholder wealth freely. Moreover, in many companies, such as IBM, there had been a long tradition of job security in exchange for employee loyalty. The sudden unilateral changing of the rules amounted to both deception and coercion on the part of management, or so it is argued.

An examination of these opposing arguments would take us far beyond the scope of this chapter. However, by framing the issue in terms of whether or not coercion and/or deception has occurred, one has adopted a Kantian approach to business ethics.

Another concern about contemporary business practice is the extent to which employees have very limited knowledge about the affairs of the company. In economic terminology, there is high information asymmetry between management and the employees. Wherever one side has information that it keeps from other side, there is a severe temptation for abuse of power and deception. A Kantian would look for ways to reduce the information asymmetry between management and employees.

In practical terms, a Kantian would endorse the practice known as open book management. Open book management was developed by Jack Stack at the Springfield Manufacturing Company. Stack and his company won a prestigious business ethics award for the technique. Under open book management, all employees are given all the financial information about the company on a regular frequent basis. With complete information and the proper incentive, employees behave responsibly without the necessity of layers of supervision.

> How does open book management do what it does? The simplest answer is this. People get a chance to act, to take responsibility, rather than just doing their

job.... No supervisor or department head can anticipate or handle all...
situations. A company that hired enough managers to do so would go broke
from the overhead. Open book management gets people on the job doing
things right. And it teaches them to make smart decisions...because they can see
the impact of their decisions on the relevant numbers (Case, L995, pp. 45–6).

The adoption of practices like open book management would go far toward
correcting the asymmetrical information that managers possess, a situation that
promotes abuse of power and deception. Under open book management, if a
firm faced a situation that might involve the layoff of employees, everyone in
the firm would have access to the same information. Deception would be very
difficult in such circumstances. Suspicion would be less and, as a result,
cooperative efforts to address the problem would be more likely.

Open book management also enhances employee self-respect. Employees
at Springfield Manufacturing Company use Kantian "respect for persons"
language when describing the impact of open book management on working
conditions. Thus, open book management lessens the opportunity for
deception and supports negative freedom.

By enhancing employee self-respect, open book management supports
positive freedom as well. What are the implications of Kant's theory of positive
freedom for business practice? To treat the humanity in a person as an end in
itself sometimes requires that we take some positive action to help a person.
This is required by the "respect for persons" formulation of the categorical
imperative, by some of Kant's own writing on the nature of work, and by the
demands of Kant's imperfect duty of beneficence to help others.

The requirement that business practice be supportive of positive freedom
has wide implications for business practice. I will focus on only one
implication here. I believe Kant's moral philosophy enables business ethicists
to develop a useful definition of meaningful work and that Kantian ethics
would require companies to provide meaningful work so defined. Although I
cannot cite all the Kantian texts in this brief chapter, I think the following
conditions for meaningful work are consistent with Kant's views. For a
Kantian, meaningful work:

- is freely chosen and provides opportunities for the worker to exercise
  autonomy on the job;
- supports the autonomy and rationality of human beings; work that lessens
  autonomy or that undermines rationality is immoral;
- provides a salary sufficient to exercise independence and provide for
  physical wellbeing and the satisfaction of some of the worker's desires;
- enables a worker to develop rational capacities; and
- does not interfere with a worker's moral development.

(Notice that these requirements are normative in the sense that they spell out
what meaningful work ought to be. There is no requirement that workers who
are provided meaningful work must themselves subjectively experience it as
meaningful.)

A manager taking the Kantian approach to business ethics would regard providing meaningful work as a moral obligation. Some management attitudes and practices are more conducive toward meeting this obligation than others. Thus, Kantian managers need to create a certain kind of organization. A discussion of what a Kantian business firm would look like leads directly to a discussion of the third formulation of the categorical imperative.

The Business Firm As A Moral Community

Kant's third formulation of the categorical imperative roughly says that you should act as if you were a member of an ideal kingdom of ends in which you were both subject and sovereign at the same time. Organizations are composed of persons and, given the nature of persons, organizational structures must treat the humanity in persons with dignity and respect (as an end). Moreover, the rules that govern an organization must be rules that can be endorsed by everyone in the organization. This universal endorsement by rational persons is what enables Kant to say that everyone is both subject and sovereign with respect to the rules that govern them. I believe a Kantian approach to the organizational design of a business firm would endorse these principles:

1 The business firm should consider the interests of all the affected stakeholders in any decision it makes.
2 The firm should have those affected by the firm's rules and policies participate in the determination of those rules and policies before they are implemented.
3 It should not be the case that, for all decisions, the interests of one stakeholder automatically take priority.
4 When a situation arises where it appears that the interest of one set of stakeholders must be subordinated to the interests of another set of stakeholders, that decision should not be made solely on the grounds that there is a greater number of stakeholders in one group than in another.
5 No business rule or practice can be adopted which is inconsistent with the first two formulations of the categorical imperative.
6 Every profit-making firm has a limited, but genuine, duty of beneficence.
7 Every business firm must establish procedures designed to ensure that relations among stakeholders are governed by rules of justice.

I think the rationale for most of these principles can be derived from the explanation of Kant's ethics already provided. Principle 1 seems like a straightforward requirement for any moral theory that takes respect for persons seriously. Since autonomy is what makes humans worthy of respect, a commitment to principle 2 is required. Principle 3 provides a kind of organizational legitimacy; it ensures that those involved in the firm receive some minimum benefits from being a part of it. Principle 4 rules out utilitarianism as a criterion for decision-making in the moral firm. The justification for principle 6 is based on an extension of the individual's imperfect obligation of beneficence which Kant defended in the *Metaphysics of Morals*. There Kant (1994, p. 52) says:

> That beneficence is a duty results from the fact that since our self-love cannot be separated from our need to be loved by others (to obtain help from them in the case of need) we thereby make ourselves an end for others...hence the happiness of others is an end which is at the same time a duty.

The strategy here is to extend this argument to the corporate level. If corporations have benefited from society, they have a duty of beneficence to society in return. And corporations have benefited. Society protects corporations by providing the means for enforcing business contracts. It provides the infrastructure which allows the corporation to function – such as roads, sanitation facilities, police and fire protection – and, perhaps most importantly, an educated work force with both the skills and attitudes required to perform well in a corporate setting. Few would argue that corporate taxes pay the full cost of these benefits. Finally, principle 7 is a procedural principle designed to ensure that whatever rules the corporation adopts conform to the basic principles of justice.

A Kantian views an organization as a moral community. Each member of the organization stands in a moral relationship to all the others. On one hand, the managers of a business firm should respect the humanity in all the persons in the organization. On the other hand, each individual in a business firm, managed as a Kantian moral community, should view the organization other than purely instrumentally, that is, as merely a means for achieving individual goals. Organizations are created as ways of achieving common goals and shared ends. An individual who views the organization purely instrumentally is acting contrary to the "respect for persons" principle.

A manager who adopts the Kantian principles of a moral firm must also look at human nature in a certain way. In management terms, the theory Y view of human nature must be adopted rather than a theory X view. (The distinction between theory X and theory Y was made prominent by McGregor (1960).) Theory X assumed that people had an inherent dislike of work and would avoid it if possible. It also assumed that the average person seeks to avoid responsibility. Theory Y assumes the opposite: that employees prefer to act imaginatively and creatively and are willing to assume responsibility, Although we can debate about which theory is descriptively more accurate, as a normative matter a Kantian manager should adopt theory Y. For it is theory Y that views human beings as having the dignity Kant thinks they deserve.

Moreover, both theory X and theory Y have the tendency to become self-fulfilling prophecies, By that I mean that people will tend to behave as they are treated. If a manager treats people in accordance with theory X, employees will tend to behave as theory X predicts. Conversely with theory Y. Thus the question becomes what kind of organization should the manager and the employees, working together, create. For the Kantian, the answer is clear. People should try to create an organization where the participants in the organization behave as theory Y would predict. People should seek to create an organization where members develop their rational and moral capacities, including the capacity to take responsibility.

One of the chief implications of Kant's ethics is that it acts as a moral critique of authoritarian hierarchical organizational structures. Principle 2 demands participation in some form by all the corporate stakeholders, especially stockholders and employees. A Kantian would morally object to a hierarchical structure that requires those lower down to carry out the orders of those above, more or less without question.

Kantian moral theory also requires worker participation; indeed, it requires a vast democratization of the work place. Certainly, a necessary condition of autonomy is consent given under non-coercive and non-deceptive conditions. Consent also requires that the individuals in an organization endorse the rules that govern them. As a minimum condition of democratization, Kantian moral philosophy requires that each person in an organization be represented by the stakeholder group to which he or she belongs, and that these various stakeholder groups must consent to the rules and policies which govern the organization.

This requirement for a more democratic work place is not purely utopian; it has some support in management theory and in management practice. Teamwork is almost universally praised, and several corporations have endorsed varieties of the concept of participative management. Levi Strauss and Singapore Airlines, to name just two examples, have democratic work places.

I hope I have convinced the reader that Kant's moral philosophy has rich implications for business practice. When the three formulations of the categorical imperative are considered together as a coherent whole, they provide guidance to the manager, both in terms of negative injunctions and positive ideals. The negative injunctions prohibit actions like contract break-ing, theft, deception and coercion. The positive ideals include a more democratic work place and a commitment toward meaningful work.

However, Kantian ethics is not without its limitations and challenges. Kant had nothing to say about environmental ethics and had little understanding of the suffering of animals and thus held a truncated view of our obligations to animals. But the biggest challenge to the Kantian ethic is that the Kantian ethic is too demanding. Let us consider that objection at greater length.

The Purity of Motive

It is a central tenet of Kant's moral philosophy that an action is only truly moral if it is morally motivated. Truly moral actions cannot be contaminated by motives of self-interest. Since the good acts of even the most enlightened corporations are almost always justified in part on the grounds that such actions are profitable, it appears that even the best actions of the best corporations are not truly moral. Consider the following quotation from J. W. Marriott Jr

(Milbank, 1996, p. A1) describing the decision of the Marriott Corporation to hire welfare recipients.

> We're getting good employees for the long term but we're also helping these communities. If we don't step up in these inner cities and provide work, they'll never pull out of it. But it makes bottom line sense. If it didn't we wouldn't do it.

A strict Kantian could not call Marriott's act of hiring welfare recipients a good act. In Kantian language, the act would be done in conformity with duty but not out of duty. But doesn't that make Kant's theory too austere to apply to business? Several things can be said in response to this question.

We might say that Kant is mistaken about requiring such purity of motive. Yet even if Kant is wrong about the necessity of pure motivation for an act's being moral, he still has a lot to offer the business ethicist. Working out the implications of the three formulations of the categorical imperative provides a rich agenda for the business ethicist. However, a bit more should be said, especially in light of the fact that the general public judges business from a strict Kantian position.

In discussing this issue, people seem to assume that actions that enhance the bottom line are acts of self-interest on the part of the corporation. However, for publicly held corporations and for partnerships, this is not the case. Publicly held corporations have an obligation to make a profit based on their charters of incorporation, legal obligations to shareholders, and an implied contract with the public. It would not be stretching a point too far to say that the managers of a publicly held corporation have promised to strive for profits. If that is so, the position of the Marriott Corporation is a moral one, even for the strict Kantian. The Marriott Corporation is honoring its obligation to realize profits and its obligation of beneficence. Thus, Kant's insistence that an action must be done from a truly moral motive need not undercut acts of corporate beneficence that also contribute to the bottom line.

So far all we have shown is that Kant's insistence on the purity of a moral motive has not made his theory irrelevant to business ethics. But perhaps his insistence on the purity of the moral motive has a positive contribution to make to business ethics and is not simply a barrier to be overcome. Perhaps focusing on issues other than profits, such as meaningful work for employees, a democratic work place, non-deceptive advertising, and a non-coercive relationship with suppliers will actually enhance the bottom line. Many management theorists urge businesses to always focus on the bottom line. However, perhaps paradoxically, profits can be enhanced if we do not focus so exclusively on the bottom line. To put this in more Kantian terms, perhaps profits will be enhanced if the manager focuses on respecting the humanity in the person of all the corporate stakeholders. Perhaps we should view profits as a consequence of good business practices rather than as the goal of business.

With this standard criticism of Kantian moral philosophy addressed, we can close by considering briefly how Kant's cosmopolitan perspective provides a moral ideal for international business.

Kant's Cosmopolitanism and International Business

One of the key features of the enlightenment was its cosmopolitan perspective, and Kant was cosmopolitan in many ways. For Kant, national boundaries have, at root, derivative significance. His greatest concern was with the human community and with ways that the human community could live in peace. Contemporary capitalism is also cosmopolitan and is no respecter of national boundaries. Many have also argued that capitalism contributes to world peace. Kant would tend to agree. In addition, international economic cooperation provides the foundation for a universal morality that is consistent with Kant's philosophy.

To see how Kant's philosophy provides a foundation for a universal morality, we need to return to the first formulation of the categorical imperative. Interestingly, that formulation provides a convincing argument against a full blown ethical relativism (the doctrine that what a culture believes to be right or wrong really is right or wrong for that culture). At least within international capitalist economic relations, the maxims of certain actions if universalized, would be self-defeating. Thus, as capitalism spreads throughout the world, a certain minimum morality, what I have called the "morality of the market-place", will be universally adopted. For example, I believe that international capitalism will necessarily promote increased honesty and trust among different cultures participating in capitalist economic relations, and I believe that international capitalism will undermine certain forms of discrimination, e.g. against women. However, I will illustrate my general argument by providing an argument against bribery – an argument which enables us to predict that we will see less bribery as capitalism spreads throughout the world.

I maintain that, if a maxim permitting bribery were universalized, it could not pass the test of the categorical imperative. (For purposes of this discussion, bribery is distinguished from extortion and facilitating payments.) Put most abstractly, the argument – for which I am indebted to Robert Frederick – goes like this:

If we understand the practice of bribery to be a secret attempt to gain a special advantage over others, an advantage these others would not agree to if they knew about it, then a principle permitting bribery could not be universalized. If everybody offered bribes, then the practice of trying to make secret attempts to gain special advantages would make no sense.

Bribery involves practical inconsistencies as well. Consider a company offering a bribe. Suppose the company could have received the contract on the merits of the product without offering a bribe. If so, paying adds to its costs and it will lose out to competitors that have equally good products but incur less costs since they do not bribe. Other things being equal, companies that do not bribe have a competitive advantage that will drive companies that bribe out of business. Since companies wish to stay in business, a maxim to offer a bribe cannot be universalized.

A similar argument can be made for a company taking a bribe. It receives a product of the same or even less quality for a greater expenditure. That puts it at a competitive disadvantage and, other things being equal, it will be driven out of business. The maxim of accepting a bribe cannot be universalized.

However, bribery is, allegedly, a fact of life in many countries. In those countries, an international firm doing business in that country would have to offer bribes to stay in business. There is some merit in that reply, but the nature of the reply shifts the argument to a higher level. If a country adopts the practice of bribery, it condemns itself to a much lower standard of living and to an ever-increasing gap between those countries where bribery is widespread and those countries where it is not widespread. It is widely maintained that one reason for the lack of economic development in many countries of Africa is the high level of corruption, especially the bribery that takes place there. As Hong Kong returns to China, business writers have commented on the economic danger to Hong Kong if political influence replaces arm's-length considerations of quality and price in business transactions. These theoretical considerations receive empirical support. Research has shown that corruption, including bribery, diminishes per capita income; a study by Johns Hopkins economist, Steve Hanke, is cited in Zachary (1997, p. A8). Specific figures have been given for Italy, where it is estimated that Italy's debt has been increased $200 billion by bribery (Penner, 1993, pp. 133–8). Given this data, and the fact that decreases in per capital income are nearly universally seen as undesirable, a country that practices bribery cannot universalize its practice.

Kantians would use arguments such as this to try to show that there is a minimum market morality that capitalist countries must adhere to, if they are to gain the economic advantages of capitalism. Such arguments would be useful in undercutting the relativism that is in intellectual fashion these days. But Kant's moral philosophy has even more to offer international business ethics. It shows how international business can contribute to world peace.

The thesis that commerce supports world peace was widely held in Kant's time. Exponents of the thesis included Adam Smith, David Hume, and John Stuart Mill. Kant (1963, p. 23) had this to say:

> In the end, war itself will be seen as not only so artificial, in outcome so uncertain for both sides, in after effects so painful in the form of an ever-growing war debt (a new invention) that cannot be met, that it will be regarded as a most dubious undertaking. The impact of any revolution on all states on our continent, so clearly knit together through commerce will be so obvious that other states, driven by their own danger, but without any legal basis, will offer themselves as arbiters, and thus will prepare the way for a distant international government for which there is not precedent in world history.

For all these thinkers, commerce is a way of bringing people together rather than keeping them apart. If commerce is successful in bringing people together, then the chances for peace among nations improves. Given the exponential growth of international business, it is not surprising that this view has many adherents today. During the 1970s and 1980s, trade agreements between the USA and the former Soviet Union were defended on the grounds that they would enhance the chances of peace. Similar arguments are heard today regarding the granting of Most Favored Nation Status to China. Such arguments are not limited to US spokespersons. A Mideast Common Market has been proposed as a cure of the continuing conflicts in the Middle East.

If these arguments are right, then business ethics from a Kantian perspective is not simply a matter of following the demands of the three formulations of the categorical imperative. International business has an opportunity to contribute to an ethical ideal. International business, if done from the Kantian perspective, can contribute to the long hoped for, but elusive, goal of world peace.

This concludes our brief analysis of the implications of Kantian moral philosophy for business ethics. I hope I have shown that Kant's moral philosophy is not a system of inflexible absolute rules. The categorical imperative does rule out certain practices such as the unilateral breaking of contracts, theft, and bribery. But Kant's moral philosophy is more than a series of negative constraints. If business is to be faithful to the second and third formulations of the categorical imperative, business managers should manage so as to provide meaningful work for employees, and business firms should be organized more democratically. Finally, firms engaged in international business can contribute to the goal of world peace. Kant's moral philosophy has rich implications for business ethics.

References

Bowie, N. E. 1999: *Business Ethics: A Kantian Perspective*. Oxford: Blackwell Publishers.

Case, J. 1995: *Open Book Management*. New York: Harper Collins Publishers.

Kant, I. 1963: What is enlightenment (1784). in L. White Beck (ed. and trans.) *On History*. Trans. Indianapolis: The Bobbs Merrill Company.

Kant, I. 1990: *Foundations of the Metaphysics of Morals* (1785). Trans. by Lewis White Beck. New York: Macmillan Publishing Company.

Kant, I. 1994: *The metaphysics of moral; The metaphysical principles of virtue* (1797). In I. Kant *Ethical Philosophy* 2nd edn, Trans. by James W. Ellington. Indianapolis/ Cambridge, MA: Hackett Publishing Company.

Korsgaard, C. 1996: *Creating the Kingdom of Ends*. New York: Cambridge University Press.

McGregor D. 1960: *The Human Side of Enterprise*. New York: McGraw Hill Book Company.

Milbank, D. 1996: Hiring welfare people, hotel chain finds, is tough but rewarding. *The Wall Street Journal*, October 31.

Penner. K. 1993: The destructive costs of greasing palms. *Business Week*, December 6.

Zachary, G. P. 1997: Global growth attains a higher level that could be lasting. *The Wall Street Journal*, March 13.

UNIT TWO
DISTRIBUTIVE JUSTICE

10

Excerpts from "Leviathan"

Thomas Hobbes

T homas Hobbes (1588–1679), a crucial figure in the history of political philosophy, was a leading exponent of social contract theory.

Chapter 13 – Of the Natural Condition of Mankind as Concerning Their Felicity, and Misery

Nature hath made men so equal, in the faculties of body, and mind; as that though there be found one man sometimes manifestly stronger in body, or of quicker mind than another; yet when all is reckoned together, the difference between man, and man, is not so considerable, as that one man can thereupon claim to himself any benefit, to which another may not pretend, as well as he. For as to the strength of body, the weakest has strength enough to kill the strongest, either by secret machination, or by confederacy with others, that are in the same danger as himself.

And as to the faculties of the mind, (setting aside the arts grounded upon words, and especially that skill of proceeding upon general, and infallible rules, called science; which very few have, and but in few things; as being not a native faculty, born with us; nor attained, (as prudence,) while we look after someone else,) I find yet a greater equality amongst men, than that of strength. For prudence, is but experience; which equal time, equally bestows on all men, in those things they equally apply themselves unto. That which may perhaps make such equality incredible, is but a vain conceit of one's own wisdom, which almost all men think they have in a greater degree, than the vulgar; that is, than all men but themselves, and a few others, whom by fame, or for concurring with themselves, they approve. For such is the nature of men, that howsoever they may acknowledge many others to be more witty, or more eloquent, or more learned; yet they will hardly believe there be many so wise

Source: Edwin Curley (ed.), *Leviathan* (Indianapolis, IN: Hackett Publishing, 1994).

as themselves: For they see their own wit at hand, and other men's at a distance. But this proveth rather that men are in that point equal, than unequal. For there is not ordinarily a greater sign of the equal distribution of any thing, than that every man is contented with his share.

From this equality of ability, ariseth equality of hope in the attaining of our ends. And therefore if any two men desire the same thing, which nevertheless they cannot both enjoy, they become enemies; and in the way to their end, (which is principally their own conservation, and sometimes their delectation only,) endeavour to destroy, or subdue one another. And from hence it comes to pass, that where an invader hath no more to fear, than another man's single power; if one plant, sow, build, or possess a convenient seat, others may probably be expected to come prepared with forces united, to dispossess, and deprive him, not only of the fruit of his labour, but also of his life, or liberty. And the invader again is in the like danger of another.

And from this diffidence of one another, there is no way for any man to secure himself, so reasonable, as anticipation; that is, by force, or wiles, to master the persons of all men he can, so long, till he see no other power great enough to endanger him: and this is no more than his own conservation requireth, and is generally allowed. Also because there be some, that taking pleasure in contemplating their own power in the acts of conquest, which they pursue farther than their security requires; if others, that otherwise would be glad to be at ease within modest bounds, should not by invasion increase their power, they would not be able, long time, by standing only on their defence, to subsist. And by consequence, such augmentation of dominion over men, being necessary to a man's conservation, it ought to be allowed him.

Again, men have no pleasure, (but on the contrary a great deal of grief) in keeping company, where there is no power able to over-awe them all. For every man looketh that his companion should value him, at the same rate he sets upon himself: and upon all signs of contempt, or undervaluing, naturally endeavours, as far as he dares (which amongst them that have no common power to keep them in quiet, is far enough to make them destroy each other,) to extort a greater value from his contemners, by damage; and from others, by the example.

So that in the nature of man, we find three principal causes of quarrel. First, competition; secondly, diffidence; thirdly, glory.

The first, maketh man invade for gain; the second, for safety; and the third, for reputation. The first use violence, to make themselves masters of other men's persons, wives, children, and cattle; the second, to defend them; the third, for trifles, as a word, a smile, a different opinion, and any other sign of undervalue, either direct in their persons, or by reflection in their kindred, their friends, their nation, their profession, or their name.

Hereby it is manifest, that during the time men live without a common power to keep them all in awe, they are in that condition which is called war; and such a war, as is of every man, against every man. For WAR, consisteth not in battle only, or the act of fighting; but in a tract of time, wherein the will to contend by battle is sufficiently known: and therefore the notion of time, is to be considered in the nature of war; as it is in the nature of weather. For as the nature of foul weather, lieth not in a shower or two of rain; but in an inclination thereto of many days together: so the nature of war, consisteth not in actual fighting; but in the known disposition thereto, during all the time there is no assurance to the contrary. All other time is PEACE.

Whatsoever therefore is consequent to a time of war, where every man is enemy to every man; the same is consequent to the time, wherein men live without other security, than what their own strength, and their own invention shall furnish them withal. In such condition, there is no place for industry; because the fruit thereof is uncertain: and consequently no culture of the earth; no navigation, nor use of the commodities that may be imported by sea; no commodious building; no instruments of moving, and removing such things as require much force; no knowledge of the face of the earth; no account of time; no arts; no levers; no society; and which is worst of all, continual fear, and danger of violent death; and the life of man, solitary, poor, nasty, brutish, and short.

It may seem strange to some man, that has not well weighted these things; that nature should thus dissociate, and render men apt to invade, and destroy one another: and he may therefore, not trusting to this inference, made from the passions, desire perhaps to have the same confirmed by experience. Let him therefore consider with himself, when taking a journey, he arms himself, and seeks to go well accompanied; when going to sleep, he locks his doors; when even in his house he locks his chests; and this when he knows there be laws, and public officers, armed, to revenge all injuries shall be done him; what opinion he has of his fellow subjects, when he rides armed; of his fellow citizens, when he locks his doors; and of his children, and servants, when he locks his chests. Does he not there as much accuse mankind by his actions, as I do by my words? But neither of us accuse man's nature in it. The desires, and other passions of man, are in themselves no sin. No more are the actions, that proceed from those passions;, till they know a law that forbids them: which till laws be made they cannot know: nor can any law be made, till they have agreed upon the person that shall make it.

It may peradventure be thought, there was never such a time, nor condition of war as this; and I believe it was never generally so, over all the world: but there are many places, where they live so now. For the savage people in many places of *America*, except the government of small families, the concord whereof dependeth on natural lust, have no government at all; and live at this day in that brutish manner, as I said before. Howsoever, it may be perceived what manner of life there would be, where there were no common power to fear; by the manner of life, which men that have formerly lived under a peacefull government, use to degenerate into, in a civil war.

But though there had never been any time, wherein particular men were in a condition of war one against another; yet in all times, kings, and persons of sovereign authority, because of their independency, are in continual jealousies, and in the state and posture of gladiators; having their weapons pointing, and their eyes fixed on one another; that is, their forts, garrisons, and guns upon the frontiers of their kingdoms; and continual spies upon their neighbours; which is a posture of war. But because they uphold thereby, the industry of their subjects; there does not follow from it, that misery, which accompanies the liberty of particular men.

To this war of every man against every man, this also is consequent; that nothing can be unjust. The notions of right and wrong, justice and injustice have there no place. Where there is no common power, there is no law: where no law, no injustice. Force, and fraud, are in war the two cardinal virtues. Justice, and injustice are none of the faculties neither of the body, nor mind. If they were, they might be in a man that were alone in the world, as well as his senses, and passions. They are qualities, that relate to men in society, not in solitude. It is consequent also to the same condition, that there be no propriety, no dominion, no *mine* and *thine* distinct; but only that to be every man's, that he can set; and for so long, as he can keep it. And thus much for the ill condition, which many by mere nature is actually placed in; though with a possibility to come out of it, consisting partly in the passions, partly in his reason.

The passions that incline men to peace, are fear of death; desire of such things as are necessary to commodious living; and a hope by their industry to obtain them. And reason suggesteth convenient articles of peace, upon which men may be drawn to agreement. These articles, are they, which otherwise are called the Laws of Nature; whereof I shall speak more particularly, in the two following chapters.

Chapter 14. Of the First and Second Natural Laws, and of Contracts

The RIGHT OF NATURE, which writers commonly call *jus naturale*, is the liberty each man hath, to use his own power, as he will himself, for the presentation of his own nature; that is to say, of his own life; and consequently, of doing any thing, which in his own judgment, and reason, he shall conceive to be the aptest means thereunto.

By LIBERTY, is understood, according to the proper signification of the word, the absence of external impediments: which impediments, may oft take away part of a man's power to do what he would; but cannot hinder him from using the power left him, according as his judgment, and reason shall dictate to him.

A LAW OF NATURE, (*lex naturalis*,) is a precept, or general rule, found out by reason, by which a man is forbidden to do that, which is destructive of his life, or taketh away the means of preserving the same; and to omit that, by which he thinketh it may be best preserved. For though they that speak of this subject, use to confound *jus*, and *lex*, *right* and *law*; yet they ought to be distinguished; because RIGHT, consisteth in liberty to do, or to forbear; whereas LAW, determineth, and bindeth to one of them: so that law, and right, differ as much, as obligation, and liberty; which in one and the same matter are inconsistent.

And because the condition of man, (as hath been declared in the precedent chapter) is a condition of war of every one against every one; in which case every one is governed by his own reason; and there is nothing he can make use of, that may not be a help unto him, in preserving his life against his enemies; it followeth, that in such a condition, every man has a right to every thing: even to one another's body. And therefore, as long as this natural right of every man to every thing endureth, there can be no security to any man, (how strong or wise soever he be,) of living out the time, which nature ordinarily alloweth men to live. And consequently it is a precept, or general rule of reason, *that every man, ought to endeavour peace, as far as he has hope of obtaining it; and when he cannot obtain it, that he may seek and use, all helps, and advantages of war.* The first branch of which rule, containeth the first, and fundamental law of nature; which is, *to seek peace, and follow it.* The second, the sum of the right of nature; which is, *by all means we can, to defend ourselves.*

From this fundamental law of nature, by which men are commanded to endeavor peace, is derived this second law; *that a man be willing when others are so too, as farforth, as for peace, and defence of himself he shall think it necessary, to lay down this right to all things; and be contented with so much liberty against other men, as he would allow other men against himself.* For as long as every man holdeth this right, of doing any thing he liketh; so long are all men in the condition of war. But if other men will not lay down their right, as well as he; then there is no reason for any one, to divest himself of his: for that were to expose himself to prey, (which no man is bound to) rather than to dispose himself to peace. This is that law of the Gospel; *whatsoever you require that others should do for you, that do ye to them.* And that law of all men, *quod tibi fieri non vis, alteri ne feceris.*

To *lay down* a man's *right* to any thing, is to *divest* himself of the *liberty*, of hindering another of the benefit of his own right to the same. For he that renounceth, or passeth away his right, giveth not to any other man a right which he had not before; because there is nothing to which every man had not right by nature: but only standeth out of his way, that he may enjoy his own original right, without hindrance from him; not without hindrance from another so that the effect which redoundeth to one man, by another man's defect of right, is but so much diminution of impediments to the use of his own right original.

Right is laid aside, either by simply renouncing it; or by transferring it to another. By *simply* RENOUNCING; when he cares not to whom the benefit thereof redoundeth. By TRANSFERRING; when he intendeth the benefit thereof to some certain person, or persons And when a man hath in either manner abandoned, or granted away his right; then is he said to be OBLIGED, or BOUND, not to hinder those, to whom such right is granted, or abandoned, from the benefit of it: and that he *ought*, and it is his DUTY, not to make void that voluntary act of his own: and that such hindrance is INJUSTICE, and INJURY, as being *sine jure*, the right being before renounced, or transferred. So that *injury*, or *injustice*, in the controversies of the world, is somewhat like to that, which in the disputations of scholars is called *absurdity*. For as it is there called an absurdity, to contradict what one maintained in the beginning so in the world, it is called injustice, and injury, voluntarily to undo that, which from the beginning he had voluntarily done. The way by which a man either simply renounceth, or transferreth his right, is a declaration, or signification, by some voluntary and sufficient sign, or signs, that he doth so renounced, or transfer; or hath so renounced, or transferred the same, to him that accepteth it. And these signs are either words only, or actions only; or (as it happeneth most often) both words, and actions. And the same are the BONDS, by which men are bound, and obliged: bonds, that have their strength, not from their own nature, (for nothing is more easily broken than a man's word) but from fear of some evil consequence upon the rupture.

Whensoever a man transferreth his right, or renounceth it; it is either in consideration of some right reciprocally transferred to himself; or for some other good he hopeth for thereby. For it is a voluntary act: and of the voluntary acts of every man, the object is some *good to himself.* And therefore there be some rights, which no man can be understood by any words, or other signs, to have abandoned or transferred. As first a man cannot lay down the right of resisting them, that assault him by force, to take away his life; because he cannot be understood to aim thereby, at any good to himself. The same may be said of wounds, and chains, and imprisonment; both because there is no benefit consequent to such patience; as there is to the patience of suffering another to be wounded, or imprisoned: as also because a man cannot tell, when he seeth men proceed against him by violence, whether they intend his death or not. And lastly the motive, and end for which this renouncing, and transferring of right is introduced, is nothing else but the security of a man's person, in his life, and in the means of so preserving life, as not to be weary of it. And therefore if a man by words, or other signs, seem to despoil himself of the end, for which those signs were intended; he is not to be understood as if he meant it, or that it was his will; but that he was ignorant of how such words and actions were to be interpreted.

The mutual transferring of right, is that which men call CONTRACT.

There is difference between transferring of right to the thing; and transferring, or tradition, that is, delivery of the thing it self. For the thing may be delivered together with the translation of the right; as in buying and selling with ready money; or exchange of goods, or lands: and it may be delivered some time after.

Again, one of the contractors, may deliver the thing contracted for on his part, and leave the other to perform his part at some determinate time after, and in the mean time be trusted; and then the contract on his part, is called PACT, or COVENANT: or both parts may contract now, to perform hereafter: in which cases, he that is to perform in time to come, being trusted, his performance is called *keeping of promise,* or faith; and the failing of performance (if it be voluntary) *violation of faith.*

When the transferring of right, is not mutual; but one of the parties transferreth, in hope to gain thereby friendship, or service from another, or from his friends; or in hope to gain the reputation of charity, or magnanimity; or to deliver his mind from the pain of compassion; or in hope of reward in heaven; this is not contract, but GIFT, FREE-GIFT, GRACE: which words signify one and the same thing....

If a covenant be made, wherein neither of the parties perform presently, but trust one another; in the condition of mere nature, (which is a condition of war of every man against every man,) upon any reasonable suspicion, it is void: but if there be a common power set over them both, with right and force sufficient to compel performance, it is not void. For he that performeth first, has no assurance the other will perform after; because the bonds of words are too weak to bridle men's ambition, avarice, anger, and other passions, without the fear of some coercive power; which in the condition of mere nature, where all men are equal, and judges of the justness of their own fears, cannot possibly be supposed. And therefore he which performeth first, does but betray himself to his enemy; contrary to the right (he can never abandon) of defending his life, and means of living.

But in a civil estate, where there is a power set up to constrain those that would otherwise violate their faith, that fear is no more reasonable; and for that cause, he which by the covenant is to perform first, is obliged so to do.

The cause of fear, which maketh such a covenant invalid, must be always something arising after the covenant made; as some new fact, or other sign of the will not to perform: else it cannot make the covenant void. For that which could not hinder a man from promising, ought not to be admitted as a hindrance of performing....

The matter, or subject of a covenant, is always something that falleth under deliberation; (for to covenant, is an act of the will; that is to say an act, and the last act, of deliberation;) and is therefore always understood to be something to come, and which is judged possible for him that covenanteth, to perform.

And therefore, to promise that which is known to be impossible, is no covenant. But if that prove impossible afterwards, which before was thought possible, the covenant is valid, and bindeth, (though not to the thing it self,) yet to the value, or if that also be impossible, to the unfeigned endeavour of performing as much as is possible: for to more no man can be obliged.

Men are freed of their covenants two ways; by performing; or by being forgiven. For performance, is the natural end of obligation; and forgiveness, the restitution of liberty; as being a retransferring of that right, in which the obligation consisted.

Covenants entered into by fear, in the condition of mere nature, are obligatory. For example, if I covenant to pay a ransom, or service for my life, to an enemy; I am bound by it. For it is a contract, wherein one receiveth the benefit of life; the other is to receive money, or service for it; and consequently, where no other law (as in the condition, of mere nature) forbiddeth the performance, the covenant is valid. There are prisoners of war, if trusted with the payment of their ransom, are obliged to pay it, and if a weaker prince, make a disadvantageous peace with a stronger, for fear; he is bound to keep it; unless (as hath been said before) there ariseth some new, and just cause of fear, to renew the war. And even in commonwealths, if I be forced to redeem myself from a thief by promising him money, I am bound to pay it, till the civil law discharge me. For whatsoever I may lawfully do without obligation, the same I may lawfully covenant to do through fear: and what I lawfully covenant, I cannot lawfully break.

A former covenant, makes void a later. For a man that hath passed away his right to one may today, hath it not to pass tomorrow to another: and therefore the later promise passeth no right, but is null.

A covenant not to defend myself from force, by force, is always void. For (as I have showed before) no man can transfer, or lay down his right to save himself from death, wounds, and imprisonment, (the avoiding whereof is the only end of laying down any right, and therefore the promise of not resisting force, in no covenant transferreth any right; nor is obliging. For though a man may covenant thus, *unless I do so, or so, kill me*; he cannot covenant thus, *unless I do so, or so, I will nor resist you, when you come to kill me.* For man by nature chooseth the lesser evil, which is danger of death in resisting; rather than the greater, which is certain and present death in not resisting. And this is granted to be true by all men, in that they lead criminals to execution, and prison, with armed men, notwithstanding that such criminals have consented to the law, by which they are condemned.

A covenant to accuse one self, without assurance of pardon, is likewise invalid. For in the condition of nature, where every man is judge, there is no place for accusation: and in the civil state, the accusation is followed with punishment; which being force, a man is not obliged not to resist. The same is also true, of the accusation of those, by whose condemnation a man falls into misery; as of a father, wife, or benefactor. For the testimony of such an accuser, if it be not willingly given, is presumed to be corrupted by nature; and therefore not to be received: and where a man's testimony is not to be credited, he is not bound to give it. Also accusations upon torture, are not to be reputed as testimonies. For torture is to be used but as means of conjecture, and light, in the further examination, and search of truth: and what is in that case confessed, tendeth to the ease of him that is tortured, not to the informing of the torturers: and therefore ought not to have the credit of a sufficient testimony: for whether he deliver himself by true, or false accusation, he does it by the right of preserving his own life.

The force of words, being (as I have formerly noted) too weak to hold men to the performance of their covenants; there are in man's nature, but two imaginable helps to strengthen it And those are either a fear of the consequence of breaking their word; or a glory, or pride in appearing not to need to break it. This latter is a generosity too rarely found to be presumed on, especially in the pursuers of wealth, command, or sensual pleasure; which are the greatest part of mankind. The passion to be reckoned upon, is fear; whereof there be two very general objects: one, the power of spirits invisible; the other, the power of those men they shall therein offend. Of these two, though the former be the greater power, yet the fear of the latter is commonly the greater fear. The fear of the former is in every man, his own religion: which hath place in the nature of man before civil society. The latter hath not so; at least not place enough, to keep men to their promises; because in the condition of mere nature, the inequality of power is not discerned, but by the event of battle. So that before the time of civil society, or in the interruption thereof by war, there is nothing can strengthen a covenant of peace agreed on, against the temptations of avarice, ambition, lust, or other strong desire, but the fear of that invisible power, which they every one worship as God; and fear as a revenger of their perfidy. All therefore that can be done between two men not subject to civil power, is to put one another to swear by the God he feareth: which *swearing*, or OATH, is a *form of speech, added to a promise; by which he that promiseth, signifieth, that unless he perform, he renounceth the mercy of his God, or calleth to him for vengeance on himself.* Such was the heathen form, *Let* Jupiter *kill me else, as I kill this beast.* So is our form, *I shall do thus, and thus, so help me God.* And this, with the rites and ceremonies, which every one useth in his own religion, that the fear of breaking faith might be the greater.

By this it appears, that an oath taken according to any other form, or rite, than his, that sweareth, is in vain; and no oath: and that there is no swearing by any thing which the swearer thinks not God. For though men have sometimes used to swear by their kings, for fear, or flattery; yet they would have it thereby understood, they attributed to them divine honour. And that swearing unnecessarily by God, is but prophaning of his name: and swearing by other things, as men do in common discourse, is not swearing, but an impious custom, gotten by too much vehemence of talking.

It appears also, that the oath adds nothing to the obligation. For a covenant, if lawful, binds in the sight of God, without the oath, as much as with it: if unlawful, bindeth not at all; though it be confirmed with an oath.

Chapter 15. Of Other Laws of Nature

From that law of nature, by which we are obliged to transfer to another, such rights, as being retained, hinder the peace of mankind, there followeth a third; which is this, *that men perform their covenants made*: without which, covenants are in vain, and but empty words; and the right of all men to all things remaining, we are still in the condition of war.

And in this law of nature, consisteth the fountain and original of JUSTICE. For where no covenant hath preceded, there hath no right been transferred and every man has right to every thing; and consequently, no action can be unjust. But when a covenant is made, then to break it is *unjust*; and the definition of INJUSTICE, is no other than *the not performance of covenant.* And whatsoever is not unjust, is *just.*

But because covenants of mutual trust, where there is fear of not performance on either part, (as hath been said in the former chapter,) are invalid; though the original of justice be the making of covenants; yet injustice actually there can be none, till the cause of such fear be taken away; which while men are in the natural condition of war, cannot be done. Therefore before the names of just, and unjust can have place, there must be some coercive power, to compel men equally to the performance of their covenants, by the terror of some punishment, greater than the benefit they expect by the breach of their covenant; and to make good that propriety, which by mutual contract men acquire, in recompense of the universal right they abandon: and such power there is none before the erection of a commonwealth. And this is also to be gathered out of the ordinary definition of justice in the Schools: for they say, that *justice is the constant will of giving to every man his own.* And therefore where there is no *own,* that is, no propriety, there is no injustice; and where there is no coercive power erected, that is, where there is no commonwealth, there is no propriety; all men having right to all things: therefore where there is no commonwealth, there nothing is unjust. So that the nature of justice, consisteth in keeping of valid covenants: but the validity of covenants begins not but with the constitution of a civil power, sufficient to compel men to keep them: and then it is also that propriety begins.

The fool hath said in his heart, there is no such thing as justice; and sometimes also with his tongue; seriously alleging, that every man's conservation, and contentment, being committed to his own care, there could be no reason, why every man might not do what he thought conducted thereunto: and therefore also to make, or not make; keep, or not keep covenants, was not against reason, when it conduced to one's benefit. He does not therein deny, that there be covenants; and that they are sometimes broken, sometimes kept; and that such breach of them may be called injustice, and the observance of them justice: but he questioneth, whether injustice, taking away the fear of God, (for the same fool hath said in his heart there is no God,) may not sometimes stand with that reason, which dictateth to every man his own good; and particularly then, when it conduceth to such a benefit, as shall put a man in a condition, to neglect not only the dispraise, and revilings, but also the power of other men. The kingdom of God is gotten by violence: but what if it could be gotten by unjust violence? were it against reason so to get it, when it is impossible to receive hurt by it? and if it be not against reason, it is not against justice; or else justice is not to be approved for good. From such reasoning as this, successful wickedness hath obtained the name of virtue: and some that in all other things have disallowed the violation of faith; yet have allowed it, when it is for the getting of a kingdom. And the heathen that believed, that *Saturn* was deposed by his son *Jupiter,* believed nevertheless the same *Jupiter* to be the avenger of injustice: somewhat like to a piece of law in *Coke's Commentaries on Littleton;* where he says, if the right heir of the crown be attainted of treason; yet the crown shall descend to him, and *eo instante* the attainder be void: from which instances a man will be very prone to infer; that when the heir apparent of a kingdom, shall kill him that is in possession, though his father; you may call it injustice, or by what other name you will; yet it can never be against reason, seeing all the voluntary actions of men tend to the benefit of themselves; and those actions are most reasonable, that conduce most to their ends. This specious reasoning is nevertheless false.

For the question is not of promises mutual, where there is no security of performance on either side; as when there is no civil power erected over the parties promising; for such promises are no covenants: but either where one of the parties has performed already; or where there is a power to make him perform; there is the question whether it be against reason, that is, against the benefit of the other to perform, or not. And I say it is not against reason. For the manifestation whereof, we are to consider; first, that when a man doth a thing, which notwithstanding any thing can be foreseen, and reckoned on, tendeth to his own destruction, howsoever some accident which he could not expect, arriving may turn it to his benefit; yet such events do not make it reasonably or wisely done. Secondly, that in a condition of war, wherein every man to every man, for want of a common power to keep them all in awe, is an enemy, there is no man can hope by his own strength, or wit, to defend himself from destruction, without the help of confederates; where every one expects the same defence by the confederation, that any one else does: and therefore he which declares he thinks it reason to deceive those that help him, can in reason expect no other means of safety, than what can be had from his own single power. He therefore that breaketh his covenant, and consequently declareth that he thinks he may with reason do so, cannot be received into any society, that unite themselves for peace and defence, but by the error of them that receive him; nor when he is received, be retained in it, without seeing the danger of their error; which errors a man cannot reasonably reckon upon as the means of his security: and therefore if he be left, or cast out of society, he perisheth; and if he live in society, it is by the errors of other men, which he could not foresee, nor reckon upon; and consequently against the reason of his preservation; and so, as all men that contribute not to his destruction, forbear him only out of ignorance of what is good for themselves.

As for the instance of gaining the secure and perpetual felicity of heaven, by any way; it is frivolous: there being but one way imaginable; and that is not breaking, but keeping of covenant.

And for the other instances of attaining sovereignty by rebellion; it is manifest, that though the event follow, yet because it cannot reasonably be expected, but rather the contrary; and because by gaining it so, others are taught to gain the same in like manner, the attempt thereof is against reason. Justice therefore, that is to say, keeping of covenant, is a rule of reason, by which we are forbidden to do any thing destructive to our life; and consequently a law of nature.

There be some that proceed further; and will not have the law of nature to be those rules which conduce to the preservation of man's life on earth; but to the attaining of an eternal felicity after death; to which they think the breach of covenant may conduce; and consequently be just and reasonable; (such are they that think it a work of merit to kill, or depose, or rebel against, the sovereign power constituted over them by their own consent.) But because there is no natural knowledge of man's estate after death; much less of the reward that is then to be given to breach of faith; but only a belief grounded upon other men's saying, that they know it supernaturally, or that they know those, that knew them, that knew others, that knew it supernaturally; breach of faith cannot be called a precept of reason or nature.

11

The Justification of Property

John Locke

. . . God, who hath given the world to men in common, hath also given them reason to make use of it to the best advantage of life and convenience. The earth and all that is therein is given to men for the support and comfort of their being. And though all the fruits it naturally produces, and beasts it feeds, belong to mankind in common, as they are produced by the spontaneous hand of nature; and nobody has originally a private dominion exclusive of the rest of mankind in any of them as they are thus in their natural state; yet being given for the use of men, there must of necessity be a means to appropriate them some way or other before they can be of any use at all beneficial to any particular man. The fruit or venison which nourishes the wild Indian, who knows no enclosure, and is still a tenant in common, must be his, and so his, i.e., a part of him, that another can no longer have any right to it, before it can do any good for the support of his life.

Though the earth and all inferior creatures be common to all men, yet every man has a property in his own person; this nobody has any right to but himself. The labor of his body and the work of his hands we may say are properly his. Whatsoever, then, he removes out of the state that nature hath provided and left it in, he hath mixed his labor with, and joined to it something that is his own, and thereby makes it his property. It being by him removed from the common state nature placed it in, it hath by this labor something annexed to it that excludes the common right of other men. For this labor being the unquestionable property of the laborer, no man but he can have a right to what this is once joined to, at least where there is enough, and as good left in common for others.

He that is nourished by the acorns he picked up under an oak, or the apples he gathered from the trees in the wood, has certainly appropriated them to himself. Nobody can deny but the nourishment is his. I ask, then, When did they begin to be his—when he digested, or when he ate, or when he boiled, or

Source: John Locke, *The Second Treatise of Government* (New York: Macmillan, 1956, first published, 1764).

when he brought them home, or when he picked them up? And 'tis plain if the first gathering made them not his, nothing else could. That labor put a distinction between them and common; that added something to them more than nature, the common mother of all, had done, and so they became his private right. And will anyone say he had no right to those acorns or apples he thus appropriated, because he had not the consent of all mankind to make them his? Was it robbery thus to assume to himself what belonged to all in common? If such a consent as that was necessary, man had starved, notwithstanding the plenty God had given him. We see in common which remains so by compact that 'tis the taking any part of what is common and removing it out of the state nature leaves it in, which begins the property; without which the common is of no use. And the taking of this or that does not depend on the express consent of all the commoners. Thus the grass my horse has bit, the turfs my servant has cut, the ore I have dug in any place where I have a right to them in common with others, become my property without the assignation or consent of anybody. The labor that was mine removing them out of that common state they were in, hath fixed my property in them....

It will perhaps be objected to this, that if gathering the acorns, or other fruits of the earth, etc., makes a right to them, then anyone may engross as much as he will. To which I answer, Not so. The same law of nature that does by this means give us property, does also bound that properly too. "God has given us all things richly" (1 Tim. vi. 17), is the voice of reason confirmed by inspiration. But how far has He given it us? To enjoy. As much as anyone can make use of any advantage of life before it spoils, so much he may by his labor fix a property in; whatever is beyond this, is more than his share, and belongs to others. Nothing was made by God for man to spoil or destroy. And thus considering the plenty of natural provisions there was a long time in the world, and the few spenders, and to how small a part of that provision the industry of one man could extend itself, and engross it to the prejudice of others—especially keeping within the bounds, set by reason, of what might serve for his use—there could be then little room for quarrels or contentions about property so established.

But the chief matter of property being now not the fruits of the earth, and the beasts that subsist on it, but the earth itself, as that which takes in and carries with it all the rest, I think it is plain that property in that, too, is acquired as the former. As much land as a man tills, plants, improves, cultivates, and can use the product of, so much is his property. He by his labor does as it were enclose it from the common. Nor will it invalidate his right to say, everybody else has an equal title to it; and therefore he cannot appropriate, he cannot enclose, without the consent of all his fellow-commoners, all mankind. God, when He gave the world in common to all mankind, commanded man also to labor, and the penury of his condition required it of him. God and his reason commanded him to subdue the earth, i.e., improve it for the benefit of life, and therein lay out something upon it that was his own, his labor. He that, in obedience to this command of God, subdued, tilled, and sowed any part of it, thereby annexed to it something that was his property, which another had no title to, nor could without injury take from him.

Nor was this appropriation of any parcel of land, by improving it, any prejudice to any other man, since there was still enough and as good left; and more than the yet unprovided could use. So that in effect, there was never the less left for others because of his enclosure for himself. For he that leaves as much as another can make use of, does as good as take nothing at all. Nobody could think himself injured by the drinking of another man, though he took a good draught, who had a whole river of the same water left him to quench his thirst; and the case of land and water, where there is enough of both, is perfectly the same. God gave the world to men in common; but since He gave it them for their benefit, and the greatest conveniences of life they were capable to draw from it, it cannot be supposed He meant it should always remain common and uncultivated. He gave it to the use of the industrious and rational (and labor was to be his title to it), not to the fancy or coveteousness of the quarrelsome and contentious. He that had as good left for his improvement as was already taken up, needed not complain, ought not to meddle with what was already improved by another's labor; if he did, it is plain he desired the benefit of another's pains, which he had no right to, and not the ground which God had given him in common with others to labor on, and whereof there was as good left as that already possessed, and more than he knew what to do with, or his industry could reach to.

It is true, in land that is common in England, or any other country where there is plenty of people under Government, who have money and commerce, no one can enclose or appropriate any part without the consent of all his fellow-commoners: because this is left common by compact, i.e., by the law of the land, which is not to be violated. And though it be common in respect of some men, it is not so to all mankind; but is the joint property of this country, or this parish. Besides, the remainder, after such enclosure, would not be as good to the rest of the commoners as the whole was, when they could all make use of the whole, whereas in the beginning and first peopling of the great common of the world it was quite otherwise. The law man was under was rather for appropriating. God commanded, and his wants forced him, to labor. That was his property, which could not be taken from him wherever he had fixed it. And hence subduing or cultivating the earth, and having dominion, we see are joined together. The one gave title to the other. So that God, by commanding to subdue, gave authority so far to appropriate. And the condition of human life, which requires labor and materials to work on, necessarily introduces private possessions. The measure of property nature has well set by the extent of men's labor and the conveniency of life. No man's labor could subdue or appropriate all, nor could his enjoyment consume more than a small part; so that it was impossible for any man, this way, to entrench upon the right of another or acquire to himself a property to the prejudice of his neighbor, who would still have room for as good and as large a possession (after the other had taken out his) as before it was appropriated. Which measure did confine every man's possession to a very moderate proportion, and such as he might appropriate to himself without injury to anybody in the first ages of the world, when men were more in danger to be lost, by wandering from their company, in the then vast wilderness of the earth than to be straitened for want of room to plant in....

And thus, without supposing any private dominion and property in Adam over all the world, exclusive of all other men, which can no way be proved, nor any one's property be made out from it, but supposing the world, given as it was to the children of men in common, we see how labor could make men distinct titles to several parcels of it for their private uses, wherein there could be no doubt of right, no room for quarrel.

Nor is it so strange, as perhaps before consideration it may appear, that the property of labor should be able to overbalance the community of land. For it is labor indeed that puts the difference of value on everything; and let anyone consider what the difference is between an acre of land planted with tobacco or sugar, sown with wheat or barley, and an acre of the same land lying in common without any husbandry upon it, and he will find that the improvement of labor makes the far greater part of the value. I think it will be but a very modest computation to say that of the products of the earth useful to the life of man nine-tenths are the effects of labor; nay, if we will rightly estimate things as they come to our use, and cast up the several expenses about them—what in them is purely owing to nature, and what to labor—we shall find that in most of them ninety-nine hundredths are wholly to be put on the account of labor....

From all which it is evident that, though the things of nature are given in common, yet man, by being master of himself and proprietor of his own person and the actions or labor of it, had still in himself the great foundation of property; and that which made up the great part of what he applied to the support or comfort of his being, when invention and arts had improved the conveniences of life, was perfectly his own, and did not belong in common to others.

Thus labor, in the beginning, gave a right of property, wherever anyone was pleased to employ it upon what was common, which remained a long while the far greater part, and is yet more than mankind makes use of. Men at first, for the most part, contented themselves with what unassisted nature offered to their necessities; and though afterwards, in some parts of the world (where the increase of people and stock, with the use of money, had made land scarce, and so of some value), the several communities settled the bounds of their distinct territories, and by laws within themselves, regulated the properties of the private men of their society, and so, by compact and agreement, settled the property which labor and industry began—and the leagues that have been made between several states and kingdoms, either expressly or tacitly disowning all claim and right to the land in the other's possession, have, by common consent, given up their pretenses to their natural common right, which originally they had to those countries; and so have, by positive agreement, settled a property amongst themselves in distant parts of the world—yet there are still great tracts of ground to be found which, the inhabitants thereof not having joined with the rest of mankind in the consent of the use of their common money, lie waste, and more than the people who dwell on it do or can make use of, and so still lie in common; though this can scarce happen amongst that part of mankind that have consented to the use of money.

The greatest part of things really useful to the life of man, and such as the necessity of subsisting made the first commoners of the world look after, as it doth the Americans now, are generally things of short duration, such as, if they are not consumed by use, will decay and perish of themselves- gold, silver, and diamonds are things that fancy or agreement have put the value on more than real use and the necessary support of life. Now of those good things which nature hath provided in common, everyone hath a right, as hath been said, to as much as he could use, and had a property in all he could effect with his labor–all that his industry could extend to, to alter from the state nature had put it in, was his. He that gathered a hundred bushels of acorns or apples had thereby a property in them; they were his goods as soon as gathered. He was only to look that he used them before they spoiled, else he took more than his share, and robbed others; and, indeed, it was a foolish thing, as well as dishonest, to hoard up more than he could make use of. If he gave away a part to anybody else, so that it perished not uselessly in his possession, these he also made use of; and if he also bartered away plums that would have rotted in a week, for nuts that would last good for his eating a whole year, he did no injury; he wasted not the common stock, destroyed no part of the portion of goods that belonged to others, so long as nothing perished uselessly in his hands. Again, if he would give his nuts for a piece of metal, pleased with its color, or exchange his sheep for shells, or wool for a sparkling pebble or a diamond, and keep those by him all his life, he invaded not the right of others; he might heap up as much as these durable things as he pleased, the exceeding of the bounds of his just property not lying in the largeness of his possessions, but the perishing of anything uselessly in it.

And thus came in the use of money–some lasting thing that men might keep without spoiling, and that, by mutual consent, men would take in exchange for the truly useful but perishable supports of life.

And as different degrees of industry were apt to give men possessions in different proportions, so this invention of money gave them the opportunity to continue and enlarge them; for supposing an island, separate from all possible commerce with the rest of the world, wherein there were but a hundred families–but there were sheep, horses, and cows, with other useful animals, wholesome fruits, and land enough for corn for a hundred thousand times as many, but nothing in the island, either because of its commonness or perishableness, fit to supply the place of money–what reason could anyone have there to enlarge his possessions beyond the use of his family and a plentiful supply to its consumption, either in what their own industry produced, or they could barter for like perishable useful commodities with others? Where there is not something both lasting and scarce, and so valuable to be hoarded up, there men will not be apt to enlarge their possessions of land, were it never so rich, never so free for them to take; for I ask, what would a man value ten thousand or a hundred thousand acres of excellent land, ready cultivated, and well stocked too with cattle, in the middle of the inland parts of

America, where he had no hopes of commerce with other parts of the world, to draw money to him by the sale of the product? It would not be worth the enclosing, and we should see him give up again to the wild common of nature whatever was more than would supply the conveniences of life to be had there for him and his family.

Thus in the beginning all the world was America, and more so than that is now, for no such thing as money was anywhere known. Find out something that hath the use and value of money amongst his neighbors, you shall see the same man will begin presently to enlarge his possessions.

But since gold and silver, being little useful to the life of man in proportion to food, raiment, and carriage, has its value only from the consent of men, whereof labor yet makes, in great part, the measure, it is plain that the consent of men have agreed to a disproportionate and unequal possession of the earth— I mean out of the bounds of society and compact; for in governments the laws regulate it; they having, by consent, found out and agreed in a way how a man may rightfully and without injury possess more than he himself can make use of by receiving gold and silver, which may continue long in a man's possession, without decaying for the overplus, and agreeing those metals should have a value.

And thus, I think, it is very easy to conceive without any difficulty how labor could at first begin a title of property in the common things of nature, and how the spending it upon our uses bounded it; so that there could then be no reason of quarrelling about title, nor any doubt about the largeness of possession it gave. Right and conveniency went together; for as a man had a right to all he could employ his labor upon, so he had no temptation to labor for more than he could make use of. This left no room for controversy about the title, nor for encroachment on the right of others; what portion a man carved to himself was easily seen, and it was useless, as well as dishonest, to carve himself too much, or take more than he needed.

12

Excerpts from "The Wealth of Nations"

Adam Smith

Book I

O f the causes of improvement in the productive powers of labor and of the order according to which its produce is naturally attributed among the different ranks of the people

Chapter I Of the Division of Labor

The greatest improvement in the productive powers of labor, and the greater part of the skill, dexterity, and judgment with which it is anywhere directed, or applied, seem to have been the effects of the division of labor....

To take an example, therefore, from a very trifling manufacture; but one in which the division of labor has been very often taken notice of, the trade of the pin-maker; a workman not educated to this business (which the division of labor has rendered a distinct trade), nor acquainted with the use of the machinery employed in it (to the invention of which the same division of labor has probably given occasion), could scarce, perhaps, with his utmost industry, make one pin in a day, and certainly could not make twenty. But in the way in which this business is now carried on, not only the whole work is a peculiar trade, but it is divided into a number of branches, of which the greater part are likewise peculiar trades. One man draws out the wire, another straights it, a third cuts it, a fourth points it, a fifth grinds it at the top for receiving the head; to make the head requires two or three distinct operations; to put it on is a peculiar business, to whiten the pins is another; it is even a trade by itself to put them into the paper; and the important business of making a pin is, in this manner, divided into about eighteen distinct operations, which in some manufactories, are all performed by distinct hands, though in others the same man will sometimes perform two or three of them. I have seen a small

Source: Adam Smith, *The Wealth of Nations,* Books I and IV (Chicago, IL: Chicago University Press, 1976, first published 1776).

manufactory of this kind where ten men only were employed, and where some of them consequently performed two or three distinct operations. But though they were very poor, and therefore but indifferently accommodated with the necessary machinery, they could, when they exerted themselves, make among them about twelve pounds of pins a day. There are in a pound upwards of four thousand pins of a middling size. Those ten persons, therefore, could make among them upwards of forty-eight thousand pins in a day. Each person, therefore, making a tenth part of forty-eight thousand pins, might be considered as making four thousand eight hundred pins in a day. But if they had all wrought separately and independently, and without any of them having been educated to this peculiar business, they certainly could not each of them have made twenty, perhaps not one pin in a day; that is, certainly, not the two hundred and fortieth, perhaps not the four thousand eight hundredth part, of what they are at present capable of performing in consequence of a proper division and combination of their different operations.

In every other art and manufacture, the effects of the division of labor are similar to what they are in this very trifling one; though in many of them, the labor can neither be so much subdivided, nor reduced to so great a simplicity of operation. The division of labor, however, so far as it can be introduced, occasions, in every art, a proportionate increase of the productive powers of labor....

This great increase of the quantity of work, which in consequence of the division of labor, the same number of people are capable of performing, is owing to three different circumstances: first, to the increase of dexterity in every particular workman; secondly, to the saving of the time which is commonly lost in passing from one species of work to another; and lastly, to the invention of a great number of machines which facilitate and abridge labor, and enable one man to do the work of many.

First, the improvement of the dexterity of the workman necessarily increases the quantity of the work he can perform; and the division of labor, by reducing every man's business to some one simple operation and by making this operation the sole employment of his life, necessarily increases very much the dexterity of the workman. A common smith, who, though accustomed to handle the hammer, has never been used to make nails, if upon some particular occasion he is obliged to attempt it, will scarce, I am assured, be able to make about two or three hundred nails in a day, and those too very bad ones. A smith who has been accustomed to make nails, but whose sole or principal business has not been that of a nailer, can seldom with his utmost diligence make more than eight hundred or a thousand nails in a day. I have seen several boys under twenty years of age who had never exercised any other trade but that of making nails, and who, when they exerted themselves, could make, each of them, upwards of two thousand three hundred nails in a day. The making of a nail, however, is by no means one of the simplest operations. The same person blows the bellows, stirs or mends the fire as there is occasion, heats the iron, and forges every part of the nail: In forging the head too he is obliged to change his tools. The different operations into which the making of a pin or of a metal button is subdivided, are all of them much more simple; and the dexterity of the person, of whose life it has been the sole business to perform them, is usually much greater. The rapidity with which some of the operations of those manufacturers are performed exceeds what the human hand could, by those who had never seen them, be supposed capable of acquiring.

Secondly, the advantage which is gained by saving the time commonly lost in passing from one sort of work to another is much greater than we should at first view be apt to imagine it. It is impossible to pass very quickly from one kind of work to another, that is carried on in a different place, and with quite different tools. A country weaver who cultivates a small farm must lose a good deal of time in passing from his loom to the field, and from the field to his loom. When the two trades can be carried on in the same workhouse, the loss of time is no doubt much less. It is even in this case, however, very considerable....

Thirdly, and lastly, every body must be sensible how much labor is facilitated and abridged by the application of proper machinery....

... A great part of the machines made use of in those manufactures in which labor is most subdivided were originally the inventions of common workmen, who, being each of them employed in some very simple operation, naturally turned their thoughts toward finding out easier and readier methods of performing it. Whoever has been much accustomed to visit such manufacturers must frequently have been shown very pretty machines which were inventions of such workmen in order to facilitate and quicken their own particular part of the work. In the first fire-engines, a boy was constantly employed to open and shut alternately the communication between the boiler and the cylinder, according as the piston either ascended or descended. One of those boys, who loved to play with his companions, observed that, by tying a string from the handle of the valve which opened this communication to another part of the machine, the valve would open and shut without his assistance, and leave him at liberty to divert himself with his play-fellows. One of the greatest improvements that has been made upon this machine, since it was first invented, was in this manner the discovery of a boy who wanted to save his own labor....

It is the great multiplication of the productions of all the different arts, in consequence of the division of labor, which occasions, in a well-governed society, that universal opulence which extends itself to the lowest ranks of the people. Every workman has a great quantity of his own work to dispose of beyond what he himself has occasion for; and every other workman being exactly in the same situation, he is enabled to exchange a great quantity of his own goods for a great quantity, or, what comes to the same thing, for the price of a great quantity of theirs. He supplies them abundantly with what they have occasion for, and they accommodate him as amply with what he has occasion for, and a general plenty diffuses itself through all the different ranks of the society....

Chapter II Of the Principle which Gives Occasion to the Division of Labor

This division of labor, from which so many advantages are derived, is not originally the effect of any human wisdom which forsees and intends that general opulence to which it gives occasion. It is the necessary, though very slow and gradual, consequence of a certain propensity in human nature which has in view no such extensive utility: the propensity to truck, barter, and exchange one thing for another.

... In almost every other race of animals each individual, when it is grown up to maturity, is entirely independent, and in its natural state has occasion for the assistance of no other living creature. But man has almost constant occasion for the help of his brethren, and it is in vain for him to expect it from their benevolence only. He will be more likely to prevail if he can interest their self-love in his favor, and show them that it is for their own advantage to do for him what he requires of them. Whoever offers to another a bargain of any kind, proposes to do this. Give me that which I want, and you shall have this which you want, is the meaning of every such offer; and it is in the manner that we obtain from one another the far greater part of those good offices which we stand in need of. It is not from the benevolence of the butcher, the brewer, or the baker, that we expect our dinner, but from their regard to their own interest. We address ourselves, not to their humanity but to their self-love, and never talk to them of our own necessities but of their advantages. Nobody but a beggar chooses to depend chiefly upon the benevolence of his fellow-citizens. Even a beggar does not depend upon it entirely. The charity of well-disposed people, indeed, supplies him with the whole fund of his subsistence. But though this principle ultimately provides him with all the necessaries of life which he has occasion for, it neither does nor can provide him with them as he has occasion for them. The greater part of his occasional wants are supplied in the same manner as those of other people, by treaty, by barter, and by purchase. With the money which one man gives him he purchases food. The old clothes which another bestows upon him he exchanges for other old clothes which suit him better, or for lodging, or for food, or for money, with which he can buy either food, clothes, or lodging, as he has occasion.

As it is by treaty, by barter, and by purchase that we obtain from one another the greater part of those mutual good offices which we stand in need of, so it is this same trucking disposition which originally gives occasion to the division of labor. In a tribe of hunters or shepherds a particular person makes bows and arrows, for example, with more readiness and dexterity than any other. He frequently exchanges them for cattle or for venison with his companions; and he finds at last that he can in this manner get more cattle and venison than if he himself went to the field to catch them. From a regard to his own interest, therefore, the making of bows and arrows grows to be his chief business, and he becomes a sort of armorer. Another excels in making the frames and covers of their little huts or moveable houses. He is accustomed to be of use in this way to his neighbors, who reward him in the same manner with cattle and with venison till at last he finds it his interest to dedicate himself entirely to this employment, and to become a sort of house carpenter. In the same manner a third becomes a smith or a brazier; a fourth a tanner or dresser of hides or skins, the principal part of the clothing of savages. And thus the certainty of being able to exchange all that surplus part of the produce of his own labor, which is over and above his own consumption, for such parts of the produce of other men's labor as he may have occasion for, encourages every man to apply himself to a particular occupation, and to cultivate and bring to perfection whatever talent or genius he may possess for that particular species of business. The difference of natural talents in different men is, in reality, much less than we are aware of; and the very different genius which appears to distinguish men of different professions, when grown up to maturity, is not upon many occasions so much the cause as the effect of the division of labor. The difference between the most dissimilar characters, between a philosopher and a common street porter, for example, seems to arise not so much from nature as from habit, custom, and education. When they came into the world, and for the first six or eight years of their existence, they were, perhaps, very much alike, and neither their parents nor play-fellows could perceive any remarkable difference. About that age or soon after, they come to be employed in very different occupations. The difference of talents comes then to be taken notice of, and widens by degrees, till at last the vanity of the philosopher is willing to acknowledge scarce any resemblance. But without the disposition to truck, barter, and exchange, every man must have procured to himself every necessary and conveniency of life which he wanted. All must have had the same duties to perform, and the same work to do, and there could have been no such difference of employment as could alone give occasion to any great difference of talents....

BOOK IV

Chapter II Of Restraints upon the Importation from Foreign Countries

Every individual is continually exerting himself to find out the most advantageous employment for whatever capital he can command. It is his own advantage, indeed, and not that of the society, which he has in view. But the study of his own advantage, naturally, or rather necessarily, leads him to prefer that employment which is most advantageous to the society....

As every individual, therefore, endeavours as much as he can both to employ his capital in the support of domestic industry, and so to direct that industry that its produce may be of the greatest value, every individual necessarily labors to render the annual revenue of the society as great as he can. He generally, indeed, neither intends to promote the public interest, nor knows how much he is promoting it. By preferring the support of domestic to that of foreign industry, he intends only his own securing and by directing that industry in such a manner as its produce may be of the greatest value, he intends only his own gain, and he is in this, as in many other cases, led by an invisible hand to promote an end which was no part of his intention. Nor is it always the worse for society that it was no part of it. By pursuing his own interest he frequently promotes that of the society more effectually than when he really intends to promote it. I have never known much good done by those who affected to trade for the public good. It is an affectation, indeed, not very common among merchants, and very few words need be employed in dissuading them from it.

13

Alienated Labor and Private Property Communism

Karl Marx

Alienated Labour

We have proceeded from the presuppositions of political economy. We have accepted its language and its laws. We presupposed private property, the separation of labor, capital and land, hence of wages, profit of capital and rent, likewise the division of labor, competition, the concept of exchange value, etc. From political economy itself, in its own words, we have shown that the worker sinks to the level of a commodity, the most miserable commodity; that the misery of the worker is inversely proportional to the power and volume of his production; that the necessary result of competition is the accumulation of capital in a few hands and thus the revival of monopoly in a more frightful form; and finally that the distinction between capitalist and landowner, between agricultural laborer and industrial worker, disappears and the whole society must divide into the two classes of *proprietors* and propertyless *workers*.

Political economy proceeds from the fact of private property. It does not explain private property. It grasps the actual, *material* process of private property in abstract and general formulae which it then takes as *laws*. It does not *comprehend* these laws, that is, does not prove them as proceeding from the nature of private property. Political economy does not disclose the reason for the division between capital and labor, between capital and land. When, for example, the relation of wages to profits is determined, the ultimate basis is taken to be the interest of the capitalists; that is, political economy assumes what it should develop. Similarly, competition is referred to at every point and explained from external circumstances. Political economy teaches us nothing about the extent to which these external, apparently accidental circumstances are simply the expression of a necessary development. We have seen how

Source: Karl Marx, *Selected Writings*, Lawrence H. Simon (ed.) (Indianapolis, IN: Hackett Publishing, 1994).

political economy regards exchange itself as an accidental fact. The only wheels which political economy puts in motion are *greed* and the *war among the greedy, competition.*

Just because political economy does not grasp the interconnections within the movement, the doctrine of competition could stand opposed to the doctrine of monopoly, the doctrine of freedom of craft to that of the guild, the doctrine of the division of landed property to that of the great estate. Competition, freedom of craft, and division of landed property were developed and conceived only as accidental, deliberate, forced consequences of monopoly, the guild, and feudal property, rather than necessary, inevitable, natural consequences.

We now have to grasp the essential connection among private property, greed, division of labor, capital and landownership, and the connection of exchange with competition, of value with the devaluation of men, of monopoly with competition, etc., and of this whole alienation with the *money*-system.

Let us not put ourselves in a fictitious primordial state like a political economist trying to clarify things. Such a primordial state clarifies nothing. It merely pushes the issue into a gray, misty distance. It acknowledges as a fact or event what it should deduce, namely, the necessary relation between two things for example, between division of labor and exchange. In such a manner theology explains the origin of evil by the fall of man. That is, it asserts as a fact in the form of history what it should explain.

We proceed from a *present* fact of political economy.

The worker becomes poorer the more wealth he produces, the more his production increases in power and extent. The worker becomes a cheaper commodity the more commodities he produces. The *increase in value* of the world of things is directly proportional to the *decrease in value* of the human world. Labor not only produces commodities. It also produces itself and the worker as a *commodity*, and indeed in the same proportion as it produces commodities in general.

This fact simply indicates that the object which labor produces, its product, stands opposed to it as an *alien thing*, as a *power independent* of the producer. The product of labor is labor embodied and made objective in a thing. It is the *objectification* of labor. The realization of labor is its objectification. In the viewpoint of political economy this realization of labor appears as the *diminution* of the worker, the objectification *as the loss of and subservience to the object*, and the appropriation as *alienation [Entfremdung]*, as externalization [*Entäusserung*].

So much does the realization of labor appear as diminution that the worker is diminished to the point of starvation. So much does objectification appear as loss of the object that the worker is robbed of the most essential objects not only of life but also of work. Indeed, work itself becomes a thing of which he can take possession only with the greatest effort and with the most unpredictable interruptions. So much does the appropriation of the object appear as alienation that the more objects the worker produces, the fewer he can own and the more he falls under the domination of his product, of capital.

All these consequences follow from the fact that the worker is related to the *product of his labor* as to an *alien* object. For it is clear according to this premise: The more the worker exerts himself, the more powerful becomes the alien objective world which he fashions against himself, the poorer he and his inner world become, the less there is that belongs to him. It is the same in religion. The more man attributes to God, the less he retains in himself. The worker puts his life into the object; then it no longer belongs to him but to the object. The greater this activity, the poorer is the worker. What the product of his work is, he is not. The greater this product is, the smaller he is himself. The *externalization* of the worker in his product means not only that his work becomes an object, an *external* existence, but also that it exists *outside him* independently, alien, an autonomous power, opposed to him. The life he has given to the object confronts him as hostile and alien.

Let us now consider more closely the *objectification*, the worker's production and with it the *alienation* and *loss* of the object, his product.

The worker can make nothing without *nature*, without the *sensuous external world*. It is the material wherein his labor realizes itself, wherein it is active, out of which and by means of which it produces.

But as nature furnishes to labor the *means of life* in the sense that labor cannot *live* without objects upon which labor is exercised, nature also furnishes the *means of life* in the narrower sense, namely, the means of physical subsistence of the *worker* himself.

The more the worker *appropriates* the external world and sensuous nature through his labor, the more he deprives himself of the *means of life* in two respects: first, that the sensuous external world gradually ceases to be an object belonging to his labor, a *means of life* of his work; secondly, that it gradually ceases to be a *means of life* in the immediate sense, a means of physical subsistence of the worker.

In these two respects, therefore, the worker becomes a slave to his objects; first, in that he receives an *object of labor*, that is, he receives labor, and secondly that he receives the *means of subsistence*. The first enables him to exist as a *worker* and the second as a *physical subject*. The terminus of this slavery is that he can only maintain himself as a *physical subject* so far as he is a worker, and only as a physical subject is he a worker.

(The alienation of the worker in his object is expressed according to the laws of political economy as follows: the more the worker produces, the less he has to consume; the more values he creates the more worthless and unworthy he becomes; the better shaped his product, the more misshapen is he; the more civilized his product, the more barbaric is the worker; the more powerful the work, the more powerless becomes the worker; the more intelligence the work has, the more witless is the worker and the more he becomes a slave of nature.)

Political economy conceals the alienation in the nature of labor by ignoring the direct relationship between the worker (labor) *and production.* To be sure, labor produces marvels for the wealthy but it produces deprivation for the worker. It produces palaces, but hovels for the worker. It produces beauty, but mutilation for the worker. It displaces labor through machines, but it throws some workers back into barbarous labor and turns others into machines. It produces intelligence, but for the worker it produces imbecility and cretinism.

The direct relationship of labor to its products is the relationship of the worker to the objects of his production. The relationship of the rich to the objects of production and to production itself is only a *consequence* of this first relationship and confirms it. Later we shall observe the latter aspect.

Thus, when we ask, What is the essential relationship of labor? we ask about the relationship of the *worker* to production.

Up to now we have considered the alienation, the externalization of the worker only from one side: his *relationship to the products of his labor.* But alienation is shown not only in the result but also in the *process of production,* in the *producing activity* itself. How could the worker stand in an alien relationship to the product of his activity if he did not alienate himself from himself in the very act of production? After all, the product is only the resume of activity, of production. If the product of work is externalization, production itself must be active externalization, externalization of activity, activity of externalization. Only alienation–and externalization in the activity of labor itself–is summarized in the alienation of the object of labor.

What constitutes the externalization of labor?

First is the fact that labor is *external* to the laborer–that is, it is not part of his nature–and that the worker does not affirm himself in his work but denies himself, feels miserable and unhappy, develops no free physical and mental energy but mortifies his flesh and ruins his mind. The worker, therefore feels at ease only outside work, and during work he is outside himself. He is at home when he is not working and when he is working he is not at home. His work, therefore, is not voluntary, but coerced, *forced labor.* It is not the satisfaction of a need but only a *means* to satisfy other needs. Its alien character is obvious from the fact that as soon as no physical or other pressure exists, labor is avoided like the plague. External labor, labor in which man is externalized, is labor of self-sacrifice, of penance. Finally, the external nature of work for the worker appears in the fact that it is not his own but another person's, that in work he does not belong to himself but to someone else. In religion the spontaneity of human imagination, the spontaneity of the human brain and heart, acts independently of the individual as an alien, divine or devilish activity. Similarly, the activity of the worker is not his own spontaneous activity. It belongs to another. It is the loss of his own self.

The result, therefore, is that man (the worker) feels that he is acting freely only in his animal functions–eating, drinking, and procreating, or at most in his shelter and finery–while in his human functions he feels only like an animal. The animalistic becomes the human and the human the animalistic.

To be sure, eating, drinking, and procreation are genuine human functions. In abstraction, however, and separated from the remaining sphere of human activities and turned into final and sole ends, they are animal functions.

We have considered labor, the act of alienation of practical human activity, in two aspects: (1) the relationship of the worker to the *product of labor* as an alien object dominating him. This relationship is at the same time the relationship to the sensuous external world, to natural objects as an alien world hostile to him; (2) the relationship of labor to the act of production in labor. This relationship is that of the worker to his own activity as alien and not belonging to him, activity as passivity, power as weakness, procreation as emasculation, the worker's *own* physical and spiritual energy, his personal life— for what else is life but activity—as an activity turned against him, independent of him, and not belonging to him. *Self-alienation*, as against the alienation of the *object*, stated above.

We have now to derive a third aspect of *alienated labor* from the two previous ones.

Man is a species-being [*Gattungswesen*] not only in that he practically and theoretically makes his own species as well as that of other things his object, but also—and this is only another expression for the same thing—in that as present and living species he considers himself to be a universal and consequently free being.

The life of the species in man as in animals is physical in that man, (like the animal) lives by inorganic nature. And as man is more universal than the animal, the realm of inorganic nature by which he lives is more universal. As plants, animals, minerals, air, light, etc., in theory form a part of human consciousness, partly as objects of natural science, partly as objects of art—his spiritual inorganic nature or spiritual means of life which he first must prepare for enjoyment and assimilation—so they also form in practice a part of human life and human activity. Man lives physically only by these products of nature, they may appear in the form of food, heat, clothing, housing, etc. The universality of man appears in practice in the universality which makes the whole of nature his *inorganic* body: (1) as a direct means of life, and (2) as the matter, object, and instrument of his life activity. Nature is the *inorganic body* of man, that is, nature insofar as it is not the human body. Man *lives* by nature. This means that nature is his *body* with which he must remain in perpetual process in order not to die. That the physical and spiritual life of man is tied up with nature is another way of saying that nature is linked to itself, for man is a part of nature.

In alienating (1) nature from man, and (2) man from himself, his own active function, his life activity, alienated labor also alienates the *species* from him; it makes *species-life* the means of individual life. In the first place it alienates species-life and the individual life, and secondly it turns the latter in its abstraction into the purpose of the former, also in its abstract and alienated form.

For labor, *life activity*, and *productive life* appear to man at first only as a means to satisfy a need, the need to maintain physical existence. Productive life, however, is species-life. It is life begetting life. In the mode of life activity lies the entire character of a species, its species-character; and free conscious activity is the species-character of man. Life itself appears only as a *means of life*.

The animal is immediately one with its life activity, not distinct from it. The animal is its *life activity*. Man makes his life activity itself into an object of will and consciousness. He has conscious life activity. It is not a determination with which he immediately identifies. Conscious life activity distinguishes man immediately from the life activity of the animal. Only thereby is he a species-being. Or rather, he is only a conscious being–that is, his own life is an object for him–since he is a species-being. Only on that account is his activity free activity. Alienated labor reverses the relationship in that man, since he is a conscious being, makes his life activity, his *essence*, only a means for his *existence*.

The practical creation of an *objective world*, the *treatment* of inorganic nature, is proof that man is a conscious species-being, that is, a being which is related to its species as to its own essence or is related to itself as a species-being. To be sure animals also produce. They build themselves nests, dwelling places, like the bees, beavers, ants, etc. But the animal produces only what is immediately necessary for itself or its young. It produces in a one-sided way while man produces universally. The animal produces under the domination of immediate physical need while man produces free of physical need and only genuinely so in freedom from such need. The animal only produces itself while man reproduces the whole of nature. The animal's product belongs immediately to its physical body while man is free when he confronts his product. The animal builds only according to the standard and need of the species to which it belongs while man knows how to produce according to the standard of any species and at all times knows how to apply an intrinsic standard to the object. Thus man creates also according to the laws of beauty.

In the treatment of the objective world, therefore, man proves himself to be genuinely a *species-being*. This production is his active species-life. Through it nature appears as his work and his actuality. The object of labor is thus the *objectification of man's species-life*: he produces himself not only intellectually, as in consciousness, but also actively in a real sense and sees himself in a world he made. In taking from man the object of his production, alienated labor takes from his *species-life*, his actual and objective existence as a species. It changes his superiority to the animal to inferiority, since he is deprived of nature, his inorganic body.

By degrading free spontaneous activity to the level of a means, alienated labor makes the species-life of man a means of his physical existence.

The consciousness which man has from his species is altered through alienation, so that species-life becomes a means for him.

(3) Alienated labor hence turns the *species-existence of man*, and also nature as his mental species-capacity, into an existence *alien* to him, into the *means* of his *individual existence*. It alienates his spiritual nature, his *human essence*, from his own body and likewise from nature outside him.

(4) A direct consequence of man's alienation from the product of his work, from his life activity, and from his species-existence, is the *alienation of man* from *man*. When man confronts himself, he confronts other men. What holds true of man's relationship to his work, to the product of his work, and to himself, also holds true of man's relationship to other men, to their labor, and the object of their labor.

In general, the statement that man is alienated from his species-existence means that one man is alienated from another just as each man is alienated from human nature.

The alienation of man, the relation of man to himself, is realized and expressed in the relation between man and other men. Thus in the relation of alienated labor every man sees the others according to the standard and the relation in which he finds himself as a worker.

We began with an economic fact, the alienation of the worker and his product. We have given expression to the concept of this fact: *alienated, externalized* labor. We have analyzed this concept and have thus analyzed merely a fact of political economy.

Let us now see further how the concept of alienated, externalized labor must express and represent itself in actuality.

If the product of labor is alien to me, confronts me as an alien power, to whom then does it belong?

If my own activity does not belong to me, if it is an alien and forced activity, to whom then does it belong?

To a being *other* than myself.

Who is this being?

Gods? To be sure, in early times the main production, for example, the building of temples in Egypt, India, and Mexico, appears to be in the service of the gods, just as the product belongs to the gods. But gods alone were never workmasters. The same is true of *nature.* And what a contradiction it would be if the more man subjugates nature through his work and the more the miracles of gods are rendered superfluous by the marvels of industry, man should renounce his joy in producing and the enjoyment of his product for love of these powers.

The *alien* being who owns labor and the product of labor, whom labor serves and whom the product of labor satisfies can only be man himself.

That the product of labor does not belong to the worker and an alien power confronts him is possible only because this product belongs to *a man other than the worker.* If his activity is torment for him, it must be the pleasure and the life-enjoyment for another. Not gods, not nature, but only man himself can be this alien power over man.

Let us consider the statement previously made, that the relationship of man to himself is *objective* and *actual* to him only through his relationship to other men. If man is related to the product of his labor, to his objectified labor, as to an alien, hostile, powerful object independent of him, he is so related that another *alien*, hostile, powerful man independent of him is the lord of this object. If he is unfree in relation to his own activity, he is related to it as bonded activity, activity under the domination, coercion, and yoke of another man.

Every self-alienation of man, from himself and from nature, appears in the relationship which he postulates between other men and himself and nature. Thus religious self-alienation appears necessarily in the relation of laity to priest, or also to a mediator, since we are here now concerned with the spiritual world. In the practical real world self-alienation can appear only in the practical real relationships to other men. The means whereby the alienation proceeds is a *practical* means. Through alienated labor man thus not only produces his relationship to the object and to the act of production as an alien man at enmity with him. He also creates the relation in which other men stand to his production and product, and the relation in which he stands to these other men. Just as he begets his own production as loss of his reality, as his punishment; just as he begets his own product as a loss, a product not belonging to him, so he begets the domination of the non-producer over production and over product. As he alienates his own activity from himself, he confers upon the stranger an activity which is not his own.

Up to this point, we have investigated the relationship only from the side of the worker and will later investigate it also from the side of the non-worker.

Thus through *alienated externalized labor* does the worker create the relation to this work of man alienated to labor and standing outside it. The relation of the worker to labor produces the relation of the capitalist to labor, or whatever one wishes to call the lord of labor. *Private property* is thus product, result, and necessary consequence of *externalized labor*, of the external relation of the worker to nature and to himself.

Private property thus is derived, through analysis, from the concept of *externalized labor*, that is, *externalized man*, alienated labor, alienated life, and *alienated* man.

We have obtained the concept of *externalized labor* (*externalized life*) from political economy as a result of the *movement of private property*. But the analysis of this idea shows that though private property appears to be the ground and cause of externalized labor, it is rather a consequence of externalized labor, just as gods are *originally* not the cause but the effect of an aberration of the human mind. Later this relationship reverses.

Only at the final culmination of the development of private property does this, its secret, reappear—namely, that on the one hand it is the *product* of externalized labor and that secondly it is the *means* through which labor externalizes itself, the *realization of this externalization.*

This development throws light on several conflicts hitherto unresolved.

(1) Political economy proceeds from labor as the very soul of production and yet gives labor nothing, private property everything. From this contradiction Proudhon decided in favor of labor and against private property. We perceive, however, that this apparent contradiction is the contradiction of *alienated labor* with itself and that political economy has only formulated the laws of alienated labor.

Therefore we also perceive that *wages* and *private property* are identical: for when the product, the object of labor, pays for the labor itself, wages are only a necessary consequence of the alienation of labor. In wages labor appears not as an end in itself but as the servant of wages. We shall develop this later and now only draw some conclusions.

An enforced *raising of wages* (disregarding all other difficulties, including that this anomaly could only be maintained forcibly) would therefore be nothing but a better *slave-salary* and would not achieve either for the worker or for labor human significance and dignity.

Even the *equality of wages*, as advanced by Proudhon, would only convert the relation of the contemporary worker to his work into the relation of all men to labor. Society would then be conceived as an abstract capitalist.

Wages are a direct result of alienated labor, and alienated labor is the direct cause of private property. The downfall of one is necessarily the downfall of the other.

(2) From the relation of alienated labor to private property it follows further that the emancipation of society from private property, etc., from servitude, is expressed in its *political* form as the *emancipation of workers*, not as though it is only a question of their emancipation but because in their emancipation is contained universal human emancipation. It is contained in their emancipation because the whole of human servitude is involved in the relation of worker to production, and all relations of servitude are only modifications and consequences of the worker's relation to production.

As we have found the concept of *private property* through *analysis* from the concept of *alienated, externalized labor,* so we can develop all the categories of political economy with the aid of these two factors, and we shall again find in each category—for example, barter, competition, capital, money—only a *particular* and *developed expression* of these primary foundations.

Before considering this configuration, however, let us try to solve two problems.

(1) To determine the general *nature of private property* as a result of alienated labor in its relation to *truly human* and *social property.*

(2) We have taken the *alienation of labor* and its *externalization* as a fact and analyzed this fact. How, we ask now, does it happen that *man externalizes* his *labor*, alienates it? How is this alienation rooted in the nature of human development? We have already achieved much in resolving the problem by *transforming* the question concerning the *origin of private property* into the question concerning the relationship of *externalized labor* to evolution of humanity. In talking about *private property* one believes he is dealing with something external to man. Talking of labor, one is immediately dealing with man himself. This new formulation of the problem already contains its solution.

On (1) *The general nature of private property and its relation to truly human property.*

We have resolved alienated labor into two parts which mutually determine each other or rather are only different expressions of one and the same relationship. *Appropriation* appears as *alienation,* as *externalization; externalization* as *appropriation; alienation* as the *true naturalization.*

We considered the one side, *externalized* labor, in relation to the *worker* himself, that is, the *relation of extentalized labor to itself* we have found the *property relation of the non-worker* to the *worker* and *labor* to be the product, the necessary result, of this relationship. *Private property* as the material, summarized expression of externalized labor embraces both relationships—the *relationship of worker to labor, the product of his work, and the non-worker,* and the relationship of the non-worker to the worker and the *product of his labor.*

As we have seen that in relation to the worker who *appropriates* nature through his labor the appropriation appears as alienation—self-activity as activity for another and of another, living as the sacrifice of life, production of the object as loss of it to an alien power, an *alien* man—we now consider the relationship of this *alien* man to the worker, to labor and its object.

It should be noted first that everything which appears with the worker as an *activity of externalization* and an *activity of alienation* appears with the non-worker as a *condition of externalization,* a *condition of alienation.*

Secondly, that the *actual, practical attitude* of the worker in production and to his product (as a condition of mind) appears as a *theoretical* attitude in the non-worker confronting him.

Thirdly, the non-worker does everything against the worker which the worker does against himself, but he does not do against his own self what he does against the worker.

Let us consider more closely these three relationships. [Here the manu-script breaks off, unfinished.]

Private Property and Communism

The antithesis between *propertylessness* and *property,* however, still remains indifferent, not grasped in its *active connection* with its *internal* relationship as *contradiction,* so long as it is not understood as the antithesis of *labor* and *capital.* This antithesis can be expressed in the *first* form even without the advanced development of private property as in ancient Rome, in Turkey, etc. It does not yet *appear* as instituted by private property itself. But labor, the subjective essence of private property as exclusion of property, and capital, objective labor as the exclusion of labor, is *private property* as its developed relation of contradiction, hence a dynamic relation driving toward resolution.

The overcoming [*Aufhebung*] of self-alienation follows the same course as self-alienation. *Private property* is first considered only in its objective aspect—but still with labor as its essence. Its form of existence is therefore capital which is to be overcome "as such" (Proudhon). Or the *particular form* of labor—leveled down, parceled, and thus unfree labor—is taken as the source of the *perniciousness* of private property and its humanly alienated existence. *Fourier,* agreeing with the physiocrats, thus regards *agricultural labor* as being at least *exemplary,* while *Saint-Simon* on the other hand holds *industrial labor* as such to be the essence of labor and thus seeks the *exclusive* predominance of the industrialists and the improvement of the workers' condition. *Communism* is ultimately the *positive* expression of private property as overcome [*aufgehoben*]. Immediately it is *universal* private property. In taking this relation in its *universality* communism is: (1) In its first form only a *universalization* and *completion* of this relationship. As such it appears in a double pattern: On the one hand the domination of *material* property bulks so large that it wants to destroy *everything* which cannot be possessed by everyone as *private property.* It wants to abstract from talent, etc., by *force.* Immediate, physical *possession* is for it the sole aim of life and existence. The condition of the *laborer* is not overcome but extended to all men. The relationship of private property remains the relationship of the community to the world of things. Ultimately this movement which contrasts universal private property to private property is expressed in the animalistic form that *marriage* (surely a *form* of *exclusive private property*) is counterposed to the *community of women* where they become *communal* and *common property.* We might say that this idea of the *community of women* is the *open secret* of this still very crude, unthinking communism. As women go from marriage into universal prostitution, so the whole world of wealth–that is, the objective essence of man–passes from the relationship of exclusive marriage with the private owner into the relationship of universal prostitution with the community. This communism–in that it negates man's *personality* everywhere–is only the logical expression of the private property which is this negation. Universal *envy* establishing itself as a power is only the disguised form in which *greed* reestablishes and satisfies itself in *another* way. The thought of every piece of private property as such is *at the very least* turned against *richer* private property as envy and the desire to level so that envy and the desire to level in fact constitute the essence of competition. Crude communism is only the fulfillment of this envy and leveling on the basis of a *preconceived* minimum. It has a *definite delimited* measure. How little this overcoming of private property is an actual appropriation is shown precisely by the abstract negation of the entire world of culture and civilization, the reversion to the *unnatural* simplicity of the *poor* and wantless man who has not gone beyond private property, has not yet even achieved it.

The community is only a community of *labor* and an equality of *wages* which the communal capital, the *community* as universal capitalist, pays out. Both sides of the relationship are raised to a *supposed* universality–*labor* as the condition in which everyone is put, *capital* as the recognized universality and power of the community.

In the relationship with *woman,* as the spoil and handmaid of communal lust, is expressed the infinite degradation in which man exists for himself since the secret of this relationship has its *unambiguous,* decisive, *plain,* and revealed expression in the relationship of *man* to *woman* and in the way in which the *immediate, natural* species-relationship is conceived. The immediate, natural, necessary relationship of human being to human being is the *relationship* of *man* to *woman.* In this *natural* species-relationship man's relationship to nature is immediately his relationship to man, as his relationship to man is immediately his relationship to nature, to his own *natural* condition. In this relationship the extent to which the human essence has become nature for man or nature has become the human essence of man is *sensuously manifested,* reduced to a perceptible *fact.* From this relationship one can thus judge the entire level of mankind's development. From the character of this relationship follows the extent to which *man* has become and comprehended himself as a *generic being,* as *man;* the relationship of man to woman is the most natural relationship of human being to human being. It thus indicates the extent to which man's *natural* behavior has become *human* or the extent to which his *human* essence has become a *natural* essence for him, the extent to which his *human nature* has become *nature* to him. In this relationship is also apparent the extent to which man's *need* has become *human*, thus the extent to which the *other* human being, as human being, has become a need for him, the extent to which he in his most individual existence is at the same time a social being.

The first positive overcoming of private property—*crude* communism—is thus only an *apparent form* of the vileness of private property trying to set itself up as the *positive community.*

(2) Communism (a) still of political nature, democratic or despotic; (b) with the overcoming of the state, but still incomplete and influenced by private property, that is, by the alienation of man. In both forms communism already knows itself as the reintegration or return of man to himself, as the overcoming of human self-alienation, but since it has not yet understood the positive essence of private property and just as little the *human* nature of needs, it still remains captive to and infected by private property. It has, indeed, grasped its concept but still not its essence.

(3) *Communism* as *positive* overcoming of *private property* as *human self-alienation*, and thus as the actual *appropriation of the human* essence through and for man; therefore as the complete and conscious restoration of man to himself within the total wealth of previous development, the restoration of man as a social, that is, human being. This communism as completed naturalism is humanism, as completed humanism it is naturalism. It is the *genuine* resolution of the antagonism between man and nature and between man and man; it is the true resolution of the conflict between existence and essence, objectification and self-affirmation, freedom and necessity, individual and species. It is the riddle of history solved and knows itself as this solution.

The entire movement of history is therefore both its *actual* genesis—the birth of its empirical existence—and also for its thinking awareness the *conceived* and *conscious* movement of its *becoming* whereas the other yet undeveloped communism seeks in certain historical forms opposed to private property a *historical* proof, a proof in what explicitly exists. It thereby tears particular moments out of the movement (Cabet, Villegardelle, etc., particularly ride this horse) and marks them as proofs of its historical pedigree. Thus it makes clear that the far greater part of this movement contradicts its claims and that if it once existed, its *past* existence refutes the pretension of its *essence.*

It is easy to see the necessity that the whole revolutionary movement finds both its empirical as well as theoretical basis in the development of *private property*—in the economy, to be exact.

This *material*, immediately *perceptible* private property is the material, sensuous expression of *alienated human life*. Its movement—production and consumption—is the *sensuous* manifestation of the movement of all previous production, that is, the realization or actuality of man. Religion, family, state, law, morality, science, art, etc., are only *particular* forms of production and fall under its general law. The positive overcoming of *private property* as the appropriation of *human* life is thus the positive overcoming of all alienation and the return of man from religion, family, state, etc., to his *human*, that is, *social* existence. Religious alienation as such occurs only in the sphere of the inner human *consciousness*, but economic alienation belongs to *actual life*—its overcoming thus includes both aspects. It is obvious that the movement has its *first* beginning among different peoples depending on whether their true *acknowledged* life proceeds more in consciousness or in the external world, is more ideal or real. Communism thus begins (*Owen*) with atheism, but atheism is at the beginning still far from being *communism* since it is mostly an *abstraction.**–The philanthropy of atheism is at first therefore only a *philosophical,* abstract philanthropy; that of communism is at once real and immediately bent toward *action.*

On the assumption that private property has been positively overcome we have seen how man produces man, himself, and other men; how the object, the immediate activity of his individuality, is at the same time his own existence for other men, their existence, and their existence for him. Similarly, however, both the material of labor and man as subject are equally the result and beginning of the movement (and the historical *necessity* of private property lies precisely in the fact that they must be this *beginning*). Thus is the *social* character the general character of the whole movement; *as* society itself produces *man* as *man,* so it is *produced* by him. Activity and satisfaction [*Genuss*], both in their content and *mode of existence,* are *social,* social activity and *social* satisfaction. The *human* essence of nature primarily exists only for social man, because only here is nature a *link* with *man,* as his existence for others and their existence for him, as the life-element of human actuality–only here is nature the *foundation* of man's own *human* existence. Only here has the *natural* existence of man become his *human* existence and nature become human. Thus *society* is the completed, essential unity of man with nature, the true resurrection of nature, the fulfilled naturalism of man and humanism of nature.

Social activity and satisfaction by no means exist *merely* in the form of an *immediate* communal activity and immediate *communal* satisfaction. Nevertheless such activity and satisfaction, expressed and confirmed immediately in *actual association* with other men, will occur wherever that *immediate* expression of sociality is essentially grounded in its content and adequate to its nature.

Even as I am *scientifically active,* etc.–an activity I can seldom pursue in direct community with others–I am *socially* active because I am active as a *man.* Not only is the material of my activity–such as the language in which the thinker is active–given to me as a social product, but my *own* existence *is* social activity; what I make from myself I make for society, conscious of my nature as social.

My *general* consciousness is only the *theoretical* form of that whose *living* form is the *real* community, the social essence, although at present *general* consciousness is an abstraction from actual life and antagonistically opposed to it. Consequently the activity of my general consciousness is thus, as activity, my *theoretical* existence as a social being.

To be avoided above all is establishing "society" once again as an abstraction over against the individual. The individual *is* the *social being.* The expression of his life–even if it does not appear immediately in the form of a *communal* expression carried out together with others–is therefore an expression and assertion of *social life.* The individual and generic life of man are not *distinct*, however much–and necessarily so–the mode of existence of individual life is either a more *particular* or more *general* mode of generic life, or generic life a more *particular* or *universal* mode of individual life.

As *generic consciousness* man asserts his real *social life* and merely repeats his actual existence in thought just as, conversely, generic existence asserts itself in generic consciousness and in its universality exists explicitly as a thinking being. Though man is therefore a *particular* individual–and precisely his particularity makes him an individual, an actual *individual* communal being– he is equally the totality, the ideal *totality*, the subjective existence of society explicitly thought and experienced. Likewise he also exists in actuality both as perception and actual satisfaction of social existence and as a totality of human expression of life.

Thinking and being, to be sure, are thus *distinct* but at the same time in *unity* with one another.

Death seems to be a harsh victory of the species over the particular individual and to contradict the species' unity, but the particular individual is only a *particular generic being* and as such mortal.

(((4) Just as *private property* is only the sensuous expression of the fact that man becomes *objective* for himself and at the same time becomes an alien and inhuman object for himself, that his expression of life is his externalization of life and his realization a loss of reality, an *alien* actuality, so the positive overcoming of private property–that is, the *sensuous* appropriation of the human essence and life, of objective man and of human *works* by and for man– is not to be grasped only as *immediate*, exclusive *satisfaction* or as *possession*, as *having*. Man appropriates to himself his manifold essence in an all-sided way, thus as a whole man. Every one of his *human* relations to the world–seeing, hearing, smelling, tasting, feeling, thinking, perceiving, sensing, wishing, acting, loving–in short, all the organs of his individuality, which are immediately communal in form, are an appropriation of the object in their *objective* relation [*Verhalten*] or their *relation to it*. This appropriation of *human* actuality and its relation to the object is the *confirmation of human actuality*. It is therefore as varied as are the *determinations* of the human essence and activities. It is human *efficacy* and human *suffering*, for suffering, humanly conceived, is a satisfaction of the self in man.

Private property has made us so stupid and one-sided that an object is *ours* only if we have it, if it exists for us as a capital or is immediately possessed by us, eaten, drunk, worn, lived in, etc., in short, *used*; but private property grasps all these immediate forms of possession only as *means of living*, and the life they serve is the *life* of *private property*, labor, and capitalization.

Hence *all* the physical and spiritual senses have been replaced by the simple alienation of them *all*, the sense of *having*. Human nature had to be reduced to this absolute poverty so that it could give birth to its inner wealth. (On the category of *having*, see *Hess* in *Twenty-one Sheets*.)

The overcoming of private property means therefore the complete *emancipation* of all human senses and aptitudes [*Eigenschaften*], but it means this emancipation precisely because these senses and aptitudes have become *human* both subjectively and objectively. The eye has become a *human* eye, just as its *object* has become a social, *human* object derived from and for man. The *senses* have therefore become *theoreticians* immediately in their *praxis*. They try to relate themselves to their *subject matter* [*Sache*] for its own sake, but the subject matter itself is an *objective human* relation to itself and to man,* and vice versa. Need or satisfaction have thus lost their *egoistic* nature, and nature has lost its mere *utility* by use becoming *human* use.

Similarly the senses and satisfactions of other men have become my *own* appropriation. Besides these immediate organs, *social* organs are therefore developed in the *form* of society; for example, activity in direct association with others, etc., has become an organ of a *life-expression* and a way of appropriating *human* life.

It is obvious that the *human* eye appreciates differently from the crude, inhuman eye, the human *ear* differently from the crude ear, etc.

Only if man's object, we have seen, becomes for him a *human* object or objective man, is he not lost in it. This is possible only when the object becomes *social* and he himself becomes social just as society becomes essential for him in this object.

On the one hand, therefore, it is only when objective actuality generally becomes for man in society the actuality of essential human capacities, human actuality, and thus the actuality of his *own* capacities that all *objects* become for him the *objectification* of himself, become objects which confirm and realize *his* individuality as his objects, that is, *he himself* becomes the object. *How* they become his depends on the nature of the *object* and the nature of the *essential capacity* corresponding to *it*, for it is precisely the *determinateness* of this relationship which shapes the particular, *actual* mode of affirmation. For the *eye* an object is different than for the *ear*, and the object of the eye *is* another object than that of the *ear*. The peculiarity of each essential capacity is precisely its *characteristic essence* and thus also the characteristic mode of its objectification, of its *objectively actual*, living *being*. Thus man is affirmed in the objective world not only in thought but with *all* his senses.

On the other hand and from the subjective point of view, as music alone awakens man's musical sense and the most beautiful music has *no* meaning for the unmusical ear–is no object for it, because my object can only be the confirmation of one of my essential capacities and can therefore only be so for me insofar as my essential capacity exists explicitly as a subjective capacity, because the meaning of an object for me reaches only as far as my senses go (only makes sense for a corresponding sense)–for this reason the *senses* of social man *differ* from those of the unsocial. Only through the objectively unfolded wealth of human nature is the wealth of the subjective *human* sensibility either cultivated or created–a musical ear, an eye for the beauty of form, in short, *senses* capable of human satisfaction, confirming themselves as essential *human* capacities. For not only the five senses but also the so-called spiritual and moral senses (will, love, etc.), in a word, *human* sense and the humanity of the senses come into being only through the existence of *their* object, through nature *humanized*. The *development* of the five senses is a labor of the whole previous history of the world. ((*Sense* subordinated to crude, practical need has only a *narrow* meaning.)) For the starving man food does not exist in its human form but only in its abstract character as food. It could be available in its crudest form and one could not say wherein the starving man's eating differs from that of *animals*. The careladen, needy man has no mind for the most beautiful play. The dealer in minerals sees only their market value but not their beauty and special nature; he has no mineralogical sensitivity. Hence the objectification of the human essence, both theoretically and practically, is necessary to *humanize* man's *senses* and also create a *human sense* corresponding to the entire wealth of humanity and nature.

((Just as the coming society finds at hand all the material for this *cultural development* [*Bildung*] through the movement of *private property*, its wealth as well as its poverty both material and spiritual, *so* the fully *constituted* society produces man in this entire wealth of his being, produces the *rich*, deep, and *entirely sensitive* man as its enduring actuality.))

It is apparent how subjectivism and objectivism, spiritualism and materialism, activity and passivity lose their opposition and thus their existence as antitheses only in the social situation; ((it is apparent how the resolution of *theoretical* antitheses is possible *only* in a *practical* way, only through man's practical energy, and hence their resolution is in no way merely a problem of knowledge but a *real* problem of life which *philosophy* could not solve because it grasped the problem as *only* theoretical.))

((It is apparent how the history of *industry*, industry as *objectively* existing, is the *open* book of man as *essential powers*, the observably present human *psychology*, which has not been thus far grasped in its connection with man's *essential* nature but only in an external utilitarian way because in the perspective of alienation only the general existence of man—religion or history in its abstract-general character as politics, art, literature, etc.—was grasped as the actuality of man's essential powers and his *human generic action*. We have before us the *objectified essential powers* of man in the form of *sensuous, alien, useful objects*—in the form of alienation—in *ordinary material industry* (which can be conceived as a part of that general movement just as that movement can be grasped as a *particular* part of industry since all human activity up to the present has been labor, industry, activity alienated from itself). A *psychology* for which this book, that is, the most observably present and accessible part of history, remains closed cannot become an actual, substantial, and *real* science.)) What indeed should one think of a science which *arbitrarily* abstracts from this large area of human labor and is unaware of its own incompleteness while such an extended wealth of human activity means no more to it than can be expressed in one word—"*need*," "*common need*"?

The *natural sciences* have become enormously active and have accumulated an ever growing subject-matter. But philosophy has remained as alien to them as they have to it. Their momentary unity was only a *fantastic illusion*. The will was there, but the means were missing. Historiography itself only occasionally takes account of natural science as a moment of enlightenment, utility, some particular great discoveries. But natural science has penetrated and transformed human life all the more *practically* through industry, preparing for human emancipation however much it immediately had to accentuate dehumanization. *Industry* is the *actual* historical relationship of nature, and thus of natural science, to man. If it is grasped as the *exoteric* manifestation of man's *essential powers*, the *human* essence of nature or the natural essence of man can also be understood. Hence, natural science will lose its abstract material–or rather idealistic–tendency and become the basis of *human* science as it has already become, though in an alienated form, the basis of actual human life. One basis for life and *another* for *science* is in itself a lie. ((Nature developing in human history–the creation of human society–is the *actual* nature of man; hence nature as it develops through industry, though in an *alienated* form, is true *anthropological* nature.))

Sense perception (see Feuerbach) must be the basis of all science. Science is only *actual* when it proceeds from sense perception in the twofold form of both *sensuous* awareness and *sensuous* need, that is, from nature. The whole of history is a preparation for "*man*" to become the object of *sensuous* awareness and for the needs of "man as man" to become sensuous needs. History itself is an *actual* part of *natural history*, of nature's development into man. Natural science will in time include the science of man as the science of man will include natural science: There will be *one* science.

Man is the immediate object of natural science because immediately *perceptible nature* is for man, immediately, human sense perception (an identical statement) as the other man immediately perceptible for him. His own sense perception only exists as human sense perception for himself through the *other* man. But *nature* is the direct object of the *science of man*. The first object for man–man himself–is nature, sense perception; and the particular, perceptible, and essential powers of man can attain self-knowledge only in natural science because they are objectively developed only in *natural* objects. The element of thought itself, the element of the life-expression of thought, *language*, is perceptible nature. The *social* actuality of nature and *human* natural science or the *natural science of man* are identical expressions.

((It is apparent how the *rich man* and wide *human* need appear in place of economic *wealth* and *poverty*. The rich man is simultaneously one who *needs* a totality of human manifestations of life and in whom his own realization exists as inner necessity, as *need*. Not only the *wealth* but also the *poverty* of man equally acquire–under the premise of socialism–a *human* and thus social meaning. It is the passive bond which lets man experience the greatest wealth, the *other* human being, as need. The domination of the objective essence within me, the sensuous eruption of my essential activity, is *emotion* which thereby becomes the *activity* of my nature.))

(5) A *being* only regards himself as independent when he stands on his own feet, and he stands on his own feet only when he owes his *existence* to himself. A man who lives by the favor of another considers himself dependent. But I live entirely by the favor of another if I owe him not only the maintenance of my life but also its *creation*, its *source*. My life necessarily has such an external ground if it is not my own creation. The notion of *creation* is thus very difficult

to expel from popular consciousness. For such consciousness the self-subsistence of nature and man is *inconceivable* because it contradicts all the *palpable facts* of practical life.

The creation of the *earth* has been severely shaken by *geognosy* [rather: by *geogony*], the science which presents the formation and development of the earth as a self-generative process. Generatio aequivoca is the only practical refutation of the theory of creation.

It is easy indeed to tell a particular individual what Aristotle said: You were begotten by your father and mother, so in you the mating of two human beings, a generic act of mankind, produced another. You see therefore that man owes even his physical existence to another. Here you must not keep in view only *one* of the two aspects, the *infinite* progression, and ask further, Who begot my father? Who his grandfather? etc. You must also keep in mind the *circular atonement* sensibly apparent in that process whereby man reproduces himself in procreation; thus *man* always remains the subject. But you will answer: I grant this circular movement but you must allow the progression which leads even further until I ask, Who created the first man and nature as a whole? I can only answer: Your question is itself a product of abstraction. Ask yourself how you arrive at that question, whether it does not arise from a standpoint to which I cannot reply because it is twisted. Ask yourself whether that progression exists as such for rational thought. If you ask about the creation of nature and man, you thus abstract from man and nature. You assert them as *nonexistent* and yet want me to prove them to you as *existing*. I say to you: Give up your abstraction and you will also give up your question. Or if you want to maintain your abstraction, be consistent and if you think of man and nature as *non-existent*, think of yourself as non-existent as you too are nature and man. Do not think, do not question me, for as soon as you think and question, your *abstraction* from the existence of nature and man makes no sense. Or are you such an egoist that you assert everything as nothing and yet want yourself to exist?

You may reply to me: I do not want to assert the nothingness of nature, etc. I only ask about its *genesis* as I ask the anatomist about the formation of bones etc.

Since for socialist man, however, the *entire so-called world history* is only the creation of man through human labor and the development of nature for man, he has evident and incontrovertible proof of his *self-creation*, his own *formation process*. Since the *essential dependence* of man in nature—man for man as the existence of nature and nature for man as the existence of man—has become practical, sensuous and perceptible, the question about an *alien* being beyond man and nature (a question which implies the unreality of nature and man) has become impossible in practice. *Atheism* as a denial of this unreality no longer makes sense because it is a *negation of God* and through this negation asserts the *existence of man*. But socialism as such no longer needs such mediation. It begins with the *sensuous perception, theoretically and practically*, of man and nature as *essential beings*. It is man's *positive self-consciousness*, no longer attained through the overcoming of religion, just as *actual life* is positive actuality no longer attained through the overcoming of private property, through *communism*. The position of communism is the negation of the negation and hence, for the next stage of historical development, the necessary *actual* phase of man's emancipation and rehabilitation. *Communism* is the necessary form and dynamic principle of the immediate future but not as such the goal of human development—the form of human society.

Notes

*Prostitution is only a *particular* expression of the *general prostitution* of the laborer, and since prostitution is a relationship which includes not only the prostituted but also the prostitutor—whose vileness is still greater—so also the capitalist, etc. falls in this category [Marx's footnote]

*I can practically relate myself to the subject matter in a human way only if it is itself humanly related to man [Marx's footnote]

14

Excerpts from "A Theory of Justice"

John Rawls

The Main Idea of the Theory of Justice

My aim is to present a conception of justice which generalizes and carries to a higher level of abstraction the familiar theory of the social contract as found, say, in Locke, Rousseau, and Kant.[1] In order to do this we are not to think of the original contract as one to enter a particular society or to set up a particular form of government. Rather, the guiding idea is that the principles of justice for the basic structure of society are the object of the original agreement. They are the principles that free and rational persons concerned to further their own interests would accept in an initial position of equality as defining the fundamental terms of their association. These principles are to regulate all further agreements; they specify the kinds of social cooperation that can be entered into and the forms of government that can be established. This way of regarding the principles of justice I shall call justice as fairness.

Thus we are to imagine that those who engage in social cooperation choose together, in one joint act, the principles which are to assign basic rights and duties and to determine the division of social benefits. Men are to decide in advance how they are to regulate their claims against one another and what is to be the foundation charter of their society. Just as each person must decide by rational reflection what constitutes his good, that is, the system of ends which it is rational for him to pursue, so a group of persons must decide once and for all what is to count among them as just and unjust. The choice which rational men would make in this hypothetical situation of equal liberty, assuming for the present that this choice problem has a solution, determines the principles of justice.

In justice as fairness the original position of equality corresponds to the state of nature in the traditional theory of the social contract. This original position is not, of course, thought of as an actual historical state of affairs, much

Source: John Rawls, *A Theory of Justice: Revised Edition* (Cambridge, MA: Harvard University Press, 1999). Copyright © 1999 by the President and Fellows of Harvard College.

less as a primitive condition of culture. It is understood as a purely hypothetical situation characterized so as to lead to a certain conception of justice.[2] Among the essential features of this situation is that no one knows his place in society, his class position or social status, nor does any one know his fortune in the distribution of natural assets and abilities, his intelligence, strength, and the like. I shall even assume that the parties do not know their conceptions of the good or their special psychological propensities. The principles of justice are chosen behind a veil of ignorance. This ensures that no one is advantaged or disadvantaged in the choice of principles by the outcome of natural chance or the contingency of social circumstances. Since all are similarly situated and no one is able to design principles to favor his particular condition, the principles of justice are the result of a fair agreement or bargain. For given the circumstances of the original position, the symmetry of everyone's relations to each other, this initial situation is fair between individuals as moral persons, that is, as rational beings with their own ends and capable, I shall assume, of a sense of justice. The original position is, one might say, the appropriate initial status quo, and thus the fundamental agreements reached in it are fair. This explains the propriety of the name "justice as fairness."...

Further Cases of Priority

I now wish to give the final statement of the two principles of justice for institutions....

First principle

Each person is to have an equal right to the most extensive total system of equal basic liberties compatible with a similar system of liberty for all.

Second principle

Social and economic inequalities are to be arranged so that they are both:

(a) to the greatest benefit of the least advantaged, consistent with the just savings principle, and
(b) attached to offices and positions open to all under conditions of fair equality of opportunity.

First priority rule (the priority of liberty)

The principles of justice are to be ranked in lexical order and therefore the basic liberties can be restricted only for the sake of liberty. There are two cases:

(a) a less extensive liberty must strengthen the total system of liberties shared by all;

(b) a less than equal liberty must be acceptable to those with the lesser liberty.

Second priority rule (the priority of justice over efficiency and welfare)

The second principle of justice is lexically prior to the principle of efficiency and to that of maximizing the sum of advantages; and fair opportunity is prior to the difference principle. There are two cases:

(a) an inequality of opportunity must enhance the opportunities of those with the lesser opportunity;
(b) an excessive rate of saving must on balance mitigate the burden of those bearing this hardship.

The Veil of Ignorance

The idea of the original position is to set up a fair procedure so that any principles agreed to will be just. The aim is to use the notion of pure procedural justice as a basis of theory. Somehow we must nullify the effects of specific contingencies which put men at odds and tempt them to exploit social and natural circumstances to their own advantage. Now in order to do this I assume that the parties are situated behind a veil of ignorance. They do not know how the various alternatives will affect their own particular case and they are obliged to evaluate principles solely on the basis of general considerations.[3]

It is assumed, then, that the parties do not know certain kinds of particular facts. First of all, no one knows his place in society, his class position or social status; nor does he know his fortune in the distribution of natural assets and abilities, his intelligence and strength, and the like. Nor, again, does anyone know his conception of the good, the particulars of his rational plan of life, or even the special features of his psychology such as his aversion to risk or liability to optimism or pessimism. More than this, I assume that the parties do not know the particular circumstances of their own society. That is, they do not know its economic or political situation, or the level of civilization and culture it has been able to achieve. The persons in the original position have no information as to which generation they belong. These broader restrictions on knowledge are appropriate in part because questions of social justice arise between generations as well as within them, for example, the question of the appropriate rate of capital saving and of the conservation of natural resources and the environment of nature. There is also, theoretically anyway, the question of a reasonable genetic policy. In these cases too, in order to carry through the idea of the original position, the parties must not know the contingencies that set them in opposition. They must choose principles the consequences of which they are prepared to live with whatever generation they turn out to belong to.

As far as possible, then, the only particular facts which the parties know is that their society is subject to the circumstances of justice and whatever this implies. It is taken for granted, however, that they know the general facts about human society. They understand political affairs and the principles of economic theory; they know the basis of social organization and the laws of human psychology. Indeed, the parties are presumed to know whatever general facts affect the choice of the principles of justice. There are no limitations on general information, that is, on general laws and theories, since conceptions of justice must be adjusted to the characteristics of the systems of social cooperation which they are to regulate, and there is no reason to rule out these facts. It is, for example, a consideration against a conception of justice that, in view of the laws of moral psychology, men would not acquire a desire to act upon it even when the institutions of their society satisfied it. For in this case there would be difficulty in securing the stability of social cooperation. An important feature of a conception of justice is that it should generate its own support. Its principles should be such that when they are embodied in the basic structure of society men tend to acquire the corresponding sense of justice and develop a desire to act in accordance with its principles. In this case a conception of justice is stable. This kind of general information is admissible in the original position.

The notion of the veil of ignorance raises several difficulties. Some may object that the exclusion of nearly all particular information makes it difficult to grasp what is meant by the original position. Thus it may be helpful to observe that one or more persons can at any time enter this position, or perhaps better, simulate the deliberations of this hypothetical situation, simply by reasoning in accordance with the appropriate restrictions. In arguing for a conception of justice we must be sure that it is among the permitted alternatives and satisfies the stipulated formal constraints. No considerations can be advanced in its favor unless they would be rational ones for us to urge were we to lack the kind of knowledge that is excluded. The evaluation of principles must proceed in terms of the general consequences of their public recognition and universal application, it being assumed that they will be complied with by everyone. To say that a certain conception of justice would be chosen in the original position is equivalent to saying that rational deliberation satisfying certain conditions and restrictions would reach a certain conclusion. If necessary the argument to this result could be set out more formally. I shall, however, speak throughout in terms of the notion of the original position. It is more economical and suggestive, and brings out certain essential features that otherwise one might easily overlook.

These remarks show that the original position is not to be thought of as a general assembly which includes at one moment everyone who will live at some time; or, much less, as an assembly of everyone who could live at some time. It is not a gathering of all actual or possible persons. If we conceived of the original position in either of these ways, the conception would cease to be a natural guide to intuition and would lack a clear sense. In any case, the original position must be interpreted so that one can at any time adopt its perspective. It must make no difference when one takes up this viewpoint, or who does so: the restrictions must be such that the same principles are always chosen. The veil of ignorance is a key condition in meeting this requirement. It insures not only that the information available is relevant, but that it is all times the same.

It may be protested that the condition of the veil of ignorance is irrational. Surely, some may object, principles should be chosen in the light of all the knowledge available. There are various replies to this intention. Here I shall sketch those which emphasize the simplifications that need to be made if one is to have any theory at all.... To begin with, it is clear that since the differences among the parties are unknown to them, and everyone is equally rational and similarly situated, each is convinced by the same arguments. Therefore, we can view the agreement in the original position from the standpoint of one person selected at random. If anyone after due reflection prefers a conception of justice to another, then they all do, and a unanimous agreement can be reached. We can, to make the circumstances more vivid, imagine that the parties are required to communicate with each other through a referee as intermediary, and that he is to announce which alternatives have been suggested and the reasons offered in their support. He forbids the attempt to form coalitions, and he informs the parties when they have come to an understanding. But such a referee is actually superfluous, assuming that the deliberations of the parties must be similar.

Thus there follows the very important consequence that the parties have no basis for bargaining in the usual sense. No one knows his situation in society nor his natural assets, and therefore no one is in a position to tailor principles to his advantage. We might imagine that one of the contractees threatens to hold out unless the others agree to principles favorable to him. But how does he know which principles are especially in his interests? The same holds for the formation of coalitions: if a group were to decide to band together to the disadvantage of the others, they would not know how to favor themselves in the choice of principles. Even if they could get everyone to agree to their proposal, they would have no assurance that it was to their advantage, since they cannot identify themselves either by name or description. The one case where this conclusion fails is that of saving. Since the persons in the original position know that they are contemporaries (taking the present time of entry interpretation), they can favor their generation by refusing to make any sacrifices at all for their successors; they simply acknowledge the principle that no one has a duty to save for posterity. Previous generations have saved or they have not; there is nothing the parties can now do to affect that. So in this instance the veil of ignorance fails to secure the desired result. Therefore, to handle the question of justice between generations, I modify the motivation assumption and add a further constraint. With these adjustments, no generation is able to formulate principles especially designed to advance its own cause and some significant limits on savings principles can be derived. Whatever a person's temporal position, each is forced to choose for all.[4]

The restrictions on particular information in the original position are, then, of fundamental importance. Without them we would not be able to work out any definite theory of justice at all. We would have to be content with a vague formula stating that justice is what would be agreed to without being able to say much, if anything, about the substance of the agreement itself. The formal constraints of the concept of right, those applying to principles directly, are not sufficient for our purpose. The veil of ignorance makes possible a unanimous choice of a particular conception of justice. Without these limitations on knowledge the bargaining problem of the original position would be hopelessly complicated. Even if theoretically a solution were to exist, we would not, at present anyway, be able to determine it.

The notion of the veil of ignorance is implicit, I think, in Kant's ethics. Nevertheless the problem of defining the knowledge of the parties and of characterizing the alternatives open to them has often been passed over, even by contract theories. Sometimes the situation definitive of moral deliberation is presented in such an indeterminate way that one cannot ascertain how it will turn out. Thus Perry's doctrine is essentially contractarian: he holds that social and personal integration must proceed by entirely different principles, the latter by rational prudence, the former by the concurrence of persons of good will. He would appear to reject utilitarianism on much the same grounds suggested earlier: namely, that it improperly extends the principle of choice for one person to choices facing society. The right course of action is characterized as that which best advances social aims as these would be formulated by reflective agreement, given that the parties have full knowledge of the circumstances and are moved by a benevolent concern for one another's interests. No effort is made, however, to specify in any precise way the possible outcomes of this sort of agreement. Indeed, without a far more elaborate account, no conclusions can be drawn.[5] I do not wish here to criticize others; rather, I want to explain the necessity for what may seem at times like so many irrelevant details.

Now the reasons for the veil of ignorance go beyond mere simplicity. We want to define the original position so that we get the desired solution. If a knowledge of particulars is allowed, then the outcome is biased by arbitrary contingencies. As already observed, to each according to his threat advantage is not a principle of justice. If the original position is to yield agreements that are just, the parties must be fairly situated and treated equally as moral persons. The arbitrariness of the world must be corrected for by adjusting the circumstances of the initial contractual situation. Moreover, if in choosing principles we required unanimity even when there is full information, only a few rather obvious cases could be decided. A conception of justice based on unanimity in these circumstances would indeed be weak and trivial. But once knowledge is excluded, the requirement of unanimity is not out of place and the fact that it can be satisfied is of great importance. It enables us to say of the preferred conception of justice that it represents a genuine reconciliation of interests.

A final comment. For the most part I shall suppose that the parties possess all general information. No general facts are closed to them. I do this mainly to avoid complications. Nevertheless a conception of justice is to be the public basis of the terms of social cooperation. Since common understanding necessitates certain bounds on the complexity of principles, there may likewise be limits on the use of theoretical knowledge in the original position. Now clearly it would be very difficult to classify and to grade the complexity of the various sorts of general facts. I shall make no attempt to do this. We do however recognize an intricate theoretical construction when we meet one. Thus it seems reasonable to say that other things equal one conception of justice is to be preferred to another when it is founded upon markedly simpler general facts, and its choice does not depend upon elaborate calculations in the light of a vast array of theoretically defined possibilities. It is desirable that the grounds for a public conception of justice should be evident to everyone when circumstances permit. This consideration favors, I believe, the two principles of justice over the criterion of utility.

The Rationality of the Parties

I have assumed throughout that the persons in the original position are rational. But I have also assumed that they do not know their conception of the good. This means that while they know that they have some rational plan of life, they do not know the details of this plan, the particular ends and interests which it is calculated to promote. How, then, can they decide which conceptions of justice are most to their advantage? Or must we suppose that they are reduced to mere guessing? To meet this difficulty, I postulate that they accept the account of the good touched upon in the preceding chapter: they assume that they normally prefer more primary social goods rather than less. Of course, it may turn out, once the veil of ignorance is removed, that some of them for religious or other reasons may not, in fact, want more of these goods. But from the standpoint of the original position, it is rational for the parties to suppose that they do want a larger share, since in any case they are not compelled to accept more if they do not wish to. Thus even though the parties are deprived of information about their particular ends, they have enough knowledge to rank the alternatives. They know that in general they must try to protect their liberties, widen their opportunities, and enlarge their means for promoting their aims whatever these are. Guided by the theory of the good and the general facts of moral psychology, their deliberations are no longer guesswork. They can make a rational decision in the ordinary sense.

The concept of rationality invoked here, with the exception of one essential feature, is the standard one familiar in social theory.[6] Thus in the usual way, a rational person is thought to have a coherent set of preferences between the options open to him. He ranks these options according to how well they further his purposes; he follows the plan which will satisfy more of his desires rather than less, and which has the greater chance of being successfully executed. The special assumption I make is that a rational individual does not suffer from envy. He is not ready to accept a loss for himself if only others have less as well. He is not downcast by the knowledge or perception that others have a larger index of primary social goods. Or at least this is true as long as the differences between himself and others do not exceed certain limits, and he does not believe that the existing inequalities are founded on injustice or are the result of letting chance work itself out for no compensating social purpose.

The assumption that the parties are not moved by envy raises certain questions. Perhaps we should also assume that they are not liable to various other feelings such as shame and humiliation. Now a satisfactory account of justice will eventually have to deal with these matters too, but for the present I shall leave these complications aside. Another objection to our procedure is that it is too unrealistic. Certainly men are afflicted with these feelings. How can a conception of justice ignore this fact? I shall meet this problem by dividing the argument for the principles of justice into two parts. In the first part, the principles are derived on the supposition that envy does not exist; while in the second, we consider whether the conception arrived at is feasible in view of the circumstances of human life.

One reason for this procedure is that envy tends to make everyone worse off. In this sense it is collectively disadvantageous. Presuming its absence amounts to supposing that in the choice of principles men should think of themselves as having their own plan of life which is sufficient for itself. They have a secure sense of their own worth so that they have no desire to abandon any of their aims provided others have less means to further theirs. I shall work out a conception of justice on this stipulation to see what happens. Later I shall try to show that when the principles adopted are put into practice, they lead to social arrangements in which envy and other destructive feelings are not likely to be strong. The conception of justice eliminates the conditions that give rise to disruptive attitudes. It is, therefore, inherently stable.

The assumption of mutually disinterested rationality, then, comes to this: the persons in the original position try to acknowledge principles which advance their system of ends as far as possible. They do this by attempting to win for themselves the highest index of primary social goods, since this enables them to promote their conception of the good most effectively whatever it turns out to be. The parties do not seek to confer benefits or to impose injuries on one another; they are not moved by affection or rancor. Nor do they try to gain relative to each other; they are not envious or vain. Put in terms of a game, we might say: they strive for as high an absolute score as possible. They do not wish a high or a low score for their opponents, nor do they seek to maximize or minimize the difference between their successes and those of others. The idea of a game does not really apply, since the parties are not concerned to win but to get as many points as possible judged by their own system of ends.

There is one further assumption to guarantee strict compliance. The parties are presumed to be capable of a sense of justice and this fact is public knowledge among them. This condition is to insure the integrity of the agreement made in the original position. It does not mean that in their deliberations the parties apply some particular conception of justice, for this would defeat the point of the motivation assumption. Rather, it means that the parties can rely on each other to understand and to act in accordance with whatever principles are finally agreed to. Once principles are acknowledged the parties can depend on one another to conform to them. In reaching an agreement, then, they know that their undertaking is not in vain: their capacity for a sense of justice insures that the principles chosen will be respected. It is essential to observe, however, that this assumption still permits the consideration of men's capacity to act on the various conceptions of justice. The general facts of human psychology and the principles of moral learning are relevant matters for the parties to examine. If a conception of justice is unlikely to generate its own support, or lacks stability, this fact must not be overlooked. For then a different conception of justice might be preferred. The assumption only says that the parties have a capacity for justice in a purely formal sense: taking everything relevant into account, including the general facts of moral psychology, the parties will adhere to the principles eventually chosen. They are rational in that they will not enter into agreements they know they cannot keep, or can do so only with great difficulty. Along with other considerations, they count the strains of commitment. Thus in assessing conceptions of justice the persons in the original position are to assume that the one they adopt will be strictly complied with. The consequences of their agreement are to be worked out on this basis....

We can turn now to the choice of principles. But first I shall mention a few misunderstandings to be avoided. First of all, we must keep in mind that the parties in the original position are theoretically defined individuals. The grounds for their consent are set out by the description of the contractual situation and their preference for primary goods. Thus to say that the principles of justice would be adopted is to say how these persons would decide being moved in ways our account describes. Of course, when we try to simulate the original position in everyday life, that is, when we try to conduct ourselves in moral argument as its constraints require, we will presumably find that our deliberations and judgments are influenced by our special inclinations and attitudes. Surely it will prove difficult to correct for our various propensities and aversions in striving to adhere to the conditions of this idealized situation. But none of this affects the contention that in the original position rational persons so characterized would make a certain decision. This proposition belongs to the theory of justice. It is another question how well human beings can assume this role in regulating their practical reasoning.

Since the persons in the original position are assumed to take no interest in one another's interests (although they may have a concern for third parties), it may be thought that justice as fairness is itself an egoistic theory. It is not, of course, one of the three forms of egoism mentioned earlier, but some may think, as Schopenhauer thought of Kant's doctrine, that it is egoistic nevertheless.[7] Now this is a misconception. For the fact that in the original position the parties are characterized as mutually disinterested does not entail that persons in ordinary life, or in a well-ordered society, who hold the principles that would be agreed to are similarly disinterested in one another. Clearly the two principles of justice and the principles of obligation and natural duty require us to consider the rights and claims of others. And the sense of justice is a normally effective desire to comply with these restrictions. The motivation of the persons in the original position must not be confused with the motivation of persons in everyday life who accept the principles of justice and who have the corresponding sense of justice. In practical affairs an individual does have a knowledge of his situation and he can, if he wishes, exploit contingencies to his advantage. Should his sense of justice move him to act on the principles of right that would be adopted in the original position, his desires and aims are surely not egoistic. He voluntarily takes on the limitations expressed by this interpretation of the moral point of view. Thus, more generally, the motivation of the parties in the original position does not determine directly the motivation of people in a just society. For in the latter case, we assume that its members grow up and live under a just basic structure, as the two principles require; and then we try to work out what kind of conception of the good and moral sentiments people would acquire. Therefore the mutual disinterestedness of the parties determines other motivations only indirectly, that is, via its effects on the agreement on principles. It is these principles, together with the laws of psychology (as these work under the conditions of just institutions), which shape the aims and moral sentiments of citizens of a well-ordered society.

Once we consider the idea of a contract theory it is tempting to think that it will not yield the principles we want unless the parties are to some degree at least moved by benevolence, or an interest in one another's interests. Perry, as I mentioned before, thinks of the right standards and decisions as those promoting the ends reached by reflective agreement under circumstances making for impartiality and good will. Now the combination of mutual disinterest and the veil of ignorance achieves much the same purpose as benevolence. For this combination of conditions forces each person in the original position to take the good of others into account. In justice as fairness, then, the effects of good will are brought about by several conditions working jointly. The feeling that this conception of justice is egoistic is an illusion fostered by looking at but one of the elements of the original position. Furthermore, this pair of assumptions has enormous advantages over that of benevolence plus knowledge. As I have noted, the latter is so complex that no definite theory at all can be worked out. Not only are the complications caused by so much information insurmountable, but the motivational assumption requires clarification. For example, what is the relative strength of benevolent desires? In brief, the combination of mutual disinterestedness plus the veil of ignorance has the merits of simplicity and clarity while at the same time insuring the effects of what are at first sight morally more attractive assumptions.

Finally, if the parties are conceived as themselves making proposals, they have no incentive to suggest pointless or arbitrary principles. For example, none would urge that special privileges be given to those exactly six feet tall or born on a sunny day. Nor would anyone put forward the principle that basic rights should depend on the color of one's skin or the texture of one's hair. No one can tell whether such principles would be to his advantage. Furthermore, each such principle is a limitation of one's liberty of action, and such restrictions are not to be accepted without a reason. Certainly we might imagine peculiar circumstances in which these characteristics are relevant.

Those born on a sunny day might be blessed with a happy temperament, and for some positions of authority this might be a qualifying attribute. But such distinctions would never be proposed in first principles, for these must have some rational connection with the advancement of human interests broadly defined. The rationality of the parties and their situation in the original position guarantees that ethical principles and conceptions of justice have this general content.[8] Inevitably, then, racial and sexual discrimination presupposes that some hold a favored place in the social system which they are willing to exploit to their advantage. From the standpoint of persons similarly situated in an initial situation which is fair, the principles of explicit racist doctrines are not only unjust. They are irrational. For this reason we could say that they are not moral conceptions at all, but simply means of suppression. They have no place on a reasonable list of traditional conceptions of justice.[9] Of course, this contention is not at all a matter of definition. It is rather a consequence of the conditions characterizing the original position, especially the conditions of the rationality of the parties and the veil of ignorance. That conceptions of right have a certain content and exclude arbitrary and pointless principles is, therefore, an inference from the theory.

The Reasoning Leading to the Two Principles of Justice

In this and the next two sections I take up the choice between the two principles of justice and the principle of average utility. Determining the rational preference between these two options is perhaps the central problem in developing the conception of justice as fairness as a viable alternative to the utilitarian tradition. I shall begin in this section by presenting some intuitive remarks favoring the two principles. I shall also discuss briefly the qualitative structure of the argument that needs to be made if the case for these principles is to be conclusive.

Now consider the point of view of anyone in the original position. There is no way for him to win special advantages for himself. Nor, on the other hand, are there grounds for his acquiescing in special disadvantages. Since it is not reasonable for him to expect more than an equal share in the division of social primary goods, and since it is not rational for him to agree to less, the sensible thing is to acknowledge as the first step a principle of justice requiring an equal distribution. Indeed, this principle is so obvious given the symmetry of the parties that it would occur to everyone immediately. Thus the parties start with a principle requiring equal basic liberties for all, as well as fair equality of opportunity and equal division of income and wealth.

But even holding firm to the priority of the basic liberties and fair equality of opportunity, there is no reason why this initial acknowledgment should be final. Society should take into account economic efficiency and the requirements of organization and technology. If there are inequalities in income and wealth, and differences in authority and degrees of responsibility, that work to make everyone better off in comparison with the benchmark of equality, why not permit them? One might think that ideally individuals should want to serve one another. But since the parties are assumed to be mutually disinterested, their acceptance of these economic and institutional inequalities is only the recognition of the relations of opposition in which men stand in the circumstances of justice. They have no grounds for complaining of one another's motives. Thus the parties would agree to these differences only if they would be dejected by the bare knowledge or perception that others are better situated; but I suppose that they decide as if they are not moved by envy. Thus the basic structure should allow these inequalities so long as these improve everyone's situation, including that of the least advantaged, provided that they are consistent with equal liberty and fair opportunity. Because the parties start from an equal division of all social primary goods, those who benefit least have, so to speak, a veto. Thus we arrive at the difference principle. Taking equality as the basis of comparisons those who have gained more must do so on terms that are justifiable to those who have gained the least.

By some such reasoning, then, the parties might arrive at the two principles of justice in serial order. I shall not try to justify this ordering here, but the following remarks may convey the intuitive idea. I assume that the parties view themselves as free persons who have fundamental aims and interests in the name of which they think it legitimate for them to make claims on one another concerning the design of the basic structure of society. The religious interest is a familiar historical example; the interest in the integrity of the person is another. In the original position the parties do not know what particular forms these interests take; but they do assume that they have such interests and that the basic liberties necessary for their protection are guaranteed by the first principle. Since they must secure these interests, they rank the first principle prior to the second. The case for the two principles can be strengthened by spelling out in more detail the notion of a free person. Very roughly the parties regard themselves as having a highest-order interest in how all their other interests, including even their fundamental ones, are shaped and regulated by social institutions. They do not think of themselves as inevitably bound to, or as identical with, the pursuit of any particular complex of fundamental interests that they may have at any given time, although they want the right to advance such interests (provided they are admissible). Rather, free persons conceive of themselves as beings who can revise and alter their final ends and who give first priority to preserving their liberty in these matters. Hence, they not only have final ends that they are in principle free to pursue or to reject, but their original allegiance and continued devotion to these ends are to be formed and affirmed under conditions that are free. Since the two principles secure a social form that maintains these conditions, they would be agreed to rather than the principle of utility. Only by this agreement can the parties be sure that their highest-order interest as free persons is guaranteed.

The priority of liberty means that whenever the basic liberties can be effectively established, a lesser or an unequal liberty cannot be exchanged for an improvement in economic well-being. It is only when social circumstances do not allow the effective establishment of these basic rights that one can concede their limitation; and even then these restrictions can be granted only to the extent that they are necessary to prepare the way for the time when they are no longer justified. The denial of the equal liberties can be defended only when it is essential to change the conditions of civilization so that in due course these liberties can be enjoyed. Thus in adopting the serial order of the two principles, the parties are assuming that the conditions of their society, whatever they are, admit the effective realization of the equal liberties. Or that if they do not, circumstances are nevertheless sufficiently favorable so that the priority of the first principle points out the most urgent changes and identifies the preferred path to the social state in which all the basic liberties can be fully instituted. The complete realization of the two principles in serial order is the long-run tendency of this ordering, at least under reasonably fortunate conditions.

It seems from these remarks that the two principles are at least a plausible conception of justice. The question, though, is how one is to argue for them more systematically. Now there are several things to do. One can work out their consequences for institutions and note their implications for fundamental social policy. In this way they are tested by a comparison with our considered judgments of justice.... But one can also try to find arguments in their favor that are decisive from the standpoint of the original position. In order to see how this might be done, it is useful as a heuristic device to think of the two principles as the maximin solution to the problem of social justice. There is a relation between the two principles and the maximin rule for choice under uncertainty.[10] This is evident from the fact that the two principles are those a person would choose for the design of a society in which his enemy is to assign him his place. The maximin rule tells us to rank alternatives by their worst possible outcomes: we are to adopt the alternative the worst outcome of which is superior to the worst outcomes of the others.[11] The persons in the original position do not, of course, assume that their initial place in society is decided by a malevolent opponent. As I note below, they should not reason from false premises. The veil of ignorance does not violate this idea, since an absence of information is not misinformation. But that the two principles of justice would be chosen if the parties were forced to protect themselves against such a contingency explains the sense in which this conception is the maximin solution. And this analogy suggests that if the original position has been described so that it is rational for the parties to adopt the conservative attitude expressed by this rule, a conclusive argument can indeed be constructed for these principles. Clearly the maximum rule is not, in general, a suitable guide for choices under uncertainty. But it holds only in situations marked by certain special features. My aim, then, is to show that a good case can be made for the two principles based on the fact that the original position has these features to a very high degree.

Notes

1. As the text suggests, I shall regard Locke's *Second Treatise of Government*, Rousseau's *The Social Contract* and Kant's ethical works beginning with *The Foundations of the Metaphysics of Morals* as definitive of the contract tradition. For all of its greatness, Hobbes's *Leviathan* raises special problems. A general historical survey is provided by J. W. Gough, *The Social Contract*, 2nd ed. (Oxford, The Clarendon Press, 1957), and Otto Gierke, *Natural Law and the Theory of Society*, trans. with an introduction by Ernest Barker (Cambridge, The University Press, 1934). A presentation of the contract view as primarily an ethical theory is to be found in G. R. Grice, T*he Grounds of Moral Judgment* (Cambridge, The University Press, 1967).

2. Kant is clear that the original agreement is hypothetical. See *The Metaphysics of Morals*. pt. I (*Rechtslehre*), especially §§47,52; and pt: II of the essay "Concerning the Common Saying: This May Be True in Theory but it Does Not Apply in Practice," in *Kant's Political Writings*, ed. Hans Reiss and trans. by H. B. Nisbet (Cambridge, The University Press, 1970), pp. 73–87. See Georges Vlachos, *La Pensée politique de Kant* (Paris, Presses Universitaires de France, 1962), pp. 326–335; and J. G. Murphy, *Kant: The Philosophy of Right* (London, Macmillan, 1970), pp. 109–112, 133–136, for a further discussion.

3. The veil of ignorance is so natural a condition that something like it must have occurred to many. The formulation in the text is implicit, I believe, in Kant's doctrine of the categorical imperative, both in the way this procedural criterion is defined and the use Kant makes of it. Thus when Kant tells us to test our maxim by considering what would be the case were it a universal law of nature, he must suppose that we do not know our place within this imagined system of nature. See, for example, his discussion of the topic of practical judgment in *The Critique of Practical Reason*, Academy Edition, vol. 5, pp. 68–72. A similar restriction on information is found in J. C. Harsanyi, "Cardinal Utility in Welfare Economics and in the Theory of Risk-taking", *Journal of Political Economy*, vol. 61 (1953). However, other aspects of Harsanyi's view are quite different, and he uses the restriction to develop a utilitarian theory....

4. Rousseau, *The Social Contract*, bk. II ch. IV, par. 5.

5. See R. B. Perry, *The General Theory of Value* (New York, Longmans, Green and Company, 1926), pp. 674–682.

6. For this notion of rationality, [see the references to Sen and Arrow above, §23, note 9.] The discussion in I. M. D. Little, *The Cntique of Welfare Economics*, 2nd ed. (Oxford, Clarendon Press, 1957), ch. 11, is also relevant here.... H. A. Simon discusses the limitations of the classical conceptions of rationality and the need for a more realistic theory in "A Behavioral Model of Rational Choice," *Quarterly Journal of Economics*, vol. 69 (1955). See also his essay in *Surveys of Economic Theory*, vol. 3 (London, Macmillan, 1967). For philosophical discussions see Donald Davidson, "Actions, Reasons, and Causes," *Journal of Philosophy*, vol. 60 (1963); C. G. Hempel, *Aspects of Scientific Explanation* (New York, The Free Press, 1965), pp. 463–486; Jonathan Bennett, *Rationality* (London, Routledge and Kegan Paul,1964), and J. D. Mabbott, "Reason and Desire," *Philosophy*, vol. 28 (1953).

7. See *On the Basis of Ethics* (1840), trans. E. E J. Payne (New York, The Liberal Arts Press, Inn., 1965), pp. 89–92.

8. For a different way of reaching this conclusion, see Philippa Foot, "Moral Arguments," *Mind*, vol. 67 (1958), and "Moral Beliefs," *Proceedings of the Aristotelian Society*, vol. 59 (1958–1959); and R. W. Beardsmore, *Moral Reasoning* (New York, Schocken Books, 1969), especially ch. IV. The problem of content is discussed briefly

in G. E Warnock, *Contemporary Moral Philosophy* (London, Macmillan, 1967), pp. 55–61.

9. For a similar view, see B. A. O. Williams, "The Idea of Equality," *Philosophy, Politics, and Society,* Second Series, ed. Peter Laslett and W. G. Runciman (Oxford, Basil Blackwell, 1962), p. 113.

10. An accessible discussion of this and other rules of choice under uncertainty can be found in W. J. Baumol, *Economic Theory and Operations Analysis*, 2nd ed. (Englewood Cliffs, N.J., Prentice-Hall Inc., 1965), ch. 24. Baumol gives a geometric interpretation of these rules.... See pp. 558–562. See also R. D. Lure and Howard Raiffa, *Games and Decisions* (New York, John Wiley and Sons, Inn., 1957), ch. XIII, for a fuller account.

11. Consider the gain-and-loss table below. It represents the gains and losses for a situation which is not a game of strategy. There is no one playing against the person making the decision; instead he is faced with several possible circumstances which may or may not obtain. Which circumstances happen to exist does not depend upon what the person choosing decides or whether he announces his moves in advance. The numbers in the table are monetary values (in hundreds of dollars) in comparison with some initial situation. The gain (g) depends upon the individual's decision (d) and the circumstances (c). Thus $g = f(d, c)$. Assuming that there are three possible decisions and three possible circumstances, we might have this gain-and-loss table.

| | *Circumstances* | | |
Decisions	c_1	c_2	c_3
d_1	-7	8	12
d_2	-8	7	14
d_3	5	6	8

The maximin rule requires that we make the third decision. For in this case the worst that can happen is that one gains five hundred dollars, which is better than the worst for the other actions. If we adopt one of these we may lose either eight or seven hundred dollars. Thus, the choice of d_3 maximizes $f(do)$ for that value of c, which for a given d, minimizes f. The term "maximin" means the *maximum minimorum*; and the rule directs our attention to the worst that can happen under any proposed course of action, and to decide in the light of that.

John Rawls is James B. Conant University Professor, Emeritus, at Harvard University. After publishing *A Theory of Justice* in 1971 he continued to rethink his views on justice, resulting in his later books *Political Liberalism* and *The Law of Peoples.*

15

Excerpts from "Anarchy, State, and Utopia"

Robert Nozick

Section I

The entitlement theory

The subject of justice in holdings consists of three major topics. The first is the *original acquisition of holdings*, the appropriation of unheld things. This includes the issues of how unheld things may come to be held, the process, or processes, by which unheld things may come to be held, the things that may come to be held by these processes, the extent of what comes to be held by a particular process, and so on. We shall refer to the complicated truth about this topic, which we shall not formulate here, as the principle of justice in acquisition. The second topic concerns the *transfer of holdings* from one person to another. By what processes may a person transfer holdings to another? How may a person acquire a holding from another who holds it? Under this topic come general descriptions of voluntary exchange, and gift and (on the other hand) fraud, as well as reference to particular conventional details fixed upon in a given society. The complicated truth about this subject (with placeholders for conventional details) we shall call the principle of justice in transfer. (And we shall suppose it also includes principles governing how a person may divest himself of a holding, passing it into an unheld state.)

If the world were wholly just, the following inductive definition would exhaustively cover the subject of justice in holdings.

1. A person who acquires a holding in accordance with the principle of justice in acquisition is entitled to that holding.
2. A person who acquires a holding in accordance with the principle of justice

Source: Robert Nozick, *Anarchy, State, and Utopia* (New York: Basic Books, Inc., 1974).

in transfer, from someone else entitled to the holding, is entitled to the holding.

3. No one is entitled to a holding except by (repeated) applications of 1 and 2.

The complete principle of distributive justice would say simply that a distribution is just if everyone is entitled to the holdings they possess under the distribution.

A distribution is just if it arises from another just distribution by legitimate means. The legitimate means of moving from one distribution to another are specified by the principle of justice in transfer. The legitimate first "moves" are specified by the principle of justice in acquisition.[1] Whatever arises from a just situation by just steps is itself just. The means of change specified by the principle of justice in transfer preserve justice. As correct rules of inference are truth-preserving, and any conclusion deduced via repeated application of such rules from only true premises is itself true, so the means of transition from one situation to another specified by the principle of justice in transfer are justice-preserving, and any situation actually arising from repeated transitions in accordance with the principle from a just situation is itself just. The parallel between justice-preserving transformations and truth-preserving transformations illuminates where it fails as well as where it holds. That a conclusion could have been deduced by truth-preserving means from premises that are true suffices to show its truth. That from a just situation a situation *could* have arisen via justice-preserving means does not suffice to show its justice. The fact that a thief's victims voluntarily *could* have presented him with gifts does not entitle the thief to his ill-gotten gains. Justice in holdings is historical; it depends upon what actually has happened. We shall return to this point later.

Not all actual situations are generated in accordance with the two principles of justice in holdings: the principle of justice in acquisition and the principle of justice in transfer. Some people steal from others, or defraud them, or enslave them, seizing their product and preventing them from living as they choose, or forcibly exclude others from competing in exchanges. None of these are permissible modes of transition from one situation to another. And some persons acquire holdings by means not sanctioned by the principle of justice in acquisition. The existence of past injustice (previous violations of the first two principles of justice in holdings) raises the third major topic under justice in holdings: the rectification of injustice in holdings. If past injustice has shaped present holdings in various ways, some identifiable and some not, what now, if anything, ought to be done to rectify these injustices? What obligations do the performers of injustice have toward those whose position is worse than it would have been had the injustice not been done?...

The general outlines of the theory of justice in holdings are that the holdings of a person are just if he is entitled to them by the principles of justice in acquisition and transfer, or by the principle of rectification of injustice (as specified by the first two principles). If each person's holdings are just, then the total set (distribution) of holdings is just. To turn these general outlines into a specific theory we would have to specify the details of each of the three principles of justice in holdings: the principle of acquisition of holdings, the principle of transfer of holdings, and the principle of rectification of violations of the first two principles. I shall not attempt that task here.

Historical principles and end-result principles

The general outlines of the entitlement theory illuminate the nature and defects of other conceptions of distributive justice. The entitlement theory of justice in distribution is *historical*; whether a distribution is just depends upon how it came about. In contrast, *current time-slice principles* of justice hold that the justice of a distribution is determined by how things are distributed (who has what) as judged by some *structural* principle(s) of just distribution. A utilitarian who judges between any two distributions by seeing which has the greater sum of utility and, if the sums tie, applies some fixed equality criterion to choose the more equal distribution, would hold a current time-slice principle of justice. As would someone who had a fixed schedule of trade-offs between the sum of happiness and equality. According to a current time-slice principle, all that needs to be looked at, in judging the justice of a distribution, is who ends up with what; in comparing any two distributions one need look only at the matrix presenting the distributions. No further information need be fed into a principle of justice. It is a consequence of such principles of justice that any two structurally identical distributions are equally just. (Two distributions are structurally identical if they present the same profile, but perhaps have different persons occupying the particular slots. My having ten and your having five, and my having five and your having ten are structurally identical distributions.) Welfare economics is the theory of current time-slice principles of justice. The subject is conceived as operating on matrices representing only current information about distribution. This, as well as some of the usual conditions (for example, the choice of distribution is invariant under relabeling of columns), guarantees that welfare economics will be a current time-slice theory, with all of its inadequacies.

Most persons do not accept current time-slice principles as constituting the whole story about distributive shares. They think it relevant in assessing the justice of a situation to consider not only the distribution it embodies, but also how that distribution came about. If some persons are in prison for murder or war crimes, we do not say that to assess the justice of the distribution in the society we must look only at what this person has, and that person has, and that person has, ... at the current time. We think it relevant to ask whether someone did something so that he deserved to be punished, deserved to have a lower share. Most will agree to the relevance of further information with regard to punishments and penalties. Consider also desired things. One traditional socialist view is that workers are entitled to the product and full fruits of their labor; they have earned it; a distribution is unjust if it does not give the workers what they are entitled to. Such entitlements are based upon some past history. No socialist holding this view would find it comforting to be told that because the actual distribution *A* happens to coincide structurally with the one he desires *D*, *A* therefore is no less just than *D*; it differs only in that the "parasitic" owners of capital receive under *A* what the workers are entitled to under *D*, and the workers receive under *A* what the owners are entitled to under *D*, namely very little. This socialist rightly, in my view, holds onto the notions of earning, producing, entitlement, desert, and so forth, and he rejects current time-slice principles that look only to the structure of the resulting set of holdings. (The set of holdings resulting from what? Isn't it implausible that how holdings are produced and come to exist has no effect at all on who should hold what?) His mistake lies in his view of what entitlements arise out of what sorts of productive processes.

We construe the position we discuss too narrowly by speaking of *current* time-slice principles. Nothing is changed if structural principles operate upon a time sequence of current time-slice profiles and, for example, give someone more now to counterbalance the less he has had earlier. A utilitarian or an egalitarian or any mixture of the two over time will inherit the difficulties of his more myopic comrades. He is not helped by the fact that *some* of the information others consider relevant in assessing a distribution is reflected, unrecoverably, in past matrices. Henceforth, we shall refer to such unhistorical principles of distributive justice, including the current time-slice principles, as *end-result principles* or *end-state principles*.

In contrast to end-result principles of justice, *historical principles* of justice hold that past circumstances or actions of people can create differential entitlements or differential deserts to things. An injustice can be worked by moving from one distribution to another structurally identical one, for the second, in profile the same, may violate people's entitlements or deserts; it may not fit the actual history.

Patterning

The entitlement principles of justice in holdings that we have sketched are historical principles of justice. To better understand their precise character, we shall distinguish them from another subclass of the historical principles. Consider, as an example, the principle of distribution according to moral merit. This principle requires that total distributive shares vary directly with moral merit; no person should have a greater share than anyone whose moral merit is greater. (If moral merit could be not merely ordered but measured on an interval or ratio scale, stronger principles could be formulated.) Or consider the principle that results by substituting "usefulness to society," for "moral merit" in the previous principle. Or instead of "distribute according to moral merit," or "distribute according to usefulness to society," we might consider "distribute according to the weighted sum of moral merit, usefulness to society, and need," with the weights of the different dimensions equal. Let us call a principle of distribution *patterned* if it specifies that a distribution is to vary along with some natural dimension, weighted sum of natural dimensions, or lexicographic ordering of natural dimensions. And let us say a distribution is patterned if it accords with some patterned principle. (I speak of natural dimensions, admittedly without a general criterion for them, because for any set of holdings some artificial dimensions can be gimmicked up to vary along with the distribution of the set.) The principle of distribution in accordance with moral merit is a patterned historical principle, which specifies a patterned distribution. "Distribute according to I.Q." is a patterned principle that looks to information not contained in distributional matrices. It is not historical, however, in that it does not look to any past actions creating differential entitlements to evaluate a distribution; it requires only distributional matrices whose columns are labeled by I.Q. scores. The distribution in a society, however, may be composed of such simple patterned distributions, without itself being simply patterned. Different sectors may operate different patterns, or some combination of patterns may operate in different proportions across a society. A distribution composed in this manner, from a small number of patterned distributions, we also shall term "patterned." And we extend the use of "pattern" to include the overall designs put forth by combinations of end-state principles.

Almost every suggested principle of distributive justice is patterned: to each according to his moral merit, or needs, or marginal product, or how hard he tries, or the weighted sum of the foregoing, and so on. The principle of entitlement we have sketched is not patterned.[2] There is no one natural dimension or weighted sum or combination of a small number of natural dimensions that yields the distributions generated in accordance with the principle of entitlement. The set of holdings that results when some persons receive their marginal products, others win at gambling, others receive a share of their mate's income, others receive gifts from foundations, others receive interest on loans, others receive gifts from admirers, others receive returns on investment, others make for themselves much of what they have, others find things, and so on, will not be patterned. Heavy strands of patterns will run through it; significant portions of the variance in holdings will be accounted for by pattern-variables. If most people most of the time choose to transfer some of their entitlements to others only in exchange for something from them, then a large part of what many people hold will vary with what they held that others wanted. More details are provided by the theory of marginal productivity. But gifts to relatives, charitable donations, bequests to children, and the like, are not best conceived, in the first instance, in this manner. Ignoring the strands of pattern, let us suppose for the moment that a distribution actually arrived at by the operation of the principle of entitlement is random with respect to any pattern. Though the resulting set of holdings will be unpatterned, it will not be incomprehensible, for it can be seen as arising from the operation of a small number of principles. These principles specify how an initial distribution may arise (the principle of acquisition of holdings) and how distributions may be transformed into others (the principle of transfer of holdings) The process whereby the set of holdings is generated will be intelligible, though the set of holdings itself that results from this process will be unpatterned...

How liberty upsets patterns

It is not clear how those holding alternative conceptions of distributive justice can reject the entitlement conception of justice in holdings. For suppose a distribution favored by one of these nonentitlement conceptions is realized. Let us suppose it is your favorite one and let us call this distribution D_1; perhaps everyone has an equal share, perhaps shares vary in accordance with some dimension you treasure. Now suppose that Wilt Chamberlain is greatly in demand by basketball teams, being a great gate attraction. (Also suppose contracts run only for a year, with players being free agents.) He signs the following sort of contract with a team: in each home game, twenty-five cents from the price of each ticket of admission goes to him. (We ignore the question of whether he is "gouging" the owners, letting them look out for themselves.) The season starts, and people cheerfully attend his team's games; they buy their tickets, each time dropping a separate twenty-five cents of their admission price into a special box with Chamberlain's name on it. They are excited about seeing him play; it is worth the total admission price to them. Let us suppose that in one season one million persons attend his home games, and Wilt Chamberlain winds up with $250,000, a much larger sum than the average income and larger even than anyone else has. Is he entitled to this income? Is this new distribution D_2, unjust? If so, why? There is no question about whether each of the people was entitled to the control over the resources they held in D_1; because that was the distribution (your favorite) that (for the purposes of argument) we assumed was acceptable. Each of these persons *chose* to give twenty-five cents of their money to Chamberlain. They could have spent it on going to the movies, or on candy bars, or on copies of *Dissent* magazine, or of *Monthly Review.* But they all, at least one million of them, converged on giving it to Wilt Chamberlain in exchange for watching him play basketball. If D_1 was a just distribution, and people voluntarily moved from it to D_2, transferring parts of their shares they were given under D_1 (what was it for if not to do something with?), isn't D_2 also just? If the people were entitled to dispose of the resources to which they were entitled (under D_1), didn't this include their being entitled to give it to, or exchange it with, Wilt Chamberlain? Can anyone else complain on grounds of justice? Each other person already has his legitimate share under D_1. Under D_1, there is nothing that anyone has that anyone else has a claim of justice against. After someone transfers something to Wilt Chamberlain, third parties *still* have their legitimate shares; *their* shares are not changed. By what process could such a transfer among two persons give rise to a legitimate claim of distributive justice on a portion of what was transferred, by a third party who had no claim of justice on any holding of the others before the transfer?[3]...

The general point illustrated by the Wilt Chamberlain example and the example of the entrepreneur in a socialist society is that no end-state principle or distributional patterned principle of justice can be continuously realized without continuous interference with people's lives. Any favored pattern would be transformed into one unfavored by the principle, by people choosing to act in various ways; for example, by people exchanging goods and services with other people, or giving things to other people, things the transferrers are entitled to under the favored distributional pattern. To maintain a pattern one must either continually interfere to stop people from transferring resources as they wish to, or continually (or periodically) interfere to take from some persons resources that others for some reason chose to transfer to them. (But if some time limit is to be set on how long people may keep resources others voluntarily transfer to them, why let them keep these resources for any period of time? Why not have immediate confiscation?) It might be objected that all persons voluntarily will choose to refrain from actions which would upset the pattern. This presupposes unrealistically (1) that all will most want to maintain the pattern (are those who don't, to be "reeducated" or forced to undergo "self-criticism"?), (2) that each can gather enough information about his own actions and the ongoing activities of others to discover which of his actions will upset the pattern, and (3) that diverse and far-flung persons can coordinate their actions to dovetail into the pattern. Compare the manner in which the market is neutral among persons' desires, as it reflects and transmits widely scattered information via prices, and coordinates persons' activities.

Redistribution and property rights

... Patterned principles of distributive justice necessitate *re*distributive activities. The likelihood is small that any actual freely-arrived-at set of holdings fits a given pattern; and the likelihood is nil that it will continue to fit the pattern as people exchange and give. From the point of view of an entitlement theory, redistribution is a serious matter indeed, involving, as it does, the violation of people's rights. (An exception is those takings that fall under the principle of the rectification of injustices.) From other points of view, also, it is serious.

Taxation of earnings from labor is on a par with forced labor.[4] Some persons find this claim obviously true: taking the earnings of n hours labor is like taking n hours from the person; it is like forcing the person to work n hours for another's purpose. Others find the claim absurd. But even these, *if* they object to forced labor, would oppose forcing unemployed hippies to work for the benefit of the needy.[5] And they would also object to forcing each person to work five extra hours each week for the benefit of the needy. But a system that takes five hours' wages in taxes does not seem to them like one that forces someone to work five hours, since it offers the person forced a wider range of choice in activities than does taxation in kind with the particular labor specified. (But we can imagine a gradation of systems of forced labor, from one that specifies a particular activity, to one that gives a choice among two activities, to...; and so on up.) Furthermore, people envisage a system with something like a proportional tax on everything above the amount necessary for basic needs. Some think this does not force someone to work extra hours, since there is no fixed number of extra hours he is forced to work, and since he can avoid the tax entirely by earning only enough to cover his basic needs. This is a very uncharacteristic view of forcing for those who *also* think people are forced to do something *whenever* the alternatives they face are considerably worse. However, neither view is correct. The fact that others intentionally intervene, in violation of a side constraint against aggression, to threaten force to limit the alternatives, in this case to paying taxes or (presumably the worse alternative) bare subsistence, makes the taxation system one of forced labor and distinguishes it from other cases of limited choices which are not forcings.[6] ...

Locke's theory of acquisition

... [W]e must introduce an additional bit of complexity into the structure of the entitlement theory. This is best approached by considering Locke's attempt to specify a principle of justice in acquisition. Locke views property rights in an unowned object as originating through someone's mixing his labor with it. This gives rise to many questions. What are the boundaries of what labor is mixed with? If a private astronaut clears a place on Mars, has he mixed his labor with (so that he comes to own) the whole planet, the whole uninhabited universe, or just a particular plot? Which plot does an act bring under ownership? The minimal (possibly disconnected) area such that an act decreases entropy in that area, and not elsewhere? Can virgin land (for the purposes of ecological investigation by high-flying airplane) come under ownership by a Lockean process? Building a fence around a territory presumably would make one the owner of only the fence (and the land immediately underneath it).

Why does mixing one's labor with something make one the owner of it? Perhaps because one owns one's labor, and so one comes to own a previously unowned thing that becomes permeated with what one owns. Ownership seeps over into the rest. But why isn't mixing what I own with what I don't own a way of losing what I own rather than a way of gaining what I don't ? If I own a can of tomato juice and spill it in the sea so that its molecules (made radioactive, so I can check this) mingle evenly throughout the sea, do I thereby come to own the sea, or have I foolishly dissipated my tomato juice? Perhaps the idea, instead, is that laboring on something improves it and makes it more valuable; and anyone is entitled to own a thing whose value he has created. (Reinforcing this, perhaps, is the view that laboring is unpleasant. If some people made things effortlessly, as the cartoon characters in *The Yellow Submarine* trail flowers in their wake, would they have lesser claim to their own products whose making didn't cost them anything?) Ignore the fact that laboring on something may make it less valuable (spraying pink enamel paint on a piece of driftwood that you have found). Why should one's entitlement extend to the whole object rather than just to the *added value* one's labor has produced? (Such reference to value might also serve to delimit the extent of ownership; for example, substitute "increases the value of" for "decreases entropy in" in the above entropy criterion.) No workable or coherent value-added property scheme has yet been devised, and any such scheme presumably would fall to objections (similar to those) that fell the theory of Henry George.

It will be implausible to view improving an object as giving full ownership to it, if the stock of unowned objects that might be improved is limited. For an object's coming under one person's ownership changes the situation of all others. Whereas previously they were at liberty (in Hohfeld's sense) to use the object, they now no longer are. This change in the situation of others (by removing their liberty to act on a previously unowned object) need not worsen their situation. If I appropriate a grain of sand from Coney Island, no one else may now do as they will with *that* grain of sand. But there are plenty of other grains of sand left for them to do the same with. Or if not grains of sand, then other things. Alternatively, the things I do with the grain of sand I appropriate might improve the position of others, counterbalancing their loss of the liberty to use that grain. The crucial point is whether appropriation of an unowned object worsens the situation of others.

Locke's proviso that there be "enough and as good left in common for others" (sect. 27) is meant to ensure that the situation of others is not worsened. (If this proviso is met is there any motivation for his further condition of nonwaste?) It is often said that this proviso once held but now no longer does. But there appears to be an argument for the conclusion that if the proviso no longer holds, then it cannot ever have held so as to yield permanent and inheritable property rights. Consider the first person Z for whom there is not enough and as good left to appropriate. The last person Y to appropriate left Z without his previous liberty to act on an object, and so worsened Z's situation. So Y's appropriation is not allowed under Locke's proviso. Therefore the next to last person X to appropriate left Y in a worse position, for X's act ended permissible appropriation. Therefore X's appropriation wasn't permissible. But then the appropriator two from last, W, ended permissible appropriation and so, since it worsened X's position, W's appropriation wasn't permissible. And so on back to the first person A to appropriate a permanent property right.

This argument, however, proceeds too quickly. Someone may be made worse off by another's appropriation in two ways: first, by losing the opportunity to improve his situation by a particular appropriation or any one; and second, by no longer being able to use freely (without appropriation) what he previously could. A *stringent* requirement that another not be made worse off by an appropriation would exclude the first way if nothing else counterbalances the diminution in opportunity, as well as the second. A weaker requirement would exclude the second way though not the first. With the weaker requirement, we cannot zip back so quickly from Z to A, as in the above argument; for though person Z can no longer *appropriate*, there may remain some for him to use as before. In this case Y's appropriation would not violate the weaker Lockean condition. (With less remaining that people are at liberty to use, users might face more inconvenience, crowding, and so on; in that way the situation of others might be worsened, unless appropriation stopped far short of such a point.) It is arguable that no one legitimately can complain if the weaker provision is satisfied. However, since this is less clear than in the case of the more stringent proviso, Locke may have intended this stringent proviso by "enough and as good" remaining, and perhaps he meant the nonwaste condition to delay the end point from which the argument zips back.

Is the situation of persons who are unable to appropriate (there being no more accessible and useful unowned objects) worsened by a system allowing appropriation and permanent property? Here enter the various familiar social considerations favoring private property: it increases the social product by putting means of production in the hands of those who can use them most efficiently (profitably); experimentation is encouraged, because with separate persons controlling resources, there is no one person or small group whom someone with a new idea must convince to try it out; private property enables people to decide on the pattern and types of risks they wish to bear, leading to specialized types of risk bearing; private property protects future persons by leading some to hold back resources from current consumption for future markets; it provides alternate sources of employment for unpopular persons who don' t have to convince any one person or small group to hire them, and so on. These considerations enter a Lockean theory to support the claim that appropriation of private property satisfies the intent behind the "enough and as good left over" proviso, not as a utilitarian justification of property. They enter to rebut the claim that because the proviso is violated no natural right to private property can arise by a Lockean process. The difficulty in working such an argument to show that the proviso is satisfied is in fixing the appropriate base line for comparison. Lockean appropriation makes people no worse off than they could be *how*? This question of fixing the baseline needs more detailed investigation than we are able to give it here. It would be desirable to have an estimate of the general economic importance of original appropriation in order to see how much leeway there is for differing theories of appropriation and of the location of the baseline. Perhaps this importance can be measured by the percentage of all income that is based upon untransformed raw materials and given resources (rather than upon human actions), mainly rental income representing the unimproved value of land, and the price of raw material *in situ*, and by the percentage of current wealth which represents such income in the past.[7]

We should note that it is not only persons favoring *private* property who need a theory of how property rights legitimately originate. Those believing in collective property, for example those believing that a group of persons living in an area jointly own the territory, or its mineral resources, also must provide a theory of how such property rights arise; they must show why the persons living there have rights to determine what is done with the land and resources there that persons living elsewhere don't have (with regard to the same land and resources).

The proviso

Whether or not Locke's particular theory of appropriation can be spelled out so as to handle various difficulties, I assume that any adequate theory of justice in acquisition will contain a proviso similar to the weaker of the ones we have attributed to Locke. A process normally giving rise to a permanent bequeathable property right in a previously unowned thing will not do so if the position of others no longer at liberty to use the thing is thereby worsened. It is important to specify *this* particular mode of worsening the situation of others, for the proviso does not encompass other modes. It does not include the worsening due to more limited opportunities to appropriate (the first way above, corresponding to the more stringent condition), and it does not include how I "worsen" a seller's position if I appropriate materials to make some of what he is selling, and then enter into competition with him. Someone whose appropriation otherwise would violate the proviso still may appropriate provided he compensates the others so that their situation is not thereby worsened; unless he does compensate these others, his appropriation will violate the proviso of the principle of justice in acquisition and will be an illegitimate one.[8] A theory of appropriation incorporating this Lockean proviso will handle correctly the cases (objections to the theory lacking the proviso) where someone appropriates the total supply of something necessary for life.[9]

A theory which includes this proviso in its principle of justice in acquisition must also contain a more complex principle of justice in transfer. Some reflection of the proviso about appropriation constrains later actions. If my appropriating all of a certain substance violates the Lockean proviso, then so does my appropriating some and purchasing all the rest from others who obtained it without otherwise violating the Lockean proviso. If the proviso excludes someone's appropriating all the drinkable water in the world, it also excludes his purchasing it all. (More weakly, and messily, it may exclude his charging certain prices for some of his supply.) This proviso (almost?) never will come into effect; the more someone acquires of a scarce substance which others want, the higher the price of the rest will go, and the more difficult it will become for him to acquire it all. But still, we can imagine, at least, that something like this occurs: someone makes simultaneous secret bids to the separate owners of a substance, each of whom sells assuming he can easily purchase more from the other owners; or some natural catastrophe destroys all of the supply of something except that in one person's possession. The total supply could not be permissibly appropriated by one person at the beginning. His later acquisition of it all does not show that the original appropriation violated the proviso (even by a reverse argument similar to the one above that tried to zip back from Z to A). Rather, it is the combination of the original appropriation *plus* all the later transfers and actions that violates the Lockean proviso.

Each owner's title to his holding includes the historical shadow of the Lockean proviso on appropriation. This excludes his transferring it into an agglomeration that does violate the Lockean proviso and excludes his using it in a way, in coordination with others or independently of them, so as to violate the proviso by making the situation of others worse than their baseline situation. Once it is known that someone's ownership runs afoul of the Lockean proviso, there are stringent limits on what he may do with (what it is difficult any longer unreservedly to call) "his property." Thus a person may not appropriate the only water hole in a desert and charge what he will. Nor may he charge what he will if he possesses one, and unfortunately it happens that all the water holes in the desert dry up, except for his. This unfortunate circumstance, admittedly no fault of his, brings into operation the Lockean proviso and limits his property rights.[10] Similarly, an owner's property right in the only island in an area does not allow him to order a castaway from a shipwreck off his island as a trespasser, for this would violate the Lockean proviso.

Notice that the theory does not say that owners do have these rights, but that the rights are overridden to avoid some catastrophe. (Overridden rights do not disappear; they leave a trace of a sort absent in the cases under discussion.)[11] There is no such external (and ad hoc?) overriding. Considerations internal to the theory of property itself, to its theory of acquisition and appropriation, provide the means for handling such cases. The results, however, may be coextensive with some condition about catastrophe, since the baseline for comparison is so low as compared to the productiveness of a society with private appropriation that the question of the Lockean proviso being violated arises only in the case of catastrophe (or a desert-island situation).

The fact that someone owns the total supply of something necessary for others to stay alive does not entail that his (or anyone's) appropriation of anything left some people (immediately or later) in a situation worse than the baseline one. A medical researcher who synthesizes a new substance that effectively treats a certain disease and who refuses to sell except on his terms does not worsen the situation of others by depriving them of whatever he has appropriated. The others easily can possess the same materials he appropriated; the researcher's appropriation or purchase of chemicals didn't make those chemicals scarce in a way so as to violate the Lockean proviso. Nor would someone else's purchasing the total supply of the synthesized substance from the medical researcher. The fact that the medical researcher uses easily available chemicals to synthesize the drug no more violates the Lockean proviso than does the fact that the only surgeon able to perform a particular operation eats easily obtainable food in order to stay alive and to have the energy to work. This shows that the Lockean proviso is not an "end-state principle"; it focuses on a particular way that appropriative actions affect others, and not on the structure of the situation that results.

Intermediate between someone who takes all of the public supply and someone who makes the total supply out of easily obtainable substances is someone who appropriates the total supply of something in a way that does not deprive the others of it. For example, someone finds a new substance in an out-of-the-way place. He discovers that it effectively treats a certain disease and appropriates the total supply. He does not worsen the situation of others; if he did not stumble upon the substance no one else would have, and the others would remain without it. However, as time passes, the likelihood increases that others would have come across the substance; upon this fact might be based a limit to his property right in the substance so that others are not below their baseline position; for example, its bequest might be limited. The theme of someone worsening another's situation by depriving him of something he otherwise would possess may also illuminate the example of patents. An inventor's patent does not deprive others of an object which would not exist if not for the inventor. Yet patents would have this effect on others who independently invent the object. Therefore, these independent inventors, upon whom the burden of proving independent discovery may rest, should not be excluded from utilizing their own invention as they wish (including selling it to others). Furthermore, a known inventor drastically lessens the chances of actual independent invention. For persons who know of an invention usually will not try to reinvent it, and the notion of independent discovery here would be murky at best. Yet we may assume that in the absence of the original invention, sometime later someone else would have come up with it. This suggests placing a time limit on patents, as a rough rule of thumb to approximate how long it would have taken, in the absence of knowledge of the invention, for independent discovery.

I believe that the free operation of a market system will not actually run afoul of the Lockean proviso.... If this is correct, the proviso will not play a very important role in the activities of protective agencies and will not provide a significant opportunity for future state action. Indeed, were it not for the effects of previous *illegitimate* state action, people would not think the possibility of the proviso's being violated as of more interest than any other logical possibility. (Here I make an empirical historical claim; as does someone who disagrees with this.) This completes our indication of the complication in the entitlement theory introduced by the Lockean proviso.

Notes

1. Applications of the principle of justice in acquisition may also occur as part of the move from one distribution to another. You may find an unheld thing now and appropriate it. Acquisitions also are to be understood as included when, to simplify, I speak only of transitions by transfers.

2. One might try to squeeze a patterned conception of distributive justice into the framework of the entitlement conception, by formulating a gimmicky obligatory "principle of transfer" that would lead to the pattern. For example, the principle that if one has more than the mean income one must transfer everything one holds above the mean to persons below the mean so as to bring them up to (but not over) the mean. We can formulate a criterion for a "principle of transfer" to rule out such obligatory transfers, or we can say that no correct principle of transfer, no principle of transfer in a free society will be like this. The former is probably the better course, though the latter also is true.

Alternatively, one might think to make the entitlement conception instantiate a pattern, by using matrix entries that express the relative strength of a person's entitlements as measured by some real-valued function. But even if the limitation to natural dimensions failed to exclude this function, the resulting edifice would *not* capture our system of entitlements to *particular* things.

3. Might not a transfer have instrumental effects on a third party, changing his feasible options? (But what if the two parties to the transfer independently had used

their holdings in this fashion?) I discuss this question below, but note here that this question concedes the point for distributions of ultimate intrinsic noninstrumental goods (pure utility experiences, so to speak) that are transferrable. It also might be objected that the transfer might make a third party more envious because it worsens his position relative to someone else. I find it incomprehensible how this can be thought to involve a claim of justice....

Here and elsewhere in this chapter, a theory which incorporates elements of pure procedural justice might find what I say acceptable, *if* kept in its proper place; that is, if background institutions exist to ensure the satisfaction of certain conditions on distributive shares. But if these institutions are not themselves the sum or invisible-hand result of people's voluntary (nonaggressive) actions, the constraints they impose require justification. At no point does *our* argument assume any background institutions more extensive than those of the minimal night-watchman state, a state limited to protecting persons against murder, assault, theft, fraud, and so forth.

4. I am unsure as to whether the arguments I present below show that such taxation merely *is* forced labor; so that "is on a par with" means "is one kind of." Or alternatively, whether the arguments emphasize the great similarities between such taxation and forced labor, to show it is plausible and illuminating to view such taxation in the light of forced labor. This latter approach would remind one of how John Wisdom conceives of the claims of metaphysicians.

5. Nothing hangs on the fact that here and elsewhere I speak loosely of *needs*, since I go on, each time, to reject the criterion of justice which includes it. If, however, something did depend upon the notion, one would want to examine it more carefully. For a skeptical view, see Kenneth Minogue, *The Liberal Mind*, (New York: Random House, 1963), pp. 103–112.

6. Further details which this statement should include are contained in my essay "Coercion," in *Philosophy, Science, and Method*, ed. S. Morgenbesser, P. Suppes, and M. White (New York: St. Martin, 1969).

7. I have not seen a precise estimate. David Friedman, *The Machinery of Freedom* (N.Y.: Harper & Row, 1973), pp. XIV, XV, discusses this issue and suggests 5 percent of U.S. national income as an upper limit for the first two factors mentioned. However he does not attempt to estimate the percentage of current wealth which is based upon such income in the past. (The vague notion of "based upon" merely indicates a topic needing investigation.)

8. Fourier held that since the process of civilization had deprived the members of society of certain liberties (to gather, pasture, engage in the chase), a socially guaranteed minimum provision for persons was justified as compensation for the loss (Alexander Gray, *The Socialist Tradition* (New York: Harper & Row, 1968), p. 188). But this puts the point too strongly. This compensation would be due those persons, if any, for whom the process of civilization was a *net loss*, for whom the benefits of civilization did not counterbalance being deprived of these particular liberties.

9. For example, Rashdall's case of someone who comes upon the only water in the desert several miles ahead of others who also will come to it and appropriates it all. Hastings Rashdall, "The Philosophical Theory of Property," in *Property, its Duties and Rights* (London: MacMillan, 1915). We should note Ayn Rand's theory of property rights ("Man's Rights" in *The Virtue of Selfishness* (New York: New American Library, 1964), p. 94), wherein these follow from the right to life, since people need physical things to live. But a right to life is not a right to whatever one needs to live; other people may have rights over these other things (see Chapter 3 of this book). At most, a right to life would be a right to have or strive for whatever one needs to live, provided that

having it does not violate anyone else's rights. With regard to material things, the question is whether having it does violate any right of others. (Would appropriation of all unowned things do so? Would appropriating the water hole in Rashdall's example?) Since special considerations (such as the Lockean proviso) may enter with regard to material property, one *first* needs a theory of property rights before one can apply any supposed right to life (as amended above). Therefore the right to life cannot provide the foundation for a theory of property rights.

10. The situation would be different if his water hole didn't dry up, due to special precautions he took to prevent this. Compare our discussion of the case in the text with Hayek, *The Constitution of Liberty*, p. 136; and also with Ronald Hamowy, "Hayek's Concept of Freedom; A Critique," *New Individualist Review*, April 1961, pp. 28–31.

11. I discuss overriding and its moral traces in "Moral Complications and Moral Structures," *Natural Law Forum*, 1968, pp. 1–50.

Robert Nozick (1938–2002) was Pellegrino University Professor at Harvard University. The book from which this selection is taken won the National Book Award in 1975.

16

Capitalism and Morality

James Q. Wilson

Twenty-five years ago, the two founding editors of this magazine published important essays on the cultural and moral status of capitalism.[a] Irving Kristol worried that the most intelligent contemporary defenders of capitalism were now mostly libertarians who praised the market because it produced material benefits and enhanced human freedom but who denied that markets had anything to do with morality. Friedrich Hayek, for example, had written that "in a free society it is neither desirable nor practicable that material rewards should be made generally to correspond to what men recognize as merit." It is not practicable because no one can supply a non-arbitrary definition of merit (or justice); it is not desirable because any attempt to impose such a definition would create a despotism. Kristol worried that people would not support any economic order in which "the will to success and privilege was severed from its moral moorings." Capitalism could not survive if, quoting George Fitzhugh, "none but the selfish virtues are in repute" because in such a society "virtue loses all her loveliness" and social order becomes impossible.

In the same issue, Daniel Bell published his famous essay on "The Cultural Contradictions of Capitalism" in which he suggested that the bourgeois culture–rational, pragmatic, and moral–that had created capitalism was now being destroyed by the success of capitalism. As capitalism replaced feudal stagnation with material success, it replaced tradition with materialism; as privation was supplanted by abundance, prudence was displaced by prodigality. Capitalism created both a parvenu class of rich plutocrats and corporate climbers and a counterculture of critical intellectuals and disaffected youth. The latter began to have a field day exposing what they took to be the greed, hypocrisy, and Philistinism of the former.

Source: *The Public Interest* 121 (Fall, 1995), 42–61.

Capitalism's Great Test

Both Kristol and Bell were amplifying on a theme first developed by Joseph Schumpeter: Contrary to what Marx had taught, capitalism would be destroyed not by its failures but by its successes. Their views did not go unchallenged; a decade later George Gilder, in *Wealth and Poverty*, launched a frontal attack on the Schumpeterian theory (and its development by Kristol and Bell) by arguing that capitalism was, in fact, a highly moral enterprise because it "begins with giving" and requires "faith."

However one judges that debate, it is striking that in 1970–at a time when socialism still had many defenders, when certain American economists (and the CIA!) were suggesting that the Soviet economy was growing faster than the American, when books were being written explaining how Fidel Castro could achieve by the use of "moral incentives" what other nations achieved by employing material ones–Kristol and Bell saw that the great test of capitalism would not be economic but moral. Time has proved them right. Except for a handful of American professors, everyone here and abroad now recognizes that capitalism produces greater material abundance for more people than any other economic system ever invented. The evidence is not in dispute. A series of natural experiments were conducted on a scale that every social scientist must envy: Several nations–China, Germany, Korea, and Vietnam-were sawed in two, and capitalism was installed in one part and "socialism" in the other. In every case, the capitalist part out-produced, by a vast margin, the non-capitalist one.

Moreover, it has become clear during the last half century that democratic regimes only flourish in capitalist societies. Not every nation with something approximating capitalism is democratic, but every nation that is democratic is, to some significant degree, capitalist. (By "capitalist," I mean that production is chiefly organized on the basis of privately owned enterprises, and exchange takes place primarily through voluntary markets.)

If capitalism is an economic success and the necessary (but not sufficient) precondition for democracy, it only remains vulnerable on cultural and moral grounds. That is, of course, why today's radical intellectuals have embraced the more extreme forms of multiculturalism and postmodernism. These doctrines are an attack on the hegemony of bourgeois society and the legitimacy of bourgeois values. The attack takes various forms–denying the existence of any foundation for morality, asserting the incommensurability of cultural forms, rejecting the possibility of textual meaning, or elevating the claims of non-Western (or non-white or non-Anglo) traditions. By whatever route it travels, contemporary radicalism ends with a rejection of the moral claims of capitalism: Because morality is meaningless, because capitalism is mere power, or because markets and corporations destroy culture, capitalism is arbitrary, oppressive, or corrupting.

Most critics of capitalism, of course, are not radicals. Liberal critics recognize, as postmodernists pretend not to, that, if you are going to offer a moral criticism of capitalism, you had better believe that moral judgments are possible and can be made persuasive. To liberals, the failure of capitalism lies in its production of unjustifiable inequalities of wealth and its reckless destruction of the natural environment. Capitalism may produce material abundance, the argument goes, but at too high a price in human suffering and social injustice.

I do not deny that capitalism has costs; every human activity has them. (It was a defender of Capitalism, after all, who reminded us that there is no such thing as a free lunch.) For people worried about inequality or environmental degradation, the question is not whether capitalism has consequences but whether its consequences are better or worse than those of some feasible economic alternative. (I stress "feasible" because I tire of hearing critics compare capitalist reality to socialist–or communitarian or cooperative–ideals. When ideals are converted into reality, they tend not to look so ideal.) And, in evaluating consequences, one must reckon up not simply the costs but the costs set against the benefits. In addition, one must count as benefits the tendency of an economic system to produce beliefs and actions that support a prudent concern for mitigating the unreasonable costs of the system.

Capitalism and Public Policy

By these tests, practical alternatives to capitalism do not seem very appealing. Inequality is a feature of every modern society; Adam Smith expected that it would be a particular feature of what we call capitalism. Indeed, he began *The Wealth of Nations* by setting forth a puzzle that he hoped to solve. It was this: in "the savage nations of hunters and fishers" (what we later learned to call euphemistically "native cultures" or "less-developed nations"), everyone works and almost everyone acquires the essentials of human sustenance, but they tend to be "so miserably poor" that they are reduced, on occasion, to killing babies and abandoning the elderly and the infirm. Among prosperous nations, by contrast, many people do not work at all and many more live lives of great luxury, yet the general level of prosperity is so high that even the poorest people are better off than the richest person in a primitive society. His book was an effort to explain why "the system of natural liberty" would produce both prosperity and inequality and to defend as tolerable the inequality that was the inevitable (and perhaps necessary) corollary of prosperity.

Smith certainly succeeded in the first task but was less successful in the second, at least to judge by the number of people who believe that inequality can be eliminated without sacrificing prosperity. Many nations have claimed to eliminate market-based inequalities, but they have done so only by creating non-market inequalities–a Soviet nomenklatura, a ruling military elite, an elaborate black market, or a set of non-cash perks. Between unconstrained market inequality and the lesser inequality achieved by some redistribution, there is much to discuss and decide, and so the welfare-state debate proceeds. Participants in this debate sometimes forget that the only societies in which such a debate can have much meaning are those that have produced wealth that can be redistributed and that have acquired a government that will do so democratically–in short, capitalist societies.

Similarly with respect to the environment: Only rich (that is, capitalist) nations can afford to worry much about the environment, and only democratic (that is, capitalist) nations have governments that will listen to environmentalists. As with inequality, environmental policies in capitalist systems will vary greatly–from the inconsequential through the prudent to the loony–but they will scarcely exist in non-capitalist ones. If anyone doubted this, they were surely convinced when the Iron Curtain was torn down in 1989, giving the West its first real look at what had been hidden behind the Berlin Wall. Eastern Europe had been turned into a vast toxic waste dump. Vaclav Havel explained why: A government that commands the economy will inevitably command the polity; given a commanding position, a government will distort or destroy the former and corrupt or oppress the latter.

To compel people engaged in production and exchange to internalize all of the costs of production and exchange without destroying production and exchange, one must be able to make proposals to people who do not want to hear such proposals, induce action among people who do not want to act, and monitor performance by people who do not like monitors, and do all of this only to the extent that the gains in human welfare are purchased at acceptable costs. No regime will make this result certain, but only democratic capitalist regimes make it at all possible.

Capitalism creates what are often called "post-material values" that lead some private parties to make environment-protecting proposals. Capitalism, because it requires private property, sustains a distinction between the public and the private sphere and thereby provides a protected place for people to stand who wish to make controversial proposals. And capitalism permits (but does not require) the emergence of democratic institutions that can (but may not) respond to such proposals. Or to put it simply: environmental action arises out of the demands of journalists, professors, foundation executives, and private-sector activists who, for the most part, would not exist in a non-capitalist regime.

Capitalism and the Good Life

Many readers may accept the view that capitalism permits, or possibly even facilitates, the making of desirable public policies but reject the idea that this is because there is anything moral about it. At best, it is amoral, a tool for the achievement of human wants that is neither good nor bad. At worst, it is an immoral system that glorifies greed but, by happy accident, occasionally makes possible popular government and pays the bills of some public-interest lobbies that can get on with the business of doing good. Hardly anyone regards it as moral.

People with these views can find much support in *The Wealth of Nations*. They will recall the famous passage in which Smith points out that it is from the "interest," not the "benevolence," of the butcher, the brewer, or the baker that we expect our dinner. An "invisible hand" leads him to promote the public good, though this is "no part of his intention." Should they study the book more carefully, they will come across passages predicting the degradation of the human spirit that is likely to occur from the division of labor, the incessant seeking after monopoly benefits and political privilege that will follow from the expansion of manufacturing, and the "low profligacy and vice" that will attend upon the growth of large cities. The average worker employed in repetitive tasks will become "stupid and ignorant," the successful merchant living in a big city will become personally licentious and politically advantaged.

Karl Marx, a close student of Smith's writings, had these passages in mind (and, indeed, referred to them) when he drew his picture of the alienation man would suffer as a consequence of private property and capitalism. But Marx (and, in some careless passages, even Smith) had made an error. They had confused the consequences of modernization (that is, of industrialization and urbanization) with the consequences of capitalism. The division of labor can be furthered and large industrial enterprises created by statist regimes as well as by free ones; people will flock to cities to seek opportunities conferred by socialist as well as capitalist economies; a profligate and self-serving elite will spring up to seize the benefits supplied by aristocratic or socialist or authoritarian or free-market systems. Show people the road to wealth, status, or power, and they will rush down that road; many will do some rather unattractive things along the way.

Among the feasible systems of political economy, capitalism offers the best possibility for checking some, but not all, of these tendencies toward degradation and depravity. When Smith suggested that the increased division of labor would turn most workers into unhappy copies of Charlie Chaplin in *Modern Times*, he thought that only public education could provide a remedy. Because he wrote long before the advent of modern technology, he can be forgiven for not having foreseen the tendency of free markets to substitute capital for labor in ways that relieve many workers of precisely those mindlessly repetitive tasks that Smith supposed would destroy the human spirit.

Urbanization is the result of modernity–that is, of the weakening of village ties, the advent of large-scale enterprise, the rise of mass markets, and an improvement in transportation and modernity may have non-capitalist as well as capitalist sources. Mexico City, Sao Paulo, Rio de Janeiro, and Moscow have long been among the dozen largest cities in the world, but, until quite recently (and still quite uncertainly), none of these was located in a nation that could be fairly described as capitalist. They were state-dominated economies, either socialist or mercantilist, and Smith would have had no use for any of them. And, being non-capitalist, most of these states were barely democratic (the USSR not at all). Lacking either a truly private sector or a truly democratic regime, reformist and meliorist tendencies designed to counteract the adverse consequences of massive urbanization were not much in evidence. Americans who rightly think that high rates of crime are characteristic of big cities, but wrongly suppose that this is especially true of capitalist cities, need to spend some time in Moscow, Rio, and Mexico City.

Capitalism creates privilege; socialism creates privilege; mercantilism creates privilege; primitivism creates privilege. Men and women everywhere will seek advantage, grasp power, and create hierarchies. But to the extent that a society is capitalist, it is more likely than its alternatives to sustain challenges to privilege. These arise from economic rivals, privately financed voluntary associations, and democratically elected power-holders; they operate through market competition, government regulation, legal action, and moral suasion. But they operate clumsily and imperfectly, and, in the routine aspects of ordinary morality, they may not operate well enough.

Capitalism and the Morality of Everyday Life

By this point, I may have persuaded a few readers that a system of rival interests has some beneficial moral effects, at least in comparison to statist economies in which the playing field is tilted by one set of greedy actors having decisive power over another. But nothing I have said is inconsistent with the view that capitalism rests on greed and therefore with the view that, at best, capitalism is amoral.

This was not, I think, the view of either Smith or many of the other earlier defenders of capitalism. In *The Wealth of Nations*, he certainly gives an unflinchingly honest account of how self-interest drives economic decisions. But, as Albert Hirschman has suggested, eighteenth-century thinkers did not divide human motives into reason and interests, they divided them into reason, passions, and interests. Having seen the failures of unaided reason and the perils of unguided passions, they hoped that calm interests would inform reason and temper passion.

This was the argument about the beneficial effects of doux commerce–sweet (or gentle) commerce–and it was implicitly taken up by the American Founders when they made their case for a commercial republic. It has been repeated of late by the British anthropologist and philosopher Ernest Gellner who, in reflecting on the failure of European communism, observes that no society can avoid finding a way to channel the desire men have to advance themselves. In traditional and in statist societies, the way to attain wealth is first to attain power, usually by force. But, in market societies, "production becomes a better path to wealth than domination."

Critics of capitalism argue that wealth confers power, and indeed it does, up to a point. But this is not a decisive criticism unless one supposes, fancifully, that there is some way to arrange human affairs so that the desire for wealth vanishes. The real choice is between becoming wealthy by first acquiring political or military power or by getting money directly without bothering with conquest or domination. Max Weber put it this way. All economic systems rest on greed, but capitalism, because it depends on profit, is the one that disciplines greed.

In the process of imposing that discipline, capitalism contributes to self-discipline. It encourages civility, trust, self-command, and cosmopolitanism by first making these traits useful and then making them habitual.

Smith alluded to this when he observed that "commerce and manufactures gradually introduced order and good government, and with them, the liberty and security of individuals...who had before lived almost in a continual state of war with their neighbours and of servile dependency upon their superiors." Lest Smith be interpreted as arguing in favor of central government, he makes clear in other places that the beneficial effects of free and orderly commerce operate chiefly on the character of individuals, especially would-be lords and conquerors now converted into merchants. Nor is he, in the passage quoted above, contradicting his account of the baleful effects on ordinary people of an extreme division of labor; capitalism may bring liberty and security, but it also brings temerity, narrowness, and profligacy. To Smith, sweet commerce was sweet-and-sour.

Smith's ambivalence reflected his analysis of the class structure of society. Commerce would create a middle class whose new members would mostly be decent people. "In the middling and inferior stations of life," he wrote, "the road to virtue and that to fortune...are, happily, very nearly the same." Among people engaged in middle-class occupations, "real and solid professional abilities, joined to prudent, just, firm, and temperate conduct, can very seldom fail of success." In this circumstance, the proverb that "honesty is the best policy" proves true. But matters are very different in "the superior stations of life," in part, because the rich and wellborn live in a self-constructed world of privilege that isolates them from the effective judgment of ordinary (and ordinarily decent) men, and, in part, because merchants and manufacturers will move to cities where they will have countless opportunities to acquire political privileges–monopolies, loopholes, and subsidies–that insulate them from fair market judgments about their products, services, and practices.

Smith's worries, so often quoted, about the affluent few detract, I think, from the much more important impact of capitalism on the not-so-affluent many. An economic system that provides many alternative suppliers for any desired product or service creates an incentive for each supplier to act as if he or she cared about the interests of the customer. Everyone has heard enough stories about surly waiters in Soviet restaurants to acknowledge that communist managers never took customers as seriously as they took commissars, but perhaps this was simply the extreme result of doing business in a pathological society. I doubt that. There has been comparable evidence available in the United States for many years. Until recently, most big airports supplied food to travelers by giving an exclusive franchise to a single vendor. Of late many airports are giving franchises to several rival vendors–McDonald's, Burger King, Taco Bell, and the like–to offer food competitively in airports. Without question, the quality of food and service has gone up.

A skeptic will rejoin that competition merely requires suppliers to act as if they cared about the customer. But, as any economist will note, a firm's reputation has a capital value (it is sometimes measured on the balance sheet as good will) and so business executives who wish to maximize that value will devote a great deal of effort to inculcating a service ethic in their employees. One cannot do that cynically. "If you can fake sincerity, you've got it made," someone once said. That may be true for a few individuals, but organizing such fakery on a large scale is impossible–the teaching will be unconvincing, and the lesson will be ignored.

But acting as if one cared has more than economic significance. Our characters are formed, as Aristotle observed, by the process of habituation. Any process that makes a personal disposition habitual is character forming. Parents know this, which is why they teach good manners to their children by means of constant small reminders and an insistence on routine observances. Though I am aware of no evidence bearing on it, there is little reason to suppose that habituation ends with adulthood or cannot occur outside the family. Are young people who have worked for three years at McDonald's and been taught to parrot learned phrases ("How may I serve you?" "Will that be all?" "Thank you.") more likely on leaving for better jobs to be civil than are similar youngsters who worked in a company that attached no value to civility? I don't know, but I think so.

When Smith wrote that the "understandings of the greater part of men are necessarily formed by their ordinary employments," he was worrying about the harmful effect on the mind of dull and exhausting labor. But the shortened work day and the use of machinery have made this effect much less likely than it was in the eighteenth century. Today, it may be that it is the manners of people that are formed in part by their daily employment.

Capitalist Virtues

Capitalism requires some measure of trust. In any economic system, buying and selling occurs, but voluntary buying and selling on a large scale among strangers requires confidence in fair dealing that cannot depend on one party having much detailed knowledge about the other. Routinized exchanges present some of the same problems as a "Prisoner's Dilemma" in which both participants have an incentive to cheat if they assume they will only play the game–or engage in the exchange–once. The solution to the dilemma lies in repeating the game in conformity with this rule: do to the other party what he has just done to you ("tit for tat," in political scientist Robert Axelrod's phrase), but make your first move a "nice" one in order to encourage the other party to do the same. In some societies, mainly Western ones, this rule is enforced by contract law; in others, notably Eastern ones, by group affiliations. Capitalism takes advantage of this rule in order to create large, permanent markets among strangers that can operate without incessant recourse to retribution. In so doing, it strengthens conformity to the premise on which it depends: some minimum level of trust. This is a moralizing activity even though every customer knows that another rule–caveat emptor–also operates.

In a recent paper, John Mueller of the University of Rochester has observed that price haggling–once a common feature of most markets and still characteristic of some–has been abandoned even though it conferred short-term advantages on the seller. (This was true because sellers, knowing more about their wares than customers, had an advantage over most casual shoppers.) But some sellers discovered that, in the long run, they did more business by setting attractive, fixed prices. This practice lowered transaction costs for customers, thereby enlarging the number of customers.[1] Mueller notes that, as early as 1727, businessman-turned-novelist Daniel Defoe argued against haggling because it encouraged both parties to lie. The rise of fixed-price dealing has shifted misrepresentation from price to quality (or at least to advertising about quality).

Another premise on which capitalism depends is self-command. Smith understood that investment was required for capital to be accumulated and that investment, in turn, required that some people be willing to postpone immediate gratification for later (and larger) benefits. Smith did not explain why we should assume that the number of savers will be sufficient to produce the necessary investment. He observed that "prodigality," the result of a "passion for present enjoyment," will diminish the capital available for economic growth, and so it will be necessary for the "frugal man" to save enough to spare the rest of us from the consequences of our own prodigality. But will this occur? Smith predicts that "the profusion or imprudence of some" will be "always more than compensated for by the frugality and good conduct of others." Why? Well, the desire to save comes from an innate desire to better our condition. But, since only a few save a lot, the desire must be limited to a few. Will they be too few?

People differ in their degree of self-command but are alike in the high regard in which they hold people who display self-command (provided the display is not excessive, as it is with personalities that are miserly or rigid). Self-command is, in short, regarded (up to a point) as a virtue, one that is essential to capitalism and that capitalism strengthens to the extent that it induces more and more people to think about the future. (Indeed, economic growth requires that people have a concept of a secular future, a notion that may well have been absent or meaningless in feudal Europe.) The recent decline in the rate of American private savings corresponds to a period in which self-indulgence has been conspicuous. I have no idea what to make of this parallel except to suggest that a complete understanding will almost surely require a cultural, as well as economic, analysis. If all that mattered were net yields on savings, the Japanese would not be saving anything. Their banks pay very low interest rates, yet their customers save at world-record rates.

Finally, capitalism contributes to cosmopolitanism. This remark will be laughable to any reader who, when hearing the word "capitalist," conjures up an image of George Babbitt or Henry Ford. Capitalism, having been linked by artists to bourgeois culture, has forever been linked to narrow Philistinism. But, long ago, Gary Becker explained why markets are the enemy of racial or ethnic discrimination. Prejudice is costly: it cuts a supplier off from potential customers and an employer off from potential workers, thus reducing sales and raising factor costs.

Embedded in a thoroughly racist community, capitalism can easily exist side by side with prejudice because there are no competitive disadvantages to acting on the basis of prejudice: Since white workers and customers will not mingle with black workers and customers, all employers are on the same footing. But let a crack develop in the unanimity of racist sentiment; let some workers and some customers become indifferent to the racial identity of their colleagues; let nationwide enterprises discover that some customers dislike racism and will make their purchasing decisions on that basis; let this happen, and market pressures will swiftly penalize employers who think that they can, without cost, cater to prejudice.

None of this is to deny the important role played by law, court order, and the example of desegregated government agencies. But imagine rapid desegregation occurring if only law, order, and example were operating. It would be slow, uneven, and painful. Public schools desegregated more slowly than hotels and restaurants not only because white parents cared more about who their children went to school with than about who was in the next hotel room or at the next cafe table but also because school authorities lacked any market incentive to admit more or different pupils. Indeed, a statist economy would not only resist desegregation, it would allocate economic benefits– franchises, licenses, credit–precisely on the basis of political, class, ethnic, or racial status.

Capitalism Against Slavery

In a remarkable essay, historian Thomas L. Haskell of Rice University has connected capitalism to the attack on slavery in a bold and new way. The conventional view among historians of the social-control school has been that reform efforts, including the attack on slavery, were intended to further the hegemonic interests of the bourgeoisie. When abolishing slavery was the most rational way to insure the docility of the workers and enhance the legitimacy of the bourgeoisie, slavery was abolished.

This argument is not crudely Marxist; sophisticated control theorists do not necessarily say that businessmen stood to benefit immediately and materially from an end to slavery. They are even prepared to concede that the business classes deceived themselves about what they were doing. But, what they insist upon is that the bourgeoisie could not really have acted out of altruistic motives. And it does seem strange to think that they might have done so. After all, British capitalists were practicing profitable large-scale agriculture in the West Indies. They had many allies, including customers, in London. Then, all of a sudden, slavery was ended after a public debate that rested almost entirely, as far as I can tell, on humanitarian principles. Control theorists suggest that it came about because the capitalists wanted to enhance their legitimacy by abolishing slave labor so that labor for slave wages would not be suspect. As David Brion Davis put it, the abolitionist movement "helped clear an ideological path for British industrialists" that, by exaggerating the harshness of slavery, "gave sanction to less barbarous modes of social discipline."

Haskell finds this a somewhat tortured argument. Can capitalist opponents of slavery, notably the successful Quaker businessmen of the late eighteenth century, really have thought that their "ideological hegemony" (whatever they thought that might be) would be enhanced by attacking the slave system, and that this was more important to them than what they repeatedly and eloquently said was their motive–namely, the horror they felt toward involuntary servitude?

In place of the social-control theory, Haskell suggests that capitalism supported, and was wholly consistent with, the religious convictions of the Quaker abolitionists. As capitalism spread, it carried with it a universalistic message. An important part was the new, high value attached to keeping promises and the concordant development and enforcement of contract law. As commerce spread, promise keeping and contract writing were increasingly carried on with strangers and foreigners, including Jews, heathens, and Levantines. Capitalism sharpened one's sense of, and commitment to, the future, and it equipped its more skillful practitioners with experience in dealing with contingencies. Successful capitalists learned to deal fairly with distant strangers and thus learned to attach greater importance to individual reliability than to group membership.

Commerce across cultures can be profitable, but it is risky. In coping with the risks, capitalists learned ways of dealing with remote circumstances. They acquired, in Haskell's phrase, "recipes for intervention," or what a social scientist would call a sense of efficacy. By this route, some came to believe that it was possible, as well as desirable, to challenge slavery. Haskell does not argue that capitalism was inherently a moral argument against slavery, only that it was a cultural, as well as economic, movement that contained within its assumptions and practices certain preconditions–beliefs, experiences, recipes– for expanding the humanitarian sensibility to strangers. This cultural change made possible, in about the length of one man's life, the abolition of a practice supported by custom, profits, argument, and property rights.

Capitalism and Bureaucracy

Capitalism is a system of action, but it is also one in which large-scale institutions operate. Like politics, economics creates bureaucracies, and bureaucracies have a logic different from that of either markets or politics. A large enterprise, whether private or public, tends to generate commitments to co-workers and subunits rather than to the enterprise as a whole, to separate employees from the customers or citizens affected by employee actions, and to operate on the basis of standard operating procedures that seem instrumentally rational even when they are substantively irrational. In short, bureaucracy diffuses or displaces the sense of personal responsibility. Firms differ from government agencies in many important respects, but this does not mean that they are free from the vices attendant on large-scale organization. There may be economic returns to scale, but not moral ones.

With all the talk about white-collar crime, we have remarkably little information about what kinds of organizational arrangements stimulate or impede misconduct. Big firms probably are more likely than smaller ones to obey certain laws and regulations because they have a more visible reputation to protect and the financial resources to hire specialists to do the protecting (for example, by discovering and complying with government rules). But big firms may be less inclined to right conduct of a different sort–that is, fair play in the most general sense.

One meaning of fairness is the Golden Rule: Treat customers, workers, and suppliers as you would wish to be treated under the same circumstances. That rule, however, will operate differently when the other party is dealt with at second or third hand, invisibly and impersonally, than when he is confronted personally. Even when we deal with a person face to face, we often find it quite easy to invent rationales for discounting their interests or rejecting their claims: "This guy is (take your pick) different, insincere, or unworthy." But it is much easier to conceive of other people as convenient abstractions when they are known only by labels, words, or numbers, as is likely the case when we are members of a large organization.

Fairness can also be defined as receiving rewards proportional to effort. In face-to-face transactions, effort is the product delivered or the service rendered, and rewards are the cash received or the thanks expressed. In impersonal transactions, effort may be the skill displayed at currying favor from one's superiors and rewards the promotions and preferment that result from successful currying. Bureaucratization not only insulates some parts of a firm from market forces but also isolates them from human forces. Bureaucratization involves specialization that often implies encapsulation, reducing the proportion of workers who deal intimately and regularly with other specialists. (In sociological jargon, there is a decline in boundary-spanning roles.)

Bureaucratization also requires measures of employee achievement that are poor proxies for market success. In a firm, a successful accountant, lawyer, or personnel officer is rarely the one who has increased profits or sales for the enterprise (managers rarely can know whether these people have materially helped or hurt profits); it is the person who has best conformed with higher-level expectations as to how an accountant, lawyer, or personnel officer is supposed to behave (and these may be reasonable, unreasonable, or self-serving expectations).

Robert Jackall, in his book *Moral Mazes*, explores how managers in two large corporations define the rules, and thus implicitly the moral requirements, of their jobs. In both firms, he found struggles for status and dominance, perceived gaps between reward and merit, and a preoccupation with the maintenance of good public relations over sound policy. Managers seeking advancement had to keep their eye out for "the main chance," and that, in turn, meant, among other things, "unrelenting attentiveness to the social intricacies of one's organization." The tone of Jackall's book suggests that he is no friend of corporations, but his detailed observations cannot for that reason be ignored.

Corporate executives are aware that they live at a time when great attention is paid to "corporate responsibility" and "business ethics." Observers who are well-disposed toward capitalism and suspicious of elite fads may dismiss these preoccupations as mere catering to a hostile media. That would be a mistake. Though much of this talk may be fatuous or superficial, the problem of imbuing large-scale enterprise with a decent moral life is fundamental. Chester Barnard made this clear nearly 60 years ago in *The Functions of the Executive*. However ready people are to comply with the self-regarding demands of a group and conform to the narrow culture of an organization, most people know the difference between doing things they are proud to tell their children about and things they hope their children never find out about.

Serious executives know this and worry about it. The emergence of codes of corporate ethics and the emphasis on fashioning a defensible corporate culture are not, I think, merely public relations (though they are sometimes just that). They are, at their best, a recognition that people want to believe that they live and work in a reasonably just and decent world. Americans are gloomy about the decency of their culture and the justice of their politics; it may be one of the supreme ironies of our time that they are often more satisfied with their employer than with their community. If true, Marx has been stood squarely on his head: Life has become more alienating than work.

As Michael Novak has observed, the corporation is an important mediating structure that stands, like the family and the church, between the individual and the state. It constitutes not simply a utilitarian arrangement but a community of sorts that shapes human conduct. People, of course, know the difference between a profit-making firm, on the one hand, and a child-rearing family or a soul-comforting church, on the other. They have different expectations from each. But no economist should suppose that since firms are about profits, that is all they are about, anymore than he should imagine that because families are about sex, that is all they are about. Corporations are not vehicles for realizing the ideal society; one of their good features, as Paul Johnson has noted, is that they attach little value to Utopian causes. But they are systems of human action that cannot for long command the loyalty of their members if their standards of collective action are materially lower than those of their individual members.

Capitalism is not irrelevant to morality: it assumes the existence of certain moral dispositions, strengthens some of these, and threatens still others. The problem for capitalists is to recognize that, while free markets will ruthlessly eliminate inefficient firms, the moral sentiments of man will only gradually and uncertainly penalize immoral ones. But, while the quick destruction of inefficient corporations threatens only individual firms, the slow anger at immoral ones threatens capitalism–and thus freedom–itself.

Notes

a *The Public Interest*, Number 21, Fall 1970.

1 Why, then, does price haggling still occur in the sale of automobiles? In part, it is

because the purchaser, as well as the dealer, has something to sell. The purchaser usually has a used car to trade in and has little incentive to set a fixed price for it. He bargains over what the trade-in is worth and so the dealer must bargain over what the new car is worth. Even here, however, some dealers are experimenting with fixed-price sales.

17

Illusions about Private Property and Freedom

Gerald A. Cohen

1.

In capitalist societies everyone owns something, be it only his own labour power, and each is free to sell what he owns and to buy whatever the sale of it enables him to buy.[1] Many claims made on capitalism's behalf may reasonably be doubted, but here is a freedom which it certainly bestows.

It is clear that under capitalism everyone has this freedom, unless being free to sell something is incompatible with being forced to sell it but I do not think it is. For one is in general free to do anything which one is forced to do.

There are several reasons for affirming this possibly surprising thesis. The most direct argument in favour of it is as follows: you cannot be forced to do what you are not able to do, and you are not able to do what you are not free to do. Hence you are free to do what you are forced to do.

I am not, in the foregoing argument, equating being free to do something with being able to do it.[2] Being free to do *A* is a necessary but not a sufficient condition of being able to do *A*. I may be unable to do something not because I am unfree to, but because I lack the relevant capacity. Thus I am no doubt free to swim across the English Channel, but I am nevertheless unable to. If I were a much better swimmer, but forbidden by well-enforced law to swim it, then, again, I would be unable to swim it. The argument of the last paragraph goes through on what is often called the "negative" or "social" conception of freedom, according to which I am free to do whatever nobody would prevent me from doing. I have no quarrel with that conception in this paper.

A second argument for the claim that I am free to do what I am forced to do is that one way of frustrating someone who would force me to do something is by rendering myself not free to do it: it follows, by contraposition, that if I am forced to do it, I am free to do it. To illustrate: I commit a crime, thereby causing myself to be gaoled, so that I cannot be forced by you to do something

Source: John Mepham and David Hillil Rubin (eds), *Issues in Marxist Philosophy*, *IV* (Atlantic Highlands, NJ: Humanities Press 1979).

I abhor. If you still hope to force me to do it you will have to make me free to do it (by springing me from jail).

Look at it this way: before you are forced to do A, you are, at least in standard cases, free to do A and free not to do A. The force removes the second freedom, but why suppose that it removes the first? It puts no obstacle in the path of your doing A, and you therefore remain free to do it.

We may conclude, not only that being free to do A is compatible with being forced to do A, but that being forced to do A *entails* being free to do A. Resistance to this odd-sounding but demonstrable result reflects failure to distinguish the idea of *being free to do something* from other ideas, such as the idea of *doing something freely*. I am free to do what I am forced to do even if, as is usually true,[3] I do not do it freely, and even though, as is always true, I am not free with respect to whether or not I do it.

I labour this truth—that one is free to do what one is forced to do—because it, and failure to perceive it, help to explain the character and the persistence of a certain ideological disagreement. Marxists say that working class people are forced to sell their labour power. Bourgeois thinkers celebrate the freedom of contract manifest not only in the capitalist's purchase of labour power but also in the worker's sale of it. If Marxists are right[4] working class people are importantly unfree: they are not free not to sell their labour power. But it remains true that (unlike chattel slaves) they are free to sell their labour power. The unfreedom asserted by Marxists is compatible with the freedom asserted by bourgeois thinkers. Indeed: if the Marxists are right the bourgeois thinkers are right, unless they also think, as characteristically they do, that the truth they emphasise refutes the Marxist claim. The bourgeois thinkers go wrong not when they say that the worker is free to sell his labour power, but when they infer that the Marxist cannot therefore be right in his claim that the worker is forced to. And Marxists[5] share the bourgeois thinkers' error when they think it necessary to deny what the bourgeois thinkers say. If the worker is not free to sell his labour power, of what freedom is a foreigner whose work permit is removed deprived?

2. Freedom to buy and sell is one freedom, of which in capitalism there is a great deal. It belongs to capitalism's essential nature. But many think that capitalism is, quite as essentially, a more comprehensively free society. Very many people, including philosophers, who try to speak carefully, use the phrase "free society" as an alternative name for societies which are capitalist.[6] And many contemporary English-speaking philosophers and economists call the doctrine which recommends a purely capitalist society "libertarianism," not, as might be thought more apt, "libertarianism with respect to buying and selling."

It is not only the libertarians themselves who think that is the right name for their party. Many who reject their aims concede the name to them: they agree that unmodified capitalism is comprehensively a realm of freedom. This applies to *some* of those who call themselves "liberals."

These liberals assert, plausibly, that liberty is a good thing, but they say that it is not the only good thing so far, libertarians will agree. But liberals also believe that libertarians wrongly sacrifice other good things in too total defence of the one good of liberty. They agree with libertarians that pure capitalism is liberty pure and simple, or anyway *economic*[7] liberty pure and simple, but they think the various good things lost when liberty pure and simple is the rule justify restraints on liberty. They want a capitalism modified by welfare legislation and state intervention in the market. They advocate, they say, not unrestrained liberty, but liberty restrained by the demands of social and economic security. They think that what they call a free economy is too damaging to those, who, by nature or circumstance, are ill placed to achieve a minimally proper standard of life within it, so they favour, within limits, taxing the better off for the sake of the worse off, although they believe that such taxation reduces liberty. They also think that what they call a free economy is subject to fluctuations in productive activity and misallocations of resources which are potentially damaging to everyone, so they favour measures of interference in the market, although, again, they believe that such interventions diminish liberty. They do not question the libertarian's description of capitalism as the (economically) free society. But they believe that economic freedom may rightly and reasonably be abridged. They believe in a compromise between liberty and other values, and that what is known as the welfare state mixed economy achieves the right compromise.

I shall argue that libertarians, and liberals of the kind described, misuse the concept of freedom. This is not a comment on the attractiveness of the institutions they severally favour, but on the rhetoric they use to describe them. If, however, as I contend, they misdescribe those institutions, then that is surely because the correct description of them would make them less attractive, so my critique of the defensive rhetoric is indirectly a critique of the institutions the rhetoric defends.

My central contention is that liberals and libertarians see the freedom which is intrinsic to capitalism, but do not give proper notice to the unfreedom which necessarily accompanies it.

To expose this failure of perception, I shall criticise a description of the libertarian position provided by Antony Flew in his *Dictionary of Philosophy.* It is there said to be "whole-hearted political and economic liberalism, opposed to any social or legal constraints on individual freedom."[8] Liberals of the kind I described above would avow themselves unwholehearted in the terms of this definition. For they would say that they support certain (at any rate) legal constraints on individual freedom.

Now a society in which there are *no* "social and legal constraints on individual freedom" is perhaps imaginable, at any rate by people who have highly anarchic imaginations. But, be that as it may, the Flew definition misdescribes libertarians, since it does not apply to defenders of capitalism, which is what libertarians profess to be, and are.

For consider. If the state prevents me from doing something I want to do, it evidently places a constraint on my freedom. Suppose, then, that I want to perform an action which involves a legally prohibited use of your property. I want, let us say, to pitch a tent in your large back garden, because I have no home or land of my own, but I have got hold of a tent, legitimately or otherwise. If I now try to do what I want to do, the chances are that the state will intervene on your behalf. If it does, I shall suffer a constraint on my freedom. The same goes for all unpermitted uses of a piece of private property by those who do not own it, and there are always those who do not own it, since "private ownership by one person...presupposes non-ownership on the part of other persons."[9] But the free enterprise economy advocated by libertarians rests upon private property: you can sell and buy only what you respectively own and come to own. It follows that the Flew definition is untrue to its *definiendum*, and that 'libertarianism' is a questionable name for the position it now standardly denotes.

How could Flew publish the definition I have criticised? I do not think he was being dishonest I would not accuse him of appreciating the truth of this particular matter and deliberately falsifying it. Why then is it that Flew, and libertarians like him,[10] see the unfreedom in prospective state interference with your use of your property, but do not see the unfreedom in the standing intervention against my use of it entailed by the fact that it *is* your private property? What explains their monocular vision?

One explanation is a tendency to take as part of the structure of human existence in general, and therefore as no "social or legal constraint" on freedom, any structure around which, *merely as things are*, much of our activity is organised. In capitalist society the institution of private property is such a structure. It is treated as so *given* that the obstacles it puts on freedom are not perceived, while any impingement on private property itself is immediately noticed. Yet private property pretty well *is* a distribution of freedom *and* unfreedom. It is necessarily associated with the liberty of private owners to do as they wish with what they own, but it no less necessarily withdraws liberty from those who do not own it. To think of capitalism as a realm of freedom is to overlook half of its nature. (I am aware that the tendency to this failure of perception is stronger, other things being equal, the more private property a person has. I do not think really poor people need to have their eyes opened to the simple conceptual truth I emphasis I also do not claim that anyone of sound mind will for long deny that private property places restrictions on freedom, once the point has been made. What is striking is that the point so often needs to be made, against what should be *obvious* absurdities, such as Flew's definition of "libertarianism").

I have supposed that to prevent someone from doing something he wants to do is to make him, in that respect, unfree: I am unfree whenever someone interferes, *justifiably or otherwise*, with my actions. But there is a definition of freedom which is implicit in much libertarian writing,[11] and which entails that interference is *not* a sufficient condition of unfreedom. On that definition, which I shall call the *moralised* definition, I am unfree only when someone does or would *unjustifiably* interfere with me. If one now combines this moralised definition of freedom with a moral endorsement of private property, one reaches the result that the protection of legitimate private property cannot restrict anyone's freedom. It will follow from the moral endorsement of private property that you and the police are justified in preventing me from pitching my tent on your land, and, because of the moralised definition of freedom, it will then further follow that you and the police do not thereby restrict my freedom. So here we have another explanation of how intelligent philosophers are able to say that they do about capitalism, private property and freedom. But the characterization of freedom which figures in the explanation is unacceptable. For it entails that a properly convicted murderer is not rendered unfree when he is justifiably imprisoned.

Even justified interference reduces freedom. But suppose for a moment that, as libertarians say or imply, it does not. On that supposition one cannot readily argue that interference with private property is wrong *because* it reduces freedom. For one can no anger take for granted, what is evident on a morally neutral account of freedom, that interference with private property *does* reduce freedom. Under a moralised account of freedom one must abstain from that assertion until one has shown that private property is morally defensible. Yet libertarians tend both to use a moralised definition *and* to take it for granted that interference with private property diminishes the owner's freedom. Yet they can take that for granted only on an account of freedom in which it is equally obvious that the protection of private property diminishes the freedom of nonowners, to avoid which consequence they retreat to a moralised definition of the concept.

Still, libertarians who embrace the moralised definition of freedom need not occupy this inconsistent position. They can escape it by justifying private property on grounds other than considerations of freedom. They can contrive, for example, to represent interference with rightfully held private property as unjust, and *therefore*, by virtue of the moralised definition, invasive of freedom. This is a consistent position.[12] But it still incorporates an unacceptable definition of freedom, and the position is improved[13] if that is eliminated we then have a defence of private property on grounds of justice. Freedom falls out of the picture.[14]

3. I now want to consider a possible response to what I said about pitching a tent on your land. It might be granted that the prohibition on my doing so restricts my freedom, but not, so it might be said, my *economic* freedom. If the connection between capitalism and freedom is overstated by libertarians and others, the possibility that capitalism is *economic* freedom still requires consideration.

The resurrected identification will survive only if the unavailability to me of your garden is no restriction on my economic freedom. I can think of only one reason for saying so. It is that I am not here restricted with respect to whether I may sell something I own, or buy something in exchange for what I own. If that is economic freedom, then my lack of access to your garden does not limit my economic freedom.

A different definition of economic freedom would include in it freedom to use goods and services. It is hard to say whether such a definition is superior to the less inclusive one just considered, since "neither the tradition of political philosophy nor common understanding provides us with a...set of categories of economic liberty" comparable to the acknowledged set of categories of political liberty,[15] perhaps because the boundary of the economic domain is unclear.[16] A reasoned attempt to construct a clear concept of economic freedom might be a valuable exercise, but it is not one which I can report having completed. I am accordingly unable to recommend any particular characterization of economic freedom.

I can nevertheless reply to the present claim, as follows: either economic freedom includes the freedom to use goods and services, or it does not. If it does, then capitalism withholds economic freedom wherever it grants it, as the tent case shows. If, on the other hand, economic freedom relates only to buying and selling, then the case for identifying economic freedom and free enterprise looks better. But we have to define "economic freedom" narrowly to obtain this result. On a wide but eligible definition of economic freedom, capitalism offers a particular limited form of it. On a narrow definition, the limitations recede, but we are now talking about a much narrower freedom.

To those who do not think this freedom is narrow, I offer three comments, which may move them a little:

(i) The freedom in question is, fully described, freedom to sell what I own and to buy whatever the sale of what I own enables me to buy. Importantly, that freedom is not identical with freedom to buy and sell just anything at all, which is much broader, and which is not granted by capitalism. For first, one is evidently not free to sell what belongs to somebody else. This is, to be sure, true by definition: there logically *could* not be that freedom, in any society. But this does not diminish the importance of noticing that capitalism does not offer it.[17] And secondly, one is free to buy, not anything at all, but only that which the sale of what one owns enables one to buy. A poor man is not free to buy a grand piano, even if one necessary condition of that freedom–he is not legally forbidden to do so–is satisfied.

(ii) It is an important fact about freedom in general, and hence about the freedom under discussion, that it comes in degrees. That 1 am free to do something does not say *how* free I am to do that thing, which might be more or less. To cite just one dimension in which freedom's degree varies, my freedom to do A is, other things equal, smaller, the greater is the cost to me of doing A. It might be true of both a poor man and a rich man that each is free to buy an £8 ticket to the opera, yet the rich man's freedom to do so is greater, since, unlike the poor man, he will not have to give up a few decent meals, for example, in order to buy the ticket. Since it is consistent with the capitalist character of a society that it should contain poor people, the buying and selling freedom which capitalism grants universally can be enjoyed in very limited degrees.

Now some will disagree with my claim that freedom varies in degree in the manner just described. They will deny that some people have a higher degree of a certain freedom than others (who also have that freedom), and will say, instead, that for some people it is relatively easy to exercise a freedom which others, who also have it, find it difficult to exercise. But even if they are right, the substance of my case is unweakened. For it is scarcely intelligible that one should be interested in how much freedom people have in a certain form of society without being interested in how readily they are able to exercise it.

(iii) Finally, we should consider the *point* of the freedom to buy and sell, as far as the individual who has it is concerned. For most citizens, most of the time, that point is to obtain goods and services of various sorts. When, therefore, goods and services are available independently of the market, the individual might not feel that his lack of freedom to *buy* them is a particularly significant lack. A lack of freedom to buy medical services is no serious restriction on liberty in a society which makes them publicly available on a decent scale. In a socialist society certain things will be unbuyable, and, consequently, unsellable. But, as long as they are obtainable by other means, one should not exaggerate the gravity of the resulting restrictions on freedom.

Still, restrictions on freedom do result. I may not *want* to buy a medical or an educational service, but I am nevertheless unfree to, if the transaction is forbidden. Note that I would not be unfree to if a certain popular account of freedom were correct, according to which I am unfree only when what I *want* to do is something I shall or would be prevented from doing. But that account is false.[18] There are important connections between freedom and desire, but the straightforward one maintained in the popular account is not among them. Reference to a man's desires is irrelevant to the question "What is he free to do?" but it is, I believe, relevant to the question "How much freedom (comprehensively) does he have?" and consequently to the politically crucial question of comparing the amounts of freedom enjoyed in different societies. As far as I know, the vast philosophical literature on freedom contains no sustained attempt to formulate criteria for answering questions about quantity of freedom. I attempted a discussion of such criteria in an earlier draft of this paper, but the response to it from many friends was so skeptical that I decided to abandon it. I hope to return to it one day, and I hope that others will address it too.

4. I have wanted to show that private property, and therefore capitalist society, limit liberty, but I have not shown that they do so more than communal property and socialist society. Each *form* of society is by its nature congenial and hostile to various sorts of liberty, for variously placed people. And *concrete* societies exemplifying either form will offer and withhold additional liberties whose presence or absence may not be inferred from the nature of the form itself. Which form is better for freedom, all things considered, is a question which may have no answer in the abstract: it may be that which form is better for freedom depends entirely on the historical circumstances.

I am here separating two questions about capitalism, socialism, and freedom. The first, or *abstract* question, is which form of society is, just as such, better for freedom, not, and this is the second, and *concrete* question, which form is better for freedom in the conditions of a particular place and time.[19] The first question is interesting, but difficult and somewhat obscure. I shall try to clarify it presently. I shall then indicate that two distinct ranges of consideration bear on the second question, about freedom in a particular case, considerations which must be distinguished not only for theoretical but also for political reasons.

Though confident that the abstract interpretation of the question, which form, if any, offers more liberty, is meaningful, I am not at all sure what its meaning is. I do not think we get an answer to it favouring one form if and only if that form would in all circumstances provide more freedom than the other. For I can understand the claim that socialism is by nature a freer society than capitalism even though it would be a less free society under certain conditions.

Consider a possible analogy. It will be agreed that sports cars are faster than jeeps, even though jeeps are faster on certain kinds of terrain. Does the abstract comparison, in which sports cars outclass jeeps, mean, therefore, that sports cars are faster on *most* terrains? I think not. It seems sufficient for sports cars to be faster in the abstract that there is some unbizarre terrain on which their maximum speed exceeds the maximum speed of jeeps on any terrain. Applying the analogy, if socialism is said to be freer than capitalism in the abstract, this would mean that there are realistic concrete conditions under which a socialist society would be freer than any concrete capitalist society would be. This, perhaps, is what some socialists mean when they say that socialism is a freer society, for some who say that would acknowledge that in some conditions socialism, or what would pass for it,[20] would be less free than at any rate some varieties of capitalism.

There are no doubt other interesting abstract questions, which do not yield to the analysis just given. Perhaps, for example, the following intractably rough prescription could be made more useable: consider, with respect to each form of society, the sum of liberty which remains when the liberties it withholds by its very nature are subtracted from the liberties it guarantees by its very nature. The society which is freer in the abstract is the one where that sum is larger.

So much for the abstract issue. I said that two kinds of consideration bear on the answer to concrete questions, about which form of society would provide more freedom in a particular here and now. We may look upon each form of society as a set of rates which generates, in particular cases, particular enjoyments and deprivations of freedom. Now the effect of the rules in a particular case will depend, in the first place, on the resources and traditions which prevail in the society in question. But secondly, and distinctly, it will also depend on the ideological and political views of the people concerned. (This distinction is not always easy to make, but it is never impossible to make it). To illustrate the distinction, it could be that in a given case collectivization of agriculture would provide more freedom on the whole for rural producers, were it not for the fact that they do not *believe* it would, and would therefore resist collectivization so strongly that it could be introduced only at the cost of enormous repression. It could be that though socialism might distribute more liberty in Britain now, capitalist ideology is now here so powerful, and the belief that socialism would reduce liberty is, accordingly, so strong, that conditions *otherwise* propitious for realising a socialism with a great deal of liberty are not favourable in the final reckoning, since the final reckoning must take account of the present views of people about how free a socialist society would be.

I think it is theoretically and politically important to attempt a reckoning independent of that final reckoning.

It is theoretically important because there exists a clear question about whether a socialist revolution would expand freedom whose answer is not determined by people's beliefs about what its answer is. *Its* answer might be "yes" even though most people think its answer is "no" and even though, as a result, "no" is the correct answer to the further, "final reckoning" question, for whose separateness I am arguing. Unless one separates the questions, one cannot coherently evaluate the ideological answers to the penultimate question which help to cause the ultimate question to have the answer it does.

It is also politically necessary to separate the questions, because it suits our rulers not to distinguish the two levels of assessment. The Right can often truly say that, all things considered, socialism would diminish liberty, where, however, the chief reason why this is so is that the Right, with its powerful ideological arsenal, have convinced enough people that it is so. Hence one needs to argue for an answer which does not take people's convictions into account, partly of course, in order to combat and transform those convictions. If, on the other hand, you want to defend the status quo, then I recommend that you confuse the questions I have distinguished.

The distinction between concrete questions enables me to make a further point about the abstract question, which *form* of society provides more freedom. We saw above that a plausible strategy for answering it involves asking concrete questions about particular cases. We may now add that the concrete questions relevant to the abstract one are those which prescind from people's beliefs about their answers.

I should add, finally, that people's beliefs about socialism and freedom affect not only how free an achieved socialist society would be, but also how much restriction on freedom would attend the process of achieving it. (Note that there is a somewhat analogous distinction between how much freedom we have in virtue of the currently maintained capitalist arrangements, and how much we have, or lose, because of the increasingly repressive measures used to maintain them). Refutation of bourgeois ideology is an imperative task for socialists, not as an alternative to the struggle for socialism, but as part of the struggle for a socialism which will justify the struggle which led to it.

5. I said above that capitalism and socialism offer different sets of freedoms, but I emphatically do not say that they provide freedom in two different senses of that term. To the claim that capitalism gives people freedom some socialists respond that what they get is *merely bourgeois* freedom. Good things can be meant by that response: that there are important particular liberties which capitalism does not confer; and/or that I do not have freedom, but only a necessary condition of it, when a course of action (for example, skiing) is, though not *itself* against the law, unavailable to me anyway, because other laws (for example, those of private property, which prevent a poor man from using a

rich man's unused skis) forbid me the means to perform it. But when socialists suggest that there is no "real" freedom under capitalism, at any rate for the workers, or that socialism promises freedom of a higher and as yet unrealised kind, then I think their line is theoretically incorrect and politically disastrous. For there is freedom under capitalism, in a plain, good sense, and if socialism will not give us more of it, we shall rightly be disappointed. If the socialist says he is offering a new variety of freedom, the advocate of capitalism will carry the day with his reply that he prefers freedom of the known variety to an unexplained and unexemplified rival. But if, as I would recommend, the socialist argues that capitalism is, all things considered, inimical to freedom *in the very sense* of "freedom" in which, as he should concede, a person's freedom is diminished when his private property is tampered with, then he presents a challenge which the advocate of capitalism, by virtue of his own commitment, cannot ignore.

For it is a contention of socialist thought that capitalism does not live up to its own professions. A fundamental socialist challenge to the libertarian is that pure capitalism does not protect liberty in general, but rather those liberties which are built into private property, an institution which also limits liberty. And a fundamental socialist challenge to the liberal is that the modifications of modified capitalism modify not liberty, but private property, often in the interest of liberty itself. Consequently, transformations far more revolutionary than a liberal would contemplate might be justified on the very same grounds as those which support liberal reform.

A homespun example shows how communal property offers a differently shaped liberty, in no different sense of that term, and, in certain circumstances, more liberty than the private property alternative. Neighbours A and B own sets of household tools. Each has some tools which the other lacks. If A needs tools of a kind which only B has, then, private property being what it is, he is not free to take B's one for a while, even if B does not need it during that while. Now imagine that the following rule is imposed, bringing the tools into partly common ownership: each may take and use a tool belonging to the other without permission provided that the other is not using it and that he returns it when he no longer needs it, or when the other needs it, whichever comes first. *Things being what they are* (a substantive qualification: we are talking, as often we should, about the real world, not about remote possibilities) the communising rule would, l contend, increase tool-using freedom, on any reasonable view. To be sure, some freedoms are removed by the new rule. Neither neighbour is as assured of the same easy access as before to the tools that were wholly his. Sometimes he has to go next door to retrieve one of them. Nor can either now charge the other for use of a tool he himself does not then require. But these restrictions probably count for less than the increase in the range of tools available. No one is as sovereign as before over any tool, so the privateness of the property is reduced. But freedom is probably expanded.

It is true that each would have more freedom still if he were the sovereign owner of *all* the tools. But that is not the relevant comparison. I do not deny that full ownership of a thing gives greater freedom than shared ownership of that thing. But no one did own all the tools before the modest measure of communism was introduced. The kind of comparison we need to make is between, for example, sharing ownership with ninety-nine others in a hundred things and fully owning just one of them. I submit that which arrangement nets more freedom is a matter of cases. There is little sense in one hundred people sharing control over one hundred toothbrushes. There is an overwhelming case, from the point of view of freedom, in favour of our actual practice of public ownership of street pavements. Denationalising the pavements in favour of private ownership of each piece by the residents adjacent to it would be bad for freedom of movement.

But someone will say: ownership of private property is the only example of *full* freedom. Our practice with pavements may be a good one, but no one has full freedom with respect to any part of the pavement, since he cannot, for instance, break it up and put the result to a new use, and he cannot prevent others from using it (except, perhaps, by the costly means of indefinitely standing on it himself, and he cannot even do that when laws against obstruction are enforced). The same holds for all communal possessions. No one is fully free with respect to anything in which he enjoys a merely shared ownership. Hence even if private property entails unfreedom, and even if there is freedom without private property, *there is no case of full freedom which is not a case of private property.* The underlined thesis is unaffected by the arguments against libertarianism in sections 2 and 3 of this paper.

There are two things wrong with this fresh attempt to associate freedom and private property. First, even if it is true that every case of full freedom is a case of private property, a certain number of full freedoms need not add up to more freedom overall than a larger number of partial freedoms: so it is not clear that the underlined thesis supports any interesting conclusion.

The thesis is, moreover, questionable in itself. It is a piece of bourgeois ideology masquerading as a conceptual insight. The argument for the thesis treats freedom fetishistically, as control over *material things.* But freedom, in the central sense of the term with which we have been occupied, is freedom to act, and if there is a concept of full freedom in that central sense, then it is inappropriate, if we want to identify it, to focus, from the start, on control over *things.* I can be fully free to walk to your home when and because the pavement is communally owned, even though I am not free to destroy or to sell a single square inch of that pavement. To be sure, action requires the use of matter, or at least space,[21] but it does not follow that to be fully free to perform an action with certain pieces of matter in a certain portion of space I need full control over the matter and the space, since some forms of control will be unnecessary to the action in question. The rights I need over things to perform a given action depend on the nature of that action.

The thesis under examination is, then, either false, or reducible to the truism that one has full freedom *with respect to a thing* only if one privately owns that thing. But why should we be especially interested in full freedom with respect to a *thing*, unless, of course, we are already ideologically committed to the over-riding importance of private property?

6. Recall the example of the tools, described above. An opponent might say: the rules of private property allow neighbours to *contract* in favour of the stated arrangement. If both would gain from the change, and they are rational, they will agree to it. No communist property rule, laid down independently of contract, is needed.

This is a good reply with respect to the case at hand. For that case my only counter is the weakish one that life under capitalism tends to generate an irrationally strong attachment to purely private use of purely private property, which can lead to neglect of mutually gainful and freedom-expanding options.

That point aside, it must be granted that contracts often establish desirably communal structures, sometimes with transaction costs which communist rules would not impose, but also without the administrative costs which often attach to public regulation.

But the stated method of achieving communism cannot be generalised. We could not by contract bring into shared ownership those non-household tools and resources which Marxists call means of production. They will never be won for socialism by contract,[22] since they belong to a small minority, to whom the rest can offer no quid pro quo. Most of the rest must lease their labour power to members of that minority, in exchange for some of the proceeds of their labour on facilities in whose ownership they do not share.

So we reach, at length, a central charge with respect to freedom which Marxists lay against capitalism, and which is, in my view, well founded: that in capitalist society the great majority of people are forced, because of the character of the society, to sell their labour power to others. In properly refined form, this important claim about capitalism and liberty is, I am sure, correct. I have attempted to refine it elsewhere.[23]

Notes

1. The present paper rewrites and extends arguments first presented on pp. 9–17 of "Capitalism, Freedom and the Proletariat" which appeared in Alan Ryan (ed.), *The Idea of Freedom: Essays in Honour of Isaiah Berlin*, Oxford, 1979. The position of the proletariat with respect to freedom, discussed on pp. 17–25 of that paper, is not treated here. I return to that issue in a forthcoming article on "The Structure of Proletarian Unfreedom".

2. I point this out because the argument was thus misinterpreted by Galen Strawson in a review of *The Idea of Freedom* which appeared in Lycidas, the journal of Wolfson College, Oxford. See *Lycidas*, 7, 1978–9, pp. 35–6.

3. It is not true that whenever I am forced to do something I act unfreely, not, at any rate, if we accept Gerald Dworkin's well-defended claim that "*A* does *X* freely if...*A* does *X* for reasons which he doesn't mind acting from" ("Acting Freely," *Nous*, 1970, p. 381) On this view some forced action is freely performed: if, for example, I am forced to do something which I had wanted to do and had fully intended to do, then, unless I resent the supervenient coercion, I do it freely.

4. I consider whether they are right in the latter half of "Capitalism, Freedom and the Proletariat," and in "The Structure of Proletarian Unfreedom."

5. Such as Ziyad Husami, if he is a Marxist, who says of the wage worker. "Deprived of the ownership of means of production and means of livelihood, he is forced (not free) to sell his labour power to the capitalist." ("Marx on Distributive Justice," *Philosophy and Public Affairs*, Fall, 1978, pp. 51–2). I contend that the phrase in parentheses introduces a falsehood into Husami's sentence, a falsehood which Karl Marx avoided when he said of the worker that "the time for which he is free to sell his labour power is the time for which he is forced to sell it." (*Capital*, I, Moscow, 1961, p. 302).

6. See, for example, Jan Narveson, "A Puzzle about Economic Justice in Rawls' Theory" *Social Theory and Practice*, 1976, p. 3; James Rachels, "What People Deserve," in J. Arthur and W. Shaw (eds.), *Justice and Economic Distribution*, Englewood Cliffs, 1978, p. 151.

7. See p. 229 below on what might be meant by *economic* liberty.

8. *A Dictionary of Philosophy*, London 1979, p. 188.

9. Karl Marx, *Capital* III, Moscow, 1970, p. 812.

10. The question also applies to anti-libertarian liberals of the kind described on pp. 225–226, such as Isaiah Berlin and H. L A. Hart. See "Capitalism, Freedom and the Proletariat," p. 13, on Berlin, and my forthcoming essay "Respecting Private Property," on Hart.

11. And sometimes also explicit: see Robert Nozick, *Anarchy, State and Utopia*, New York, 1974, p. 262.

12. I argued elsewhere that, unlike libertarians, liberals of the kind described on pp. 225–226 *necessarily* proceed inconsistently, that their idea of compromise between freedom and other values requires vacillation between neutral and moralised versions of freedom. But Bill Shaw and Tim Scanlon have convinced me that my argument is inconclusive. See "Capitalism, Freedom and the Proletariat," p. 13.

13. It is improved intellectually in that a certain objection to it no longer applies, but ideologically speaking it is weakened, since there is more ideological power in a recommendation of private property on grounds of justice and freedom—however confused the relationship between them may be—than in a recommendation of private property on grounds of justice alone.

14. The justice argument for private property is not examined in what follows. I deal with it at length in "Respecting Private Property."

15. Thomas Scanlon, "Liberty, Contract and Contribution," in G. Dworkin et al. (eds.), *Markets and Morals*, Washington, 1977, p. 54; and see also p. 57.

16. This suggestion is due to Chris Provis.

17. Cheyney Ryan's discussion of "capacity rights" is relevant here. See his "The Normative Concept of Coercion," *Mind*, forthcoming.

18. See Isaiah Berlin, *Four Essays on Liberty*, Oxford, 1969, pp. xxxviii ff., 139–40. The point was originally made by Richard Wollheim, in a review of Berlin's *Two Concepts of Liberty*. See too Hillel Steiner, "Individual Liberty,' *Proceedings of the Aristotelian Society*, 1974–5, p. 34.

19. One may also distinguish not, as above, between the capitalist form of society and a particular capitalist society, but between the capitalist form in general and specific forms of capitalism, such as competitive capitalism, monopoly capitalism, and so on (I provide a systematic means of generating specific forms in Karl Marx's *Theory of History*, Oxford, 1978, Chapter III, sections (6) and (8)). This further distinction is at the abstract level, rather than between abstract and concrete. I prescind from it here to keep my discussion relatively uncomplicated. The distinction would have to be acknowledged, and employed, in any treatment which pretended to be definitive.

20. Which way they would put it depends on how they would define socialism. If it

is defined as public ownership of the means of production, and this is taken in a narrowly juridical sense, then it is compatible with severe restrictions on freedom. But if, to go to other extreme, it is defined as a condition in which the free development of each promotes, and is promoted by, the free development of all, then only the attempt to institute socialism, not socialism, could have negative consequences for freedom.

21. This fact is emphasised by Hillel Steiner in section III of his "Individual Liberty," but he goes too far when he says: "My theorem is...that *freedom is the personal possession of physical objects*" (p. 48). I claim that the "theorem" is just bourgeois ideology. For further criticism of Steiner, see Onora O'Neill, 'The Most Extensive Liberty:' *Proceedings of the Aristotelian Society,* 1979–80, p. 48.

22. Unless the last act of this scenario qualifies as a contract: in the course of a general strike a united working class demands that private property in major means of production be socialized, as a condition of resumption of work, and a demoralised capitalist class meets the demand. (How, by the way, could "libertarians" object to such a revolution? For hints see Robert Nozick, "Coercion," in P. Laslett *et al.,* (eds.) *Philosophy, Politics and Society,* Fourth Series, Oxford, 1972).

23. See note I above.

G. A. Cohen is Chichele Professor of Social and Political Theory and Fellow of All Souls College, Oxford University. Among his books are *If You're An Egalitarian, How Come You're so Rich?, Karl Marx's Theory of History: A Defense,* and *Labor and Freedom.*

18

Excerpts from "Ethics and Society"

Milton Fisk

Defenders of the capitalist form of society do not defend a right to economic equality. Economic inequality is, they argue, to everyone's advantage. Yet some of these defenders of capitalism are also supporters of liberal democracy. They must then recognize limits to economic inequality beyond which even capitalism should not go. Vast concentrations of economic wealth are sources of political power that strangle the basic liberties of a democratic society. But many defenders of capitalist society maintain that in the US at least these limits to economic inequality have not been reached.

The purpose of this [paper] is to show that the arguments justifying the existing high degree of economic inequality fall apart. To show this it will not be necessary to defend, or to reject, the right to complete economic equality. Nonetheless, this [paper] points in an egalitarian direction. For it shows also that the degree of economic inequality inevitable within even a reformed capitalist society cannot be justified from the perspective of working-class morality.

1 Economic Inequality

According to many writers on US society, the stage of widespread affluence has been reached within the US. There is, on the one hand, a reduced level of economic inequality, and there is, on the other hand, an elimination of the lower classes as a majority in favour of a large and prosperous middle class. The misery and inequality that characterized nineteenth- and early twentieth-century capitalism have been redeemed with the arrival of the "affluent society." This picture, however, conceals the urgent problem of economic inequality within the US. As Gabriel Kolko notes in his pathbreaking dissenting work on income distribution, "The predominantly middle-class society is only an image in the minds of isolated academicians."[1]

Source: Milton Fisk, *Ethics and Society* (New York: New York University Press, 1980).

First let us look at the distribution of before-tax personal, as opposed to corporate, income during the period 1910–70 to get some idea as to whether there has been a significant trend toward equality. To do this we can consider families as broken up into five groups of equal size, ranging from those with the highest to those with the lowest income. (People living in families make up roughly 90 per cent of the US population.) *In the sixty-year period considered, families in the highest fifth received between 40 and 45 per cent of all family income.* That is, they received at least two times more than they would have if every family received the same income. Despite variations from year to year, there is no overall trend in this period toward a significantly smaller share of the national income for the richest fifth. The middle fifth has received between 15 and 18 per cent of all family income. This means that it received over the entire sixty-year period less than it would have if income were egalitarian. For this group the trend, within these narrow limits, has been for a slight rise in its share of income, but after World War II that rise stopped completely. Finally, what about the families in the poorest quintile? That group has received between 4 and 6 per cent of the national personal income, which runs up to five times less than it would receive under equality. The overall trend has been for families in this bottom group to get proportionately the same during the sixty-year period. As regards income in the US, then, there is significant and continuing inequality.[2] The top fifth as a whole takes six to ten times more of the national family income than does the bottom fifth. (Data for non-family persons shows even greater inequality.)

Our data has so far been taken on before-tax income. Will not taxation make the picture one of greater equality? It does change the picture as regards equality but only in an insignificant way. Many taxes are regressive: they are a larger fraction of lower than of higher incomes. Social security taxes, property taxes, and sales taxes are all regressive. It cannot be expected that these would provide a shift toward equality. But even the federal income tax, which is progressive, has failed to do more than decrease by two per cent the share of national income of the top fifth. The increase in the share of the bottom fifth resulting from federal income taxes has remained a fraction of a per cent. Moreover, the percentage of all taxes coming from the non-owning classes has been rising steadily since World War II. Taxes have, then, failed to equalize income significantly.[3]

We are dealing with a society in which private ownership of the means of production is a fundamental feature. Some personal income comes from ownership, to be sure, but one cannot say exactly how wealth is distributed simply on the basis of knowing how income is distributed. For one thing, a significant but variable share of returns from ownership is invested in new means of production and does not appear as dividend income. Nonetheless, in a capitalist society we can predict that wealth, like income, is unevenly distributed. It is highly concentrated in the hands of a very few owners: they own the plants, the trucks, the warehouses, the mines, the office buildings, the large estates, and the objects of art. The poor are often net holders of "negative wealth" because of their debts. *Between 1810 and 1969, the concentration of wealth has remained remarkably constant; the top one per cent as regards wealth has held between 20 and 30 per cent of all the wealth in the US.* In 1962 the poorest 20 per cent held less than one-half of one per cent of the nation's wealth.[4]

Nonetheless, some currency has been given to the view that corporate ownership has become widespread and that workers are now significant owners. Stock ownership is, indeed, more widespread, but this has not seriously affected the high degree of concentration of stock ownership in the hands of the wealthiest.

By 1962, the wealthiest one percent of the population still held 72 percent of the nation's corporate stock. In that year, the wealthiest one percent also held 48 percent of the nation's bonds, 24 percent of the loans, and 16 percent of the real estate.[5] Clearly then wealth is even less equitably distributed than income in the US, and the inequality has been one of long duration. Pensions for workers account for nearly ten percent of corporate stock. This may provide workers with security after retirement, but it does not give them the power of wealth holders. The reason is that they have no control over these pension funds, which merely add power to the financial institutions that manage them....

A large prosperous middle class has by no means replaced the struggling lower classes as the majority class. With more than half of the people living below the modest but adequate budget of the BLS, the underbelly of US capitalist society is a deprived majority, just as it was fifty years ago. "In advanced capitalist societies, the costs of staying out of poverty (i.e., of satisfying invariant subsistence needs) grows as the economy grows. Consequently, there is no long-term tendency in advanced capitalist societies for the incidence of poverty to decrease significantly as the economy grows."[6] The economic inequality of US society is not just relative inequality, for it is an inequality that means deprivation for a sizeable chunk of the society.

2 Ownership and Productivity

There are several strategies used by spokespersons of the ruling class to defend the situation of inequality described above. The first defence rests on the rights of ownership. The second rests on the need for inequality in order to increase productivity. In the next section, a third strategy will be discussed: it rests on the notion of a fair wage.

According to the *first defence* of inequality, those who have put their hard-earned money into a business enterprise have the right to appropriate the fruits of that enterprise and divide them according to their own decisions. Thus the product that workers have made is controlled by owners and not by the workers. Owners are within their rights to divide the product in such a way that inequality is great and poverty widespread. An entire web of ideology has been woven on this basic frame of the rights of ownership. Part of that web is the system of law, backed by police force, entitling the owner to the fruits of the worker. From the perspective of members of the working class, there are several holes in this defence. These holes show that what is built on the frame of ownership rights is indeed only ideology.

On the one hand, if ownership rights lead to continued inequality and poverty, then from a working-class perspective there simply are no such rights. The attitude that ownership of the means of production is sacred merely protects the owners at the expense of those who suffer the resulting inequality. A right is more than such an attitude; it must be justified and indeed justified from a class standpoint. Economic inequality can be justified by ownership rights only if there are such rights. There may well be such rights from the perspective of the ruling class. Yet the continued inequality and poverty resulting from ownership are evidence favouring the view that relative to the working class owners have no legitimate right to the fruits of enterprise.

On the other hand, the basis given for the justification of the owner's right to the fruits of enterprise is not adequate. That basis was the hard work of the investor. Investment, however, is an on-going process in a viable firm. The initial investment is followed by many subsequent investments. Let us grant that the owner has worked hard—whether in the form of the honest toil of the self-employed person or in the form of the forcible plunder of the syndicated criminal—to accumulate the initial investment. But when the plant is rebuilt or expanded, the new investment will be possible only because of the hard work of the workers. Once new investment has been made, there is no longer the same basis for saying that the original owner has the right to control the entire product of the new investment. The logic of "hard work" applies here too. If the owner worked hard to accumulate the initial investment it is equally true that the workers worked hard to make the new investment possible. Thus, in a viable firm, the workers should, on the logic of hard work, have a right to appropriate an ever increasing share of the product. The capitalist's own logic backfires!...

According to the *second defence* of inequality, significant inequality with poverty at the bottom is a necessary condition for making the society as affluent as it is. In a widely published newspaper article entitled "Morality and the Pursuit of Wealth" appearing in July 1974, the President of the US Chamber of Commerce, Arch Booth, said the realization of equality by the transfer of wealth from the haves to the have-nots would lessen the "work incentive of the most productive members of society" and endanger "the ability of the economic system to accumulate capital for new productive facilities." Booth's solution is to let the rich keep on investing in productive facilities thereby increasing the share the poor get through better wages and higher employment.

There is one glaring fallacy in this argument. It is the logical fallacy of an "incomplete disjunction." The disjunction Booth offers us is that *either* we have a forced redistribution of income within capitalism *or* we let the income of the non-owners rise naturally by increasing investment. But the disjunction needs to be expanded to include at least one more alternative: beyond capitalism, it is possible to expand productive facilities through the investment of collective rather than of private capital. In one form of collective ownership, workers would manage the investment of collective capital in order to advance their interests. In this case, the inequality in both wealth and income needed for growth under private capitalism becomes unnecessary. Without significant inequality, private capitalism would lack the centres of economic power needed to put large amounts of labour to work in order to produce a surplus for growth. The model here for a system of collective ownership of the means of production is not that of nationalized industry run by a bunch of officials who are not controlled by workers. This would be the bureaucratic model found in places like the USSR which are no longer private capitalist societies. Rather, the model is that of a workers' democracy in which democracy extends down to the workplace and in which workplaces are coordinated by a council of representatives from each. This socialist alternative is sufficient to make Booth's disjunction incomplete....

3 A Fair Wage

A *third strategy* for defending the inequality and the poverty that is to be found today in the US introduces the concept of compensation for work. The defence is that labour is sold on the free market and, on the whole, the free market determines a *just* price for things. Thus, since inequality and poverty are, in part, a result of the free market for labour, there is no right to economic equality or even to a "modest budget." A free market must not involve the use of power by those who exchange their goods and services within it to coerce those with whom they exchange.

This argument seems to leave open the possibility that wages should mount and thus that the worker should come closer to the owner in economic status. But in fact this possibility is not open. As pointed out in Section I, the range of inequality and the degree of poverty in the US have remained remarkably constant. The majority of the people are at or below the level of existence provided by the modest budget. Because of the greater power and organization of the owning class, the wages and salaries of workers remain at a level that allows them merely to perform their jobs well and to raise a new generation of workers. (Differences between the wages of, say, industrial and clerical workers need to be viewed against the background of a general pull toward this subsistence level.) To perform well and to reproduce themselves they have been forced to purchase the ever more elaborate and hence more expensive means of satisfying survival needs and the needs specific to their jobs. Short-term variations in the supply of and demand for labour are only part of this long-term pattern of compensating workers at a subsistence level. At this level, there is nothing much left over for savings and investments that might narrow the gap between them and the owning class....

What, then, is a fair wage from the perspective of the working class? Suppose we are calves who face the prospect of going to slaughter as one-year olds. The farmers who send us to slaughter find that this is the age at which to realize a maximum profit on us. So one year is the 'fair' time, from the perspective of the farmers, for calves to enjoy themselves before slaughter. An inquisitive calf poses the question, "What is the true 'fair' time for cattle to live before slaughter? Is it two years, or even three?" A selfish calf who has no regard for the farmer and the future of cattle farming generally shouts, "Stop quibbling; we should demand a moratorium on beef eating. An end to the slaughter of cattle!" Similarly, Marx said that the slogan, "A fair day's wage for a fair day's work!" should be replaced by the slogan, "An end to the wage system!"[7] Instead of the wage system, work should be done in such a way that the workers' compensation is not just a function of the greater power of a non-working ruling class.

The wage system is a system that in advanced industrial countries has been central to the domination of lower classes by a ruling class. Through that system people are set to work in order to preserve or increase the control of wealth by and, thus, the power of a minority class. They are thus given from what they produce only what is needed to reproduce their labour. When part of the product of workers is used in this way to perpetuate and strengthen the domination of a non-working class, workers are properly said to be "exploited." Acceptance of the wage system and plans to reform it from within do not face up to the key role wages play in domination. When workers themselves decide how they are to be compensated out of what they produce, the wage system has ceased to exist and along with it exploitation....

The struggle for higher income begins the organization of people for the collective action that is needed to abolish the wage system itself. This long-term perspective has for some time been forgotten by trade unions everywhere. Their leaders advocate accommodation with the existing system of domination of working people. These leaders talk about a fair wage but they mean only the wages and benefits they think they can wheedle out of the owners. Their conception of fairness and of rights is no longer a class conception. A class conception makes overthrowing the wage system a right of working people.

4 A Just Distribution

Let us leave defences of present economic inequality and take up a proposal for limiting inequality. If capitalist arguments justifying present inequality fail, then where is the line to be drawn for an acceptable degree of inequality? Our problem is how to distribute a product that has come about through the combined efforts of people in different roles. Since isolated producers are the exception, we cannot start with the assumption that there is a product to which an individual producer is "entitled" because he or she is "responsible" for that product.[8] In deciding on a principle of just distribution there are two factors to be considered.

On the one hand, there is the average amount of goods per individual in the population, and, on the other hand, there is the degree of inequality with which goods are actually parceled out to individuals. Increasing the average amount of goods per individual might increase the inequality of distribution, whereas decreasing the inequality in distribution might decrease the average per individual. In capitalism we saw that inequality of wealth is a condition of economic growth. Also, inequality of income within the working class weakens solidarity, making possible a greater surplus and hence greater growth. If strict equality means poverty all around, we might recoil from strict equality and look for a balance between a large average amount and considerable equality. But so far we have no clue as to where to strike this balance.

John Rawls has recently proposed an interesting way of balancing a high average amount of goods with a low degree of inequality.[9] The idea is that we are to avoid demanding such a low degree of inequality that the worst off are penalized by getting less than they would with a higher degree of inequality. We are to avoid only those high degrees of inequality that are arrived at by preventing the worst off from getting the most they could get.

Rawls formulated this in his Principle of Difference which tells us to "maximize the expectations of the least favoured position"....

[But] Rawls talks about distribution without relating it to production. He assumes wrongly that the validity of his principle is absolute, rather than relative to circumstances within production. One thing is certain: In capitalist society there is not the least chance that the Rawlsian scheme could be put into practice. The reason is simply that the organization of production in a capitalist society centres around increasing productive facilities through the making of profits. The class of owners would not advance the interests characteristic of their class by agreeing to maximize the expectations of the least favoured. Given its power, this class would block the realization of the scheme. Suppose, though, that some mode of production would allow for distribution in accordance with the Principle of Difference. Should not one simply choose to bring about such a mode of production? Certainly–if the Principle of Difference is valid. But its validity is relative to production in the following way. Validity in general is relative to classes, and classes are essential roles in a given mode of production. One should, then, choose to realize the principle only if it is valid relative to one's class. Nonetheless, that class might have to change the existing mode of production in order to realize the new distribution. Even though the capitalist mode of production excludes the application of the Principle of Difference, it may be a valid principle for one of the lower classes within capitalism.

A distributional plan is not just because it is elegant or intuitive but because it answers to needs arising in production. Not only the actual but also the just distribution is dependent on production.

Notes

1. Gabriel Kolko, *Wealth and Power in America* (Praeger, New York, 1962), p. 108.

2. These data are based on tables in Kolko, *Wealth and Power in America*, p. 14, and in Frank Ackerman and Andrew Zimbalist, "Capitalism and Inequality in the United States," in *The Capitalist System*, 2nd ed., p. 298.

3. Kolko, *Wealth and Power in America*, Ch. II, and Ackerman and Zimbalist

"Capitalism and Inequality in the United States," in *The Capitalist System*, 2nd ed., p. 303. In Sweden, by contrast, taxes change the ratio of the bottom third to that of the top third from 38 to 48 percent.

4. Lititia Upton and Nancy Lyons, *Basic Facts: Distribution of Personal Income and Wealth in the United States* (Cambridge Institute, 1878 Massachusetts Ave., Cambridge, Mass., 1972), p. 67 and Ackerman and Zimbalist, "Capitalism and Inequality in the United States," in *The Capitalist System*, 2nd ed., p. 301.

5. Upton and Lyons, *Basic Facts*, p. 31

6. Bernard Gendron, "Capitalism and Poverty," *Radical Philosophers' Newsjournal*, 4, January 1975, p. 13. This essay appears as Ch. XII of Gendron's *Technology and the Human Condition* (St. Martin's Press, New York, 1977).

7. Karl Marx, *Wages, Price, and Profit* (1865) (Foreign Language Press, Peking, 1970), Ch. XIV.

8. On entitlement, see Robert Nozick, *Anarchy, State, and Utopia* (Basic Books, New York, 1974), Ch. VII.

9. Rawls, *A Theory of Justice*, pp. 78–80.

19

Justifying Intellectual Property

Edwin C. Hettinger

Property institutions fundamentally shape a society. These legal relationships between individuals, different sorts of objects, and the state are not easy to justify. This is especially true of intellectual property. It is difficult enough to determine the appropriate kinds of ownership of corporeal objects (consider water or mineral rights); it is even more difficult to determine what types of ownership we should allow for noncorporeal, intellectual objects, such as writings, inventions, and secret business information. The complexity of copyright, patent, and trade secret law reflects this problem.

According to one writer "patents are the heart and core of property rights, and once they are destroyed, the destruction of all other property rights will follow automatically, as a brief postscript."[1] Though extreme, this remark rightly stresses the importance of patents to private competitive enterprise. Intellectual property is an increasingly significant and widespread form of ownership. Many have noted the arrival of the "post-industrial society"[2] in which the manufacture and manipulation of physical goods is giving way to the production and use of information. The result is an ever-increasing strain on our laws and customs protecting intellectual property.[3] Now, more than ever, there is a need to carefully scrutinize these institutions.

As a result of both vastly improved information handling technologies and the larger role information is playing in our society, owners of intellectual property are more frequently faced with what they call "piracy" or information theft (that is, unauthorized access to their intellectual property). Most readers of this article have undoubtedly done something considered piracy by owners of intellectual property. Making a cassette tape of a friend's record, videotaping television broadcasts for a movie library, copying computer programs or using them on more than one machine, photocopying more than one chapter of a book, or two or more articles by the same author–all are examples of alleged infringing activities. Copyright, patent, and trade secret

Source: *Philosophy and Public Affairs* 18 (1989), 31–32. Copyright © The Johns Hopkins University Press.

violation suits abound in industry, and in academia, the use of another person's ideas often goes unacknowledged. These phenomena indicate widespread public disagreement over the nature and legitimacy of our intellectual property institutions. This article examines the justifiability of those institutions.

Copyrights, Patents, and Trade Secrets

It is commonly said that one cannot patent or copyright ideas. One copyrights "original works of authorship," including writings, music, drawings, dances, computer programs, and movies; one may not copyright ideas, concepts, principles, facts, or knowledge. Expressions of ideas are copyrightable; ideas themselves are not.[4] While useful, this notion of separating the content of an idea from its style of presentation is not unproblematic.[5] Difficulty in distinguishing the two is most apparent in the more artistic forms of authorship (such as fiction or poetry), where style and content interpenetrate. In these mediums, more so than in others, *how* something is said is very much part of *what* is said (and vice versa).

A related distinction holds for patents. Laws of nature, mathematical formulas, and methods of doing business, for example, cannot be patented. What one patents are inventions—that is, processes, machines, manufacturers, or compositions of matter. These must be novel (not previously patented); they must constitute nonobvious improvements over past inventions; and they must be useful (inventions that do not work cannot be patented). Specifying what sorts of "technological recipes for production"[6] constitute patentable subject matter involves distinguishing specific applications and utilizations from the underlying unpatentable general principles.[7] One cannot patent the scientific principle that water boils at 212 degrees, but one can patent a machine (for example, a steam engine) which uses this principle in a specific way and for a specific purpose.[8]

Trade secrets include a variety of confidential and valuable business information, such as sales, marketing, pricing, and advertising data, lists of customers and suppliers, and such things as plant layout and manufacturing techniques. Trade secrets must not be generally known in the industry, their nondisclosure must give some advantage over competitors, and attempts to prevent leakage of the information must be made (such as pledges of secrecy in employment contracts or other company security policies). The formula for Coca-Cola and bids on government contracts are examples of trade secrets.

Trade secret subject matter includes that of copyrights and patents: anything which can be copyrighted or patented can be held as a trade secret, though the converse is not true. Typically a business must choose between patenting an invention and holding it as a trade secret. Some advantages of trade secrets are

1. they do not require disclosure (in fact they require secrecy), whereas a condition for granting patents (and copyrights) is public disclosure of the

invention (or writing);

2. they are protected for as long as they are kept secret, while most patents lapse after seventeen years; and

3. they involve less cost than acquiring and defending a patent.

Advantages of patents include protection against reverse engineering (competitors figuring out the invention by examining the product which embodies it) and against independent invention. Patents give their owners the *exclusive* right to make, use, and sell the invention no matter how anyone else comes up with it, while trade secrets prevent only improper acquisition (breaches of security).

Copyrights give their owners the right to reproduce, to prepare derivative works from, to distribute copies of, and to publicly perform or display the "original work of authorship." Their duration is the author's life plus fifty years. These rights are not universally applicable, however. The most notable exception is the "fair use" clause of the copyright statute, which gives researchers, educators, and libraries special privileges to use copyrighted material.[9]

Intellectual Objects as Nonexclusive

Let us call the subject matter of copyrights, patents, and trade secrets "intellectual objects."[10] These objects are nonexclusive: they can be at many places at once and are not consumed by their use. The marginal cost of providing an intellectual object to an additional user is zero, and though there are communications costs, modern technologies can easily make an intellectual object unlimitedly available at a very low cost.

The possession or use of an intellectual object by one person does not preclude others from possessing or using it as well.[11] If someone borrows your lawn mower, you cannot use it, nor can anyone else. But if someone borrows your recipe for guacamole, that in no way precludes you, or anyone else, from using it. This feature is shared by all sorts of intellectual objects, including novels, computer programs, songs, machine designs, dances, recipes for Coca-Cola, lists of customers and suppliers, management techniques, and formulas for genetically engineered bacteria which digest crude oil. Of course, sharing intellectual objects does prevent the original possessor from selling the intellectual object to others, and so this sort of use is prevented. But sharing in no way hinders *personal* use.

This characteristic of intellectual objects grounds a strong *prima facie* case against the wisdom of private and exclusive intellectual property rights. Why should one person have the exclusive right to possess and use something which all people could possess and use concurrently? The burden of justification is very much on those who would restrict the maximal use of intellectual objects. A person's right to exclude others from possessing and using a physical object can be justified when such exclusion is necessary for this person's own possession and unhindered use. No such justification is available for exclusive possession and use of intellectual property.

One reason for the widespread piracy of intellectual property is that many people think it is unjustified to exclude others from intellectual objects.[12] Also, the unauthorized taking of an intellectual object does not feel like theft. Stealing a physical object involves depriving someone of the object taken, whereas taking an intellectual object deprives the owner of neither possession nor personal use of that object–though the owner is deprived of potential profit. This nonexclusive feature of intellectual objects should be kept firmly in mind when assessing the justifiability of intellectual property.

Owning Ideas and Restrictions on the Free Flow of Information

The fundamental value our society places on freedom of thought and expression creates another difficulty for the justification of intellectual property. Private property enhances one person's freedom at the expense of everyone else's. Private intellectual property restricts methods of acquiring ideas (as do trade secrets), it restricts the use of ideas (as do patents), and it restricts the expression of ideas (as do copyrights)–restrictions undesirable for a number of reasons. John Stuart Mill argued that free thought and speech are important for the acquisition of true beliefs and for individual growth and development.[13] Restrictions on the free flow and use of ideas not only stifle individual growth, but impede the advancement of technological innovation and human knowledge generally.[14] Insofar as copyrights, patents, and trade secrets have these negative effects, they are hard to justify. Since a condition for granting patents and copyrights is public disclosure of the writing or invention, these forms of intellectual ownership do not involve the exclusive right to possess the knowledge or ideas they protect. Our society gives its inventors and writers a legal right to exclude others from certain uses of their intellectual works in return for public disclosure of these works. Disclosure is necessary if people are to learn from and build on the ideas of others. When they bring about disclosure of ideas which would have otherwise remained secret, patents and copyrights enhance rather than restrict the free flow of ideas (though they still restrict the idea's widespread use and dissemination). Trade secrets do not have this virtue. Regrettably, the common law tradition which offers protection for trade secrets encourages secrecy. This makes trade secrets undesirable in a way in which copyrights or patents are not.[15]

Labor, Natural Intellectual Property Rights, and Market Value

Perhaps the most powerful intuition supporting property rights is that people are entitled to the fruits of their labor. What a person produces with her own intelligence, effort, and perseverance ought to belong to her and to no one else. "Why is it mine? Well, it's mine because I made it, that's why. It wouldn't have existed but for me."

John Locke's version of this labor justification for property derives property rights in the product of labor from prior property rights in one's body.[16] A person owns her body and hence she owns what it does, namely, its labor. A person's labor and its product are inseparable, and so ownership of one can be secured only by owning the other. Hence, if a person is to own her body and thus its labor, she must also own what she joins her labor with–namely, the product of her labor.

This formulation is not without problems. For example, Robert Nozick wonders why a person should gain what she mixes her labor with instead of losing her labor. (He imagines pouring a can of tomato juice into the ocean and asks whether he thereby ought to gain the ocean or lose his tomato juice.)[17] More importantly, assuming that labor's fruits are valuable, and that laboring gives the laborer a property right in this value, this would entitle the laborer only to the value she added, and not to the *total* value of the resulting product. Though exceedingly difficult to measure, these two components of value (that attributable to the object labored on and that attributable to the labor) need to be distinguished.

Locke thinks that until labored on, objects have little human value, at one point suggesting that labor creates 99 percent of their value.[18] This is not plausible when labor is mixed with land and other natural resources. One does not create 99 percent of the value of an apple by picking it off a tree, though some human effort is necessary for an object to have value for us.

What portion of the value of writings, inventions, and business information is attributable to the intellectual laborer? Clearly authorship, discovery, or development is necessary if intellectual products are to have value for us; we could not use or appreciate them without this labor. But it does not follow from this that all of their value is attributable to that labor. Consider, for example, the wheel, the entire human value of which is not appropriately attributable to its original inventor.[19]

The value added by the laborer and any value the object has on its own are by no means the only components of the value of an intellectual object. Invention, writing, and thought in general do not operate in a vacuum; intellectual activity is not creation *ex nihilo*. Given this vital dependence of a person's thoughts on the ideas of those who came before her, intellectual products are fundamentally social products. Thus even if one assumes that the value of these products is entirely the result of human labor, this value is not entirely attributable to *any particular laborer* (or small group of laborers).

Separating out the individual contribution of the inventor, writer, or manager from this historical/social component is no easy task. Simply identifying the value a laborer's labor adds to the world with the market value or the resulting product ignores the vast contributions of others. A person who relies on human intellectual history and makes a small modification to produce something of great value should no more receive what the market will bear than should the last person needed to lift a car receive full credit for lifting it. If laboring gives the laborer the right to receive the market value of the resulting product, this market value should be shared by all those whose ideas contributed to the origin of the product. The fact that most of these contributors are no longer present to receive their fair share is not a reason to give the entire market value to the last contributor.[20]

Thus an appeal to the market value of a laborer's product cannot help us here. Markets work only after property rights have been established and enforced, and our question is what sorts of property rights an inventor, writer, or manager should have, given that the result of her labor is a joint product of human intellectual history.

Even if one could separate out the laborer's own contribution and determine its market value, it is still not clear that the laborer's right to the fruits of her labor naturally entitles her to receive this. Market value is a socially created phenomenon, depending on the activity (or nonactivity) of other producers, the monetary demand of purchasers, and the kinds of property rights, contracts, and markets the state has established and enforced. The market value of the same fruits of labor will differ greatly with variations in these social factors.

Consider the market value of a new drug formula. This depends on the length and the extent of the patent monopoly the state grants and enforces, on the level of affluence of those who need the drug, and on the availability and price of substitutes. The laborer did not produce these. The intuitive appeal behind the labor argument—"I made it, hence it's mine"—loses its force when it is used to try to justify owning something others are responsible for (namely, the market value). The claim that a laborer, in virtue of her labor, has a "natural right" to this socially created phenomenon is problematic at best.

Thus, there are two different reasons why the market value of the product of labor is not what a laborer's labor naturally entitles her to. First, market value is not something that is produced by those who produce a product, and the labor argument entitles laborers only to the products of their labor. Second, even if we ignore this point and equate the fruits of labor with the market value of those fruits, intellectual products result from the labor of many people besides the latest contributor, and they have claims on the market value as well.

So even if the labor theory shows that the laborer has a natural right to the fruits of labor, this does not establish a natural right to receive the full market value of the resulting product. The notion that a laborer is naturally entitled as a matter of right to receive the market value of her product is a myth. To what extent individual laborers should be allowed to receive the market value of their products is a question of social policy; it is not solved by simply insisting on a moral right to the fruits of one's labor.[21]

Having a moral right to the fruits of one's labor might also mean having a right to possess and personally use what one develops. This version of the labor theory has some force. On this interpretation, creating something through labor gives the laborer a *prima facie* right to possess and personally use it for her own benefit. The value of protecting individual freedom guarantees this right as long as the creative labor, and the possession and use of its product, does not harm others.

But the freedom to exchange a product in a market and receive its full market value is again something quite different. To show that people have a right to this, one must argue about how best to balance the conflicts in freedoms which arise when people interact. One must determine what sorts of property rights and markets are morally legitimate. One must also decide when society should enforce the results of market interaction and when it should alter those results (for example, with tax policy). There is a gap—requiring extensive argumentative filler—between the claim that one has a natural right to possess and personally use the fruits of one's labor and the claim that one ought to receive for one's product whatever the market will bear.

Such a gap exists as well between the natural right to possess and personally use one's intellectual creations and the rights protected by copyrights, patents, and trade secrets. The natural right of an author to personally use her writings is distinct from the right, protected by copyright, to make her work public, sell it in a market, and then prevent others from making copies. An inventor's natural right to use the invention for her own benefits is not the same as the right, protected by patent, to sell this invention in a market and exclude others (including independent inventors) from using it. An entrepreneur's natural right to use valuable business information or techniques that she develops is not the same as the right, protected by trade secret, to prevent her employees from using these techniques in another job.

In short, a laborer has a *prima facie* natural right to possess and personally use the fruits of her labor. But a right to profit by selling a product in the market is something quite different. This liberty is largely a socially created phenomenon. The "right" to receive what the market will bear is a socially created privilege, and not a natural right at all. The natural right to possess and personally use what one has produced is relevant to the justifiability of such a privilege, but by itself it is hardly sufficient to justify that privilege.

Deserving Property Rights Because of Labor

The above argument that people are naturally entitled to the fruits of their labor is distinct from the argument that a person has a claim to labor's fruits based on desert. If a person has a natural right to something–say her athletic ability–and someone takes it from her, the return of it is something she is *owed* and can rightfully demand. Whether or not she deserves this athletic ability is a separate issue. Similarly, insofar as people have natural property rights in the fruits of their labor, these rights are something they are owed, and not something they necessarily deserve.[22]

The desert argument suggests that the laborer deserves to benefit from her labor, at least if it is an attempt to do something worthwhile. This proposal is convincing, but does not show that what the laborer deserves is property rights in the object labored on. The mistake is to conflate the created object which makes a person deserving of a reward with what that reward should be.

Property rights in the created object are not the only possible reward. Alternatives include fees, awards, acknowledgment, gratitude, praise, security, power status, and public financial support.

Many considerations affect whether property rights in the created object are what the laborer deserves. This may depend, for example, on what is created by labor. If property rights in the very things created were always an appropriate reward for labor, then as Lawrence Becker notes, parents would deserve property rights in their children.[23] Many intellectual objects (scientific laws, religious and ethical insights, and so on) are also the sort of thing that should not be owned by anyone.

Furthermore, as Becker also correctly points out, we need to consider the purpose for which the laborer labored. Property rights in the object produced are not a fitting reward if the laborer does not want them. Many intellectual laborers produce beautiful things and discover truths as ends in themselves.[24] The appropriate reward in such cases is recognition, gratitude, and perhaps public financial support, not full-fledged property rights, for these laborers do not want to exclude others from their creations.

Property rights in the thing produced are also not a fitting reward if the value of these rights is disproportional to the effort expended by the laborer. "Effort" includes

1. how hard someone tries to achieve a result,
2. the amount of risk voluntarily incurred in seeking this result, and
3. the degree to which moral consideration played a role in choosing the result intended.

The harder one tries, the more one is willing to sacrifice, and the worthier the goal, the greater are one's deserts.

Becker's claim that the amount deserved is proportional to the value one's labor produces is mistaken.[25] The value of labor's results is often significantly affected by factors outside a person's control, and no one deserves to be rewarded for being lucky. Voluntary past action is the only valid basis for determining desert.[26] Here only a person's effort (in the sense defined) is relevant. Her knowledge, skills, and achievements insofar as they are based on natural talent and luck, rather than effort expended, are not. A person who is born with extraordinary natural talents, or who is extremely lucky, *deserves* nothing on the basis of these characteristics. If such a person puts forward no greater effort than another, she deserves no greater reward. Thus, two laborers who expend equal amounts of effort deserve the same reward, even when the value of the resulting products is vastly different.[27] Giving more to workers whose products have greater social value might be justified if it is needed as an incentive. But this has nothing to do with giving the laborer what she deserves.

John Rawls considers even the ability to expend effort to be determined by factors outside a person's control and hence a morally impermissible criterion for distribution.[28] How hard one tries, how willing one is to sacrifice and incur risk, and how much one cares about morality are to *some extent* affected by natural endowments and social circumstances. But if the ability to expend effort is taken to be entirely determined by factors outside a person's control, the result is a determinism which makes meaningful moral evaluation impossible. If people are responsible for anything, they are responsible for how hard they try, what sacrifices they make, and how moral they are. Because the effort a person expends is much more under her control than her innate intelligence, skills, and talents, effort is a far superior basis for determining desert. To the extent that a person's expenditure of effort is under her control, effort is the proper criterion for desert.[29]

Giving an inventor exclusive rights to make and sell her invention (for seventeen years) may provide either a greater or a lesser reward than she deserves. Some inventions of extraordinary market value result from flashes of genius, while others with little market value (and yet great social value) require significant effort.

The proportionality requirement may also be frequently violated by granting copyright. Consider a five-hundred-dollar computer program. Granted, its initial development costs (read "efforts") were high. But once it has been developed, the cost of each additional program is the cost of the disk it is on–approximately a dollar. After the program has been on the market several years and the price remains at three or four hundred dollars, one begins to suspect that the company is receiving far more than it deserves. Perhaps this is another reason so much illegal copying of software goes on: the proportionality requirement is not being met, and people sense the unfairness of the price. Frequently, trade secrets (which are held indefinitely) also provide their owners with benefits disproportional to the effort expended in developing them.

The Lockean Provisos

We have examined two versions of the labor argument for intellectual property, one based on desert, the other based on a natural entitlement to the fruits of one's labor. Locke himself put limits on the conditions under which labor can justify a property right in the thing produced. One is that after the appropriation there must be "enough and as good left in common for others."[30] This proviso is often reformulated as a "no loss to others" precondition for property acquisition.[31] As long as one does not worsen another's position by appropriating an object, no objection can be raised to owning that with which one mixes one's labor.

Under current law, patents clearly run a foul of this proviso by giving the original inventor an exclusive right to make, use, and sell the invention. Subsequent inventors who independently come up with an already patented invention cannot even personally use their invention, much less patent or sell it. They clearly suffer a great and unfair loss because of the original patent grant. Independent inventors should not be prohibited from using or selling their inventions. Proving independent discovery of a publicly available patented invention would be difficult, however. Nozick's suggestion that the length of patents be restricted to the time it would take for independent invention may be the most reasonable administrative solution.[32] In the modern world of highly competitive research and development, this time is often much shorter than the seventeen years for which most patents are currently granted.

Copyrights and trade secrets are not subject to the same objection (though they may constitute a loss to others in different ways). If someone independently comes up with a copyrighted expression or a competitor's business technique, she is not prohibited from using it. Copyrights and trade secrets prevent only mimicking of other people's expressions and ideas.

Locke's second condition on the legitimate acquisition of property rights prohibits spoilage. Not only must one leave enough and as good for others, but one must not take more than one can use.[33] So in addition to leaving enough apples in the orchard for others, one must not take home a truckload and let them spoil. Though Locke does not specifically mention prohibiting waste, it is the concern to avoid waste which underlies his proviso prohibiting spoilage. Taking more than one can use is wrong because it is wasteful. Thus Locke's concern here is with appropriations of property which are wasteful.

Since writings, inventions, and business techniques are nonexclusive, this requirement prohibiting waste can never be completely met by intellectual property. When owners of intellectual property charge fees for the use of their expressions or inventions, or conceal their business techniques from others, certain beneficial uses of these intellectual products are prevented. This is clearly wasteful, since everyone could use and benefit from intellectual objects concurrently. How wasteful private ownership of intellectual property is depends on how beneficial those products would be to those who are excluded from their use as a result.

Sovereignty, Security, and Privacy

Private property can be justified as a means to sovereignty. Dominion over certain objects is important for individual autonomy. Ronald Dworkin's liberal is right in saying that "some sovereignty over a range of personal possessions is essential to dignity."[34] Not having to share one's personal possessions or borrow them from others is essential to the kind of autonomy our society values. Using or consuming certain objects is also necessary for survival. Allowing ownership of these things places control of the means of survival in the hands of individuals, and this promotes independence and security (at least for those who own enough of them). Private ownership of life's necessities lessens dependence between individuals, and takes power from the group and gives it to the individual. Private property also promotes privacy. It constitutes a sphere of privacy within which the individual is sovereign and less accountable for her actions. Owning one's own home is an example of all of these: it provides privacy, security, and a limited range of autonomy.

But copyrights and patents are neither necessary nor important for achieving these goals. The right to exclude others from using one's invention or copying one's work of authorship is not essential to one's sovereignty. Preventing a person from personally using her own invention or writing, on the other hand, would seriously threaten her sovereignty. An author's or inventor's sense of worth and dignity requires public acknowledgment by those who use the writing or discovery, but here again, giving the author or inventor the exclusive right to copy or use her intellectual product is not necessary to protect this.

Though patents and copyrights are not directly necessary for survival (as are food and shelter), one could argue that they are indirectly necessary for an individual's security and survival when selling her inventions or writings is a person's sole means of income. In our society, however, most patents and copyrights are owned by institutions (businesses, universities, or governments). Except in unusual cases where individuals have extraordinary bargaining power, prospective employees are required to give the rights to their inventions and works of authorship to their employers as a condition of employment. Independent authors or inventors who earn their living by selling their writings or inventions to others are increasingly rare.[35] Thus arguing that intellectual property promotes individual security makes sense only in a minority of cases. Additionally, there are other ways to ensure the independent intellectual laborer's security and survival besides copyrights and patents (such as public funding of intellectual workers and public domain property status for the results).

Controlling who uses one's invention or writing is not important to one's privacy. As long as there is no requirement to divulge privately created intellectual products (and as long as laws exist to protect people from others taking information they choose not to divulge—as with trade secret laws), the creator's privacy will not be infringed. Trying to justify copyrights and patents on grounds of privacy is highly implausible given that these property rights give the author or inventor control over certain uses of writings and inventions only after they have been publicly disclosed.

Trade secrets are not defensible on grounds of privacy either. A corporation is not an individual and hence does not have the personal features privacy is intended to protect.[36] Concern for sovereignty counts against trade secrets, for they often directly limit individual autonomy by preventing employees from changing jobs. Through employment contracts, by means of gentlemen's agreements among firms to respect trade secrets by refusing to hire competitors' employees, or simply because of the threat of lawsuits, trade secrets often prevent employees from using their skills and knowledge with other companies in the industry.

Some trade secrets, however, are important to a company's security and survival. If competitors could legally obtain the secret formula for Coke, for example, the Coca-Cola Company would be severely threatened. Similar points hold for copyrights and patents. Without some copyright protection, companies in the publishing, record, and movie industries would be severely threatened by competitors who copy and sell their works at lower prices (which need not reflect development costs). Without patent protection, companies with high research and development costs could be underpriced and driven out of business by competitors who simply mimicked the already developed products. This unfair competition could significantly weaken incentives to invest in innovative techniques and to develop new products.

The next section considers this argument that intellectual property is a necessary incentive for innovation and a requirement for healthy and fair competition. Notice, however, that the concern here is with the security and survival of private companies, not of individuals. Thus one needs to determine whether, and to what extent, the security and survival of privately held companies is a goal worth promoting. That issue turns on the difficult question of what type of economy is most desirable. Given a commitment to capitalism, however, this argument does have some force.

The Utilitarian Justification

The strongest and most widely appealed to justification for intellectual property is a utilitarian argument based on providing incentives. The constitutional justification for patents and copyrights–"to promote the progress of science and the useful arts"[37]–is itself utilitarian. Given the shortcomings of the other arguments for intellectual property, the justifiability of copyrights, patents) and trade secrets depends, in the final analysis, on this utilitarian defense.

According to this argument, promoting the creation of valuable intellectual worlds requires that intellectual laborers be granted property rights in those works. Without the copyright, patent, and trade secret property protections, adequate incentives for the creation of a socially optimal output of intellectual products would not exist. If competitors could simply copy books, movies, and records, and take one another's inventions and business techniques, there would be no incentive to spend the vast amounts of time, energy, and money necessary to develop these products and techniques. It would be in each firm's self-interest to let others develop products, and then mimic the result. No one would engage in original development, and consequently no new writings, inventions, or business techniques would be developed. To avoid this disastrous result, the argument claims, we must continue to grant intellectual property rights.

Notice that this argument focuses on the users of intellectual products, rather than on the producers. Granting property rights to producers is here seen as necessary to ensure that enough intellectual products (and the countless other goods based on these products) are available to users. The grant of property rights to the producers is a mere means to this end.

This approach is paradoxical. It establishes a right to restrict the current availability and use of intellectual products for the purpose of increasing the production and thus future availability and use of new intellectual products. As economist Joan Robinson says of patents: "A patent is a device to prevent the diffusion of new methods before the original investor has recovered profit adequate to induce the requisite investment. The justification of the patent system is that by slowing down the diffusion of technical progress it ensures that there will be more progress to diffuse.... Since it is rooted in a contradiction, there can be no such thing as an ideally beneficial patent system, and it is bound to produce negative results in particular instances, impeding progress unnecessarily even if its general effect is favorable on balance."[38] Although this strategy may work, it is to a certain extent self-defeating. If the justification for intellectual property is utilitarian in this sense, then the search for alternative incentives for the production of intellectual products takes on a good deal of importance. It would be better to employ equally powerful ways to stimulate the production and thus use of intellectual products which did not also restrict their use and availability.

Government support of intellectual work and public ownership of the result may be one such alternative. Governments already fund a great deal of basic research and development, and the results of this research often become public property. Unlike private property rights in the results of intellectual labor, government funding of this labor and public ownership of the result stimulate new inventions and writings without restricting their dissemination and use. Increased government funding of intellectual labor should thus be seriously considered.

This proposal need not involve government control over which research projects are to be pursued. Government funding of intellectual labor can be divorced from government control over what is funded. University research is an example. Most of this is supported by public funds, but government control over its content is minor and indirect. Agencies at different governmental levels could distribute funding for intellectual labor with only the most general guidance over content, leaving businesses, universities, and private individuals to decide which projects to pursue.

If the goal of private intellectual property institutions is to maximize the dissemination and use of information, to the extent that they do not achieve this result, these institutions should be modified. The question is not whether copyrights, patents, and trade secrets provide incentives for the production of original works of authorship, inventions, and innovative business techniques. Of course they do. Rather, we should ask the following questions: Do copyrights, patents, and trade secrets increase the availability and use of intellectual products more than they restrict this availability and use? If they do, we must then ask whether they increase the availability and use of intellectual products more than any alternative mechanism would. For example, could better overall results be achieved by shortening the length of copyright and patent grants, or by putting a time limit on trade secrets (and on the restrictions on future employment employers are allowed to demand of employees)? Would eliminating most types of trade secrets entirely and letting patents carry a heavier load produce improved results? Additionally, we must determine whether and to what extent public funding and ownership of intellectual products might be a more efficient means to these results.[39]

We should not expect an across-the-board answer to these questions. For example, the production of movies is more dependent on copyright than is academic writing. Also, patent protection for individual inventors and small beginning firms makes more sense than patent protection for large corporations (which own the majority of patents). It has been argued that patents are not important incentives for the research and innovative activity of large corporations in competitive markets.[40] The short-term advantage a company gets from developing a new product and being the first to put it on the market may be incentive enough.

That patents are conducive to a strong competitive economy is also open to question. Our patent system, originally designed to reward the individual inventor and thereby stimulate invention, may today be used as a device to monopolize industries. It has been suggested that in some cases "the patent position of the big firms makes it almost impossible for new firms to enter the industry"[41] and that patents are frequently bought up in order to suppress competition.[42]

Trade secrets as well can stifle competition, rather than encourage it. If a company can rely on a secret advantage over a competitor, it has no need to develop new technologies to stay ahead. Greater disclosure of certain trade secrets—such as costs and profits of particular product lines would actually increase competition, rather than decrease it, since with this knowledge firms would then concentrate on one another's most profitable products.[43] Furthermore, as one critic notes, trade secret laws often prevent a former employee "from doing work in just that field for which his training and experience have best prepared him. Indeed, the mobility of engineers and scientists is often severely limited by the reluctance of new firms to hire them for fear of exposing themselves to a lawsuit."[44] Since the movement of skilled workers between companies is a vital mechanism in the growth and spread of technology, in this important respect trade secrets actually slow the dissemination and use of innovative techniques.

These remarks suggest that the justifiability of our intellectual property institutions is not settled by the facile assertion that our system of patents, copyrights, and trade secrets provides necessary incentives for innovation and ensures maximally healthy competitive enterprise. This argument is not as easy to construct as one might at first think; substantial empirical evidence is needed. The above considerations suggest that the evidence might not support this position.

Conclusion

Justifying intellectual property is a formidable task. The inadequacies of the traditional justifications for property become more severe when applied to intellectual property. Both the nonexclusive nature of intellectual objects and the presumption against allowing restrictions on the free flow of ideas create special burdens in justifying such property.

We have seen significant shortcomings in the justifications for intellectual property. Natural rights to the fruits of one's labor are not by themselves sufficient to justify copyrights, patents, and trade secrets, though they are relevant to the social decision to create and sustain intellectual property institutions. Although intellectual laborers often deserve rewards for their labor, copyrights, patents, and trade secrets may give the laborer much more or much less than is deserved. Where property rights are not what is desired, they may be wholly inappropriate. The Lockean labor arguments for intellectual property also run afoul of one of Locke's provisos–the prohibition against spoilage or waste. Considerations of sovereignty, security, and privacy are inconclusive justifications for intellectual property as well.

This analysis suggests that the issue turns on considerations of social utility. We must determine whether our current copyright, patent, and trade secret statutes provide the best possible mechanisms for ensuring the availability and widespread dissemination of intellectual works and their resulting products. Public financial support for intellectual laborers and public ownership of intellectual products is an alternative which demands serious consideration. More modest alternatives needing consideration include modifications in the length of intellectual property grants or in the strength and scope of the restrictive rights granted. What the most efficient mechanism for achieving these goals is remains an unresolved empirical question.

This discussion also suggests that copyrights are easier to justify than patents or trade secrets. Patents restrict the actual usage of an idea (in making a physical object), while copyrights restrict only copying an expression of an idea. One can freely use the ideas in a copyrighted book in one's own writing, provided one acknowledges their origin. One cannot freely use the ideas a patented invention represents when developing one's own product. Furthermore, since inventions and business techniques are instruments of production in a way in which expressions of ideas are not, socialist objections to private ownership of the means of production apply to patents and trade secrets far more readily than they do to copyrights. Trade secrets are suspect also because they do not involve the socially beneficial public disclosure which is part of the patent and copyright process. They are additionally problematic to the extent that they involve unacceptable restrictions on employee mobility and technology transfer.

Focusing on the problems of justifying intellectual property is important not because these institutions lack any sort of justification, but because they are not so obviously or easily justified as many people think. We must begin to think more openly and imaginatively about the alternative choices available to us for stimulating and rewarding intellectual labor.

Notes

1 Ayn Rand, *Capitalism: The Unknown Ideal* (New York: New American Library, 1966), p. 128.

2 See, for example, John Naisbitt's *Megatrends* (New York: Warner Books, 1982), chap. 1.

3 See R. Salaman and E. Hettinger, *Policy Implications of Information Technology.* NTIA Report 84–144, U.S. Department of Commerce, 1984, pp. 28–29.

4 For an elaboration of this distinction see Michael Brittin, "Constitutional Fair Use," in *Copyright Law Symposium*, no. 28 (New York: Columbia University Press, 1982), pp. 142ff.

5 For an illuminating discussion of the relationships between style and subject, see Nelson Goodman's *Ways of Worldmaking* (Indianapolis: Hackett, 1978), chap. II, esp. sec. 2.

6 This is Fritz Machlup's phrase. See his *Production and Distribution of Knowledge in the United States* (Princeton: Princeton University Press, 1962), p. 163.

7 For one discussion of this distinction, see Deborah Johnson, *Computer Ethics* (Englewood Cliffs, N.J.: Prentice-Hall, 1985), pp. 100–101.

8 What can be patented is highly controversial. Consider the recent furor over patenting genetically manipulated animals or patenting computer programs.

9 What constitutes fair use is notoriously bewildering. I doubt that many teachers who sign copyright waivers at local copy shops know whether the packets they make available for their students constitute fair use of copyrighted material.

10 "Intellectual objects," "information," and "ideas" are terms I use to characterize the "objects" of this kind of ownership. Institutions which protect such "objects" include copyright, patent, trade secret, and trademark laws, as well as socially enforced customs (such as sanctions against plagiarism) demanding acknowledgment of the use of another's ideas. What is owned here are objects only in a very abstract sense.

11 There are intellectual objects of which this is not true, namely, information whose usefulness depends precisely on its being known only to a limited group of people. Stock tips and insider trading information are examples.

12 Ease of access is another reason for the widespread piracy of intellectual property. Modern information technologies (such as audio and video recorders, satellite dishes, photocopiers, and computers) make unauthorized taking of intellectual objects far easier than ever before. But it is cynical to submit that this is the major (or the only) reason piracy of information is widespread. It suggests that if people could steal physical objects as easily as they can take intellectual ones, they would do so to the same extent. That seems incorrect.

13 For a useful interpretation of Mill's argument, see Robert Ladenson, "Free Expression in the Corporate Workplace," in *Ethical Theory and Business*, 2d ed., ad. T. Beauchamp and N. Bowie (Englewood Cliffs, N.J.: Prentice-Hall, 1983), pp. 162–69.

14 This is one reason the recent dramatic increase in relationships between universities and businesses is so disturbing: it hampers the disclosure of research results.

15 John Snapper makes this point in "Ownership of Computer Programs," available from the Center for the Study of Ethics in the Professions at the Illinois Institute of Technology. See also Sissela Bok, "Trade and Corporate Secrecy," in *Ethical Theory and Business*, p. 176.

16 John Locke, *Second Treatise of Government*, chap. 5. There are several strands to the Lockean argument. See Lawrence Becker, *Property Rights* (London: Routledge and Kegan Paul, 1977), chap. 4, for a detailed analysis of these various versions.

17 Robert Nozick, *Anarchy, State, and Utopia* (New York: Basic Books, 1974), p. 175.

18 Locke, *Second Treatise*, chap. 5, sec. 40.

19 Whether ideas are discovered or created affects the plausibility of the labor argument for intellectual property. "I discovered it, hence it's mine" is much less

persuasive than "I made it, hence it's mine." This issue also affects the cogency of the notion that intellectual objects have a value of their own not attributable to intellectual labor. The notion of mixing one's labor with something and thereby adding value to it makes much more sense if the object preexists.

20 I thank the Editors of *Philosophy & Affairs* for this way of making the point.

21 A libertarian might respond that although a natural right to the fruits of labor will not by itself justify a right to receive the market value of the resulting product, that right plus the rights of free association and trade would justify it. But marketplace interaction presupposes a set of social relations, and parties to these relations must jointly agree on their nature. Additionally, market interaction is possible only when property rights have been specified and enforced, and there is no a "natural way" to do this (that is, no way independent of complex social judgments concerning the rewards the laborer deserves and the social utilities that will result from granting property rights). The sorts of freedoms one may have in a marketplace are thus socially agreed-upon privileges rather than natural rights.

22 For a discussion of this point) see Joel Feinberg, *Social Philosophy* (Englewood Cliffs, N.J.: Prentice-Hall, 1973), p. 116.

23 Becker, *Property Rights*, p. 46.

24 This is becoming less and less true as the results of intellectual labor are increasingly treated as commodities. University research in biological and computer technologies is an example of this trend.

25 Becker, *Property Rights*, p. 52. In practice it would be easier to reward laborers as Becker suggests, since the value of the results of labor is easier to determine than the degree of effort expended.

26 This point is made nicely by James Rachels in "What People Deserve," in *Justice and Economic Distribution*, ed. J. Arthur and W. Shaw (Englewood Cliffs, N.J.: Prentice-Hall, 1978), pp. 150–63.

27 Completely ineffectual efforts deserve a reward provided that there were good reasons beforehand for thinking the efforts would pay off. Those whose well-intentioned efforts are silly or stupid should be rewarded the first time only and then counseled to seek advice about the value of their efforts.

28 See John Rawls, *A Theory of Justice* (Cambridge: Harvard University Press, 1971), p. 104: "The assertion that a man deserves the superior character that enables him to make the effort to cultivate his abilities is equally problematic; for his character depends in large part upon fortunate family and social circumstances for which he can claim no credit." See also p. 312: "the effort a person is willing to make is influenced by his natural abilities and skills, and the alternatives open to him. The better endowed are more likely, other things equal, to strive conscientiously."

29 See Rachels, "What People Deserve," pp. 157–58, for a similar resistance to Rawl's determinism.

30 Locke, *Second Treatise*, chap. 5, sec. 27.

31 See Nozick, *Anarchy*, pp. 175-82, and Becker, *Property Rights*, pp. 42–43.

32 Nozick, *Anarchy*, p. 182.

33 Locke, *Second Treatise*, chap. 5, sec. 31.

34 Ronald Dworkin, "Liberalism," in *Public and Private Morality*, ed. Stuart Hampshire (Cambridge: Cambridge University Press, 1978), p. 139.

35 "In the United States about 60 per cent of all patents are assigned to corporations" (Machlup, *Production*, p. 168). This was the case twenty-five years ago, and I assume the percentage is even higher today.

36 Very little (if any) of the sensitive information about individuals that corporations have is information held as a trade secret. For a critical discussion of the attempt to defend corporate secrecy on the basis of privacy see Russell B. Stevenson, Jr., *Corporations and Information* (Baltimore: Johns Hopkins University Press, 1980), chap. 5.

37 U.S. Constitution sec. 8, para. 8.

38 Quoted in Dorothy Nelkin, *Science as Intellectual Property* (New York: Macmillan, 1984), p. 15.

39 Even supposing our current copyright, patent, and trade secret laws did maximize the availability and use of intellectual products, a thorough utilitarian evaluation would have to weigh all the consequences of these legal rights. For example, the decrease in employee freedom resulting from trade secrets would have to be considered, as would the inequalities in income, wealth, opportunity, and power which result from these socially established and enforced property rights.

40 Machlup, *Production*, pp. 168–69.

41 Ibid., p. 170.

42 See David Noble, *America by Design* (New York: Knopf, 1982) chap. 6.

43 This is Stevenson's point in *Corporations*, p. 11.

44 Ibid., p. 23. More generally, see ibid., chap. 2, for a careful and skeptical treatment of the claim that trade secrets function as incentives.

20

Trade Secrets and the Justification of Intellectual Property: A Comment on Hettinger

Lynn Sharp Paine

I n a recent article Edwin Hettinger considers various rationales for recognizing intellectual property.[1] According to Hettinger, traditional justifications for property are especially problematic when applied to intellectual property because of its nonexclusive nature.[2] Since possessing and using intellectual objects does not preclude their use and possession by others, there is, he says a "strong prima facie case against the wisdom of private and exclusive intellectual property rights." There is, moreover, a presumption against allowing restrictions on the free flow of ideas.

After rejecting several rationales for intellectual property, Hettinger finds its justification in an instrumental, or "utilitarian,"[3] argument based on incentives.[4] Respecting rights in ideas makes sense, he says, if we recognize that the purpose of our intellectual property institutions is to promote the dissemination and use of information. To the extent that existing institutions do not achieve this result, they should be modified.[5] Skeptical about the effectiveness of current legal arrangements, Hettinger concludes that we must think more imaginatively about structuring our intellectual property institutions—in particular, patent, copyright, and trade secret laws—so that they increase the availability and use of intellectual products. He ventures several possibilities for consideration: eliminating certain forms of trade secret protections, shortening the copyright and patent protection periods, and public funding and ownership of intellectual objects.

Hettinger's approach to justifying our intellectual property institutions rests on several problematic assumptions. It assumes that all of our intellectual property institutions rise or fall together—that the rationale for trade secret protection must be the same as that for patent and copyright protection.[6] This

Source: *Philosophy and Public Affairs* 20 (1991), 247–63.

assumption, I will try to show, is unwarranted. While it may be true that these institutions all promote social utility or wellbeing, the web of rights and duties understood under the general heading of "intellectual property rights" reflects a variety of more specific rationales and objectives.[7]

Second, Hettinger assumes that the rights commonly referred to as "intellectual property rights" are best understood on the model of rights in tangible and real property. He accepts the idea, implicit in the terminology, that intellectual property is like tangible property, only less corporeal. This assumption leads him to focus his search for the justification of intellectual property on the traditional arguments for private property. I will try to show the merits of an alternative approach to thinking about rights in ideas—one that does not depend on the analogy with tangible property and that recognizes the role of ideas in defining personality and social relationships.

The combined effect of these assumptions is that trade secret law comes in for particular serious criticism. It restricts methods of acquiring ideas; it encourages secrecy; it places unacceptable restrictions on employee mobility and technology transfer; it can stifle competition; it is more vulnerable to socialist objections. In light of these deficiencies, Hettinger recommends that we consider the possibility of "eliminating most types of trade secrets entirely and letting patents carry a heavier load." He believes that trade secrets are undesirable in ways that copyrights and patents are not.

Without disagreeing with Hettinger's recommendation that we reevaluate and think more imaginatively about our intellectual property institutions, I believe we should have a clearer understanding of the various rationales for these institutions than is reflected in Hettinger's article. If we unbundle the notion of intellectual property into its constituent rights,[8] we find that different justifications are appropriate for different clusters of rights.[9] In particular, we find that the rights recognized by trade secret law are better understood as rooted in respect for individual liberty, confidential relationships, common morality, and fair competition than in the promotion of innovation and the dissemination of ideas. While trade secret law may serve some of the same ends as patent and copyright law, it has other foundations which are quite distinctive.[10]

In this article, I am primarily concerned with the foundations of trade secret principles. However, my general approach differs from Hettinger's in two fundamental ways. First, it focuses on persons and their relationships rather than property concepts. Second, it reverses the burden of justification, placing it on those who would argue for treating ideas as public goods rather than those who seek to justify private rights in ideas. Within this alternative framework, the central questions are how ideas may be legitimately acquired from others, how disclosure obligations arise, and how ideas become part of the common pool of knowledge. Before turning to Hettinger's criticisms of trade secret principles, it will be useful to think more broadly about the rights of individuals over their undisclosed ideas. This inquiry will illustrate my approach to thinking about rights in ideas and point toward some of the issues at stake in the trade secret area.

The Right to Control Disclosure

If a person has any right with respect to her ideas, surely it is the right to control their initial disclosure.[11] A person may decide to keep her ideas to herself, to disclose them to a select few, or to publish them widely. Whether those ideas are best described as views and opinions, plans and intentions, facts and knowledge, or fantasies and inventions is immaterial. While it might in some cases be socially useful for a person to be generous with her ideas, and to share them with others without restraint, there is no general obligation to do so. The world at large has no right to the individual's ideas.[12]

Certainly, specific undertakings, relationships, and even the acquisition of specific information can give rise to disclosure obligations. Typically, these obligations relate to specific types of information pertinent to the relationship or the subject matter of the undertaking. A seller of goods must disclose to potential buyers latent defects and health and safety risks associated with the use of the goods. A person who undertakes to act as an agent for another is obliged to disclose to the principal information she acquires that relates to the subject matter of the agency. Disclosure obligations like these, however, are limited in scope and arise against a general background right to remain silent.

The right to control the initial disclosure of one's ideas is grounded in respect for the individual. Just as a person's sense of herself is intimately connected with the stream of ideas that constitutes consciousness, her public persona is determined in part by the ideas she expresses and the way she expresses them. To require public disclosure of one's ideas and thoughts–whether about "personal" or other matters–would distort one's personality and, no doubt, alter the nature of one's thoughts.[13] It would seriously interfere with the liberty to live according to one's chosen life plans. This sort of thought control would be an invasion of privacy and personality of the most intrusive sort. If anything is private, one's undisclosed thoughts surely are.[14]

Respect for autonomy, respect for personality, and respect for privacy lie behind the right to control disclosure of one's ideas, but the right is also part of what we mean by freedom of thought and expression. Frequently equated with a right to speak, freedom of expression also implies a *prima facie* right not to express one's ideas or to share them only with those we love or trust or with whom we wish to share.[15] These observations explain the peculiarity of setting up the free flow of ideas and unrestricted access as an ideal. Rights in ideas are desirable insofar as they strengthen our sense of individuality and undergird our social relationships. This suggests a framework quite different from Hettinger's, one that begins with a strong presumption against requiring disclosure and is in favor of protecting people against unconsented-to acquisitions of their ideas.[16] This is the moral backdrop against which trade secrecy law is best understood.

Consequences of Disclosure

Within this framework, a critical question is how people lose rights in their ideas. Are these rights forfeited when people express their ideas or communicate them to others? Surely this depends on the circumstances of disclosure. Writing down ideas in a daily journal to oneself or recording them on a cassette should not entail such a forfeiture. Considerations of individual autonomy, privacy, and personality require that such expressions not be deemed available for use by others who may gain access to them.[17]

Likewise, communicating an idea in confidence to another should not render it part of the common pool of knowledge. Respect for the individual's desire to limit the dissemination of the idea is at stake, but so is respect for the relationship of trust and confidence among the persons involved. If *A* confides in *B* under circumstances in which *B* gives *A* reason to believe she will respect the confidence, A should be able to trust that *B* will not reveal or misuse the confidence and that third parties who may intentionally or accidentally discover the confidence will respect it.[18]

The alternative possibility is that by revealing her ideas to *B*, *A* is deemed to forfeit any right to control their use or communication. This principle is objectionable for a couple of reasons. First, it would most certainly increase reluctance to share ideas since our disclosure decisions are strongly influenced by the audience we anticipate. If we could not select our audience, that is, if the choice were only between keeping ideas to ourselves and sharing them with the world at large, many ideas would remain unexpressed, to the detriment of individual health as well as the general good.

Second, the principle would pose an impediment to the formation and sustenance of various types of cooperative relationships—relationships of love and friendship, as well as relationships forged for specific purposes such as education, medical care, or business. It might be thought that only ideas of an intimate or personal nature are important in this regard. But it is not only "personal" relationships, but cooperative relationships of all types, that are at stake. Shared knowledge and information of varying types are central to work relationships and communities—academic departments and disciplines, firms, teams—as well as other organizations. The possession of common ideas and information, to the exclusion of those outside the relationship or group, contributes to the group's self-definition and to the individual's sense of belonging. By permitting and protecting the sharing of confidences, trade secret principles, among other institutions, permit "special communities of knowledge" which nurture the social bonds and cooperative efforts through which we express our individuality and pursue common purposes.[19]

Of course, by disclosing her idea to *B*, *A* runs the risk that *B* or anyone else who learns about the idea may use it or share it further. But if *B* has agreed to respect the confidence, either explicitly or by participating in a relationship in which confidence is normally expected, she has a *prima facie* obligation not to disclose the information to which she is privy.[20] Institutions that give *A* a remedy against third parties who appropriate ideas shared in confidence reduce the risk that *A*'s ideas will become public resources if she shares them with *B*. Such institutions thereby support confidential relationships and the cooperative undertakings that depend on them.

Yet another situation in which disclosure should not be regarded as a license for general use is the case of disclosures made as a result of deceit or insincere promises. Suppose *A* is an entrepreneur who has created an unusual software program with substantial sales potential. Another party, *B*, pretending to be a potential customer, questions *A* at great length about the code and other details of her program. *A*'s disclosures are not intended to be, and should not be deemed, a contribution to the general pool of knowledge, nor should *B* be permitted to use *A*'s ideas.[21] Respect for *A*'s right to disclose her ideas requires that involuntary disclosures–such as those based on deceit, coercion, and theft of documents containing expressions of those ideas–not be regarded as forfeitures to the common pool of knowledge and information. In recognition of *A*'s right to control disclosure of her ideas and to discourage appropriation of her ideas against her wishes, we might expect our institutions to provide *A* with a remedy against these sorts of appropriation. Trade secret law provides such a remedy.

Competitive fairness is also at stake if *B* is in competition with *A*. Besides having violated standards of common morality in using deceit to gain access to *A*'s ideas, *B* is in a position to exploit those ideas in the marketplace without having contributed to the cost of their development. *B* can sell her version of the software more cheaply since she enjoys a substantial cost advantage compared to *A*, who may have invested a great deal of time and money in developing the software. Fairness in a competitive economy requires some limitations on the rights of firms to use ideas developed by others. In a system based on effort, it is both unfair and ultimately selfdefeating to permit firms to have a free ride on the efforts of their competitors.[22]

Problematic Issues

Respect for personal control over the disclosure of ideas, respect for confidential relationships, common morality, and fair competition all point toward recognizing certain rights in ideas. Difficult questions will arise within this system of rights. If *A* is not an individual but an organization or group, should *A* have the same rights and remedies against *B* or third parties who use or communicate information shared with *B* in confidence? For example, suppose *A* is a corporation that hires an employee, *B*, to develop a marketing plan. If other employees of *A* reveal in confidence to *B* information they have created or assembled, should *A* be able to restrain *B* from using this information to benefit herself (at *A*'s expense)? Does it matter if *A* is a two-person corporation or a corporation with 100,000 employees? What if *A* is a social club or a private school?

Hettinger seems to assume that corporate *A*'s should not have such rights–on the grounds that they might restrict *B*'s employment possibilities. It is certainly true that giving *A* a right against *B* if she reveals information communicated to her in confidence could rule out certain jobs for *B*. However, the alternative rule–that corporate *A*'s should have no rights in ideas they reveal in confidence to others–has problems as well.

One problem involves trust. If our institutions do not give corporate A's certain rights in ideas they reveal in confidence to employees, A's will seek other means of ensuring that competitively valuable ideas are protected. They may contract individually with employees for those rights, and if our legal institutions do not uphold those contracts, employers will seek to hire individuals in whom they have personal trust. Hiring would probably become more dependent on family and personal relationships and there would be fewer opportunities for the less well connected. Institutional rules giving corporate A's rights against employees who reveal or use information given to them in confidence are a substitute for personal bonds of trust. While such rules are not cost-free and may have some morally undesirable consequences, they help sustain cooperative efforts and contribute to more open hiring practices.

Contrary to Hettinger's suggestion, giving corporate A's rights in the ideas they reveal in confidence to others does not always benefit the strong at the expense of the weak, or the large corporation at the expense of the individual, although this is surely sometimes the case.[23] Imagine three entrepreneurs who wish to expand their highly successful cookie business. A venture capitalist interested in financing the expansion naturally wishes to know the details of the operation–including the prized cookie recipe–before putting up capital. After examining the recipe, however, he decides that it would be more profitable for him to sell the recipe to CookieCo, a multinational food company, and to invest his capital elsewhere. Without money and rights to prevent others from using the recipe, the corporate entrepreneurs are very likely out of business. CookieCo, which can manufacture and sell the cookies much more cheaply, will undoubtedly find that most of the entrepreneurs' customers are quite happy to buy the same cookies for less at their local supermarket.

Non-Property Foundations of Trade Secret Law

To a large extent, the rights and remedies mentioned in the preceding discussion are those recognized by trade secret law. As this discussion showed, the concept of property is not necessary to justify these rights. Trade secret law protects against certain methods of appropriating the confidential and commercially valuable ideas of others. It affords a remedy to those whose commercially valuable secrets are acquired by misrepresentation, theft, bribery, breach or inducement of a breach of confidence, espionage or other improper means.[24] Although the roots of trade secret principles have been variously located, respect for voluntary disclosure decisions and respect for confidential relationships provide the best account of the pattern of permitted and prohibited appropriations and use of ideas.[25] As Justice Oliver Wendell Holmes noted in a 1917 trade secret case, "The property may be denied but the confidence cannot be."[26] Trade secret law can also be seen as enforcing ordinary standards of morality in commercial relationships, thus ensuring some consistency with general social morality.[27]

It may well be true, as Hettinger and others have claimed, that the availability of trade secret protection provides an incentive for intellectual labor and the development of ideas. The knowledge that they have legal rights against those who "misappropriate" their ideas may encourage people to invest large amounts of time and money in exploring and developing ideas. However, the claim that trade secret protection promotes invention is quite different from the claim that it is grounded in or justified by this tendency. Even if common law trade secret rights did not promote intellectual labor or increase the dissemination and use of information, there would still be reasons to recognize those rights. Respect for people's voluntary disclosure decisions, respect for confidential relationships, standards of common morality, and fair competition would still point in that direction.

Moreover, promoting the development of ideas cannot be the whole story behind trade secret principles, since protection is often accorded to information such as customer data or cost and pricing information kept in the ordinary course of doing business. While businesses may need incentives to engage in costly research and development, they would certainly keep track of their customers and costs in any event. The rationale for giving protection to such information must be other than promoting the invention, dissemination, and use of ideas. By the same token, trade secret principles do not prohibit the use of ideas acquired by studying products available in the marketplace. If the central policy behind trade secret protection were the promotion of invention, one might expect that trade secret law, like patent law, which was explicitly fashioned to encourage invention, would protect innovators from imitators.

The fact that Congress has enacted patent laws giving inventors a limited monopoly in exchange for disclosure of their ideas without at the same time eliminating state trade secret law may be a further indication that trade secret and patent protection rest on different grounds.[28] By offering a limited monopoly in exchange for disclosure, the patent laws implicitly recognize the more fundamental right not to disclose one's ideas at all or to disclose them in confidence to others.[29]

Reassessing Hettinger's Criticism of Trade Secret Law

If we see trade secret law as grounded in respect for voluntary disclosure, confidential relationships, common morality, and fair competition, the force of Hettinger's criticisms diminishes somewhat. The problems he cites appear not merely in their negative light as detracting from an ideal "free flow of ideas," but in their positive role as promoting other important values.

Restrictions on acquiring ideas

Hettinger is critical, for example, of the fact that trade secret law restricts methods of acquiring ideas. But the prohibited means of acquisition–

misrepresentation, theft, bribery, breach of confidence, and espionage—all reflect general social morality. Lifting these restrictions would undoubtedly contribute to the erosion of important values outside the commercial context.

How much trade secrecy laws inhibit the development and spread of ideas is also open to debate. Hettinger and others have claimed that trade secrecy is a serious impediment to innovation and dissemination because the period of permitted secrecy is unlimited. Yet, given the fact that trade secret law offers no protection for ideas acquired by examining or reverse-engineering products in the marketplace, it would appear rather difficult to maintain technical secrets embodied in those products while still exploiting their market potential. A standard example used to illustrate the problem of perpetual secrecy, the Coke formula, seems insufficient to establish that this is a serious problem. Despite the complexity of modern technology, successful reverse-engineering is common. Moreover, similar technical advances are frequently made by researchers working independently. Trade secret law poses no impediment: in either case independent discoverers are free to exploit their ideas even if they are similar to those of others.

As for nontechnical information such as marketing plans and business strategies, the period of secrecy is necessarily rather short since implementation entails disclosure. Competitor intelligence specialists claim that most of the information needed to understand what competitors are doing is publicly available.[30] All of these considerations suggest that trade secret principles are not such a serious impediment to the dissemination of information.

Competitive effects

Hettinger complains that trade secret principles stifle competition. Assessing this claim is very difficult. On one hand, it may seem that prices would be lower if firms were permitted to obtain cost or other market advantages by using prohibited means to acquire protected ideas from others. Competitor access to the Coke formula would most likely put downward pressure on the price of "the real thing." Yet, it is also reasonable to assume that the law keeps prices down by reducing the costs of self-protection. By giving some assurance that commercially valuable secrets will be protected, the law shields firms from having to bear the full costs of protection. It is very hard to predict what would happen to prices if trade secret protection were eliminated. Self-protection would be more costly and would tend to drive prices up, while increased competition would work in the opposite direction. There would surely be important differences in morale and productivity. Moreover, as noted, any price reductions for consumers would come at a cost to the basic moral standards of society if intelligence-gathering by bribery, misrepresentation, and espionage were permitted.

Restrictions on employee mobility

Among Hettinger's criticisms of trade secret law, the most serious relate to restrictions on employee mobility In practice, employers often attempt to protect information by overrestricting the postemployment opportunities of employees. Three important factors contribute to this tendency: vagueness about which information is confidential; disagreement about the proper allocation of rights to ideas generated by employees using their employers' resources; and conceptual difficulties in distinguishing general knowledge and employers specific knowledge acquired on the job. Courts, however, are already doing what Hettinger recommends, namely, limiting the restrictions that employers can place on future employment in the name of protecting ideas.[31] Although the balance between employer and employee interests is a delicate one not always equitably struck, the solution of eliminating trade secret protection altogether is overbroad and undesirable, considering the other objectives at stake.

Hypothetical Alternatives

Hettinger's discussion of our intellectual property institutions reflects an assumption that greater openness and sharing would occur if we eliminated trade secret protection. He argues that trade secret principles encourage secrecy. He speaks of the "free flow of ideas" as the ideal that would obtain in the absence of our intellectual property institutions. This supposition strikes me as highly unlikely. People keep secrets and establish confidential relationships for a variety of reasons that are quite independent of any legal protection these secrets might have. The psychology and sociology of secrets have been explored by others. Although much economic theory is premised on complete information, secrecy and private information are at the heart of day-to-day competition in the marketplace.

In the absence of something like trade secret principles, I would expect not a free flow of ideas but greater efforts to protect information through contracts, management systems designed to limit information access, security equipment, and electronic counterintelligence devices. I would also expect stepped-up efforts to acquire intelligence from others through espionage, bribery, misrepresentation, and other unsavory means. By providing some assurance that information can be shared in confidence and by protecting against unethical methods of extracting information and undermining confidentiality, trade secret principles promote cooperation and security, two important conditions for intellectual endeavor. In this way, trade secret principles may ultimately promote intellectual effort by limiting information flow.

The Burden of Justification

We may begin thinking about information rights, as Hettinger does, by treating all ideas as part of a common pool and then deciding whether and how to allocate to individuals rights to items in the pool. Within this framework, ideas are conceived on the model of tangible property.[32] Just as, in the absence of social institutions, we enter the world with no particular relationship to its tangible assets or natural resources, we have no particular claim on the world's ideas. In this scheme, as Hettinger asserts, the "burden of justification is very much on those who would restrict the maximal use of intellectual objects."

Alternatively, we may begin, as I do, by thinking of ideas in relation to their originators, who may or may not share their ideas with specific others or contribute them to the common pool. This approach treats ideas as central to personality and the social world individuals construct for themselves. Ideas are not, in the first instance, freely available natural resources. They originate with people, and it is the connections among people, their ideas, and their relationships with others that provides a baseline for discussing rights in ideas. Within this conception, the burden of justification is on those who would argue for disclosure obligations and general access to ideas.

The structure of specific rights that emerges from these different frameworks depends not only on where the burden of justification is located, but also on how easily it can be discharged.[33] It is unclear how compelling a case is required to overcome the burden Hettinger sets up and, consequently, difficult to gauge the depth of my disagreement with him.[34] Since Hettinger does not consider the rationales for trade secret principles discussed here, it is not clear whether he would dismiss them altogether, find them insufficiently weighty to override the presumption he sets up, or agree that they satisfy the burden of justification.

One might suspect, however, from the absence of discussion of the personal and social dimension of rights in ideas that Hettinger does not think them terribly important, and that his decision to put the burden of justification on those who argue for rights in ideas reflects a fairly strong commitment to openness. On the assumption that our alternative starting points reflect seriously held substantive views (they are not just procedural devices to get the argument started) and that both frameworks require strong reasons to overcome the initial presumption, the resulting rights and obligations are likely to be quite different in areas where neither confidentiality nor openness is critical to immediate human needs. Indeed, trade secrecy law is an area where these different starting points would be likely to surface.

The key question to ask about these competing frameworks is which is backed by stronger reasons. My opposition to Hettinger's allocation of the burden of justification rests on my rejection of his conception of ideas as natural resources and on different views of how the world would look in the absence of our intellectual property institutions. In contrast, my starting point acknowledges the importance of ideas to our sense of ourselves and the communities (inducting work communities) of which we are a part. It is also more compatible with the way we commonly talk about ideas. Our talk about disclosure obligations presupposes a general background right not to reveal ideas. If it were otherwise, we would speak of concealment rights. To use the logically interesting feature of nonexclusiveness as a starting point for moral reasoning about rights in ideas seems wholly arbitrary.

Conclusion

Knives, forks, and spoons are all designed to help us eat. In a sense, however, the essential function of these tools is to help us cut, since without utensils, we could still consume most foods with our hands. One might be tempted to say that since cutting is the essential function of eating utensils, forks and spoons should be designed to facilitate cutting. One might even say that insofar as forks and spoons do not facilitate cutting, they should be redesigned. Such a modification, however, would rob us of valuable specialized eating instruments.

Hettinger's train of thought strikes me as very similar. He purports to examine the justification of our various intellectual property institutions. However, he settles on a justification that really only fits patent and, arguably, copyright institutions. He then suggests that other intellectual property rights be assessed against the justification he proposes and redesigned insofar as they are found wanting. In particular, he suggests that trade secret principles be modified to look more like patent principles. Hettinger fails to appreciate the various rationales behind the rights and duties understood under the heading "intellectual property," especially those recognized by trade secret law.

I agree with Hettinger that our intellectual property institutions need a fresh look from a utilitarian perspective.[35] The seventeen-year monopoly granted through patents is anachronistic given the pace of technological development today. We need to think about the appropriate balance between employer and employee rights in ideas developed jointly. Solutions to the problem of the unauthorized copying of software may be found in alternative pricing structures rather than in fundamental modifications of our institutions. Public interest considerations could be advanced for opening access to privately held information in a variety of areas. As we consider these specific questions) however, I would urge that we keep firmly in mind the variety of objectives that intellectual property institutions have traditionally served.[36] If, following Hettinger's advice, we single-mindedly reshape these institutions to maximize the short-term dissemination and use of ideas, we run the risk of subverting the other ends these institutions serve.

Notes

1 Edwin C. Hettinger, "Justifying Intellectual Property," *Philosophy & Public Affairs* 18, no. 1 (Winter 1989): 31–52.

2 Thomas Jefferson agrees. See Jefferson's letter to Isaac McPherson, 13 August 1813, in *The Founder's Constitution*, ed. Philip B. Kurland and Ralph Lerner (Chicago: University of Chicago Press, 1987), 3:42.

3 Hettinger uses the term *utilitarian* in a very narrow sense to refer to a justification in terms of maximizing the use and dissemination of information. Some utilitarians might see intellectual property institutions as promoting objectives other than information dissemination. My discussion of the roots of trade secret principles is perfectly consistent with a utilitarian justification of those principles. Indeed, a utilitarian could argue (as many economists do) that giving people certain rights in

ideas they generate through their own labor advances social well-being by promoting innovation. See, e.g., Robert U. Ayres, "Technological Protection and Piracy: Some Implications for Policy," *Technological Forecasting and Social Change* 30 (1986):5–18.

4 In Hettinger's paper and in mine, the terms *justification, goal, purpose, rationale,* and *objective* are used loosely and somewhat interchangeably. But, of course, identifying the purpose or goal of our intellectual property institutions does not automatically justify them. Some further legitimating idea or ultimate good, such as the general welfare or individual liberty, must be invoked. A difficulty with Hettinger's argument is that he identifies an objective for our intellectual property institutions–promoting the use and dissemination of ideas–and concludes that he has justified them. However, unless maximizing the use and dissemination of ideas is an intrinsic good, we would expect a further step in the argument linking this objective to an ultimate good. Hettinger may think this step can be made or is self-evident from his terminology. However, it is not clear whether he calls his justification "utilitarian" because of its consequentialist form or because he means to appeal to social wellbeing or some particular good he associates with utilitarianism.

5 Hettinger seems to think that he has provided a clear-cut objective against which to measure the effectiveness of our intellectual property institutions. Yet, a set of institutions that maximized the "dissemination and use of information" would not necessarily be most effective at "promoting the creation of valuable intellectual works" or promoting "the progress of science and the useful arts." A society might be quite successful at disseminating information, but rather mediocre at creating valuable intellectual works.

There is an inevitable tension between the objectives of innovation and dissemination. The same tension is present in other areas of law concerned with rights in information–insider trading, for example. For discussion of this tension, see Frank H. Easterbrook, "Insider Trading, Secret Agents, Evidentiary Privileges, and the Production of Information," *1981 Supreme Court Review,* p. 309. While we struggle to piece together a system of information rights that gives due consideration to both objectives, we must be wary of the notion that there is a single optimal allocation of rights.

Indeed, the very idea of a "socially optimal output of intellectual products" is embarrassingly imprecise. What is a socially optimal output of poems, novels, computer programs, movies, cassette recordings, production processes, formulations of matter, stock tips, business strategies, etc.? How we allocate rights in ideas may affect the quality and kinds of intellectual products that are produced as well as their quantity and dissemination. Hettinger seems concerned primarily with quantity. The use of general terms like *intellectual product* and *socially optimal output* obscures the complexity of the empirical assessment that Hettinger proposes.

6 Hettinger mentions trademark as another of our intellectual property institutions, along with our social sanction on plagiarism, but his central discussion focuses on copyright, patent, and trade secret concepts. Neither trademark principles nor the prohibition on plagiarism fits comfortably with his justification in terms of increasing the dissemination and use of ideas. Both are more closely related to giving recognition to the source or originator of ideas and products.

7 It may be helpful to think of two levels of justification: (1) an intermediate level consisting of objectives, purposes, reasons, and explanations for an institution or practice; and (2) an ultimate level linking those objectives and purposes to our most basic legitimating ideas such as the general good or individual liberty. Philosophers generally tend to be concerned with the ultimate level of justification while

policymakers and judges more frequently operate at the intermediate level. Hettinger has, I think, mistaken an intermediate-level justification of patents and copyrights (promoting the dissemination and use of ideas) for an ultimate justification of intellectual property institutions.

8 Hettinger, of course, recognizes that various rights are involved. He speaks of rights to possess, to personally use, to prevent others from using, to publish, and to receive the market value of one's ideas. And he notes that one might have a natural right to possess and personally use one's ideas even if one might not have a natural right to prevent others from copying them. But he does not consider the possibility that the different rights involved in our concept of intellectual property may rest on quite varied foundations, some firmer than others.

9 It is generally accepted that the concept of property is best understood as a "bundle of rights." Just as the bundle of rights involved in home ownership differs substantially from the bundle of rights associated with stock ownership, the bundle of rights involved in patent protection differs from the bundle of rights involved in trade secret protection.

10 Today we commonly speak of copyright protection as providing incentives for intellectual effort, while at the same time ensuring widespread dissemination of ideas. As Hettinger notes, the effectiveness of copyright protection in achieving these aims may depend partly on the period of the copyright grant. Historically, at least before the first English copyright act, the famous 1710 Act of Anne, it appears that the dissemination of ideas was not so central. The common law gave the author an exclusive first right of printing or publishing her manuscript on the grounds that she was entitled to the product of her labor. The common law's position on the author's right to prohibit subsequent publication was less clear. See generally Wheaton v. Peters, 8 Pet. 591 (1834), reprinted in *The Founders' Constitution* 3:44–60.

11 Hettinger recognizes a right not to divulge privately created intellectual products, but he does not fit this right into his discussion. If the right is taken seriously, however, it will, I believe, undermine Hettinger's own conclusions.

12 We would hope that the right to control disclosure would be exercised in a morally responsible way and that, for example, people with socially useful ideas would share them and that some types of harmful ideas would be withheld. But the potential social benefits of certain disclosures cannot justify a general requirement that ideas be disclosed.

13 Here, I am using the term *personal* to refer to ideas about intimate matters, such as sexual behavior.

14 The right to control disclosure of one's thoughts might be thought to be no more than a reflection of technical limitations. Enforcing a general disclosure requirement presupposes some way of identifying the undisclosed thoughts of others. Currently, we do not have the technology to do this. But even if we did–or especially if we did–respect for the individual would preclude any form of monitoring people's thoughts.

15 On the relation between privacy and intimate relationships, see Charles Fried, "Privacy," *Yale Law Journal* 77 (1968):475–93. Below, I will argue that confidentiality is central to other types of cooperative relationships as well.

16 Whether the presumption is overcome will depend on the importance of the objectives served by disclosure, and the degree of violence done to the individual or the relationship at stake.

17 Technically, of course, others have access to ideas that have been expressed whereas they do not have access to undisclosed thoughts. But ease of access is not the criterion for propriety of access.

18 This is the fundamental principle behind the prohibition on insider trading.

19 The phrase "special communities of knowledge" comes from Kim Lane Scheppele, *Legal Secrets* (Chicago: University of Chicago Press, 1988), p. 14.

20 In practice, this *prima facie* obligation may sometimes be overridden when it conflicts with other obligations, e.g., the obligation to prevent harm to a third party.

21 An actual case similar to this was litigated in Pennsylvania. See *Continental Data Systems, Inc. v. Eaton Corporation,* 638 F. Supp. 432 (D.C.E.D. Pa. 1986).

22 For the view that fair and honest business competition is the central policy underlying trade secret protection, see Ramon A. Klitzke, "Trade Secrets: Importing Quasi-Property Rights," *Business Lawyer* 41 (1986):557–70.

23 It appears that Hettinger is using the term *private company* in contrast to individuals rather than to public companies—those whose shares are sold to the public on national stock exchanges. If one wishes to protect individuals, however, it might be more important to distinguish small, privately held companies from large, publicly held ones than to distinguish individuals from companies. Many individuals, however, are dependent on large, publicly held companies as their livelihood.

24 *Uniform Trade Secrets Act with 1985 Amendments,* sec. 1, in *Uniform Laws Annotated,* vol. 14 (1980 with 1988 Pocket Part). The Uniform Trade Secrets Act seeks to codify and standardize the common law principles of trade secret law as they have developed in different jurisdictions.

25 See Klitzke, "Trade Secrets." Different theories of justification are discussed in Ridsdale Ellis, *Trade Secrets* (New York: Baker, Voorhis, 1953). Kim Lane Scheppele is another commentator favoring the view that breach of confidence is what trade secret cases are all about. See *Legal Secrets,* p. 241. In their famous article on privacy, Warren and Brandeis find the roots of trade secret principles in the right to privacy. Samuel D. Warren and Louis D. Brandeis, *Harvard Law Review* 4 (1890):212.

26 E. I. DuPont de Nemours Powder Co. v. Masland, 244 U.S. 100 (1917).

27 One commentator has said, "The desire to reinforce 'good faith and honest, fair dealing' in business is the mother of the law of trade secrets." Russell B. Stevenson, Jr., *Corporations and Information* (Baltimore: Johns Hopkins University Press, 1980), p. 19.

28 Support for this interpretation is found in Justice Thurgood Marshall's concurring opinion in *Kewanee Oil Co. v. Bicron Corp.,* 416 U.S. 470, 494 (1974). The court held that the federal patent laws do not preempt state trade secret laws.

29 Congress may have realized that trying to bring about more openness by eliminating trade secret protection, even with the added attraction of a limited monopoly for inventions that qualify for patent protection, would be inconsistent with fundamental moral notions such as respect for confidential relationships, and would probably not have worked anyway.

30 See. e.g., the statement of a *manager* of a competitor surveillance group quoted in Jerry L. Wall, "What the Competition Is Doing: Your Need to Know," *Harvard Business Review* 52 (November–December 1974):34. See generally Leonard M. Fuld, Competitor Intelligence: How to Get It–How to Use It (New York: John Wiley and Sons, 1985).

31 See e.g., John Burgess, "Unlocking Corporate Shackles," *Washington Business,* 11 December 1989, p. 1.

32 Hettinger speaks of ideas as objects, and of rights in ideas as comparable to water or mineral rights. Indeed, according to Hettinger, the difficulty in justifying intellectual property rights arises because ideas are not in all respects like tangible property, which he thinks is more easily justified.

33 The Editors of *Philosophy & Public Affairs* encouraged me to address this point.

34 His argument from maximizing the production and dissemination of ideas

suggests that the presumption in favor of free ideas is not terribly strong: it can be overridden by identifying some reasonable objective likely to be served by assigning exclusive rights.

35 That is, we should look at the effects of these institutions on social well-being in general and select the institutions that are best on the whole.

36 A utilitarian assessment will also include consideration of the various interests that would be affected by alternative allocations of intellectual property rights. For example, denying authors copyright in their works may increase the power and profit of publishers and further impair the ability of lesser-known writers to find publication outlets. One scholar has concluded that America's failure to recognize the copyrights of aliens before 1891 stunted the development of native literature. For fifty years before the passage of the Platt-Simmonds Act, publishing interests vigorously and successfully opposed recognition of international copyright. This is understandable since the works of well-known British authors were available to publishers free of charge. Publishers were not terribly concerned with the artistic integrity of these works. They sometimes substituted alternative endings, mixed the works of different authors, and edited as economically necessary. There were few reasons to take the risks involved in publishing the works of unknown and untested American writers who might insist on artistic integrity. See generally Aubert J. Clark, *The Movement for International Copyright in Nineteenth Century America* (Westport, Conn.: Greenwood Press, 1973).

UNIT THREE
CORPORATE SOCIAL RESPONSIBILITY

21

The Social Responsibility of Business Is to Increase Its Profits

Milton Friedman

When I hear businessmen speak eloquently about the "social responsibilities of business in a free-enterprise system," I am reminded of the wonderful line about the Frenchman who discovered at the age of 70 that he had been speaking prose all his life. The businessmen believe that they are defending free enterprise when they declaim that business is not concerned "merely" with profit but also with promoting desirable "social" ends; that business has a "social conscience" and takes seriously its responsibilities for providing employment, eliminating discrimination, avoiding pollution and whatever else may be the catchwords of the contemporary crop of reformers. In fact they are – or would be if they or anyone else took them seriously – preaching pure and unadulterated socialism. Businessmen who talk this way are unwitting puppets of the intellectual forces that have been undermining the basis of a free society these past decades.

The discussions of the "social responsibilities of business" are notable for their analytical looseness and lack of rigor. What does it mean to say that "business" has responsibilities? Only people can have responsibilities. A corporation is an artificial person and in this sense may have artificial responsibilities, but "business" as a whole cannot be said to have responsibilities, even in this vague sense. The first step toward clarity in examining the doctrine of the social responsibility of business is to ask precisely what it implies for whom.

Presumably, the individuals who are to be responsible are businessmen, which means individual proprietors or corporate executives. Most of the discussion of social responsibility is directed at corporations, so in what follows I shall mostly neglect the individual proprietors and speak of corporate executives.

Source: *New York Times Magazine*, September 13, 1970. Copyright © by The New York Times Company.

In a free-enterprise, private-property system, a corporate executive is an employee of the owners of the business. He has direct responsibility to his employers. That responsibility is to conduct the business in accordance with their desires, which generally will be to make as much money as possible while conforming to the basic rules of the society, both those embodied in law and those embodied in ethical custom. Of course, in some cases his employers may have a different objective. A group of persons might establish a corporation for an eleemosynary purpose – for example, a hospital or a school. The manager of such a corporation will not have money profit as his objective but the rendering of certain services.

In either case, the key point is that, in his capacity as a corporate executive, the manager is the agent of the individuals who own the corporation or establish the eleemosynary institution, and his primary responsibility is to them.

Needless to say, this does not mean that it is easy to judge how well he is performing his task. But at least the criterion of performance is straightforward, and the persons among whom a voluntary contractual arrangement exists are clearly defined.

Of course, the corporate executive is also a person in his own right. As a person, he may have many other responsibilities that he recognizes or assumes voluntarily – to his family, his conscience, his feelings of charity, his church, his clubs, his city, his country. He may feel impelled by these responsibilities to devote part of his income to causes he regards as worthy, to refuse to work for particular corporations, even to leave his job, for example, to join his country's armed forces. If we wish, we may refer to some of these responsibilities as "social responsibilities." But in these respects he is acting as a principal, not an agent; he is spending his own money or time or energy, not the money of his employers or the time or energy he has contracted to devote to their purposes. If these are "social responsibilities," they are the social responsibilities of individuals, not of business.

What does it mean to say that the corporate executive has a "social responsibility" in his capacity as businessman? If this statement is not pure rhetoric, it must mean that he is to act in some way that is not in the interest of his employers. For example, that he is to refrain from increasing the price of the product in order to contribute to the social objective of preventing inflation, even though a price increase would be in the best interests of the corporation. Or that he is to make expenditures on reducing pollution beyond the amount that is in the best interests of the corporation or that is required by law in order to contribute to the social objective of improving the environment. Or that, at the expense of corporate profits, he is to hire "hardcore" unemployed instead of better qualified available workmen to contribute to the social objective of reducing poverty.

In each of these cases, the corporate executive would be spending someone else's money for a general social interest. Insofar as his actions in accord with his "social responsibility" reduce returns to stockholders, he is spending their money. Insofar as his actions raise the price to customers, he is spending the customers' money. Insofar as his actions lower the wages of some employees, he is spending their money.

The stockholders or the customers or the employees could separately spend their own money on the particular action if they wished to do so. The executive is exercising a distinct "social responsibility," rather than serving as an agent of the stockholders or the customers or the employees, only if he spends the money in a different way than they would have spent it.

But if he does this, he is in effect imposing taxes, on the one hand, and deciding how the tax proceeds shall be spent, on the other.

This process raises political questions on two levels: principle and consequences. On the level of political principle, the imposition of taxes and the expenditure of tax proceeds are governmental functions. We have established elaborate constitutional, parliamentary, and judicial provisions to control these functions, to assure that taxes are imposed so far as possible in accordance with the preferences and desires of the public — after all, "taxation without representation" was one of the battle cries of the American Revolution. We have a system of checks and balances to separate the legislative function of imposing taxes and enacting expenditures from the executive function of collecting taxes and administering expenditure programs and from the judicial function of mediating disputes and interpreting the law.

Here the businessman — self-selected or appointed directly or indirectly by stockholders — is to be simultaneously legislator, executive, and jurist. He is to decide whom to tax by how much and for what purpose, and he is to spend the proceeds — all this guided only by general exhortations from on high to restrain inflation, improve the environment, fight poverty and so on and on.

The whole justification for permitting the corporate executive to be selected by the stockholders is that the executive is an agent sensing the interests of his principal. This justification disappears when the corporate executive imposes taxes and spends the proceeds for "social" purposes. He becomes in effect a public employee, a civil servant, even though he remains in name an employee of a private enterprise. On grounds of political principle, it is intolerable that such civil servants — insofar as their actions in the name of social responsibility are real and not just window-dressing — should be selected as they are now. If they are to be civil servants, then they must be elected through a political process. If they are to impose taxes and make expenditures to foster "social" objectives, then political machinery must be set up to make the assessment of taxes and to determine through a political process the objectives to be served.

This is the basic reason why the doctrine of "social responsibility" involves the acceptance of the socialist view that political mechanisms, not market mechanisms, are the appropriate way to determine the allocation of scarce resources to alternative uses.

On the grounds of consequences, can the corporate executive in fact discharge his alleged "social responsibilities?" On the other hand, suppose he could get away with spending the stockholders' or customers' or employees' money. How is he to know how to spend it? He is told that he must contribute to fighting inflation. How is he to know what action of his will contribute to that end? He is presumably an expert in running his company – in producing a product or selling it or financing it. But nothing about his selection makes him an expert on inflation. Will his holding down the price of his product reduce inflationary pressure? Or, by leaving more spending power in the hands of his customers, simply divert it elsewhere? Or, by forcing him to produce less because of the lower price, will it simply contribute to shortages? Even if he could answer these questions, how much cost is he justified in imposing on his stockholders, customers, and employees for this social purpose? What is his appropriate share and what is the appropriate share of others?

And, whether he wants to or not, can he get away with spending his stockholders', customers' or employees' money? Will not the stockholders fire him? (Either the present ones or those who take over when his actions in the name of social responsibility have reduced the corporation's profits and the price of its stock.) His customers and his employees can desert him for other producers and employers less scrupulous in exercising their social responsibilities.

This facet of "social responsibility" doctrine is brought into sharp relief when the doctrine is used to justify wage restraint by trade unions. The conflict of interest is naked and clear when union officials are asked to subordinate the interest of their members to some more general purpose. If the union officials try to enforce wage restraint, the consequence is likely to be wildcat strikes, rank-and-file revolts, and the emergence of strong competitors for their jobs. We thus have the ironic phenomenon that union leaders – at least in the U.S. – have objected to Government interference with the market far more consistently and courageously than have business leaders.

The difficulty of exercising "social responsibility" illustrates, of course, the great virtue of private competitive enterprise – it forces people to be responsible for their own actions and makes it difficult for them to "exploit" other people for either selfish or unselfish purposes. They can do good – but only at their own expense.

Many a reader who has followed the argument this far may be tempted to remonstrate that it is all well and good to speak of Government's having the responsibility to impose taxes and determine expenditures for such "social" purposes as controlling pollution or training the hard-core unemployed, but that the problems are too urgent to wait on the slow course of political processes, that the exercise of social responsibility by businessmen is a quicker and surer way to solve pressing current problems.

Aside from the question of fact – I share Adam Smith's skepticism about the benefits that can be expected from "those who affected to trade for the public good" – this argument must be rejected on grounds of principle. What it amounts to is an assertion that those who favor the taxes and expenditures in question have failed to persuade a majority of their fellow citizens to be of like mind and that they are seeking to attain by undemocratic procedures what they cannot attain by democratic procedures. In a free society, it is hard for "evil" people to do "evil," especially since one man's good is another's evil.

I have, for simplicity, concentrated on the special case of the corporate executive, except only for the brief digression on trade unions. But precisely the same argument applies to the newer phenomenon of calling upon stockholders to require corporations to exercise social responsibility (the recent G.M. crusade for example). In most of these cases, what is in effect involved is some stockholders trying to get other stockholders (or customers or employees) to contribute against their will to "social" causes favored by the activists. Insofar as they succeed, they are again imposing taxes and spending the proceeds.

The situation of the individual proprietor is somewhat different. If he acts to reduce the returns of his enterprise in order to exercise his "social responsibility," he is spending his own money, not someone else's. If he wishes to spend his money on such purposes, that is his right, and I cannot see that there is any objection to his doing so. In the process, he, too, may impose costs on employees and customers. However, because he is far less likely than a large corporation or union to have monopolistic power, any such side effects will tend to be minor.

Of course, in practice, the doctrine of social responsibility is frequently a cloak for actions that are justified on other grounds rather than a reason for those actions.

To illustrate, it may well be in the long-run interest of a corporation that is a major employer in a small community to devote resources to providing amenities to that community or to improving its government. That may make it easier to attract desirable employees, it may reduce the wage bill or lessen losses from pilferage and sabotage or have other worthwhile effects. Or it may be that, given the laws about the deductibility of corporate charitable contributions, the stockholders can contribute more to charities they favor by having the corporation make the gift than by doing it themselves, since they can in that way contribute an amount that would otherwise have been paid as corporate taxes.

In each of these – and many similar – cases, there is a strong temptation to rationalize these actions as an exercise of "social responsibility." In the present climate of opinion, with its wide-spread aversion to "capitalism," "profits," the "soulless corporation," and so on, this is one way for a corporation to generate goodwill as a by-product of expenditures that are entirely justified in its own self-interest.

It would be inconsistent of me to call on corporate executives to refrain from this hypocritical window-dressing because it harms the foundations of a free society. That would be to call on them to exercise a "social responsibility"! If our institutions, and the attitudes of the public make it in their self-interest to cloak their actions in this way, I cannot summon much indignation to denounce them. At the same time, I can express admiration for those individual proprietors or owners of closely held corporations or stock-holders of more broadly held corporations who disdain such tactics as approaching fraud.

Whether blameworthy or not, the use of the cloak of social responsibility, and the nonsense spoken in its name by influential and prestigious business-men, does clearly harm the foundations of a free society. I have been impressed time and again by the schizophrenic character of many business-men. They are capable of being extremely far-sighted and clear-headed in matters that are internal to their businesses. They are incredibly short-sighted and muddle-headed in matters that are outside their businesses but affect the possible survival of business in general. This shortsightedness is strikingly exemplified in the calls from many businessmen for wage and price guidelines or controls or income policies. There is nothing that could do more in a brief period to destroy a market system and replace it by a centrally controlled system than effective governmental control of prices and wages.

The shortsightedness is also exemplified in speeches by businessmen on social responsibility. This may gain them kudos in the short run. But it helps to strengthen the already too prevalent view that the pursuit of profits is wicked and immoral and must be curbed and controlled by external forces. Once this view is adopted, the external forces that curb the market will not be the social consciences, however highly developed, of the pontificating executives; it will be the iron fist of Government bureaucrats. Here, as with price and wage controls, businessmen seem to me to reveal a suicidal impulse.

The political principle that underlies the market mechanism is unanimity. In an ideal free market resting on private property, no individual can coerce any other, all cooperation is voluntary, all parties to such cooperation benefit or they need not participate. Where are no values, no "social" responsibilities in any sense other than the shared values and responsibilities of individuals. Society is collection of individuals and of the various groups they voluntarily form.

The political principle that underlies the political mechanism is con-formity. The individual must serve a more general social interest – whether that be determined by a church or a dictator or a majority. The individual may have a vote and say in what is to be done, but if he is overruled, he must conform. It is appropriate for some to require others to contribute to a general social purpose whether they wish to or not.

Unfortunately, unanimity is not always feasible. There are some respects in which conformity appears unavoidable, so I do not see how one can avoid the use of the political mechanism altogether.

But the doctrine of "social responsibility" taken seriously would extend the scope of the apolitical mechanism to every human activity. It does not differ in philosophy from the most explicitly collectivist doctrine. It differs only by professing to believe that collectivist ends can be attained without collectivist means. That is why, in my book *Capitalism and Freedom*, I have called it a "fundamentally subversive doctrine" in a free society, and have said that in such a society, "there is one and only one social responsibility of business – to use its resources and engage in activities designed to increase its profits so long as it stays within the rules of the game, which is to say, engages in open and free competition without deception or fraud."

22

A Stakeholder Theory of the
Modern Corporation

R. Edward Freeman

Introduction

Corporations have ceased to be merely legal devices through which the private business transactions of individuals may be carried on. Though still much used for this purpose, the corporate form has acquired a larger significance. The corporation has, in fact, become both a method of property tenure and a means of organizing economic life. Grown to tremendous proportions, there may be said to have evolved a "corporate system" – which has attracted to itself a combination of attributes and powers, and has attained a degree of prominence entitling it to be dealt with as a major social institution.[1]

Despite these prophetic words of Berle and Means (1932), scholars and managers alike continue to hold sacred the view that managers bear a special relationship to the stockholders in the firm. Since stockholders own shares in the firm, they have certain rights and privileges, which must be granted to them by management, as well as by others. Sanctions, in the form of "the law of corporations," and other protective mechanisms in the form of social custom, accepted management practice, myth, and ritual, are thought to reinforce the assumption of the primacy of the stockholder.

The purpose of this paper is to pose several challenges to this assumption, from within the framework of managerial capitalism, and to suggest the bare bones of an alternative theory, *a stakeholder theory of the modern corporation*. I do not seek the demise of the modern corporation, either intellectually or in fact. Rather, I seek its transformation. In the words of Neurath, we shall attempt to "rebuild the ship, plank by plank, while it remains afloat."[2]

My thesis is that I can revitalize the concept of managerial capitalism by

Source: Excerpts from R. Edward Freeman, 'The Politics of Stakeholder Theory', in *Business Ethics Quarterly*, 4 (1994), 409–21.

replacing the notion that managers have a duty to stockholders with the concept that managers bear a fiduciary relationship to stakeholders. Stakeholders are those groups who have a stake in or claim on the firm. Specifically I include suppliers, customers, employees, stockholders, and the local community, as well as management in its role as agent for these groups. I argue that the legal, economic, political, and moral challenges to the currently received theory of the firm, as a nexus of contracts among the owners of the factors of production and customers, require us to revise this concept. That is, each of these stakeholder groups has a right not to be treated as a means to some end, and therefore must participate in determining the future direction of the firm in which they have a stake.

The crux of my argument is that we must reconceptualize the firm around the following question: For whose benefit and at whose expense should the firm be managed? I shall set forth such a reconceptualization in the form of a *stakeholder theory of the firm.* I shall then critically examine the stakeholder view and its implications for the future of the capitalist system.

The Attack on Managerial Capitalism

The legal argument

The basic idea of managerial capitalism is that in return for controlling the firm, management vigorously pursues the interests of stockholders. Central to the managerial view of the firm is the idea that management can pursue market transactions with suppliers and customers in an unconstrained manner.

The law of corporations gives a less clearcut answer to the question: in whose interest and for whose benefit should the modern corporation be governed? While it says that the corporations should be run primarily in the interests of the stockholders in the firm, it says further that the corporation exists "in contemplation of the law" and has personality as a "legal person," limited liability for its actions, and immortality, since its existence transcends that of its members. Therefore, directors and other officers of the firm have a fiduciary obligation to stockholders in the sense that the "affairs of the corporation" must be conducted in the interest of the stockholders. And stockholders can theoretically bring suit against those directors and managers for doing otherwise. But since the corporation is a legal person, existing in contemplation of the law, managers of the corporation are constrained by law.

Until recently, this was no constraint at all. In this century, however, the law has evolved to effectively constrain the pursuit of stockholder interests at the expense of other claimants on the firm. It has, in effect, required that the claims of customers, suppliers, local communities, and employees be taken into consideration, though in general they are subordinated to the claims of stockholders.

For instance, the doctrine of "privity of contract," as articulated in *Winterbottom v. Wright* in 1842, has been eroded by recent developments in products liability law. Indeed, *Greenman v. Yuba Power* gives the manufacturer strict liability for damage caused by its products, even though the seller has exercised all possible care in the preparation and sale of the product and the consumer has not bought the product from nor entered into any contractual arrangement with the manufacturer. Caveat emptor has been replaced, in large part, with caveat venditor.[3] The Consumer Product Safety Commission has the power to enact product recalls, and in 1980 one U.S. automobile company recalled more cars than it built. Some industries are required to provide information to customers about a product's ingredients, whether or not the customers want and are willing to pay for this information.[4]

The same argument is applicable to management's dealings with employees. The National Labor Relations Act gave employees the right to unionize and to bargain in good faith. It set up the National Labor Relations board to enforce these rights with management. The Equal Pay Act of 1963 and Title VII of the Civil Rights Act of 1964 constrain management from discrimination in hiring practices; these have been followed with the Age Discrimination in Employment Act of 1967.[5] The emergence of a body of administrative case law arising from labor-management disputes and the historic settling of discrimination claims with large employers such as AT&T have caused the emergence of a body of practice in the corporation that is consistent with the legal guarantee of the rights of the employees. The law has protected the due process rights of those employees who enter into collective bargaining agreements with management. As of the present, however, only 30 percent of the labor force are participating in such agreements; this has prompted one labor law scholar to propose a statutory law prohibiting dismissals of the 70 percent of the work force not protected.[6]

The law has also protected the interests of local communities. The Clean Air Act and Clean Water Act have constrained management from "spoiling the commons." In an historic case, *Marsh v. Alabama*, the Supreme Court ruled that a company owned town was subject to the provisions of the U.S. Constitution, thereby guaranteeing the rights of local citizens and negating the "property rights" of the firm. Some states and municipalities have gone further and passed laws preventing firms from moving plants or limiting when and how plants can be closed. In sum, there is much current legal activity in this area to constrain management's pursuit of stockholders' interests at the expense of the local communities in which the firm operates.

I have argued that the result of such changes in the legal system can be viewed as giving some rights to those groups that have a claim on the firm, for example, customers, suppliers, employees, local communities, stockholders, and management. It raises the question, at the core of a theory of the firm: in whose interest and for whose benefit should the firm be managed? The answer proposed by managerial capitalism is clearly "the stockholders," but I have argued that the law has been progressively circumscribing this answer.

The economic argument

In its pure ideological form managerial capitalism seeks to maximize the interests of stockholders. In its perennial criticism of government regulation, management espouses the "invisible hand" doctrine. It contends that it creates the greatest good for the greatest number, and therefore government need not intervene. However, we know that externalities, moral hazards, and monopoly power exist in fact, whether or not they exist in theory. Further, some of the legal apparatus mentioned above has evolved to deal with just these issues.

The problem of the "tragedy of the commons" or the free-rider problem pervades the concept of public goods such as water and air. No one has an incentive to incur the cost of clean-up or the cost of nonpollution, since the marginal gain of one firm's action is small. Every firm reasons this way, and the result is pollution of water and air. Since the industrial revolution, firms have sought to internalize the benefits and externalize the costs of their actions. The cost must be borne by all, through taxation and regulation; hence we have the emergence of the environmental regulations of the 1970s.

Similarly, moral hazards arise when the purchaser of a good or service can pass along the cost of that good. There is no incentive to economize, on the part of either the producer or the consumer, and there is excessive use of the resources involved. The institutionalized practice of third-party payment in health care is a prime example.

Finally, we see the avoidance of competitive behavior on the part of firms, each seeking to monopolize a small portion of the market and not compete with one another. In a number of industries, oligopolies have emerged, and while there is questionable evidence that oligopolies are not the most efficient corporate form in some industries, suffice it to say that the potential for abuse of market power has again led to regulation of managerial activity. In the classic case, AT&T, arguably one of the great technological and managerial achievements of the century, was broken up into eight separate companies to prevent its abuse of monopoly power.

Externalities, moral hazards, and monopoly power have led to more external control on managerial capitalism. There are de facto constraints, due to these economic facts of life, on the ability of management to act in the interests of stockholders.

A Stakeholder Theory of the Firm

The stakeholder concept

Corporations have stakeholders, that is, groups and individuals who benefit from or are harmed by, and whose rights are violated or respected by, corporate actions. The concept of stakeholders is a generalization of the notion of stockholders, who themselves have some special claim on the firm. Just as stockholders have a right to demand certain actions by management, so do other stakeholders have a right to make claims. The exact nature of these claims is a difficult question that I shall address, but the logic is identical to that of the stockholder theory. Stakes require action of a certain sort, and conflicting stakes require methods of resolution.

Freeman and Reed (1983)[7] distinguish two senses of *stakeholder*. The "narrow definition" includes those groups who are vital to the survival and success of the corporation. The "wide-definition" includes any group or individual who can affect or is affected by the corporation. I shall begin with a modest aim: to articulate a stakeholder theory using the narrow definition.

Stakeholders in the modern corporation

Figure 1 depicts the stakeholders in a typical large corporation. The stakes of each are reciprocal, since each can affect the other in terms of harms and benefits as well as rights and duties. The stakes of each are not univocal and would vary by particular corporation. I merely set forth some general notions that seem to be common to many large firms.

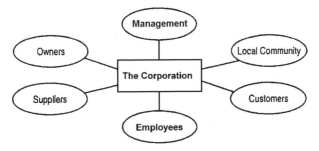

Figure 1. A Stakeholder Model of the Corporation.

Owners have financial stake in the corporation in the form of stocks, bonds, and so on, and they expect some kind of financial return from them. Either they have given money directly to the firm, or they have some historical claim made through a series of morally justified exchanges. The firm affects their livelihood or, if a substantial portion of their retirement income is in stocks or bonds, their ability to care for themselves when they can no longer work. Of course, the stakes of owners will differ by type of owner, preferences for money, moral preferences, and so on, as well as by type of firm. The owners of AT&T are quite different from the owners of Ford Motor Company, with stock of the former company being widely dispersed among 3 million stockholders and that of the latter being held by a small family group as well as by a large group of public stockholders.

Employees have their jobs and usually their livelihood at stake; they often have specialized skills for which there is usually no perfectly elastic market. In return for their labor, they expect security, wages, benefits, and meaningful work. In return for their loyalty, the corporation is expected to provide for them and carry them through difficult times. Employees are expected to follow the instructions of management most of the time, to speak favorably about the company, and to be responsible citizens in the local communities in which the company operates. Where they are used as means to an end, they must participate in decisions affecting such use. The evidence that such policies and values as described here lead to productive company-employee relationships is compelling. It is equally compelling to realize that the opportunities for "bad faith" on the part of both management and employees are enormous. "Mock participation" in quality circles, singing the company song, and wearing the company uniform solely to please management all lead to distrust and unproductive work.

Suppliers, interpreted in a stakeholder sense, are vital to the success of the firm, for raw materials will determine the final product's quality and price. In turn the firm is a customer of the supplier and is therefore vital to the success and survival of the supplier. When the firm treats the supplier as a valued member of the stakeholder network, rather than simply as a source of materials, the supplier will respond when the firm is in need. Chrysler traditionally had very close ties to its suppliers, even to the extent that led some to suspect the transfer of illegal payments. And when Chrysler was on the brink of disaster, the suppliers responded with price cuts, accepting late payments, financing, and so on. Supplier and company can rise and fall together. Of course, again, the particular supplier relationships will depend on a number of variables such as the number of suppliers and whether the supplies are finished goods or raw materials.

Customers exchange resources for the products of the firm and in return receive the benefits of the products. Customers provide the lifeblood of the firm in the form of revenue. Given the level of reinvestment of earnings in large corporations, customers indirectly pay for the development of new products and services. Peters and Waterman (1982)[8] have argued that being close to the customer leads to success with other stakeholders and that a distinguishing characteristic of some companies that have performed well is their emphasis on the customer. By paying attention to customers' needs, management automatically addresses the needs of suppliers and owners. Moreover, it seems that the ethic of customer service carries over to the community. Almost without fail the "excellent companies" in Peters and Waterman's study have good reputations in the community. I would argue that Peters and Waterman have found multiple applications of Kant's dictum, "treat persons as ends unto themselves," and it should come as no surprise that persons respond to such respectful treatment, be they customers, suppliers, owners, employees, or members of the local community. The real surprise is the novelty of the application of Kant's rule in a theory of good management practice.

The local community grants the firm the right to build facilities and, in turn, it benefits from the tax base and economic and social contributions of the firm. In return for the provision of local services, the firm is expected to be a good citizen, as is any person, either "natural or artificial." The firm cannot expose the community to unreasonable hazards in the form of pollution, toxic waste, and so on. If for some reason the firm must leave a community, it is expected to work with local leaders to make the transition as smoothly as possible. Of course, the firm does not have perfect knowledge, but when it discovers some danger or runs afoul of new competition, it is expected to inform the local community and to work with the community to overcome any problem. When the firm mismanages its relationship with the local community, it is in the same position as a citizen who commits a crime. It has violated the implicit social contract with the community and should expect to be distrusted and ostracized. It should not be surprised when punitive measures are invoked.

I have not included "competitors" as stakeholders in the narrow sense, since strictly speaking they are not necessary for the survival and success of the firm; the stakeholder theory works equally well in monopoly contexts. However, competitors and government would be the first to be included in an extension of this basic theory. It is simply not true that the interests of competitors in an industry are always in conflict. There is no reason why trade associations and other multi-organizational groups cannot band together to solve common problems that have little to do with how to restrain trade. Implementation of stakeholder management principles, in the long run, mitigates the need for industrial policy and an increasing role for government intervention and regulation.

The role of management

Management plays a special role, for it too has a stake in the modern corporation. On the one hand, management's stake is like that of employees, with some kind of explicit or implicit employment contract. But, on the other hand, management has a duty of safeguarding the welfare of the abstract entity that is the corporation. In short, management, especially top management, must look after the health of the corporation, and this involves balancing the multiple claims of conflicting stakeholders. Owners want higher financial returns, while customers want more money spent on research and development. Employees want higher wages and better benefits, while the local community wants better parks and day-care facilities.

The task of management in today's corporation is akin to that of King Solomon. The stakeholder theory does not give primacy to one stakeholder group over another, though there will surely be times when one group will benefit at the expense of others. In general, however, management must keep the relationships among stakeholders in balance. When these relationships become imbalanced, the survival of the firm is in jeopardy.

When wages are too high and product quality is too low, customers leave, suppliers suffer, and owners sell their stocks and bonds, depressing the stock price and making it difficult to raise new capital at favorable rates. Note, however, that the reason for paying returns to owners is not that they "own" the firm, but that their support is necessary for the survival of the firm, and that they have a legitimate claim on the firm. Similar reasoning applies in turn to each stakeholder group.

A stakeholder theory of the firm must define the purpose of the firm. The stockholder theory claims that the purpose of the firm is to maximize the welfare of the stockholders, perhaps subject to some moral or social constraints, either because such maximization leads to the greatest good or because of property rights. The purpose of the firm is quite different in my view.

"The stakeholder theory" can be unpacked into a number of stakeholder theories, each of which has a "normative core," inextricably linked to the way that corporations should be governed and the way that managers should act. So, attempts to more fully define, or more carefully define, a stakeholder theory are misguided. Following Donaldson and Preston, I want to insist that the normative, descriptive, instrumental, and metaphorical (my addition to their framework) uses of "stakeholder" are tied together in particular political constructions to yield a number of possible "stakeholder theories." "Stakeholder theory" is thus a genre of stories about how we could live. Let me be more specific.

A "normative core" of a theory is a set of sentences that includes among others, sentences like:

(1) Corporations ought to be governed...
(2) Managers ought to act to...

where we need arguments or further narratives which include business and moral terms to fill in the blanks. This normative core is not always reducible to a fundamental ground like the theory of property, but certain normative cores are consistent with modern understandings of property. Certain elaborations of the theory of private property plus the other institutions of political liberalism give rise to particular normative cores. But there are other institutions, other political conceptions of how society ought to be structured, so that there are different possible normative cores.

So, one normative core of a stakeholder theory might be a feminist standpoint one, rethinking how we would restructure "value-creating activity" along principles of caring and connection.[9] Another would be an ecological (or several ecological) normative cores. Mark Starik has argued that the very idea of a stakeholder theory of the *firm* ignores certain ecological necessities.[10] Exhibit 1 is suggestive of how these theories could be developed.

Exhibit 1. A Reasonable Pluralism

	A. Corporations ought to be governed...	B. Managers ought to act...	C. The background disciplines of "value creation" are...
Doctrine of... Fair Contracts	in accordance with... the six principles.	in the interests of stakeholders.	– business theories – theories that explain stakeholder behavior
Feminist Standpoint Theory	...in accordance with the principles of caring/connection and relationships.	...to maintain and care for relationships and networks of stakeholders.	– business theories – feminist theory – social science understanding of networks
Ecological Principles	...in accordance with the principle of caring for the earth.	...to care for the earth.	– business theories – ecology – other

In the next section I shall sketch the normative core based on pragmatic liberalism. But, any normative core must address the questions in columns A or B, or explain why these questions may be irrelevant, as in the ecological view. In addition, each "theory," and I use the word hesitantly, must place the normative core within a more full-fledged account of how we could understand value-creating activity differently (column C). The only way to get on with this task is to see the stakeholder idea as a metaphor. The attempt to prescribe one and only one "normative core" and construct "a stakeholder theory" is at best a disguised attempt to smuggle a normative core past the unsophisticated noses of other unsuspecting academics who are just as happy to see the end of the stockholder orthodoxy.

If we begin with the view that we can understand value-creation activity as a contractual process among those parties affected, and if for simplicity's sake we initially designate those parties as financiers, customers, suppliers, employees, and communities, then we can construct a normative core that reflects the liberal notions of autonomy, solidarity, and fairness as articulated by John Rawls, Richard Rorty, and others.[11] Notice that building these moral notions into the foundations of how we understand value creation and contracting requires that we eschew separating the business part of the process from the "ethical" part, and that we start with the presumption of equality among the contractors, rather than the presumption in favor of financier rights.

The normative core for this redesigned contractual theory will capture the liberal idea of fairness if it ensures a basic equality among stakeholders in terms of their moral rights as these are realized in the firm, and if it recognizes that inequalities among stakeholders are justified if they raise the level of the least well-off stakeholder. The liberal ideal of autonomy is captured by the realization that each stakeholder must be free to enter agreements that create value for themselves and solidarity is realized by the recognition of the mutuality of stakeholder interests.

One way to understand fairness in this context is to claim *a la* Rawls that a contract is fair if parties to the contract would agree to it in ignorance of their actual stakes. Thus, a contract is like a fair bet, if each party is willing to turn the tables and accept the other side. What would a fair contract among corporate stakeholders look like? If we can articulate this ideal, a sort of corporate constitution, we could then ask whether actual corporations measure up to this standard, and we also begin to design corporate structures which are consistent with this Doctrine of Fair Contracts.

Imagine if you will, representative stakeholders trying to decide on "the rules of the game." Each is rational in a straightforward sense, looking out for its own self-interest. At least *ex ante*, stakeholders are the relevant parties since they will be materially affected. Stakeholders know how economic activity is organized and could be organized. They know general facts about the way the corporate world works. They know that in the real world there are or could be transaction costs, externalities, and positive costs of contracting. Suppose they are uncertain about what other social institutions exist, but they know the range of those institutions. They do not know if government exists to pick up the tab for any externalities, or if they will exist in the nightwatchman state of libertarian theory. They know success and failure stories of businesses around the world. In short, they are behind a Rawls-like veil of ignorance, and they do not know what stake each will have when the veil is lifted. What groundrules would they choose to guide them?

The first groundrule is "The Principle of Entry and Exit." Any contract that is the corporation must have clearly defined entry, exit, and renegotiation conditions, or at least it must have methods or processes for so defining these conditions. The logic is straightforward: each stakeholder must be able to determine when an agreement exists and has a chance of fulfillment. This is not to imply that contracts cannot contain contingent claims or other methods for resolving uncertainty, but rather that it must contain methods for determining whether or not it is valid.

The second groundrule I shall call "The Principle of Governance," and it says that the procedure for changing the rules of the game must be agreed upon by unanimous consent. Think about the consequences of a majority of stakeholders systematically "selling out" a minority. Each stakeholder, in ignorance of its actual role, would seek to avoid such a situation. In reality this principle translates into each stakeholder never giving up its right to participate in the governance of the corporation, or perhaps into the existence of stakeholder governing boards.

The third groundrule I shall call "The Principle of Externalities," and it says that if a contract between A and B imposes a cost on C, then C has the option to become a party to the contract, and the terms are renegotiated. Once again the rationality of this condition is clear. Each stakeholder will want insurance that it does not become C.

The fourth groundrule is "The Principle of Contracting Costs," and it says that all parties to the contract must share in the cost of contracting. Once again the logic is straightforward. Any one stakeholder can get stuck.

A fifth groundrule is "The Agency Principle" that says that any agent must serve the interests of all stakeholders. It must adjudicate conflicts within the bounds of the other principals. Once again the logic is clear. Agents for any one group would have a privileged place.

A sixth and final groundrule we might call, "The Principle of Limited Immortality." The corporation shall be managed as if it can continue to serve the interests of stakeholders through time. Stakeholders are uncertain about the future but, subject to exit conditions, they realize that the continued existence of the corporation is in their interest. Therefore, it would be rational to hire managers who are fiduciaries to their interest and the interest of the collective. If it turns out the collective interests is the empty set, then this principle simply collapses into the Agency Principle.

Thus, the Doctrine of Fair Contracts consists of these six groundrules or principles:

(1) The Principle of Entry and Exit
(2) The Principle of Governance

(3) The Principle of Externalities
(4) The Principle of Contracting Costs
(5) The Agency Principle
(6) The Principle of Limited Immortality

Think of these groundrules as a doctrine which would guide actual stake holders in devising a corporate constitution or charter. Think of management as having the duty to act in accordance with some specific constitution or charter.

Obviously, if the Doctrine of Fair Contracts and its accompanying background narratives are to effect real change, there must be requisite changes in the enabling laws of the land. I propose the following three principles to serve as constitutive elements of attempts to reform the law of corporations.

The stakeholder enabling principle

Corporations shall be managed in the interests of its stakeholders, defined as employees, financiers, customers, employees, and communities.

The principle of director responsibility

Directors of the corporation shall have a duty of care to use reasonable judgment to define and direct the affairs of the corporation in accordance with the Stakeholder Enabling Principle.

The principle of stakeholder recourse

Stakeholders may bring an action against the directors for failure to perform the required duty of care.

Obviously, there is more work to be done to spell out these principles in terms of model legislation. As they stand, they try to capture the intuitions that drive the liberal ideals. It is equally plain that corporate constitutions which meet a test like the doctrine of fair contracts are meant to enable directors and executives to manage the corporation in conjunction with these same liberal ideals.[12]

Notes

1. Cf. A. Berle and C. Means, *The Modern Corporation and Private Property* (New York: Commerce Clearing House, 1932), 1. For a reassessment of Berle and Means' argument after 50 years, see *Journal of Law and Economics* 26 (June 1983), especially C. Stigler and C. Friedland, "The Literature of Economics: The Case of Berle and Means," 237–68; D. North, "Comment on Stigler and Friedland," 269–72; and C. Means, "Corporate Power in the Marketplace," 467–85.

2. The metaphor of rebuilding the ship while afloat is attributed to Neurath by W. Quine, *Word and Object* (Cambridge: Harvard University Press, 1960), and W. Quine

and J. Ullian, *The Web of Belief* (New York: Random House, 1978). The point is that to keep the ship afloat during repairs we must replace a plank with one that will do a better job. Our argument is that stakeholder capitalism can so replace the current version of managerial capitalism.

3. See R. Charan and E. Freeman, "Planning for the Business Environment of the 1980s," *The Journal of Business Strategy* 1 (1980): 9–19, especially p. 15 for a brief account of the major developments in products liability law.

4. See S. Breyer, *Regulation and Its Reform* (Cambridge: Harvard University Press, 1983), 133, for an analysis of food additives.

5. See I. Millstein and S. Katsh, *The Limits of Corporate Power* (New York: Macmillan, 1981), Chapter 4.

6. Cf. C. Summers, "Protecting All Employees Against Unjust Dismissal," *Harvard Business Review* 58 (1980): 136, for a careful statement of the argument.

7. See E. Freeman and D. Reed, "Stockholders and Stakeholders: A New Perspective on Corporate Governance," in G. Huizinga, ed., *Corporate Governance: A Definitive Exploration of the Issues* (Los Angeles: UCLA Extension Press, 1983).

8. See T. Peters and R. Waterman, *In Search of Excellence* (New York: Harper and Row, 1982).

9. See, for instance, A. Wicks, D. Gilbert, and E. Freeman, "A Feminist Reinterpretation of the Stakeholder Concept," *Business Ethics Quarterly*, Vol. 4, No. 4, October 1994; and E. Freeman and J. Liedtka, "Corporate Social Responsibility: A Critical Approach," *Business Horizons*, Vol. 34, No. 4, July–August 1991, pp. 92–98.

10. At the Toronto workshop Mark Starik sketched how a theory would look if we took the environment to be a stakeholder. This fruitful line of work is one example of my main point about pluralism.

11. J. Rawls, *Political Liberalism*, New York: Columbia University Press, 1993; and R. Rorty, "The Priority of Democracy to Philosophy" in *Reading Rorty: Critical Responses to Philosophy and the Mirror of Nature (and Beyond)*, ed. Alan R. Malachowski (Cambridge, MA: Blackwell, 1990).

23

Economics, Business Principles, and Moral Sentiments

Amartya Sen

Abstract

This essay discusses the place of business principles and of moral sentiments in economic success, and examines the role of cultures in influencing norms of business behavior. Two presumptions held in standard economic analysis are disputed: the rudimentary nature of business principles (essentially restricted, directly or indirectly, to profit maximization), and the allegedly narrow reach of moral sentiments (often treated to be irrelevant to business and economics). In contrast, the author argues for the need to recognize the complex structure of business principles and the extensive reach of moral sentiments by using theoretical considerations, a thorough analysis of Adam Smith's work, and a careful interpretation of Japan's remarkable economic success. Referring to the economic corruption in Italy and the "grabbing culture" in Russia, he further shows how deeply the presence or absence of particular features of business ethics can influence the operation of the economy, and even the nature of the society and its politics. Being an Indian himself he warns against grand generalizations like the superiority of "Asian values" over traditional Western morals. To conclude, it is diversity – over space, over time, and between groups – that makes the study of business principles and moral sentiments a rich source of understanding and explanation.

Claims and Disclaimers

There is an interesting asymmetry between the treatments of business principles and moral sentiments in standard economic analysis. Business principles are taken to be very *rudimentary* (essentially restricted, directly or

Source: Georges Enderle (ed.), *International Business Ethics* (Notre Dame, IN: University of Notre Dame Press, 1999), pp 15–29.

indirectly, to profit maximization), but with a very *wide reach* in economic matters (covering effectively all economic transactions). In contrast, moral sentiments are seen to be quite *complex* (involving different types of ethical systems), but it is assumed, that at least in economic matters, they have a very *narrow reach* (indeed, it is often presumed that such sentiments have no real influence on economic behavior).

The purpose of this essay is to discuss the place of business principles and of moral sentiments in economic success, and in that context, to examine the role of cultures in influencing norms of business behavior. If this lecture is seen in terms of the theses that I would like to present, then the first two theses consist of disputing the presumptions, respectively, of (1) the rudimentary nature of business principles, and (2) the allegedly narrow reach of moral sentiments.

Business principles cannot escape being influenced by conceptions of "good business behavior," and thus involve the standard complexities connected with multiple goals.[1] Multiple objectives can lead to competing demands made by conflicting goals, which have to be resolved in practice by some kind of compromise. Sometimes the multiplicity of normative demands may not take the explicit form of multiple objectives, but of a combination of objectives and constraints. For example, it may involve the pursuit of some unified objective (may be even maximization of profits), but subject to some self-imposed choice constraints that qualify and restrain the pursuit of that unified objective. Such constraints can reflect rules and conventions of "proper" behavior which the person involved chooses to follow. The restraints that bind the maximization of profits would, then, include not only the "feasibility constraints" that reflect the limits of what one *can* do, but also "self-imposed constraints" that the person *chooses* to obey on moral or conventional or even strategic grounds.

Since moral ideas are among the influences that affect the formulation and operation of objectives and obligations, including the demands of ethical behavior and social convention, they can be quite critical in terms of impact on the world of economics and business. The standard model of simple profit maximization as the dominant (perhaps even *exclusive*) principle covering all economic activities fails to do justice both to the content of business principles, which can be much broader, and to the domain of moral sentiments, which can be quite far-reaching.

However, these general claims must not be confused with two other beliefs which often go with the rejection of the presumption of universally self-seeking behavior. There is a need for "disclaimers" to prevent misunderstandings of what is being claimed here. First, it would be, I would argue, a great mistake to try to replace the hypothesis of universal profit maximization with another hypothesis of similar, unconditional uniformity (such as ubiquitous altruism, or universal human sympathy, or some other form of non-contingent high-mindedness). The connections are dependent on many social, cultural, and interactive considerations, and the resulting behavioral principles would tend to be complex as well as variable with respect to time, place, and group.

Second, a departure from profit maximization need not necessarily be benign, nor need moral sentiments be invariably noble. Some of the worst barbarities in the contemporary world have been committed by self-sacrificing racists – ready to do harm to some people even at great cost or risk to themselves. Indeed, this process continues today with relentless persistence – in Bosnia, Ireland, Rwanda, and many other parts of the world. The rejection of a self-centered life can go with the attempted advancement – sometimes violent promotion – of the perceived interests only of a particular group or community (excluding others), and even with willfully inflicting damages on another group or community.

Just as the reading of business principles has to be raised a notch or two from the gross presumption – standard in much of modern economics – of universal profit maximization, the role of moral sentiments may have to be lowered a notch or two from the lofty presumption – standard in some of contemporary ethics – of universal pursuit of the respective conceptions of "the good."[2] The world in which we live is very mixed, and our sentiments, principles, passions, and irritations come in many shapes and forms. The acknowledgment of diversity is the first big step we have to take in departing from the on-going traditions of self-centered economics and self-less ethics.

The conditional variability of our principles and sentiments often does have a regional component and can be linked with history and culture. In some of the social sciences, insufficient attention is paid to these variations; economics is an obvious example of this, with quite a common use of the assumption of universal profit maximization. It is, in fact, important to take serious note of the contingent and variable nature of our values.

But once again, this thesis must not be confused with the idea that the divisions in the world come in very neat and large categories – with the world population being partitioned into grand classes of followers of big ideas. Rapid generalizations of this kind have, of course, been widely made and used in social analysis, for example in praising the role of "Protestant ethics" (emphasized by many Western scholars, most notably Max Weber), or "Asian values" (much championed lately by some political leaders in Asia). In fact, the variations are more finely contingent, more forcefully local, more dependent on exact history, and much influenced by social, political, and economic experiences of the groups in question. Also, the divisions are not static, and cultural mores do shift and alter over time, sometimes quite rapidly. Once again, the appreciation of diversity is central to a realistic understanding of the varying nature of business principles and of the divergent reach of moral sentiments.

The Assumption of Universal Self-Seeking

To see business behavior exclusively in terms of profit maximization misses out many subtleties of commercial conduct, including the influence of social conventions and mores, and the roles played by dialogue, compromise, and the acceptance of "give and take." Business activities involve social interactions, and despite a possibly strong, continuing interest in making economic gains, the interactions inescapably involve much else.

The standard economic models set the focus on *exchange*, but apply that mainly to the exchange of *commodities*, as opposed to exchange of speech, claims, proposals, and settlements. The focus on "silent traders" is frequently modeled on an often-repeated interpretation of Adam Smith's analysis of exchange of commodities. The model takes off from Smith's argument that it "is not from the benevolence of the butcher, the brewer, or the baker that we expect our dinner, but from their regard to their own interest." (Smith, *Wealth of Nations*, 26–27.) There is not much here for which a complex or a sophisticated value system would be of great use. The butcher, the brewer, and the baker have to determine how much meat, beer, and bread the consumer in question would want, and a clear implicit contract can now emerge between the parties, ending with the exchange of commodities and money. The "business principles" involved in such activities would indeed be rather rudimentary.

What would go wrong in taking this to be the "model of economic behavior" is the limited nature of the particular exercise discussed in Smith's over-quoted passage. Adam Smith himself had not presented this case as being the microcosm of all economic activities, but just as an example of a case of pure exchange of commodities, for which the pursuit of self-interest entirely suffices as a motivation. But many exchanges are not like this; for example, the acceptance of a particular settlement in a wage dispute, or the emergence of agreed terms for a business partnership, can require a lot of negotiation, involving exchange of talks, claims, and concerns.

Furthermore not all economic activities are matters of exchange. There are issues of production and distribution, in which economic reasoning and business principles may, again, have to take much broader forms. Smith himself had occasion to discuss – both in *The Wealth of Nations* (1776) and in *The Theory of Moral Sentiments* (1759) – the complexity of human relations in economic as well as social matters, and the variety of motivations, principles, and ground rules that may be involved. Indeed, even the general reliability of the exchange mechanism and the use of implicit contracts (including the fact that in an on-going cultural tradition, the butcher or the brewer or the baker can accept the consumer's oral "order" without a written contract) turns ultimately on a rich history of norms, mores, trust, and convention.

Behavior of this kind is much more structured than the simple and silent pursuit of self-interest. Business principles play a central role in influencing the behavior of economic agents, and these principles can extend well beyond the straightforward seeking of individual advantage. This is not to deny that individual advantage may be a crucial motivating concern that helps to drive the engine of economic enterprise, and can also seriously influence the forms and limits of communication and agreement involved in economic and business activities. The "rawness" of the pursuit of self-interest can differ from culture to culture, and the types of principles explicitly invoked or implicitly presumed can also similarly vary. Indeed, the inter-regional and inter-cultural variations in business behavior, which we actually observe, illustrate well the fact that business principles can take much richer – and very diverse – forms, with differently structured multiple objectives. We do not have to deny the importance of self-interest to accept that many business decisions and economic activities are motivationally much more complex than the single and simple pursuit of self-interest alone.

The moral sentiments that last and flourish are, of course, influenced by – and may to a considerable extent be selected by an – evolutionary process. That aspect of the emergence of values and norms is beginning to receive serious attention in evolutionary game theory (see Binmore 1994 and Weibull 1995). This is a useful supplement to the focus on reflective ethics that we find in the works of Immanuel Kant and Adam Smith, among others. Selection by *individual reasoning* and that by *systemic survival* are two routes that can work together, rather than exclude each other. But no matter what the balance of importance is between these two different routes, the end-result is the use of substantive ethical principles and moral sentiments in business and economic behavior. They exist, they are important, they are productive, and we can ignore them only by impoverishing economic analysis and by demeaning the sophistication and breadth of human conduct.

Variations of Norms and Their Significance

Business principles that are taken for granted in one commercial environment may be very far from standard in another. This variability not only is an observed characteristic of the world as we see it, but also it affects the successes and failures – and the strengths and the weaknesses – of different economies. Indeed, the presence or absence of particular features of business ethics can deeply influence the operation of the economy and even the nature of the society and its politics.

One example is the prevalence of economic corruption in some economies, say, Italy. Parts of business ethics that may be standard in the commerce of, say, Switzerland, may be far less common in Italy, or indeed in many other financial environments. In explaining the differences, it is important to see the role played by conventions of good behavior, and how these conventions have emerged and been sustained in different regions and societies.

The issue of corruption relates also to the weakness of mutual trust. Transactions and trade are much facilitated by the trust that people have in each other's words. Confidence in the reliability of offers and promises made by others helps the efficiency of exchanges in a way that relentless self-seeking cannot. In fact, had self-interest been the only determinant of behavior, there would be many occasions in which letting the other side down (for example, by reneging on earlier arrangements) would be sensible enough. Preventing such reneging through legal means (involving suing, convicting, and penalizing) may be both expensive and painfully slow, and much of the work is done by behavioral codes and morals. The force of that code often varies sharply between different commercial environments.

When the sense of mutual trust – and corresponding standards of market ethics – are not yet well established, an outside organization can deal with the breach and provide a socially valued service in the form of strong-armed enforcement. An organization like the Mafia has been able to play an economic role here in parts of Italy, and this can be particularly important in pre-capitalist economies being drawn rapidly into capitalist transactions. Enforcement of this type, through "bandit" organizations, can be, in practice, contingently useful for different parties, even though they have no direct interest at all in corruption or crime. The respective contracting parties may each need the "assurance" that the other economic agents are also doing the appropriate thing.[3]

The flourishing of strong-armed organizations, which guarantee such "assurance," depends on the absence of behavioral codes that would reduce the need for external enforcement. The business function of enforcement through extra-legal organizations would shrink with an increase in trusting and trust-generating behavior. Complementarity between behavioral norms and institutional reform can, thus, be very strong indeed. Even though the Mafia is one of the most detestable organizations in the world (responsible for so much violence and murder), we still have to understand the economic basis of the influence of the Mafia to understand their hold on the society and their surviving power. We have to supplement our recognition of the power of guns and bombs with an understanding of some of the economic activities that make the Mafia a functionally relevant part of the economy. That functional attraction would cease as and when the combined influence of legal enforcement and behavioral development makes the Mafia economically redundant.

There is, thus, a general connection between the limited emergence of business norms and the hold of organized crime. More generally, variations in norms and values can have quite a profound effect on the functioning of the respective economies.[4] The codes of business and professional behavior are parts of the "productive resources" of a society. Variations in these resources can be seen over time as well as between regions – even between localities. Not only is Italy very diverse in terms of the modalities of behavior – indeed the contrast between North Italy and South Italy has received much attention lately – but variations can be seen *within* North Italy itself and also between one region or another *within* the South.

Variations can also be quite sharp and fast over time. A recent example includes the breakdown of law-abiding behavior in Russia as it went for tremendously rapid economic reform and marketization. The process was no doubt helped by the absence, in pre-reform Russia, of institutional patterns of behavior and codes of business ethics that are central to successful capitalism. There was a strong need at the time of institutional reform for the development of an alternative system of codes and conventions with its own logic and loyalties, which would have to play a central role in post-reform Russia. Instead of that, there clearly was quite an outburst of economic opportunism and breathless attempts to "grab the gravy that could be grabbed." Some of the difficulty in bringing about a smooth transition arose from such counter-productive developments in patterns of business behavior. Instead of a smooth emergence of mainstream business virtues of established capitalism, Russia experienced an intensification of behavioral problems, fed by the rapid development of a "grabbing culture," which hindered rather than helped the process of reform.

Also the "grabbing culture" made the emergence of mutual business trust that much more difficult. The growth of Mafia style operations in the former Soviet Union has recently received considerable attention, and it has certainly been a significant development. To place this development in its context, we have to examine its behavioral antecedents, and the interconnections between (1) the breakdown of law, order, and economic discipline; (2) the emergence of extra-legal organizations (as supplements to business activities); and (3) the intensification of behavioral malaise.

The challenge that is faced is not that of policing only. The combined role of business principles and of moral sentiments, in the form of social conventions and mores, cannot be overemphasized in this context. There are some hopeful indications now that more stable and less counterproductive behavioral norms are gradually emerging in Russia, and if this proceeds smoothly, the development of a prosperous business economy there would be substantially easier.

Similar variations between regions and cultures, and over time, can be analyzed in the context of many other economic and social concerns, such as:

- variations in *industrial productivity* (the operation of codes of duty and loyalty within the firm can be very important in this);
- differences in the smoothness of *market relations* (basic standards of honesty and trust can play an important role here);
- dissimilar treatments of the *environment* and *industrial and social pollution* (environmental values are nearly absent in some communities and quite well-developed in others);
- diversities in the use and abuse of *public goods* (for example, in the operational possibilities of urban transport on an "honor system," with little or no checking of tickets).

The importance of economic ethics and of business principles relates both to their reach and effectiveness, and to their variability over time, space, and group. They constitute a crucial aspect of inter-regional and inter-temporal variations in economic performance and social achievement.

Limits of Grand Generalizations: The Example of Asian Values

While regional variations are extremely important, there is a real danger of over-simplifying the contrasts by concentrating on immense categories such as "Asian values versus Western values," or "Confucian ethics versus Protestant ethics." Generalizations of such heroic simplicity used to come earlier from scholars in the Western tradition (Max Weber's attributions to Protestant ethics was an extremely influential example), but increasingly we now see such generalizations coming from Asia.

The recent emergence of Asia as the most economically dynamic region in the world has prepared the ground for the same kind of value-arrogance that was characteristic of Europe in the nineteenth century. Asian economic growth is now very far in excess of any other region in the world, and the domain of high growth has persistently expanded in Asia, and continues to do so right now. Can these contrasts be explained by the superiority of an Asian value system that has great advantages over traditional Western morals?

I would argue that one must be deeply skeptical of such grand contrasts. Asia is where about 60 per cent of the total world population live. There are no quintessential values that apply to this immensely large and heterogeneous population, which separate them out as a group from people in the rest of the world. The internal diversity of Asia is simply tremendous. Indeed, even *East Asia*, including Japan, China, and Korea, among other countries, has too many different cultural traditions to permit any easy generalization of "east Asian values." The analysis of values has to be much finer than that.

If geography and the largeness of Asia give us one reason to doubt the helpfulness of the concept of "Asian values," the historical instability of the assessment of Asian culture provides another reason. As the balance of economic development has shifted, the reading of "Asian values" has persistently and radically altered.

It was in Europe that the Industrial Revolution occurred first, not in Asia, and even earlier, the developments that constituted the European Renaissance had been changing the face of Europe before similar things were occurring in Asia. This was a time when questions were frequently asked about what made the European values so productive of great social results, in contrast with which Asian values seemed – to Europeans – to be very primitive. The question that was repeatedly asked, then, was: what values, what knowledge have made Europe go so far ahead of Asia and the rest of the world?[5] The Asians evidently "lacked" something or other that made capitalism work in Europe, but not in Asia, and economists as distinguished as Alfred Marshall speculated on what behavior patterns kept Asian cultures economically down. It was in this context that Max Weber diagnosed that it was the "rational ethic of activity" that was missing in Asia, but plentifully provided by Judeo-Christian heritage in general and Protestant ethics in particular.

This line of reasoning had to be adjusted when things in Asia started moving. There was, first of all, the remarkable economic success and progress of Japan, and its emergence as a major military and financial power. The question now shifted, with remarkable rapidity, to include Japan in the world of privileged values. By the middle of the twentieth century, the contrast took the form of asking why Japan was "the only non-Western country to have become a major industrial nation?" (Moulder 1977, vii.) And more specifically: "Why did modern industrial capitalism arise in one East Asian society (Japan) and not in another (China)?" (Jacobs 1958, ix.) Special norms, traditions, and values of Japan – from the martial Samurai heritage to its family-centered business traditions – began receiving very special attention.

In the second half of the century, east Asian countries and regions *other than* Japan – South Korea, Singapore, Taiwan, Hong Kong – also started doing very well, and the "specialness" story had to be extended to them too. As a result, the Samurai had to give way to shared traditions on the eastern edge of Asia. This has more recently been followed by mainland China itself becoming a country with very fast economic growth and a rapid industrial transformation of its economy. The theses now shifted to special virtues of Confucianism – the cultural tie that binds China and Japan and much of east Asia – and even today this is the dominant story of "Asian values" and its great successes.

Meanwhile, however, Thailand has started forging ahead at remarkable speed, and its cultural background is Buddhist rather than Confucian. Indonesia, too, with an Islamic culture and much Buddhist and Hindu influences in its past, has begun to grow impressively fast. And, then, even more recently, adding to the cacophony, the large economy of India has started to move forward quite rapidly, and right now South Asia as a whole has a substantially faster rate of GNP growth than any other region of the world (including, of course, Europe and America), except for further East. Old explanations of sluggishness based on the debilitating values of these regions are giving way, at this very moment, to explanations of economic dynamism, with identification of other values, connections, and other achievements.

There are, clearly, strong elements of arbitrariness and "ad-hocism" taking Asian values to be particularly favorable to economic growth and rapid progress. Putting the issue somewhat differently, we can ask: if indeed Asian values have been so important in the recent economic success of these regions, a success which is getting increasingly larger in scope and coverage, *what took it so long*? Did Asian values change radically, and if so, why? Value explanations are much easier to give *ex post* than *ex ante*, and the ease of these answers hides the questions that have to be asked to scrutinize the answers critically.

Exposing the weakness of an earlier grand contrast and a big pro-European prejudice was much overdue, and it is good that the glib generalizations about Protestant ethics and "the rational ethic of activity" have, by now, been largely rejected (see Goody 1996). But the disestablishment of an earlier grand contrast must not be confused with the establishment of a new and different grand contrast, with another massive asymmetry of values – this time in favor of Asia, against Europe. There are things to learn from the recent Asian experiences, and at a less grand level, even the values and value changes in particular Asian regions are very worth studying. There are many things to be learned about the role of values from the Japanese experience itself, but the analysis has to be more detailed and richer in information about local history and tradition.

In a negative sense, Japan's remarkable success does point to the need to modify the admiration for exclusive reliance on profit maximization as the "royal road" to economic success (a royal road much explored in contemporary economics). Certainly, there are many non-individualist values – more geared to social norms and loyalties – that play significant parts in Japan's economic performance, and these have to be understood in their full detail, rather than being drowned in some aggregative story of "Asian values." There is quite a literature on this subject, and different commentators have emphasized distinct aspects of Japanese motivational specialness. Michio Morishima has focused on the special characteristics of the "Japanese ethos" as emerging from its particular history of rule-based behavior patterns (Morishima 1982). Ronald Dore has seen the influence of "Confucian ethics" (Dore 1987). Masahiko Aoki has seen cooperation and behavioral codes in terms that are more responsive to strategic reasoning (Aoki 1989). Kotaro Suzumura has emphasized the combination of commitment with a competitive atmosphere (Suzumura 1995). Eiko Ikegami has stressed the influence of Samurai culture (Ikegami 1995). There are other behavior based accounts as well. All these need serious attention as well as careful scrutiny, armed with detailed local knowledge about values and their roles. There is an excellent case for probing the role of values, focusing on the particularities rather than over-grand generalities.

There is, of course, a shared element in these stories, to wit, the presence of motives and modes of reasoning that go well beyond narrow profit-maximization in the operation of firms and individual workers and managers. There may, in fact, be some truth even in the apparently puzzling claim made on the front page of *The Wall Street Journal* that Japan is "the only communist nation that works." (*Wall Street Journal*, 30 January 1989, 1.) The witticism does stress the importance of non-profit motivations underlying many economic and business activities in Japan. Attention has to be paid to the peculiar fact that what is arguably the most successful capitalist nation in the world flourishes economically with a motivation structure that departs in crucial respects from the pursuit of self interest, which – we had been told – is the bedrock of capitalism.

It is, thus, important to see the role of complex business principles (not just profit maximization) and the influence of shared moral sentiments (rather than treating them to be irrelevant to business and economics), and at the same time, to recognize that value analysis has to be geared to the particular rather than to grand generalities. In fact, even within Japan there are considerable variations, and there have been many exposures lately of lapses from noble business behavior, and even of straightforward corruption. What is needed is not a general praise of Japanese value systems (not to mention sweeping generalizations about the wonders of "Asian values"), but information-rich analysis of various parts of Japanese traditions and conventions, and their respective bearing on the working and performance of the Japanese economy.

Similar remarks can be made about the other, more recent cases of Asian economic success. The recognition of local variability has to be supplemented by an understanding of temporal change. The answer to the question (asked earlier) "what took it so long?" – includes the fact that values in Asian countries are not static and stationary, and we have to consider not merely the nature of the indigenous cultures, but also the influence of Western ideas and organizational thoughts. It is diversity–over space, over time, and between groups – that makes the study of business principles and moral sentiments a rich source of understanding and explanation.

A Concluding Remark

The need to recognize the complex structure of business principles and the extensive reach of moral sentiments has been the motivating theme of this essay. The assumption of universal profit maximization as the only business principle – common in many economic analysis – militates against both. But this assumption has little empirical support, nor much analytical plausibility, and there is a strong case for going beyond that rudimentary structure.

The need to displace profit maximization as the sole business principle does not call for the placing of another simple and uniform rule as an alternative general system, with the same level of universality. Rather, there is a strong case for analyzing more complex structures, involving diverse concerns, and varying over time, space, and culture. A promising – and versatile – framework is that of *multiple objectives*, which can very plausibly include the search for profits as one important objective *among others*. The other objectives can compete with profit maximization in influencing business behavior, and can sometimes work as constraints reflecting established moral codes and social conventions. The force of profit maximization may have to work subject to these constraints.

In understanding the content and operation of social conventions and behavioral constraints, a richer comprehension of particular cultures can be very important. Indeed, cultural differences can have a crucial influence on business behavior. But we must not take the cultural parameters to be static and immutable, nor see them in terms of monumental and magnificent contrasts across very broad regions. These grand generalizations hide more than they reveal. I have argued for the simultaneous recognition of:

1. the significance of cultural variations;
2. the need to avoid cultural stereotypes and sweeping generalizations;
3. the importance of taking a dynamic rather than a static view of cultures; and
4. the necessity of recognizing heterogeneity within given communities.

The recognition of diversity over time and space – involving local variations as well as historical shifts – can be very important in understanding the practical nature and role of business principles and moral sentiments. This may look a little complex, compared with easy generalizations about "Western rationality" and "Asian values," but that complexity is, I believe, inescapable given the nature of the subject. Simplicity is not, after all, the only virtue.

Endnotes

1. I have tried to discuss these issues in *Resources, Values and Development* (1984), and in *On Economics and Ethics* (1987).

2. An excellent model of a community of persons with each pursuing their "comprehensive conception of the good" has been illuminatingly analyzed by John Rawls, *A Theory of Justice* (1971). Rawls does not claim that actual communities are exactly like this, and a substantial part of modern ethics seems to be primarily concerned with using that presumption to explore the "possibility" of "just social arrangements" (without committing itself on the nature of the observed world).

3. On this, see Stefano Zamagni, ed., *Mercati Illegali e Mafie* (1993), particularly his own paper on the economic circumstances that facilitate the persistence of a Mafia-inclusive equilibrium. See also my "On Corruption and Organized Crime," address to the Italian Parliament's Anti-Mafia Commission, Rome, 1993; Italian translation in Luciano Violante, ed., *Economic e criminalità* (1993).

4. On these issues, see Armando Massarenti and Antonio Da Re, *L'Etica de Applicare*, with an introduction by Angelo Ferro, and comments of Giovanni Agnelli and Salvatore Veca (Milano: Il Sole 24 Ore Libri, 1991).

5. In Samuel Johnson's *Rasselas*, Imlac identifies "the northern and western nations of Europe" as being "in possession of all power and all knowledge, whose armies are irresistible, and whose fleets command the remotest parts of the globe" (Johnson, *Rasselas*, 1759, 47).

References

Aoki, Masahiko, *Information, Incentive and Bargaining in the Japanese Economy* (Cambridge: Cambridge University Press, 1989).

Binmore, Ken, *Playing Fair* (Cambridge, Mass.: MIT Press, 1994).

Dore, Ronald, *Taking Japan Seriously: A Confucian Perspective on Leading Economic Issues* (Stanford: Stanford University Press, 1987).

Goody, Jack, *East in the West* (Cambridge: Cambridge University Press, 1996).

Ikegami, Eiko, *The Taming of the Samurai: Honorific Individualism and the Making of Modern Japan* (Cambridge MA: Harvard University Press, 1995).

Jacobs, H. Norman, *The Origin of Modern Capitalism and Eastern Asia* (Hong Kong, 1958).

Johnson, Samuel, *Rasselas: The Prince of Abissinia: A Tale* (London: Dodsley, 1759).

Massarenti, Armando, and Da Re, Antonio, *L'Etica de Applicare*, intro. Angelo Ferro, and comments of Giovanni Agnelli and Salvatore Veca (Milano: Il Sole 24 Ore Libri, 1991).

Morishima, Michio, *Why Has Japan "Succeeded"? Western Technology and Japanese Ethos* (Cambridge: Cambridge University Press, 1982).

Moulder, F. V., *Japan. China, and the Modern World Economy: Toward a Reinterpretation of East Asian Development (c.1600 to c.1918)* (Cambridge: Cambridge University Press, 1977).

Rawls, John, *A Theory of Justice* (Cambridge, Mass.: Harvard University Press, 1971).

Sen, Amartya, *On Ethics and Economics* (Oxfords: Blackwell, 1987).

Sen, Amartya, *Resources, Values and Development* (Oxford: Blackwell, and Cambridge, Mass.: Harvard University Press, 1984).

Sen, Amarya, "On Corruption and Organized Crime," address to the Italian Parliament's AntiMafia Commission, Rome, 1993; Italian translation in Luciano Violante, ed., *Economia e criminalità* (Roma: Camera dei deputati, 1993).

Smith, Adam, *The Theory of Moral Sentiments* (1759, 6th revised edition, 1790; republished, eds. D.D. Raphael and A.L. Macfie, Oxford: Clarendon Press, 1975).

Smith, Adam, *An Inquiry into the Nature and Causes of the Wealth of Nations* (1776; republished, edited by R.H. Campbell and A.S. Skinner, Oxford: Clarendon Press, 1976).

Suzumura, Kotaro, *Competition, Commitment and Welfare* (Oxford: Clarendon Press, 1995).

The Wall Street Journal, 30 January 1989.

Weibull, Jorgen, *Evolutionary Game Theory* (Cambridge, Mass.: MIT Press, 1995).

Zamagni, Stefano, ed., *Mercati Illegali e Mafie* (Bologna: Il Mulino, 1993).

24

The Normative Theories of Business Ethics: A Guide for the Perplexed[1]

John Hasnas[2]

Abstract

The three leading normative theories of business ethics are the stockholder theory, the stakeholder theory, and the social contract theory. Currently, the stockholder theory is somewhat out of favor with many members of the business ethics community. The stakeholder theory, in contrast, is widely accepted, and the social contract theory appears to be gaining increasing adherents. In this article, I undertake a critical review of the supporting arguments for each of the theories, and argue that the stockholder theory is neither as outdated nor as flawed as it sometimes made to seem and that there are significant problems with the grounding of both the stakeholder and social contract theory. I conclude by suggesting that a truly adequate normative theory of business ethics must ultimately be grounded in individual consent.

I. Introduction

A charge that is frequently lodged against the practical utility of business ethics as a field of study concerns the apparent failure of communication between the theorist and the business practitioner.[3] Critics of the discipline often point out that business ethicists are usually academics, and worse, philosophers, who speak in the language of abstract ethical theory. Thus, they are accused of expressing their ideas in terms of 'deontological requirements,' 'consequentialist considerations,' 'the categorical imperative,' 'rule utilitarianism,' 'the hedonistic calculus,' 'human flourishing' and other locutions that are essentially meaningless to the ordinary business person who possesses little or no philosophical training. Business people, it is pointed out, express themselves in

Source: *Business Ethics Quarterly* 8(1) (1998), 19–43.

ordinary language and tend to resist dealing in abstractions. What they want to know is how to resolve the specific problems that confront them.

To the extent that this criticism is justified, it places the business ethicist on the horns of a dilemma. Without the guidance of principles, ethical discussion is mere casuistry. Thus, general principles are necessary if business ethics is to constitute a substantive normative discipline. However, if the only principles available are expressed in language unfamiliar to those who must apply them, they can have no practical effect. This suggests that the task of the business ethicist is to produce a set of ethical principles that can be both expressed in language accessible to and conveniently applied by an ordinary business person who has no formal philosophical training.

The search for such principles has led to the development of several normative theories that have been specifically tailored to fit the business environment; theories that, for purposes of this article, I shall refer to as the normative theories of business ethics.[4] These theories attempt to derive what might be called "intermediate level" principles to mediate between the highly abstract principles of philosophical ethics and the concrete ethical dilemmas that arise in the business environment. Philosophical ethics must provide human beings with guidance in all aspects of their lives. A normative theory of business ethics is an attempt to focus this general theory exclusively upon those aspects of human life that involve business relationships. By thus limiting its range of application and translating the language of philosophical ethics into the everyday language of the business world, such a theory is specifically designed to provide human beings with ethical guidance while they are functioning in their capacity as business people.

Currently, the three leading normative theories of business ethics are the stockholder, stakeholder, and social contract theories. These theories present distinct and incompatible accounts of a business person's ethical obligations, and hence, at most one of them can be correct. The stockholder theory is the oldest of the three, and it would be fair to characterize it as out of favor with many contemporary business ethicists. To them, the stockholder theory represents a disreputable holdover from the bad old days of rampant capitalism. In contrast, the past decade and a half has seen the stakeholder theory gain such widespread adherence that it currently may be considered the conventionally-accepted position within the business ethics community.[5] In recent years, however, the social contract theory has been cited with considerable approbation and might accurately be characterized as challenging the stakeholder theory for preeminence among normative theorists.[6]

In this article, I propose to present a contrarian review of these theories. I will suggest that the stockholder theory is neither as outdated nor as unacceptable as it is often made to seem, and, further, that there are significant problems with both the stakeholder and the social contract theories. To do this, I propose to summarize each theory, analyze its supporting rationale, and canvass the chief objections against it. I will then draw a tentative conclusion regarding the adequacy of each theory. Finally, on the basis of these conclusions, I will attempt to suggest what the contours of a truly adequate normative theory of business ethics must be. Before turning to this, however, I feel compelled to say a word about the meaning of the phrase, 'social responsibility.'

In the business setting, 'social responsibility' is often employed as a synonym for a business's or business person's ethical obligations. This is unfortunate because this loose, generic use of the phrase can often obscure or prejudice the issue of what a business's or business person's ethical obligations truly are. To see why, one must appreciate that the phrase is also used to contrast a business's or business person's "social" responsibilities with its or his or her ordinary ones.

A business's or business person's ordinary responsibilities are to manage the business and expend business resources so as to accomplish the specific purposes for which the business was organized. Thus, in the case of a business organized for charitable or socially beneficial purposes (e.g., nonprofit corporations such as the Red Cross or the Nature Conservancy and for-profit corporations in which the stockholders pass resolutions compelling charitable contributions), it is a manager's ordinary responsibility to attempt to accomplish these goals. Even when a business is organized strictly for profit, it may be part of a manager's ordinary responsibilities to expend business resources for socially beneficial purposes when he or she believes that such expenditures will enhance the firm's long-term profitability (e.g., through the creation of customer goodwill). When the phrase 'social responsibility' is used in contradistinction to this, the claim that businesses or business persons have social responsibilities indicates that they are obligated to expend business resources for socially beneficial purposes even when such expenditures are not designed to help the business achieve the ends for which it was organized.

When 'social responsibility' in this narrow sense is conflated with 'social responsibility' as a synonym for a business's or business person's ethical obligations in general, it groundlessly implies that businesses or business persons do, in fact, have ethical obligations to expend business resources in ways that do not promote the business's fundamental purposes. Since not all theorists agree that this is the case, a definition that carries such an implication should be scrupulously avoided. For this reason, I intend to employ 'social responsibility' to refer exclusively to those ethical obligations, if any, that businesses or business persons have to expend business resources in ways that do not promote the specific purposes for which the business is organized. When the phrase is used in this way, it can make perfect sense to say that a business or business person has no social responsibilities. In fact, the first normative theory of business ethics that I will examine, the stockholder theory, makes precisely this claim.

II. The Stockholder Theory

The first normative theory of business ethics to be examined is the stockholder theory.[7] According to this theory, businesses are merely arrangements by which one group of people, the stockholders, advance capital to another group, the managers, to be used to realize specified ends and for which the stockholders receive an ownership interest in the venture.[8] Under this view, managers act as agents for the stockholders. They are empowered to manage the money advanced by the stockholders, but are bound by their agency relationship to do so exclusively for the purposes delineated by their stockholder principals.[9] The existence of this fiduciary relationship implies that managers cannot have an obligation to expend business resources in ways that have not been authorized by the stockholders regardless of any societal benefits that could be accrued by doing so. Of course, both stockholders and managers are free to spend their personal funds on any charitable or socially beneficial project they wish, but when functioning in their capacity as officers of the business, managers have a duty not to divert business resources away from the purposes expressly authorized by the stockholders. This implies that a business can have no social responsibilities.

Strictly speaking, the stockholder theory holds that managers are obligated to follow the (legal) directions of the stockholders, whatever these may be. Thus, if the stockholders vote that the business should not close a plant without giving its employees 90 days notice, should have no dealings with a country with a racist regime, or should endow a local public library, the management would be obligated to carry out such a directive regardless of its effect on the business's bottom line. In most cases, however, the stockholders issue no such explicit directives and purchase stock for the sole purpose of maximizing the return on their investment. When this is the purpose for which the stockholders have advanced their money, the managers' fiduciary obligation requires them to apply it to this end. For this reason, the stockholder theory is often imprecisely expressed as requiring managers to maximize the financial returns of the stockholders. The most famous statement of this shorthand description of the stockholder theory has been given by Milton Friedman who ironically refers to this as a "social responsibility." As he expresses it, "there is one and only one social responsibility of business—to use its resources and engage in activities designed to increase its profits so long as it stays within the rules of the game, which is to say, engages in open and free competition, without deception or fraud."[10]

It is important to note that even in this imprecise form, the stockholder theory does not instruct managers to do anything at all to increase the profitability of the business. It does not assert that managers have a moral blank check that allows them to ignore all ethical constraints in the pursuit of profits. Rather, it states that managers are obligated to pursue profit *by all legal, nondeceptive means.*[11] Far from asserting that there are no ethical constraints on a manager's obligation to increase profits, the stockholder theory contends that the ethical constraints society has embodied in its laws plus the general ethical tenet in favor of honest dealing constitute the ethical boundaries within which managers must pursue increased profitability.[12] A significant amount of the criticism that is directed against the stockholder theory results from over-looking these ethical limitations.[13]

For whatever reason, the stockholder theory has come to be associated with the type of utilitarian argument frequently advanced by free market economists.[14] Thus, supporting arguments often begin with the claim that when individual actors pursue private profit in a free market, they are led by Adam Smith's invisible hand to promote the general interest as well. It is then claimed that since, for each individual, "[b]y pursuing his own interest he frequently promotes that of the society more effectually than when he really intends to promote it,"[15] it is both unnecessary and counterproductive to exhort businesses or business persons to act directly to promote the common good. From this it is concluded that there is no justification for claiming that businesses or business persons have any social responsibilities other than to legally and honestly maximize the profits of the firm.

Although this consequentialist argument is the one most frequently cited in support of the stockholder theory, it must be noted that there is another, quite simple deontological argument for it as well. This argument is based on the observation that stockholders advance their money to business managers on the condition that it be used in accordance with their wishes. If the managers accept the money on this condition and then proceed to spend it to accomplish social goals not authorized by the stockholders, they would be violating their agreement and spending other people's money without their consent, which is wrong.[16]

The stockholder theory has been subjected to some harsh criticism by several of the leading business ethicists working today. It has been described as an outmoded relic of corporate law that even the law itself has evolved beyond,[17] as containing a "myopic view of corporate responsibility" that is unfortunately held by a significant number of business practitioners, and, more pointedly, as "corporate Neanderthalism...with morally pernicious consequences,"[18] and as "not only foolish in theory, but cruel and dangerous in practice" and misguided "from its nonsensically one-sided assumption of responsibility to his pathetic understanding of stockholder personality as *Homo economicus*."[19] For a significant number of theorists, the stockholder theory is introduced into discussion not as a serious candidate for the proper ethical standard for the business environment, but merely as a foil for other, putatively more enlightened normative theories.

At least part of the explanation for this harsh treatment seems to be the stockholder theory's association with the utilitarian supporting argument described above. Few contemporary business ethicists have the kind of faith in the invisible hand of the market that neoclassical economists do. Most take for granted that a free market produces coercive monopolies, results in damaging externalities, and is beset by other instances of market failure such as the free rider and public goods problems, and thus cannot be relied upon to secure the common good.[20] Accordingly, to the extent that it is associated with this line of economic reasoning, the stockholder theory becomes tarred with the brush of these standard objections to laissez faire capitalism.

It should be pointed out, however, that it is not necessary to join the debate over the theoretical viability of laissez faire to demonstrate the vulnerability of the utilitarian defense of the stockholder theory. This is because contemporary economic conditions are so far removed from those of a true free market as to render the point essentially moot. Regardless of the adequacy of the stockholder theory in a world of ideal markets, the world in which we currently reside is one where businesses may gain competitive advantages by obtaining government subsidies, tax breaks, protective tariffs, and state-conferred monopoly status (e.g., utilities, the Baby Bells, cable television franchises); having health, safety or environmental regulations written so as to burden small competitors; and otherwise purchasing governmental favor. In such a world, it is extremely unlikely that the pursuit of private profit will truly be productive of the public good. There is ample reason to be suspicious of such a claim in an environment in which 65 percent of the chief executive officers of the top 200 Fortune firms come to Washington, D.C. at least once every two weeks.[21]

It is important to note that the fact that the utilitarian argument for the stockholder theory may be seriously flawed does not mean that the theory is untenable. This is because the deontological argument for the theory, which has frequently been overlooked, is, in fact, the superior argument. To the extent that it has received serious consideration, the primary objection against it seems to consist in the contention that it is not wrong to spend other people's money without their consent *as long as it is being done to promote the public interest.*[22] This contention is usually bolstered by the observation that this is precisely what democratic governments do all the time (at least, in theory). Since such action is presumably justified in the political realm, so the objection goes, there is no reason to think that it is not equally justified in the business realm.

There are two serious problems with this objection, however. The first is that it misses the essential point of the argument. As stated above, this argument is deontological in character. It is based on an underlying assumption that there are certain principles of conduct that must be observed regardless of the generalized benefits that must be foregone by doing so. One of the most fundamental of these principles states that individuals must honor the commitments they voluntarily and knowingly undertake. Hence, the essence of the argument is the claim that it is morally wrong to violate one's freely-assumed agreement to use the stockholders' resources only as specified even though society could be made a somewhat better place by doing so. To assert that a manager may violate his or her agreement with the stockholders whenever doing so would promote the public interest is simply to deny this claim. It is to declare that one's duty to advance the common good overrides one's duty to honor one's agreements, and that the moral quality of one's actions must ultimately be judged according to a utilitarian standard. While some ethicists argue that the principle of utility is indeed the supreme ethical principle, this is far from obviously true, and any contention that merely assumes that it is cannot serve as a compelling objection to a deontological argument.

The second problem is that the objection is based on a false analogy. The assumption that democratic governments are morally justified in spending *taxpayers'* money without their consent to promote the general interest does not imply that businesses or business persons are justified in spending *stockholders'* money without their consent for the same reason. Consider that once the citizens have made their required contribution to governmental efforts to benefit society, all should be equally entitled to the control of their remaining assets. Should a citizen elect to invest them in a savings account to provide for his or her children's education or his or her old age, a banker who diverted some of these assets to other purposes, no matter how worthy, would clearly be guilty of embezzlement. For that matter, should the citizen elect to use his or her assets to purchase a new car, go on an extravagant vacation, or even take a course in business ethics, a car dealer, travel agent, or university that failed to deliver the bargained-for product in order to provide benefits to others would be equally guilty. Why should it be any different if the citizen elects to invest in a business? At least superficially, it would appear that citizens have a right to control their after-tax assets that is not abrogated merely because they elect to purchase stock and that would be violated were business managers to use these assets in unauthorized ways. If this is not the case, some showing is required to demonstrate why not.

Of course, these comments in no way establish that the stockholder theory is correct. The most that they can demonstrate is that some of the objections that are frequently raised against it are ill-founded. Other, more serious objections remain to be considered.[23] However, they do suggest that the cavalier dismissal the stockholder theory sometimes receives is unjustified, and that, at least at present, it should continue to be considered a serious candidate for the proper normative theory of business ethics.[24]

III. The Stakeholder Theory

The second of the leading normative theories of business ethics is the stakeholder theory. Unfortunately, 'stakeholder theory' is somewhat of a troublesome label because it is used to refer to both an empirical theory of management and a normative theory of business ethics, often without clearly distinguishing between the two.[25] As an empirical theory of management, the stakeholder theory holds that effective management requires the balanced consideration of and attention to the legitimate interests of all stakeholders,[26] defined as anyone who has "a stake in or claim on the firm."[27] This has been interpreted in both a wide sense that includes "any group or individual who can affect or is affected by the corporation," and a more narrow sense that includes only "those groups who are vital to the survival and success of the corporation."[28] It is perhaps more familiar in its narrow sense in which the stakeholder groups are limited to stockholders, customers, employees, suppliers, management, and the local community. Thus, as an empirical theory, the stakeholder theory asserts that a business's financial success can best be achieved by giving the interests of the business's stockholders, customers, employees, suppliers, management, and local community proper consideration and adopting policies which produce the optimal balance among them.[29]

When viewed as an empirical theory of management designed to prescribe a method for improving a business's performance, the stakeholder theory does not imply that businesses have any social responsibilities. In this sense, it is perfectly consistent with the normative stockholder theory since what is being asserted is the empirical claim that the best way to enhance the stockholders' return on their investment is to pay attention to the legitimate interests of all stakeholders. The essence of the stakeholder theory of *management* is that stakeholder management is required for managers to successfully meet their fiduciary obligation to the stockholders. For the purposes of this article, however, we are concerned with the stakeholder theory not as an empirical theory of management, but as a normative theory of business ethics.

When viewed as a normative theory, the stakeholder theory asserts that, regardless of whether stakeholder management leads to improved financial performance, managers *should* manage the business for the benefit of all stakeholders. It views the firm not as a mechanism for increasing the stockholders' financial returns, but as a vehicle for coordinating stakeholder interests and sees management as having a fiduciary relationship not only to the stockholders, but to all stakeholders. According to the normative stakeholder theory, management must give equal consideration to the interests of all stakeholders[30] and, when these interests conflict, manage the business so as to attain the optimal balance among them. This, of course, implies that there will be times when management is obligated to at least partially sacrifice the interests of the stockholders to those of other stakeholders. Hence, in its normative form, the stakeholder theory does imply that businesses have true social responsibilities.

The stakeholder theory holds that management's fundamental obligation is not to maximize the firm's financial success, but to ensure its survival by balancing the conflicting claims of multiple stakeholders. This obligation is to be met by acting in accordance with two principles of stakeholder management. The first, called the principle of corporate legitimacy, states that "the corporation should be managed for the benefit of its stakeholders: its customers, suppliers, owners, employees, and the local communities. The rights of these groups must be ensured and, further, the groups must participate, in some sense, in decisions that substantially affect their welfare."[31] The second, called the stakeholder fiduciary principle, states that "management bears a fiduciary relationship to stakeholders and to the corporation as an abstract entity. It must act in the interests of the stakeholders as their agent, and it must act in the interests of the corporation to ensure the survival of the firm, safeguarding the long-term stakes of each group."[32]

The stakeholder theory enjoys a considerable degree of approbation from both theorists and practitioners. In fact, it is probably fair to say that the stakeholder theory currently enjoys a breadth of acceptance equal to that the stockholder theory was said to have enjoyed in the past. To some extent, this may result from the fact that the theory seems to accord well with many people's moral intuitions, and, to some extent, it may simply be a spillover effect of the high regard in which the empirical version of the stakeholder theory is held as a theory of management. It is clear, however, that the normative theory's widespread acceptance does not derive from a careful examination of the arguments that have been offered in support of it. In fact, it is often remarked that the theory seems to lack a clear normative foundation.[33]

An argument that is frequently cited in support of the stakeholder theory is the one offered by Ed Freeman and William Evan in their 1988 article.[34] That argument asserts that management's obligation to the stakeholders can be derived from Immanuel Kant's principle of respect for persons. This fundamental ethical principle holds that every human being is entitled to be treated not merely as a means to the achievement of the ends of others, but as a being valuable in his or her own right; that each person is entitled to be respected as an end in himself or herself. Since to respect someone as an end is to recognize that he or she is an autonomous moral agent, i.e., a being with desires of his or her own and the free will to act upon those desires, the principle of respect for persons requires respect for others' autonomy.

Freeman and Evan apply this principle to the world of business by claiming that businesses are bound to respect it as much as anyone else. Thus, businesses may not treat their stakeholders merely as means to the business's ends, but must recognize that as moral agents, all stakeholders are entitled "to agree to and hence participate (or choose not to participate) in the decisions to be used as such."[35] They then claim that it follows from this that all stakeholders are entitled to "participate in determining the future direction of the firm in which they have a stake."[36] However, because it is impossible to consult with all of a firm's stakeholders on every decision, this participation must be indirect. Therefore, the firm's management has an obligation to "represent" the interests of all stakeholders in the business's decision-making process. Accordingly, management is obligated to give equal consideration to the interests of all stakeholders in developing business policy and to manage the business so as to optimize the balance among these interests.

The main problem with this argument is that there is a gap in the reasoning that leads from the principle of respect for persons to the prescriptions of the stakeholder theory. It may readily be admitted that businesses are ethically bound to treat all persons, and hence all stakeholders, as entities worthy of respect as ends in themselves. It may further be admitted that this requires businesses to treat their stakeholders as autonomous moral agents, and hence, that stakeholders are indeed entitled "to agree to and hence participate (or choose not to participate) in the decisions to be used"[37] as means to business ends. The problem is that this implies only that no stakeholder may be forced to deal with the business without his or her consent, not that all stakeholders are entitled to a say in the business's decision-making process or that the business must be managed for their benefit.

It is certainly true that respect for the autonomy of others requires that one keep one's word. To deceive someone into doing something he or she would not otherwise agree to do would be to use him or her merely as a means to one's own ends. For this reason, the principle of respect for persons requires businesses to deal honestly with all of their stakeholders. This means that businesses must honor the contracts they enter into with their customers, employees, suppliers, managers, and stockholders and live up to any representations they freely make to the local community. However, it is simply incorrect to say that respect for another's autonomy requires that the other have a say in any decision that affects his or her interests. A student's interests may be crucially affected by what grade he or she receives in a course as may a Republican's by the decision of whom the Democrats nominate for President. But the autonomy of neither the student nor the Republican is violated when he or she is denied a say in these decisions.

An adherent of the stockholder theory could point out that employees (including managers), suppliers, and customers negotiate for and autonomously accept wage and benefit packages, purchasing arrangements, and sales contracts, respectively. It does not violate their autonomy or treat them with a lack of the respect they are due as persons to fail to provide them with benefits in excess of those they freely accept. However, if managers were to break their agreement with the stockholders to use business resources only as authorized in order to provide other stakeholders with such benefits, the managers would be violating the autonomy of the stockholders. Therefore, the stockholder theorist could contend that not only is the stakeholder theory not entailed by the principle of respect for persons, but to the extent that it instructs managers to use the stockholders' money in ways they have not approved, it is, in fact, violative of it.

Perhaps because of the problems with this argument, efforts have recently been made to provide a more adequate normative justification for the stakeholder theory. Indeed, Freeman and Evan have themselves offered an alternative argument that claims that changes in corporate law imply that businesses consist in sets of multilateral contracts among stakeholders that must be administered by managers.[38] Asserting that "all parties that are affected by a contract have a right to bargain about the distribution of those effects,"[39] they then apply a Rawlsian "veil of ignorance" decision procedure to deduce that "fair contracting" requires that all stakeholders be entitled to "participate in monitoring the actual effects of the firm on them,"[40] i.e. have a say in the business's decision-making process.

Unfortunately, this argument seems to have even more problems than the one it replaces. In the first place, Rawls' decision procedure was specifically designed to guide the construction of the basic structure of society and it is at least open to question whether it may be appropriately employed in the highly specific context of business governance issues. Further, deriving ethical conclusions from observations of the state of the law comes dangerously close to the classic fallacy of assuming that what is legally required must be ethically correct. More significantly, however, this new argument seems to suffer from the same defect as its predecessor since the assumption that all parties that are affected by a contract have a right to bargain about the distribution of those effects is virtually equivalent to the earlier argument's problematic assumption that all parties affected by a business's actions have a right to participate in the business's decision-making process. As in the earlier argument, this is the assertion that must be established, not assumed.[41]

Another recent attempt at justification has been undertaken by Donaldson and Preston who claim to base the stakeholder theory on a theory of property. After asserting that the stockholder theory is "normatively unacceptable,"[42] they contend that because 1) property rights must be based on an underlying principle of distributive justice, 2) among theorists, "the trend is toward theories that are pluralistic, allowing more than one fundamental principle to play a role," and 3) "all critical characteristics underlying the classic theories of distributive justice are present among the stakeholders of a corporation," it follows that "the normative principles that underlie the contemporary theory of property rights also provide the foundation for the stakeholder theory as well."[43] However, because the authors have failed to provide any specification for what "the contemporary theory of property rights" is, this can be regarded as, at best, a preliminary sketch rather than a fully developed justificatory argument. Further, because premise 1 is open to serious question,[44] premise 2 seems to confuse academic opinion with evidence of truth, and premise 3 seems, at first glance, to be wholly unconnected to the conclusion, much work remains to be done before this argument can serve as an adequate basis for the stakeholder theory.

In sum, the lacunae in each of these supporting arguments suggest that, despite its widespread acceptance, the normative version of the stakeholder theory is simply not wellgrounded. At this point, its adequacy as a normative theory of business ethics must be regarded as open to serious question.[45]

IV. The Social Contract Theory

The third normative theory of business ethics, the social contract theory, really comprises a family of closely related theories and, in some ways, is still in the process of formation.[46] However, in its most widely accepted form, the social contract theory asserts that all businesses are ethically obligated to enhance the welfare of society by satisfying consumer and employee interests without violating any of the general canons of justice.[47] Because the specific nature of this obligation can best be appreciated in the context of the theory's derivation, let us turn our attention immediately to the theory's supporting rationale.

The social contract theory is based on the traditional concept of a social contract, an implicit agreement between society and an artificial entity in which society recognizes the existence of the entity on the condition that it serves the interests of society in certain specified ways. As a normative theory of business ethics, the social contract theory is explicitly modeled on the political social contract theories of thinkers such as Thomas Hobbes, John Locke, and Jean-Jacques Rousseau. These political theorists each attempted to imagine what life would be like in the absence of a government, i.e., in the "state of nature," and asked what conditions would have to be met for citizens to agree to form one. The obligations of the government toward its citizens were then derived from the terms of this agreement.

The normative social contract theory of business ethics takes much the same approach toward deriving the social responsibilities of businesses. It begins by imagining a society in which there are no complex business organizations, i.e., a state of "individual production," and proceeds by asking what conditions would have to be met for the members of such a society to agree to allow businesses to be formed. The ethical obligations of businesses toward the individual members of society are then derived from the terms of this agreement. Thus, the social contract theory posits an implicit contract between the members of society and businesses in which the members of society grant businesses the right to exist in return for certain specified benefits.

In granting businesses the right to exist, the members of society give them legal recognition as single agents and authorize them to own and use land and natural resources and to hire the members of society as employees.[48] The question then becomes what the members of society would demand in return. The minimum would seem to be "that the benefits from authorizing the existence of productive organizations outweigh these detriments of doing so."[49] In general, this would mean that businesses would be required to "enhance the welfare of society...in a way which relies on exploiting corporations' special advantages and minimizing disadvantages"[50] while remaining "within the bounds of the general canons of justice."[51]

This generalization may be thought of as giving rise to a social contract with two terms: the social welfare term and the justice term. The social welfare term recognizes that the members of society will be willing to authorize the existence of businesses only if they gain by doing so. Further, there are two distinct capacities in which the members of society stand to gain from businesses: as consumers and as employees. As consumers, people can benefit from the existence of businesses in at least three ways. First, businesses provide increased economic efficiency by maximizing the advantages of specialization, improving decision-making resources, and increasing the capacity to use and acquire expensive technology and resources. Second, businesses provide stable levels of output and channels of distribution. And third, they provide increased liability resources from which to compensate injured consumers. As employees, people can benefit from the existence of businesses by receiving increased income potential, diffused personal legal liability for harmful errors, and the ability to participate in "income-allocation schemes...detached from the vicissitudes of [their] capacity to produce."[52] However, businesses can also have negative effects on consumers and employees. People's interests as consumers can be harmed when businesses pollute the environment and deplete natural resources, undermine the personal accountability of their constituent members, and misuse political power. People's interests as employees can be harmed when they are alienated from the product of their labor, suffer from lack of control over their working conditions, and are subjected to monotonous and dehumanizing working conditions. These, then, constitute the respective advantages and disadvantages that businesses can provide to and impose upon society. Therefore, when fully specified, the social welfare term of the social contract requires that businesses act so as to 1) benefit consumers by increasing economic efficiency, stabilizing levels of output and channels of distribution, and increasing liability resources; 2) benefit employees by increasing their income potential, diffusing their personal liability, and facilitating their income allocation; while 3) minimizing pollution and depletion of natural resources, the destruction of personal accountability, the misuse of political power, as well as worker alienation, lack of control over working conditions, and dehumanization.

The justice term recognizes that the members of society will be willing to authorize the existence of businesses only if businesses agreed to remain within the bounds of the general canons of justice. Admittedly, precisely what these canons require is far from settled. However, since there seems to be general agreement that the least they require is that businesses "avoid fraud and deception,...show respect for their workers as human beings, and...avoid any practice that systematically worsens the situation of a given group in society," [53] it is reasonable to read the justice term as requiring at least this much.

In general, then, the social contract theory holds that managers are ethically obligated to abide by both the social welfare and justice terms of the social contract. Clearly, when fully specified, these terms impose significant social responsibilities on the managers of business enterprises.

The social contract theory is often criticized on the ground that the "social contract" is not a contract at all. To appreciate the nature of this criticism, let us borrow some terminology from the legal realm. The law recognizes three types of contracts: express contracts, implied contracts, and quasi-contracts. An express contract consists in an explicit agreement made in speech or writing. In this case, there is a true meeting of the minds of the parties that is expressly memorialized through language. An implied contract consists in an agreement that is manifested in some other way. For example, continuing to deal with another party under the terms of an expired contract can imply an agreement to renew or, perhaps more familiarly, failing to return an invoice marked 'cancel' following a trial membership can imply a contract to buy four books in the next twelve months. As with express contracts, in such cases, there is a true meeting of the minds. However, in implied contracts, that agreement is manifested through action rather than language. A quasi-contract, on the other hand, consists in the legal imposition of a contractual relationship where there has been no meeting of the minds because such is necessary to avoid injustice. For example, a doctor who expends resources aiding an unconscious patient in an emergency situation is said to have a quasi-contract for reasonable compensation even though there was no antecedent agreement between the parties. In quasi-contracts, the law acts as though there has been a meeting of the minds where none in fact exists in order to do justice.

Critics of the social contract theory point out that the social contract is neither an express nor an implied contract. This is because there has been no true meeting of the minds between those who decide to form businesses and the members of the society in which they do so. Most people who start businesses do so by simply following the steps prescribed by state law and would be quite surprised to learn that by doing so they had contractually agreed to serve society's interests in ways that were not specified in the law and that can significantly reduce the profitability of the newly formed firm.[54] To enter a contractual arrangement, whether expressly or by implication, one has to at least be aware that one is doing so. Thus, the critics maintain that the social contract must be a quasi-contract, which is merely a fiction rather than a true contract.

This objection is not very distressing to social contract theorists, however. They freely admit that the social contract is a fictional or hypothetical contract, but go on to claim that this is precisely what is required to identify managers' ethical obligations. As Thomas Donaldson has put it, "if the contract were something *other* than a 'fiction,' it would be inadequate for the purpose at hand: namely revealing the moral foundations of productive organizations."[55] What the social contract theorists are admitting here is that the moral force of the social contract is not derived from the consent of the parties. Rather, they are advancing a moral theory that holds that "[p]roductive organizations should behave as if they had struck a deal, the kind of deal that would be acceptable to free, informed parties acting from positions of equal moral authority..."[56]

This seems perfectly adequate as a response to the objection. It does suggest, however, that much of the psychological appeal of the social contract theory is based on a confusion. This is because a great deal of the theory's appeal to ordinary (philosophically untrained) business practitioners derives from their natural, intuitive identification of contract terminology with consent. To the extent that the language of contract suggests that one has given consent, it has a strong emotive force. People generally accept consent as a source of moral obligation, and this is especially true of the business practitioner who makes contracts every day and whose success or failure often turns on his or her reputation for upholding them. Most people would agree that when one voluntarily gives one's word, one is ethically bound to keep it. Thus, business practitioners as well as people generally are psychologically more willing to accept obligations when they believe they have consented to them. By employing contract terminology when consent plays no role in grounding the posited social responsibilities of business, the social contract theory inappropriately benefits from the positive psychological attitude that this terminology engenders. For this reason, it is not unreasonable to suggest that the social contract theory trades upon the layperson's favorable attitude toward consent with no intention of delivering the goods.

This, of course, casts no aspersions on the theory's philosophical adequacy. However, the admission that the social contract is actually a quasi-contract does provide good reason to believe that the social contract theory has not been adequately supported. Once consent has been abandoned as the basis for the posited social responsibilities, the acceptability of the social contract theory rests squarely on the adequacy of the moral theory that undergirds it. This theory asserts that justice requires businesses and business managers to behave as though they had struck a deal "that would be acceptable to free, informed parties acting from positions of equal moral authority."[57] This may be correct, but it is not patently so. It is far from obvious that justice demands that managers behave *as if* they had made an agreement with hypothetical people, especially when doing so would violate real-world agreements made with actual people (e.g., the company's stockholders). It seems equally reasonable to assert that justice demands only that managers abide by the will of the people as it has been expressed by their political representatives in the commercial law of the state, or perhaps merely that they deal honestly with all parties and refrain from taking any illegal or harmful actions. Until the theory of justice on which the social contract theory rests has been fully articulated and defended, there is simply no reason to prefer it to any other putative normative theory of business ethics.[58] At present, therefore, this version of the social contract theory cannot be regarded as established.

There is, however, another version of the social contract theory that is genuinely consent-based and thus cannot be criticized on this ground.[59] This version asserts that the business enterprise is characterized by a myriad of "extant social contracts," informal agreements that embody "actual behavioral norms which derive from shared goals, beliefs and attitudes of groups or communities of people."[60] These extant social contracts are not quasi-contracts, but true agreements which, although sometimes express, are usually "implied from [*sic*] certain characteristics, attitudes and patterns of the group"[61] and "represent the view of the community concerning what constitutes proper behavior within the confines of the community."[62] According to this version of the theory, whenever the extant social contracts pass a "filtering test," i.e., are found not to be violative of the tenets of general ethical theory, they give rise to "genuine ethical norms" that managers are ethically obligated to obey.

There is nothing patently objectionable about this version of the social contract theory. However, it is so underdeveloped that it is difficult to know what to make of it. For example, it is not clear whether the theory contains an implicit norm against entering into social contracts that give rise to incompatible obligations or are incompatible with obligations that arise from one's earlier voluntary agreements. If it does, the theory seems to collapse into the stockholder theory which instructs managers to deal honestly with others and honor all agreements *that do not violate their antecedent voluntary agreement to use the stockholders' resources only as authorized.* If it does not, it seems to prescribe a host of incompatible obligations.[63] Furthermore, because the filtering test has not been specified, this version of the social contract theory reduces to the claim that one is obligated to abide by the informal agreements one has entered into as long as doing so is ethically acceptable. Although this does not say nothing, it says very little. For example, if the filtering test places primacy on a deontological obligation to honor one's agreements, the theory becomes coextensive with the stockholder theory and implies that businesses have no social responsibilities. However, if it places primacy on the principle of utility, the theory may produce a set of social responsibilities very much like that prescribed by the stakeholder theory. Finally, if it prescribes a general obligation to behave as though one had made an agreement with perfectly rational, self-interested, free and equal hypothetical people, the theory might produce a set of social responsibilities equivalent to those prescribed by the earlier version of the social contract theory. As this diversity of outcome suggests, in its present skeletal form, this version of the social contract theory is, at best, of limited usefulness.[64]

V. Conclusion

In this article, I have subjected each of the three leading normative theories of business ethics to critical examination. I have argued that the stockholder theory is not as obviously flawed as it is sometimes supposed to be and that several of the objections conventionally raised against it are misdirected. I have also suggested that the deontological argument in support of the stockholder theory is not obviously unsound, although I have admittedly not subjected this argument to the scrutiny that would be necessary to establish its soundness. Further, I have argued that the supporting arguments for the stakeholder theory are significantly flawed and that the social contract theory either has not been adequately supported or is too underdeveloped to be useful. Thus, I have suggested that the amount of confidence that is currently placed in the stakeholder theory and is coming to be placed in the social contract theory is not well founded.

Although it may appear surprising given these conclusions, I do not view this article as a brief for the stockholder theory. Rather, I view it as a compass that can point us in the direction of a truly adequate normative theory of business ethics. I should add, however, that I also believe it points to a serious difficulty that must be overcome in order to arrive at any such theory.

To see what I mean, I would ask you to consider that all three normative theories share a common feature; they all either explicitly or implicitly recognize the preeminent moral value of individual consent. The stockholder theory is explicitly based on consent. The ethical obligations it posits are claimed to derive directly from the voluntary agreement each business officer makes on accepting his or her position to use the stockholders' resources strictly in accordance with their wishes. Similarly, the stakeholder theory is at least implicitly based on consent. The ethical obligation it places on business officers to manage the firm in the interest of all stakeholders is supposed to derive from the claim that every stakeholder is entitled to a say in decisions that affect his or her interests, which itself contains the implicit recognition of each individual's right to control his or her own destiny.[65] Finally, consent resides at the heart of the social contract theory as well. This is clear with regard to the extant social contract variant of the theory in which the manager's ethical obligations are explicitly based on consent. However, even the hypothetical social contract variant indirectly recognizes the moral significance of consent. For although it derives managers' ethical obligations from a depersonalized, morally sanitized, hypothetical form of consent, there would be no reason to cast the theory in terms of a contract at all if consent were not recognized as a fundamental source of ethical obligation.

The fact that all three normative theories of business ethics rely on the moral force of individual consent should come as no surprise given a proper understanding of what a business is, i.e., "a voluntary association of individuals, united by a network of contracts"[66] organized to achieve a specified end.[67] Because businesses consist in nothing more than a multitude of voluntary agreements among individuals, it is entirely natural that the ethical obligations of the parties to these agreements, including those of the managers of the business, should derive from the individual consent of each. Clearly, any attempt to provide a general account of the ethical obligations of businesses and business people must ultimately rely on the moral force of the individual's freely-given consent.[68]

Recognizing this tells us much about what an adequate normative theory of business ethics must look like. If businesses are merely voluntary associations of individuals, then the ethical obligations of business people will be the ethical obligations individuals incur by joining voluntary associations, i.e., the ordinary ethical obligations each has as a human being plus those each has voluntarily assumed by agreement. Just as individuals do not take on ethical obligations beyond those they agree to by joining a chess club, a political party, or a business school faculty, so too individuals do not become burdened with unagreed upon obligations by going into or joining a business. There is no point in time at which the collection of individuals that constitutes a business is magically transformed into a new, separate and distinct entity that is endowed with rights or laden with obligations not possessed by the individual human beings that comprise it.

This implies that an adequate normative theory of business ethics must capture the ethical obligations generated when an individual voluntarily enters the complex web of contractual agreements that constitutes a business. Of the three theories I have examined, the stockholder theory comes closest to achieving this because it focuses on the actual agreement that exists between the stockholders and managers. It is woefully incomplete, however, because it 1) does not adequately address the limits managers' ordinary ethical obligations as human beings place on the actions they may take in the business environment, and 2) entirely fails to address the managerial obligations that arise out of the actual agreements made with the non-stockholder participants in the business enterprise.[69] Of course, recognizing these deficiencies of the stockholder theory also highlights the essential difficulty in constructing a satisfactory normative theory of business ethics; the need to generalize across the myriad of individual contractual agreements that are the constituent elements of the business.

Can an adequate consent-based normative theory of business ethics be devised? Can the ethical obligations arising from the agreements that characterize the typical business as well as those that individuals carry with them when they enter the business venture be captured in a manageable set of principles expressed in language accessible to the ordinary business person? Considering the differing nature of the relationships and agreements involved in a business of any complexity, devising such a set of principles may appear to be a daunting, if not hopeless, task.[70] Nevertheless, I believe the present survey indicates that this is a challenge that must be undertaken if a supportable normative theory of business ethics is to be devised. Undertaking this challenge, however, must remain the project of another day.[71]

Notes

1 Apologies to Maimonides.

2 J.D., Ph.D., Philosophy, Duke University, LL.M. Temple University School of Law. Assistant General Counsel, Koch Industries, Inc., Wichita, Kansas. This paper has greatly benefitted from the thoughtful comments and suggestions of Thomas Donaldson, Dennis Quinn, and Tom Beauchamp of Georgetown University, Thomas Dunfee of the Wharton School, Thomas Jones of the University of Washington, Ian Maitland of the University of Minnesota, Jeff Nesteruk of Franklin & Marshall College, Douglas Den Uyl of Bellarmine College, Patricia Werhane of the Darden Graduate School of Business Administration, Ann C. Tunstall, and my anonymous reviewers. I am sincerely grateful to each of them for their assistance. An earlier version of this article was presented as part of the John F. Connelly Business Ethics Seminar Series at Georgetown University.

3 For a famous example of this, see Andrew Stark, "What's the Matter with Business Ethics?", 71 *Harv. Bus. Rev.* 38 (1993). See also Thomas Donaldson and Thomas W. Dunfee, "Integrative Social Contracts Theory: A Communitarian Conception of Business Ethics," 11 *Econ. & Phil.* 85, 87 (1995).

4 I am employing this phrase in an effort to avoid the confusion engendered by referring to strictly normative theories as "theories of corporate social responsibility." The latter phrase has been used to refer to not only normative theories, which attempt to identify the philosophically verifiable ethical obligations of businesses and business persons, but also to theories that are either purely or partially descriptive or instrumental in nature, such as those that focus on businesses' or business person's responsiveness to societal expectations or demands. Indeed, historically speaking, the concept of corporate social responsibility arose as a response to an increasing level of criticism of the business system in general and the power and privilege of large corporations in particular, see Thomas M. Jones. "Corporate Social Responsibility: Revisited, Redefined," 22 *Cal. Bus. Rev.* 59, 59 (1980), and, to some extent, as a reaction against the stockholder theory, one of the normative theories to be examined in the body of this article. As a result, the theories of corporate social responsibility should probably be seen as a genus of which what I am calling the normative theories of business ethics are a species.

5 Evidence for this may be found not only in the inordinately large percentage of business ethics journal articles that discuss the stakeholder theory favorably, but in the increasing number of textbooks that are being written from the stakeholder perspective. See, e.g., Ronald M. Green, *The Ethical Manager* (1994), Joseph W. Weiss, *Business Ethics: A Managerial, Stakeholder Approach* (1994), Archie B. Carroll, Business and Society: *Ethics and Stakeholder Management* (1996).

6 Consider, for example, the recent special issue of *Business Ethics Quarterly* devoted to the social contract theory. 5 *Business Ethics Quarterly* 167 (Thomas W. Dunfee, ed.,

1995).

7 In this article, I intentionally speak in terms of 'the stockholder theory' rather than 'agency theory' to emphasize that I am discussing a normative theory. 'Agency theory' seems to be used ambiguously to refer to both the attempt to produce an empirical description of the relationship between managers and stockholders and the normative implications that would flow from such a relationship. See Norman E. Bowie and R. Edward Freeman, "Ethics and Agency Theory: An Introduction," in *Ethics and Agency Theory* 3, 3–4 (Norman E. Bowie and R. Edward Freeman, eds., 1992). In order to avoid this ambiguity in the present context, I employ the label 'stockholder theory' to indicate that I am referring strictly to a theory of how businesses or business people should behave.

8 Historically, the normative theories of business ethics grew out of the literature on corporate social responsibility. As a result, they are often expressed as though they apply only to corporations rather than to businesses generally. This is certainly the case with regard to the stockholder theory. To be adequate, however, a normative theory of business ethics should apply to businesses of all types.

For ease of expression, I intend to follow the convention and employ the terminology of the corporate form in my representation of the theories. However, I will attempt to show how each of the theories may be generalized to apply to other forms of business as well. See *infra* notes 24, 45, 64.

9 I wish to emphasize again that the stockholder theory is a normative and not a descriptive theory. As such, it asserts not that managers are, in fact, the agents of the stockholders, but that they are ethically obligated to act as though they were.

10 Milton Friedman, *Capitalism and Freedom* 133 (1962). I should point out that Friedman does not always describe the constraints on the pursuit of profit this precisely. Often, he merely states that businesses should "make as much money as possible while conforming to the basic rules of society, both those embodied in law and those embodied in ethical custom." Milton Friedman, "The Social Responsibility of Business is to Increase Its Profits," *N.Y. Times Magazine*, September 13, 1970 at 32–33. Of course, when stated this broadly, Friedman's injunction becomes a triviality asserting nothing more than that one should pursue profits ethically. Although this has been the source of much criticism of Friedman's particular expression of the stockholder theory, it need not concern us in the present context. The more specific statement given in the text does define a substantive position worthy of serious consideration, and so, that is the formulation that will be used in this article.

11 The additional restriction of Friedman's formulation that requires managers to engage solely in open and free competition is usually ignored. In today's regulatory environment, it is not regarded as unethical to lobby the government for favor. In many cases, such activities are necessary as a matter of corporate self-defense.

12 It may be accurate to characterize the stockholder theory as proposing an "ethical division of labor." According to the stockholder theory, the nature of the business environment itself imposes a basic duty of honest dealing on business people. However, the theory also claims that for there to be any more extensive restrictions on managers, it is the job of society as a whole to impose them through the legislative process.

It is, of course, true that this approach defines managers' ethical obligations partially in terms of their legal obligations and implies that their ethical obligations will change as the legislation that defines and regulates the business environment changes. This, in turn, implies that the stockholder theory is not self-sufficient, but is dependent upon the political theory (which delimits the scope of the state's power to legislate) within which it is embedded. This dependence does not render the theory unintelligible, however. At any particular point in time, the theory can be understood as asserting that a business or business person must refrain from engaging in deceptive practices and violating the laws of the land *as they exist at that time*.

13 It must be kept in mind at all times that the version of the stockholder theory that asserts that the manager is ethically obliged to increase the company's profits is true only for those for-profit companies in which it is reasonable to interpret the stockholders' wishes as the maximization of profit. Whenever the stockholders have indicated that they wish their resources to be used for other purposes, the stockholder theory requires managers to attempt to fulfill those purposes, even if doing so comes at the expense of profits.

14 See, e.g., Dennis P. Quinn and Thomas M. Jones, "An Agent Morality View of Business Policy," 20 *Acad. Mgmt. Rev.* 22, 24 (1995); William M. Evan and R. Edward Freeman, "A Stakeholder Theory of the Modern Corporation: Kantian Capitalism," in *Ethical Theory and Business* 75, 77 (Tom L. Beauchamp and Norman E. Bowie, eds., 4th ed., 1993).

15 Adam Smith, *The Wealth of Nations*, bk. IV, ch. 2, para. 9.

16 This argument can be expressed in more philosophically sophisticated language by stating that one who breaches an agreement that induced another to deal with him or her is treating the other merely as a means to his or her own ends, and is thus violating the Kantian principle of respect for persons.

It is useful to note that Friedman himself offers this deontological argument in support of the stockholder theory, not the utilitarian argument described previously. See Milton Friedman, *The Social Responsibility of Business is to Increase Its Profits*, *supra* note 10. See also Friedman, *Capitalism and Freedom*, *supra* note 10, at 135.

17 See Evan and Freeman, *supra* note 14, at 76–7; Thomas Donaldson and Lee E. Preston, "The Stockholder Theory of the Corporation: Concepts, Evidence, and Implications," 20 *Acad. Mgmt Rev.* 65, 81–2 (1995).

18 Thomas Donaldson, *The Ethics of International Business* 45 (1989).

19 Robert C. Solomon, *Ethics and Excellence* 45 (1992).

20 Evan and Freeman, *supra* note 14, at 77–8.

21 See James D. Gwartney and Richard E. Wagner, "Public Choice and the Conduct of Representative Government," in *Public Choice and Constitutional Economics* 3, 23 (James D. Gwartney and Richard E. Wagner, eds., 1988).

22 This highly telescoped formulation of what is, in truth, a considerably more sophisticated consequentialist argument is employed strictly in the interest of conciseness. The fuller articulation it deserves must await a more detailed consideration of the stockholder theory than the present overview of the normative theories of business ethics permits.

23 For two examples, see *infra* p. 35.

24 As mentioned previously, see *supra* note 8, because of its historical association with debate over *corporate* social responsibility, the stockholder theory is expressed in language that suggests the corporate form, e.g., stock, stockholders. Despite this, the stockholder theory can be applied to all forms of business. In its generalized form, the theory would simply state that managers are ethically obligated to use business resources that have been advanced to them under condition that they be used for specified purposes to accomplish only those purposes. Thus, whether the managers are officers of a public corporation funded by stockholders, managing partners of a limited partnership funded by the limited partners, or sole proprietors funded by investors, they are obligated to use the business's resources in accordance with the agreements

they entered into with the stockholders, limited partners, or investors.

25 Unlike 'agency theory,' however, the phrase 'stakeholder theory' cannot be avoided.

Various attempts have been made to clarify the distinction between the normative and non-normative variants of the stakeholder theory. For example, Kenneth Goodpaster distinguishes non-normative "strategic stakeholder synthesis" from normative "multi-fiduciary stakeholder synthesis." Kenneth E. Goodpaster, "Business Ethics and Stakeholder Analysis," 1 *Business Ethics Quarterly* 53 (1991). Recently, Thomas Donaldson and Lee Preston have further clarified the situation by identifying and distinguishing three different "types" of stakeholder theory; descriptive/empirical, instrumental, and normative. See Donaldson and Preston, *supra* note 17, at 69–73.

For purposes of simplicity and because in this article I will not be commenting on the distinction between the descriptive/empirical and instrumental versions of the theory, I will employ the term 'empirical' in a generic sense to refer to the non-normative versions of the stakeholder theory.

26 See R. E. Freeman, *Strategic Management: A Stakeholder Approach* (1984); Donaldson and Preston, *supra* note 17, at 71.

27 See Evan and Freeman, *supra* note 14, at 76.

28 *Id.* at 79. See also E. Freeman and D. Reed, "Stockholders and Stakeholders: A New Perspective on Corporate Governance," in *Corporate Governance: A Definitive Exploration of the Issues* (C. Huizinga, ed., 1983).

29 This corresponds to Goodpaster's strategic stakeholder synthesis and Donaldson and Preston's instrumental stakeholder theory. See *supra* note 25.

30 In stating that management must give *equal* consideration to the interests of *all* stakeholders, I am not ignoring the work being done to distinguish among different classes of stakeholders. See, e.g., Max B.E. Clarkson, "A Stakeholder Framework for Analyzing and Evaluating Corporate Social Performance," 20 *Acad. Mgmt Rev.* 92, 105–8 (1995). On this point, it is essential to distinguish between the stakeholder theory as a normative theory of business ethics on the one hand and as either a theory of corporate social responsibility or a theory of management on the other. See *supra* note 4 and the material immediately preceding this note. For purposes of either evaluating a business's responsiveness to societal demands or describing effective management techniques, it can make perfect sense to distinguish among different classes of stakeholders. However, given the arguments that have been provided in support of the stakeholder theory as a normative theory of business ethics (to be discussed below), it can not. The logic of these arguments, whether Kantian, Rawlsian, or derived from property rights, makes no allowance for stakeholders of differing moral status. Each implies that all stakeholders are entitled to equal moral consideration. In my opinion, this represents a major difference between the normative and non-normative versions of the stakeholder theory, and one that is likely to generate confusion if not carefully attended to.

31. Evan and Freeman, *supra* note 14, at 82.

32 *Id.* Clearly, this is Goodpaster's multi-fiduciary stakeholder synthesis. See *supra* note 25.

This feature of the normative stakeholder theory immediately gives rise to the objection that it is based on an oxymoron. Given the meaning of the word 'fiduciary,' it is impossible to have a fiduciary relationship to several parties who, like the stakeholders of a corporation, have potentially conflicting interests. Further, even if this did make sense, placing oneself in such a position would appear to be unethical. For example, an attorney who represented two parties with conflicting interests would clearly be guilty of a violation of the canon of ethics.

This objection clearly deserves a fuller treatment than it can be given in a footnote. However, because the purpose of the present work is limited to the critical examination of the arguments offered in support of the three main normative theories of business ethics, an attempt to fully evaluate the theories' adequacy would clearly be beyond its scope. Hence, a more detailed examination of this objection must be deferred until a later time.

33 See, e.g., Donaldson and Preston, *supra* note 17, at 72, who point out that in most of the stakeholder literature "the fundamental normative principles involved are often unexamined."

34 Evan and Freeman, *supra* note 14. This was not the earliest attempt to provide a normative grounding for the stakeholder theory. See, e.g., Thomas M. Jones and Leonard D. Goldberg, "Governing the Large Corporation: More Arguments for Public Directors," 7 *Acad. Mgmt. Rev.* 603 (1982). However, it does appear to be the first effort to derive the stakeholder theory directly from a widely accepted principle of philosophical ethics. This apparently accounts for the widespread attention it has commanded among the commentators.

35 Evan and Freeman, *supra* note 14.

36 *Id.* at 76.

37 *Id.* at 78.

38 R. Edward Freeman and William Evan, "Corporate Governance: A Stakeholder Interpretation," 19 *J. Behav. Econ.* 337 (1990).

39 *Id.* at 352.

40 *Id.* at 353.

41 The unsupported and counter-intuitive assumption that people are ethically entitled to a say in any decision which affects their interests appears to lie at the heart of most attempts to ground the stakeholder theory, and can be found even in those that predate the ones presently under consideration. For an early example of this, consider Jones and Goldberg's 1982 assertion that "if legitimacy centers on the consent of the governed, the legitimacy of corporate decisions made by managers would hinge on the willingness of people *affected* by these decisions to recognize the right of the managers to make them. Because several groups are affected by managerial decisions, legitimacy depends on acceptance of this authority by several types of 'stake holders.'" Jones and Goldberg, *supra* note 34, at 606 (emphasis added).

42 Donaldson and Preston, *supra* note 17, at 82. The rationale underlying this claim is, at best, somewhat murky. The sentence which immediately follows it is: "Changes in state incorporation laws to reflect a constituency's perspective have already been mentioned." *Id.* Professor Donaldson has assured me that this is not intended as an appeal to the ethical authority of the law, but rather to the normative reasons behind the change in the law as indicated by the article's next sentence: "The normative basis for these changes in current mainstream legal thinking is articulated in the recent American Law Institute report, *Principles of Corporate Governance* (1992)." *Id.* However, the sections of the ALI report that the authors cite state nothing more than that corporate officials are *legally permitted* to take ethical considerations into account even where doing so would not enhance corporate profit or shareholder gain and that they are "subject to the same ethical considerations as other members of society." *Id.* This, however, is wholly consistent with the stockholder theory which asserts that corporate managers are not only legally permitted, but ethically required to restrict the means by which they seek to carry out the instructions of their stockholder principals to those which fall within the ethical boundaries set by the law and the principles of honest dealing and open and free competition. The ALI report is indeed inconsistent with the

claim that corporate managers should pursue profit by any means without regard to legal or ethical constraints. It hardly needs repeating, however, that this is not the claim made by the stockholder theory, but that of the straw man the theory's opponents trot out to stand in its stead. At any rate, it is entirely unclear how the comments cited by Donaldson and Preston provide any support for the assertion that the stockholder theory is normatively unacceptable.

43 Donaldson and Preston, *supra* note 17, at 82–4.

44 Philosophers such as Robert Nozick would not accept this contention nor would anyone who argues from a classical liberal perspective. Further, as a matter of purely historical fact, the assertion is clearly false.

45 Like the other theories, the stakeholder theory is expressed in language suggesting the corporate form. However, the theory is clearly perfectly general. Whether the business concerned is a corporation, partnership, or sole proprietorship, the business's stakeholders, those who are vital to its survival and success, can be identified. The stakeholder theory requires the managers to manage the business for the benefit of these stakeholders, regardless of the business's form.

46 Professors Thomas Donaldson and Thomas Dunfee have recently introduced a complex and highly sophisticated version of social contract theory that they call Integrative Social Contracts Theory (ISCT). See Thomas Donaldson and Thomas W. Dunfee, "Toward a Unified Conception of Business Ethics: Integrative Social Contracts Theory," 19 *Acad. Mgmt. Rev.* 252 (1994). The authors are presently in the process of developing a book length exposition of this theory. Although this theory is beyond the scope of the present work and hence will not be directly addressed, it should be noted that ISCT constitutes an attempt to marry the individual social contract theories of Donaldson and Dunfee, both of which are addressed. Therefore, to some extent, the comments made in this article may be extrapolated to apply to ISCT as well.

47 See Thomas Donaldson, *Corporations and Morality*, ch. 2 (1982).

48 See Donaldson, *Corporations and Morality*, *supra* note 47, at 43. The specific description of the social contract theory that follows is taken from this source.

49 *Id.* at 44.

50 *Id.* at 54.

51 *Id.* at 53.

52 *Id.* at 48–9.

53 *Id.* at 53. This last requirement is apparently intended as an antidiscrimination provision.

54 Indeed, many entrepreneurs forum-shop, electing to go into business in the state whose legal regime appears least burdensome to them. Such individuals would clearly be shocked to be told that regardless of which state they chose, they had agreed to abide by the restrictions described by the social contract theory.

55 Thomas Donaldson, *The Ethics of International Business* 56 (1989).

56 *Id.* at 61.

57 *Id.*

58 Because this version of the social contract theory appears to be based on what is essentially a Rawlsian theory of justice, this task would indeed be a formidable one. It would require an examination not only of the relative merits of a Rawlsian conception of justice as opposed to Nozickian and other conceptions, but also of whether such a conception is appropriate in the present limited realm of application. However, once consent has been abandoned as the basis for the social contract, there seems to be no avoiding this. Currently, the best that can be said about this version of the social contract theory is that it is, at most, as well established as John Rawls' theory of justice.

59 See Thomas W. Dunfee, "Business Ethics and Extant Social Contracts," 1 *Business Ethics Quarterly* 23 (1991).

60 *Id.* at 32.

61 *Id.* In fact, there is some question whether all extant social contracts are true agreements since it is claimed that consent is implied by "merely enjoying the benefits of the community or even engaging in transactions within the realm of the community." *Id.* This raises the thorny problem of how one can be said to consent to an agreement without being aware one is doing so. However, because any attempt to resolve this point is beyond the scope of the current work, I will assume for purposes of the present discussion that all extant social contracts are true, consent-based agreements.

62 *Id.* at 33.

63 This may be an unfair characterization. The theory contemplates the possibility of one simultaneously belonging to several communities with incompatible social contracts and asserts that such conflicts must be resolved on the basis of an unspecified "priority rule." (It should be noted that, like the filtering test discussed below, as long as the priority rule remains unspecified, it is impossible to fully evaluate this theory.) However, the theory does not seem to address the situation in which one has entered into incompatible agreements within a single community. It is the latter point that I am presently addressing.

64 As was the case with the stakeholder theory, although the social contract theory is sometimes expressed in the language of the corporation, it clearly applies to businesses generally. Under a social contract approach, the members of society authorize the existence of not merely corporations, but businesses of any form. Thus, all businesses are bound by the terms of the social contract. As a matter of fact, Donaldson's early version of the theory was expressed in perfectly general terms, speaking not about corporations, but about "productive organizations."

65 I have argued in the body of this article that there is, in fact, no ethical entitlement to have a say in any decision that affects one's interests and that the attempts of stakeholder theorists to derive one from Kant's principle of respect for persons, Rawls' theory of justice, and a contemporary theory of property rights have been unsuccessful. However, assuming *arguendo* that the stakeholder theorists are correct and that such an entitlement does exist, it would certainly imply that individuals are ethically entitled to control their own lives.

66 Robert Hessen, "A New Concept of Corporations: A Contractual and Private Property Model," 30 *Hastings L.J.* 1327, 1330 (1979).

67 This is as true of corporations as it is of any other type of business organization. The claim that a corporation is a "creature of the state," endowed by the government with special privileges not available to other freely-organized forms of business is asserted so frequently that it is typically regarded as a truism. That this is not, in fact, the case, is amply demonstrated by Robert Hessen in the article cited in the immediately preceding note. I heartily recommend it to those unfamiliar with the history and law of corporations.

I should add that I am not claiming either that the idea of a business as a network of contracts is a new or original insight (its long lineage is indicated by the source I cite in support of it in the immediately preceding note) or that it commands universal acceptance. I am suggesting, however, that it is an accurate characterization of the ethical nature of business, and further, that support for it can be found in the centrality of consent to each of the three previously examined theories. I am also suggesting that it is an observation that deserves more consideration than it has yet received from those working on the normative theories of business ethics.

68 In this context, I am clearly referring to actual, as opposed to hypothetical or tacit, consent. Hypothetical or tacit consent is, in fact, not consent at all, but the presumption of consent where none has actually been given. It follows that in describing a business as a voluntary association of individuals united by a network of contracts, the contracts being referred to are actual interpersonal agreements, not hypothetical social contracts.

69 It may be more precise to say that the stockholder theory fails to address the obligations arising out of those agreements *that are not inconsistent with the managers' antecedent agreement with the stockholders.* However, it is at least arguable that what should be done when managers have made inconsistent commitments is itself an issue that would have to be addressed by an adequate normative theory of business ethics.

70 This may well be an understatement. Given the wide variety of enterprises that are described by the word 'business,' from the smallest closely-held family business to the largest publicly-traded multinational conglomerate, and from the most mission-oriented nonprofit to the most bottom-line-oriented entrepreneurial venture, it is reasonable to doubt whether this term has a definite enough referent for the construction of a general normative theory of business ethics to even be possible. If it does not, we will simply have to content ourselves with the recognition that ethically proper behavior necessarily depends on the particular agreements the actor has entered into, and leave it at that.

71 Actually, some promising preliminary steps in meeting this challenge have already been taken by Professors Dennis Quinn and Thomas Jones in their article *An Agent Morality View of Business Policy, supra* note 14. This may serve as a useful starting point for those who believe that an adequate general normative theory of business ethics can, in fact, be formulated.

25

Arguments For and Against
Corporate Social Responsibility

N. Craig Smith

There are five principal arguments against corporate social responsibility: the problem of competing claims (the role of profit), competitive disadvantage, competence, fairness, and legitimacy. Each will be considered in turn.

Competing Claims – The Role of Profit

Friedman argues that the notion of social responsibility in business 'shows a fundamental misconception of the character and nature of a free economy'. Business's function is economic, not social. Accordingly, it should be guided and judged by economic criteria alone. Action dictated by anything other than profit maximisation, within the rules of the game, impairs economic efficiency and represents a taxation on those bearing the costs of such inefficiency, most notably the stockholders. The role of the corporation is to make a profit and maximise social welfare through the efficiency which that entails, and as Simon *et al.* put it, 'Consideration of any factors other than profit-maximising ones either results in a deliberate sacrifice of profits or muddies the process of corporate decision-making so as to impair profitability' . So, to quote Silk and Vogel, 'In short, the corporation will best fulfill its obligation to society by fulfilling its obligation to itself'. However, this argument falls down in a number of ways. Simon *et al.* identify four reasons. First, it emphasises the profits of the individual firm as opposed to the corporate sector, which may not mean the highest efficiency from society's point of view. Second, there is the distinction between the short term and the long term. Social goals may be profitable in the long term, for the reasons...of enlightened self-interest. Third, there are other indicators of well-being besides profitability. Because of the uncertainty about

Source: N. Craig Smith, *Morality and The Market* (New York: Routledge, 1990), pp 69–76.

what will be profitable, corporate goals in practice place profitability second, seeking an assurance of a required minimum profit. Fourth, and finally, there is the concern for the efficient use of national resources. Because of social costs, profitability is not necessarily the best measure of effectiveness. Indeed, they argue, 'the argument for efficient allocation of resources would appear to require the corporation to locate and regulate the social consequences of its own conduct'.

Furthermore, Simon *et al.* suggest that if these arguments are not accepted, the negative injunction against social injury would, at least, have to be respected. In other words, Friedman ignores the moral minimum: 'Most of the debate on corporate responsibility, by rather carelessly focusing on what we have termed affirmative duties...has obscured what seems to be the funda- mental point: that economic activity...can have unwanted and injurious side effects, and that the correction of these indirect consequences require self- regulation'. (There are some similarities here with Heilbroner's point that pure profit-maximisation could amount to social irresponsibility.... Essentially, the main criticism of this argument against corporate social responsibility—the need for profit maximisation—is its basis in an inappropriate economic model, the competitive model of capitalism; particularly because of social costs and the question of who the profits are for. Noting the argument about the separation of ownership and control and the consequent limited influence of shareholders over the conduct of professional managers, Ackerman quotes a statement by the chairman of Xerox which pointedly illustrates the inapplicability of the notion of profit-maximisation for shareholders: 'If we ran this business Wall Street's way, we'd run it into the ground...We're in this business for a hell of a long time and we're not going to try to maximise earnings over the short run'.

Competitive Disadvantage

The competitive disadvantage argument against corporate social responsibility suggests that because social action will have a price for the firm it also entails a competitive disadvantage. So, either such works should be carried out by government or, at least, legislated for so that all corporations or industries will be subject to the same requirements. Mintz and Cohen show that such a consideration was paramount in Alfred Sloan's 1929 decision not to fit safety glass to Chevrolets, 'one of the single most important protections ever devised against avoidable automotive death, disfigurement and injury'. Sloan was concerned about public anxiety over automobile safety and did not wish to publicise hazards. In his correspondence with Lammont du Pont over the possible supply of safety glass he observes that despite General Motors' La Salles and Cadillacs being equipped with safety glass, sales by Packard, one of their competitors, had not been materially affected. So Sloan wrote, 'I do not think that from the stockholder's standpoint the move on Cadillac's part has been justified'. Sloan was still reluctant even when he recognized that such a feature would come in the end, he did not want to hurry it along: 'The net result would be that both competition and ourselves would have reduced the return on our capital'. Even when Du Pont noted that Ford had started to fit safety glass in the windshields of all their cars, Sloan observed: 'It is not my responsibility to sell safety glass'.

Green notes that Sloan's rejection of safety glass because it would add slightly to price and because his competitors lacked the 'lifesaving technology' should not be possible today because companies could go to the government to urge minimum standards and thereby avoid placing the firm at a competitive disadvantage. And as Simon *et al.* observe, the competitive disadvantage argument against social responsibility is difficult to accept when the social injury is caused by one firm but not its industry peers–as in Sloan's refusal to fit safety glass after it was fitted to the windshields of all Ford cars. But if the social injury is not unique to one firm then 'the individual corporation can at least be expected to work for industrywide self-regulation within the limits of anti-trust laws; or the individual firm can work for government regulation'. What this ignores, however, is that many industries are ultimately in competition with other industries and there may then be a competitive disadvantage for the industry as a whole in relation to substitution goods. This issue of inter-industry competition aside, the criticism of the competitive disadvantage argument is essentially sound. In approbation of his position, Friedman quotes Adam Smith's comment: 'I have never known much good done by those who affected to trade for the public good.' While healthy skepticism might be desirable, the oligopolistic form of most markets and increased consumer knowledge and awareness makes such a position inappropriate. There are other reasons besides. Ackerman's observations on the advantages and disadvantages of early corporate response to social demands suggest that an early response, while it may seem unnecessary, does provide flexibility. Perhaps more significant, though, is his recognition that the area of discretion within which managers act is quite broad and as competition is conducted on many fronts there is scope for an early response, particularly when the potential benefits are also considered.

Competence

Friedman asks, 'If businessmen do have a social responsibility other than making maximum profits for stockholders, how are they to know what it is?' This implies the competence argument against corporate social responsibility. Simon *et al.* identify three ways in which, it may be claimed, a firm is not competent to deal with social issues. First, there is the claim that corporations do not have the technical skills to deal with social issues. This, they suggest, will vary from case to case and, given the notion of last resort in the Kew Gardens Principle...can only be valid if some other party can do the job better. Second, there is the claim that corporations do not know what is good for society and some other institution, such as government, knows better. But, they observe, 'a corporation's alleged lack of insight into the nature of the good is not a reason for objecting to its social activities unless they are deliberately coercive'. Third, there is the claim that incompetent attempts to resolve social issues waste shareholders' money. But, suggest Simon *et al.*, this is only true if management needs to be made more accountable to the shareholder. Alternatively, such a claim could be countered by pointing to the separation of ownership and control and the role of the professional manager. These factors notwithstanding, the argument of competence can only be applicable to affirmative actions; there is still, as Simon *et al.* note, the moral minimum of the negative injunction against social injury, for which competence cannot be an issue.

Bradshaw, a practitioner writing in this area (as President of Atlantic Richfield Company), does point out that 'corporations cannot cure all social ills, and, indeed, in many areas should not even try...This nation is richly endowed with many and varied institutions. Social change is, I believe, accomplished through these many institutions and not through any one'. He goes on to argue that business people should stick to their competencies, but, bearing in mind his observation that the rules of the game are changing, work 'within those competencies [and] become a prime mover for change at the rule-making level, whether it is in national government, regional areas or states'. Similarly, Silk and Vogel report the comments of the executives at the Conference Board meetings who contended that if they try to operate outside their special area of competence they will invariably get into trouble: 'We shouldn't accept responsibility for what we don't know about'. Elsewhere, Vogel observes that many social issues do not present much scope for solution by business. Moreover, it is not realistic to expect the business community to assume a leading role in balancing social needs with economic imperatives, because it would be inconsistent with the political views of business: 'The social reforms whose enactment have so dramatically improved the lot of the average American over the last 75 years mostly were adopted in spite of business lobbying, not because of it...if business is to perform as well as it can, it requires pressure from those outside it'..

So on the competency argument one must conclude that while there is the moral minimum, social actions beyond this are constrained by what business is able, competent, and willing to do. As Rockefeller notes: 'No one sector of our society is competent to deal with these problems...The only answer is that all sections must become involved, each in its own distinctive way, but in full and collaborative relationship with the others'.

Fairness–Domination By Business

Friedman asks, 'Is it tolerable that these public functions of taxation, expenditure, and control be exercised by the people who happen at the moment to be in charge of particular enterprises, chosen for those posts by strictly private groups?' This is the fairness argument against corporate social responsibility. Heilbroner's concern about corporations playing God has already been noted. In a similar vein, Davis and Blomstrom observe, 'combining social activities with the established economic activities of business would give business an excessive concentration of power...[which] would threaten the pluralistic division of powers which we now have among institutions, probably reducing the viability of our free society'. As Levitt notes, 'The corporation would eventually invest itself with all-embracing duties, obligations, and finally powers–ministering to the whole man and molding him and society in the image of the corporation's narrow ambitions and its essentially unsocial needs'. Big business acting in accord with notions of social responsibility gives managers more discretionary power over the lives of others in three ways, as Simon *et al.* observe: by political action (lobbying), the creation of private government (within the organization), and by a smothering effect–domination by business values.

However, they counter, if business does have this power then the problem is to control it, not think it presents a problem only in the social policy context. One must also consider what is worse: a lack of self-regulation may be more arbitrary in its effects:

> We grant that even corporate self-regulation may have some spill-over effect–
> that the attempt to avoid or correct a self-caused social injury may have some
> influence on the freedom of action of others. Such effects will, we think, be
> relatively insignificant when compared to the benefits of self-correction.

Moreover, they ask that even if affirmative modes of corporate social responsibility involve manipulation, should one fault genuine efforts to help? Besides which, the distinction between leadership and manipulation is a fine one. They conclude on this issue: 'We are convinced that the type of corporate self-regulation we have proposed will help to limit the arbitrary and oppressive impact of corporate activity, rather than the opposite, and therefore does not present a fairness problem'.

Legitimacy–The Role Of Government

The final principal argument against corporate social responsibility is legitimacy: social issues are the concern of government. Or, as one executive commented at the Conference Board meetings: 'We pay the government well. It should do its job and leave us alone to do ours.' As Silk and Vogel comment, the business person feels 'non business' contributions should be voluntary and government has legitimate social concerns which business supports in the payment of taxes. Simon *et al.* identify three positions in this argument. First, unless business acts then government will act, with all the attendant disadvantages of government intervention cited by critics of government encroachment of private spheres. Moreover, corporate social problem-solving may be preferable because it is pluralistic and is therefore likely to be preferred by the people. This position seeks to minimise the role of government. Second, as Levitt and Friedman suggest, corporate involvement in social problems is likely to be bungled, which in itself will lead to government intervention. This has the disadvantages of both government and business interference in the private sphere: again, a position which can be employed to support business action to minimise government's role. The third position claims that only government can deal with market imperfections. This is because some encroachment is viewed as necessary (the mixed market position) and there needs to be an orderly division of labour. They counter that again these positions against corporate social responsibility reflect only on the affirmative duty and not on the negative injunction against social injury. In any event, there is still a case for self-regulation because the duplication of effort cannot in itself be harmful, federal agencies tend to represent industry interests anyway, and much corporate activity is overseas and outside government jurisdiction.

Simon *et al.* conclude on these five principal arguments against corporate social responsibility:

> These points do carry weight with respect to some affirmative modes of corporate social action, but we find these objections unpersuasive in application to self-regulating activity. Whatever debate there may be over more expansive notions of corporate responsibility, a self-policing attempt to take into account the social consequences of business activity and at least an attempt to avoid or correct social injury represents a basic obligation.

The problem of competing claims, competitive disadvantage, competency, fairness, and legitimacy are the principal arguments against corporate social responsibility. Other arguments include: the public being misled about who bears the cost of corporate social action, believing it to be free; the problem of determining benefits, costs, and priorities; the weakened international balance of payments—reduced efficiency raises costs and may put companies at a competitive disadvantage internationally; and the lack of a broad base of support among all groups in society. Also, as Beesley and Evans observe, Friedman's argument must be seen within the context in which it is presented, as 'part of an argument holding that property rights, as for instance manifest in company shareholdings, and, more fundamentally, the right to engage freely in economic activity, are necessary (but admittedly not sufficient) conditions for the maintenance of Western-style political freedom'.... Essentially this argument, the others briefly mentioned, and the principal arguments have been answered and found to be lacking. This is due mainly to their dependence on an inappropriate socioeconomic model of contemporary society, and their failure to account for social costs and the moral minimum of the negative injunction against social injury.

The arguments for corporate social responsibility are implied above. They emphasise changes in public expectations of business; enlightened self-interest; the avoidance of government intervention; the extent of corporate power and the need to balance this with responsibility in self-regulation; and business resources. It is worth concluding this chapter by quoting Steiner and Steiner's summary in review of the arguments for and against corporate social responsibility:

Business decision making today is a mixture of altruism, self-interest, and good citizenship. Managers do take actions that are in the social interest even though there is a cost involved and the connection with long-range profits is quite remote. These actions traditionally were considered to be in the category of 'good deeds'. The issue today is that some people expect—and some managers wonder whether they should respond to the expectation—that business should assume a central role in resolving major social problems of the day in the name of social responsibility...Business cannot do this, nor should it try. Larger corporations, however, clearly feel that the old-fashioned single-minded lust for profits tempered with a few 'good deeds' must be modified in favour of a new social concern. Society also expects its business leaders to be concerned. The issue is not whether business has social responsibilities. It has them. The fundamental issue is to identify them for business in general and for the individual company.

The identification of these responsibilities and ensuring they are met—as well as the continuing problem of corporate power ignored by Steiner and Steiner—demand social control of business....

26

Smith and Friedman on the Pursuit of Self-interest and Profit

Harvey S. James, Jr., and Farhad Rassekh

The purpose in the following essay is to delineate Adam Smith's doctrine and Milton Friedman's thesis as they relate to business ethics. The authors analyze the economics of the pursuit of self-interest and profit as well as the moral constraints that Smith and Friedman impose on business conduct. A careful reading of both economists reveals that Smith's doctrine and Friedman's thesis embody ethical and other regarding considerations, which have important implications for business activity. The authors describe these implications and provide examples and applications of the moral constraints Smith and Friedman advocate.

I. Introduction

The modern market system owes its intellectual roots to the writings of the Scottish moral philosopher and political economist Adam Smith. Smith designed a social system in which markets, where people ostensibly pursue their self-interest, assume a central role. Smith used the metaphor "invisible hand" to show how the pursuit of self-interest unintentionally and unknowingly promotes the public interest. The invisible hand doctrine is one of the most influential ideas in history.

A major theme in the field of business ethics concerns the "social responsibility of corporations," which has attracted considerable attention in recent years. In this regard, the economist and Nobel laureate Milton Friedman has argued that the only social responsibility of business is to maximize its profit. Friedman's thesis, which is an extension of Smith's doctrine, represents one of the most controversial arguments in business ethics.

Source: Laura P. Hartman (ed.), *Perspectives in Business Ethics*, 3rd edn (New York: McGraw-Hill, 2002), pp. 248–56.

II. The Economics and Ethics of Self-Interest

Adam Smith (1723–1790), a leading figure of the Enlightenment, set out to discover the rules and laws that govern a civil and prosperous society. He began his inquiry with his first book, *The Theory of Moral Sentiments* (TMS), in 1759 in which he analyzed, among other things, the motives behind moral behavior. As a part of his social design, Smith in 1776 published his treatise on political economy, *An Inquiry into the Nature and Causes of the Wealth of Nations* (WN). Although it is in the latter book that Smith focused on the requisites for a viable and prosperous economy, to understand the moral constraints Smith places on economic behavior completely and accurately one must study both books.[1]

Smith predicates his system on the observation that we are naturally endowed with a powerful "desire of bettering our condition, a desire which...comes with us from the womb, and never leaves us till we go into grave" (WN, p. 709). Smith also observes "a certain propensity in human nature...the propensity to truck, barter, and exchange one thing for another" (WN, p. 25). These natural impulses lead to division of labor because specializing in production and trading in the marketplace improve our living standards.

Further, Smith delves into the motivation behind market exchanges. Here the choice is between self-interest and benevolence. Although Smith believes benevolence is a praiseworthy virtue, he does not think humans are capable of being benevolent all the time. In this regard, he notes:

> Benevolence may, perhaps, be the sole principle of action in the Deity, and there are several, not improbable, arguments which tend to persuade us that it is so. It is not easy to conceive what other motive an independent and all-perfect Being, who stands in need of nothing external, and whose happiness is complete in himself, can act from. But whatever may be the case with the Deity, so imperfect a creature as man, the support of whose existence requires so many things external to him, must often act from many other motives. (TMS, p. 305)

If human beings are too imperfect and too weak to act out of benevolence, then self-interest is the inevitable choice when an exchange occurs within the market. Moreover, as the economic historian Jacob Viner observed, Smith maintains that virtues such as sympathy and benevolence rule non-market and familial relationships. But since market exchanges are anonymous and mechanical, sympathy and benevolence are "insufficiently strong as a disciplinary force" and thus self-interest "would be the dominant psychological force" in the market.[2] In the following passage, Smith explains why markets operate on self-interest:

> Man has almost constant occasion for the help of his brethren, and *it is in vain for him to expect it from their benevolence only.* He will be more likely to prevail if he can interest their self-love in his favour, and skew them that it is for their own advantage to do for him what he requires of them...and it is this manner that we obtain from one another the far greater part of those good offices which we

stand in need of. It is not from benevolence of the butcher, the brewer, or the baker, that we expect our dinner, but from their regard to their own interest, we address ourselves, not to their humanity but to their self-love, and never talk to them of our own necessities but of their advantages. *Nobody but a begger chuses (sic) to depend chiefly upon the benevolence of his fellow-citizens.* (WN, pp. 26–27, emphasis added)

The last sentence of Smith's remarks suggests that it would be undignified for human beings to appeal to the benevolence of others for their needs. Far more importantly, though, Smith argues that the unintended consequences of self-interested actions frequently benefit society. This analysis leads to the invisible hand doctrine. Here are Smith's remarks:

As every individual, therefore, endeavors as much as he can to employ his capital in the support of domestick industry, and so to direct that industry that its produce may be of the greatest value; every individual necessarily labours to render the annual revenue of the society as great as he can. He generally, indeed, neither intends to promote the publick interest, nor knows how much he is promoting it. By preferring the support of domestick to that of foreign industry, he intends only his own security; and by directing that industry in such a manner as its produce may be of the greatest value, he intends only his own gain, and he is in this, as in many other cases, led by an invisible hand to promote an end which was no part of his intention. Nor is it always the worse for the society that it was no part of it. By pursuing his own interest he frequently promotes that of the society more effectually than when he really intends to promote it. (WN, p. 456)

How does the pursuit of individual self-interest promote that of the society? Consider the following chain of events in the computer industry: The proliferation of computers in the early 1970s increased demand for computer operators, programmers, and engineers. College students quickly realized the promising opportunities in the computer industry and. in large numbers majored in computer-related fields. Thus, students' pursuit of their own interests (i.e., majoring in computers because of job opportunities) met the needs of the computer industry, which in turn met the needs of the society. The evolution of the computer industry, of course, has continued over the years because businesses and individuals benefit enormously from computers. Our demand for computers (i.e., our pursuit of self-interest) continues to attract investment and talents into this industry. The people who enter the computer business also pursue their own interests. *The Wall Street Journal* reports that the U.S. computer industry attracts people from all over the world. For example, it reports, "nearly one third of start-up companies in Silicon Valley are headed by an Indian or Chinese immigrant."[3]

The operation of the invisible hand (i.e., promoting the common good while pursuing self-interest), Smith observes however, is bound by ethical constraints. First and foremost, he distinguishes between self-interest and selfishness. In the introduction to TMS, two noted scholars of Smith point out that "Smith recognizes a variety of motives, not only for actions in general but also for virtuous action. These motives include self-interest or, to use the eighteenth-century term, self-love. It is this, not 'selfishness,' that comes to the fore in EN. Smith distinguished the two expressions, using 'selfishness' in the pejorative sense for such self-love as issues in harm or neglect of other people."[4] The depth of Smith's disapproval of selfish behavior can be discerned from the following passage:

> that to feel much for others and little for ourselves, that to restrain our selfish, and to indulge our benevolent affections, constitutes the perfection of human nature; and can alone produce among mankind that harmony of sentiments and passions in which consists their whole grace and propriety. (TMS, p. 25)

In fact, Smith sets the parameters within which one may pursue self-interest and compete with others. To distinguish right from wrong, Smith introduces an imaginary figure, a moral judge, which he calls the "impartial spectator." Consider the following passage:

> There can be no proper motive for hurting our neighbor.... To disturb his happiness merely because it stands in the way of our own, to take from him what is of real use to him merely because it may be of equal or of more use to us, is what no impartial spectator can go along with.... *In the race for wealth, honors, and preferments, he may run as hard as he can, and strain every nerve and every muscle, in order to outstrip all his competitors. But if he should justle, or throw down any of them, the indulgence of the spectators is entirely at an end. It is a violation of fair play, which they cannot admit of.* (TMS, pp. 82–83, emphasis added)

Therefore, one may work hard to outcompete others, but one ought not to justle to get ahead. In business, "justling," or selfish behavior, includes fraud, deception, lack of concern for public welfare, mistreatment of employees, etc. Although these actions may be illegal, there are legal actions that are ethically questionable. For example, suppose some firms in the computer industry lobby the government for restrictions on immigration because they wish to limit the number of competitors. Such action amounts to justling and throwing down potential competitors, rather than straining every nerve to improve quality and productivity. A restriction on immigration would benefit the existing firms at the expense of consumers and potential entrepreneurs. Smith would consider such policy to be unjust because, in his words, "to hurt in any degree the interest of one order of citizens for no other purpose but to promote that of some other, is evidently contrary to that justice and equality of treatment which the sovereign owes to all different orders of his subjects" (WN, p. 654).

For self-interested actions not to turn selfish, Smith believes that justice must rule business conduct. He notes:

> All systems either of preferences or restraint, therefore, being thus completely taken away, the obvious and simple system of natural liberty establishes itself of its own accord. *Every man, as long as he does not violate the laws of justice, is left perfectly free to pursue his own interest his own way,* and to bring both his industry

and capital into competition with those of any man, or order of men. (WN, p. 687, emphasis added)

In an analysis of the Smithian system, Viner remarks that to Smith "justice is a negative virtue; it consists of refraining from injury to another person and from taking or withholding from another what belongs to him.... Smith considered justice, so understood, to be the necessary foundation of a viable society."[5]

In summary, a careful reading of Smith makes it clear that while he condones the pursuit of self-interest in the marketplace, he argues that we ought to refrain from injuring others. In particular, Smith believes that self-interest should be moderated by a sense of justice toward others in the marketplace. The application of Smith's philosophy to business conduct may be explained as the distinction between self-interest and selfishness as well as the observation and administration of justice in the sense of avoiding harm to others.

III. The Economics and Ethics of Profit

Although Friedman was awarded the Nobel Prize for his work on economic stabilization policy and monetary history, his most influential and controversial writings concern the philosophical subjects of freedom, corporate responsibility, and the role of government in society.[6] Here we focus on his thesis that the only social responsibility of corporations is to maximize profit. To understand Friedman's thesis, one must study carefully his philosophy of economic activity, particularly his books *Capitalism and Freedom* (CF) and *Free to Choose* (FC), and his article "The Social Responsibility of Business is to Increase its Profits" (SRB).[7]

One of Friedman's principal objectives in these writings is to delineate the proper roles of government and individual responsibility in society. Specifically, he seeks to demonstrate what he calls the "fecundity of freedom" (FC, p. 3)–that is, the overriding significance of individual freedom in both the political and economic realms. Friedman takes the "freedom of the individual, or perhaps the family, as [the] ultimate goal in judging social arrangements" (CF, p. 12). For him, freedom is the fundamental criterion by which one should judge individual actions. Thus, social processes that increase individual freedom should be encouraged while those that are restrictive or coercive should be avoided.

Because Friedman values individual freedom so highly, he strongly advocates market mechanisms characterized by voluntary exchanges between individuals. For this reason, he draws heavily on the philosophy and analysis of Adam Smith in the *Wealth of Nations*. According to Friedman:

Adam Smith's key insight was that both parties to an exchange can benefit and that, *so long as cooperation is strictly voluntary*, no exchange will take place unless both parties do benefit. No external force, no coercion, no violation of freedom is necessary to produce cooperation among individuals all of whom can benefit

(FC, pp. 1–2; emphasis in original)

Indeed, Friedman's thesis that corporations should maximize profit is derived from Smith's account of the benefits to society of individuals and corporations freely trading in the marketplace. In fact, Friedman advances a number of teleological arguments in support of his thesis. For instance, one advantage to a society characterized by economic freedom (i.e., voluntary exchange) in the pursuit of profit is that it "provides an offset to whatever concentration of political power may arise" (FC, p. 3). According to Friedman, competitive, profit-driven capitalism is a means of ensuring that political freedom endures. Another benefit is economic prosperity, not just to society but also to groups that otherwise are disadvantaged due to racial or other prejudices. In this regard, Friedman states that it is a

> striking historical fact that the development of capitalism has been accompanied by a major reduction in the extent to which particular religious, racial, or social groups have operated under special handicaps in respect of their economic activities; have, as the saying goes, been discriminated against.... [A] free market separates economic efficiency from irrelevant characteristics.... [T]he purchaser of bread does not know whether it was made from wheat grown by a white man or a Negro, by a Christian or a Jew. In consequence, the producer of wheat is in a position to use resources as effectively as he can, regardless of what the attitudes of the community may be toward the color, the religion, or other characteristics of the people he hires. (CF, pp. 108, 109)

When individuals and corporations maximize profits, resources are used most effectively because the pursuit of profit requires the minimization of all (social) costs of engaging in economic activity. The social cost of producing, say A, is the forgone benefit to) society of the next best alternative, say B, that the same amount of resources could produce. Firms, in attempting to maximize profit while producing A, end up minimizing what society has to sacrifice (i.e., B), an important benefit to a society faced with limited resources. The concept and the process here are akin to Smith's invisible hand. By maximizing profits (i.e., pursuing self-interest) business owners and managers minimize the social cost without knowing or intending it.

Furthermore, Friedman argues that corporate executives who pursue any goal other than profit maximization, such as advancing social causes, may not know what constitutes society's best interest, and they may do it at the expense of some other people. "Can self-selected private individuals decide what the social interest is? Can they decide how great a burden they are justified in placing on themselves or their stockholders to serve that social interest?" (CF, pp. 133–34). Hence, Friedman is skeptical of the net social benefits of business executives trying to act in the social (rather than corporate) interest. As an illustration, Friedman observes that "during the 1930s, German businessmen used some corporate money to support Hitler and the Nazis. Was that a proper exercise of social responsibility?"[8]

Friedman also advances deontological arguments in support of his thesis.

For example, he asserts that corporate executives who pursue any goal other than profit maximization (and thus necessarily reduce profit) violate their specific responsibilities and duties. He states:

> In a free-enterprise, private-property system, a corporate executive is an employee of the owners of the business. He has a direct responsibility to his employers. That responsibility is to conduct the business in accordance with their desires, which generally will be to make as much money as possible. (SRB, p. 33)

A corporate executive who forgoes maximum profit by spending corporate money on social causes is "imposing taxes" on the stockholders and is "deciding how the tax proceeds shall be spent" (SRB, pp. 33, 122). When this occurs, Friedman reasons, the executive ceases to be an employee of a private enterprise and instead becomes a "self-selected" public employee or civil servant (SRB, p. 122), who seeks "to attain by undemocratic procedures what [he] cannot attain by democratic procedures" (SRB, p. 124). Moreover, even if the actions can be justified as serving the corporate interest because they promote the company's product, Friedman rejects such actions as "hypocritical window-dressing" and considers them to be "approaching fraud" (SRB, 124).

Although business executives and managers have an obligation to the corporation, in SRB Friedman clearly states that the pursuit of profit must be constrained by both legal and ethical considerations. Business executives should maximize profits "while conforming to the basic rules of the society, both those embodied in law and those embodied in ethical custom" (SRB, p. 33). For example, Friedman believes that the pursuit of profit should *not* be interpreted narrowly to mean that one might do *whatever* action will result in greater economic returns (even if it is technically legal). In this respect Friedman is consistent with Smith's view that there is a distinction between self-interest and selfishness. According to Friedman, there is a

> broad meaning that must be attached to the concept of "self-interest". Narrow preoccupation with the economic market has led to a narrow interpretation of self-interest as myopic selfishness, as exclusive concern with immediate material rewards. Economics has been berated for allegedly drawing far-reaching conclusions from a wholly unrealistic "economic man" who is little more than a calculating machine, responding only to monetary stimuli. That is a great mistake. *Self-interest is not myopic selfishness.* It is whatever it is that interests the participants, whatever they value, whatever goals they pursue. (FC, p. 27, emphasis added)

Furthermore, individuals have a profound obligation "to wrestle with" the ethical implications of the choices they make, as expressed in this passage by Friedman:

> [In] a society freedom has nothing to say about what an individual does with his freedom, it is not an all-embracing ethic. Indeed, a major aim...is to leave the ethical problem for the individual to wrestle with. The "really" important ethical

> problems are those that face an individual in a free society—what he should do
> with his freedom. There are thus two sets of values...the values that are relevant
> to relations among people, which is the context in which he assigns first priority
> to freedom; and the values that are relevant to the individual in the exercise of
> his freedom, which is the realm of individual ethics and philosophy. (CF, p. 12)

In addition to these ethical considerations, Friedman places two other important restrictions on the pursuit of profit: Business people must commit no deception or fraud, and they must maintain open and free competition (see CF, p. 133).[9] These restrictions mean that individuals are free to pursue their interests (such as making a profit) as long as they do not interfere with the economic (and political) freedom of others. Such interference occurs when individuals in business, for instance, breach contracts, cheat customers, misrepresent the efficacy of their products, withhold important information on product safety, sabotage a competitor's operations, or monopolize markets by political means, such as lobbying the government for protection against imports.

For an illustration of Friedman's thesis, consider the following example. Suppose a company president learns that the firm's manufacturing operations, and those of competitors, discharge a harmful pollutant, and suppose the pollutant is not subject to the country's environmental regulations (i.e., continuing to pollute is not illegal). Should the company president conceal that information and continue manufacturing the product? Certainly, keeping the knowledge secret would increase company profits, at least in the short run. But, Friedman would argue the company president ought to inform the public and accept the consequences of the environmental problem because failing to do so would be tantamount to deception. And, if the pollutant causes harm to others, then it violates the important principle of freedom because others are involuntarily affected by the action of the company president. That is, costs, or "negative externalities," are imposed on others.

Friedman recognizes that "[a]lmost everything we do has some third-party [negative] effects, however small and however remote" (FC, p. 31). Hence, he distinguishes between two types of harms: Harm as a consequence of decisions individuals make when they freely enter into risky transactions, and harm caused by such "external" effects as deception and illegal and unethical actions. Friedman accepts harm of the first type as a necessary by-product of a free society; but he maintains that individuals, in pursuit of profits (or any other reward from one's activities), should not cause harm of the second type. The pursuit of profit ought to be constrained—not by the desire to exercise social responsibility (i.e., to do good), but rather by respect for the rights of others to enter into mutually profitable transactions. The principal constraints Friedman advocates, which Michael Novak describes as "no small moral agenda,"[10] are that executives should obey the law, observe society's ethical customs, commit no deception and fraud, and maintain an open and competitive environment.

VI. Applications

Cases in business ethics can be analyzed by applying the criteria that Smith and Friedman have proposed and we reviewed above. Here we analyze two well-known cases.[11] The first case involves the selling of fire-retardant but cancer-causing children pajamas in the third world countries. In the mid-1970s, millions of pairs of children pajamas containing a new flame-retardant chemical were manufactured and sold in the U.S. Then, in 1977, the Consumer Product Safety Commission banned the sale of the pajamas in the U.S. because the fire-retardant fabric had been linked to kidney cancer in children. Prohibited from selling in the U.S. the pajamas already produced, manufacturers sold millions of pairs to exporters, who resold them in Third World countries where the sale of the product had not been banned.

Should the manufacturers sell the pajamas to exporters in order to minimize their losses (or even turn a profit), knowing they are banned in the U.S. for health reasons? Should the exporters market the pajamas in the Third World? A superficial reading of Smith and Friedman might suggest that they would condone the marketing of the pajamas in the Third World countries because they believe in the pursuit of self-interest and profit. However, as we saw in the analysis of the Smithian system, the manufacturers and exporters must carefully distinguish between self-interest and selfishness. That is, they must ask if they are causing harm to others for personal gain. If the manufacturers and exporters acted selfishly and unjustly, Smith would condemn the action as unethical.

Friedman would state that the manufacturers and exporters are free to take actions that minimize losses or that produce profits for the firms so long as the actions are legal, do not involve deception or fraud, and do not interfere with the competitive processes of the market. According to Friedman's moral constraints on profit maximization, the manufacturers must ensure that the exporters and potential customers are fully informed of the possible carcinogenic effects of the pajamas. If the producers (and exporters) failed to inform the Third World countries that the product had been banned in the U.S., Friedman would denounce the sale as unethical.

The second case involves the action of Raybestos-Manhattan and Johns-Manville towards their employees who were infected with asbestosis, a lung disease. During the early 1930s, executives at the two companies became aware of the hazards their employees faced from inhaling asbestos dust. Here we may ask: Should the companies inform their workers of the health-related effects of inhaling asbestos dust, even though workers who contracted the disease were still able to work? Dr. K. Smith, the medical director of a Johns-Manville facility, testified that "as long as the man is not disabled, it is felt that he should not be told of his condition so that he can live and work in peace and the Company can benefit by his many years of experience."[12] Of course, the companies may find it in their own interest (i.e., profit maximizing) to keep their workers in the dark. In fact, Dr. Smith explained, "the corporation is in business to make products, to provide jobs for people and to make money for stockholders...and if the application of a caution label identifying a product as hazardous would cut out sales, there would be serious financial implications." However, it should be quite clear that both Smith and Friedman would argue that the companies acted unethically because they allowed harm to come upon their employees. Furthermore, Friedman would stress that the companies have an ethical obligation to disclose the information to their workers and to the public, since to do otherwise would constitute deception.

Notes

1 Adam Smith's books are *The Theory of Moral Sentiments* (Indianapolis: Liberty Classics, 1984), and *An Inquiry into the Nature and Causes of the Wealth of Nations* (Indianapolis: Liberty Classics, 1981).

2 Jacob Viner, "The 'Economic Man,' or the Place of Self-Interest in a 'Good society,'" reprinted in Douglas Irwin (ed.), Jacob Viner, *Essays on the Intellectual History of Economics* (Princeton: Princeton University Press, 1991), p. 74 (originally published in 1959).

3 Stephen Gotz-Richter and Daniel Bachman, "Welcome More Immigrants" *Wall Street Journal,* July 22, 1999, p. A26.

4 D. D. Raphael and A. L. Macfie, "Introduction" in Smith, *The Theory of Moral Sentiments,* Indianapolis: Liberty Classics, 1984, p. 22.

5 Jacob Viner, "Adam Smith," reprinted in Irwin (ed.), *Jacob Viner, Essays on the Intellectual History of Economics,* p. 262.

6 It is remarkable that Milton Friedman won the Nobel Prize in Economics in 1976, the bicentennial anniversary of the signing of the Declaration of Independence in the United States as well as the publication of Smith's *Wealth of Nations.*

7 Milton Friedman's books are *Capitalism and Freedom* (Chicago: University of Chicago Press, 1962) (republished in 1982), and *Free to Choose: A Personal Statement* (New York: Harcourt, Brace, and Jovanovich, 1980), published with his wife, Rose Friedman. The article is "The Social Responsibility of Business is to Increase its Profits," *New York Times Magazine,* September 13, 1970, pp. 32–33, 122–26.

8 Milton Friedman, "Milton Friedman Responds: A Business and Society Review Interview," *Business and Society Review* 1, 1972, p. 6.

9 Friedman repeats these two restrictions at the end of his SRB article.

10 Michael Novak, *Business as a Calling* (New York: Free Press, 1996), p. 141.

11 The source of both cases is William Shaw and Vincent Barry, *Moral Issues in Business* (Belmont, CA: Wadsworth, 1998), pp. 25–27, 211–13.

12 Shaw and Barry, p. 212.

27

Does Business Ethics Make Economic Sense?

Amartya Sen[1]

1. Introduction

I begin not with the need for business ethics, but at the other end—the idea that many people have that there is no need for such ethics. That conviction is quite widespread among practitioners of economics, though it is more often taken for granted implicitly rather than asserted explicitly. We have to understand better what the conviction rests on, to be able to see its inadequacies. Here, as in many other areas of knowledge, the importance of a claim depends to a great extent on what it denies.

How did this idea of the redundancy of ethics get launched in economics? The early authors on economic matters, from Aristotle and Kautilya (in ancient Greece and ancient India respectively—the two were contemporaries, as it happens) to medieval practitioners (including Aquinas, Ockham, Maimonides, and others), to the economists of the early modern age (William Petty, Gregory King, Francois Quesnay, and others) were all much concerned, in varying degrees, with ethical analysis. In one way or another, they saw economics as a branch of "practical reason," in which concepts of the good, the right and the obligatory were quite central.

What happened then? As the "official" story goes, all this changed with Adam Smith, who can certainly be described—rightly—as the father of modern economics. He made, so it is said, economics scientific and hardheaded, and the new economics that emerged in the 19th and 20th centuries was already to do business, with no ethics to keep it tied to "morals and moralizing." That view of what happened—with Smith doing the decisive shooting of business and economic ethics—is not only reflected in volumes of professional economic writings, but has even reached the status of getting into the English literature via a limerick by Stephen Leacock, who was both a literary writer

Source: *Business Ethics Quarterly* 3 (1) (1993), 245–51.

and an economist:

> Adam, Adam, Adam Smith
> Listen what I charge you with!
> Didn't you say
> In a class one day
> That selfishness was bound to pay?
> Of all doctrines that was the Pith.
> Wasn't it, wasn't it, wasn't it, Smith?[2]

The interest in going over this bit of history–or alleged history–does not lie, at least for this conference, in scholastic curiosity. I believe it is important to see how that ethics-less view of economics and business emerged in order to understand what it is that is being missed out. As it happens, that bit of potted history of "who killed business ethics" is altogether wrong, and it is particularly instructive to understand how that erroneous identification has come about.

2. Exchange, Production and Distribution

I get back, then, to Adam Smith. Indeed, he did try to make economics scientific, and to a great extent was successful in this task, within the limits of what was possible then. While that part of the alleged history is right (Smith certainly did much to enhance the scientific status of economics), what is altogether mistaken is the idea that Smith demonstrated–or believed that he had demonstrated–the redundancy of ethics in economic and business affairs. Indeed, quite the contrary. The Professor of Moral Philosophy at the University of Glasgow–for that is what Smith was–was as interested in the importance of ethics in behavior as anyone could have been. It is instructive to see how the odd reading of Smith–as a "no-nonsense" sceptic of economic and business ethics–has come about.

Perhaps the most widely quoted remark of Adam Smith is the one about the butcher, the brewer and the baker in *The Wealth of Nations*: "It is not from the benevolence of the butcher, the brewer, or the baker that we expect our dinner, but from their regard to their own interest. We address ourselves, not to their humanity but to their self-love..."[3] The butcher, the brewer and the baker want our money, and we want their products, and the exchange benefits us all. There would seem to be no need for any ethics–business or otherwise–in bringing out this betterment of all the parties involved. All that is needed is regard for our respective interests, and the market is meant to do the rest in bringing about the mutually gainful exchanges.

In modern economics this Smithian tribute to self-interest is cited again and again–indeed with such exclusivity that one is inclined to wonder whether this is the only passage of Smith that is read these days. What did Smith really suggest? Smith did argue in this passage that the pursuit of self-interest would do fine to motivate the exchange of commodities. But that is a very limited claim, even though it is full of wonderful insights in explaining why it is that we seek exchange and how come exchange can be such a beneficial thing for all. But to understand the limits of what is being claimed here, we have to ask, first: Did Smith think that economic operations and business activities consist only of exchanges of this kind? Second, even in the context of exchange, we have to question: Did Smith think that the result would be just as good if the businesses involved, driven by self-interest, were to try to defraud the consumers, or the consumers in question were to attempt to swindle the sellers?

The answers to both these questions are clearly in the negative. The butcher-brewer-baker simplicity does not carry over to problems of production and distribution (and Smith never said that it did), nor to the problem as to how a system of exchange can flourish institutionally. This is exactly where we begin to see why Smith could have been right in his claim about the *motivation for exchange* without establishing or trying to establish *the redundancy of business or ethics* in general (or even in exchange). And this is central to the subject of this conference.

The importance of self-interest pursuit is a helpful part of understanding many practical problems, for example, the supply problems in the Soviet Union and East Europe. But it is quite unhelpful in explaining the success of, say, Japanese economic performance *vis-à-vis* West Europe or North America (since behavior modes in Japan are often deeply influenced by other conventions and pressures). Elsewhere in *The Wealth of Nations*, Adam Smith considers other problems which call for a more complex motivational structure. And in his *The Theory of Moral Sentiments*, Smith goes extensively into the need to go beyond profit maximization, arguing that "humanity, justice, generosity, and public spirit, are the dualities most useful to others."[4] Adam Smith was very far from trying to deny the importance of ethics in behavior in general and business behavior in particular.[5]

Overlooking everything else that Smith said in his wide-ranging writings and concentrating only on this one butcher-brewer-baker passage, the father of modern economics is too often made to look like an ideologue. He is transformed into a partisan exponent of an ethics-free view of life which would have horrified Smith. To adapt a Shakespearian aphorism, while some men are born small and some achieve smallness, the unfortunate Adam Smith has had much smallness thrust upon him.

It is important to see how Smith's whole tribute to self-interest as a motivation for exchange (best illustrated in the butcher-brewer-baker passage) can co-exist peacefully with Smith's advocacy of ethical behavior elsewhere. Smith's concern with ethics was, of course, extremely extensive and by no means confined to economic and business matters. But since this is not the occasion to review Smith's ethical beliefs, but only to get insights from his combination of economic and ethical expertise to understand better the exact role of business ethics, we have to point our inquiries in that particular direction.

The butcher-brewer-baker discussion is all about *motivation for exchange*, but Smith was—as any good economist should be—deeply concerned also with production as well as distribution. And to understand how exchange might itself actually work in practice, it is not adequate to concentrate only on the motivation that makes people seek exchange. It is necessary to look at the behavior patterns that could sustain a flourishing system of mutually profitable exchanges. The positive role of intelligent self-seeking in motivating exchange has to be supplemented by the motivational demands of production and distribution, and the systemic demands on the organization of the economy.

These issues are taken up now, linking the general discussion with practical problems faced in the contemporary world. In the next three sections I discuss in turn (1) the problem of organization (especially that of exchange), (2) the arrangement and performance of production, and (3) the challenge of distribution.

3. Organization and Exchange: Rules and Trust

I come back to the butcher-brewer-baker example. The concern of the different parties with their own interests certainly can adequately *motivate* all of them to take part in the exchange from which each benefits. But whether the exchange would operate well would depend also on organizational conditions. This requires institutional development which can take quite some time to work—a lesson that is currently being learned rather painfully in East Europe and the former Soviet Union. That point is now being recognized, even though it was comprehensively ignored in the first flush of enthusiasm in seeking the magic of allegedly automatic market processes.

But what must also be considered now is the extent to which the economic institutions operate on the basis of common behavior patterns, shared trusts, and a mutual confidence in the ethics of the different parties. When Adam Smith pointed to the motivational importance of "regard to their own interest," he did not suggest that this motivation is all that is needed to have a flourishing system of exchange. If he cannot trust the householder, the baker may have difficulty in proceeding to produce bread to meet orders or in delivering bread without prepayment. And the householder may not be certain whether he would be sensible in relying on the delivery of the ordered bread if the baker is not always altogether reliable. These problems of mutual confidence— discussed in a very simple form here—can be incomparably more complex and more critical in extended and multifarious business arrangements.

Mutual confidence in certain rules of behavior is typically implicit rather than explicit—indeed so implicit that its importance can be easily overlooked in situations in which confidence is unproblematic. But in the context of economic development across the Third World, and also of institutional reform now sweeping across what used to be the Second World, these issues of behavioral norms and ethics can be altogether central.

In the Third World there is often also a deep-rooted scepticism of the reliability and moral quality of business behavior. This can be directed both at local businessmen and the commercial people from abroad. The latter may sometimes be particularly galling to well-established business firms including well-known multinationals. But the record of some multinationals and their unequal power in dealing with the more vulnerable countries have left grounds for much suspicion, even though such suspicion may be quite misplaced in many cases. Establishing high standards of business ethics is certainly one way of tackling this problem.

I have been discussing problems of organization in exchange, and it would seem to be right to conclude this particular discussion by noting that the need for business ethics is quite strong even in the field of exchange (despite the near-universal presence of the butcher-brewer-baker motivation of "regard to their own interest"). If we now move on from exchange to production and distribution, the need for business ethics becomes even more forceful and perspicuous. The issue of trust is central to all economic operations. But we now have to consider other problems of interrelation in the process of production and distribution.

4. Organization of Production: Firms and Public Goods

Capitalism has been successful enough in generating output and raising productivity. But the experiences of different countries are quite diverse. The recent experiences of Eastern Asian economies—most notably Japan—raise deep questions about the modeling of capitalism on traditional economic theory. Japan is often seen—rightly in a particular sense—as a great example of successful capitalism, but it is clear that the motivation patterns that dominate Japanese business have much more content than would be provided by pure profit maximization.

Different commentators have emphasized distinct aspects of Japanese motivational features. Michio Morishima has outlined the special characteristics of "Japanese ethos" as emerging from its particular history of rule-based behavior pattern.[6] Ronald Dore has seen the influence of "Confucian ethics."[7] Recently, Eiko Ikegami has pointed to the importance of the traditional concern with "honor"—a kind of generalization of the Samurai code—as a crucial mollifier of business and economic motivation.[8]

Indeed, there is some truth, oddly enough, even in the puzzlingly witty claim made by *The Wall Street Journal* that Japan is "the only communist nation that works" (30 January 1989, p. 1). It is, as one would expect, mainly a remark about the non-profit motivations underlying many economic and business activities in Japan. We have to understand and interpret the peculiar fact that the most successful capitalist nation in the world flourishes economically with a motivation structure that departs firmly—and often explicitly—from the pursuit of self-interest, which is meant to be the bedrock of capitalism.

In fact, Japan does not, by any means, provide the only example of a powerful role of business ethics in promoting capitalist success. The productive merits of selfless work and devotion to enterprise have been given much credit for economic achievements in many countries in the world. Indeed, the need of capitalism for a motivational structure more complex than pure profit maximization has been acknowledged in various forms, over a long time, by various social scientists (though typically not by any "mainstream" economists): I have in mind Marx, Weber, Tawney, and others.[9] The basic point about the observed success of non-profit motives is neither unusual nor new, even though that wealth of historical and conceptual insights is often thoroughly ignored in professional economics today.

It is useful to try to bring the discussion in line with Adam Smith's concerns, and also with the general analytical approaches successfully developed in modern microeconomic theory. In order to understand how motives other than self-seeking can have an important role, we have to see the limited reach of the butcher-brewer-baker argument, especially in dealing with what modern economists call "public good." This becomes particularly relevant because the overall success of a modern enterprise is, in a very real sense, a public good.

But what *is* a public good? That idea can be best understood by contrasting it with a "private good," such as a toothbrush or a shirt or an apple, which either you can use or I, but not both. Our respective uses would compete and be exclusive. This is not so with public goods, such as a livable environment or the absence of epidemics. All of us may benefit from breathing fresh air, living in an epidemic-free environment, and so on. When uses of commodities are non-competitive, as in the case of public goods, the rationale of the self-interest-based market mechanism comes under severe strain. The market system works by putting a price on a commodity and the allocation between consumers is done by the intensities of the respective willingness to buy it at the prevailing price. When "equilibrium prices" emerge, they balance demand with supply for each commodity. In contrast, in the case of public goods, the uses are—largely or entirely—non-competitive, and the system of giving a good to the highest bidder does not have much merit, since one person's consumption does not exclude that of another. Instead, optimum resource allocation would require that the *combined* benefits be compared with the costs of production, and here the market mechanism, based on profit maximization, functions badly.[10]

A related problem concerns the allocation of private goods involving strong "externalities" with interpersonal interdependencies working outside the markets. If the smoke from a factory makes a neighbor's home dirty and unpleasant, without the neighbor being able to charge the factory owner for the loss she suffers, then that is an "external" relation. The market does not help in this case, since it is not there to allocate the effects—good or bad—that work outside the market.[11] Public goods and externalities are related phenomena, and they are both quite common in such fields as public health care, basic education, environmental protection, and so on.

There are two important issues to be addressed in this context in analysing the organization and performance of production. First, there would tend to be some failure in resource allocation when the commodities produced are public goods or involve strong externalities. This can be taken either (1) as an argument for having *publicly owned enterprises*, which would be governed by principles other than profit maximization, or (2) as a case for *public regulations* governing private enterprise, or (3) as establishing a need for the use of non-profit values–particularly of *social concern*–in private decisions (perhaps because of the goodwill that it might generate). Since public enterprises have not exactly covered themselves with glory in the recent years, and public regulations–while useful–are sometimes quite hard to implement, the third option has become more important in public discussions. It is difficult, in this context, to escape the argument for encouraging business ethics, going well beyond the traditional values of honesty and reliability, and taking on social responsibility as well (for example, in matters of environmental degradation and pollution).

The second issue is more complex and less recognized in the literature but also more interesting. Even in the production of private commodities there can be an important "public good" aspect in the production process itself. This is because production itself is typically a joint activity, supervisions are costly and often unfeasible, and each participant contributes to the overall success of the firm in a way that cannot be fully reflected in the private rewards that he or she gets.

The overall success of the firm, thus, is really a public good, from which all benefit, to which all contribute, and which is not parceled out in little boxes of person-specific rewards strictly linked with each person's *respective contribution*. And this is precisely where the motives other than narrow self-seeking become productively important. Even though I do not have the opportunity to pursue the point further here, I do believe that the successes of "Japanese ethos," "Confucian ethics," "Samurai codes of honor," etc., can be fruitfully linked to this aspect of the organization of production.

5. The Challenge of Distribution: Values and Incentives

I turn now to distribution. It is not hard to see that non-self-seeking motivations can be extremely important for *distributional* problems in general. In dividing a cake, one person's gain is another's loss. At a very obvious level, the contributions that can be made by ethics–business ethics and others–include the amelioration of misery through policies explicitly aimed at such a result. There is an extensive literature on donations, charity, and philanthropy in general, and also on the willingness to join in communal activities geared to social improvement. The connection with ethics is obvious enough in these cases.

What is perhaps more interesting to discuss is the fact that distributional and productional problems very often come mixed together so that how the cake is divided influences the size of the cake itself. The so-called "incentive problem" is a part of this relationship. This too is a much discussed problem, but it is important to clarify in the present context that the extent of the conflict between size and distribution depends crucially on the motivational and behavioral assumptions. The incentive problem is not an immutable feature of production technology. For example, the more narrowly profit-oriented an enterprise is, the more it would, in general, tend to resist looking after the interests of others—workers, associates, consumers. This is an area in which ethics can make a big difference.

The relevance of all this to the question we have been asked to address ("Does business ethics make economic sense?") does, of course, depend on how "economic sense" is defined. If economic sense includes the achievement of a good society in which one lives, then the distributional improvements can be counted in as parts of sensible outcomes even for business. Visionary industrialists and businesspersons have tended to encourage this line of reasoning.

On the other hand, if "economic sense" is interpreted to mean nothing other than achievement of profits and business rewards, then the concerns for others and for distributional equity have to be judged entirely instrumentally— in terms of how they indirectly help to promote profits. That connection is not to be scoffed at, since firms that treat its workers well are often very richly rewarded for it. For one thing, the workers are then more reluctant to lose their jobs, since more would be sacrificed if dismissed from this (more lucrative) employment, compared with alternative opportunities. The contribution of goodwill to team spirit and thus to productivity can also be quite plentiful.

We have then an important contrast between two different ways in which good business behavior could make economic sense. One way is to see the improvement of the society in which one lives as a reward in itself; this works directly. The other is to use ultimately a business criterion for improvement, but to take note of the extent to which good business behavior could in its turn lead to favorable business performance; this enlightened self-interest involves an indirect reasoning.

It is often hard to disentangle the two features, but in understanding whether or how business ethics make economic sense, we leave to take note of each feature. If, for example, a business firm pays inadequate attention to the safety of its workers, and this results accidentally in a disastrous tragedy, like the one that happened in Bhopal in India some years ago (though I am not commenting at present on the extent to which Union Carbide was in fact negligent there), that event would be harmful both for the firm's profits and for the general objectives of social well-being in which the firm may be expected to take an interest. The two effects are distinct and separable and should act cumulatively in an overall consequential analysis. Business ethics has to relate to both.

Notes

1. Lamont University Professor, and Professor of Economics and Philosophy, at Harvard University.

2. Stephen Leacock, *Hellements of Hickonomics* (New York: Dodd, Mead & Co.,

1936), p. 75.

3. Adam Smith, *An Inquiry into the Nature and Causes of the Wealth of Nations* (1776; republished, London: Dent, 1910), vol. 1, p. 13.

4. Adam Smith, *The Theory of Moral Sentiments* (revised edition, 1890; reprinted, Oxford: Clarendon Press, 1976), p.189.

5. On this and related manners, see my *On Ethics and Economics* (Oxford: Blackwell, 1987); Patricia H. Werhane, *Adam Smith and His Legacy for Modern Capitalism* (New York: Oxford University Press, 1991); Emma Rothschild, "Adam Smith and Conservative Economics," *Economic History Review,* 45 (1992).

6. Michio Morishima, *Why Has Japan 'Succeeded'? Western Technology and Japanese Ethos* (Cambridge: Cambridge University Press, 1982).

7. Ronald Dore, "Goodwill and the Spirit of Market Capitalism," *British Journal of Sociology,* 34 (1983), and *Taking Japan Seriously: A Confucian Perspective on Leading Economic Issues* (Stanford: Stanford University Press, 1987).

8. Eiko Ikegami, "The Logic of Cultural Change: Honor, State-Making, and the Samurai," mimeographed, Department of Sociology, Yale University, 1991.

9. Karl Marx (with F. Engels), *The German Ideology* (1945–46), English translation, New York: International Publishers, 1947); Richard Henry Tawney, *Religion and the Rise of Capitalism* (London: Murray, 1926); Max Weber, *The Protestant Ethic and the Spirit of Capitalism* (London: Allen & Unwin, 1930).

10. The classic treatment of public goods was provided by Paul. A. Samuelson, "The Pure Theory of Public Expenditure," *Review of Economics and Statistics,* 35 (1954).

11. For a classic treatment of external effects, see A. C. Pigou, *The Economics of Welfare* (London: Macmillan, 1920). There are many different ways of defining "externalities," with rather disparate bearings on policy issues; on this see the wide-ranging critical work of Andreas Papandreou (*Jr.,* I should add to avoid an ambiguity, though I don't believe he uses that clarification), *Ideas of Externality,* to be published by Clarendon Press, Oxford, and Oxford University Press, New York.

28

New Directions in Corporate Social Responsibility

Norman Bowie

Among philosophers writing in business ethics, something of a consensus has emerged in the past ten years regarding the social responsibility of business. Although these philosophers were critical of the classical view of Milton Friedman (the purpose of the corporation is to make profits for stockholders), the consensus view had much in common with Friedman, so much so that I referred to my own statement of this position as the neoclassical view of corporate responsibility (Bowie 1982). The heart of the neoclassical view was that the corporation was to make a profit while avoiding inflicting harm. In other formulations the corporation was to make a profit while (1) honoring the moral minimum or (2) respecting individual rights and justice. Tom Donaldson arrived at a similar neoclassical description of the purpose of the corporation by arguing that such a view is derived from the social contract that business has with society (1989).

The stakeholder theory made popular by Ed Freeman does seem to represent a major advance over the classical view (Freeman 1984; Evan and Freeman 1988). It might seem inappropriate to refer to the stakeholder position as neoclassical. Rather than argue that the job of the manager was to maximize profits for stockholders, Freeman argued that the manager's task was to protect and promote the rights of the various corporate stakeholders. Stakeholders were defined by Freeman as members of groups whose existence was necessary for the survival of the firm–stockholders, employees, customers, suppliers, the local community, and managers themselves.

Despite the vast increase in scope of managerial obligations, a Friedmanite might try to bring stakeholder theory under his or her umbrella. Of course, the managers must worry about the rights and interests of the other corporate stakeholders. If you don't look after them, these other stakeholders will not be as productive and profits will fall. A good manager is concerned with all

Source: *Business Horizons* (July–August, 1991), 56–65.

stakeholders while increasing profits for stockholders. In the Friedmanite view, the stakeholder theorist does not give us an alternative theory of social responsibility; rather, he or she reminds us how an enlightened Friedmanite, as opposed to an unenlightened one, is supposed to manage. The unenlightened Friedmanite exploits stakeholders to increase profits. Although that strategy might succeed in the short run, the morale and hence the productivity of the other stakeholders plummets, and as a result long-run profits fall. To protect long-run profits, the enlightened manager is concerned with the health, safety, and family needs (day care) of employees, a no-question-asked return policy, stable long-term relations with suppliers, and civic activities in the local community. In this way, long-run profitability is protected or even enhanced. In the classical view, the debate between Milton Friedman and Ed Freeman is not a debate about corporate ends, but rather about corporate means to that end.

Moreover, some classicists argue the neoclassical concern with avoiding harm or honoring the moral minimum does not add anything to Friedman's theory. In *Capitalism and Freedom* (1962) he argues that the manager must obey the law and moral custom. The quotation goes like this:

> In such an economy, there is one and only one social responsibility of business—
> to use its resources and engage in activities designed to increase its profits so
> long as it stays within the rules of the game, which is to say, engages in open and
> free competition, without deception or fraud.

If there really is a social contract that requires business to honor a moral minimum, then a business manager on the Friedmanite model is duty-bound to obey it. To the extent that the moral minimum involves duties to not cause avoidable harm, or to honor individual stakeholder rights, or to adhere to the ordinary canons of justice, then the Friedmanite manager has these duties as well. Even if Friedman didn't emphasize the manager's duties to law and common morality, the existence of the duties are consistent with Friedman's position. Unfortunately, the compatibility of the classical Friedmanite position with obedience to law and morality is undercut by some of Friedman's most well-known followers. The late Albert Carr (1968) substituted the morality of poker for ordinary morality. Indeed he argued that ordinary morality was inappropriate in business:

> Poker's own brand of ethics is different from the ethical ideals of civilized
> human relationships. The game calls for distrust of the other fellow. It ignores
> the claim of friendship. Cunning deception and concealment of one's strength
> and intentions, not kindness and openheartedness, are vital in poker. No one
> thinks any the worse of poker on that account. And no one should think the
> worse of the game of business because its standards of right and wrong differ
> from the prevailing traditions of morality in our society....

Even more pervasive has been the influence of former *Harvard Business Review* editor Theodore Levitt. He defends various deceptive practices in advertising, which seem to be in violation of ordinary morality, as something consumers really like after all (1970):

> Rather than deny that distortion and exaggeration exist in advertising, in this article I shall argue that embellishment and distortion are among advertising's legitimate and socially desirable purpose; and that illegitimacy in advertising consists only of falsification with larcenous intent.... But the consumer suffers from an old dilemma. He wants "truth," but he also wants and needs the alleviating imagery and tantalizing promise of the advertiser and designer.

The writings of these authors give Friedman's theory that "anything for profit" ring that its critics hear. But Friedman need not be interpreted in that way. Many profit-oriented business people do not espouse that interpretation; neither do some academic Friedmanites. What needs to be done is for the Friedmanite school to declare Carr and Levitt heretics and excommunicate them from the faith. The Friedmanites also need to include as part of their canon some statement of the moral minimum idea so the phrase "rules of the game" in *Capitalism and Freedom* has some flesh and bone. On one important point the neoclassical theorists and the Friedmanites are already in explicit agreement. Both positions argue that it is not the purpose of business to do good. The neoclassicists agree with Levitt that providing for the general welfare is the responsibility of government. A business is not a charitable organization.

> Business will have a much better chance of surviving if there is no nonsense about its goals—that is, if long-run profit maximization is one dominant objective in practice as well as in theory. Business should recognize what government's functions are and let it go at that, stopping only to fight government where government directly intrudes itself into business. It should let government take care of the general welfare so that business can take care of the more material aspects of welfare. (Levitt 1958)

Both the classicists and the neoclassicists have elaborate arguments to support their views. The classicist arguments focus on legitimacy. Corporate boards and managers are not popularly elected. Politicians are. Hence government officials have a legitimacy in spending tax dollars for public welfare that corporate managers don't. Moreover, the corporate board and managers are agents of the stockholders. Unless the stockholders authorize charitable contributions, the corporate officers have no right to give the stockholders' money away and violate their fiduciary responsibility in doing so.

Levitt (1958) gives the legitimacy argument a final twist. It is the job of the government to provide for the general welfare; but if business starts doing the government's job, the government will take over business. As a result, business and government will coalesce into one powerful group at the expense of our democratic institutions. Levitt seems to hold the traditional American view, adopted from Montesquieu, that the existence of a democracy requires a balance of competing powers among the main institutions of society. Levitt and Friedman both see the competing institutions as business, government, and labor, each with its distinct and competing interests. If business starts to take on the task of government, the balance of power is upset.

The neoclassical arguments are much more pragmatic. Corporations don't have the resources to solve social problems. Moreover, since the obligation to do good is an open-ended one, society cannot expect corporations to undertake it. A corporation that tries to solve social problems is an institutional Mother Teresa. What it does is good, but its actions, in the language of ethics, are supererogatory.

Some of the neoclassicists add a little sophistication to the argument by showing that competitive pressure will prevent corporations from doing good, even if the competitors all want to. If company X spends more of its money solving social problems than company Y, company Y gains a competitive advantage. Even if company Y wants to contribute to solving social problems, it will try to get company X to contribute even more. Company X has thought this all through; as a result it can't contribute (or contribute as much as it would like). The conclusion is that all competitive companies believe they can't focus on solving social problems even if they want to.

As a result of the arguments, a fairly orthodox position has developed both in theory and in practice. American corporations do not have an obligation to solve social problems. Whatever the notion of corporate responsibility means, it does not mean that. However, the orthodox position does have its critics, and these critics have arguments of their own.

Perhaps the three strongest arguments are based on the duties of gratitude and citizenship and the responsibilities of power. With respect to gratitude, defenders of a duty to help solve social problems argue that society provides tremendous resources to corporations. The local community provides public education that trains workers, a legal system complete with police and courts to enforce corporate contracts, and a huge infrastructure of highways, sewage and garbage disposal, and public health facilities. Corporate taxes are not sufficient payment for the corporations' share of these resources, therefore corporations have a duty out of gratitude to help solve social problems. Moreover, even if corporate taxes did cover their fair share, corporations are citizens morally similar to individual citizens; as a result, they have a similar obligation to help solve social problems. Thus, corporations have a duty based on citizenship to help solve social problems. Finally, the moral use of power requires that power be used responsibly. The term "stewardship" is often used to describe the responsibilities of those who have great power and resources. Individual corporate leaders make reference to the duties of stewardship when they establish private foundations. Carnegie and Rockefeller are two prominent examples.

In addition to the intellectual arguments on behalf of a duty to help solve social problems, there are many actual cases where corporations have acted on that duty. It is part of the corporate culture in the Twin Cities (Minneapolis and St. Paul). Indeed, it seems to be part of the Minnesota corporate culture. Three chambers of commerce annually compile a list of the corporations who give 2 to 5 percent of their pre-tax profits to charitable organizations. The list contains a number of *Fortune* 500 companies including General Mills, Honeywell, Pillsbury, and the H.B. Fuller Co. The Minneapolis offices at the accounting firms of Arthur Andersen, Price Waterhouse, Peat Marwick and Mitchell, and Touche Ross and Company are also on the list.

The number of academics who support the view that corporate responsibility involves an obligation to help solve social problems is even smaller than the number of corporations who support the view. Moreover, the corporate culvert of the Minnesota business community is considered unique. The orthodox view is that a socially responsible corporation pursues profit while respecting the moral minimum. I have been an adherent of that position, but I now think the position is mistaken. Part of what it means for a corporation to be socially responsible is cooperation with other corporations and with nonprofit social and government agencies to help solve social problems.

Social Responsibility and the Duty to Solve Social Problems

I begin this section with an argument for a duty to solve social problems. This argument resembles one a Friedmanite could use to defend an obligation on the part of corporate managers to honor the needs and rights of corporate stakeholders. As you recall, a Friedmanite could argue that a concern with the needs and rights of corporate stakeholders is required for long-term profits. Treating one's customers, employees, and suppliers well is a means to profit.

That theme provides a rationale for an instrumental duty of business to solve social problems. The argument I shall make rests on a number of complicated and controversial empirical claims, and I have neither the expertise nor the space to argue for these empirical claims here. However, these empirical claims constitute something of a conventional wisdom on this subject.

Among the social problems the U.S. faces, most of the more important ones have a severe impact on the quality of the work force. The problem of drug use and other forms of substance abuse, the abysmal quality of public education, the decline in work ethic values, the instability of the family, and the short-term orientation of all corporate stakeholders all affect the firm negatively. The impact is especially acute on employees and suppliers. If the work force is poorly educated, affected with substance abuse, poorly motivated, and short-term oriented, productivity suffers both in quantity and quality.

In future international competition, the quality of the work force is the most important asset a company can have. If capital markets are open, the cost of capital will even out, so any advantage a country might gain through lower costs of capital is short-term. If a country gains an advantage through a technological discovery, highly developed technological competitors will reverse engineer the discovery so the advantage is short-term as well. The one advantage that is relatively long lasting is the quality of one's work force.

In that respect America is at a disadvantage. All the problems pointed out earlier have affected the quality of our work force more severely than in other countries. In addition, racial, religious, and ethnic tensions in our pluralistic work force affect productivity, putting us at a disadvantage against industrial societies with a more homogeneous work force. Thus if America is to remain competitive, social problems that affect workforce productivity must be addressed.

However, the traditional institutional source for resolving social problems– government– seems to have neither the will nor the power to do so. After all, the costs are high and Americans–as events in the past decade have demonstrated–don't like taxes. In addition to being high, the costs are also immediate. However, the benefits, though higher, are very distant. Politicians have difficulty with a time frame beyond the next election. Therefore, there is little incentive for a politician to pay the costs now. A well worked-out statement of this view can be found in Alan Blinder's *Hard Heads Soft Hearts* (1987).

To make matters worse, our high national debt, the recent war with Iraq, the S&L debacle, and our aging infrastructure will only drain resources from social problems. If international competition requires that such problems be solved, but government is unwilling and perhaps unable to do so, it would seem that business has no choice but to become involved. The long-term competitiveness and hence long-term profitability of business is at stake. If the scenario I have painted is at all accurate, then even a Friedmanite could argue that business should help solve social problems. Business initiative in that area is justified on the grounds that such action is necessary to increase profits.

There certainly is nothing inconsistent with a Friedmanite arguing that business should help solve social problems to increase profit, so long as the dangers from not doing so outweigh the dangers discussed earlier. But I doubt that people like Levitt would ever agree that the increase in profitability would be worth the cost of lost independence now enjoyed by the business community. Even though Friedmanites in theory could support a view of corporate responsibility that included a corporate duty to help solve social problems, in all probability they would not.

On the chance some Friedmanite might support such an expanded concept of social responsibility, let me argue why a Friedmanite approach to an obligation to help solve social problems would probably fail. My argument here is tied up with issues of motivation and intentionality.

Consider what philosophers call "the hedonic paradox": the more people consciously seek happiness the less likely they are to achieve it. The reader is invited to test this assertion by getting up tomorrow and framing his or her activities with a conscious goal of happiness. In other words, do everything to be happy. If you do, almost certainly you will fail to achieve happiness.

To understand the paradox, we must distinguish between the intended end of an action and the feelings we get when we succeed (achieve the goal). If you are thirsty, you seek a glass of water to extinguish the thirst. When you quench your thirst you feel pleasure or contentment. But you didn't get the glass of water to get the contentment that goes with quenching your thirst. And you generally don't act to be happy. You are happy when you succeed in obtaining the goals that constitute the basis of your actions. Happiness is not one of those goals; it is a state one achieves when one successfully gains one's other goals.

What does this have to do with profit? Should profit be a conscious goal of the firm, or the result of achieving other corporate goals? For simplicity's sake let us say there is some relation between providing meaningful work for employees, quality products for customers, and corporate profits. What is the nature of that relationship? Do you achieve meaningful work for employees and quality products for customers by aiming at profits (by making profits your goal), or do you aim at providing meaningful work for employees and quality products for customers (make them your goal) and achieve profits as a result? A Friedmanite is committed to making profits the goal. As we saw in the discussion of stakeholder theory, a Friedmanite will respect the needs and rights of the other stakeholders to increase profits for the stockholders. But for a genuine stakeholder theorist, the needs and rights of the various stakeholders take priority. Management acts in response to those needs; profits are often the happy result.

Both Friedmanites and non-Friedmanites can posit a relationship between profits and meeting stakeholder needs. What divides them is the strength of the casual arrow, a difference over which one should be the conscious objective of management. A Friedmanite argues for profit. A stakeholder theorist argues for the needs and rights of stakeholders. A Friedmanite argues that you treat employees and customers well to make a profit; good treatment is a means to an end. A stakeholder theorist argues that a manager should treat employees and customers well because it is the right thing to do; the needs and rights of the corporate stakeholders are the ends the manager should aim at. Profits are the happy results that usually accompany these ends.

American corporations have thought like Friedmanites even when they speak the language of stakeholder theorists. They introduce quality circles or ESOPS to increase profits. Some of our international competitors have thought like stakeholder theorists even though they have achieved Friedman-like results.

With respect to the duty to help solve social problems, should that duty be taken on because by doing so profits may be increased, or because it is a moral responsibility to do so? To answer that question, I suggest we visit the work of Cornell economist Robert Frank (1988) and consider the spotty success of the introduction of quality circles and other forms of "enlightened" labor management in the U.S.

Frank's point, buttressed by a large amount of empirical evidence from psychology, sociology, and biology, is that an altruistic person (a person who will not behave opportunistically even when he or she can get away with it) is the most desirable person to make a deal with. After all, if you have a contractual relationship with someone, the best person you can deal with is someone you know will honor the terms of the contract even if he or she could get away with not honoring them. An employer wants employees who won't steal or cheat even if they could. A marriage partner wants a spouse who won't cheat even if he or she could. Altruists rather than profit maximizers make the best business partners.

Frank then goes on to make the point Immanuel Kant would make. You can't adopt altruism as a strategy like "honesty is the best policy" and gain the advantages of altruism. After all, if I knew you were being an altruist because it paid, I would conclude that in any case where altruism didn't pay, you would revert to opportunism. My ideal business partner is someone who doesn't merely adopt altruism because it pays but adopts it because he or she is committed to it. She or he is not an opportunist because opportunism is wrong. As Frank says:

> For the model to work, satisfaction from doing the right thing must not be premised on the fact that material gains may later follow; rather it must be *intrinsic* to the act itself. Otherwise a person will lack the necessary motivation to make self-sacrificing choices, and once others sense that, material gains will not, in fact, follow. Under the commitment model, moral sentiments do not lead to material advantage unless they are heartfelt.

Frank's theoretical account of the advantages of committed altruism over reciprocal altruism as the best payoff strategy helps explain the spotty record of "enlightened" employee management techniques. Techniques like quality circles that work very well in Japan and Sweden don't work as well in the U.S. Why? Cultural difference is not a sufficiently specific answer. What cultural differences make the transfer difficult? I hypothesize that since labor/ management relations in the U.S. are opportunistically based, labor assumes— probably correctly–that such reforms are motivated not by employer concern for employees but by profit. If that is the motivation, labor reasons, why should labor embrace the reforms? The elements of trust created by genuine concern for employees are missing in the American context. Indeed, both labor and management assume the other will behave opportunistically. Academics assume that too, and agency theory provides a model for the opportunistic framework. Given that cultural and intellectual context, it is no surprise that labor would distrust an employer whose concern with an improved working environment was not genuinely altruistic.

This discussion affects the duty to help solve social problems. If the resolution of these problems would improve America's human capital, that result would be most likely to occur if the investment in human capital were altruistically motivated. The one good thing about corporate efforts to solve social problems is that it is easy to show that with respect to the individual firm, such efforts must be altruistic. After all, an improved labor force is a classic case of a public good. There is no guarantee that the money spent by an individual firm will benefit that firm. If a firm adopts an inner city elementary school and pours resources into it, there is no reason to think that firm will get its investment back. The reason need not be that many of the students of that elementary school won't work for the supporting firm. After all, it might gain employees from other schools supported by other firms. Rather, the reason is that some firms will ride free off the expenditures of the moral firms. Thus, employees who understand these considerations can be sure that the employers who give money to solve social problems are altruistic.

If this analysis is correct the following conclusions can be drawn:

1. It is in the interest of business to adopt an extended view of corporate social responsibility that includes a duty to help solve social problems.

2. If business adopts that duty because it thinks it will benefit, its actions will be viewed cynically.

3. Moreover, because an improved labor force is a public good for business, the only real reason for an individual firm to help solve social problems is altruistic.

4. Thus, employees and other corporate stakeholders have a good reason to believe that corporate attempts to solve social problems are altruistic.

Obligations of Various Stakeholders in a Socially Responsible Corporation

In the previous section I gave an argument to show that everyone has good reason to believe that corporate attempts to solve social problems are genuinely altruistic. What are the implications of this for the various corporate stakeholders, especially customers?

Our ordinary way of speaking is to say the corporation ought to respect stakeholder needs and rights. Thus, we say that the corporation should produce quality products for customers, or that the corporation should not subject its employees to lie detector tests. We speak of the obligation of the firm (firm's management) to employees, customers, and local community. However, this way of speaking tends to give a one-sided emphasis to the moral obligations of the corporation.

My concern is that within the firm conceived of as a moral community, we speak as if all the obligations fall on the firm, or its managers and stockholders. In a previous article, "The Firm as a Moral Community" (Bowie 1991), I argued that Kant's third formulation of the categorical imperative best captures the moral relations that exist among corporate stakeholders. Kant would view a corporation as a moral community in which all of the stakeholders would both create the rules that govern them and be bound to one another by these same rules.

Moral relations are reciprocal. In addition to the obligations of managers, what of the obligations of the employees, customers, or local community to the firm (firm's management)? For example, business ethicists are critical of the so-called employment-at-will doctrine under which employees can be let go for "any reason, no reason, or reason immoral." Such a doctrine is unresponsive to the needs and rights of employees; it permits a manager to ignore both the quality of an employee's work performance and the number of years he or she has been with the firm.

Similarly, business ethicists are critical of the noneconomic layoffs that often accompany a hostile takeover. An example of noneconomic layoffs is when people are fired just because they worked for the old company. The new managers simply want their people in those positions–an understandable view, but one that does not take into account the interests of the employees let go. Those people might have served the target company for 20 years with great loyalty and distinction. Now they find themselves out of work through no fault of their own.

However, these business ethicists seldom criticize employees who leave a corporation on short notice simply to get a better job. Business firms argue that they invest huge amounts of money in training new employees, and losses from turnover are very high. Sometimes the employee might have been given educational benefits or even paid leave to resolve personal problems such as alcohol and drug abuse. Others may have received company financial support for further education—perhaps even an M.B.A. Yet these employees think nothing of leaving the proven loyal employer for a better job elsewhere. As managers often remind us, loyalty is not a one-way street.

What needs to be decided is the nature of the employment relationship. Because it is among people, it cannot be merely an economic relationship. Although some currently refer to it as such, they are mistaken. All employment relationships have some contractual elements attached to them. A contract represents a kind of promise; even the standard employment relationship is in part moral. Some argue that legally the employment contract is nothing more than an agreement that the employer can let the employee go whenever he or she wants, and the employee can leave whenever he or she wants. There is true reciprocity here, even if the relationship is rather limited morally.

However, in the world of actual business practice one side or the other often behaves in ways that go far beyond the limited legal contractual relationship, thus adding moral capital to the relationship. Loyal employees who may have passed up other jobs are let go; employees leave loyal employers who have invested heavily in their welfare for a slightly better-paying job. Both actions are morally wrong because the duties of reciprocity and gratitude have been breached. Social responsibility under a stakeholder model requires that each stakeholder has reciprocal duties with others. Thus, if an employee has a duty of loyalty to an employer, an employer has a duty of loyalty to an employee.

Let us apply this analysis to a triadic stakeholder relationship—the firm's management, its customers, and the local community. One of the moral problems facing any community is environmental pollution. As with the employment-at-will doctrine, most business ethicists focus on the obligations of the firm. But what of the obligations of the consumers who buy and use the firm's products?

Consider the following instances reported by Alicia Swasy in a recent *Wall Street Journal* article (1988). Wendy's tried to replace foam plates and cups with paper, but customers in the test markets balked.

Procter and Gamble offered Downy fabric softener in a concentrated form that requires less packaging than ready-to-use products. However, the concentrate version is less convenient because it has to be mixed with water. Sales have been poor. Procter and Gamble also manufactures Vizir and Lenor brands of detergents in concentrate form. Europeans will take the trouble; Americans will not.

Kodak tried to eliminate its yellow film boxes but met customer resistance. McDonald's has been testing mini-incinerators that convert trash into energy but often meets opposition from community groups that fear the incinerators will pollute the air. A McDonald's spokesperson points out that the emissions are mostly carbon dioxide and water vapor and are "less offensive than a barbecue."

And Jerry Alder reports in *Newsweek* (1989) that Exxon spent approximately $40,000 each to "save" 230 otters. Otters in captivity cost $800. Fishermen in Alaska are permitted to shoot otters as pests.

Recently environmentalists have pointed out the environmental damage caused by the widespread use of disposable diapers. However, are Americans ready to give up Pampers and go back to cloth diapers and the diaper pail? Most observers think not.

If environmentalists want business to produce products that are more friendly to the environment, they must convince Americans to purchase them. Business will respond to the market. It is the consuming public that has the obligation to make the trade-off between cost and environmental integrity.

Yet another example involved corporate giving. Earlier I cited the Twin Cities, Minnesota business community as providing an example of a local community where many of the firms gave either 2 percent or 5 percent of their pretax profits hack to the community. I have never heard anyone argue that on the principle of reciprocity citizens of the Twin Cities have obligations to these firms. Yet I would argue that these citizens have an obligation to support socially responsible firms over firms that are either socially irresponsible or indifferent to social responsibility. The relation of a local citizen to the companies that do business locally is again not simply economic. Citizens who consider only price in choosing between two department stores are behaving in a socially irresponsible way. If one department store contributes to the local community and the other doesn't, that factor should be taken into account when citizens in that community decide on where to shop. It's more than a matter of price.

The Target department store chain is a branch of the Dayton Hudson Company. It has a special program for hiring the disabled, and even assists these people with up to one-third of their rent. At Christmas it closes its stores to the general public and opens them to the elderly and disabled. These people receive an additional 10 percent discount and free gift wrapping. In many stores 75 percent of the trash generated is recycled. Target is a member of the 5 percent club. The list of its activities that support the community goes on and on. Target's competitors, WalMart and K mart, have nothing comparable. I maintain that Target's superior social performance creates an obligation for members of the community to shop at Target.

All these examples lead to a general point. For too long corporate responsibility has been analyzed simply in terms of the responsibilities of the firm (firm's management) to all other corporate stakeholders except stockholders. I exclude stockholders because the cost of honoring stakeholder obligations comes almost exclusively from their profits. If we are to have a truly comprehensive theory of corporate social responsibility, we must develop a theory for determining the appropriate reciprocal duties that exist among corporate stakeholders. If the managers and stockholders have a duty to customers, suppliers, employees, and the local community, then the local community, employees, suppliers, and customers have a duty to managers and stockholders. What these duties are has barely been discussed.

The Complications of Moral Pluralism

A great complication that exists for any attempt to determine reciprocal stakeholder duties occurs when the existence of moral pluralism is taken into account. For purposes of this paper, moral pluralism is a descriptive term that applies to the widespread disagreement about moral matters that exists among the American people. People disagree as to what is right and wrong. Some consider drug testing to be right. Others think it's wrong. People also disagree about the priorities given to various rights and responsibilities. For example, does the firm's obligation to protect its customers override its obligation to protect the privacy of its employees? And suppose it is decided that the safety of the customers does take priority? Is testing all employees or random testing more fair? The general point is this: If people cannot agree as to what is right and wrong and how to set priorities when our duties conflict, what advice can be given to managers and other corporate stakeholders regarding what their duties are?

The unhappy situation that befell Dayton Hudson in late 1990 illustrates the point exactly. Dayton Hudson has long been a member of the Twin Cities 5 percent club. The funds are distributed through the Dayton Hudson Foundation. For many years Planned Parenthood has been the recipient of relatively small grants of a few thousand dollars. Abortion opponents have charged Planned Parenthood with various degrees of complicity in abortion activities. In 1990 Dayton Hudson announced that to avoid becoming embroiled in the abortion debate, it would no longer support Planned Parenthood. No decision could have gotten it more embroiled in the debate. Pro-choice forces announced an immediate boycott of Dayton Hudson and its Target stores; hundreds of people cut up their Dayton Hudson credit cards and mailed them back to the company. In a few days Dayton Hudson relented and agreed to provide a grant to Planned Parenthood as it had done in the past. Now the anti-abortion forces were enraged. They organized boycotts and demonstrations that continued into the holiday season.

Dayton Hudson officials were both embarrassed and angry, but they indicated they would not retreat from their position to give 5 percent of their pretax income to charity. Although little was said publicly, the Dayton Hudson public relations disaster gave many executives pause. Perhaps the Friedmanites were right. They were giving away stockholder money for causes deemed inappropriate. Obviously some stockholders would not approve of the company's choices, just as some of Dayton's customers and citizens of the local community didn't.

In addition some executives were rumored to have taken the following position:

1. The money is ours;

2. If people don't like how we spend our money, then we won't spend it on charity at all.

These corporate officials saw Dayton Hudson's protesting customers and citizens in the Twin Cities as ungrateful and unappreciative of the largesse Dayton Hudson had given over the years. These ingrates did not deserve corporate support. Whether corporate support for charities in the Twin Cities will fall off over the next few years remains to be seen.

Should the Dayton Hudson problem become more widespread, a serious impediment toward any corporation's decision to help solve social problems will have arisen. How should such difficulties be resolved? To answer that question we need to return to our model of the firm as a nexus of moral relationships among stakeholders. From that perspective I might suggest some principles that can be used to help resolve the problems created by moral pluralism.

First, if a corporation really has a duty to help solve social problems, we can ask whether the corporation, through its managers, should have sole say as to how the money is to be spent. I think the answer to that question must be "no." A firm as constituted by its stakeholders is not narrowly defined. To let the managers have the sole say is to allow one stakeholder to make the decisions on behalf of all. How can that be justified?

Some argue that legal ownership justifies the decision. On this view the decision should be made by the stockholders, because they are the legal owners. To my knowledge, no corporation decides either the amount of charity or determines those organizations that receive charity by taking a vote of the stockholders. Of course, the matter could be settled in this way, but I have argued elsewhere (Bowie 1990) that the limited short-term view of most stockholders undercuts any moral claim that ownership might have to make the sole decision here.

These arguments, if valid, also count against any view that would justify the manager making this decision as the agent of the stockholder. If the stockholders have no right to make the sole determination in these matters, neither do the stockholders' agents. If no one stakeholder should settle these issues, it seems reasonable to think that all stakeholders should have a voice. How this voice is exercised can be aided in a number of ways.

Some corporations might focus on providing funds to groups that have broad public support, such as the United Way. Agencies like the United Way reflect community decisions concerning which charities are considered worthwhile. Undoubtedly some people in the community will object to the list, and agencies like the United Way have been criticized for leaving out controversial nonprofits that really fight social problems while keeping "middle class" charities such as the Boy Scouts. Despite these objections, deferring to local agencies recognizes the voice of the local community in decisions that are made. Alternatively, a corporation might put community people on its foundation board or community affairs council. I would recommend the first approach. The latter approach runs the risk of filling a board or council with individuals who speak only to narrow interests.

Moreover, in line with my argument that moral duties fall on all corporate stakeholders, I would argue that it is the moral responsibility of the community to structure the United Way and other social agencies to meet genuine social needs. It is up to the local community to find a place for unpopular but socially concerned and effective nonprofits. It is up to the local community to solve the problems of representation.

Many corporations have given voice to their employees by matching employee contributions to charity. If an employee gives $100 to his or her college alma mater, the company will kick in $100 as well. Corporations also support charitable organizations in cities and towns where they have plants. They might extend this to cities and towns where their suppliers are located as well. These strategies should be adopted as policy by other corporations unless other defensible ways of giving voice to employees and suppliers can be found.

As for customers, they are part of the local community; unless there are some special circumstances that should be taken into account, I think our analysis will suffice. Customers are given voice the same way the local community is–by supporting local agencies through the United Way or some other similar organization.

Finally, I turn to stockholders. Although I have argued that the amount and type of corporate support given to help solve social problems should not be decided by the stockholders alone, they certainly should have some say in the decisions. Management might poll stockholders to determine their interests or get them to specifically approve the company's program in this area when they cast their annual proxy vote for the election of the board and other matters.

As the tenor of these remarks suggest, we are further along than might have been suspected with regard to giving all stakeholders a voice in corporate decisions. However we have a way to go, and I have made some suggestions as to the directions we might take.

Let me close by making a point that will seem obvious to philosophers but less obvious to others. In essence I have approached the issues raised by ethical pluralism by process rather than substance. I have not tried to argue that one position on these matters is morally correct and the others morally flawed. Rather, I have tried to elucidate a just process so the various stakeholder voices in these matters can be heard and have some influence on the decision. To put my perspective in Rawls's language (1971), I think the issues presented by ethical pluralism can only be handled by just procedures rather than aiming at just results. In Rawls's language, I am suggesting a system of imperfect procedural justice to address this issue.

References

Jerry Alder, "Alaska After Exxon," *Newsweek*, September 18, 1989, pp. 50–62.
Alan S. Blinder, *Hard Heads Soft Hearts* (Reading, Mass.: Addison Wesley, 1987).
Norman Bowie, *Business Ethics* (Englewood Cliffs, NJ.: Prentice Hall Inc., 1982).
Norman Bowie with Ronald Duska, *Business Ethics*, 2nd ed. (Englewood Cliffs, NJ.: Prentice Hall Inc., 1990).

Norman Bowie, "The Firm as a Moral Community," in Richard M. Coughlin, ed., *Perspectives on Socio-Economics* (White Plains, N.Y.: M.E. Sharpe, Inc., 1991; forthcoming).

Albert Carr, "Is Business Bluffing Ethical?" *Harvard Business Review*, January–February 1968, pp. 143–146.

Thomas Donaldson, *The Ethics of International Business* (New York: Oxford University Press, 1989).

William E. Evan and R. Edward Freeman, "A Stakeholder Theory of the Modern Corporation: Kantian Capitalism," in Tom L. Beauchamp and Norman E. Bowie, eds., *Ethical Theory and Business*, 3rd ed. (Englewood Cliffs, N.J.: Prentice Hall, 1988).

Robert Frank, *Passions Within Reason* (New York: W.W. Norton & Co., 1988).

R. Edward Freeman, *Strategic Management: A Stakeholder Approach* (Marshfield, Mass.: Pitman, 1984).

Milton Friedman, *Capitalism & Freedom* (Chicago: University of Chicago Press, 1962).

Milton Friedman, "The Social Responsibility of Business Is to Increase Its Profits," *New York Times Magazine*, September 13, 1970, pp. 32–34, 122–126.

Immanuel Kant, *Foundations of the Metaphysics of Morals* (Lewis White Beck, trans.) (Indianapolis: Bobbs Merrill, 1969).

Theodore Levitt, "The Dangers of Social Responsibility," *Harvard Business Review*, September–October 1958, pp. 41–50.

Theodore Levitt, "The Morality(?) of Advertising," *Harvard Business Review*, July-August 1970, pp. 84–92.

John Rawls, *A Theory of Justice* (Cambridge, Mass.: Harvard University Press, 1971).

Alicia Swasy, "For Consumers, Ecology Comes Second," *Wall Street Journal*, August 23, 1988, p. B1.

Norman Bowie is a professor of management at the Curtis L. Carlson School of Management, University of Minnesota, Minneapolis.

29

Globalization and its Impact on the Full Enjoyment of All Human Rights

Preliminary Report of the Secretary-General

I. Introduction

1. In its resolution 54/165 of 17 December 1999, the General Assembly requested the Secretary-General, taking into account the different views of Member States, to submit a comprehensive report on globalization and its impact on the full enjoyment of all human rights to the General Assembly at its fifty-fifth session.

2. The present preliminary report is submitted in response to that request. It is the intention of the Secretary-General to explore the issues and solicit the initial reactions of States before submitting the final report. For the preparation of that report, the written views of Member States will be sought and partner agencies will be brought into the process.

3. The present preliminary report has been written on the basis of reports of United Nations departments, programmes and funds, as well as the outcome document adopted at the twenty-fourth special session of the General Assembly, entitled "World Summit for Social Development and beyond: achieving social development for all in a globalizing world" (A/S-24/8/Rev. 1, chap. III).

4. In particular, the report draws on paragraph 4 of the political declaration of the twenty-fourth special session as expressing the views of Member States concerning globalization. Specifically, in paragraph 4, it is noted that:

> "Globalization and continuing rapid technological advances offer unprecedented opportunities for social and economic development. At the same time, they continue to present serious challenges, including widespread financial crises, insecurity, poverty, exclusion and inequality within and among societies. Considerable obstacles to further integration and full participation in the global economy remain for developing countries, in particular the least developed

Source: *United Nations General Assembly* 31 (2000), 1–12.

countries, as well as for some countries with economies in transition. Unless the benefits of social and economic development are extended to all countries, a growing number of people in all countries and even entire regions will remain marginalized from the global economy."

II. Globalization – Issues and Challenges

5. Globalization is a term often used without any formal definition. The United Nations Development Programme *Human Development Report* 1999 noted that globalization is not new, but that the present era of globalization has distinctive features. Shrinking space, shrinking time and disappearing borders are linking people's lives more deeply, more intensely, more immediately than ever before.[1] The present report assumes that globalization is multidimensional. It can be broken down into numerous complex and interrelated processes that have a dynamism of their own, resulting in both varied and often unpredictable effects. While there have been previous eras that have experienced globalization, the present era has certain distinctive features, including, although not limited to, advances in new technology, in particular information and communications technology, cheaper and quicker transport, trade liberalization, the increase in financial flows and the growth in the size and power of corporations. In order to advance a constructive exchange of views on globalization, States might consider conveying to the Secretary-General their views on how globalization might best be defined and approached from the perspective of human rights.

6. While many people are benefiting from new opportunities for travel and from new communications technology, new levels of wealth through increased trade, investment and capital flows, others are being left behind, in poverty, effectively marginalized from the hopes that globalization holds out.

7. Globalization therefore presents an important challenge to the international community. Over 50 years ago, the international community agreed, within the framework of the Universal Declaration of Human Rights, that, "Everyone is entitled to a social and international order in which the rights and freedoms set forth in this Declaration can be fully realized". According to the norms and standards of international human rights law, such an international and social order is one that promotes the inherent dignity of the human person, respects the right of people to self-determination and seeks social progress through participatory development and by promoting equality and non-discrimination in a peaceful, interdependent and accountable world.

8. The norms and standards of international human rights law have an important role in providing principles for globalization. At the same time, the international rules established under the General Agreement on Tariffs and Trade (GATT) and the World Trade Organization (WTO), and the macro-economic policies of the International Monetary Fund (IMF) and the World Bank play a significant role in shaping and directing globalization. While the norms and standards of international human rights law stress participation, non-discrimination, empowerment and accountability, the global economy stresses economic objectives of free trade, growth, employment and sustain-

able development. The challenge facing the international community is to ensure that these two sets of objectives can be brought together to meet the commitment to a social and international order conducive to the enjoyment of all human rights. "The Global Compact" with business proposed by the Secretary-General in 1999 is an example of a strategy designed to address issues such as these.

9. The present report begins with an examination of the framework of international economic rules and policies from the perspective of the principles and goals of human rights law. This examination is followed by an overview of the principal effects of globalization as they have so far been identified by the reports of United Nations organizations, programmes and agencies, specifically as a result of trade liberalization, the increase in international financial flows, the advances in information and communications technology and the growth in the size and power of transnational corporations. The report concludes that the norms and standards of human rights are crucial to a full assessment of the cultural, political, social, environmental and economic dimensions of globalization.

III. The Global Economy and Human Rights

10. While various national, regional as well as international rules and policies drive many of the processes of globalization, in particular liberalization, deregulation and privatization, the trade rules established within the framework of the World Trade Organization (WTO) Agreement (the WTO agreements) and the macroeconomic policies of international financial institutions have a particularly strong influence in shaping the workings of the global economy. A review of the global economy as it functions within the framework of the policies of the international financial institutions and the rules of WTO will assist in establishing the extent to which an enabling environment supportive of the enjoyment of human rights exists.

11. The global economy is of course only one aspect in the creation of a social and international order conducive to the enjoyment of human rights. A just, efficient and equitable social order must also exist at the national level. Good governance at the national level is therefore an essential element. Good governance is important, not only from the perspective of ensuring respect for human rights at the national level, but as a means of incorporating and implementing international norms faithfully. The following issues are raised to solicit responses from States on the diverse effects of globalization at the national, regional and international levels, as a means of developing understanding for a constructive exchange of views on globalization.

A. The World Trade Organization agreements

12. On 15 April 1995, the Members of the General Agreement on Tariffs and Trade (GATT) signed the Final Act of the Uruguay Round of Multilateral Trade Negotiations, a document including the various agreements setting rules

relevant to trade in goods, services and intellectual property. The various agreements set the principles for trade liberalization, as well as the permitted exceptions, and established a procedure for settling disputes. As a result of the Uruguay Round, WTO, the organization responsible for strengthening the rule of law governing international trade, was created.

13. There is an unavoidable link between the international trading regime and the enjoyment of human rights. Economic growth through free trade can increase the resources available for the realization of human rights. However, economic growth does not automatically lead to greater promotion and protection of human rights. From a human rights perspective, questions are raised: does economic growth entail more equitable distribution of income, more and better jobs, rising wages, more gender equality and greater inclusiveness? From a human rights perspective, the challenge posed is how to channel economic growth equitably to ensure the implementation of the right to development and fair and equal promotion of human well-being.

14. There are points of potential convergence between trade principles and objectives and the norms and standards of international human rights law. Looking at the WTO agreements themselves, the guiding principles can be said to mirror, to some extent, the principles of human rights law and, as such, to provide an opening for a human rights approach to the international trade regime.

15. The WTO agreements seek to create a liberal and rules-based multilateral trading system under which enterprises from Member States can trade with each other under conditions of fair competition. The goals of WTO itself link the objectives of increasing living standards, full employment, the expansion of demand, production and trade in goods and services with the optimal use of the world's resources, in accordance with the objective of sustainable development. The agreements seek to achieve these ends by establishing rules geared towards reducing barriers to trade and ensuring respect for the principle of non-discrimination among Member States. The WTO agreements also encourage preferential treatment in favour of developing countries and least developed countries in the form of special assistance and longer implementation periods, the non-prohibition on export subsidies and the obligation to consider constructive remedies in anti-dumping actions against imports from developing countries.

16. The goals and principles of the WTO agreements and those of human rights law do, therefore, share much in common. Goals of economic growth, increasing living standards, full employment and the optimal use of the world's resources are conducive to the promotion of human rights, in particular the right to development.[3] Parallels can also be drawn between the principles of fair competition and non-discrimination under trade law and equality and non-discrimination under human rights law. Furthermore, the special and differential treatment offered to developing countries under the WTO rules reflects notions of affirmative action under human rights law.

17. These parallels can even be traced to the origins of GATT. It will be recalled that, in 1945, the United Nations was established to uphold peace on

the foundations of respect for human rights and economic and social progress and development. The International Trade Organization, which was envisaged in the Havana Charter for an International Trade Organization of 1947, included the International Bank for Reconstruction and Development (IBRD) and IMF as part of that vision. Article XX of the original GATT recognized non-trade public interest values in particular cases where values and rules conflict. Article XX provided that nothing in the Agreement should be construed to prevent the adoption or enforcement by any contracting party of measures necessary to protect public morals, necessary to protect human, animal or plant life or health, relating to the products of prison labour, relating to the conservation of exhaustible natural resources if such measures were made effective in conjunction with restrictions on domestic production or consumption or essential to the acquisition or distribution of products in general or local short supply. The exceptions referred to call to mind the protection of the right to life, the right to a clean environment, the right to food and to health, the right to self-determination over the use of natural resources and the right to development and freedom from slavery, to mention a few. The exceptions under GATT give rise to the question: to what extent does article XX indicate a point of convergence between trade rules and international human rights law? The challenge ahead is to develop the human rights aspects incorporated in international trade law, in particular as a result of the inclusion of article XX, so that the development and implementation of trade rules promote the social and international order envisaged under article 28 of the Universal Declaration of Human Rights.

18. While the goals and principles of the WTO agreements and international human rights law converge to some extent, the rules which have been adopted to achieve the goals of the former do not always produce results that are consistent with human rights imperatives. To take a case in point, specific issues arise in relation to the standards set concerning intellectual property rights.

19. First, the minimum standards for the protection and enforcement of intellectual property rights included under the Agreement on Trade-Related Aspects of Intellectual Property Rights (the TRIPS agreement) have led to the expression of concerns of balance and fairness.[4] Issues have been raised in relation to the protection of the intellectual property of indigenous peoples and local communities. It has been said that, while some of the standards in the TRIPS agreement are relevant to the protection of the knowledge and technology of these groups, the question arises whether the standards established under the TRIPS agreement are sufficient to provide comprehensive protection to the intellectual property of indigenous peoples and local communities. It has been pointed out, for example, that, in spite of the relevance of intellectual property of indigenous peoples to the development of modern technology, including biotechnology and technology relevant to the protection of the environment, universities and companies have taken and developed traditional medicines and other knowledge, protecting the resulting technology with intellectual property rights, without the equitable sharing of

the benefits and profits with the original holders of that knowledge. It has also been contended that the TRIPS agreement, in its present form, has not been effective in preventing such uses of culture and technology. One question that has been raised from a human rights perspective is: how can international rules be adapted to protect and promote the cultural rights of indigenous peoples and other groups?[5]

20. Similarly, questions have been raised over the adequacy of the TRIPS agreement in addressing the needs of developing countries, generally technology users, to access needed technology for development and the protection of the environment.[6] Figures related to patent applications demonstrate an overwhelming presence of technology holders in developed countries.[7] Furthermore, an examination of the flow of royalty fees indicates that the overwhelming proportion of payments and receipts of royalties and licence fees flow between countries with high incomes. For example, in 1998, while sub-Saharan Africa paid US$ 273 million in royalty and licensing fees, and Europe and Central Asia paid US$ 723 million, high-income countries paid US$ 53,723 million. To put this in perspective, high-income countries dwarf the rest of the world in royalty and licensing fee receipts, with high-income countries receiving US$ 63,051 million and the rest of the world only US$ 1,283 million.[8]

21. While there are many complex reasons explaining the concentration of technology holders and technology transfer in and among developed countries, the figures are significant. Given the importance of technology to development, the TRIPS agreement has implications for the enjoyment of human rights, in particular the right to development, which need to be explored further.

22. The Committee on Economic, Social and Cultural Rights issued a statement to the Third Ministerial Conference of WTO noting that human rights norms must shape the process of international economic policy formulation so that the benefits for human development of the evolving international trading regime will be shared equitably by all, in particular the most vulnerable sectors.[9] The Committee stated its willingness to collaborate with WTO in the realization of economic, social and cultural rights.

B. The policies of international financial institutions

23. The implementation of macroeconomic policies, in particular through the projects and programmes of the international financial institutions, has also played a significant role in shaping globalization. The design and implementation of structural adjustment programmes has heightened concerns that macroeconomic policies do not sufficiently accommodate the need to promote and protect human rights. The special rapporteur of the working group on structural adjustment programmes established by the Economic and Social Council has noted that, while such programmes might be necessary and in fact beneficial for economic growth and social development, their design has generally been motivated by the objective of ensuring repayment of interest on

debts owed to international creditor institutions and not by the promotion and protection of human rights.[10] The Committee on Economic and Social Rights has underlined the importance of including the promotion and protection of human rights within the framework of structural adjustment programmes.[11]

IV. The Effects of Globalization: Preliminary Remarks

24. While the rules and policies of the global economy are important in shaping an international and social order conducive to the protection of human rights, the active features of globalization, the growth in trade and financial flows, the new information and communication technology and the growth in size and power of corporations, have a dynamism of their own which affect human rights in ways beyond the rules and policies referred to above. The following section identifies issues needing further research concerning some of the possible impacts of these processes on the enjoyment of human rights. The summary of issues is built on recognition of the many positive effects that the processes of globalization have on the enjoyment of human rights for many. However, from a human rights perspective, the principles of equality and nondiscrimination underline the importance of promoting the human rights of all. This concern forms the basis for the identification of the issues that follow. The issues are identified in order to assist States in identifying factors relevant for a continuing dialogue on globalization.

A. Advances in communications and information technology

25. One of the most influential elements in the globalization process has been the explosion of information and communications technology. The Internet has enabled people from different regions and cultures to communicate rapidly and across great distances and to access information quickly. Indeed, the Internet is the fastest growing communications tool, with more than 140 million users as at mid-1998, and the number of users expected to pass 700 million by 2001.[12]

26. In addition, communications networks can foster advances in health and education. The Internet has enabled the interconnection of civil society, which has had a direct impact on the promotion and protection of human rights. The successful organization of civil society has been assisted by the interconnection of individuals and interested groups made possible through modern telecommunication and information technology.

27. In spite of the benefits flowing from information and communications technology, the uneven spread of new technology can also result in the marginalization of people. World Bank figures indicate that while in high-income countries there are 607 Internet hosts per 10,000 people, in sub-Saharan Africa and in South Asia there are, respectively, only 2 and 0.17 hosts per 10,000 people. Similarly, while in high-income countries, there are, on average, 311 people per 1,000 with personal computers, in Latin America and the Caribbean, there are only 34, and in South Asia there are only 2.9 per

1,000.[13] In the *Human Development Report*, 1999, it has been noted that, in spite of the positive effects of the new technology, it also introduces problems of marginalization. The report characterizes marginalization in the form of divisions by geographical location (countries of the Organisation for Economic Cooperation and Development (OECD) have 91 percent of connections), education (30 per cent of users have at least one university degree), income (only wealthy people and countries can afford Internet connections) and language (80 per cent of web sites are in English).[14]

28. The new technology can also be used to abuse human rights, in particular through the spread of hate speech. The Internet, in particular, has been used for the propagation of racism, child pornography and religious intolerance through the spread of violent, sexist, pornographic, anti-minority and anti-religious hate speech and images. The technical difficulty of regulating the content of messages broadcast through the Internet makes it a particularly effective means of misusing the freedom of expression and inciting discrimination and other abuses of human rights. This aspect of the Internet poses particular problems for Governments as protectors of human rights. It will be one of the key issues at the World Conference against Racism, Racial Discrimination, Xenophobia and Related Intolerance, which is to be held in Durban, South Africa, in 2001.

B. Liberalization of trade and financial flows

29. In recent years, many countries, spurred on by liberalizing international and regional trade policies, have based their development strategies on increasing integration into the global financial and trading systems. This has led to a dramatic increase in world exports of goods and services, from $4.7 trillion in 1990 to $7.5 trillion in 1998.[15] Today, nearly one fifth of all goods and services produced are being traded internationally. The results have generally been an increase in capital inflows and outflows and a growth in the share of external trade relative to national income.

30. Increased trade and investment has brought significant benefits to many nations and people. There is evidence to suggest that increased trade and investment are related to higher rates of economic growth and productivity.[17] A recent WTO study suggests that trade provides an important contribution to the economic growth of nations and may ultimately lead to the alleviation of poverty.[18]

31. However, dismantling trade barriers and the growth of international trade does not always have a positive impact on human rights.[19]

32. For example, while some nations have benefited from impressive increases in trade and financial flows over the past decade, other countries have not fared so well.[20] *The Human Development Report* 2000 noted that, in 1998, least developed countries, with 10 per cent of the world population, accounted for only 0.4 per cent of global exports, representing a consistent fall from 0.6 per cent in 1980 and 0.5 per cent in 1990. Sub-Saharan Africa's share declined to 1.4 per cent, down from 2.3 per cent in 1980 and 1.6 per cent in 1990.[21]

Similarly, capital flows tended to remain highly concentrated between developed countries, or to a limited number of developing countries. For example, in 1998, the 10 top developing country recipients accounted for 70 per cent of foreign direct investment (FDI) flows.[22] In 1998, the 48 least developed countries received only $3 billion of the total FDI flow of $600 billion that year.

33. These figures raise several questions for further consideration: to what extent are the figures connected to trade and financial liberalization? To what extent are they related to a failure to liberalize trade and finance effectively? What other factors cause the low rates of foreign direct investment? To what extent do they identify the benefits of globalization being shared unevenly or at different rates? Finally, how could a human rights approach to trade liberalization correct perceived inequalities in international trade and investment?

34. It should be recognized that the trade protectionism, which the liberalization of trade is now replacing, can have a negative impact on the promotion and protection of human rights. The uneven distribution of trade and finance is not helped by the significant restrictions on trade that often face developing countries. Indeed, as developing countries open up their economies, they are often faced with significant trade barriers or restricted access in their areas of natural comparative advantage, such as agriculture or textiles.[23] For example, a report of the Department of Economic and Social Affairs notes that, in the agricultural sector, the total level of support in the form of subsidies for agriculture in OECD countries averaged $350 billion during the period from 1996 to 1998, a figure that represents double the agricultural exports from developing countries over the same period. This makes it difficult for developing countries to compete, which is particularly harmful, given the importance of the agricultural sector as a source of income and employment. Ironically, sub-Saharan Africa has one of the most liberal agricultural sectors in the world, in spite of its small share of the global market.[24]

35. While dismantling barriers to trade and investment opens up markets to new opportunities, a recent study on the social impact of globalization carried out by the International Labour Organization (ILO) found that it can also leave countries vulnerable to global economic changes in exchange rates, wages and commodity prices.[25] This vulnerability to external shocks is exacerbated by a lack of sophisticated economic and social structures in many developing countries.

36. Ultimately, trade liberalization and financial deregulation have diverse impacts that are often difficult to assess. Country studies undertaken by ILO also indicate that, while it has the potential to improve people's welfare, globalization occurs in a context of rising inequalities.[26] For example, the final ILO report on country studies states that there is a trend towards wider income inequalities, not only in most of the countries under study, but also in other member States. The report goes on to state that there is little evidence that trade is the main direct factor at work.[27] Further research is needed to clarify

any linkages between the processes of globalization, trade liberalization and inequality.

37. While globalization has led to the dismantling of barriers to the trade in goods and services, labour is increasingly restricted inside national and ethnic boundaries. The increasing barriers to trade in labour, and migration in general, have been coupled with a resistance to promote and protect the human rights of migrants. Although the General Assembly adopted the International Convention on the Protection of the Rights of All Migrant Workers and Their Families in 1990, 10 years ago, it still lacks the sufficient number of ratifications by States for it to come into force.

38. The effect of the growth in trade on workers rights is difficult to assess. A study of nine countries undertaken by the Department of Economic and Social Affairs noted that trade liberalization was accompanied by reduced wages, underemployment, informalization of labour and adverse impacts on unskilled labour, particularly in the manufacturing sector.[28] In relation to women's workers' rights, globalization seems to have had the effect of repeating existing patterns of discrimination against women, but on an international scale. The *World Survey on the Role of Women in Development* indicates that, on the positive side, the orientation of manufacturing production towards exports has led to a significant increase in the share of female workers in export industries. In the international financial services sector, women enjoy high rates of employment, increasingly even at higher levels. However, the report also shows that, in the export manufacturing sector, women workers are generally confined to low skill wage occupations, and it appears that, as jobs and wages improve in quality, women tend to be excluded from them.[29] In the informal sector, it appears that women suffer as a result of the growth of trade with imports displacing women, as workers and as small entrepreneurs, disproportionately to men.[30] This is occurring, in spite of the significant role that women play in the globalization process. As the survey states, "it is now a well-known fact that industrialization in the context of globalization is as much female-led as it is export led".[31]

39. It is also important to highlight certain negative aspects of international trade in a globalizing world. In doing so, a distinction is made between the rules and policies of the international community concerning trade liberalization and particular international trade practices in a globalizing world. While the globalization of trade has been accompanied by the growth in particular types of trade that lead to human rights abuses, these should not be confused with international rules and policies that are intended to produce trade liberalization. Nonetheless, a report of the Subcommission on the Promotion and Protection of Human Rights notes that, in some instances, and particularly in impoverished and undemocratic societies, globalization has facilitated trade in the form of international arms transfers, which, in turn, provide the necessary tools for armed conflict.[32] The same report links globalization with an increase in the dumping of environmental waste near the homes of low income or minority groups and notes significant dumping in developing countries. Globalization has also been accompanied by the rise in

the international trafficking of drugs, diamonds and even human beings, including children. Such aspects of international trade raise issues of the right to life, the right to a clean environment, and the right to development. Further research is needed into the links between the processes of globalization and negative aspects of international trade and the ways in which policies may be formulated to promote and protect human rights in this regard.

40. The growth of trafficking in women and girls and the sex industry are causes of major concern. Each year, millions of individuals, the vast majority of them women and children, are tricked, sold or coerced into situations of exploitation from which they cannot escape.[33] The causes and effects of trafficking are complex, however several observations are relevant to the discussion of trafficking. First, trafficking in women and girls reflects global inequalities, as it invariably involves movement from a poorer country to a wealthier one.[34] Secondly, trafficking, in particular for prostitution, is becoming more widespread. Crime cartels, operating transnationally, are often the mediator for trafficking, and trafficking for prostitution can be traced to the demand caused by the rapidly expanding global sex industry.[35] As a result, trafficked people suffer abuses of their human rights, in particular freedom from slavery, freedom of movement, freedom from fear, discrimination and injustice.

C. Growth of corporations

41. The need to compete in new and often distant markets has led to a wave of mergers and acquisitions, which have enabled companies to specialize in core competencies that ensure international competitive advantages in particular areas. This, in turn, has led to the phenomenon of the mega-corporation, with crossborder mergers and acquisitions exceeding the value of $1,100 billion in 1999. As a result, some transnational corporations have greater economic wealth than States. A report by the United Nations Research Institute for Social Development (UNRISD) noted that the annual sales of one transnational corporation exceeds the combined gross domestic product of Chile, Costa Rica and Ecuador.[36]

42. The comparative size and power of transnational corporations raises issues that need to be considered. In a worst case scenario, transnational corporations may be able to use their position of comparative power over States to play nations and communities off against each other in an effort to receive the most advantageous benefits.[37] The relative power of transnational corporations must not detract from the enjoyment of human rights.

43. Questions have been raised about the social costs of schemes to attract foreign investment such as economic processing zones. Questions have also been raised about the employment practices of transnational corporations and their effects on the human rights of their employees. Greater attention is needed in order to devise strategies that link investment policy with the protection of workers' rights. In this regard, ILO has been active in developing strategies for the protection of workers rights, in particular through the

development and implementation of the Declaration on Fundamental Principles and Rights at Work, as well as the ILO Convention (No. 182) concerning the Prohibition and Immediate Action for the Elimination of the Worst Forms of Child Labour. In the outcome document of the World Summit for Social Development of July 2000, States committed themselves to improving the quality of work in the context of globalization, including through the promotion of these and other ILO initiatives.[38]

44. Concerns about the impact of the operations of transnational corporations in relation to the protection of cultural diversity were also expressed in the *Human Development Report* 1999.[39] Some commentators fear that failure to give appropriate attention and support to the cultures of local and indigenous peoples, as a counterbalance to foreign influence, could result in pressures on local cultures.[40] Moreover, media control in the hands of a limited number of transnational media corporations can also have implications for the freedom of expression. Highly concentrated media ownership vests powers of censorship in the hands of media owners to determine where and what they publish.[41]

45. At the same time, transnational corporations can play an important role in promoting and protecting human rights. The Global Compact initiative of the Secretary-General, was first proposed in 1999 to challenge business leaders to promote and apply, within their own domains, nine principles derived from international instruments, including the Universal Declaration of Human Rights, to advance human rights, labour and environmental standards.[42] At a meeting held at United Nations Headquarters on 26 July 2000, global leaders from business, labour and civil society met with the Secretary-General to formally launch this initiative. They agreed to work together within the common framework of the Global Compact to strengthen responsible corporate citizenship and the social pillars of globalization through dialogue and operational activities. While the Global Compact is not a substitute for effective action by Governments, or for the implementation of existing or future international agreements, it is a significant step in the direction of voluntary cooperation between the United Nations and the private sector in order to ensure that corporations have a positive impact on the enjoyment of human rights.

V. Conclusions

A. Poverty

46. The above preliminary overview of globalization identifies evidence to suggest that while globalization provides potential for the promotion and protection of human rights through economic growth, increased wealth, greater interconnection between peoples and cultures and new opportunities for development, its benefits are not being enjoyed evenly at the current stage. Indeed, many people are still living in poverty. On the positive side, World Bank figures indicate that the number of people living on less than $1 a day has

been relatively stable in the past decade, in spite of an increase in the world's population, and, as a percentage rate, the percentage of people living in extreme poverty decreased from 29 per cent to 24 per cent between 1990 and 1998. Nonetheless, poverty alleviation is uneven. While East Asia and the Pacific, the Middle East and North Africa have had significant reductions in poverty, poverty rates in South Asia, Latin America and the Caribbean and sub-Saharan Africa have remained relatively stable, while Europe and Central Asia have experienced significant increases in poverty.[43] Statistics also reveal that 790 million people suffer from malnutrition, 880 million have no access to basic health services, 900 million adults are illiterate and 20 per cent of the world's population lacks access to safe drinking water. In sub-Saharan Africa, 51 per cent of the population lives in absolute poverty. The majority of people living in poverty are women.[44]

47. Poverty is both a cause and effect of human rights abuses. The Vienna Declaration and Programme of Action, adopted at the World Conference on Human Rights in 1993, affirmed that extreme poverty and social exclusion constitute a violation of human dignity. It is difficult to assess the extent to which the various agents of globalization, trade liberalization, deregulation of finance and the growth of corporations and new technology, lead to or alleviate poverty. A study commissioned by WTO indicates that domestic policy in areas such as education and health has a greater impact on poverty than trade does, and concludes that trade liberalization is generally a positive contributor to poverty alleviation.[45] Nonetheless, it is clear that poverty is still a part of the present era of globalization. Given the potential for growth that is offered by globalization, there is a need for more effective strategies to harness this potential as a means of alleviating poverty for all nations and regions.

B. A social and international order

48. The challenge of article 28 of the Universal Declaration of Human Rights, to ensure the entitlement of everyone to a social and international order supportive of the realization of human rights, remains. At the heart of the challenge is the need to examine the social, political, cultural and economic, dimensions of globalization, and the impact they have on the rights of every human being. As the Secretary-General said in his report to the Millennium Assembly:

> "The economic sphere cannot be separated from the more complex fabric of social and political life, and sent shooting off on its own trajectory. To survive and thrive, a global economy must have a more solid foundation in shared values and institutional practices – it must advance broader, and more inclusive, social purposes".[46]

49. The keys to achieving these goals exist. The world conferences of the 1990's set out commitments and programmes for the promotion and protection of human rights, the advancement of women and social development. In June 2000, States agreed on new initiatives to achieve social development during the

present era of globalization, including through the constant monitoring of the social impacts of economic policies, the reduction of negative impacts of international financial turbulence on social and economic development, the strengthening of the capacities of developing countries, in particular through the strengthening of capacities for trade as it relates to health, and the integration of social as well as economic aspects in the design of structural adjustment and reform programmes.[47]

50. The goals and programmes are already formulated. The strategy to achieve them lies in acknowledging that the principles and standards of human rights should be adopted as an indispensable framework for globalization. Human rights embody universal shared values and are the common standard of achievement for all peoples and all nations.[48] By adopting a human rights approach, globalization can be examined in its civil, cultural, political, social and economic contexts so that the international community can meet its commitment to an international and social order conducive to respect for human rights. This must be the strategy of governance at all levels - to secure respect of all human rights for everyone.

Notes

1 United Nations Development Programme (UNDP), *Human Development Report 1999*, Oxford University Press, New York, 1999, p. 1. The report goes on to note that globalization is not a new phenomenon in historical terms, but that it is different today. Some of the characteristics are new markets − foreign exchange and capital markets linked globally, operating 24 hours a day, with dealings at a distance in real time; new tools − Internet links, cellular phones, media networks; new actors − the World Trade Organization (WTO) with authority over national Governments, the multinational corporations with more economic power than many States, the global network of non-governmental organizations (NGOs) and other groups that transcend national boundaries; new rules − multilateral agreements on trade, services and intellectual property, backed by strong enforcement mechanisms and more binding for national governments reducing the scope for national policy.

2 See articles 1, 2 and 28 of the Universal Declaration of Human Rights, parts I and II of the International Covenant on Economic, Social and Cultural Rights and the International Covenant on Civil and Political Rights and article I of the United Nations Declaration on the Right to Development.

3 See also articles 3 (Right to life), 23 (Right to work) and 25 (Right to an adequate standard of living) of the Universal Declaration of Human Rights.

4 It should be noted that the protection of intellectual property is a human right under article 27 of the Universal Declaration of Human Rights and article 15 of the International Covenant on Economic, Social and Cultural Rights. In particular, article 15 (1) (c) notes that "The States Parties to the present Covenant recognize the right of everyone ... to benefit from the protection of the moral and material interests resulting from any scientific, literary or artistic production of which he is the author". Intellectual property rights themselves, as for example those established according to the minimum standards contained in the TRIPS agreement, are not themselves human rights. However they could be a means of promoting and protecting the human right to intellectual property, so long as the granting of such intellectual property rights achieves

the balance and fairness required by article 27 of the Universal Declaration and article 15 of the Covenant.

5 There is of course nothing in the TRIPS agreement that prevents States taking individual action to protect the technology and knowledge of indigenous peoples and local communities.

6 While article 7 of the TRIPS agreement states that the protection and enforcement of intellectual property rights should contribute to the transfer and dissemination of technology, the agreement does not develop any mechanism to achieve this.

7 For example: in 1997, patent applications numbered 2,785,420 in high-income countries, while in East Asia and the Pacific they numbered 290,630; in the Middle East and North Africa there were only 1,716 applications; and in sub-Saharan Africa, 392,959, with only 38 of those being filed by residents. See World Bank, *World Development Indicators 2000*, World Bank, Washington, D.C., 2000, table 5.12.

8 World Bank, op. cit., table 5.12.

9 See E/CN.12/1999/9, para. 5.

10 See E/CN.4/1999/47.

11 See E/1999/22, paras. 378-393. See also, E/C.12/1/Add.7/Rev.l, para. 21.

12 UNDP, op. cit., p. 5.

13 World Bank, op. cit., table 5.12.

14 UNDP, 1999, op. cit., p. 6.

15 UNDP, *Human Development Report 2000*, Oxford University Press, New York, 2000, p. 82.

16 UNDP, 1999, op. cit., p. 1.

17 International Labour Office, *Country studies on the social impact of globalization: final report*, ILO, Governing Body, 276th Session, GB. 276/WP/SDL/I, para. 30.

18 Ben-David, D. and L. Alan Winters, "Trade, Income Disparity and Poverty", *Special Studies No. 5*, World Trade Organization, WTO Publications, Geneva, 1999.

19 See E/CN.4/Sub.2/1999/11, para. 3.

20 Even those countries that have experienced impressive increases in trade and financial flows have suffered downturns and reversals in fortune as a result of financial crises, such as the Asian financial crisis of 1997.

21 UNDP, 2000, op. cit., p. 82.

22 A/AC.253125, para. 41.

23 See the comments of Joseph Stiglitz, former World Bank chief economist, quoted in E/CN.4/Sub.2/2000/13, para. 14.

24 A/AC.253125, para. 21.

25 International Labour of Vice, op. cit., para. 68 (f).

26 Ibid, para 3.

27 Ibid.

28 See Janine Berg and Lance Taylor, "External liberalization, economic performance and social policy", New School for Social Research, Working Paper Series: Globalization, Labour Markets and Social Policy, February 2000. Cited in AIAC.253125, para. 9.

29 See E/1999/44, para. 52.

30 Ibid., para. 55.

31 Ibid, para 50

32 E/CN.4/Sub.2/1999/8, para. 16.

33 E/ECE/RW.2/2000/3, para. 1.

34 Ibid., para. 11.

35 Ibid., para. 17.

36 United Nations Research Institute for Social Development, *States of Disarray: The Social Effects of Globalization*, report on the World Summit for Social Development, Geneva, March 1995, p. 153. Similarly, according to the *Human Development Report 1999*, the assets of the top three billionaires are more than the combined gross national product of all least developed countries.

37 See E/CN.4/Sub.2/1995/11, para. 53.

38 AIS 24/8/Rev.1, para 38

39 UNDP, 1999, op. cit., para. 4 (f).

40 E/CN.4/Sub.2/1999/8, para. 19. Also, UNDP 1999, op. cit., p. 5.

41 Ghai, Y., "Rights, Markets and Globalization: East Asian Experience", *Report of the Symposium on Human Development and Human Rights*, UNDP and the Office of the United Nations High Commissioner for Human Rights, Royal Ministry of Foreign Affairs, Oslo, Norway, 2–3 October 1998, p. 130.

42 See Mary Robinson, United Nations High Commissioner for Human Rights, *Putting principles into practice: creating a Global Compact with the business sector, 2000.*

43 World Bank, 2000, op. cit., p. 4.

44 See UNDP, 1999, op. cit.; *United Nations Action Strategy for Halving Poverty* (25 May 2000); and United Nations Bulletin on the Eradication of Poverty (Nos. 1–5).

45 Ben-David, D. and L. Alan Winters, op. cit.

46 A/54/2000, para. 25.

47 See A/S-24/2/Add.2 (Parts I and 111), paras. 6 bis, 10, 82, 82 bis and 103 ter.

48 See *Universal Declaration of Human Rights*, preamble.

30

Rights in the Global Market

Thomas J. Donaldson

Rights we take for granted are sometimes trampled abroad. Child labor plagues Central America, and dozens of interviews with workers in Central America conducted in the fall of 1987 reveal that most respondents started working between the ages of 12 and 14.[1] In other countries the rights to minimal education, free speech, basic nutrition, and freedom from torture are little more than dreams. What obligations do multinational corporations have in such contexts? Are they obliged not only to honor but to encourage the protection of such rights? Consider the claim that persons everywhere have a right to adequate food. What are we to say when a multinational corporation, working in a country where malnutrition is rampant, buys a parcel of land and converts it from the production of a staple food source to one for cash export? If the land is purchased from a wealthy landowner and converted from growing black beans to coffee, has the company indirectly violated a right to adequate food if it turns out that the purchase lowers the food supply?

These questions exist in a class of questions concerned with establishing minimal conditions upon the behavior of multinational corporations. They are ones that have been largely neglected by academic researchers. Business academics have contributed significantly to understanding the problems of international business; they have offered a bounty of empirical analysis relevant to multinational corporations, and have conducted detailed inquiries into the structure of global markets and the strategies of multinational corporations.[2] Yet few of their efforts highlight the moral element. The notable exceptions are academics working out of the so-called social issues and business environment perspectives,[3] yet even here only a fraction of such normative work from academic business researchers has found application to multinational corporations, and when it has, the context has tended to be issue-specific, for example, Bhopal, or South African divestment.[4]

Source: R. Edward Freeman (ed.), *Business Ethics: The State of the Art* (Oxford: Oxford University Press, 1991).

This paper will attempt to develop a list of fundamental human rights serviceable for international business. Ten specific rights are advanced to establish bottom-line moral considerations for multinational corporations. The paper concludes that corporations, individuals, and governments must respect these 10 rights, although it argues that the correlative duties that corporations must shoulder in honoring those rights are different from those of nation states and individuals. Much of the analysis is drawn from a more extensive treatment offered in my recent book, *The Ethics of International Business.*[5]

Rights Establish Minimal Corporate Responsibilities

We should first distinguish those corporate responsibilities that hold as minimal conditions from those that exceed the minimum."Minimal" duties for multinational corporations are similar to Kant's "perfect" duties; that is, they are mandatory and allow no discretion as to when or how they are performed. A "maximal" duty, on the other hand, is one whose fulfillment would be praiseworthy but not absolutely mandatory. Our concern, in turn, is with "minimal," rather than "maximal" duties. Our aim is to inquire, for example, whether a foreign corporation's minimal duties include refusing to hire children in a Honduran assembly plant, even if doing so harms the company's competitive position. It is not to establish guidelines for exemplary or "model" multinational behavior.

Our strategy will be to assume that most if not all minimal responsibilities can be framed through the language of rights, a language recognized for establishing minimal moral obligations. Rights may be seen to lie at the rock bottom of modern moral deliberation. Maurice Cranston writes that the litmus test for whether or not something is a right is whether it protects something of "paramount importance."[6] If I have a right not to be tortured, then in violating that right you threaten something of paramount value to me. It would be splendid if you did even more–if, for example, you treated me with love and charity; but at *a minimum* you must respect my rights

The flip side of a right typically is a duty,[7] a fact that gives aptness to Joel Feinberg's well-known definition of a right as a "justified entitlement to something from someone."[8] It is the "from someone" part of the definition that reflects the assumption of a duty, for without a correlative duty that attaches to some moral agent or group of agents, a right is weakened–if not beyond the status of a right entirely, then significantly. If we cannot say that a multinational corporation has a duty to keep the levels of arsenic low in the workplace, then the worker's right not to be poisoned means little.

Often, duties fall upon more than one class of moral agent. Consider, for example, the furor over the dumping of toxic waste in West Africa by multinational corporations. During 1988, virtually every country from Morocco to Zaire on Africa's west coast received offers from companies seeking cheap sites for dumping waste.[9] In the years prior, toxic waste dumping had become enormously expensive in the United States and Europe, in large part because of the costly safety measures mandated by U.S. and European governments. In February 1988 officials in Guinea Bissau, one of the world's poorest nations, agreed to bury 15 million tons of toxic wastes from European tanneries and pharmaceutical companies. The companies agreed to pay about $120 million, which is only slightly less than the country's entire gross national product. And in Nigeria, in 1987, five European ships unloaded toxic waste containing dangerous poisons such as polychlorinated biphenyls, or PCBs. Workers wearing thongs and shorts unloaded the barrels for $2.50 a day, and placed them in a dirt lot in a residential area in the town of Kiko.[10] They were not told about the contents of the barrels.[11] Who bears responsibility for protecting the workers' and inhabitants' rights to safety in such instances? It would be wrong to place it entirely upon a single group of agents such as the governments of West African nations. As it happens, the toxic waste dumped in Nigeria entered under an import permit for "non-explosive, non-radioactive and non-self-combusting chemicals." But the permit turned out to be a loophole; Nigeria had not meant to accept the waste and demanded its removal once word about its presence filtered into official channels. The example reveals the difficulty many developing countries have in generating the sophisticated language and regulatory procedures necessary to control high-technology hazards. It seems reasonable in such instances, then, to place the responsibility not upon a single class of agents but upon a broad collection of them, including governments, corporate executives, host country companies and officials, and international organizations. The responsibility for not violating the rights of people living in West Africa from the dangers of toxic waste then potentially falls upon every agent whose actions might harm, or contribute to harming, West African inhabitants. Nor is one agent's responsibility always mitigated when another "accepts" responsibility. To take a specific instance, corporate responsibility may not be eliminated if a West African government explicitly agrees to accept toxic waste. There is always the possibility—said to be a reality by some critics—that corrupt government officials will agree to accept and handle waste that threatens safety in order to fatten their own Swiss bank accounts.

Rights with international relevance should be viewed as occupying an intermediary zone between abstract moral principles such as liberty or fairness on the one hand, and national specifications of rights on the other.[12] International rights must be more specific than abstract principles if they are to facilitate practical implication, but be less specific than the entries on lists of rights whose duties fall on national governments if they are to preserve cosmopolitan relevance. One nation's particular social capacities or social traditions may favor the recognition of certain rights that are inappropriate to other nations. Citizens of a rich, technologically advanced nation, for example, but not of a poor, developing one, may be viewed as possessing a right to a certain technological level of health care. You, as a citizen of the United States, may have the right to kidney dialysis; but a citizen of Bangladesh may not.

As a first approximation, then, let us interpret a multinational's obligations by asking which international rights it should respect, where we understand *international rights* to be sort of moral precepts that lie in a zone between abstract moral principles and national rights specifications. Multinationals, we shall assume, should respect the international rights of those whom they affect, especially when those rights are of the most fundamental sort.

But whose list of international rights shall we choose? Libertarians tend to endorse well-pruned lists of liberty-centered rights, ones that look like the first 10 amendments to the U.S. Constitution (the Bill of Rights) without the subsequent constitutional amendments, while welfare liberals frequently endorse lush, well-tangled structures that include entitlements as well as freedoms. Who is to say that a given person's list, or a given country's list, for that matter, is preferable to another's?

One list receiving significant international attention, a list bearing the signatures of most of the world's nations, is the "Universal Declaration of Human Rights."[13] However, it and the subsequent "International Covenant on Social, Economic and Cultural Rights," have spawned controversy despite the fact that the Universal Declaration was endorsed by virtually all of the important post-World War II nations in 1948 as part of the affirmation of the U.N. Charter. What distinguishes these lists from their predecessors, and what serves also as the focus of controversy, is their inclusion of rights that have come to be called alternatively "social," "economic," "positive," or "welfare" rights. Nuances separate these four concepts, but they need not detain us; all formulations share the feature of demanding more than forbearance from those upon whom the right's correlative duties fall. All four refer to rights that entail claims by rights holders to specific goods, where such goods must at least sometimes be provided by other persons (although sometimes by unspecified others). The goods at issue are typically such things as food, education, and shelter. For convenience, we shall use the term "welfare rights" to refer to all claims of this kind. Some international rights documents even specify as welfare rights claims to goods that are now regarded as standard benefits of the modern welfare state. For example, Articles 22 through 27 of the Universal Declaration assert rights to social security insurance, employment, protection against unemployment, health care, education, and limits on working hours.[14]

Many have balked when confronted with such lists, arguing that no one can have a right to a specific supply of an economic good. Can anyone be said to have a "right" for example, to 128 hours of sleep and leisure each week? And, in the same spirit, some international documents have simply refused to adopt the welfare-affirming blueprint established in the Universal Declaration.[15] The issue is critical for establishing the minimal responsibilities of multinational corporations, for it is only to the extent that, say, the right to adequate food exists, that multinationals can be chided for violating it.

Henry Shue advances a compelling notion of welfare rights–one with special relevance to our task–in his book, *Basic Rights.*[16] Shue's guiding concept of a "basic right" entails the existence of welfare rights. The essence of a basic right, says Shue, is "something the deprivation of which is one standard threat to rights generally."[17] Basic rights include the right to subsistence, or "minimal economic security," to freedom of physical movement, security, and political participation By way of explanation, the right to *subsistence* entails a claim to, e.g., "unpolluted air, unpolluted water, adequate food, adequate clothing, adequate shelter, and minimal preventative public health care."[18] The right to *freedom of physical movement* is a right to not have "arbitrary constraints upon parts of one's body, such as ropes, chains, ...and the absence of arbitrary constraints upon the movement from place to place of one's whole body, such as ...pass laws (as in South Africa)."[19] The right to security is a right not to be subjected to "murder, torture, mayhem, rape, or assault"; and the right to *political participation* is the right to have "genuine influence upon the fundamental choices among the societal institutions and the societal policies that control security and subsistence and, where the person is directly affected, genuine influence upon the operation of institutions and the implementation of policy."[20] The key to understanding a basic right for Shue is recognizing that it is a prerequisite for the enjoyment of other rights. Thus being secure from beatings is a prerequisite for the enjoyment of, e.g., the right to freedom of assembly, since one's freedom to hold political meetings is dependent upon one's freedom from the fear of beatings in the event one chooses to assemble. Shue insists correctly that benevolent despotism cannot ensure basic rights. One's rights are not protected even by the most enlightened despot in the absence of social institutions that guarantee that basic rights will be preserved in the event such benevolence turns to malevolence.[21] Illusions, as the saying goes, are not liberties.

Shue's analysis, moreover, provides a formidable argument on behalf of such rights. The argument is successful because it unpacks the sense in which it is contradictory to support any list of rights without at the same time supporting those specific rights upon whose preservation the list can be shown to depend. It is a strategy with direct application to the controversy between defenders and critics of welfare rights, for if Shue is correct, even a list of non-welfare rights ultimately depends upon certain basic rights, some of which are welfare rights. His argument utilizes the following, simple propositions:

1. Everyone has a right to something.
2. Some other things are necessary for enjoying the first thing as a right, whatever the first right is.
3. Therefore, everyone also has rights to the other things that are necessary for enjoying the first thing as a right.[22]

We shall grasp Shue's point even better by considering, on the one hand, a standard objection to welfare rights, and on the other, a response afforded by Shue's theory. Now many who criticize welfare rights utilize a traditional philosophical distinction between so-called negative and positive rights. A "positive" right is said to be one that requires persons to act positively to do something, and a "negative" right requires only that people not deprive directly. Hence, the right to liberty is said to be a negative right, whereas the right to enough food is said to be a positive one. With this distinction in hand, it is common to conclude that no one can be bound to improve the welfare of another (unless, say, that person has entered into an agreement to do so); rather, at most they can be bound to *refrain* from damaging the welfare of another.

Shue's argument, however, reveals the implausibility of the very distinction between native and positive rights. Perhaps the most celebrated and best accepted example of a negative right is the right to freedom. Yet the meaningful preservation of freedom requires a variety of positive actions: for example, on the part of the government it requires the establishment and maintenance of a police force, courts, and the military, and on the part of the citizenry it requires ongoing cooperation and diligent (not merely passive) forbearance. And the protection of another so-called negative right, the right to physical security, necessitates "police forces; criminal rights; penitentiaries; schools for training police, lawyers, and guards; and taxes to support an enormous system for the prevention, detention, and punishment of violations of personal security."[23]

This is compelling. The maintenance and preservation of many non-welfare rights (where, again, such maintenance and preservation is the key to a right's status as "basic") requires the support of certain basic welfare rights. For example, certain liberties depend upon the enjoyment of subsistence, just as subsistence sometimes depends upon the enjoyment of some liberties. One's freedom to speak freely is meaningless if one is weakened by hunger to the point of silence.

The Problem with "Basic" Rights

But while establishing the legitimacy of some welfare rights, Shue's argument is nonetheless flawed. To begin with, from the standpoint of moral logic, his methodology appears to justify the more important in terms of the less important. That is to say, insofar as a basic right is defined as one whose preservation is necessary for the preservation of all rights generally, the determination of what counts as "basic" will occur by a process that takes as fundamental all rights, including non-basic ones, and then asks which among those rights are rights such that their absence would constitute a threat to the others. Not only does this fail to say anything about the moral grounding or rights in general, it also hinges the status of the basic rights on their ability to support all rights, including non-basic rights, and this appears to place the hierarchical cart before the horse.[24] This problem enlarges when we notice that many of the so-called non-basic rights such as freedom of speech appear to be of equal importance to some so-called basic rights. One wonders why a few of the world's most important rights, such as the rights to property, free speech, religious freedom, and education, are regarded as non-basic. One can see why, given Shue's concept of a basic right, they are non-basic, but then one wonders whether they might be basic in an even more important sense.

Shue himself acknowledges that status as a basic right does not guarantee that the right in question is more important. At one point, while contrasting a non-basic right, such as the right to education, to a basic right, such as the right to security, he states, "I do not mean by this to deny that the enjoyment of the right to education is much greater and richer–more distinctively human, perhaps–than merely going through life without ever being assaulted." But he next asserts the practical priority of basic rights by saying, "I mean only that, if the choice must be made, the prevention of assault ought to supersede the provision of education."[25] So while denying that basic rights are necessarily more important than non-basic ones in all respects, he grants that they are more important in the sense that probably matters most: they are given priority in decisions where a choice must be made between defending one right and defending another. He concludes, "therefore, if a right is basic, other, non-basic rights may be sacrificed, if necessary, in order to secure the basic right."[26]

But what Shue leaves obscure is the matter of which rights *other* than basic rights are deserving of emphasis. For Shue, every right must occupy one of two positions on the rights hierarchy: it is either basic or not. But if so, then how are individuals, governments, and corporations to know which rights should be honored in a crunch? Shue clearly believes that individuals, governments, and corporations must honor basic rights, but how are the remaining non-basic rights to be treated? What of the right to freedom of speech, to property, or to a minimal education? Are these rights always to be given second-class status? And if they are to be given priority in some instances, then why? Then too, surely, Shue will agree that all nation states must honor the right to freedom of speech, but is the same true of all individuals and corporations? Does it follow that corporations must tolerate all speech affecting the workplace and never penalize offending workers, even when the speech is maliciously motivated and severely damages profitability? Similarly, are all states responsible for defending all other non-basic rights?

Fundamental International Rights

Let us adopt another method of approach. Let us attempt to determine which rights are most fundamental directly, i.e., by using criteria that ground fundamental rights. In other words, instead of employing an analytic argument that takes for granted a body of rights and then analyzes the logic of their interdependence (as Shue does), let us employ a normative argument that looks to the grounding of rights in general. Let us stipulate three conditions that will be independently necessary and jointly sufficient for considering a given prospective as (a) a right and (b) a right of fundamental importance. Such a right we shall label a "fundamental international right." These three conditions are that (1) the right protects something of extreme importance, that (2) it is subject to significant, recurring threats, and that (3) the obligations or burdens it imposes are economically affordable and fair with respect to the distribution of burdens generally. These three conditions resemble, although they are not identical to, three of the four conditions advanced by James Nickel, in his book, *Making Sense of Human Rights*,[27] for identifying rights imposing claims on nation-states. In the present context, however, they are advanced as having application to all three of the major classes of international actors, i.e., nation-states, individuals, and multinational corporations.

Consider each condition. The first recognizes that if claims are made to things that have little or only moderate importance, then even if those claims happen to be valid, they cannot aspire to the status of "rights." We are reminded of Maurice Cranston's "paramount importance" test cited earlier for bona fide rights. The second notes that rights also must be subject to what Shue calls "standard" threats or what Nickel has alternatively dubbed "recurrent" threats. A right must be subject to significant, recurring threats for the simple reason that the list of claims centering on interests of fundamental importance would otherwise expand indefinitely. And finally, as Nickel has shown convincingly, any right must satisfy what could be called an "affordability-fairness" criterion in that it must impose obligations or other burdens that are in Nickel's words "affordable in relation to resources, other obligations, and fairness in the distribution of burdens." Part of the justification for this condition is as simple as the time-honored dictum in moral philosophy that "ought implies can," or, in other words, that no person or entity can be held responsible for doing something if it is not in their power to do it. We need only add the reasonable proviso that sometimes a duty may be of a kind that is discouraged for moral reasons, i.e., either because it conflicts with another bona fide obligation or because it constitutes an unfairness in the distribution of burdens.

Next, consider the following list of fundamental international rights:

1. The right to freedom of physical movement
2. The right to ownership of property
3. The right to freedom from torture
4. The right to a fair trial
5. The right to non-discriminatory treatment (i.e., freedom from discrimination on the basis of such characteristics as race or sex)
6. The right to physical security
7. The right to freedom of speech and association
8. The right to minimal education
9. The right to political participation
10. The right to subsistence

This seems a minimal list. Some will wish to add entries such as the right to employment, to social security, or to a certain standard of living (say, as might be prescribed by Rawls's well-known "difference" principle). Disputes also may arise about the wording or overlapping features of some rights: for example, is not the right to freedom from torture included in the right to physical security, at least when the latter is properly interpreted? We shall not attempt to resolve such controversies here. Rather, the list as presented aims to suggest, albeit incompletely, a description of a *minimal* set of rights and to serve as a point of beginning and consensus for evaluating international conduct. If I am correct, many would wish to add entries, but few would wish to subtract them.

The list has been generated by application of the three conditions and the compatibility proviso. Readers may satisfy for themselves whether the ten entries fulfill these conditions; in doing so, however, they should remember that in constructing the list one looks for *only* those rights that can be honored in some form by all international agents, including nation-states, corporations, and individuals. Hence, to consider only the issue of affordability, each candidate for a right must be tested for "affordability" by way of the lowest common denominator by ways for example, of the poorest nation-state. If, even after receiving its fair share of charitable aid from wealthier nations, that state cannot "afford" dialysis for all citizens who need it, then the right to receive dialysis from one's nation state will not be a fundamental international right, although dialysis may contribute a bona fide right for those living within a specific nation-state, such as Japan.

Although the hope for a definitive interpretation of the list of rights is an illusion, we can add specificity by clarifying the correlative duties entailed for different kinds of international actors. Because by definition the list contains items that all three major classes of international actors must respect, the next task is to spell out the correlative duties that fall upon our targeted group of international actors, namely, multinational corporations.

Doing so requires putting the third condition from Nickel's revised list to a second, and different, use. This "affordability-fairness" condition–which, again, concerns the affordability of respecting a right from the perspective of an agent's resources, other obligations, and overall fairness in the distribution of burdens–was used first as one of the criteria for generating the original list of fundamental rights. There it demanded satisfaction of an affordability-fairness threshold for each potential respecter of a right. For example, were the burdens imposed by a given right not fair (in relation to other bona fide obligations and burdens) or affordable for nation-states, individuals, and corporations, then presumably the prospective right would not qualify as a fundamental international right. In its second use, to which it is about to be put, the condition goes beyond the judgment *that* a certain affordability-fairness threshold has been crossed to the determination of *what* the proper duties are for multinational corporations in relation to a given right. In its second use, in other words, the condition's notions of fairness and affordability are invoked to help determine *which* obligations properly fall upon corporations, in contrast to individuals and nation-states. We shall use the condition to help determine the correlative duties that attach to multinational corporations in their honoring of fundamental international rights.

As we look over the list, it is noteworthy that except for a few isolated instances multinational corporations have probably succeeded in fulfilling their duty not to *actively deprive* persons of their enjoyment of the rights at issue. But correlative duties involve more than failing to actively deprive people of the enjoyment of their rights. Shue, for example, notes that three types of correlative duties are possible for any right, namely, duties to (1) avoid depriving, (2) help protect from deprivation, and (3) aid the deprived.[28]

While it is obvious that the honoring of rights clearly imposes duties of the first kind, i.e., to avoid depriving directly, it is less obvious, but frequently true, that honoring them involves acts or omissions that help prevent the deprivation of rights. If I receive a threat from Murder, Inc., and it looks like they mean business, my right to security is clearly at risk. If a third party has relevant information that if revealed to the police would help protect my right, it is no excuse for the third party to say that it is Murder, Inc., and not they (the third party), who wishes to kill me. Hence, honoring rights sometimes involves not only duties to *avoid depriving*, but to *help protect from deprivation* as well, and it is interesting that many critics of multinationals have faulted them not for the failure to avoid depriving but for failing to take reasonable protective steps.

Similarly, the duties associated with rights can often include duties from the third category, i.e., that of *aiding the deprived*, as when a government is bound to honor the right of its citizens to adequate nutrition by distributing food in the wake of a famine or natural disaster, or when the same government in the defense of political liberty is required to demand that an employer reinstate or compensate an employee fired for voting for a particular candidate in a government election.

Nonetheless, the honoring by multinational corporations of at least *some* of the ten fundamental rights requires the adoption of only the first class of correlative duties, i.e., the duty to avoid depriving. Correlative duties do not extend either to protecting from deprivation or aiding the deprived, because of the relevance of the "fairness-affordability" condition discussed before. This condition requires, again, that the obligations or burdens imposed by a right must be affordable in relation to resources, other obligations, and fairness in the distribution of burdens. (Certain puzzles affecting the affordability-fairness condition are discussed later in the context of the "drug lord" problem.)

Corporations cannot be held to the same standards of charity and love as individuals. Nor can corporations be held to the same standards to which we hold civil governments for enhancing social welfare since frequently governments are dedicated to enhancing the welfare of, and actively preserving the liberties of, their citizens. The profit-making corporation, in contrast, is designed to achieve an economic mission and as a moral actor possesses an exceedingly narrow personality. It is an undemocratic institution, furthermore, which is ill-suited to the broader task of distributing society's goods in accordance with a conception of general welfare. The corporation is an economic animal; although one may deny that its sole responsibility is to make a profit for its investors, one will surely wish to define its responsibilities differently than for civil governments.

Let us employ a "minimal/maximal" distinction to draw the inference that duties of the third class, i.e., to aid the deprived, do not fall upon for-profit multinational corporations, except, of course, in instances where the corporations themselves have done the depriving. For example, although it would be strikingly generous for multinationals to sacrifice some of their profits to buy milk, grain, and shelter for persons in poor countries, assisting the poor is not one of the corporations' minimal moral requirements; such minimal obligations belong more properly to the people's respective governments or, perhaps, to better-off individuals. If corporations possess duties to aid those deprived of the benefits of rights (except, again, in instances where they have done the depriving), then they possess them as "maximal" not "minimal" duties, which means that a given corporation's failure to observe them does not deprive that corporation of its moral right to exist. Furthermore, since rights impose minimal, not maximal duties, it follows that whereas a corporation might have a maximal duty to aid the deprived in a given instance, their failure to honor that duty could not be claimed necessarily as a violation of someone's *rights.*

The same, however, is not true of the second class of duties, i.e., to protect from deprivation. These duties, like those in the third class, are also usually the province of government, but it sometimes happens that the rights to which they correlate are ones whose protection is a direct outcome of ordinary corporate activities. For example, the duties associated with protecting a worker from the physical threats of other workers may fall not only upon the local police but also to some extent upon the employer. These duties, in turn, are properly viewed as correlative duties of a person's right–in this instance, the worker's right–to personal security. This will become clearer in a moment when we discuss the correlative duties of specific rights.

The table of correlative duties ... reflects the application of the "afford-ability-fairness" condition to the earlier list of fundamental international rights, and indicates which rights do, and which do not, impose correlative duties upon multinational corporations of the three various kinds. A word of caution should be issued for interpreting the list: the first type of correlative obligation, i.e., of not depriving directly, is broader than might be supposed at first. It includes *cooperative* as well as exclusively individual actions. Thus, if a company has personnel policies that inhibit freedom of movement, or if a multinational corporation operating in South Africa cooperates with the

Minimal Correlative Duties of Multinational Corporations

Fundamental Rights	To Avoid Depriving	To Help Protect from Deprivation	To Aid the Deprived
Freedom of physical movement	X		
Ownership of property	X		
Freedom from torture	X		
Fair trial	X		
Non-discriminatory treatment	X	X	
Physical security	X	X	
Freedom of speech and association	X	X	
Minimal education	X	X	
Political participation	X	X	
Subsistence	X	X	

government's restrictions on pass laws, then those companies actively deprive persons of their right to freedom of movement, despite the fact that actions of other agents (in particular, of the South African government) may be essential in effecting the deprivation. Similarly, in an instance where a corporation cooperates with political groups in fighting land reforms designed to take land from a tiny aristocratic minority (a minority that, say, owns virtually all of a country's usable land) for redistribution to peasants, those corporations may well–at least under certain circumstances–violate the right to private property.

Still, the list asserts that at least six of the ten fundamental rights impose correlative duties of the second kind upon corporations, that is, to protect from deprivation.[29] What follows is a brief set of commentaries discussing sample applications of each of those six rights from the perspective of such correlative duties.

Sample Applications

Discrimination

The obligation to protect from deprivation a person's freedom from discrimination properly falls upon corporations as well as governments insofar as everyday corporate activities directly affect compliance with the right. Because employees and prospective employees possess the moral right not to be discriminated against on the basis of race, sex, caste, class, or family affiliation, it follows that multinational corporations have an obligation not only to refrain from discrimination but in some instances to protect the right to non-discriminatory treatment by establishing appropriate procedures. This may require, for example, offering notice to prospective employees of the company's policy of non-discriminatory hiring, or educating lower level managers about the need to reward or penalize on the basis of performance rather than irrelevant criteria.

Physical security

The right to physical security similarly entails duties of protection: if a Japanese multinational corporation operating in Nigeria hires shop workers to run metal lathes in an assembly factory but fails to provide them with protective goggles, then the corporation has failed to honor the workers' moral right to physical security (no matter what the local law might decree). Injuries from such a failure would be the moral responsibility of the Japanese multinational despite the fact that the company could not be said to have inflicted the injuries directly.

Free speech and association

In the same vein, the duty to protect the right of free speech and association from deprivation finds application in the ongoing corporate obligation not to bar the emergence of labor unions. Corporations are not obliged on the basis of human rights to encourage or welcome labor unions, but neither are they morally permitted to destroy them or prevent their emergence through coercive tactics; to do so would violate the workers' international right to association. Their duty to protect the right to association from deprivation, in turn, includes refraining from lobbying host governments for restrictions that would violate the right in question, and perhaps even to protesting host government measures that do violate it.[30]

Minimal education

The correlative duty to protect the right of education may be illustrated through the very example used to open this paper: namely, the prevalence of child labor in developing countries. A multinational in Central America is not entitled to hire a 10-year-old child for full-time work because, among other reasons, doing so blocks the child's ability to receive a minimally sufficient education. While what counts as a "minimally sufficient" education may be debated, and while it seems likely, moreover, that the specification of the right to a certain level of education will depend, at least in part, upon the level of economic resources available in a given country, it is reasonable to assume that any action by a corporation that has the effect of blocking the development of a child's ability to read or write will be proscribed on the basis of rights.

Political participation

In some instances corporations have failed to honor the correlative duty of protecting the right to political participation from deprivation. The most blatant examples of direct deprivation are fortunately becoming so rare as to be non-existent, namely, cases in which companies directly aid in overthrowing democratic regimes, as when United Fruit helped overthrow a democratically elected regime in Honduras during the 1950s. But a few corporations have continued indirectly to threaten this right by failing to protect it from deprivation. A few have persisted, for example, in supporting military dictatorships in countries with growing democratic sentiment, and others have blatantly bribed publicly elected officials with large sums of money. Perhaps the most celebrated example of the latter occurred when the prime minister of Japan was bribed with $7 million by the Lockheed Corporation to secure a lucrative Tri-Star Jet contract. Here, the complaint from the perspective of this right is not against bribes or "sensitive payments" in general, but to bribes in contexts where they serve to undermine a democratic system in which publicly elected officials are in a position of public trust.

Even the buying and owning of major segments of a foreign country's land and industry has been criticized in this regard. As Brian Barry has remarked, "the paranoia created in Britain and the United States by land purchases by foreigners (especially Arabs, it seems) should serve to make it understandable that the citizenry of a country might be unhappy with a state of affairs in which the most important natural resources are in foreign ownership."[31] At what point would Americans regard their democratic control threatened by foreign ownership of U.S. industry and resources? At 20 percent ownership? At 40 percent? At 60 percent? At 80 percent? The answer is debatable, yet there seems to be some point beyond which the right to national self-determination, and in turn national democratic control, is violated by foreign ownership of property.[32]

Subsistence

Corporations also have duties to protect the right to subsistence from deprivation. Consider the following scenario: a number of square miles of land in an underdeveloped country has been used for years to grow black beans. Further, the bulk of the land is owned, as it has been for centuries, by two wealthy landowners. Poorer members of the community work the land and receive a portion of the crop, a portion barely sufficient to satisfy nutritional needs. Next, imagine that a multinational corporation offers the two wealthy owners a handsome sum for the land, and does so because it plans to grow coffee for export. Now *if*—and this, admittedly, is a crucial "if"—the corporation has reason to know that a significant number of people in the community will suffer malnutrition as a result; that is, if the company has convincing reasons to believe that those persons will not be hired by the company, or that if forced to migrate to the city they will earn less than subsistence wages, i.e. inadequate to provide proper food and shelter, then the multinational may be said to have failed in its correlative duty to protect persons from the deprivation of the right to subsistence. This despite the fact that the corporation would never have stopped to take food from workers' mouths, and despite the fact that the malnourished will, in Coleridge's words, "die so slowly that none call it murder."

Disagreements: The relevance of fact and culture

The commentaries above are obviously not intended to complete the project of specifying the correlative duties associated with fundamental international rights; only to begin it. Furthermore, here—as in the matter of specifying specific correlative duties generally—disagreements are inevitable. Take the land acquisition case above. One may claim that multinationals are never capable of knowing the consequences of land purchases with sufficient certainty to predict malnutrition or starvation. The issue obviously requires debate. Furthermore, one may wish to argue for the moral relevance of predictions about the actions of other agents. If the corporation in question refrains from buying land, won't another corporation rush in with the same negative consequences? And might not such a prediction mitigate the former corporation's responsibility in buying land in the first place? Here both facts and meta-moral principles must be debated

The same point arises in the context of an even more controversial issue, one related also to the right of persons to subsistence. Critics have asserted that by promoting high technology agriculture in developing countries where wealthier farmers are preferred risks for loans to buy imported seeds and fertilizer, multinationals encourage the syndrome of land concentration and dependence upon imported food and fertilizer, leading to the situation where proceeds from cash crops buy luxuries for the rich and where poor farmers are forced to sell their small plots of land and move to the city. Whether such practices do violate rights will obviously be a subject of controversy. But what is central to the resolution of such a controversy is the empirical question of whether such practices do lead to starvation and malnourishment. That is to say, the problem may be positioned for solution, but it is certainly not solved, by establishing the right to subsistence and its correlative duties: facts remain crucial.

More generally, the solution to most difficult international problems requires a detailed understanding not only of moral precepts but of particular facts. The answer does not appear, as if by magic, simply by referencing the relevant rights and correlative duties, any more than the issue of whether welfare recipients in the United States should be required to work disappears by appealing to the state's correlative duty to aid the disadvantaged. Elsewhere I propose an "ethical algorithm" to aid multinational managers in making difficult tradeoffs between home and host country values,[33] but while that algorithm augments the appeal to fundamental international rights established in this paper, neither it nor any other theory can draw moral conclusions when key facts are in dispute. Put simply, when facts are in irreconcilable dispute, so too will be the moral outcome.[34]

It may be that some of the above rights would not be embraced, or at least not embraced as formulated here, by cultures far different from ours. Would, for example, the Fulanis, a nomadic cattle culture in Nigeria, subscribe to this list with the same eagerness as the citizens of Brooklyn, New York? What list would they draw up if given the chance? And could we, or should we, try to convince them that our list is preferable? Would such a dialogue even make sense?[35]

I want to acknowledge that rights may vary in priority and style of expression from one culture to another. Yet in line with the conclusions of the earlier discussion of cultural relativism, I maintain that the list itself is applicable to all people even if they would fail to compose an identical list. Clearly the Fulanis do not have to accept the list of ten rights in question for it to constitute a valid means of judging the Fulani culture. If the Fulanis treat women unfairly and unequally, then at least one fundamental international right remains unfulfilled in their culture, and our discussion implies that their culture is poorer for that practice. Three of the rights are especially prone to varying cultural interpretation. These include that of non-discriminatory treatment (with special reference to women), to political participation, and to the ownership of property. The latter two raise tendentious political issues for cultures with traditions of communal property and non-democratic institutions. The list has no pretensions to solve these age-old political problems. While I may (as, in fact, I do) subscribe to a modified Lockean notion of property in which certain political systems incorporating social ownership violate individual rights, the right to property advanced in our list need not be so narrowly interpreted as to rule out any instance of public ownership. For example, even primitive societies with communal property practices might be said to recognize a modified version of the right to property if those practices entail mutually agreed-upon, and fairly applied, rules of use, benefit, and liability. I am not prepared to say that each and every such instance violates the right to own property.

Even so, there will be a point beyond which the public ownership of property violates individual rights. State ownership of all land and movable property violates the individual's right to own property. Is the point passed when a country nationalizes its phone systems? Its oil industry? Is it passed when a primitive culture refuses to subordinate family to individual property? Although it is clear that such questions are of decisive significance, it is equally clear that establishing such a point is a task that cannot be undertaken satisfactorily here.

The same holds true for interpreting the right to political participation. I affirm the merits of a democratic electoral system in which representatives are chosen on the basis of one-person-one-vote; yet the list should not be interpreted to demand a photocopy of U.S. or English style democracy. For example, it is possible to imagine a small, primitive culture utilizing other fair means for reflecting participation in the political process—other than a representative electoral system—and thereby satisfying the right to political participation.

The drug lord problem

One of the most difficult aspects of the rights list proposed concerns the affordability-fairness condition. We can see it more clearly by reflecting on what might be called the "drug lord" problem.[36] Imagine that an unfortunate country has a weak government and is run by various drug lords (not, it appears, a hypothetical case). These drug lords threaten the physical security of various citizens and torture others. The government—the country—cannot afford to mount the required police or military actions that would bring these drug lords into moral line. Or, perhaps, this could be done but only by imposing terrible burdens on certain segments of the society that would be unfair to others. Does it follow that members of that society do not have the fundamental international right not to be tortured and to physical security? Surely they do, even if the country cannot afford to guarantee them. But if that is the case, what about the affordability-fairness criterion?

Let us begin by noting that the "affordability" part of the affordability-fairness condition does imply some upper limit for the use of resources in the securing of a fundamental international right (such that, for example, dialysis cannot be a fundamental international right). With this established, the crucial question becomes *how* to draw the upper limit. The preceding argument commits us to draw that limit through at least two criteria: first, compatibility with other, already recognized, international rights, and second, the level of importance of the interest (moral or otherwise) being protected by the right (the first of the three conditions). As for the former, we remember that the affordability-fairness principle already entails a "moral compatibility" condition requiring that the duties imposed be compatible with other moral duties. Hence, a *prima facie* limit may be drawn on the certification of a prospective right corresponding to the point at which other bona fide international rights are violated. As for the latter, trade-offs among members of a class of prospective rights will be made by reference to the relative importance of the interest being protected by the right. The right not to be tortured protects a more fundamental interest than the right to an aesthetically pleasing environment.

This provides a two-tiered solution for the drug lord problem. At the first tier, we note that the right of people not to be tortured by the drug lords (despite the unaffordability of properly policing the drug lords) implies that people, and especially the drug lords, have a duty not to torture. Here the solution is simple. The argument of this chapter establishes a fundamental international right not to be tortured, and it is a right that binds all parties to the duty of forbearance in torturing others. For on the first pass of applying the affordability-fairness condition, that is, when we are considering simply the issue of which fundamental international rights exist, we are only concerned about affordability in relation to *any* of the three classes of correlative duties. That is, we look to determine only whether duties of *any* of the three classes of duties are fair and affordable. And with respect to the issue of affordability, clearly the drug lords along with every other moral agent can "afford" to refrain from actively depriving persons of their right not to be tortured. That is, they can afford to refrain from torturing. It follows that people clearly have the fundamental international right not to be tortured, which imposes at least one class of duties upon all international actors, namely, those of forbearance.

At the second tier, on the other hand, we are concerned with the issue of whether the right not to be tortured includes a duty of the government to mount an effective prevention system against torture. Here the affordability-fairness criterion is used in a second pass, one that helps establish the specific kinds of correlative duties associated with the right not to be tortured. Here surely all nation states can "afford" to shoulder duties of the second and third categories, i.e., of helping prevent deprivation, and of aiding the deprived, although the specific extent of those duties may be further affected by considerations of fairness and affordability. For example, given an instance like the country described in the drug lord problem, it clearly seems questionable that all countries could "afford" to succeed completely in preventing torture, and hence the duty to help prevent torture presupposed by a fundamental international right to freedom from torture probably cannot be construed to demand complete success. Nonetheless, a fairly high level of success in preventing torture is probably demanded by virtue of international rights, because, as I have argued elsewhere,[37] the ordinary protection of civil and political rights, such as the right not to be tortured, carries a negative rather than positive economic cost. That is, the economic cost of allowing the erosion of rights to physical security and fair trial–as an empirical matter of fact–tends to exceed the cost of maintaining the rights.

Conclusion

What the list of rights and corollary corporate duties establishes is that multinational corporations frequently do have obligations derived from rights where such obligations extend beyond abstaining from depriving directly, to protecting from deprivation. It implies, in other words, that the relevant factors for analyzing a difficult issue like that of hunger and high technology agriculture include not only the degree of factual correlation existing between multinational policy and hunger but also the recognition of the existence of a right to subsistence along with a specification of the corporate correlative duties entailed.

Hence the paper has argued that the ten rights identified earlier constitute minimal and bedrock moral considerations for multinational corporations operating abroad. While the list may be incomplete, the human claims it honors, and the interests those claims represent, are globally relevant. They are, in turn, immune from the Hobbesian or relativistically inspired challenges offered by skeptics. The existence of fundamental international rights implies that no corporation can wholly neglect considerations of racism, hunger, political oppression, or freedom through appeal to its "commercial" mission. These rights are, rather, moral considerations for every international moral agent, although, as we have seen, different moral agents possess different correlative obligations. The specification of the precise correlative duties associated with such rights for corporations is an ongoing task that the paper has left incomplete. Yet the existence of the rights themselves, including the imposition of duties upon corporations to protect–as well as to refrain from directly violating–such rights, seems beyond reasonable doubt.

Notes

Portions of this essay are contained in Thomas Donaldson, *The Ethics of International Business* (New York: Oxford University Press, 1990), and are repeated here with permission.

1. James LeMoyne, "In Central America, the Workers Suffer Most," *New York Times,* October 26, 1987, p. 1.

2. Some work explores the issue of political risk (for example, Thomas Poynter, *Multinational Enterprises and Government Intervention* (New York: St. Martin's Press, 1985); Thomas Moran, ed., *Multinational Corporations; The Political Economy of Foreign Direct Investment* (Lexington, MA: Lexington Books, 1985); and J. N. Behrman, *Decision Criteria for Foreign Direct Investment in Latin America* (New York: Council of the Americas, 1974); while other work explores the nature of international corporate strategy (See W.J. Keegan, "Multinational Scanning: A Study of Information Sources Utilized by Headquarters Executives in Multinational Companies", *Administrative Science Quarterly* (1974): 411–21; and D. Cray, "Control and Coordination in Multinational Corpora-

tions," *Journal of International Business Studies* 15, no 2 (1984): 55–98); and still other work explores multinational public policy issues (See Lee Preston, "The Evolution of Multinational Public Policy Toward Business: Codes of Conduct" in Lee Preston, ed., *Research in Corporate Social Performance and Policy*, Vol. 10, Greenwich, CT: JAI Press, 1988).

3. This group has produced what is probably the best developed ethical literature from business schools. Their efforts evolve from the tradition of "business and society" research with roots in the sixties and early seventies. Contributors such as Buchholz, Cochran, Epstein, Frederick, Freeman, and Sethi have made significant advances, not only in developing descriptive studies with moral relevance, but in advancing normative hypotheses. See, for example, Rogene A. Buchholz, *Business Environment and Public Policy* (Englewood Cliffs, NJ: Prentice-Hall, 1982); Stephen L.Wartick and Philip L. Cochran, "The Evolution of the Corporate Social Performance Mode," *Academy of Management Review* 10 (1985): 758–69; Edwin Epstein, "The Corporate Social Policy Process: Beyond Business Ethics, Corporate Social Responsibility, and Corporate Social Responsiveness," *California Management Review* 29 (Spring 1987); William C. Fredericks "Toward CSR3: Why Ethical Analysis is Indispensable and Unavoidable in Corporate Affairs," *California Management Review* 28 (1986): 126–41; R. Edward Freeman, *Strategic Management: A Stakeholder Approach* (Boston: Pitman Press, 1984), and *Corporate Strategy and the Search for Ethics* (Englewood Cliffs, NJ: Prentice-Hall, 1988); and S. Prakash Sethi, "Corporate Law Violations and Executive Liability," in Lee Preston, ed., *Corporate Social Performance and Policy*, Vol. 3 (Greenwich, CT: JAI Press, 1981), pp. 72–73, and S. Prakash Sethi et al., *Corporate Governance: Public Policy Social Responsibility Committee of Corporate Board* (Richardson, TX.: Center for Research in Business and Social Policy, 1979).

4. An exception is Duane Windsor's "Defining the Ethical Obligations of the Multinational Enterprise," in W. M. Hoffman et al., eds., *Ethics and the Multinational Corporation* (Washington, DC: University Press of America, 1986).

5 Thomas Donaldson, *The Ethics of International Business* (New York: Oxford University Press, 1990). See especially Chapter 6.

6. Maurice Cranston, *What Are Human Rights?* (New York: Tamlinger, 1973), p.67.

7. H. J. McCloskey, for example, understands a right as a positive entitlement that need not specify who bears the responsibility for satisfying that entitlement. H. J. McCloskey, "Rights–Some Conceptual Issues," *Australasian Journal of Philosophy* 54 (1976): 99.

8. Joel Feinberg, "Duties, Rights, and Claims," *American Philosophical Quarterly* 3 (1966): 137–44. See also Feinberg, "The Nature and Value of Rights," *Journal of Value Inquiry* 4 (1970): 243–57

9. James Brooke, "Waste Dumpers Turning to West Africa," *New York Times,* July 17, 1988, p.1.

10. Ibid.

11. Nigeria and other countries have struck back, often by imposing strict rules against the acceptance of toxic waste. For example, in Nigeria officials now warn that anyone caught importing toxic waste will face the firing squad. Brooke, "Waste Dumpers Turning to West Africa," p.7.

12. James W: Nickel, *Making Sense of Human Rights: Philosophical Reflections on the Universal Declaration of Human Rights* (Berkeley: University of California Press,1987), pp.107–8.

13. See Ian Brownlie, *Basic Documents on Human Rights* (Oxford: Oxford University Press, 1975).

14. For a contemporary analysis of the Universal Declaration of Human Rights and companion international documents, see James W. Nickel, *Making Sense of Human Rights: Philosophical Reflections on the Universal Declaration of Human Rights* (Berkeley: University of California Press, 1987).

15 For example, the "European Convention of Human Rights" omits mention of welfare rights, preferring instead to create an auxiliary document ("The European Social Charter of 1961") which references many of what earlier had been treated as rights as "goals."

16. Henry Shue, *Basic Rights* (Princeton, NJ: Princeton University Press, 1982).

17. Ibid., p. 34.

18. Ibid., p. 20–23.

19. Ibid., p.78.

20. Ibid, p.71.

21. Ibid., p.76.

22. Ibid., p. 31.

23. Ibid., pp. 37–38.

24. I am indebted to Alan Gewirth who made this point in a conversation about Shue's theory of basic rights.

25. Shue, *Basic Rights*, p. 20.

26. Ibid., p. 19.

27. James Nickel, *Making Sense of Human Rights* (Berkeley: University of California Press, 1987), pp. 108–19. The phrasing of the third condition is derived almost directly from Nickel's condition that "the obligations or burdens imposed by the right must be affordable in relation to resources, other obligations, and fairness in the distribution of burdens."

28. Shue, *Basic Rights*, p. 57.

29. It is possible to understand even the remaining four rights as imposing correlative duties to protect from deprivation by imagining unusual or hypothetical scenarios. For example, if it happened that the secret police of a host country dictatorship regularly used corporate personnel files in their efforts to kidnap and torture suspected political opponents, then the corporation would be morally obligated to object to the practice, and to refuse to make their files available any longer. Here the corporation would have a correlative duty to protect from deprivation the right not to be tortured. The list of rights identified as imposing correlative duties of protection was lionized to six, however, on the basis of the fact that their protection is directly related to activities frequently undertaken by corporations in the real world.

30. The twin phenomena of commercial concentration and the globalization of business, both associated with the rise of the multinational, have tended to weaken the bargaining power of organized labor. It is doubtful that labor is sharing as fully as it once did in the cyclical gains of industrial productivity. This gives special significance to the right in question.

31. Brian Barry, "The Case for a New International Economic Order" in J. Roland Pennock and John W. Chapman, eds., *Ethics, Economics, and the Law: Nomos Vol. XXIV* (New York: New York University Press, 1982).

32. Companies are also charged with undermining local governments, and hence infringing on basic rights, by sophisticated tax evasion schemes. Especially when companies buy from their own subsidiaries, they can establish prices that have little connection to existing market values. This, in turn, means that profits can be shifted from high-tax to low-tax countries with the result that poor nations can be deprived of their rightful share.

33. See Donaldson, *The Ethics of International Business*, Chapter 5.

34. It is important to remember that it is "key" or "crucial" facts that are being discussed here. The ten fundamental international rights are not to be eroded in every instance by the old argument that "we don't have enough facts." Such a defense clearly has its limits, and these limits are overstepped by the demand that evidence be definitive in every sense. An excellent example of excess in this vein is that of cigarette companies denying that their products are dangerous because we do not yet understand the causal mechanism whereby cigarette smoking is correlated with cancer.

35. Both for raising these questions, and in helping me formulate answers, I am indebted to William Frederick.

36. I am indebted to George Brenkert for suggesting and formulating the "drug lord" problem.

37. Thomas Donaldson, "Trading Justice for Bread: A Reply to James W. Nickel," in Kenneth Kipnis and Diana T. Meyers, eds, *Economic Justice: Private Rights and Public Responsibilities* (Totowa, NJ: Rowman and Allenheld, 1985), pp. 226–29.

31

International Business, Morality, and the Common Good

Manuel Velasquez

During the last few years an increasing number of voices have urged that we pay more attention to ethics in international business, on the grounds that not only are all large corporations now internationally structured and thus engaging in international transactions, but that even the smallest domestic firm is increasingly buffeted by the pressures of international competition.[1] This call for increased attention to international business ethics has been answered by a slowly growing collection of ethicists who have begun to address issues in this field. The most comprehensive work on this subject to date is the recent book *The Ethics of International Business* by Thomas Donaldson.[2]

I want in this article to discuss certain realist objections to bringing ethics to bear on international transactions, an issue that, I believe, has not yet been either sufficiently acknowledged nor adequately addressed but that must be resolved if the topic of international business ethics is to proceed on solid foundations. Even so careful a writer as Thomas Donaldson fails to address this issue in its proper complexity. Oddly enough, in the first chapter where one would expect him to argue that, in spite of realist objections, businesses have international moral obligations, Donaldson argues only for the less pertinent claim that, in spite of realist objections, *states* have international moral obligations.[3] But international business organizations, I will argue, have special features that render realist objections quite compelling. The question I want to address, here, then, is a particular aspect of the question Donaldson and others have ignored: Can we say that businesses operating in a competitive international environment have any moral obligations to contribute to the international common good, particularly in light of realist objections? Unfortunately, my answer to this question will be in the negative.

Source: *Business Ethics Quarterly,* 2 (1) (1992), 27–40.

My subject, then, is international business and the common good. What I will do is the following. I will begin by explaining what I mean by the common good, and what I mean by international business. Then I will turn directly to the question whether the views of the realist allow us to claim that international businesses have a moral obligation to contribute to the common good. I will first lay out the traditional realist treatment of this question and then revise the traditional realist view so that it can deal with certain shortcomings embedded in the traditional version of realism. I will then bring these revisions to bear on the question of whether international businesses have any obligations toward the common good, a question that I will answer in the negative. My hope is that I have identified some extremely problematic issues that are both critical and disturbing and that, I believe, need to be more widely discussed than they have been because they challenge our easy attribution of moral obligation to international business organizations.

I should note that what follows is quite tentative. I am attempting to work out the implications of certain arguments that have reappeared recently in the literature on morality in international affairs. I am not entirely convinced of the correctness of my conclusions, and offer them here as a way of trying to get clearer about their status. I should also note that although I have elsewhere argued that it is improper to attribute *moral responsibility* to corporate entities, I here set these arguments aside in order to show that even if we ignore the issue of moral responsibility, it is still questionable whether international businesses have obligations toward the common good.

I. The Common Good

Let me begin by distinguishing a weak from a strong conception of the common good, so that I might clarify what I have in mind when I refer to the common good.

What I have in mind by a weak conception of the common good is essentially the utilitarian notion of the common good. It is a notion that is quite clearly stated by Jeremy Bentham:

> The interest of the community then is—what? The sum of the interests of the several members who compose it... It is vain to talk of the interest of the community, without understanding what is the interest of the individual. A thing is said to promote the interest or to be for the interest of an individual, when it tends to add to the sum total of his pleasure; or what comes to the same thing, to diminish the sum total of his pains.[4]

On the utilitarian notion of the common good, the common good is nothing more than the sum of the utilities of each individual. The reason why I call this the "weak" conception of the common good will become clear, I believe, once it is contrasted with another, quite different notion of the common good.

Let me describe, therefore, what I will call a strong conception of the common good, the conception on which I want to focus in this essay. It is a conception that has been elaborated in the Catholic tradition, and so I will refer to it as the Catholic conception of the common good. Here is how one writer, William A. Wallace, O.P., characterizes the conception:

> A common good is clearly distinct from a private good, the latter being the good of one person only, to the exclusion of its being possessed by any other. A common good is distinct also from a *collective* good, which, though possessed by all of a group, is not really participated in by the members of the group; divided up, a collective good becomes respectively the private goods of the members. A true *common* good is universal, not singular or collective, and is distributive in character, being communicable to many without becoming anyone's private good. Moreover, each person participates in the whole common good, not merely in a part of it, nor can any one person possess it wholly.[5]

In the terms used by Wallace, the utilitarian conception of the common good is actually a "collective" good. That is, it is an aggregate of the private goods (the utilities) of the members of a society. The common good in the utilitarian conception is divisible in the sense that the aggregate consists of distinct parts and each part is enjoyable by only one individual. Moreover, the common good in the utilitarian conception is not universal in the sense that not all members of society can enjoy all of the aggregate; instead, each member enjoys only a portion of the aggregate.

By contrast, in the Catholic conception that Wallace is attempting to characterize, the common good consists of those goods that (1) benefit all the members of a society in the sense that all the members of the society have access to each of these goods, and (2) are not divisible in the sense that none of these goods can be divided up and allocated among individuals in such a way that others can be excluded from enjoying what another individual enjoys. The example that Wallace gives of one common good is the "good of peace and order."[6] Other examples are national security, a clean natural environment, public health and safety, a productive economic system to whose benefits all have access, a just legal and political system, and a system of natural and artificial associations in which persons can achieve their personal fulfillment.

It is this strong notion of the common good that the Catholic tradition has had in mind when it has defined the common good as "the sum total of those conditions of social living whereby men are enabled more fully and more readily to achieve their own perfection."[7] It is also the conception that John Rawls has in mind when he writes that "Government is assumed to aim at the common good, that is, at maintaining conditions and achieving objectives that are similarly to everyone's advantage," and "the common good I think of as certain general conditions that are in an appropriate sense equally to everyone's advantage."[8]

The Catholic conception of the common good is the conception that I have in mind in what follows. It is clear from the characterization of the common good laid out above that we can think of the common good on two different levels. We can think of the common good on a national and on an international level. On a national level, the common good is that set of conditions within a certain nation that are necessary for the citizens of that nation to achieve their individual fulfillment and so in which all of the citizens have an interest.

On an international level, we can speak of the global common good as that set of conditions that are necessary for the citizens of all or of most nations to achieve their individual fulfillment, and so those goods in which all the peoples of the world have an interest. In what follows, I will be speaking primarily about the global common good.

Now it is obvious that identifying the global common good is extremely difficult because cultures differ on their views of what conditions are necessary for humans to flourish. These differences are particularly acute between the cultures of the lesser developed third world nations who have demanded a "new economic order," and the cultures of the wealthier first world nations who have resisted this demand. Nevertheless, we can identify at least some elements of the global common good. Maintaining a congenial global climate, for example is certainly part of the global common good. Maintaining safe transportation routes for the international flow of goods is also part of the global common good. Maintaining clean oceans is another aspect of the global common good, as is the avoidance of a global nuclear war. In spite of the difficulties involved in trying to compile a list of the goods that qualify as part of the global common good, then, it is nevertheless possible to identify at least some of the items that belong on the list.

II. International Business

Now let me turn to the other term in my title: international business. When speaking of international business, I have in mind a particular kind of organization: the multinational corporation. Multinational corporations have a number of well known features, but let me briefly summarize a few of them. First, multinational corporations are businesses and as such they are organized primarily to increase their profits within a competitive environment. Virtually all of the activities of a multinational corporation can be explained as more or less rational attempts to achieve this dominant end. Secondly, multinational corporations are bureaucratic organizations. The implication of this is that the identity, the fundamental structure, and the dominant objectives of the corporation endure while the many individual human beings who fill the various offices and positions within the corporation come and go. As a consequence, the particular values and aspirations of individual members of the corporation have a relatively minimal and transitory impact on the organization as a whole. Thirdly, and most characteristically, multinational corporations operate in several nations. This has several implications. First, because the multinational is not confined to a single nation, it can easily escape the reach of the laws of any particular nation by simply moving its resources or operations out of one nation and transferring them to another nation. Second, because the multinational is not confined to a single nation, its interests are not aligned with the interests of any single nation. The ability of the multinational to achieve its profit objectives does not depend upon the ability of any particular nation to achieve its own domestic objectives.

In saying that I want to discuss international business and the common good, I am saying that I want to discuss the relationship between the global common good and multinational corporations, that is, organizations that have the features I have just identified.

The general question I want to discuss is straightforward: I want to ask whether it is possible for us to say that multinational corporations with the features I have just described have an obligation to contribute toward the global common good But I want to discuss only one particular aspect of this general question. I want to discuss this question in light of the realist objection.

III. The Traditional Realist Objection in Hobbes

The realist objection, of course, is the standard objection to the view that agents–whether corporations, governments, or individuals–have moral obligations on the international level. Generally, the realist holds that it is a mistake to apply moral concepts to international activities: morality has no place in international affairs. The classical statement of this view, which I am calling the "traditional" version of realism, is generally attributed to Thomas Hobbes. I will assume that this customary attribution is correct; my aim is to identify some of the implications of this traditional version of realism even if it is not quite historically accurate to attribute it to Hobbes.

In its Hobbsian form, as traditionally interpreted, the realist objection holds that moral concepts have no meaning in the absence of an agency powerful enough to guarantee that other agents generally adhere to the tenets of morality. Hobbes held, first, that in the absence of a sovereign power capable of forcing men to behave civilly with each other, men are in "the state of nature", a state he characterizes as a "war...of every man, against every man."[9] Secondly, Hobbes claimed, in such a state of war, moral concepts have no meaning:

> To this war of every man against every man, this also is consequent; that nothing can be unjust. The notions of right and wrong, justice and injustice have there no place. Where there is no common power, there is no law: where no law, no injustice.[10]

Moral concepts are meaningless, then, when applied to state of nature situations. And, Hobbes held, the international arena is a state of nature, since there is no international sovereign that can force agents to adhere to the tenets of morality.[11]

The Hobbsian objection to talking about morality in international affairs, then, is based on two premises: (1) an ethical premise about the applicability of moral terms and (2) an apparently empirical premise about how agents behave under certain conditions. The ethical premise, at least in its Hobbsian form, holds that there is a connection between the meaningfulness of moral terms and the extent to which agents adhere to the tenets of morality: if in a given situation agents do not adhere to the tenets of morality, then in that situation moral terms have no meaning. The apparently empirical premise holds that in the absence of a sovereign, agents will not adhere to the tenets of morality: they will be in a state of war. This appears to be an empirical generalization about the extent to which agents adhere to the tenets of morality in the absence of a third-party enforcer. Taken together, the two premises imply that in situations that lack a sovereign authority, such as one finds in many international exchanges, moral terms have no meaning and so moral obligations are nonexistent.

However, there are a number of reasons for thinking that the two Hobbsian premises are deficient as they stand. I want next, therefore, to examine each of these premises more closely and to determine the extent to which they need revision.

IV. Revising the Realist Objection: The First Premise

The ethical premise concerning the meaning of moral terms, is, in its original Hobbsian form, extremely difficult to defend. If one is in a situation in which others do not adhere to any moral restraints, it simply does not logically follow that in that situation one's actions are no longer subject to moral evaluation. At most what follows is that since such an extreme situation is different from the more normal situations in which we usually act, the moral requirements placed on us in such extreme situations are different from the moral requirements that obtain in more normal circumstances. For example, morality requires that in normal circumstances I am not to attack or kill my fellow citizens. But when one of those citizens is attacking me in a dark alley, morality allows me to defend myself by counterattacking or even killing that citizen. It is a truism that what moral principles require in one set of circumstances is different from what they require in other circumstances. And in extreme circumstances, the requirements of morality may become correspondingly extreme. But there is no reason to think that they vanish altogether.

Nevertheless, the realist can relinquish the Hobbsian premise about the meaning of moral terms, replace it with a weaker and more plausible premise, and still retain much of Hobbes' conclusion. The realist or neo-Hobbsian can claim that although moral concepts can be meaningfully applied to situations in which agents do not adhere to the tenets of morality, nevertheless it is not morally wrong for agents in such situations to also fail to adhere to those tenets of morality, particularly when doing so puts one at a significant competitive disadvantage.

The neo-Hobbsian or realist, then, might want to propose this premise: When one is in a situation in which others do not adhere to certain tenets of morality, and when adhering to those tenets of morality will put one at a significant competitive disadvantage, then it is not immoral for one to likewise fail to adhere to them. The realist might want to argue for this claim, first, by pointing out that in a world in which all are competing to secure significant benefits and avoid significant costs, and in which others do not adhere to the ordinary tenets of morality, one risks significant harm to one's interests if one continues to adhere to those tenets of morality. But no one can be morally required to take on major risks of harm to oneself. Consequently, in a competitive world in which others disregard moral constraints and take any means to advance their self-interests, no one can be morally required to take on major risks of injury by adopting the restraints of ordinary morality.

A second argument the realist might want to advance would go as follows. When one is in a situation in which others do not adhere to the ordinary tenets of morality, one is under heavy competitive pressures to do the same. And, when one is under such pressures, one cannot be blamed–i.e., one is excused– for also failing to adhere to the ordinary tenets of morality. One is excused because heavy pressures take away one's ability to control oneself, and thereby diminish one's moral culpability.

Yet a third argument advanced by the realist might go as follows. When one is in a situation in which others do not adhere to the ordinary tenets of morality it is not fair to require one to continue to adhere to those tenets, especially if doing so puts one at a significant competitive disadvantage. It is not fair because then one is laying a burden on one party that the other parties refuse to carry. Thus, there are a number of arguments that can be given in defense of the revised Hobbsian ethical premise that when others do not adhere to the tenets of morality, it is not immoral for one to do likewise. The ethical premise of the Hobbsian or realist argument, then, can be restated as follows:

> In situations in which other agents do not adhere to certain tenets of morality, it is not immoral for one to do likewise when one would otherwise be putting oneself at a significant competitive disadvantage.

In what follows, I will refer to this restatement as the ethical premise of the argument. I am not altogether convinced that this premise is correct. But it appears to me to have a great deal of plausibility, and it is, I believe, a premise that underlies the feelings of many that in a competitive international environment where others do not embrace the restraints of morality, one is under no obligation to be moral.

V. Revising the Realist Objection: The Second Premise

Let us turn, then, to the other premise in the Hobbsian argument, the assertion that in the absence of a sovereign, agents will be in a state of war. As I mentioned, this is an apparently empirical claim about the extent to which agents will adhere to the tenets of morality in the absence of a third-party enforcer.

Hobbes gives a little bit of empirical evidence for this claim. He cites several examples of situations in which there is no third party to enforce civility and where, as a result, individuals are in a "state of war."[12] Generalizing from these few examples, he reaches the conclusion that in the absence of a third-party enforcer, agents will always be in a "condition of war." But the meager evidence Hobbes provides is surely too thin to support his rather large empirical generalization. Numerous empirical counterexamples can be cited of people living in peace in the absence of a third-party enforcer, so it is difficult to accept Hobbes' claim as an empirical generalization.

Recently, the Hobbsian claim, however, has been defended on the basis of some of the theoretical claims of game theory, particularly of the prisoner's dilemma. Hobbes' state of nature, the defense goes, is an instance of a prisoner's dilemma, and *rational* agents in a Prisoner's Dilemma necessarily would choose not to adhere to a set of moral norms. Rationality is here construed in the sense that is standard in social theory: having a coherent set of preferences among the objects of choice, and selecting the one(s) that has the greatest probability of satisfying more of one's preferences rather than fewer.[13] Or, more simply, always choosing so as to maximize one's interests.

A Prisoner's Dilemma is a situation involving at least two individuals. Each individual is faced with two choices: he can cooperate with the other individual or he can choose not to cooperate. If he cooperates and the other individual also cooperates, then he gets a certain payoff. If, however, he chooses not to cooperate, while the other individual trustingly cooperates, the noncooperator gets a larger payoff while the cooperator suffers a loss. And if both choose not to cooperate, then both get nothing.

It is a commonplace now that in a Prisoner's Dilemma situation, the most rational strategy for a participant is to choose not to cooperate. For the other party will either cooperate or not cooperate. If the other party cooperates, then it is better for one not to cooperate and thereby get the larger payoff on the other hand, if the other party does not cooperate, then it is also better for one not to cooperate and thereby avoid a loss. In either case, it is better for one to not cooperate.

Now Hobbes' state of nature, the neo-Hobbsian realist can argue, is in fact a prisoner's dilemma situation. In Hobbes' state of nature each individual must choose either to cooperate with others by adhering to the rules of morality (like the rule against theft), or to not cooperate by disregarding the rules of morality and attempting to take advantage of those who are adhering to the rules (e.g., by stealing from them). In such a situation it is more rational (in the sense defined above) to choose not to cooperate. For the other party will either cooperate or not cooperate. If the other party does not cooperate, then one puts oneself at a competitive disadvantage if one adheres to morality while the other party does not. On the other hand, if the other party chooses to cooperate, then one can take advantage of the other party by breaking the rules of morality at his expense. In either case, it is more rational to not cooperate.

Thus, the realist can argue that in a state of nature, where there is no one to enforce compliance with the rules of morality, it is more rational from the individual's point of view to choose not to comply with morality than to choose to comply. Assuming–and this is obviously a critical assumption–that agents behave rationally, then we can conclude that agents in a state of nature will choose not to comply with the tenets of ordinary morality. The second premise of the realist argument, then, can, tentatively, be put as follows:

> In the absence of an international sovereign, all rational agents will choose not to comply with the tenets of ordinary morality, when doing so will put one at a serious competitive disadvantage.

This is a striking, and ultimately revealing, defense of the Hobbsian claim that in the absence of a third-party enforcer, individuals will choose not to adhere to the tenets of morality in their relations with each other. It is striking because it correctly identifies, I think, the underlying reason for the Hobbsian claim. The Hobbsian claim is not an empirical claim about how most humans actually behave when they are put at a competitive disadvantage. It is a claim about whether agents that are *rational* (in the sense defined earlier) will adopt certain behaviors when doing otherwise would put them at a serious competitive disadvantage. For our purposes, this is significant since, as I claimed above, all, most, or at least a significant number of multinationals are rational agents in the required sense: all or most of their activities are rational means for achieving the dominant end of increasing profits. Multinationals, therefore, are precisely the kind of rational agents envisaged by the realist.

But this reading of the realist claim is also significant, I think, because it reveals certain limits inherent in the Hobbsian claim, and requires revising the claim so as to take these limits into account.

As more than one person has pointed out, moral interactions among agents are often quite unlike Prisoner's Dilemmas situations.[14] The most important difference is that a Prisoner's Dilemma is a single meeting between agents who do not meet again, whereas human persons in the real world tend to have repeated dealings with each other. If two people meet each other in a Prisoner's Dilemma situation, and never have anything to do with each other again, then it is rational (in the sense under discussion) from each individual's point of view to choose lot to cooperate. However, if individuals meet each other in repeated Prisoner's Dilemma situations, then they are able to punish each other for failures to cooperate, and the cumulative costs of noncooperation can make cooperation the more rational strategy.[15] One can therefore expect that when rational agents know they will have repeated interactions with each other for an indefinite future, they will start to cooperate with each other even in the absence of a third party enforcer. The two cooperating parties in effect are the mutual enforcers of their own cooperative agreements.

The implication is that the realist is wrong in relieving that in the absence of a third-party enforcer, rational individuals will always fail to adhere to the tenets of morality, presumably even when doing so would result in serious competitive disadvantage. On the contrary, we can expect that if agents know that they will interact with each other repeatedly in the indefinite future, it is rational for them to behave morally toward each other. In the international arena, then, we can expect that when persons know that they will have repeated interactions with each other, they will tend to adhere to ordinary tenets of morality with each. Others assuming that they tend to behave rationally, even when doing so threatens to put them at a competitive disadvantage.

There is a second important way in which the Prisoner's Dilemma is defective as a characterization of real world interactions. Not only do agents repeatedly interact with each other, but, as Robert Frank has recently pointed out, human agents signal to each other the extent to which they can be relied on to behave morally in future interactions.[16] We humans can determine more often than not whether another person can be relied on to be moral by observing the natural visual cues of facial expression and the auditory cues of tone of voice that tend to give us away; by relying on our experience of past dealings with the person; and by relying on the reports of others who have had past dealings with the person. Moreover, based on these appraisals of each other's reliability, we then choose to interact with those who are reliable and choose not to interact with those who are not reliable. That is, we choose to enter prisoner's dilemmas situations with those who are reliable, and choose to avoid entering such situations with those who are not reliable. As Robert Frank has shown, given such conditions it is, under quite ordinary circumstances, rational to habitually be reliable since reliable persons tend to have mutually beneficial interactions with other reliable persons, while unreliable persons will tend to have mutually destructive interactions with other unreliable persons.

The implication again is that since signaling makes it rational to habitually cooperate in the rules of morality, even in the absence of a third-party enforcer, we can expect that rational humans, who can send and receive fairly reliable signals between each other, will tend to behave morally even, presumably, when doing so raises the prospect of competitive disadvantage.

These considerations should lead the realist to revise the tentative statement of the second premise of his argument that we laid out above. In its revised form, the second premise would have to read as follows:

> In the absence of an international sovereign, all rational agents will choose not to comply with the tenets of ordinary morality, when doing so will put one at a serious competitive disadvantage, provided that interactions are not repeated and that agents are not able to signal their reliability to each other.

This, I believe, is a persuasive and defensible version of the second premise in the Hobbsian argument. It is the one I will exploit in what follows.

VI. Revised Realism, Multinationals and the Common Good

Now how does this apply to multinationals and the common good? Can we claim that it is clear that multinationals have a moral obligation to pursue the global common good in spite of the objections of the realist?

I do not believe that this claim can be made. We can conclude from the discussion of the realist objection that the Hobbsian claim about the pervasiveness of amorality in the international sphere is false when (1) interactions among international agents are repetitive in such a way that agents can retaliate against those who fail to cooperate, and (2) agents can determine the trustworthiness of other international agents.

But unfortunately, multinational activities often take place in a highly competitive arena in which these two conditions do not obtain. Moreover, these conditions are noticeably absent in the arena of activities that concern the global common good.

First, as I have noted, the common good consists of goods that are indivisible and accessible to all. This means that such goods are susceptible to the free rider problem. Everyone has access to such goods whether or not they do their part in maintaining such goods, so everyone is tempted to free ride on the generosity of others. Now governments can force domestic companies to do their part to maintain the national common good. Indeed, it is one of the functions of government to solve the free rider problem by forcing all to contribute to the domestic common good to which all have access. Moreover, all companies have to interact repeatedly with their host governments, and this leads them to adopt a cooperative stance toward their host government's objective of achieving the domestic common good.

But it is not clear that governments can or will do anything effective to force multinationals to do their part to maintain the global common good. For the governments of individual nations can themselves be free riders, and can join forces with willing multinationals seeking competitive advantages over others. Let me suggest an example. It is clear that a livable global environment is part of the global common good, and it is clear that the manufacture and use of chloroflurocarbons is destroying that good. Some nations have responded by requiring their domestic companies to cease manufacturing or using chloroflurocarbons. But other nations have refused to do the same, since they will share in any benefits that accrue from the restraint others practice, and they can also reap the benefits of continuing to manufacture and use chloroflurocarbons. Less developed nations, in particular, have advanced the position that since their development depends heavily on exploiting the industrial benefits of chloroflurocarbons, they cannot afford to curtail their use of these substances. Given this situation, it is open to multinationals to shift their operations to those countries that continue to allow the manufacture and use of chloroflurocarbons. For multinationals, too, will reason that they will share in any benefits that accrue from the restraint others practice, and that they can meanwhile reap the profits of continuing to manufacture and use chloroflurocarbons in a world where other companies are forced to use more expensive technologies. Moreover, those nations that practice restraint cannot force all such multinationals to discontinue the manufacture or use of chloroflurocarbons because many multinationals can escape the reach of their laws. An exactly parallel, but perhaps even more compelling, set of considerations can be advanced to show that at least some multinationals will join forces with some developing countries to circumvent any global efforts made to control the global warming trends (the so-called "greenhouse effect") caused by the heavy use of fossil fuels.

The realist will conclude, of course, that in such situations, at least some multinationals will seek to gain competitive advantages by failing to contribute to the global common good (such as the good of a hospitable global environment). For multinationals are rational agents, i.e. agents bureaucratically structured to take rational means toward achieving their dominant end of increasing their profits. And in a competitive environment, contributing to the common good while others do not, will fail to achieve this dominant end. Joining this conclusion to the ethical premise that when others do not adhere to the requirements of morality it is not immoral for one to do likewise, the realist can conclude that multinationals are not morally obligated to contribute to such global common goods (such as environmental goods).

Moreover, global common goods often create interactions that are not iterated. This is particularly the case where the global environment is concerned. As I have already noted, preservation of a favorable global climate is clearly part of the global common good. Now the failure of the global climate will be a one-time affair. The breakdown of the ozone layer, for example, will happen once, with catastrophic consequences for us all; and the heating up of the global climate as a result of the infusion of carbon dioxide will happen once, with catastrophic consequences for us all. Because these environmental disasters are a one-time affair, they represent a non-iterated prisoner's dilemma for multinationals. It is irrational from an individual point of view for a multinational to choose to refrain from polluting the environment in such cases. Either others will refrain, and then one can enjoy the benefits of their refraining; or others will not refrain, and then it will be better to have also not refrained since refraining would have made little difference and would have entailed heavy losses.

Finally, we must also note that although natural persons may signal their reliability to other natural persons, it is not at all obvious that multinationals can do the same. As noted above, multinationals are bureaucratic organizations whose members are continually changing and shifting. The natural persons who make up an organization can signal their reliability to others, but such persons are soon replaced by others, and they in turn are replaced by others. What endures is each organization's single-minded pursuit of increasing its profits in a competitive environment. And an enduring commitment to the pursuit of profit in a competitive environment is not a signal of an enduring commitment to morality.

VII. Conclusions

The upshot of these considerations is that it is not obvious that we can say that multinationals have an obligation to contribute to the global common good in a competitive environment in the absence of an international authority that can force all agents to contribute to the global common good. Where other rational agents can be expected to shirk the burden of contributing to the common good and where carrying such a burden will put one at a serious competitive disadvantage, the realist argument that it is not immoral for one to also fail to contribute is a powerful argument.

I have not argued, of course, nor do I find it persuasive to claim that competitive pressures automatically relieve agents of their moral obligations, although my arguments here may be wrongly misinterpreted as making that claim. All that I have tried to do is to lay out a justification for the very narrow claim that *certain very special kinds of agents, under certain very limited and very special conditions, seem to have no obligations with respect to certain very special kinds of goods.*

This is not an argument, however, for complete despair. What the argument points to is the need to establish an effective international authority capable of forcing all agents to contribute their part toward the global common good. Perhaps several of the more powerful autonomous governments of the world, for example, will be prompted to establish such an international agency by relinquishing their autonomy and joining together into a coherently unified group that can exert consistent economic, political, or military pressures on any companies or smaller countries that do not contribute to the global common good. Such an international police group, of course, would transform the present world order, and would be much different from present world organizations such as the United Nations. Once such an international force exists, of course, then both Hobbes and the neorealist would say that moral obligations can legitimately be attributed to all affected international organizations.

Of course, it is remotely possible but highly unlikely that multinationals themselves will be the source of such promptings for a transformed world order. For whereas governments are concerned with the well being of their citizens, multinationals are bureaucratically structured for the rational pursuit of profit in a competitive environment, not the pursuit of citizen well-being. Here and there we occasionally may see one or even several multinationals whose current cadre of leadership is enlightened enough to regularly steer the organization toward the global common good. But given time, that cadre will be replaced and profit objectives will reassert themselves as the enduring end built into the ongoing structure of the multinational corporation.

Notes

1. See, for example, the articles collected in W. Michael Hoffman, Ann E. Lange, and David A. Fedo, eds., *Ethics and the Multinational Enterprise* (New York: University Press of America, 1986).

2. Thomas Donaldson, *The Ethics of International Business* (New York: Oxford University Press, 1989).

3. Donaldson discusses the question whether states have moral obligations to each other in op. cit., pp. 10–29. The critical question, however, is whether *multinationals*, i.e., profit-driven types of international organizations, have moral obligations. Although Donaldson is able to point out without a great deal of trouble that the realist arguments

against morality among nations are mistaken (see pp. 20–23, where Donaldson points out that if the realist were correct, then there would be no cooperation among nations; but since there is cooperation, the realist must be wrong), his points leave untouched the arguments I discuss below which acknowledge that while much cooperation among nations is possible, nevertheless certain crucial forms of cooperation will not obtain among multinationals with respect to the global common good.

4. J. Bentham, *Principles of Morals and Legislation*, 1.4–5.

5. William A.Wallace, O.P., *The Elements of Philosophy, A Compendium for Philosophers and Theologians* (New York: Alba House, 1977), p. 166–67.

6. *Ibid*, p. 167.

7. "Common Good," *The New Catholic Encyclopedia*.

8. John Rawls, *A Theory of Justice* (Cambridge, MA: Harvard University Press, 1971), p. 233 and 246.

9. Thomas Hobbes, *Leviathan, Parts I and II*, [1651] (New York: The Bobbs-Merrill Company, Inc., 1958), p. 108.

10. *Ibid*. As noted earlier, I am simply assuming what I take to be the popular interpretation of Hobbes' view on the state of nature. As Professor Philip Kain has pointed out to me, there is some controversy among Hobbes scholars about whether or not Hobbes actually held that moral obligation exists in the state of nature. Among those who hold that moral obligation does not exist in Hobbes' state of nature is M. Oakeshott in "The Moral Life in the Writings of Thomas Hobbes" in his *Hobbes on Civil Association* (Berkeley-Los Angeles: University of California Press, 1975), pp. 95–113; among those who hold that moral obligation does exist in Hobbes' state of nature is A. E.Taylor in "The Ethical Doctrine of Hobbes" in *Hobbes Studies*, ed. K. C. Brown (Cambridge: Harvard, 1965), pp. 41ff. Kain suggests that Hobbes simply contradicts himself–holding in some passages that moral obligation does exist in the state of nature and holding in others that it does not–because of his need to use the concept of the state of nature to achieve purposes that required incompatible conceptions of the state of nature; see his "Hobbes, Revolution and the Philosophy of History," in Hobbes's '*Science of Natural Justice*,' ed. C.Walton and P.J. Johnson (Boston: Martinus Nijhoff Publishers, 1987), pp. 203–13. In the present essay I am simply assuming without argument the traditional view that Hobbes made the claim that moral obligation does not exist in the state of nature; my aim is to pursue certain implications of this claim even if I am wrong in assuming that is Hobbes'.

11. See *ibid.*, where Hobbes writes that "yet in all times kings and persons of sovereign authority, because of their independency" are in this state of war.

12. *Ibid*, pp. 107–8.

13 See Amartya K. Sen, *Collective Choice and Social Welfare* (San Francisco: Holden-Day, Inc. 1970), pp. 2–5.

14. See, for example, Gregory Kavka,"Hobbes' War of All Against All," *Ethics*, 93 (January, 1983), pp. 291–310; a somewhat different approach is that of David Gauthier, *Morals By Agreement* (Oxford: Clarendon Press, 1986) and Russell Hardin, *Morality Within the Limits of Reason* (Chicago: University of Chicago Press, 1988).

15. See Robert Axelrod, *The Evolution of Cooperation* (New York: Basic Books, Inc, 1984), pp. 27–69.

16. Robert Frank, *Passions With Reason* (New York: W. W. Norton & Company, 1988).

32

The Great Non-Debate Over International Sweatshops

Ian Maitland

I n recent years, there has been a dramatic growth in the contracting out of production by companies in the industrialized countries to suppliers in developing countries. This globalization of production has led to an emerging international division of labor in footwear and apparel in which companies like Nike and Reebok concentrate on product design and marketing but rely on a network of contractors in Indonesia, China, Central America, etc., to build shoes or sew shirts according to exact specifications and deliver a high quality good according to precise delivery schedules. As Nike's vice president for Asia has put it, "We don't know the first thing about manufacturing. We are marketers and designers."

The contracting arrangements have drawn intense fire from critics–usually labor and human rights activists. These "critics" (as I will refer to them) have charged that the companies are (by proxy) exploiting workers in the plants (which I will call "international sweatshops") of their suppliers. Specifically the companies stand accused of chasing cheap labor around the globe, failing to pay their workers living wages, using child labor, turning a blind eye to abuses of human rights, being complicit with repressive regimes in denying workers the right to join unions and failing to enforce minimum labor standards in the workplace, and so on.

The campaign against international sweatshops has largely unfolded on television and, to a lesser extent, in the print media. What seems like no more than a handful of critics has mounted an aggressive, media-savvy campaign which has put the publicity-shy retail giants on the defensive. The critics have orchestrated a series of sensational "disclosures" on prime time television exposing the terrible pay and working conditions in factories making jeans for Levi's or sneakers for Nike or Pocahontas shirts for Disney. One of the principal scourges of the companies has been Charles Kernaghan who runs

Source: *British Academy of Management Annual Conference Proceedings* (September, 1997), 240–65.

the National Labor Coalition (NLC), a labor human rights group involving 25 unions. It was Kernaghan who, in 1996, broke the news before a Congressional committee that Kathie Lee Gifford's clothing line was being made by 13- and 15-year-olds working 20-hour days in factories in Honduras. Kernaghan also arranged for teenage workers from sweatshops in Central America to testify before Congressional committees about abusive labor practices. At one of these hearings, one of the workers held up a Liz Claiborne cotton sweater identical to ones she had sewn since she was a 13-year-old working 12 hours days. According to a news report, "[t]his image, accusations of oppressive conditions at the factory and the Claiborne logo played well on that evening's network news." The result has been a circus-like atmosphere – as in Roman circus where Christians were thrown to lions.

Kernaghan has shrewdly targeted the companies' carefully cultivated public images. He has explained: "Their image is everything. They live and die by their image. That gives you a certain power over them." As a result, he says, "these companies are sitting ducks. They have no leg to stand on. That's why it's possible for a tiny group like us to take on a giant like Wal-Mart. You can't defend paying someone 31 cents an hour in Honduras..." Apparently most of the companies agree with Kernaghan. Not a single company has tried to mount a serious defense of its contracting practices. They have judged that they cannot win a war of soundbites with the critics. Instead of making a fight of it, the companies have sued for peace in order to protect their principal asset – their image.

Major U.S. retailers have responded by adopting codes of conduct on human and labor rights in their international operations. Levi-Strauss, Nike, Sears, JCPenney, WalMart, Home Depot, and Philips Van-Heusen now have such codes. As Lance Compa notes, such codes are the result of a blend of humanitarian and pragmatic impulses: "Often the altruistic motive coincides with "bottom line" considerations related to brand name, company image, and other intangibles that make for core value to the firm."[2] Peter Jacobi, President of Global Sourcing for Levi-Strauss has advised: "If your company owns a popular brand, protect this priceless asset at all costs. Highly visible companies have any number of reasons to conduct their business not just responsibly but also in ways that cannot be portrayed as unfair, illegal, or unethical. This sets an extremely high standard since it must be applied to both company-owned businesses and contractors...."[3] And according to another Levi-Strauss spokesman, "In many respects, we're protecting our single largest asset: our brand image and corporate reputation."[4] Nike recently published the results of a generally favorable review of its international operations conducted by former American U.N. Ambassador Andrew Young.

Recently a truce of sorts between the critics and the companies was announced on the White House lawn with President Clinton and Kathie Lee Gifford in attendance. A presidential task force, including representatives of labor unions, human rights groups and apparel companies like L.L. Bean and Nike, has come up with a set of voluntary standards which, it hopes, will be embraced by the entire industry. Companies that comply with the code will be entitled to use a "No Sweat" label.

Objective of This Paper

In this confrontation between the companies and their critics, neither side seems to have judged it to be in its interest to seriously engage the issue at the heart of this controversy, namely: What are appropriate wages and labor standards in international sweatshops? As we have seen, the companies have treated the charges about sweatshops as a public relations problem to be managed so as to minimize harm to their public images. The critics have apparently judged that the best way to keep public indignation at boiling point is to oversimplify the issue and treat it as a morality play featuring heartless exploiters and victimized third world workers. The result has been a great non-debate over international sweatshops. Paradoxically, if peace breaks out between the two sides, the chances that the debate will be seriously joined may recede still further. Indeed, there exists a real risk (I will argue) that any such truce may be a collusive one that will come at the expense of the very third world workers it is supposed to help.

This paper takes up the issue of what are appropriate wages and labor standards in international sweatshops. Critics charge that the present arrangements are exploitative. I proceed by examining the specific charges of exploitation from the standpoints of both (a) their factual and (b) their ethical sufficiency. However, in the absence of any well-established consensus among business ethicists (or other thoughtful observers), I simultaneously use the investigation of sweatshops as a setting for trying to adjudicate between competing views about what those standards should be. My examination will pay particular attention to (but will not be limited to) labor conditions at the plants of Nike's suppliers in Indonesia. I have not personally visited any international sweatshops, and so my conclusions are based entirely on secondary analysis of the voluminous published record on the topic.

What are Ethically Appropriate Labor Standards in International Sweatshops?

What are ethically acceptable or appropriate levels of wages and labor standards in international sweatshops? The following four possibilities just about run the gamut of standards or principles that have been seriously proposed to regulate such policies.

(1) *Home-country standards:* it might be argued (and in rare cases has been) that international corporations have an ethical duty to pay the same wages and provide the same labor standards regardless of where they operate. However, the view that home-country standards should apply in host-countries is rejected by most business ethicists and (officially at least) by the critics of international sweatshops. Thus Thomas Donaldson argues that "[b]y arbitrarily establishing U.S. wage levels as the benchmark for fairness one eliminates the role of the international market in establishing salary levels, and this in turn eliminates the incentive U.S. corporations have to

hire foreign workers."[5] Richard DeGeorge makes much the same argument: If there were a rule that said that "that American MNCs [multinational corporations] that wish to be ethical must pay the same wages abroad as they do at home,...[then] MNCs would have little incentive to move their manufacturing abroad; and if they did move abroad they would disrupt the local labor market with artificially high wages that bore no relation to the local standard or cost of living."[6]

2. *Living wage standard:* it has been proposed that an international corporation should, at a minimum, pay a "living wage." Thus DeGeorge says that corporations should pay a living wage "even when this is not paid by local firms."[7] However, it is hard to pin down what this means operationally. According to DeGeorge, a living wage should "allow the worker to live in dignity as a human being." In order to respect the human rights of its workers, he says, a corporation must pay "at least subsistence wages and as much above that as workers and their dependents need to live with reasonable dignity, given the general state of development of the society."[8] As we shall see, the living wage standard has become a rallying cry of the critics of international sweatshops. Apparently, DeGeorge believes that it is preferable for a corporation to provide no job at all than to offer one that pays less than a living wage....

3. *Classical liberal standard:* Finally, there is what I will call the classical liberal standard. According to this standard a practice (wage or labor practice) is ethically acceptable if it is freely chosen by informed workers. For example, in a recent report the World Bank invoked this standard in connection with workplace safety. It said: "The appropriate level is therefore that at which the costs are commensurate with the value that informed workers place on improved working conditions and reduced risk."[9] Most business ethicists reject this standard on the grounds that there is some sort of market failure or the "background conditions" are lacking for markets to work effectively. Thus for Donaldson full (or near-full) employment is a prerequisite if workers are to make sound choices regarding workplace safety: "The average level of unemployment in the developing countries today exceeds 40 percent, a figure that has frustrated the application of neoclassical economic principles to the international economy on a score of issues. With full employment, and all other things being equal, market forces will encourage workers to make trade-offs between job opportunities using safety as a variable. But with massive unemployment, market forces in developing countries drive the unemployed to the jobs they are lucky enough to land, regardless of the safety."[10] Apparently there are other forces, like Islamic fundamentalism and the global debt "bomb," that rule out reliance on market solutions, but Donaldson does not explain their relevance.[11] DeGeorge, too, believes that the necessary conditions are lacking for market forces to operate benignly. Without what he calls "background institutions to protect the workers and the resources of the developing country (e.g., enforceable minimum wages) and/or greater equality of bargaining power exploitation is the most likely result.[12] If

American MNCs pay workers very low wages...they clearly have the opportunity to make significant profits."[13] DeGeorge goes on to make the interesting observation that competition has developed among multi-nationals themselves, so that the profit margin has been driven down" and developing countries "can play one company against another."[14] But apparently that is not enough to rehabilitate market forces in his eyes.

The Case Against International Sweatshops

To many of their critics, international sweatshops exemplify the way in which the greater openness of the world economy is hurting workers.... Globalization means a transition from (more or less) regulated domestic economies to an unregulated world economy. The superior mobility of capital, and the essentially fixed, immobile nature of world labor, means a fundamental shift in bargaining power in favor of large international corporations. Their global reach permits them to shift production almost costlessly from one location to another. As a consequence, instead of being able to exercise some degree of control over companies operating within their borders, governments are now locked in a bidding war with one another to attract and retain the business of large multinational companies.

The critics allege that international companies are using the threat of withdrawal or withholding of investment to pressure governments and workers to grant concessions. "Today [multinational companies] choose between workers in developing countries that compete against each other to depress wages to attract foreign investment." The result is a race for the bottom–"a destructive downward bidding spiral of the labor conditions and wages of workers throughout the world..."[15] ...Thus, critics charge that in Indonesia wages are deliberately held below the poverty level or subsistence in order to make the country a desirable location. The results of this competitive dismantling of worker protections, living standards and worker rights are predictable: deteriorating work conditions, declining real incomes for workers, and a widening gap between rich and poor in developing countries. I turn next to the specific charges made by the critics of international sweatshops.

Unconscionable wages

Critics charge that the companies, by their proxies, are paying "starvation wages" and "slave wages." They are far from clear about what wage level they consider to be appropriate. But they generally demand that companies pay a "living wage." Kernaghan has said that workers should be paid enough to support their families and they should get a "living wage" and "be treated like human beings."[16] ...According to Tim Smith, wage levels should be "fair, decent or a living wage for an employee and his or her family." He has said that wages in the maquiladoras of Mexico averaged $35 to $55 a week (in or near 1993) which he calls a "shockingly substandard wage," apparently on the grounds that it "clearly does not allow an employee to feed and care for a

family adequately."[17] In 1992, Nike came in for harsh criticism when a
magazine published the pay stub of a worker at one of its Indonesian suppliers.
It showed that the worker was paid at the rage of $1.03 per day which was
reportedly less than the Indonesian government's figure for "minimum
physical need."[18]

Immiserization thesis

Former Labor Secretary Robert Reich has proposed as a test of the fairness of
development policies that "Low-wage workers should become better off, not
worse off, as trade and investment boost national income." He has written that
"[i]f a country pursues policies that...limit to a narrow elite the benefits of trade,
the promise of open commerce is perverted and drained of its rationale."[19] A
key claim of the activists is that companies actually impoverish or immiserize
developing country workers. They experience an absolute decline in living
standards. This thesis follows from the claim that the bidding war among
developing countries is depressing wages....

Widening gap between rich and poor

A related charge is that international sweatshops are contributing to the
increasing gap between rich and poor. Not only are the poor being absolutely
impoverished, but trade is generating greater inequality within developing
countries. Another test that Reich has proposed to establish the fairness of
international trade is that "the gap between rich and poor should tend to
narrow with development, not widen."[20] Critics charge that international
sweatshops flunk that test. They say that the increasing GNPs of some
developing countries simply mask a widening gap between rich and poor.
"Across the world, both local and foreign elites are getting richer from the
exploitation of the most vulnerable."[21] And, "The major adverse consequence
of quickening global economic integration has been widening income
disparity within almost all nations...[22] There appears to be a tacit alliance
between the elites of both first and third worlds to exploit the most vulnerable,
to regiment and control and conscript them so that they can create the material
conditions for the elites' extravagant lifestyles.

Collusion with repressive regimes

Critics charge that, in their zeal to make their countries safe for foreign
investment, Third World regimes, notably China and Indonesia, have stepped
up their repression. Not only have these countries failed to enforce even the
minimal labor rules on the books, but they have also used their military and
police to break strikes and repress independent unions. They have stifled
political dissent, both to retain their hold on political power and to avoid any
instability that might scare off foreign investors. Consequently, critics charge,
companies like Nike are profiting from political repression. "As unions spread
in [Korea and Taiwan], Nike shifted its suppliers primarily to Indonesia, China

and Thailand, where they could depend on governments to suppress independent union-organizing efforts."[23]

Evaluation of the Charges Against International Sweatshops

The critics' charges are undoubtedly accurate on a number of points: (1) There is no doubt that international companies are chasing cheap labor. (2) The wages paid by the international sweatshops are – by American standards – shockingly low. (3) Some developing country governments have tightly controlled or repressed organized labor in order to prevent it from disturbing the flow of foreign investment. Thus, in Indonesia, independent unions have been suppressed. (4) It is not unusual in developing countries for minimum wage levels to be lower than the official poverty level. (5) Developing country governments have winked at violations of minimum wage laws and labor rules. However, most jobs are in the informal sector and so largely outside the scope of government supervision. (6) Some suppliers have employed children or have subcontracted work to other producers who have done so. (7) Some developing country governments deny their people basic political rights. China is the obvious example; Indonesia's record is pretty horrible but had shown steady improvement until the last two years. But on many of the other counts, the critics' charges appear to be seriously inaccurate. And, even where the charges are accurate, it is not self-evident that the practices in question are improper or unethical, as we see next.

Wages and conditions

Even the critics of international sweatshops do not dispute that the wages they pay are generally higher than – or at least equal to – comparable wages in the labor markets where they operate. According to the international Labor Organization (ILO), "multinational companies often apply standards relating to wages, benefits, conditions of work, and occupational safety and health, which both exceed statutory requirements and those practiced by local firms."[24] The ILO also says that wages and working conditions in so-called Export Processing Zones (EPZs) are often equal to or higher than jobs outside. The World Bank says that the poorest workers in developing countries work in the informal sector where they often earn less than half what a formal sector employee earns. Moreover, "informal and rural workers often must work under more hazardous and insecure conditions than their formal sector counterparts."[25]

The same appears to hold true for the international sweatshops. In 1996, young women working in the plant of a Nike supplier in Serang, Indonesia were earning the Indonesian legal minimum wage of 5,200 rupiahs or about $2.28 each day. As a report in the *Washington Post* pointed out, just earning the minimum wage put these workers among higher-paid Indonesians: "In Indonesia, less than half the working population earns the minimum wage, since about half of all adults here are in farming, and the typical farmer would make only about 2,000 rupiahs each day."[26] The workers in the Serang plant reported that they save about three-quarters of their pay. A 17-year-old woman said: "I came here one year ago from central Java. I'm making more money than my father makes." This woman also said that she sent about 75 percent of her earnings back to her family on the farm.[27] Also in 1996, a Nike spokeswoman estimated that an entry-level factory worker in the plant of a Nike supplier made five times what a farmer makes.[28] Nike's chairman, Phil Knight, likes to teasingly remind critics that the average worker in one of Nike's Chinese factories is paid more than a professor at Beijing University.[29] There is also plentiful anecdotal evidence from non-Nike sources. A worker at the Taiwanese-owned King Star Garment Assembly plant in Honduras told a reporter that he was earning seven times what he earned in the countryside.[30] In Bangladesh, the country's fledgling garment industry was paying women who had never worked before between $40 and $55 a month in 1991. That compared with a national per capita income of about $200 and the approximately $1 a day earned by many of these women's husbands as day laborers or rickshaw drivers.[31]

The same news reports also shed some light on the working conditions in sweatshops. According to the *Washington Post*, in 1994 the Indonesian office of the international accounting firm Ernst & Young surveyed Nike workers concerning worker pay, safety conditions and attitudes toward the job. The auditors pulled workers off the assembly line at random and asked them questions that the workers answered anonymously. The survey of 25 workers at Nike's Serang plant found that 23 thought the hours and overtime worked were fair, and two thought the overtime hours too high. None of the workers reported that they had been discriminated against. Thirteen said the working environment was the key reason they worked at the Serang plant while eight cited salary and benefits.[32] The *Post* report also noted that the Serang plant closes for about ten days each year for Muslim holidays. It quoted Nike officials and the plant's Taiwanese owners as saying that 94 percent of the workers had returned to the plant following the most recent break....

There is also the mute testimony of the lines of job applicants outside the sweatshops in Guatemala and Honduras. According to Lucy Martinez-Mont, in Guatemala the sweatshops are conspicuous for the long lines of young people waiting to be interviewed for a job.[33] Outside the gates of the industrial park in Honduras that Rohter visited "anxious onlookers are always waiting, hoping for a chance at least to fill out a job application [for employment at one of the apparel plants]."[34]

The critics of sweatshops acknowledge that workers have voluntarily taken their jobs, consider themselves lucky to have them, and want to keep them.... But they go on to discount the workers' views as the product of confusion or ignorance, and/or they just argue that the workers' views are beside the point. Thus, while "it is undoubtedly true" that Nike has given jobs to thousands of people who wouldn't be working otherwise, they say that "neatly skirts the fundamental human-rights issue raised by these production arrangements that are now spreading all across the world."[35] Similarly the NLC's Kernaghan says that "[w]hether workers think they are better off in the assembly plants than elsewhere is not the real issue."[36] Kernaghan, and Jeff Ballinger of the AFL-CIO, concede that the workers desperately need these jobs. But "[t]hey say they're not asking that U.S. companies stop operating in these countries. They're asking that workers be paid a living wage and treated like human beings."[37] Apparently these workers are victims of what Marx called false consciousness, or else they would grasp that they are being exploited. According to Barnet and Cavanagh, "For many workers ... exploitation is not a concept easily comprehended because the alternative prospects for earning a living are so bleak."[38]

Immiserization and inequality

The critics' claim that the countries that host international sweatshops are marked by growing poverty and inequality is flatly contradicted by the record. In fact, many of those countries have experienced sharp increases in living standards – for all strata of society. In trying to attract investment in simple manufacturing, Malaysia and Indonesia and, now, Vietnam and China, are retracing the industrialization path already successfully taken by East Asian countries like Taiwan, Korea, Singapore and Hong Kong. These four countries got their start by producing labor-intensive manufactured goods (often electrical and electronic components, shoes, and garments) for export markets. Over time they graduated to the export of higher value-added items that are skill-intensive and require a relatively developed industrial base.[39]

As is well known, these East Asian countries achieved growth rates exceeding eight percent for a quarter century.... The workers in these economies were not impoverished by growth. The benefits of growth were widely diffused: These economies achieved essentially full employment in the 1960s. Real wages rose by as much as a factor of four. Absolute poverty fell. And income inequality remained at low to moderate levels. It is true that in the initial stages the rapid growth generated only moderate increases in wages. But once essentially full employment was reached, and what economists call the Fei-Ranis turning point was reached, the increased demand for labor resulted in the bidding up of wages as firms competed for a scarce labor supply.

Interestingly, given its historic mission as a watchdog for international labor standards, the ILO has embraced this development model. It recently noted that the most successful developing economies, in terms of output and employment growth, have been "those who best exploited emerging opportunities in the global economy."[40] An "export-oriented policy is vital in countries that are starting on the industrialization path and have large surpluses of cheap labour." Countries which have succeeded in attracting foreign direct investment (FDI) have experienced rapid growth in manufacturing output and exports. The successful attraction of foreign investment in plant and equipment "can be a powerful spur to rapid industrialization and employment creation." "At low levels of industrialization, FDI in garments and shoes and some types of consumer electronics can be very useful for creating employment and opening the economy to international markets; there may be some entrepreneurial skills created in simple activities like garments (as has happened in Bangladesh). Moreover, in some cases, such as Malaysia, the investors may strike deeper roots and invest in more capital-intensive technologies as wages rise."

According to the World Bank, the rapidly growing Asian economies (including Indonesia) "have also been unusually successful at sharing the fruits of their growth."[41] In fact, while inequality in the West has been growing, it has been shrinking in the Asian economies. They are the only economies in the world to have experienced high growth and declining inequality, and they also show shrinking gender gaps in education....

Profiting from repression?

What about the charge that international sweatshops are profiting from repression? It is undeniable that there is repression in many of the countries where sweatshops are located. But economic development appears to be relaxing that repression rather than strengthening its grip. The companies are supposed to benefit from government policies (e.g., repression of unions) that hold down labor costs. However, as we have seen, the wages paid by the international sweatshops already match or exceed the prevailing local wages. Not only that, but incomes in the East Asian economies, and in Indonesia, have risen rapidly....

The critics, however, are right in saying that the Indonesian government has opposed independent unions in the sweatshops out of fear they would lead to higher wages and labor unrest. But the government's fear clearly is that unions might drive wages in the modern industrial sector above market-clearing levels – or, more exactly, further above market. It is ironic that critics like Barnet and Cavanagh would use the Marxian term "reserve army of the unemployed." According to Marx, capitalists deliberately maintain high levels of unemployment in order to control the working class. But the Indonesian government's policies (e.g., suppression of unions, resistance to a higher minimum wage and lax enforcement of labor rules) have been directed at achieving exactly the opposite result. The government appears to have calculated that high unemployment is a greater threat to its hold on power. I think we can safely take at face value its claims that its policies are genuinely intended to help the economy create jobs to absorb the massive numbers of unemployed and underemployed.[42]

Labor Standards in International Sweatshops: Painful Trade-Offs

Who but the grinch could grudge paying a few additional pennies to some of the world's poorest workers? There is no doubt that the rhetorical force of the critics' case against international sweatshops rests on this apparently self-evident proposition. However, higher wages and improved labor standards are not free. After all, the critics themselves attack companies for chasing cheap labor. It follows that, if labor in developing countries is made more expensive (say, as the result of pressure by the critics), then those countries will receive less foreign investment, and fewer jobs will be created there. Imposing higher wages may deprive these countries of the one comparative advantage they enjoy, namely low-cost labor.

We have seen that workers in most "international sweatshops" are already relatively well paid. Workers in the urban, formal sectors of developing countries commonly earn more than twice what informal and rural workers get. Simply earning the minimum wage put the young women making Nike shoes in Serang in the top half of the income distribution in Indonesia. Accordingly, the critics are in effect calling for a widening of the economic disparity that already greatly favors sweatshop workers.

By itself that may or may not be ethically objectionable. But these higher wages come at the expense of the incomes and the job opportunities of much poorer workers. As economists explain, higher wages in the formal sector reduce employment there and (by increasing the supply of labor) depress incomes in the informal sector. The case against requiring above-market wages for international sweatshop workers is essentially the same as the case against other measures that artificially raise labor costs, like the minimum wage. In Jagdish Bhagwati's words: "Requiring a minimum wage in an overpopulated, developing country, as is done in a developed country, may actually be morally wicked. A minimum wage might help the unionized, industrial proletariat, while limiting the ability to save and invest rapidly which is necessary to draw more of the unemployed and nonunionized rural poor into gainful employment and income."[43] The World Bank makes the same point: "Minimum wages may help the most poverty-stricken workers in industrial countries, but they clearly do not in developing nations.... The workers whom minimum wage legislation tries to protect – urban formal workers – already earn much more than the less favored majority.... And inasmuch as minimum wage and other regulations discourage formal employment by increasing wage and nonwage costs, they hurt the poor who aspire to formal employment."[44]

The story is no different when it comes to labor standards other than wages. If standards are set too high they will hurt investment and employment. The World Bank report points out that "[r]educing hazards in the workplace is costly, and typically the greater the reduction the more it costs. Moreover, the costs of compliance often fall largely on employees through lower wages or reduced employment. As a result, setting standards too high can actually lower workers' welfare...."[45] Perversely, if the higher standards advocated by critics retard the growth of formal sector jobs, then that will trap more informal and rural workers in jobs which are far more hazardous and insecure than those of their formal sector counterparts.

The critics consistently advocate policies that will benefit better-off workers at the expense of worse-off ones. If it were within their power, it appears that they would reinvent the labor markets of much of Latin America. Alejandro Portes' description seems to be on the mark: "In Mexico, Brazil, Peru, and other Third World countries, [unlike East Asia], there are powerful independent unions representing the protected sector of the working class. Although there rhetoric is populist and even radical, the fact is that they tend to represent the better-paid and more stable fraction of the working class. Alongside, there toils a vast, unprotected proletariat, employed by informal enterprises and linked, in ways hidden from public view, with modern sector firms."...

Of course, it might be objected that trading off workers' rights for more jobs is unethical. But, so far as I can determine, the critics have not made this argument. Although they sometimes implicitly accept the existence of the trade-off (we saw that they attack Nike for chasing cheap labor), their public statements are silent on the lost or forgone jobs from higher wages and better labor standards. At other times, they imply or claim that improvements in workers' wages and conditions are essentially free....

In summary, the result of the ostensibly humanitarian changes urged by critics are likely to be (1) reduced employment in the formal or modern sector of the economy, (2) lower incomes in the informal sector, (3) less investment and so slower economic growth, (4) reduced exports, (5) greater inequality and poverty.

Conclusion: The Case for Not Exceeding Market Standards

It is part of the job description of business ethicists to exhort companies to treat their workers better (otherwise what purpose do they serve?). So it will have come as no surprise that both the business ethicists whose views I summarized at the beginning of this paper – Thomas Donaldson and Richard DeGeorge – objected to letting the market alone determine wages and labor standards in multinational companies. Both of them proposed criteria for setting wages that might occasionally "improve" on the outcomes of the market.

Their reasons for rejecting market determination of wages were similar. They both cited conditions that allegedly prevent international markets from generating ethically acceptable results. Donaldson argued that neoclassical economic principles are not applicable to international business because of high unemployment rates in developing countries. And DeGeorge argued that, in an unregulated international market, the gross inequality of bargaining power between workers and companies would lead to exploitation.

But this paper has shown that attempts to improve on market outcomes may have unforeseen tragic consequences. We saw how raising the wages of workers in international sweatshops might wind up penalizing the most vulnerable workers (those in the informal sectors of developing countries) by depressing their wages and reducing their job opportunities in the formal sector. Donaldson and DeGeorge cited high unemployment and unequal bargaining power as conditions that made it necessary to bypass or override the market determination of wages. However, in both cases, bypassing the market in order to prevent exploitation may aggravate these conditions. As we have seen, above-market wages paid to sweatshop workers may discourage further investment and so perpetuate high unemployment. In turn, the higher unemployment may weaken the bargaining power of workers vis-à-vis employers. Thus such market imperfections seem to call for more reliance on market forces rather than less. Likewise, the experience of the newly industrialized East Asian economies suggests that the best cure for the ills of sweatshops is more sweatshops. But most of the well-intentioned policies that improve on market outcomes are likely to have the opposite effect.

Where does this leave the international manager? If the preceding analysis is correct, then it follows that it is ethically acceptable to pay market wage rates in developing countries (and to provide employment conditions appropriate for the level of development). That holds true even if the wages pay less than so-called living wages or subsistence or even (conceivably) the local minimum wage. The appropriate test is not whether the wage reaches some predetermined standard but whether it is freely accepted by (reasonably) informed workers. The workers themselves are in the best position to judge whether the wages offered are superior to their next-best alternatives. (The same logic applies *mutates mutandis* to workplace labor standards).

Indeed, not only is it ethically acceptable for a company to pay market wages, but it may be ethically unacceptable for it to pay wages that exceed market levels. That will be the case if the company's above-market wages set precedents for other international companies which raise labor costs to the point of discouraging foreign investment. Furthermore, companies may have a social responsibility to transcend their own narrow preoccupation with protecting their brand image and to publicly defend a system which has greatly improved the lot of millions of workers in developing countries.

Notes

1. Steven Greenhouse, "A Crusader Makes Celebrities Tremble." *New York Times* (June 18, 1996), p. B4.

2. Lance A. Compa and Tashia Hinchliffe Darricarrere, "Enforcement Through Corporate Codes of Conduct," in Compa and Stephen F. Diamond, *Human Rights, Labor Rights, and International Trade* (Philadelphia University of Pennsylvania Press, 1996) p. 193.

3. Peter Jacobi in Martha Nichols, "Third-World Families at Work: Child Labor or Child Care." *Harvard Business Review* (Jan.–Feb., 1993).

4. David Sampson in Robin C. Givhan, "A Stain on Fashion; The Garment Industry Profits from Cheap Labor." *Washington Post* (September 12, 1995), p. B1.

5. Thomas Donaldson, *Ethics of International Business*, (New York: Oxford University Press, 1989), p. 98.

6. Richard DeGeorge, *Competing with Integrity in International Business* (New York: Oxford University Press. 1993) p. 79.

7. Ibid., pp. 356–7.

8. Ibid., p. 78.

9. World Bank, *World Development Report 1995*, *"Workers in an Integrating World Economy"* (Oxford University Press, 1995) p. 77.

10. Donaldson, *Ethics of International Business*, p. 115.

11. *Ibid.*, p. 150.

12. DeGeorge, *Competing with Integrity,* p. 48.

13. *Ibid.*, p. 358.

14. *Ibid.*

15. Terry Collingsworth, J. William Goold, Pharis J. Harvey, "Time for a Global New Deal," *Foreign Affairs* (Jan–Feb, 1994), p. 8.

16. William B. Falk, "Dirty Little Secrets," Newsday (June 16, 1996).

17. Tim Smith, "The Power of Business for Human Rights." *Business & Society Review* (January 1994), p. 36.

18. Jeffrey Ballinger, "The New Free Trade Heel." *Harper's Magazine* (August, 1992), pp. 46–7 "As in many developing countries, Indonesia's minimum wage, ..., is less than poverty level." Nina Baker, "The Hidden Hands of Nike," *Oregonian* (August 9, 1992).

19. Robert B. Reich, "Escape from the Global Sweatshop, Capitalism's Stake in Uniting the Workers of the World." *Washington Post* (May 22, 1994). Reich's test is intended to apply in developing countries "where democratic institutions are weak or absent."

20. *Ibid.*

21. Kenneth P. Hutchinson, "Third World Growth." *Harvard Business Review* (Nov.–Dec., 1994).

22. Robin Broad and John Cavanagh, "Don't Neglect the Impoverished South." Foreign Affairs (December 22, 1995).

23. John Cavanagh & Robin Broad, "Global Reach; Workers Fight the Multi-nationals." *The Nation,* (March 18, 1996), p. 21. See also Bob Herbert, "Nike's Bad Neighborhood." *New York Times* (June 14, 1996).

24. International Labor Organization, *World Employment 1995* (Geneva: ILO, 1995) p. 73.

25. World Bank, *Workers in an Integrating World Economy,* p. 5.

26. Keith B. Richburg, Anne Swardson, "U.S. Industry Overseas: Sweatshop or Job Source?: Indonesians Praise Work at Nike Factory." *Washington Post* (July 28, 1996).

27. Richburg and Swardson, "Sweatshop or Job Source?" The 17 year-old was interviewed in the presence of managers. For other reports that workers remit home large parts of their earnings see Seth Mydans, "Tangerang Journal; For Indonesian Workers at Nike Plant: Just Do It." *New York Times* (August 9, 1996), and Nina Baker, "The Hidden Hands of Nike."

28. Donna Gibbs, Nike spokeswoman on ABC's *World News Tonight,* June 6, 1996.

29. Mark Clifford, "Trading in Social Issues; Labor Policy and International Trade Regulation," *World Press Review* (June 1994), p. 36.

30. Larry Rohter, "To U.S. Critics, a Sweatshop; for Hondurans, a Better Life." *New York Times* (July 18, 1996).

31. Marcus Brauchli, "Garment Industry Booms in Bangladesh." *Wall Street Journal* (August 6, 1991)

32. Richburg and Swardson, "Sweatshop or Job Source?"

33. Lucy Martinez-Mont, "Sweatshops Are Better Than No Shops." *Wall Street Journal* (June 25, 1996).

34. Rohter, "To U.S. Critics a Sweatshop."

35. Barnet & Cavanagh, *Global Dreams,* p. 326.

36. Rohter, "To U.S. Critics a Sweatshop."

37. William B. Falk, "Dirty Little Secrets," *Newsday* (June 16, 1996).

38. Barnet and Cavanagh, "Just Undo it: Nike's Exploited Workers." *New York Times* (February 13, 1994).

39. Sarosh Kuruvilla, "Linkages Between Industrialization Strategies and Industrial Relations/Human Resources Policies: Singapore, Malaysia, The Philippines, and India." *Industrial & Labor Relations Review* (July, 1996), p. 637.

40. The ILO's Constitution (of 1919) mentions that: "... the failure of any nation to adopt humane conditions of labour is an obstacle in the way of other nations which desire to improve the conditions in their own countries." ILO, *World Employment 1995*, p. 74.

41. World Bank, *The East Asian Miracle* (New York Oxford University Press, 1993) p. 2.

42. Gideon Rachman, "Wealth in Its Grasp, a Survey of Indonesia." *Economist* (April 17, 1993), pp. 14–15.

43. Jagdish Bhagwati & Robert E. Hudec, eds. *Fair Trade and Harmonization* (Cambridge: MIT Press, 1996), vol. 1, p. 2.

44. World Bank, *Writers in an Integrating World Economy*, p. 75.

45. *Ibid.*, p. 77. As I have noted, the report proposes that the "appropriate level is therefore that at which the costs are commensurate with the value that informed workers place on improved working conditions and reduced risk...." (p. 77).

33

Should Trees Have Standing? Toward Legal Rights for Natural Objects

Christopher D. Stone

C hristopher Stone is professor of law at the University of Southern California, Los Angeles, and the author of several works in law and environmental ethics, including *Should Trees Have Standing?* from which the present selection is taken.

Stone argues that a strong case can be made for the "unthinkable idea" of extending legal rights to natural objects. Building on the models of inanimate objects, such as trusts, corporations, nation-states, and municipalities, he proposes that we extend the notion of legal guardian for legal incompetents to cover these natural objects. Note the three main ways that natural objects are denied rights under common law and how Stone's proposal addresses these considerations.

Introduction: The Unthinkable

In *Descent of Man,* Darwin observes that the history of man's moral development has been a continual extension in the objects of his "social instincts and sympathies." Originally each man had regard only for himself and those of a very narrow circle about him; later, he came to regard more and more "not only the welfare, but the happiness of all his fellow-men"; then "his sympathies became more tender and widely diffused, extending to men of all races, to the imbecile, maimed, and other useless members of society, and finally to the lower animals...."

The history of the law suggests a parallel development. Perhaps there never was a pure Hobbesian state of nature, in which no "rights" existed except in the vacant sense of each man's "right to self-defense." But it is not unlikely that so far as the earliest "families" (including extended kinship groups and clans)

Source: *Southern California Law Review* 45 (1972), 240–7.

were concerned, everyone outside the family was suspect, alien, rightless. And even within the family, persons we presently regard as the natural holders of at least some rights had none. Take, for example, children. We know something of the early rights-status of children from the widespread practice of infanticide—especially of the deformed and female. (Senicide, as among the North American Indians, was the corresponding rightlessness of the aged.) Maine tells us that as late as Patria Poteses of the Romans, the father had *jus vitae necisque*—the power of life and death—over his children. A fortiori, Maine writes, he had power of "uncontrolled corporal chastisement; he can modify their personal condition at pleasure; he can give a wife to his son; he can give his daughter in marriage; he can divorce his children of either sex; he can transfer them to another family by adoption; and he can sell them." The child was less than a person: an object, a thing.

The legal rights of children have long since been recognized in principle, and are still expanding in practice. Witness, just within recent time, *in re Gault*, guaranteeing basic constitutional protections to juvenile defendants, and the Voting Rights Act of 1970. We have been making persons of children although they were not in law, always so. And we have done the same, albeit imperfectly some would say, with prisoners, aliens, women (especially of the married variety), the insane, Blacks, foetuses, and Indians.

Nor is it only matter in human form that has come to be recognized as the possessor of rights. The world of the lawyer is peopled with inanimate right-holders: trusts, corporations, joint ventures, municipalities, Subchapter R partnerships, and nation-states, to mention just a few. Ships, still referred to by courts in the feminine gender, have long had an independent jural life, often with striking consequences. We have become so accustomed to the idea of a corporation having "its" own rights, and being a "person" and "citizen" for so many statutory and constitutional purposes, that we forget how jarring the notion was to early jurists. "That invisible, intangible and artificial being, that mere legal entity" Chief Justice Marshall wrote of the corporation in *Bank of the United States v. Deveaux*—could a suit be brought in *its* name? Ten years later, in the *Dartmouth College* case, he was still refusing to let pass unnoticed the wonder of an entity "existing only in contemplation of law." Yet, long before Marshall worried over the personifying of the modern corporation, the best medieval legal scholars had spent hundreds of years struggling with the notion of the legal nature of those great public "corporate bodies," the Church and the State. How could they exist in law, as entities transcending the living Pope and King? It was clear how a king could bind *himself*—on his honor—by a treaty. But when the king died, what was it that was burdened with the obligations of, and claimed the rights under, the treaty *his* tangible hand had signed? The medieval mind saw (what we have lost our capacity to see) how *unthinkable* it was, and worked out the most elaborate conceits and fallacies to serve as anthropomorphic flesh for the Universal Church and the Universal Empire.

It is this note of the *unthinkable* that I want to dwell upon for a moment. Throughout legal history, each successive extension of rights to some new entity has been, theretofore, a bit unthinkable. We are inclined to suppose the rightlessness of rightless "things" to be a decree of Nature, not a legal convention acting in support of some status quo. It is thus that we defer considering the choices involved in all their moral, social, and economic dimensions. And so the United States Supreme Court could straight-facedly tell us in *Dred Scott* that Blacks had been denied the rights of citizenship "as a subordinate and inferior class of beings, who had been subjugated by the dominant race...." In the nineteenth century, the highest court in California explained that Chinese had not the right to testify against white men in criminal matters because they were "a race of people whom nature has marked as inferior, and who are incapable of progress or intellectual development beyond a certain point...between whom and ourselves nature has placed an impassable difference." The popular conception of the Jew in the 13th Century contributed to a law which treated them as "men *ferae naturae*, protected by a quasi-forest law. Like the roe and the deer, they form an order apart." Recall, too, that it was not so long ago that the foetus was "like the roe and the deer." In an early suit attempting to establish a wrongful death action on behalf of a negligently killed foetus (now widely accepted practice), Holmes, then on the Massachusetts Supreme Court, seems to have thought it simply inconceivable "that a man might owe a civil duty and incur a conditional prospective liability in tort to one not yet in being." The first woman in Wisconsin who thought she might have a right to practice law was told that she did not, in the following terms:

> The law of nature destines and qualifies the female sex for the bearing and nurture of the children of our race and for the custody of the homes of the world.... [A]ll life-long callings of women, inconsistent with these radical and sacred duties of their sex, as the profession of the law, are departures from the order of nature; and when voluntary, treason against it.... The peculiar qualities of womanhood, its gentle graces, its quick sensibility, its tender susceptibility, its purity, its delicacy, its emotional impulses, its subordination of hard reason to sympathetic feeling, are surely not qualifications for forensic strife. Nature has tempered woman as little for the juridical conflicts of the court room, as for the physical conflicts of the battle field....

The fact is, that each time there is a movement to confer rights onto some new "entity," the proposal is bound to sound odd or frightening or laughable. This is partly because until the rightless thing receives its rights, we cannot see it as anything but a *thing* for the use of "us"—those who are holding rights at the time. In this vein, what is striking about the Wisconsin case above is that the court, for all its talk about women, so clearly was never able to see women as they are (and might become). All it could see was the popular "idealized" version of *an object it needed*. Such is the way the slave South looked upon the Black. There is something of a seamless web involved: there will be resistance to giving the thing "rights" until it can be seen and valued for itself; yet, it is hard to see it and value it for itself until we can bring ourselves to give it "rights"—which is almost inevitably going to sound inconceivable to a large group of people.

The reason for this little discourse on the unthinkable, the reader must know by now, if only from the title of the paper. I am quite seriously proposing that we give legal rights to forests, oceans, rivers and other so-called "natural objects" in the environment–indeed, to the natural environment as a whole.

As strange as such a notion may sound, it is neither fanciful nor devoid of operational content. In fact, I do not think it would be a misdescription of recent developments in the law to say that we are already on the verge of assigning some such rights, although we have not faced up to what we are doing in those particular terms. We should do so now, and begin to explore the implications such a notion would hold.

Toward Rights for the Environment

Now, to say that the natural environment should have rights is not to say anything as silly as that no one should be allowed to cut down a tree. We say human beings have rights, but–at least as of the time of this writing–they can be executed. Corporations have rights, but they cannot plead the fifth amendment; *In re Gault* gave 15-year-olds certain rights in juvenile proceedings, but it did not give them the right to vote. Thus, to say that the environment should have rights is not to say that it should have every right we can imagine, or even the same body of rights as human beings have. Nor is it to say that everything in the environment should have the same rights as every other thing in the environment.

What the granting of rights does involve has two sides to it. The first involves what might be called the legal-operational aspects; the second, the psychic and socio-psychic aspects. I shall deal with these aspects in turn.

The Legal-Operational Aspects

What it means to be a holder of legal rights

There is, so far as I know, no generally accepted standard for how one ought to use the term "legal rights." Let me indicate how I shall be using it in this piece.

First and most obviously, if the term is to have any content at all, an entity cannot be said to hold a legal right unless and until *some public authoritative body* is prepared to give *some amount of review* to actions that are colorably inconsistent with that "right." For example, if a student can be expelled from a university and cannot get any public official, even a judge or administrative agent at the lowest level, either (i) to require the university to justify its actions (if only to the extent of filling out an affidavit alleging that the expulsion "was not wholly arbitrary and capricious") or (ii) to compel the university to accord the student some procedural safeguards (a hearing, right to counsel, right to have notice of charges), then the minimum requirements for saying that the student has a legal right to his education do not exist.

But for a thing to be a *holder of legal rights*, something more is needed than that some authoritative body will review the actions and processes of those who threaten it. As I shall use the term, "holder of legal rights," each of three additional criteria must be satisfied. All three, one will observe, go towards making a thing *count* jurally–to have a legally recognized worth and dignity in its own right, and not merely to serve as a means to benefit "us" (whoever the contemporary group of rights-holders may be). They are, first, that the thing can institute legal actions *at its behest*; second, that in determining the granting of legal relief, the court must take injury to it into account; and, third, that relief must run to the *benefit of it*....

The rightlessness of natural objects at common law

Consider, for example, the common law's posture toward the pollution of a stream. True, courts have always been able, in some circumstances, to issue orders that will stop the pollution.... But the stream itself is fundamentally rightless, with implications that deserve careful reconsideration.

The first sense in which the stream is not a rightsholder has to do with standing. The stream itself has none. So far as the common law is concerned, there is in general no way to challenge the polluter's actions save at the behest of a lower *riparian**–another human being–able to show an invasion of *his* rights. This conception of the riparian as the holder of the right to bring suit has more than theoretical interest. The lower riparians may simply not care about the pollution. They themselves may be polluting, and not wish to stir up legal waters. They may be economically dependent on their polluting neighbor. And, of course, when they discount the value of winning by the costs of bringing suit and the chances of success, the action may not seem worth undertaking. Consider, for example, that while the polluter might be injuring 100 downstream riparians $10,000 a year *in the aggregate*, each riparian separately might be suffering injury only to the extent of $100–possibly not enough for any one of them to want to press suit by himself, or even to go to the trouble and cost of securing co-plaintiffs to make it worth everyone's while. This hesitance will be especially likely when the potential plaintiffs consider the burdens the law puts in their way: proving, *e.g.*, specific damages, the "unreasonableness" of defendant's use of the water, the fact that practicable means of abatement exist, and overcoming difficulties raised by issues such as joint causality, right to pollute by prescription, and so forth. Even in states which, like California, sought to overcome these difficulties by empowering the attorney-general to sue for abatement of pollution in limited instances, the power has been sparingly invoked and, when invoked, narrowly construed by the courts.

The second sense in which the common law denies "rights" to natural objects has to do with the way in which the merits are decided in those cases in which someone is competent and willing to establish standing. At its more primitive levels, the system protected the "rights" of the property owning human with minimal weighing of any values: "*Cujus est solum, ejus est usque ad coelum et ad infernos.*"† Today we have come more and more to make balances–

but only such as will adjust the economic best interests of identifiable humans. For example, continuing with the case of streams, there are commentators who speak of a "general rule" that "a riparian owner is legally entitled to have the stream flow by his land with its quality unimpaired" and observe that "an upper owner has, prima facie, no right to pollute the water." Such a doctrine, if strictly invoked, would protect the stream absolutely whenever a suit was brought; but obviously, to look around us, the law does not work that way. Almost everywhere there are doctrinal qualifications on riparian "rights" to an unpolluted stream. Although these rules vary from jurisdiction to jurisdiction, and upon whether one is suing for an equitable injunction or for damages, what they all have in common is some sort of balancing. Whether under language of "reasonable use," "reasonable methods of use," "balance of convenience" or "the public interest doctrine," what the courts are balancing, with varying degrees of directness, are the economic hardships on the upper riparian (or dependent community) of abating the pollution vis-à-vis the economic hardships of continued pollution on the lower riparians. What does not weigh in the balance is the damage to the stream, its fish and turtles and "lower" life. So long as the natural environment itself is rightless, these are not matters for judicial cognizance. Thus, we find the highest court of Pennsylvania refusing to stop a coal company from discharging polluted mine water into a tributary of the Lackawana River because a plaintiff's "grievance is for a mere personal inconvenience; and...mere private personal inconveniences...must yield to the necessities of a great public industry, which although in the hands of a private corporation, subserves a great public interest." The stream itself is lost sight of in "a quantitative compromise between *two* conflicting interests."

The third way in which the common law makes natural objects rightless has to do with who is regarded as the beneficiary of a favorable judgment. Here, too, it makes a considerable difference that it is not the natural object that counts in its own right. To illustrate this point, let me begin by observing that it makes perfectly good sense to speak of, and ascertain, the legal damage to a natural object, if only in the sense of "making it whole" with respect to the most obvious factors. The costs of making a forest whole, for example, would include the costs of reseeding, repairing watersheds, restocking wildlife–the sorts of costs the Forest Service undergoes after a fire. Making a polluted stream whole would include the costs of restocking with fish, waterfowl, and other animal and vegetable life, dredging, washing out impurities, establishing natural and/or artificial aerating agents, and so forth. Now, what is important to note is that, under our present system, even if a plaintiff riparian wins a water pollution suit for damages, no money goes to the benefit of the stream itself to repair *its* damages. This omission has the further effect that, at most, the law confronts a polluter with what it takes to make the plaintiff riparians whole; this may be far less than the damages to the stream, but not so much as to force the polluter to desist. For example, it is easy to imagine a polluter whose activities damage a stream to the extent of $10,000 annually, although the aggregate damage to all the riparian plaintiffs who come into the suit is only

$3000. If $3000 is less than the cost to the polluter of shutting down, or making the requisite technological changes, he might prefer to pay off the damages (*i.e.*, the legally cognizable damages) and continue to pollute the stream. Similarly, even if the jurisdiction issues an injunction at the plaintiffs' behest (rather than to order payment of damages), there is nothing to stop the plaintiffs from "selling out" the stream, *i.e.*, agreeing to dissolve or not enforce the injunction at some price (in the example above, somewhere between plaintiffs' damages–$3000–and defendant's next best economic alternative). Indeed, I take it this is exactly what Learned Hand had in mind in an opinion in which, after issuing an anti-pollution injunction, he suggests that the defendant "make its peace with the plaintiff as best it can". What is meant is a peace between *them*, and not amongst them and the river.

I ought to make clear at this point that the common law as it affects streams and rivers, which I have been using as an example so far, is not exactly the same as the law affecting other environmental objects. Indeed, one would be hard pressed to say that there was a "typical" environmental object, so far as its treatment at the hands of the law is concerned. There are some differences in the law applicable to all the various resources that are held in common: rivers, lakes, oceans, dunes, air, streams (surface and subterranean), beaches, and so forth. And there is an even greater difference as between these traditional communal resources on the one hand, and natural objects on traditionally private land, *e.g.*, the pond on the farmer's field, or the stand of trees on the suburbanite's lawn.

On the other hand, although there be these differences which would make it fatuous to generalize about a law of the natural environment, most of these differences simply underscore the points made in the instance of rivers and streams. None of the natural objects, whether held in common or situated on private land, has any of the three criteria of a rights-holder. They have no standing in their own right; their unique damages do not count in determining outcome; and they are not the beneficiaries of awards. In such fashion, these objects have traditionally been regarded by the common law, and even by all but the most recent legislation, as objects for man to conquer and master and use–in such a way as the law once looked upon "man's" relationships to African Negroes. Even where special measures have been taken to conserve them, as by seasons on game and limits on timber cutting, the dominant motive has been to conserve them *for us*–for the greatest good of the greatest number of human beings. Conservationists, so far as I am aware, are generally reluctant to maintain otherwise. As the name implies, they want to conserve and guarantee *our* consumption and *our* enjoyment of these other living things. In their own right, natural objects have counted for little, in law as in popular movements.

As I mentioned at the outset, however, the rightlessness of the natural environment can and should change; it already shows some signs of doing so.

Toward having standing in its own right

It is not inevitable, nor is it wise, that natural objects should have no rights to seek redress in their own behalf. It is no answer to say that streams and forests cannot have standing because streams and forest cannot speak. Corporations cannot speak either; nor can states, estates, infants, incompetents, municipalities or universities. Lawyers speak for them, as they customarily do for the ordinary citizen with legal problems. One ought, I think, to handle the legal problems of natural objects as one does the problems of legal incompetents— human beings who have become vegetable. If a human being shows signs of becoming senile and has affairs that he is de jure incompetent to manage, those concerned with his well being make such a showing to the court, and someone is designated by the court with the authority to manage the incompetent's affairs. The guardian (or "conservator" or "committee"–the terminology varies) then represents the incompetent in his legal affairs. Courts make similar appointments when a corporation has become "incompetent"– they appoint a trustee in bankruptcy or reorganization to oversee its affairs and speak for it in court when that becomes necessary.

On a parity of reasoning, we should have a system in which, when a friend of a natural object perceives it to be endangered, he can apply to a court for the creation of a guardianship. Perhaps we already have the machinery to do so. California law, for example, defines an incompetent as "any person, whether insane or not, who by reason of old age, disease, weakness of mind, or other cause, is unable, unassisted, properly to manage and take care of himself or his property, and by reason thereof is likely to be deceived or imposed upon by artful or designing persons." Of course, to urge a court that an endangered river is "a person" under this provision will call for lawyers as bold and imaginative as those who convinced the Supreme Court that a railroad corporation was a "person" under the fourteenth amendment, a constitutional provision theretofore generally thought of as designed to secure the rights of freedmen....

The guardianship approach, however, is apt to raise ... [the following objection]: a committee or guardian could not judge the needs of the river or forest in its charge; indeed, the very concept of "needs," it might be said, could be used here only in the most metaphorical way....

...Natural objects *can* communicate their wants (needs) to us, and in ways that are not terribly ambiguous. I am sure I can judge with more certainty and meaningfulness whether and when my lawn wants (needs) water, than the Attorney General can judge whether and when the United States wants (needs) to take an appeal from an adverse judgment by a lower court. The lawn tells me that it wants water by a certain dryness of the blades and soil–immediately obvious to the touch–the appearance of bald spots, yellowing, and a lack of springiness after being walked on; how does "the United States" communicate to the Attorney General? For similar reasons, the guardian-attorney for a smog endangered stand of pines could venture with more confidence that his client wants the smog stopped, than the directors of a corporation can assert that "the corporation" wants dividends declared. We make decisions on behalf of, and in the purported interests of, others every day; these "others" are often creatures whose wants are far less verifiable, and even far more metaphysical in conception, than the wants of rivers, trees, and land....

The argument for "personifying" the environment, from the point of damage calculations, can best be demonstrated from the welfare economics position. Every well-working legal-economic system should be so structured as to confront each of us with the full costs that our activities are imposing on society. Ideally, a paper-mill, in deciding what to produce–and where, and by what methods–ought to be forced to take into account not only the lumber, acid and labor that its production "takes" from other uses in the society, but also what costs alternative production plans will impose on society through pollution. The legal system, through the law of contracts and the criminal law, for example, makes the mill confront the costs of the first group of demands. When, for example, the company's purchasing agent orders 1000 drums of acid from the Z Company, the Z Company can bind the mill to pay for them, and thereby reimburse the society for what the mill is removing from alternative uses.

Unfortunately, so far as the pollution costs are concerned, the allocative ideal begins to break down, because the traditional legal institutions have a more difficult time "catching" and confronting us with the full social costs of our activities. In the lakeside mill example, major riparian interests might bring an action, forcing a court to weigh *their* aggregate losses against the costs to the mill of installing the anti-pollution device. But many other interests–and I am speaking for the moment of recognized homocentric interests–are too fragmented and perhaps "too remote" causally to warrant securing representation and pressing for recovery: the people who own summer homes and motels, the man who sells fishing tackle and bait, the man who rents rowboats. There is no reason not to allow the lake to prove damages to them as the prima facie measure of damages to it. *By doing so, we in effect make the natural object, through its guardian, a jural entity competent to gather up these fragmented and otherwise unrepresented damage claims, and press them before the court even where, for legal or practical reasons, they are not going to be pressed by traditional class action plaintiffs.* Indeed, one way–the homocentric way–to view what I am proposing so far, is to view the guardian of the natural object as the guardian of unborn generations, as well as of the otherwise unrepresented, but distantly injured, contemporary humans. By making the lake itself the focus of these damages, and "incorporating" it so to speak, the legal system can effectively take proof upon, and confront the mill with, a larger and more representative measure of the damages its pollution causes.

So far, I do not suppose that my economist friends (unremittent human chauvinists, every one of them!) will have any large quarrel in principle with the concept. Many will view it as a *trompe l'oeil* that comes down, at best, to effectuate the goals of the paragon class action, or the paragon water pollution control district. Where we are apt to part company is here–I propose going beyond gathering up the loose ends of what most people would presently recognize as economically valid damages. The guardian would urge before the court injuries not presently cognizable–the death of eagles and inedible crabs, the suffering of sea lions, the loss from the face of the earth of species of commercially valueless birds, the disappearance of a wilderness area. One might, of course, speak of the damages involved as "damages" to us humans, and indeed, the widespread growth of environmental groups shows that human beings do feel these losses. But they are not, at present, economically measurable losses: how can they have a monetary value for the guardian to prove in court?

The answer for me is simple. Wherever it carves out "property" rights, the legal system is engaged in the process of *creating* monetary worth. One's literary works would have minimal monetary value if anyone could copy them at will. Their economic value to the author is a product of the law of copyright; the person who copies a copyrighted book has to bear a cost to the copyright-holder because the law says he must. Similarly, it is through the law of torts that we have made a "right" of–and guaranteed an economically meaningful value to–privacy. (The value we place on gold–a yellow inanimate dirt–is not simply a function of supply and demand–wilderness areas are scarce and pretty too–, but results from the actions of the legal systems of the world, which have institutionalized that value; they have even done a remarkable job of stabilizing the price.) I am proposing we do the same with eagles and wilderness areas as we do with copyrighted works, patented inventions, and privacy: *make* the violation of rights in them to be a cost by declaring the "pirating" of them to be the invasion of a property interest. If we do so, the net social costs the polluter would be confronted with would include not only the extended homocentric costs of his pollution (explained above) but also costs to the environment *per se*.

How, though, would these costs be calculated? When we protect an invention, we can at least speak of a fair market value for it, by reference to which damages can be computed. But the lost environmental "values" of which we are now speaking are by definition over and above those that the market is prepared to bid for: they are priceless.

One possible measure of damages, suggested earlier, would be the cost of making the environment whole, just as, when a man is injured in an automobile accident, we impose upon the responsible party the injured man's medical expenses. Comparable expenses to a polluted river would be the costs of dredging, restocking with fish, and so forth. It is on the basis of such costs as these, I assume, that we get the figure of $1 billion as the cost of saving Lake Erie. As an ideal, I think this is a good guide applicable in many environmental situations. It is by no means free from difficulties, however.

One problem with computing damages on the basis of making the environment whole is that, if understood most literally, it is tantamount to asking for a "freeze" on environmental quality, even at the costs (and there will be costs) of preserving "useless" objects. Such a "freeze" is not inconceivable to me as a general goal, especially considering that, even by the most immediately discernible homocentric interests, in so many areas we ought to be cleaning up and not merely preserving the environmental status quo. In fact, there is presently strong sentiment in the Congress for a total elimination of all river pollutants by 1985, notwithstanding that such a decision would impose quite large direct and indirect costs on us all. Here one is inclined to recall the instructions of Judge Hays, in remanding Consolidated Edison's Storm King application to the Federal Power Commission in *Scenic Hudson*:

> The Commission's renewed proceedings must include as a basic concern the preservation of natural beauty and of natural history shrines, keeping in mind that, in our affluent society, the cost of a project is only one of several factors to be considered.

Nevertheless, whatever the merits of such a goal in principle, there are many cases in which the social price tag of putting it into effect are going to seem too high to accept. Consider, for example, an oceanside nuclear generator that could produce low cost electricity for a million homes at a savings of $1 a year per home, spare us the air pollution that comes of burning fossil fuels, but which through a slight heating effect threatened to kill off a rare species of temperature-sensitive sea urchins; suppose further that technological improvements adequate to reduce the temperature to present environmental quality would expend the entire one million dollars in anticipated fuel savings. Are we prepared to tax ourselves $1,000,000 a year on behalf of the sea urchins? In comparable problems under the present law of damages, we work out practicable compromises by abandoning restoration costs and calling upon fair market value. For example, if an automobile is so severely damaged that the cost of bringing the car to its original state by repair is greater than the fair market value, we would allow the responsible tortfeasor to pay the fair market value only. Or if a human being suffers the loss of an arm (as we might conceive of the ocean having irreparably lost the sea urchins), we can fall back on the capitalization of reduced earning power (and pain and suffering) to measure the damages. But what is the fair market value of sea urchins? How can we capitalize their loss to the ocean, independent of any commercial value they may have to someone else?

One answer is that the problem can sometimes be sidestepped quite satisfactorily. In the sea urchin example, one compromise solution would be to impose on the nuclear generator the costs of making the ocean whole somewhere else, in some other way, *e.g.*, reestablishing a sea urchin colony elsewhere, or making a somehow comparable contribution. In the debate over the laying of the trans-Alaskan pipeline, the builders are apparently prepared to meet conservationists' objections halfway by re-establishing wildlife away from the pipeline, so far as is feasible.

But even if damage calculations have to be made, one ought to recognize that the measurement of damages is rarely a simple report of economic facts about "the market," whether we are valuing the loss of a foot, a foetus, or a work of fine art. Decisions of this sort are always hard, but not impossible. We have increasingly taken (human) pain and suffering into account in reckoning damages, not because we think we can ascertain them as objective "facts" about the universe, but because, even in view of all the room for disagreement, we come up with a better society by making rude estimates of them than by ignoring them. We can make such estimates in regard to environmental losses fully aware that what we are really doing is making implicit normative judgments (as with pain and suffering)–laying down rules as to what the society is going to "value" rather than reporting market evaluations. In making such normative estimates decision-makers would not go wrong if they estimated on the "high side," putting the burden of trimming the figure down on the immediate human interests present. All burdens of proof should reflect common experience; our experience in environmental matters has been a continual discovery that our acts have caused more long-range damage than we were able to appreciate at the outset.

To what extent the decision-maker should factor in costs such as the pain and suffering of animals and other sentient natural objects, I cannot say; although I am prepared to do so in principle.

The Psychic and Socio-psychic Aspects

...The strongest case can be made from the perspective of human advantage for conferring rights on the environment. Scientists have been warning of the crises the earth and all humans on it face if we do not change our ways–radically–and these crises make the lost "recreational use" of rivers seem absolutely trivial. The earth's very atmosphere is threatened with frightening possibilities: absorption of sunlight, upon which the entire life cycle depends, may be diminished; the oceans may warm (increasing the "greenhouse effect" of the atmosphere), melting the polar ice caps, and destroying our great coastal cities; the portion of the atmosphere that shields us from dangerous radiation may be destroyed. Testifying before Congress, sea explorer Jacques Cousteau predicted that the oceans (to which we dreamily look to feed our booming populations) are headed toward their own death: "The cycle of life is intricately tied up with the cycle of water...the water system has to remain alive if we are to remain alive on earth." We are depleting our energy and our food sources at a rate that takes little account of the needs even of humans now living.

These problems will not be solved easily; they very likely can be solved, if at all, only through a willingness to suspend the rate of increase in the standard of living (by present values) of the earth's "advanced" nations, and by stabilizing the total human population. For some of us this will involve forfeiting material comforts; for others it will involve abandoning the hope someday to obtain comforts long envied. For all of us it will involve giving up the right to have as many offspring as we might wish. Such a program is not impossible of realization, however. Many of our so called "material comforts" are not only in excess of, but are probably in opposition to, basic biological needs. Further, the "costs" to the advanced nations is not as large as would appear from Gross National Product figures. G.N.P. reflects social gain (of a sort) without discounting for the social *cost* of that gain, *e.g.* the losses through depletion of resources, pollution, and so forth. As has well been shown, as societies become more and more "advanced," their real marginal gains become less and less for each additional dollar of G.N.P. Thus, to give up "human progress" would not be as costly as might appear on first blush.

Nonetheless, such far-reaching social changes are going to involve us in a serious reconsideration of our consciousness towards the environment....

...A few years ago the pollution of streams was thought of only as a problem of smelly, unsightly, unpotable water, *i.e.*, to us. Now we are beginning to discover that pollution is a process that destroys wondrously subtle balances of life within the water, and as between the water and its banks. This heightened awareness enlarges our sense of the dangers to us. But it also enlarges our empathy. We are not only developing the scientific capacity, but we are cultivating the personal capacities *within us* to recognize more and more the ways in which nature—like the woman, the Black, the Indian and the Alien—is like us (and we will also become more able realistically to define, confront, live with and admire the ways in which we are all different).

The time may be on hand when these sentiments, and the early stirrings of the law, can be coalesced into a radical new theory or myth—felt as well as intellectualized—of man's relationships to the rest of nature. I do not mean "myth" in a demeaning sense of the term, but in the sense in which, at different times in history, our social "facts" and relationships have been comprehended and integrated by reference to the "myths" that we are co-signers of a social contract, that the Pope is God's agent, and that all men are created equal. Pantheism, Shinto and Tao all have myths to offer. But they are all, each in its own fashion, quaint, primitive and archaic. What is needed is a myth that can fit our growing body of knowledge of geophysics, biology and the cosmos. In this vein, I do not think it too remote that we may come to regard the Earth, as some have suggested, as one organism, of which Mankind is a functional part—the mind, perhaps: different from the rest of nature, but different as a man's brain is from his lungs....

> ...As I see it, the Earth is only one organized "field" of activities—and so is the *human person*—but these activities take place at various levels, in different "spheres" of being and realms of consciousness. The lithosphere is not the biosphere, and the latter not the...ionosphere. The Earth is not *only* a material mass. Consciousness is not only "human"; it exists at animal and vegetable levels, and most likely must be latent, or operating in some form, in the molecule and the atom; and all these diverse and in a sense hierarchical modes of activity and consciousness should be seen integrated in and perhaps transcended by an all-encompassing and "eonic" planetary Consciousness.
>
> Mankind's function within the Earth-organism is to extract from the activities of all other operative systems within this organism the type of consciousness which we call "reflective" or "self"-consciousness—or, we may also say to *mentalize* and give meaning, value, and "name" to all that takes place anywhere within the Earth-field....

As radical as such a consciousness may sound today, all the dominant changes we see about us point in its direction. Consider just the impact of space travel, of world-wide mass media, of increasing scientific discoveries about the interrelatedness of all life processes. Is it any wonder that the term "spaceship earth" has so captured the popular imagination? The problems we have to confront are increasingly the world-wide crises of a global organism: not pollution of a stream, but pollution of the atmosphere and of the ocean. Increasingly, the death that occupies each human's imagination is not his own, but that of the entire life cycle of the planet earth, to which each of us is as but a cell to a body.

To shift from such a lofty fancy as the planetarization of consciousness to the operation of our municipal legal system is to come down to earth hard. Before the forces that are at work, our highest court is but a frail and feeble–a distinctly human–institution. Yet, the Court may be at its best not in its work of handing down decrees, but at the very task that is called for: of summoning up from the human spirit the kindest and most generous and worthy ideas that abound there, giving them shape and reality and legitimacy. Witness the School Desegregation Cases which, more importantly than to integrate the schools (assuming they did), awakened us to moral needs which, when made visible, could not be denied. And so here, too, in the case of the environment, the Supreme Court may find itself in a position to award "rights" in a way that will contribute to a change in popular consciousness. It would be a modest move, to be sure, but one in furtherance of a large goal: the future of the planet as we know it.

How far we are from such a state of affairs, where the law treats "environmental objects" as holders of legal rights, I cannot say. But there is certainly intriguing language in one of Justice Black's last dissents, regarding the Texas Highway Department's plan to run a six-lane expressway through a San Antonio Park. Complaining of the Court's refusal to stay the plan, Black observed that "after today's decision, the people of San Antonio and the birds and animals that make their home in the park will share their quiet retreat with an ugly, smelly stream of traffic.... Trees, shrubs, and flowers will be mowed down." Elsewhere he speaks of the "burial of public parks," of segments of a highway which "devour parkland," and of the park's heartland. Was he, at the end of his great career, on the verge of saying–just saying–that "nature has 'rights' on its own account"? Would it be so hard to do?

Notes

* Riparian–related to living on the bank of a natural waterway.
† To whosoever the soil belongs, he owns also to the sky and to the depths.

34

The Place of Nonhumans in Environmental Issues

Peter Singer

Not for Humans Only

When we humans change the environment in which we live, we often harm ourselves. If we discharge cadmium into a bay and eat shellfish from that bay, we become ill and may die. When our industries and automobiles pour noxious fumes into the atmosphere, we find a displeasing smell in the air, the longterm results of which may be every bit as deadly as cadmium poisoning. The harm that humans do the environment, however, does not rebound solely, or even chiefly, on humans. It is nonhumans who bear the most direct burden of human interference with nature.

By "nonhumans" I mean to refer to all living things other than human beings, though for reasons to be given later, it is with nonhuman animals, rather than plants, that I am chiefly concerned. It is also important, in the context of environmental issues, to note that living things may be regarded either collectively or as individuals. In debates about the environment the most important way of regarding living things collectively has been to regard them as species. Thus, when environmentalists worry about the future of the blue whale, they usually are thinking of the blue whale as a species, rather than of individual blue whales. But this is not, of course, the only way in which one can think of blue whales, or other animals, and one of the topics I shall discuss is whether we should be concerned about what we are doing to the environment primarily insofar as it threatens entire species of nonhumans, or primarily insofar as it affects individual nonhuman animals.

The general question, then, is how the effects of our actions on the environment of nonhuman beings should figure in our deliberations about what we ought to do. There is an unlimited variety of contexts in which this issue could arise. To take just one: Suppose that it is considered necessary to

Source: K. E. Goodpaster and K. M. Sayre (eds), *Ethics and Problems of the 21st Century* (Notre Dame, IN: University of Notre Dame Press, 1979), pp. 191–8.

build a new power station, and there are two sites, A and B, under consideration. In most respects the sites are equally suitable, but building the power station on site A would be more expensive because the greater depth of shifting soil at that site will require deeper foundations; on the other hand to build on site B will destroy a favored breeding ground for thousands of wildfowl. Should the presence of the wildfowl enter into the decision as to where to build? And if so, in what manner should it enter, and how heavily should it weigh?

In a case like this the effects of our actions on nonhuman animals could be taken into account in two quite different ways: directly, giving the lives and welfare of nonhuman animals an intrinsic significance which must count in any moral calculation; or indirectly, so that the effects of our actions on nonhumans are morally significant only if they have consequences for humans....

The view that the effects of our actions on other animals has no direct moral significance is not as likely to be openly advocated today as it was in the past; yet it is likely to be accepted implicitly and acted upon. When planners perform cost-benefit studies on new projects, the costs and benefits are costs and benefits for human beings only. This does not mean that the impact of the power station or highway on wildlife is ignored altogether, but it is included only indirectly. That a new reservoir would drown a valley teeming with wildlife is taken into account only under some such heading as the value of the facilities for recreation that the valley affords. In calculating this value, the cost-benefit study will be neutral between forms of recreation like hunting and shooting and those like bird watching and bush walking—in fact hunting and shooting are likely to contribute more to the benefit side of the calculations because larger sums of money are spent on them, and they therefore benefit manufacturers and retailers of firearms as well as the hunters and shooters themselves. The suffering experienced by the animals whose habitat is flooded is not reckoned into the costs of the operation; nor is the recreational value obtained by the hunters and shooters offset by the cost to the animals that their recreation involves.

Despite its venerable origins, the view that the effects of our actions on nonhuman animals have no intrinsic moral significance can be shown to be arbitrary and morally indefensible. If a being suffers, the fact that it is not a member of our own species cannot be a moral reason for failing to take its suffering into account. This becomes obvious if we consider the analogous attempt by white slaveowners to deny consideration to the interests of blacks. These white racists limited their moral concern to their own race, so the suffering of a black did not have the same moral significance as the suffering of a white. We now recognize that in doing so they were making an arbitrary distinction, and that the existence of suffering, rather than the race of the sufferer, is what is really morally significant. The point remains true if "species" is substituted for "race." The logic of racism and the logic of the position we have been discussing, which I have elsewhere referred to as "speciesism," are indistinguishable; and if we reject the former then consistency demands that we reject the latter too.[1]

It should be clearly understood that the rejection of speciesism does not imply that the different species are in fact equal in respect of such characteristics as intelligence, physical strength, ability to communicate, capacity to suffer, ability to damage the environment, or anything else. After all, the moral principle of human equality cannot be taken as implying that all humans are equal in these respects either—if it did, we would have to give up the idea of human equality. That one being is more intelligent than another does not entitle him to enslave, exploit, or disregard the interests of the less intelligent being. The moral basis of equality among humans is not equality in fact, but the principle of equal consideration of interests, and it is this principle that, in consistency, must be extended to any nonhumans who have interests.

There may be some doubt about whether any nonhuman beings have interests. This doubt may arise because of uncertainty about what it is to have an interest, or because of uncertainty about the nature of some nonhuman beings. So far as the concept of "interest" is the cause of doubt, I take the view that only a being with subjective experiences, such as the experience of pleasure or the experience of pain, can have interests in the full sense of the term; and that any being with such experiences does have at least one interest, namely, the interest in experiencing pleasure and avoiding pain. Thus consciousness, or the capacity for subjective experience, is both a necessary and a sufficient condition for having an interest. While there may be a loose sense of the term in which we can say that it is in the interests of a tree to be watered, this attenuated sense of the term is not the sense covered by the principle of equal consideration of interests. All we mean when we say that it is in the interests of a tree to be watered is that the tree needs water if it is to continue to live and grow normally; if we regard this as evidence that the tree has interests, we might almost as well say that it is in the interests of a car to be lubricated regularly because the car needs lubrication if it is to run properly. In neither case can we really mean (unless we impute consciousness to trees or cars) that the tree or car has any preference about the matter.

The remaining doubt about whether nonhuman beings have interests is, then, a doubt about whether nonhuman beings have subjective experiences like the experience of pain. I have argued elsewhere that the commonsense view that birds and mammals feel pain is well founded,[2] but more serious doubts arise as we move down the evolutionary scale. Vertebrate animals have nervous systems broadly similar to our own and behave in ways that resemble our own pain behavior when subjected to stimuli that we would find painful; so the inference that vertebrates are capable of feeling pain is a reasonable one, though not as strong as it is if limited to mammals and birds. When we go beyond vertebrates to insects, crustaceans, mollusks and so on, the existence of subjective states becomes more dubious, and with very simple organisms it is difficult to believe that they could be conscious. As for plants, though there have been sensational claims that plants are not only conscious, but even psychic, there is no hard evidence that supports even the more modest claim.[3]

The boundary of beings who may be taken as having interests is therefore not an abrupt boundary, but a broad range in which the assumption that the being has interests shifts from being so strong as to be virtually certain to being so weak as to be highly improbable. The principle of equal consideration of interests must be applied with this in mind, so that where there is a clash between a virtually certain interest and a highly doubtful one, it is the virtually certain interest that ought to prevail.

In this manner our moral concern ought to extend to all beings who have interests. Unlike race or species, this boundary does not arbitrarily exclude any being; indeed it can truly be said that it excludes nothing at all, not even "the most contemptible clod of earth" from equal consideration of interests–for full consideration of no interests still results in no weight being given to whatever was considered, just as multiplying zero by a million still results in zero.[4]

Giving equal consideration to the interests of two different beings does not mean treating them alike or holding their lives to be of equal value. We may recognize that the interests of one being are greater than those of another, and equal consideration will then lead us to sacrifice the being with lesser interests, if one or the other must be sacrificed. For instance, if for some reason a choice has to be made between saving the life of a normal human being and that of a dog, we might well decide to save the human because he, with his greater awareness of what is going to happen, will suffer more before he dies; we may also take into account the likelihood that it is the family and friends of the human who will suffer more; and finally, it would be the human who had the greater potential for future happiness. This decision would be in accordance with the principle of equal consideration of interests, for the interests of the dog get the same consideration as those of the human, and the loss to the dog is not discounted because the dog is not a member of our species. The outcome is as it is because the balance of interests favors the human. In a different situation– say, if the human were grossly mentally defective and without family or anyone else who would grieve for it–the balance of interests might favor the nonhuman.[5]

The more positive side of the principle of equal consideration is this: where interests are equal, they must be given equal weight. So where human and nonhuman animals share an interest–as in the case of the interest in avoiding physical pain–we must give as much weight to violations of the interest of the nonhumans as we do to similar violations of the human's interest. This does not mean, of course, that it is as bad to hit a horse with a stick as it is to hit a human being, for the same blow would cause less pain to the animal with the tougher skin. The principle holds between similar amounts of felt pain, and what this is will vary from case to case.

It may be objected that we cannot tell exactly how much pain another animal is suffering, and that therefore the principle is impossible to apply. While I do not deny the difficulty and even, so far as precise measurement is concerned, the impossibility of comparing the subjective experiences of members of different species, I do not think that the problem is different in kind from the problem of comparing the subjective experiences of two members of our own species. Yet this is something we do all the time, for instance when we judge that a wealthy person will suffer less by being taxed at a higher rate than a poor person will gain from the welfare benefits paid for by the tax; or when we decide to take our two children to the beach instead of to a fair, because although the older one would prefer the fair, the younger one has a stronger preference the other way. These comparisons may be very rough, but since there is nothing better, we must use them; it would be irrational to refuse to do so simply because they are rough. Moreover, rough as they are, there are many situations in which we can be reasonably sure which way the balance of interests lies. While a difference of species may make comparisons rougher still, the basic problem is the same, and the comparisons are still often good enough to use, in the absence of anything more precise....

The difficulty of making the required comparison will mean that the application of this conclusion is controversial in many cases, but there will be some situations in which it is clear enough. Take, for instance, the wholesale poisoning of animals that is euphemistically known as "pest control." The authorities who conduct these campaigns give no consideration to the suffering they inflict on the "pests," and invariably use the method of slaughter they believe to be cheapest and most effective. The result is that hundreds of millions of rabbits have died agonizing deaths from the artificially introduced disease, myxomatosis, or from poisons like "ten-eighty"; coyotes and other wild dogs have died painfully from cyanide poisoning; and all manner of wild animals have endured days of thirst, hunger, and fear with a mangled limb caught in a leg-hold trap.[6] Granting, for the sake of argument, the necessity for pest control–though this has rightly been questioned–the fact remains that no serious attempts have been made to introduce alternative means of control and thereby reduce the incalculable amount of suffering caused by present methods. It would not, presumably, be beyond modern science to produce a substance which, when eaten by rabbits or coyotes, produced sterility instead of a drawn-out death. Such methods might be more expensive, but can anyone doubt that if a similar amount of human suffering were at stake, the expense would be borne?

Another clear instance in which the principle of equal consideration of interests would indicate methods different from those presently used is in the timber industry. There are two basic methods of obtaining timber from forests. One is to cut only selected mature or dead trees, leaving the forest substantially intact. The other, known as clear-cutting, involves chopping down everything that grows in a given area, and then reseeding. Obviously when a large area is clear-cut, wild animals find their whole living area destroyed in a few days, whereas selected felling makes a relatively minor disturbance. But clear-cutting is cheaper, and timber companies therefore use this method and will continue to do so unless forced to do otherwise....[7]

It is not merely the act of killing that indicates what we are ready to do to other species in order to gratify our tastes. The suffering we inflict on the animals while they are alive is perhaps an even clearer indication of our speciesism than the fact that we are prepared to kill them.[8] In order to have meat on the table at a price that people can afford, our society tolerates methods of meat production that confine sentient animals in cramped, unsuitable conditions for the entire durations of their lives. Animals are treated like machines that convert fodder into flesh, and any innovation that results in a higher "conversion ratio" is liable to be adopted. As one authority on the subject has said, "cruelty is acknowledged only when profitability ceases."[9] So hens are crowded four or five to a cage with a floor area of twenty inches by eighteen inches, or around the size of a single page of the *New York Times.* The cages have wire floors, since this reduces cleaning costs, though wire is unsuitable for the hens' feet; the floors slope, since this makes the eggs roll down for easy collection, although this makes it difficult for the hens to rest comfortably. In these conditions all the birds' natural instincts are thwarted: They cannot stretch their wings fully, walk freely, dust-bathe, scratch the ground, or build a nest. Although they have never known other conditions, observers have noticed that the birds vainly try to perform these actions. Frustrated at their inability to do so, they often develop what farmers call "vices," and peck each other to death. To prevent this, the beaks of young birds are often cut off.

This kind of treatment is not limited to poultry. Pigs are now also being reared in cages inside sheds. These animals are comparable to dogs in intelligence, and need a varied, stimulating environment if they are not to suffer from stress and boredom. Anyone who kept a dog in the way in which pigs are frequently kept would be liable to prosecution, in England at least, but because our interest in exploiting pigs is greater than our interest in exploiting dogs, we object to cruelty to dogs while consuming the produce of cruelty to pigs. Of the other animals, the condition of veal calves is perhaps worst of all, since these animals are so closely confined that they cannot even turn around or get up and lie down freely. In this way they do not develop unpalatable muscle. They are also made anaemic and kept short of roughage, to keep their flesh pale, since white veal fetches a higher price; as a result they develop a craving for iron and roughage, and have been observed to gnaw wood off the sides of their stalls, and lick greedily at any rusty hinge that is within reach.

Since, as I have said, none of these practices cater to anything more than our pleasures of taste, our practice of rearing and killing other animals in order to eat them is a clear instance of the sacrifice of the most important interests of other beings in order to satisfy trivial interests of our own. To avoid speciesism we must stop this practice, and each of us has a moral obligation to cease supporting the practice. Our custom is all the support that the meat industry needs. The decision to cease giving it that support may be difficult, but it is no more difficult than it would have been for a white Southerner to go against the traditions of his society and free his slaves; if we do not change our dietary habits, how can we censure those slaveholders who would not change their own way of living?

Notes

1. For a fuller statement of this argument, see my *Animal Liberation* (New York: A New York Review Book, 1975), especially ch. 1.

2. *Ibid.*

3 See, for instance, the comments by Arthur Galston in *Natural History*, 83, no. 3 (March 1974): 18, on the "evidence" cited in such books as *The Secret Life of Plants.*

4. The idea that we would logically have to consider "the most contemptible clod of earth" as having rights was suggested by Thomas Taylor, the Cambridge Neo-Platonist, in a pamphlet he published anonymously, entitled *A Vindication of the Rights of Brutes* (London, 1792) which appears to be a satirical refutation of the attribution of rights to women by Mary Wollstonecroft in her *Vindication of the Rights of Women* (London, 1792). Logically, Taylor was no doubt correct, but he neglected to specify just what interests such contemptible clods of earth have.

5. Singer, *Animal Liberation*, pp. 20–23.

6. See J. Olsen, *Slaughter the Animals, Poison the Earth* (New York: Simon and Schuster, 1971), especially pp. 153–164.

7. See R. and V. Routley, *The Fight for the Forests* (Canberra: Australian National University Press, 1974), for a thoroughly documented indictment of clear-cutting in Australia; and for a recent report of the controversy about clear-cutting in America, see *Time*, May 17, 1976.

8. Although one might think that killing a being is obviously the ultimate wrong one can do to it, I think that the infliction of suffering is a clearer indication of speciesism because it might be argued that at least part of what is wrong with killing a human is that most humans are conscious of their existence over time, and have desires and purposes that extend into the future–see for instance, M. Tooley, "Abortion and Infanticide," *Philosophy and Public Affairs*, vol. 2, no. 1 (1972). Of course, if one took this view one would have to hold–as Tooley does–that killing a human infant or mental defective is not in itself wrong, and is less serious than killing certain higher mammals that probably do have a sense of their own existence over time.

9. Ruth Harrison, *Animal Machines* (Stuart, London, 1964). This book provides an eye-opening account of intensive farming methods for those unfamiliar with the subject.

35

At the Shrine of Our Lady of Fatima, or Why Political Questions Are Not All Economic

Mark Sagoff

M ark Sagoff is a research scholar at the Center for Philosophy and Public Policy, University of Maryland, College Park, and the author of several works on economic and social issues, including *The Economy of the Earth: Philosophy, Law and the Environment (1988).*

Sagoff examines and rejects the standard economic notion that the cost-benefit analysis is always the proper method for deciding social and environmental issues. Contrasting utilitarian with Kantian views of the human situation, he argues that the Kantian perspective, which treats humans as ends in themselves, should override utilitarian cost-benefit assessments. Sometimes efficiency should be sacrificed for principle.

Lewiston, New York, a well-to-do community near Buffalo, is the site of the Lake Ontario Ordnance Works, where the federal government, years ago, disposed of the residues of the Manhattan Project. These radioactive wastes are buried but are not forgotten by the residents, who say that when the wind is southerly radon gas blows through the town. Several parents at a recent conference I attended there described their terror on learning that cases of leukemia had been found among area children. They feared for their own lives as well. At the other sides of the table, officials from New York State and from local corporations replied that these fears were ungrounded. People who smoke, they said, take greater risks than people who live close to waste disposal sites. One speaker talked in terms of "rational methodologies of decision-making." This aggravated the parents' rage and frustration.

The speaker suggested that the townspeople, were they to make their

Source: *The Economy of the Earth Philosophy, Law and the Environment,* 1988: pp 13–162.
Copyright © Cambridge University Press, 1981.

decision in a free market, would choose to live near the hazardous waste facility, if they knew the scientific facts. He told me later they were irrational—he said, "neurotic"—because they refused to recognize or act upon their own interests. The residents of Lewiston were unimpressed with his analysis of their "willingness to pay" to avoid this risk or that. They did not see what risk-benefit analysis had to do with the issues they raised.

If you take the Military Highway (as I did) from Buffalo to Lewiston, you will pass through a formidable wasteland. Landfills stretch in all directions, where enormous trucks—tiny in that landscape—incessantly deposit sludge which great bulldozers, like yellow ants, then push into the ground. These machines are the only signs of life, for in the miasma that hangs in the air, no birds, not even scavengers, are seen. Along colossal power lines which criss-cross this dismal land, the dynamos at Niagara send electric power south, where factories have fled, leaving their remains to decay. To drive along this road is to feel, oddly, the mystery and awe one experiences in the presence of so much power and decadence.

Henry Adams had a similar response to the dynamos on display at the Paris Exposition of 1900. To him "the dynamo became a symbol of infinity." To Adams, the dynamo functioned as the modern equivalent of the Virgin, that is, as the center and focus of power. "Before the end, one began to pray to it; inherited instinct taught the natural expression of man before silent and infinite force."

Adams asks in his essay "The Dynamo and the Virgin" how the products of modern industrial civilization will compare with those of the religious culture of the Middle Ages. If he could see the landfills and hazardous waste facilities bordering the power stations and honeymoon hotels of Niagara Falls he would know the answer. He would understand what happens when efficiency replaces infinity as the central conception of value. The dynamos at Niagara will not produce another Mont-Saint-Michel. "All the steam in the world," Adams wrote, "could not, like the Virgin, build Chartres."

At the Shrine of Our Lady of Fatima, on a plateau north of the Military Highway, a larger than life sculpture of Mary looks into the chemical air. The original of this shrine stands in central Portugal, where in May, 1917, three children said they saw a Lady, brighter than the sun, raised on a cloud in an evergreen tree. Five months later, on a wet and chilly October day, the Lady again appeared, this time before a large crowd. Some who were skeptical did not see the miracle. Others in the crowd reported, however, that "the sun appeared and seemed to tremble, rotate violently and fall, dancing over the heads of the throng...."

The Shrine was empty when I visited it. The cult of Our Lady of Fatima, I imagine, has only a few devotees. The cult of Pareto optimality, however, has many. Where some people see only environmental devastation, its devotees perceive efficiency, utility, and maximization of wealth. They see the satisfaction of wants. They envision the good life. As I looked over the smudged and ruined terrain I tried to share that vision. I hope that Our Lady of Fatima, worker of miracles, might serve, at least for the moment, as the

Patroness of cost-benefit analysis. I thought of all the wants and needs that are satisfied in a landscape of honeymoon cottages, commercial strips, and dumps for hazardous waste. I saw the miracle of efficiency. The prospect, however, looked only darker in that light.

I

This essay concerns the economic decisions we make about the environment. It also concerns our political decisions about the environment. Some people have suggested that ideally these should be the same, that all environmental problems are problems in distribution. According to this view there is an environmental problem only when some resource is not allocated in equitable and efficient ways.

This approach to environmental policy is pitched entirely at the level of the consumer. It is his or her values that count, and the measure of these values is the individual's willingness to pay. The problem of justice or fairness in society becomes, then, the problem of distributing goods and services so that more people get more of what they want to buy. A condo on the beach. A snowmobile for the mountains. A tank full of gas. A day of labor. The only values we have, on this view, are those which a market can price.

How much do you value open space, a stand of trees, an "unspoiled" landscape? Fifty dollars? A hundred? A thousand? This is one way to measure value. You could compare the amount consumers would pay for a townhouse or coal or a landfill and the amount they would pay to preserve an area in its "natural" state. If users would pay more for the land with the house, the coal mine, or the landfill, than without—less construction and other costs of development—then the efficient thing to do is to improve the land and thus increase its value. That is why we have so many tract developments. And pizza stands. And gas stations. And strip mines. And landfills. How much did you spend last year to preserve open space? How much for pizza and gas? "In principle, the ultimate measure of environmental quality," as one basic text assures us, "is the value people place on these...services or their *willingness to pay*."

Willingness to pay. What is wrong with that? The rub is this: not all of us think of ourselves simply as *consumers*. Many of us regard ourselves as *citizens* as well. We act as consumers to get what we want *for ourselves*. We act as citizens to achieve what we think is right or best *for the community*. The question arises, then, whether what we want for ourselves individually as consumers is consistent with the goals we would set for ourselves collectively as citizens. Would I vote for the sort of things I shop for? Are my preferences as a consumer consistent with my judgments as a citizen?

They are not. I am schizophrenic. Last year, I fixed a couple of tickets and was happy to do so since I saved fifty dollars. Yet, at election time, l helped to vote the corrupt judge out of office. I speed on the highway; yet I want the police to enforce laws against speeding. I used to buy mixers in returnable bottles–but who can bother to return them? I buy only disposables now, but, to soothe my conscience, I urge my state senator to outlaw one-way containers. I love my car; I hate the bus. Yet I vote for candidates who promise to tax gasoline to pay for public transportation. I send my dues to the Sierra Club to protect areas in Alaska I shall never visit. And I support the work of the American League to Abolish Capital Punishment although, personally, I have nothing to gain one way or the other. (When I hang, I will hang myself.) And of course I applaud the Endangered Species Act, although I have no earthly use for the Colorado squawfish or the Indiana bat. I support almost any political cause that I think will defeat my consumer interests. This is because I have contempt for–although I act upon–those interests. I have an "Ecology Now" sticker on a car that leaks oil everywhere it's parked.

The distinction between consumer and citizen preferences has long vexed the theory of public finance. Should the public economy serve the same goals as the household economy? May it serve, instead, goals emerging from our association as citizens? The question asks if we may collectively strive for and achieve only those items we individually compete for and consume. Should we aspire, instead, to public goals we may legislate as a nation?

The problem, insofar as it concerns public finance, is stated as follows by R. A. Musgrave, who reports a conversation he had with Gerhard Colm.

> He [Colm] holds that the individual voter dealing with political issues has a frame of reference quite distinct from that which underlies his allocation of income as a consumer. In the latter situation the voter acts as a private individual determined by self-interest and deals with his personal wants; in the former, he acts as a political being guided by his image of a good society. The two, Colm holds, are different things.

Are these two different things? Stephen Marglin suggests that they are. He writes:

> The preferences that govern one's unilateral market actions no longer govern his actions when the form of reference is shifted from the market to the political arena. The Economic Man and the Citizen are for all intents and purposes two different individuals. It is not a question, therefore, of rejecting individual... preference maps; it is, rather, that market and political preference maps are inconsistent.

Marglin observes that if this is true, social choices optimal under one set of preferences will not be optimal under another. What, then, is the meaning of "optimality"? He notices that if we take a person's true preferences to be those expressed in the market, we may, then, neglect or reject the preferences that person reveals in advocating a political cause or position. "One might argue on welfare grounds," Marglin speculates, "for authoritarian rejection of individuals' politically revealed preferences in favor of their market revealed preferences!"

II

On February 19, 1981, President Reagan published Executive Order 12,291 requiring all administrative agencies and departments to support every new major regulation with a cost-benefit analysis establishing that the benefits of the regulation to society outweigh its costs. The Order directs the Office of Management and Budget (OMB) to review every such regulation on the basis of the adequacy of the cost-benefit analysis supporting it. This is a departure from tradition. Traditionally, regulations have been reviewed not by OMB but by the courts on the basis of their relation not to cost-benefit analysis but to authorizing legislation.

A month earlier, in January 1981, the Supreme Court heard lawyers for the American Textile Manufacturers Institute argue against a proposed Occupational Safety and Health Administration (OSHA) regulation which would have severely restricted the acceptable levels of cotton dust in textile plants. The lawyers for industry argued that the benefits of the regulation would not equal the costs. The lawyers for the government contended that the law required the tough standard. OSHA, acting consistently with Executive Order 12,291, asked the Court not to decide the cotton dust case, in order to give the agency time to complete the cost-benefit analysis required by the textile industry. The Court declined to accept OSHA's request and handed down its opinion on June 17, 1981.

The Supreme Court, in a 5–3 decision, found that the actions of regulatory agencies which conform to the OSHA law need not be supported by cost-benefit analysis. In addition, the Court asserted that Congress in writing a statute, rather than the agencies in applying it, has the primary responsibility for balancing benefits and costs. The Court said:

> When Congress passed the Occupational Health and Safety Act in 1970, it chose to place preeminent value on assuring employees a safe and healthful working environment, limited only by the feasibility of achieving such an environment. We must measure the validity of the Secretary's actions against the requirements of that Act.

The opinion upheld the finding of the Appeals Court that "Congress itself struck the balance between costs and benefits in the mandate to the agency."

The Appeals Court opinion in *American Textile Manufacturers* vs. *Donovan* supports the principle that legislatures are not necessarily bound to a particular conception of regulatory policy. Agencies that apply the law, therefore, may not need to justify on cost-benefit grounds the standards they set. These standards may conflict with the goal of efficiency and still express our political will as a nation. That is, they may reflect not the personal choices of self-interested individuals, but the collective judgments we make on historical, cultural, aesthetic, moral, and ideological grounds.

The appeal of the Reagan Administration to cost-benefit analysis, however, may arise more from political than economic considerations. The intention, seen in the most favorable light, may not be to replace political or ideological goals with economic ones but to make economic goals more apparent in regulation. This is not to say that Congress should function to reveal a collective willingness-to-pay just as markets reveal an individual willingness-to-pay. It is to suggest that Congress should do more to balance economic with ideological, aesthetic, and moral goals. To think that environmental or worker safety policy can be based exclusively on aspiration for a "natural" and "safe" world is as foolish as to hold that environmental law can be reduced to cost-benefit accounting. The more we move to one extreme, as I found in Lewiston, the more likely we are to hear from the other.

III

The labor unions won an important political victory when Congress passed the Occupational Safety and Health Act of 1970. That Act, among other things, severely restricts worker exposure to toxic substances. It instructs the Secretary of Labor to set "the standard which most adequately assures, to the extent feasible...that no employee will suffer material impairment of health or functional capacity even if such employee has regular exposure to the hazard... for the period of his working life."

Pursuant to this law, the Secretary of Labor, in 1977, reduced from ten to one part per million (ppm) the permissible ambient exposure level for benzene, a carcinogenic for which no safe threshold is known. The American Petroleum Institute thereupon challenged the new standard in court. It argued, with much evidence in its favor, that the benefits (to workers) of the one ppm standard did not equal the costs (to industry). The standard, therefore, did not appear to be a rational response to a market failure in that it did not strike an efficient balance between the interests of workers in safety and the interests of industry and consumers in keeping prices down.

The Secretary of Labor defended the tough safety standard on the ground that the law demanded it. An efficient standard might have required safety until it cost industry more to prevent a risk than it cost workers to accept it. Had Congress adopted this vision of public policy—one which can be found in many economic texts—it would have treated workers not as ends-in-themselves but as means for the production of overall utility. And this, as the Secretary saw it, was what Congress refused to do.

The United States Court of Appeals for the Fifth Circuit agreed with the American Petroleum Institute and invalidated the one ppm benzene standard. On July 2, 1980, the Supreme Court affirmed remanding the benzene standard back to OSHA for revision. The narrowly based Supreme Court decision was divided over the role economic considerations should play in judicial review. Justice Marshall, joined in dissent by three other justices, argued that the court had undone on the basis of its own theory of regulatory policy an act of Congress inconsistent with that theory. He concluded that the plurality decision of the Court "requires the American worker to return to the political arena to win a victory that he won before in 1970."

To reject cost-benefit analysis, as Justice Marshall would, as a basis for public policy making is not necessarily to reject cost-effectiveness analysis, which is an altogether different thing. "*Cost-benefit analysis*," one commentator points out, "is used by the decision maker to establish societal goals as well as the means for achieving these goals, whereas *cost-effectiveness analysis* only compares alternative means for achieving 'given' goals." Justice Marshall's dissent objects to those who would make efficiency the goal of public policy. It does not necessarily object to those who would accomplish as efficiently as possible the goals Congress sets.

IV

When efficiency is the criterion of public safety and health one tends to conceive of social relations on the model of a market, ignoring competing visions of what we as a society should be like. Yet it is obvious that there are competing conceptions of how we should relate to one another. There are some who believe, on principle, that worker safety and environmental quality ought to be protected only insofar as the benefits of protection balance the costs. On the other hand, people argue, also on principle, that neither worker safety nor environmental quality should be treated merely as a commodity, to be traded at the margin for other commodities, but should be valued for its own sake. The conflict between these two principles is logical or moral, to be resolved by argument or debate. The question whether cost-benefit analysis should play a decisive role in policymaking is not to be decided by cost-benefit analysis. A contradiction between principles–between contending visions of the good society–cannot be settled by asking how much partisans are willing to pay for their beliefs.

The role of the *legislator*, the political role, may be more important to the individual than the role of *consumer*. The person, in other words, is not to be treated as merely a bundle of preferences to be juggled in cost-benefit analyses. The individual is to be respected as an advocate of ideas which are to be judged in relation to the reasons for them. If health and environmental statutes reflect a vision of society as something other than a market by requiring protections beyond what are efficient, then this may express not legislative ineptitude but legislative responsiveness to public values. To deny this vision because it is economically inefficient is simply to replace it with another vision. It is to insist that the ideas of the citizen be sacrificed to the psychology of the consumer.

We hear on all sides that government is routinized, mechanical, entrenched, and bureaucratized; the jargon alone is enough to dissuade the most mettlesome meddler. Who can make a difference? It is plain that for many of us the idea of a national political community has an abstract and suppositious quality. We have only our private conceptions of the good, if no way exists to arrive at a public one. This is only to note the continuation, in our time, of the trend Benjamin Constant described in the essay, *De La Liberte des*

Anciens Comparee a Celle des Modernes. Constant observes that the modern world, as opposed to the ancient, emphasizes civil over political liberties, the rights of privacy and property over those of community and participation. "Lost in the multitude," Constant writes, "the individual rarely perceives the influence that he exercises," and, therefore, must be content with "the peaceful enjoyment of private independence." The individual asks only to be protected by laws common to all in his pursuit of his own self-interest. The citizen has been replaced by the consumer; the tradition of Rousseau has been supplanted by that of Locke and Mill.

Nowhere are the rights of the moderns, particularly the rights of privacy and property, less helpful than in the area of the natural environment. Here the values we wish to protect—cultural, historical, aesthetic, and moral—are public values; they depend not so much upon what each person wants individually as upon what he or she believes we stand for collectively. We refuse to regard worker health and safety as commodities; we regulate hazards as a matter of right. Likewise, we refuse to treat environmental resources simply as public goods in the economist's sense. Instead, we prevent significant deterioration of air quality not only as a matter of individual self-interest but also as a matter of collective self-respect. How shall we balance efficiency against moral, cultural, and aesthetic values in policy for the workplace and the environment? No better way has been devised to do this than by legislative debate ending in a vote. This is not the same thing as a cost-benefit analysis terminating in a bottom line.

V

It is the characteristic of cost-benefit analysis that it treats all value judgments other than those made on its behalf as nothing but statements of preference, attitude, or emotion, insofar as they are value judgments. The cost-benefit analyst regards as true the judgment that we should maximize efficiency or wealth. The analyst believes that this view can be backed by reasons; the analyst does not regard it as a preference or want for which he or she must be willing to pay. The cost-benefit analyst, however, tends to treat all other normative views and recommendations as if they were nothing but subjective reports of mental states. The analyst supposes in all such cases that "this is right" and "this is what we ought to do" are equivalent to "I want this" and "this is what I prefer." Value judgments are beyond criticism if, indeed, they are nothing but expressions of personal preference; they are incorrigible since every person is in the best position to know what he or she wants. All valuation, according to this approach, happens *in foro interno*; debate *in foro publico* has no point. On this approach, the reasons that people give for their views, unless these people are welfare economists, do not count; what counts is how much they are willing to pay to satisfy their wants. Those who are willing to pay the most, for all intents and purposes, have the right view; theirs is the more informed opinion, the better aesthetic judgment, and the deeper moral insight.

The assumption that valuation is subjective, that judgments of good and evil are nothing but expressions of desire and aversion, is not unique to economic theory. There are psychotherapists—Carl Rogers is an example—who likewise deny the objectivity or cognitivity of valuation. For Rogers, there is only one criterion of worth: it lies in "the subjective world of the individual. Only he knows it fully." The therapist shows his or her client that a "value system is not necessarily something imposed from without, but is something experienced." Therapy succeeds when the client "perceives himself in such a way that no self-experience can be discriminated as more or less worthy of positive self-regard than any other...." The client then "tends to place the basis of standards within himself, recognizing that the 'goodness' or 'badness' of any experience or perceptual object is not something inherent in that object, but is a value placed in it by himself."

Rogers points out that "some clients make strenuous efforts to have the therapist exercise the valuing function, so as to provide them with guides for action." The therapist, however, "consistently keeps the locus of evaluation with the client." As long as the therapist refuses to "exercise the valuing function" and as long as he or she practices an "unconditional positive regard" for all the affective states of the client, then the therapist remains neutral among the client's values or "sensory and visceral experiences." The role of the therapist is legitimate, Rogers suggests, because of this value neutrality. The therapist accepts all felt preferences as valid and imposes none on the client.

Economists likewise argue that their role as policymakers is legitimate because they are neutral among competing values in the client society. The political economist, according to James Buchanan, "is or should be ethically neutral: the indicated results are influenced by his own value scale only insofar as this reflects his membership in a larger group." The economist might be most confident of the impartiality of his or her policy recommendations if he or she could derive them formally or mathematically from individual preferences. If theoretical difficulties make such a social welfare function impossible, however, the next best thing, to preserve neutrality, is to let markets function to transform individual preference orderings into a collective ordering of social states. The analyst is able then to base policy on preferences that exist in society and are not necessarily his own.

Economists have used this impartial approach to offer solutions to many outstanding social problems, for example, the controversy over abortion. An economist argues that "there is an optimal number of abortions, just as there is an optimal level of pollution, or purity.... Those who oppose abortion could eliminate it entirely, if their intensity of feeling were so strong as to lead to payments that were greater at the margin than the price anyone would pay to have an abortion." Likewise economists, in order to determine whether the war in Vietnam was justified, have estimated the willingness to pay of those who demonstrated against it. Likewise it should be possible, following the same line of reasoning, to decide whether Creationism should be taught in the public schools, whether black and white people should be segregated, whether the death penalty should be enforced, and whether the square root of six is three.

All of these questions depend upon how much people are willing to pay for their subjective preferences or wants—or none of them do. This is the beauty of cost-benefit analysis: no matter how relevant or irrelevant, wise or stupid, informed or uninformed, responsible or silly, defensible or indefensible wants may be, the analyst is able to derive a policy from them—a policy which is legitimate because, in theory, it treats all of these preferences as equally valid and good.

VI

Consider, by way of contrast, a Kantian conception of value. The individual, for Kant, is a judge of values, not a mere haver of wants, and the individual judges not for himself or herself merely, but as a member of a relevant community or group. The central idea in a Kantian approach to ethics is that some values are more reasonable than others and therefore have a better claim upon the assent of members of the community as such. The world of obligation, like the world of mathematics or the world of empirical fact, is intersubjective, it is public not private, so that objective standards of argument and criticism apply. Kant recognizes that values, like beliefs, are subjective states of mind, but he points out that like beliefs they have an objective content as well; therefore they are either correct or mistaken. Thus Kant discusses valuation in the context not of psychology but of cognition. He believes that a person who makes a value judgment—or a policy recommendation—claims to know what is *right* and not just what is *preferred.* A value judgment is like an empirical or theoretical judgment in that it claims to be true, not merely to be *felt.*

We have, then, two approaches to public policy before us. The first, the approach associated with normative versions of welfare economics, asserts that the only policy recommendation that can or need be defended on objective grounds is efficiency or wealth-maximization. Every policy decision after that depends only on the preponderance of feeling or preference, as expressed in willingness to pay. The Kantian approach, on the other hand, assumes that many policy recommendations other than that one may be justified or refuted on objective grounds. It would concede that the approach of welfare economics applies adequately to some questions, e.g., those which ordinary consumer markets typically settle. How many yo-yos should be produced as compared to how many frisbees? Shall pens have black ink or blue? Matters such as these are so trivial it is plain that markets should handle them. It does not follow, however, that we should adopt a market or quasi-market approach to every public question.

A market or quasi-market approach to arithmetic, for example, is plainly inadequate. No matter how much people are willing to pay, three will never be the square root of six. Similarly, segregation is a national curse and the fact that we are willing to pay for it does not make it better but only makes us worse. Similarly, the case for abortion must stand on the merits; it cannot be priced at the margin. Similarly, the war in Vietnam was a moral debacle and this can be determined without shadow-pricing the willingness to pay of those who demonstrated against it. Similarly, we do not decide to execute murderers by asking how much bleeding hearts are willing to pay to see a person pardoned and how much hard hearts are willing to pay to see him hanged. Our failures to make the right decisions in these matters are failures in arithmetic, failures in wisdom, failures in taste, failures in morality—but not market failures. There are no relevant markets to have failed. What separates these questions from those for which markets are appropriate is this. They involve matters of knowledge, wisdom, morality, and taste that admit of better or worse, right or wrong, true or false—and these concepts differ from that of economic optimality. Surely environmental questions—the protection of wilderness, habitats, water, land, and air as well as policy toward environmental safety and health—involve moral and aesthetic principles and not just economic ones. This is consistent, of course, with cost-effectiveness and with a sensible recognition of economic constraints.

The neutrality of the economist, like the neutrality of Rogers' therapist, is legitimate if private preferences or subjective wants are the only values in question. A person should be left free to choose the color of his or her necktie or necklace—but we cannot justify a theory of public policy or private therapy on that basis. If the patient seeks moral advice or tries to find reasons to justify a choice, the therapist, according to Rogers' model, would remind him or her to trust his visceral and sensory experiences. The result of this is to deny the individual status as a cognitive being capable of responding intelligently to reasons; it reduces him or her to a bundle of affective states. What Rogers' therapist does to the patient the cost-benefit analyst does to society as a whole. The analyst is neutral among our "values"—having first imposed a theory of what value is. This is a theory that is impartial among values and for that reason fails to treat the persons who have them with respect or concern. It does not treat them even as persons but only as locations at which wants may be found. And thus we may conclude that the neutrality of economics is not a basis for its legitimacy. We recognize it as an indifference toward value—an indifference so deep, so studied, and so assured that at first one hesitates to call it by its right name.

VII

The residents of Lewiston at the conference I attended demanded to know the truth about the dangers that confronted them and the reasons for these dangers. They wanted to be convinced that the sacrifice asked of them was legitimate even if it served interests other than their own. One official from a large chemical company dumping wastes in the area told them, in reply, that corporations were people and that people could talk to people about their feelings, interests, and needs. This sent a shiver through the audience. Like Joseph K. in *The Trial*, the residents of Lewiston asked for an explanation, justice, and truth, and they were told that their wants would be taken care of. They demanded to know the reasons for what was continually happening to them. They were given a personalized response instead.

This response, that corporations are "just people serving people" is consistent with a particular view of power. This is the view that identified power with the ability to get what one wants as an individual, that is, to satisfy one's personal preferences. When people in official positions in corporations or in the government put aside their personal interests, it would follow that they put aside their power as well. Their neutrality then justifies them in directing the resources of society in ways they determine to be best. This managerial role serves not their own interests but those of their clients. Cost-benefit analysis may be seen as a pervasive form of this paternalism. Behind this paternalism, as William Simon observes of the lawyer-client relationship, lies a theory of value that tends to personalize power. "It resists understanding power as a product of class, property, or institutions and collapses power into the personal needs and dispositions of the individuals who command and obey." Once the economist, the therapist, the lawyer, or the manager abjures his own interests and acts wholly on behalf of client individuals, he appears to have no power of his own and thus justifiably manipulates and controls everything. "From this perspective it becomes difficult to distinguish the powerful from the powerless. In every case, both the exercise of power and submission to it are portrayed as a matter of personal accommodation and adjustment."

The key to the personal interest or emotive theory of value, as one commentator has rightly said, "is the fact that emotivism entails the obliteration of any genuine distinction between manipulative and non-manipulative social relations." The reason is that once the effective self is made the source of all value, the public self cannot participate in the exercise of power. As Philip Reiff remarks, "the public world is constituted as one vast stranger who appears at inconvenient times and makes demands viewed as purely external and therefore with no power to elicit a moral response." There is no way to distinguish tyranny from the legitimate authority that public values and public law create.

"At the rate of progress since 1900," Henry Adams speculates in his *Education*, "every American who lived into the year 2000 would know how to control unlimited power." Adams thought that the Dynamo would organize and release as much energy as the Virgin. Yet in the 1980s, the citizens of Lewiston, surrounded by dynamos, high tension lines, and nuclear wastes, are powerless. They do not know how to criticize power, resist power, or justify power—for to do so depends on making distinctions between good and evil, right and wrong, innocence and guilt, justice and injustice, truth and lies. These distinctions cannot be made out and have no significance within an emotive or psychological theory of value. To adopt this theory is to imagine society as a market in which individuals trade voluntarily and without coercion. No individual, no belief, no faith has authority over them. To have power to act as a nation, however, we must be able to act, at least at times, on a public philosophy, conviction, or faith. We cannot replace with economic analysis the moral function of public law. The antinomianism [*antinomian*–the rejection of law and morality] of cost-benefit analysis is not enough.

36

A Defense of Risk-Cost-Benefit Analysis

Kristin Shrader-Frechette

Kristin Shrader-Frechette is professor in both the environmental sciences and policy program and the philosophy department at the University of Notre Dame. She is the author of numerous books and articles in environmental ethics and risk assessment, including *Environmental Ethics* (1981), *Nuclear Power and Public Policy* (1983), and *Risk Analysis and Scientific Method* (1985).

In this essay, Shrader-Frechette argues that critics of science, such as William Rees and Mark Sagoff (see Readings 67 and 69), level unsound criticisms against using the cost-benefit model for making environmental decisions. After explaining the basic idea of risk-cost-benefit analysis (RCBA), she shows how it can be useful to environmentalists. Then she examines several criticisms of RCBA, including objections to it as a formal method, an economic method, and an ethical method. Shrader-Frechette argues that they all fail to undermine its value as a tool for environmentalists.

Environmentalists often criticize science. They frequently argue for a more romantic, sensitive, holistic, or profound view of the world than science provides. William Rees, for example, criticizes economics on the grounds that it falls victim to scientific materialism; in his article in this volume, he says we need a new paradigm, other than economics, for achieving sustainable development. Similarly, Mark Sagoff, also writing in this text, criticizes the economic model of benefit-cost analysis and argues that it is not always the proper method for making environmental decisions. In particular, he criticizes benefit-cost analysis as utilitarian.

This essay argues that environmentalists' criticisms of science often are misguided. The criticisms err mainly because they ignore the fact that good science can help environmental causes as well as hinder them. Economic methods, for example, can show that nuclear power is not cost effective,[1] that it makes little economic sense to bury long-lived hazardous wastes,[2] and that

Source: Louis P. Pojman (ed.), *Environmental Ethics: Readings in Theory and Application*, 3rd edn (Stamford, CT: Wadsworth, 2001).

biological conservation is extraordinarily cost effective.[3] One reason some environmentalists are antiscience or antieconomics–and ignore the way science can help environmentalism–is that they misunderstand science. They attribute flaws to science when the errors are the result of how people use, interpret, or apply science, not the result of science itself. Rees, for example, criticizes economics as guilty of scientific materialism, yet this essay will show that economics (benefit-cost analysis) can be interpreted in terms of many frameworks, not just scientific materialism. Similarly, Sagoff criticizes benefit-cost analysis as utilitarian, yet this essay will show that the technique is neither *purely* utilitarian, nor utilitarian in a flawed way, because those who use benefit-cost analysis can interpret it in terms of Kantian values, not just utilitarian ones. If this essay is right, then the ethical problems with economics are not with the science itself but with us, humans who interpret and use it in biased ways. In other words, the real problems of economics are the political and ethical biases of its users, not the science itself. To paraphrase Shakespeare: The fault, dear readers, is not with the science but with ourselves, that we are underlings who use it badly.

Consider the case of risk-cost-benefit analysis and attacks on it. Risk-cost-benefit analysis (RCBA), the target of many philosophers' and environmentalists' criticisms, is very likely the single, most used economic method, at least in the United States, for evaluating the desirability of a variety of technological actions–from building a liquefied natural gas facility to adding yellow dye number 2 to margarine. The 1969 National Environmental Policy Act requires that some form of RCBA be used to evaluate all federal environment-related projects.[4] Also, all U.S. regulatory agencies–with the exception perhaps of only the Occupational Health and Safety Administration (OSHA)–routinely use RCBA to help determine their policies.[5]

Basically, RCBA consists of three main steps. These are (1) identifying all the risks, costs, and benefits associated with a particular policy action; (2) converting those risk, cost, and benefit values into dollar figures; and (3) then adding them to determine whether benefits outweigh the risks and costs. Consider the proposed policy action of coating fresh vegetables with a waxy, carcinogenic chemical to allow them to be stored for longer periods of time. Associated with such a policy would be items such as the risk of worker carcinogenesis or the cost of labor and materials for coating the vegetables. The relevant benefits would include factors such as increased market value of the vegetables since the preservative coating would reduce spoilage and losses in storage.

Those who favor RCBA argue that this technique–for identifying, quantifying, comparing, and adding all factors relevant to an economic decision–ought to be one of the major considerations that any rational person takes into account in developing social policy. To my knowledge, no economist or policymaker ever has argued that RCBA ought to be the sole basis on which any social or environmental choice is made. Despite the fact that RCBA, an application of welfare economics, dominates U.S. decision making regarding environmental and technological issues, it continues to draw much criticism.

Economists, industrial representatives, and governmental spokespersons tend to support use of RCBA, but philosophers, environmentalists, and consumer activists tend to criticize its employment.

This essay (1) summarizes the three main lines of criticism of RCBA, (2) outlines arguments for objections to RCBA, (3) shows that the allegedly most devastating criticisms of RCBA are at best misguided and at worst incorrect, and (4) reveals the real source of the alleged deficiencies of RCBA. Let us begin with the three main criticisms of RCBA. These are objections to RCBA (1) as a formal method, (2) as an economic method, and (3) as an ethical method.

Objection 1: RCBA as a Formal Method

The most strident criticisms of RCBA (as a *formal* method for making social decisions) come from phenomenologically oriented scholars, such as Hubert and Stuart Dreyfus at Berkeley. They argue that, because it is a rigid, formal method, RCBA cannot model all instances of "human situational understanding."[6] For example, say Stuart Dreyfus, Lawrence Tribe, and Robert Socolow, whenever someone makes a decision, whether about playing chess or driving an automobile, he or she uses intuition and not some analytic, economic "point count."[7] They claim that formal models like RCBA fail to capture the essence of human decision making. The models are too narrow and oversimplified in focusing on allegedly transparent rationality and scientific know-how. Rather, say Dreyfus and others, human decision making is mysterious, unformalizable, and intuitive, something close to wisdom.[8] This is because the performance of human decision making requires expertise and human skill acquisition that cannot be taught by means of any algorithm or formal method like RCBA.[9]

Moreover, say Robert Coburn, Amory Lovins, Alasdair MacIntyre, and Peter Self, humans not only do not go through any formal routine like RCBA, but they could not, even if they wanted to. Why not? Humans, they say, often can't distinguish costs from benefits. For example, generating increased amounts of electricity represents a cost for most environmentalists, but a benefit for most economists. Lovins and his colleagues also claim that people don't know either the probability of certain events, such as energy-related accidents, or the consequences likely to follow from them; they don't know because humans are not like calculating machines; they cannot put a number on what they value.[10]

Although these criticisms of RCBA are thought provoking, they need not be evaluated in full here, in part because they are analyzed elsewhere.[11] Instead, it might be good merely to sketch the sorts of arguments that, when developed, are capable of answering these objections to the use of RCBA. There are at least six such arguments.

The first is that, since Dreyfus and others merely point to deficiencies in RCBA without arguing that there is some less deficient decision method superior to RCBA, they provide only necessary but not sufficient grounds for rejecting RCBA. A judgment about sufficient grounds for rejecting RCBA ought to be based on a relative evaluation of all methodologic alternatives because reasonable people only reject a method if they have a better alternative to it. Showing deficiencies in RCBA does not establish that a better method is available.

A second argument is that Dreyfus, Tribe, Socolow, and others have "proved too much." If human decision making is unavoidably intuitive and if benefits are indistinguishable from costs, as they say, then no rational, debatable, nonarbitrary form of technologic policymaking is possible. This is because rational policymaking presupposes at least that persons can distinguish what is undesirable from what is desirable, costs from benefits. If they cannot, then this problem does not count against only RCBA but against any method. Moreover, Dreyfus and others ignore the fact that no policy-making methods, including RCBA, are perfect. And if not, then no theory should be merely criticized separately, since such criticisms say nothing about which theory is the least desirable of all.

Another argument, especially relevant to Dreyfus's claims that RCBA is not useful for individual tasks, such as the decision making involved in driving a car, is that many of the objections to RCBA focus on a point not at issue. That RCBA is not amenable to individual decision making is not at issue. The real issue is how to take into account millions of individual opinions, to make societal decisions. This is because societal decision making presupposes some unifying perspective or method of aggregating preferences of many people, a problem not faced by the individual making choices. Of course, accomplishing RCBA is not like individual decision making, and that is precisely why social choices require some formal analytic tool like RCBA.

Criticisms of RCBA as a formal method are also questionable because Dreyfus and others provide an incomplete analysis of societal decision making in making appeals to wisdom and intuition. They fail to specify, in a political and practical context, whose wisdom and intuitions ought to be followed and what criteria ought to be used when the wisdom and intuitions of different persons conflict in an environmental controversy. RCBA answers these questions in a methodical way.

A final argument against criticisms of RCBA, as a formal method, is that Dreyfus and others are incomplete in using policy arguments that ignore the real-world importance of making decisions among finite alternatives and with finite resources. Wisdom may tell us that human life has an infinite value, but the scientific and economic reality is that attaining a zero-risk society is impossible and that there are not enough resources for saving all lives. In dismissing RCBA, Dreyfus and others fail to give their answers to the tough question of what criterion to use in distributing environmental health and safety.[12] If we do not use RCBA, what informal method is a bigger help? This realistic question they do not answer. If not, RCBA may be the best method among many bad methods.

Objection 2: RCBA as an Economic Method

Although these six argument-sketches are too brief to be conclusive in answering objections to RCBA as a formal method, let us move on to the second type of criticism so that we can get to the main focus of this essay. Philosophers of science and those who are critical of mainstream economics, like Kenneth Boulding, most often criticize RCBA as a deficient economic method. Perhaps the most powerful methodologic attack on RCBA deficiencies focuses on its central methodologic assumption: Societal welfare can be measured as the algebraic sum of compensating variations (CVs). By analytically unpacking the concept of compensating variation, one can bring many RCBA deficiencies to light.

According to RCBA theory, each individual has a CV that measures the change in his or her welfare as a consequence of a proposed policy action. For example, suppose a university was considering raising the price of student parking permits from $200 per year to $400 per year and using the additional money to build a parking garage on campus. Suppose also that the university would decide whether this act or policy was desirable on the basis of the way it affected all the students. Raising the parking fees and building a garage would affect the welfare of each student differently, depending on her (or his) circumstances. According to economic theory, the CV of each student would measure her particular change in welfare. To find exactly how each student would measure her CV, her change in welfare because of the changed parking fees, we would ask her to estimate it. For example, suppose Susan drives to campus each day and has a part-time job off campus, so she cannot carpool or ride a bus because she needs her car to move efficiently between campus and work. Susan wants to have the parking garage, however, because she has to look nice in her part-time job. If the university builds the parking garage, she will not get wet and muddy walking to her car and will not have to spend 20 minutes searching for a parking place. If someone asked Susan to put a monetary value on paying $200 more per year for parking in a garage, she might say this change was worth an additional $100, and that, even if the fees increased by $300, would rather have the parking garage. That is, Susan would say her CV was +$100 because she would gain from the new plan. However, suppose Sally also drives to campus each day and suppose her welfare is affected negatively by the increase in parking fees and the proposed parking garage. Because Sally lives at an inconvenient location two hours away, she must drive to campus and park her car every day. But because she lives so far away, has no part-time job, and is going to school with savings, Sally wants to pay as little as possible for parking and prefers the existing muddy, uncovered parking lots. If someone asks Sally to put a monetary value on paying $200 more per year for parking in a garage, she might say this change harmed her by $200. That is, Sally would say her CV was −$200. Economists who use RCBA believe that, in order to determine the desirability of building the parking garage and charging $200 more per year, they should add all the CVs of gainers (like Susan) and losers (like Sally) and see whether the gains of the action outweigh the losses.

Or consider the case of using CVs to measure the effects of building a dam. The CVs of some persons will be positive, and those of others will be negative. Those in the tourism industry might be affected positively, whereas those interested in wilderness experiences might be affected negatively. The theory is that the proposed dam is cost-beneficial if the sum of the CVs of the gainers can outweigh the sum of the CVs of the losers. In more technical language, according to economist Ezra Mishan, a CV is the sum of money that, if received or paid after the economic (or technologic) change in question, would make the individual no better or worse off than before the change. If, for example, the price of a bread loaf falls by 10 cents, the CV is the maximum sum a man would pay to be allowed to buy bread at this lower price. Per contra, if the loaf rises by 10 cents, the CV is the minimum sum the man must receive if he is to continue to feel as well off as he was before the rise in price.[13] Implicit in the notion of a CV are three basic presuppositions, all noted in standard texts on welfare economics and cost-benefit analysis: (1) the compensating variation is a measure of how gains can be so distributed to make everyone in the community better off[14]; (2) the criterion for whether one is better off is how well off feels subjectively[15]; and (3) one's feelings of being well off or better off are measured by a sum of money judged by the individual and calculated at the given set of prices on the market.[16]

According to the critics of RCBA, each of the three presuppositions built into the concept of a CV contains controversial assumptions.[17] The first presupposition, that CVs provide a measure of how to make everyone better off, is built on at least two questionable assumptions: Gains and losses, costs and benefits, for every individual in every situation can be computed numerically.[18] A second questionable assumption built into this presupposition is that employing an economic change to improve the community welfare is acceptable, even though distributional effects of this change are ignored. Many people have argued that the effect of this assumption is merely to make economic changes that let the rich get richer and the poor get poorer, thus reflecting the dominant ideologies of the power groups dominating society.

The second presupposition built into the notion of CV, that the criterion for whether one is better off is how one feels subjectively, as measured in quantitative terms, also embodies a number of doubtful assumptions. Some of these are that, as Kenneth Arrow admits, individual welfare is defined in terms of egoistic hedonism[19]; that the individual is the best judge of his welfare, that is, that preferences reveal welfare, despite the fact that utility is often different from morality[20]; that summed preferences of *individual* members of a group reveal *group* welfare[21]; and that wealthy and poor persons are equally able to judge their well-being. This last assumption has been widely criticized since willingness to pay is a function of the marginal utility of one's income. That is, rich people are more easily able to pay for improvements to their welfare than poor people are. As a consequence, poor persons obviously cannot afford to pay as much as rich persons in order to avoid the risks and other disamenities of technology-related environmental pollution.[22] That is why poor people are often forced to live in areas of high pollution, while wealthy people can afford to live in cleaner environments.

Continuing the analysis of CV, critics of RCBA point out that the third presupposition built into the notion of CV also involves a number of questionable assumptions. The presupposition that one's feelings of being better off are measured by money, and calculated in terms of market prices, includes at least one highly criticized assumption–that prices measure values. This assumption is controversial on a number of grounds. For one thing, it begs the difference between wants and morally good wants. It also ignores economic effects that distort prices. Some of these distorting effects include monopolies, externalities, speculative instabilities, and "free goods," such as clean air.[23]

Because methodologic criticisms such as these have been a major focus of much contemporary writing in philosophy of economics and in sociopolitical philosophy, discussion of them is extremely important. However, economists generally *admit* most of the preceding points but claim that they have no better alternative method to use than RCBA. If their claim is at least partially correct, as I suspect it is (see the previous section of this essay), then many of the preceding criticisms of RCBA are beside the point. Also, both economists and philosophers have devised ways of avoiding most of the troublesome presuppositions and consequences of the assumptions built into the notion of compensating variation. Chief among these ways of improving RCBA are use of alternative weighting schemes and employment of various ways to make the controversial aspects of RCBA explicit and open to evaluation. Use of a weighting scheme for RCBA would enable one, for example, to "cost" inequitably distributed risks more than equitably distributed ones. Also, if one desired, it would be possible to employ Rawlsian weighting schemes for promoting the welfare of the least-well-off persons. One of the chief reforms, important for addressing the economic deficiencies of RCBA, would be to employ a form of adversary assessment in which alternative RCBA studies would be performed by groups sharing different ethical and methodologic presuppositions. Such adversary assessment has already been accomplished, with success, in Ann Arbor, Michigan, and in Cambridge, Massachusetts.[24] Hence, at least in theory, there are ways to avoid the major economic deficiencies inherent in RCBA.

Objection 3: RCBA as an Ethical Method

The most potentially condemning criticisms of RCBA come from the ranks of moral philosophers. Most of those who criticize RCBA on ethical grounds, as one might suspect, are deontologists who employ standard complaints against utilitarians. Philosophers, such as Alasdair MacIntyre and Douglas MacLean, claim that some things are priceless and not amenable to risk-benefit costing. Alan Gewirth argues that certain commitments–for example, the right not to be caused to contract cancer–cannot be traded off (via RCBA) for some utilitarian benefit.[25] In sum, the claim of these ethicist critics of RCBA is that moral commitments, rights, and basic goods are inviolable and incommensurable and hence cannot be "bargained away" in a utilitarian scheme like RCBA, which is unable to take adequate account of them and of values like distributive justice.

Of course, the linchpin assumption of the arguments of Gewirth, MacLean, and others is that RCBA is indeed utilitarian. If this assumption can be proved wrong, then (whatever else is wrong with RCBA) it cannot be attacked on the grounds that it is utilitarian.

Misguided ethical criticism of RCBA

RCBA is not essentially utilitarian in some damaging sense for a number of reasons. First of all, let's admit that RCBA is indeed utilitarian in one crucial respect: The optimal choice is always determined by some function of the utilities attached to the consequences of all the options considered. Hence, reasoning in RCBA is unavoidably consequentialist.

Because it is unavoidably consequentialist, however, means neither that RCBA is consequentialist in some *disparaging* sense, nor that it is only consequentialist, both points that are generally begged by deontological critics of RCBA. Of course, RCBA is necessarily consequentialist, but so what? Anyone who follows some deontological theory and ignores consequences altogether is just as simplistic as anyone who focuses merely on consequences and ignores deontological elements. This is exactly the point recognized by Amartya Sen when he notes that Jeremy Bentham and John Rawls capture two different but equally important aspects of interpersonal welfare considerations.[26] Both provide necessary conditions for ethical judgments, but neither is sufficient.

Although RCBA is necessarily consequentialist, there are at least four reasons that it is not only consequentialist in some extremist or disparaging sense. *First*, any application of RCBA principles presupposes that we make some value judgments that cannot be justified by utilitarian standards alone.[27] For example, suppose we are considering which of a variety of possible actions (e.g., building a nuclear plant, a coal plant, or a solar facility) ought to be evaluated in terms of RCBA. A utilitarian value judgment would not suffice for reducing the set of options. It would not suffice for deciding which of many available chemicals to use in preserving foods in a given situation, for example, because we would not have performed the utility weighting yet. Usually we use deontological grounds for rejecting some option. For instance, we might reject chemical X as a food preservative because it is a powerful carcinogen and use of it would threaten consumers' rights to life.

Second, RCBA also presupposes another type of nonutilitarian value judgment by virtue of the fact that it would be impossible to know the utilities attached to an infinity of options because they are infinite. To reduce these options, one would have to make some nonutilitarian value judgments about which options not to consider. For example, suppose chemical Z (considered for preserving food) were known to cause death to persons with certain allergic sensitivities or to persons with diabetes. On grounds of preventing a violation of a legal right to equal protection, analysts using RCBA could simply exclude chemical Z from consideration, much as they exclude technically or economically infeasible options for consideration.

Also, in the course of carrying out RCBA calculations–one is required to make a number of nonutilitarian value judgments. Some of these are: (1) There is a cardinal or ordinal scale in terms of which the consequences may be assigned some number, (2) a particular discount rate ought to be used, (3) or certain values ought to be assigned to certain consequences. For example, if policymakers subscribed to the deontological, evaluative judgment that future generations have rights equal to our own, then they could employ a zero discount rate. Nothing in the theory underlying RCBA would prevent them from doing so and from recognizing this deontological value.

Third, one could weight the RCBA parameters to reflect whatever value system society wishes. As Ralph Keeney has noted, one could always assign the value of negative infinity to consequences alleged to be the result of an action that violated some deontological principle.[28] Thus, if one wanted to avoid any technology likely to result in violation of people's rights not to be caused to contract cancer, one could easily do so.

Fourth, RCBA is not necessarily utilitarian, as Patrick Suppes points out, because the theory could, in principle, be adopted (without change) to represent a "calculus of obligation and a theory of expected obligation"; in other words, RCBA is materially indifferent, a purely formal calculus with an incomplete theory of rationality.[29] This being so, one need not interpret only market parameters as costs. Indeed, economists have already shown that one can interpret RCBA to accommodate egalitarianism and intuitionism as well as utilitarianism.[30] More generally, Kenneth Boulding has eloquently demonstrated that economic supply-demand curves can be easily interpreted to fit even a benevolent or an altruistic ethical framework, not merely a utilitarian ethical framework.[31]

The Real Source of RCBA Problems

If these four arguments, from experts such as Suppes and Keeney, are correct, then much of the criticism of RCBA, at least for its alleged ethical deficiencies, has been misguided. It has been directed at the formal, economic, and ethical *theory* underlying RCBA, when apparently something else is the culprit. This final section will argue that there are at least two sources of the problems that have made RCBA so notorious. One is the dominant political ideology in terms of which RCBA has been interpreted, applied, and used. The second source of the difficulties associated with RCBA has been the tendency of both theorists and practitioners–economists and philosophers alike–to claim more objectivity for the conclusions of RCBA than the evidence warrants. Let's investigate both of these problem areas.

Perhaps the major reason that people often think, erroneously, that RCBA is utilitarian is that capitalist utilitarians first used the techniques. Yet, to believe that the logical and ethical presuppositions built into economic methods can be identified with the logical and ethical beliefs of those who originate or use the methods is to commit the genetic fallacy.[32] *Origins* do not necessarily determine *content*. And, if not, then RCBA has no built-in ties to utilitarianism.[33] What has happened is that, in practice, one *interpretation* of RCBA has been dominant. This interpretation, in terms of capitalist utilitarianism, is what is incompatible with nonutilitarian values. But this means that the problems associated with the dominant political ideology, in terms of which RCBA is interpreted, has been confused with RCBA problems. Were the methods interpreted according to a different ideology, it would be just as wrong to equate RCBA with that ideology.

Confusion about the real source of the problems with RCBA has arisen because of the difficulty of determining causality. The cause of the apparent utilitarian biases in RCBA is the dominant *ideology* in terms of which people interpret it. The cause is not the method itself. This is like the familiar point, which often needs reiteration, that humans, not computers, cause computer errors. Given this explanation, it is easy to see why C. B. MacPherson argues that there is no necessary incompatibility between maximizing utilities and maximizing some nonutilitarian value. The alleged incompatibility arises only after one interprets the nonutilitarian value. In this case, the alleged incompatibility arises only when one interprets utilities in terms of unlimited individual appropriations and market incentives.[34]

If the preceding view of RCBA is correct and if people have erroneously identified one—of many possible—interpretations of RCBA with the method, then obviously they have forgotten that RCBA is a formal calculus to be used with a variety of interpretations. But if they have forgotten that RCBA is open to many different interpretations, then they have identified one dominant political interpretation with RCBA itself, then they have forgotten that, because of this dominant interpretation, RCBA is politically loaded. And if they have forgotten that they are employing a utilitarian *interpretation* that is politically loaded, then they probably have assumed that RCBA is objective by virtue of its being part of science.

Utilitarian philosophers and welfare economists have been particularly prone to the errors of believing that utilitarian interpretations of decision making are objective and value-free. Utilitarian R. M. Hare argues in his book, for example, that moral philosophy can be done without ontology[35]; he also argues that moral philosophy can be done objectively and with certainty, that there are no irresolvable moral conflicts[36]; and that objective moral philosophy is utilitarian in character.[37] Hare even goes so far as to argue that a hypothetical-deductive method can be used to obtain moral evaluations and to test them.[83] Hare, one of the best moral philosophers of the century, equates utilitarian tenets with value-free, certain conclusions obtained by the scientific method of hypothesis-deduction. His error here means that we ought not be surprised that lesser minds also have failed to recognize the evaluative and interpretational component in utilitarianism and in the utilitarian interpretations of RCBA. Numerous well-known practitioners of RCBA have argued that the technique is objective, and they have failed to recognize its value component.[39] Milton Friedman calls economics objective,"[40] and Chauncey Starr, Chris Whipple, David Okrent, and other practitioners of RCBA use the same terminology; they even claim that those who do not accept their value-laden interpretations of RCBA are following merely "subjective" interpretations.[41]

Given that both moral philosophers and practitioners of RCBA claim that their utilitarian analyses are objective, they create an intellectual climate in which RCBA is presumed to be more objective, value-free, and final than it really is. Hence, one of the major problems with RCBA is not that it is inherently utilitarian but that its users erroneously assume it has a finality that it does not possess. It is one of many possible techniques, and it has many interpretations. Were this recognized, then people would not oppose it so vehemently.

Summary and Conclusions

RCBA has many problems. As a formal method, it suggests that life is more exact and precise than it really is. As an economic method, it suggests that people make decisions on the basis of hedonism and egoism. As an ethical method, people have interpreted it in utilitarian ways, in ways that serve the majority of people, but not always the minority.

Despite all these criticisms, RCBA is often better than most environmentalists believe. It is better because criticisms of RCBA often miss the point in two important ways. First, the criticisms miss the point that society needs some methodical way to tally costs and benefits associated with its activities. While it is true that RCBA has problems because of its being a formal, economic method, this criticism of it misses the point. The point is that we humans need some clear, analytic way to help us with environmental decision making. Most people would not write a blank check in some area of personal life, and no one ought to write a blank check for solving societal problems. Not using some technique like RCBA means that we would be writing a blank check, making decisions and commitments without being aware of their costs, benefits, and consequences. All that RCBA asks of us is that we add up all the risks, benefits, and costs of our actions. It asks that we not make decisions without considering all the risks, costs, and benefits. The point is that RCBA does not need to be perfect to be useful in societal and environmental decision making; it needs only to be useful, helpful, and better than other available methods for making societal decisions.

Second, criticisms of RCBA miss the point because they blame RCBA for a variety of ethical problems, mainly problems associated with utilitarianism. RCBA, however, is merely a formal calculus for problem solving. The users of RCBA are responsible for the capitalistic, utilitarian interpretation of it. If so, then what needs to be done is neither to abandon RCBA, nor to condemn it as utilitarian, but to give some philosophical lessons in the value ladenness of its interpretations. We need more ethical and epistemological sensitivity among those who interpret RCBA, and we need to recognize practical, political problems for what they are. The problem is with us, with our values, with our politics. The problem is not with RCBA methods that merely reflect our values and politics.

Notes

1. K. S. Shrader-Frechette, *Nuclear Power and Public Policy* (Boston: Kluwer, 1983), 54–60.

2. K. S. Shrader-Frechette, *Burying Uncertainty* (Berkeley: University of California Press, 1993), 239–241.

3. K. S. Shrader-Frechette and E. McCoy, *Method in Ecology* (New York: Cambridge University Press, 1993), 175–185.

4. See Ian G. Barbour, *Technology, Environment, and Human Values* (New York: Praeger, 1980), 163–164.

5. Luther J. Carter, "Dispute over Cancer Risk Quantification," *Science* 203, no. 4387 (1979): 1324–1325.

6. Stuart E. Dreyfus, "Formal Models vs. Human Situational Understanding: Inherent Limitations on the Modeling of Business Expertise," *Technology and People* 1 (1982): 133–165. See also S. Dreyfus, "The Risks! and Benefits? of Risk-Benefit Analysis," unpublished paper presented on March 24, 1983, in Berkeley, California, at the Western Division meeting of the American Philosophical Association. Stuart Dreyfus and his brother Hubert Dreyfus share the beliefs attributed to Stuart in these and other publications. They often coauthor publications. See, for example, S. Dreyfus and H. Dreyfus, "The Scope, Limits, and Training Implications of Three Models of... Behavior," ORC 79-2 (Berkeley: Operations Research Center, University of California, February 1979).

7. S. Dreyfus, "Formal Models," op. cit., note 6, 161. See also Lawrence H. Tribe, "Technology Assessment and the Fourth Discontinuity," *Southern California Law Review* 46, no. 3 (June 1973): 659; and Robert Socolow, "Failures of Discourse," in D. Scherer and T. Attig, eds., *Ethics and the Environment* (Englewood Cliffs, NJ: Prentice Hall, 1983): 152–166.

8. S. Dreyfus, "Formal Models," op. cit., note 6, 161–163; and Douglas MacLean, "Understanding the Nuclear Power Controversy," in A. L. Caplan and H. Englehardt, eds., *Scientific Controversies* (Cambridge: Cambridge University Press, 1983), Part 5.

9. S. Dreyfus, "The Risks! and Benefits?" op. cit., note 6, 2.

10. Peter Self, *Econocrats and the Policy Process: The Politics and Philosophy of Cost-Benefit Analysis* (London: Macmillan, 1975), 70; Alisdair MacIntyre, "Utilitarians and Cost-Benefit Analysis," in D. Scherer and T. Attig, eds., *Ethics and the Environment*, op. cit., note 7, 143–145; and Amory Lovins, "Cost-Risk-Benefit Assessment in Energy Policy," *George Washington Law Review* 45, no. 5 (August 1977): 913–916, 925–926. See also Robert Coburn, "Technology Assessment, Human Good, and Freedom," in K. E. Goodpaster and K. M. Sayer, eds., *Ethics and Problems of the 21st Century* (Notre Dame: University of Notre Dame Press, 1979), 108; E. J. Mishan, Cost-Benefit Analysis (New York: Praeger, 1976), 160–161; Gunnar Myrdal, *The Political Element in the Development of Economic Theory*, Paul Steeten, trans. (Cambridge: Harvard University Press, 1955), 89; and A. Radomysler, "Welfare Economics and Economic Policy," in K. Arrow and

T. Scitovsky, eds., *Readings in Welfare Economics* (Homewood, IL: Irwin, 1969), 89.

11. See K. S. Shrader-Frechette, *Science Policy, Ethics, and Economic Methodology* (Boston: Reidel, 1985), 38–54. See also K. S. Shrader-Frechette, *Risk and Rationality* (Berkeley: University of California Press, 1991), 169–196.

12. Shrader-Frechette, *Science Policy*, op. cit., note 11, 36–54; K. S. Shrader-Frechette, *Risk and Rationality*, op. cit., note 11, 169–183.

13. Mishan, *Cost-Benefit Analysis*, op. cit., note 10, 391.

14. Ibid., 390.

15. Ibid., 309.

16. E. J. Mishan, *Welfare Economics* (New York: Random House, 1969), 113; see also 107–113.

17. For a more complete analysis of these points, see K. S. Shrader-Frechette, "Technology Assessment as Applied Philosophy of Science," *Science, Technology, and Human Values* 6, no. 33 (Fall 1980), 33–50.

18. M. W. Jones-Lee, *The Value of Life* (Chicago: University of Chicago Press, 1976), 3; and R. Coburn, "Technology Assessment," in K. E. Goodpaster and K. M. Sayer, eds., *Ethics and Problems of the 21st Century*, op. cit., note 10, 109. See also Oskar Morgenstern, *On the Accuracy of Economic Observations* (Princeton, NJ: Princeton University Press, 1963), 100–101.

19. Cited in V. C. Walsh, "Axiomatic Choice Theory and Values," in Sidney Hook, ed., *Human Values and Economic Policy* (New York: New York University Press, 1967), 197.

20. See R. Coburn, "Technology Assessment," in K. E. Goodpaster and K. M. Sayer, eds., *Ethics and Problems of the 21st Century*, op. cit., note 10, 109–110; Gail Kennedy, "Social Choice and Policy Formation," in S. Hook, ed., *Human Values and Economic Policy*, op. cit., note 19, 142; and John Ladd, "The Use of Mechanical Models for the Solution of Ethical Problems," in S. Hook, ed., *Human Values and Economic Policy*, op. cit., 167–168. See also Mark Lutz and Kenneth Lux, *The Challenge of Humanistic Economics* (London: Benjamin/Cummings, 1979). Finally, see Richard Brandt, "Personal Values and the Justification of Institutions," in S. Hook, ed., *Human Values and Economic Policy*, op. cit., note 19, 37; and John Ladd, "Models," in S. Hook, ed., *Human Values and Economic Policy*, op. cit., note 19, 159–168.

21. G. Kennedy, "Social Choice," S. Hook, ed., *Human Values and Economic Policy*, op. cit., note 20, 148, makes the same point.

22. Peter S. Albin, "Economic Values and the Values of Human Life," in S. Hook, ed., *Human Values and Economic Policy*, op. cit., note 19, 97; and M. W. Jones-Lee, *Value of Life*, op. cit., note 18, 20–55.

23. See J. A. Hobson, *Confessions of an Economic Heretic* (Sussex, England: Harvester Press, 1976), 39–40; and Benjamin M. Anderson, *Social Value* (New York: A. M. Kelley, 1966), 24, 26, 31, 162. See also Kenneth Boulding, "The Basis of Value Judgments in Economics," in S. Hook, ed., *Human Values and Economic Policy*, op. cit., note 19, 67–79; and O. Morgenstern, *Accuracy of Economic Observations*, op. cit., note 18, 19. Finally, see E. J. Mishan, *Cost-Benefit Analysis*, op. cit., note 10, 393–394; and E. F. Schumacher, *Small is Beautiful* (New York: Harper, 1973), 38–49; as well as N. Georgescu Roegen, *Energy and Economic Myths* (New York: Pergamon, 1976), x, 10–14.

24. See Shrader-Frechette, *Science Policy*, op. cit., note 11, Chapters 8–9; Shrader-Frechette, *Risk and Rationality*, op. cit., note 11; and B. A. Weisbrod, "Income Redistribution Effects and Benefit-Cost Analysis," in S. Chase, ed., *Problems in Public Expenditure Analysis* (Washington, D.C.: Brookings, 1972), 177–208. See also P. Dasgupta, S. Marglin, and A. Sen, *Guidelines of Project Evaluation* (New York:

UNIDO, 1972); and A. V. Kneese, S. Ben-David, and W. Schulze, "The Ethical Foundations of Benefit-Cost Analysis," in D. MacLean and P. Brown, eds., "A Study of the Ethical Foundations of Benefit-Cost Techniques," unpublished report done with funding from the National Science Foundation, Program in Ethics and Values in Science and Technology, August 1979.

25. Lovins, "Cost-Risk-Benefit Assessment," op. cit., note 10, 929–930; Douglas MacLean, "Qualified Risk Assessment and the Quality of Life," in D. Zinberg, ed., *Uncertain Power* (New York: Pergamon, 1983), Part V; and Alan Gewirth, "Human Rights and the Prevention of Cancer," in D. Scherer and T. Attig, eds., *Ethics and the Environment*, op. cit., note 7, 177.

26. Amartya K. Sen, "Rawls Versus Bentham," in N. Daniels, ed., *Reading Rawls* (New York: Basic Books, 1981), 283–292.

27. Ronald Giere, "Technological Decision Making," in M. Bradie and K. Sayre, eds., *Reason and Decision* (Bowling Green, OH: Bowling Green State University Press, 1981), Part 3, makes a similar argument.

28. Ralph G. Keeney mentioned this to me in a private conversation at Berkeley in January 1983.

29. Patrick Suppes, "Decision Theory," in P. Edwards, ed., *Encyclopedia of Philosophy*, Vol. 1 and 2 (New York: Collier-Macmillan, 1967), 311.

30. P. S. Dasgupta and G. M. Heal, *Economic Theory and Exhaustible Resources* (Cambridge: Cambridge University Press, 1979), 269–281.

31. K. Boulding, "Value Judgments," in S. Hook, ed., *Human Values and Economic Policy*, op. cit., note 23, 67ff.

32. Alexander Rosenberg makes this point in *Macroeconomic Laws* (Pittsburgh: University of Pittsburgh Press, 1976), 203.

33. Tribe, "Technology Assessment," op. cit., note 7, 628–629; MacLean, "Qualified Risk Assessment," op. cit., note 25, Parts 5 and 6; MacIntyre, "Utilitarians and Cost-Benefit Analysis," op. cit., note 10, 139–142; Gewirth, "Human Rights," op. cit., note 25, 177; and C. B. MacPherson, "Democratic Theory: Ontology and Technology," in C. Mitcham and R. Mackey, eds., *Philosophy and Technology* (New York: Free Press, 1972), 167–168.

34. See note 33.

35. R. M. Hare, *Moral Thinking* (Oxford: Clarendon Press, 1981), 6 (see also 210–211).

36. Ibid., 26.

37. Ibid., 4.

38. Ibid., 12–14.

39. See, for example, Chauncey Starr, "Benefit-Cost Studies in Sociotechnical Systems," in Committee on Engineering Policy, *Perspectives on Benefit-Risk Decision Making* (Washington, D.C.: National Academy of Engineering, 1972), 26ff.; Chauncey Starr and Chris Whipple, "Risks of Risk Decisions," Science 208, no. 4448 (1980): 1116-1117; and D. Okrent and C. Whipple, *Approach to Societal Risk Acceptance Criteria and Risk Management*, Report no. PB-271264 (Washington, D.C.: Department of Commerce, 1977), 10.

40. Milton Friedman, "Value Judgments in Economics," in S. Hook, ed., *Human Values and Economic Policy*, op. cit., note 19, 85–88.

41. See also note 39; K. S. Shrader-Frechette, *Risk Analysis and Scientific Method* (Boston: Reidel, 1985), especially 176–189; and Shrader-Frechette, *Risk and Rationality*, op. cit., note 11, 169–196.